Praise for *Co[...]*

"*Conduct Under Fire* is an intimate and meticulous account of cruelty, courage, and extraordinary human resilience in the hellholes of Japan's WWII prison camps and more. Glusman also introduces the little-known deaths of over ten thousand American POWs by 'friendly fire,' and ends his story with the massive rain of firebombs that brought the war home to the Japanese. He has, indeed, cast an unflinching gaze on the 'fire' of hell on earth."
—John W. Dower, author of *Embracing Defeat* and *War Without Mercy*

"Glusman takes us on an extraordinary journey through the battles of the Pacific, and then into the horror of the Japanese POW camps, via the story of his father and three fellow doctors. There are moments of courage and cowardice, caring and cruelty, as these four physicians struggle under severe circumstances to preserve the bodies and heal the souls of their fellow men."
—Jerome E. Groopman, MD, Dina and Raphael Recanati Professor of Medicine, Harvard Medical School and author of *The Anatomy of Hope*

"A marvelous book, a wonderful reminder, lest we forget, that medicine is not a business, not a trade, not a degree course, but a calling. These four were called and the story of how they answered, and the tale of their suffering, their courage and their heroism is humbling, inspiring, and a wonderful read. I pray our generation is never tested in this fashion, but if we are, the standard for integrity, compassion and bravery has been set."
—Abraham Verghese, author of *My Own Country*

"A real page-turner . . . Glusman has truly done a masterful job not only researching and detailing a largely neglected story, but also putting it all in the proper context. It is beautifully written and a fitting tribute not only to his father and his father's comrades, but to all the POWs who shared their singular and horrific experience."
—Jan K. Herman, resident historian, U.S. Navy Bureau of Medicine and Surgery and editor of *Navy Medicine*

"*Conduct Under Fire* is a triumph. John Glusman has the historical breadth and literary grace of a William Manchester, but a modern even-handedness all his own."
—David Haward Bain, author of *Sitting in Darkness* and *Empire Express*

"Seldom have I read a book more committed to telling the historical truth, no matter how many inflated reputations get punctured and how much gaseous rhetoric about the 'Good War' is dispelled. [Glusman] more than balances these harsh truths with the heroism of these forgotten Americans, from the doctors to the officers and men they never ceased struggling to save. . . . *Conduct Under Fire* is a must-read."
                                    —Thomas Fleming, *Military History Quarterly*

"A moving, informative, and well-documented account of aspects of World War II that are often overlooked. . . . I highly recommend this book."
    —Harold D. Langley, Ph.D., *The New England Journal of Medicine*

"Riveting . . . A harrowing account of a brutal clash of cultures that reads like a novel."   —*Proceedings,* U.S. Naval Institute

"Masterful."   —*Parameters,* U.S. Army War College

"A compelling account of courage and sacrifice. . . . Over a third of American POWs of the Japanese died in captivity; with grace and clarity, Glusman gives a keen sense of loss to that statistic, and a heroic dignity to those that survived—a major achievement indeed."
                                    —*Publishers Weekly* (starred review)

"A thoughtful, humane meditation on war and family history, full of myth-busting truths."   —*Kirkus Reviews*

"Thoroughly absorbing . . . A very notable addition to the literature on its harrowing subject."   —*ALA Booklist*

"Interviews with veterans from the Australian, British, American, and Japanese forces, coupled with the use of diaries, letters, and war crimes testimony, make this essential."   —*Library Journal* (starred review)

PENGUIN BOOKS

CONDUCT UNDER FIRE

John A. Glusman is editor in chief of Farrar, Straus and Giroux. He has been a contributing editor to *The Paris Review* and has written for numerous publications, including *The Economist*, *The Washington Post Book World*, *The Christian Science Monitor*, and *Rolling Stone*. He lives in Glen Ridge, New Jersey, with his wife and three children.

CONDUCT UNDER FIRE

Four American Doctors
and Their Fight for Life as
Prisoners of the Japanese

1941–1945

John A. Glusman

PENGUIN BOOKS

PENGUIN BOOKS

Published by the Penguin Group

Penguin Group (USA) Inc., 375 Hudson Street, New York, New York 10014, U.S.A.
Penguin Group (Canada), 90 Eglinton Avenue East, Suite 700, Toronto,
Ontario, Canada M4P 2Y3 (a division of Pearson Penguin Canada Inc.)
Penguin Books Ltd, 80 Strand, London WC2R 0RL, England
Penguin Ireland, 25 St Stephen's Green, Dublin 2, Ireland (a division of Penguin Books Ltd)
Penguin Group (Australia), 250 Camberwell Road, Camberwell,
Victoria 3124, Australia (a division of Pearson Australia Group Pty Ltd)
Penguin Books India Pvt Ltd, 11 Community Centre,
Panchsheel Park, New Delhi - 110 017, India
Penguin Group (NZ), cnr Airborne and Rosedale Roads, Albany,
Auckland 1310, New Zealand (a division of Pearson New Zealand Ltd)
Penguin Books (South Africa) (Pty) Ltd, 24 Sturdee Avenue,
Rosebank, Johannesburg 2196, South Africa

Penguin Books Ltd, Registered Offices:
80 Strand, London WC2R 0RL, England

First published in the United States of America by Viking Penguin,
a member of Penguin Group (USA) Inc. 2005
Published in Penguin Books 2006

1 3 5 7 9 10 8 6 4 2

Portions of *Conduct Under Fire* appeared in different form in
The Virginia Quarterly Review and *Travel + Leisure*.

Excerpt from *Dusk* by F. Sionil José reprinted by permission of Random House, Inc.

Photograph credits appear on page 570.

Maps by Jeffrey L. Ward

ISBN 0 14 20.0222 4
CIP data available

Printed in the United States of America
Set in Adobe Garamond

For Jenny,
Isabel,
and Graham

Patriotism is selfless. And it is not the generals who are the bravest—they usually have the means to stay away from the battle and thereby lengthen their lives. The bravest are usually those whom we do not know or hear about. . . . It has always been the many faceless men, those foot soldiers, who have suffered most, who have died. It is they who make a nation.

—F. Sionil José, *Dusk*

A NOTE ON NAMES

Throughout *Conduct Under Fire* I have followed the Japanese custom of using family names first and given names last. In some English-language translations, the name order is reversed to conform to Western style, in which case I have referenced names in the Notes and Bibliography exactly as they appear in print.

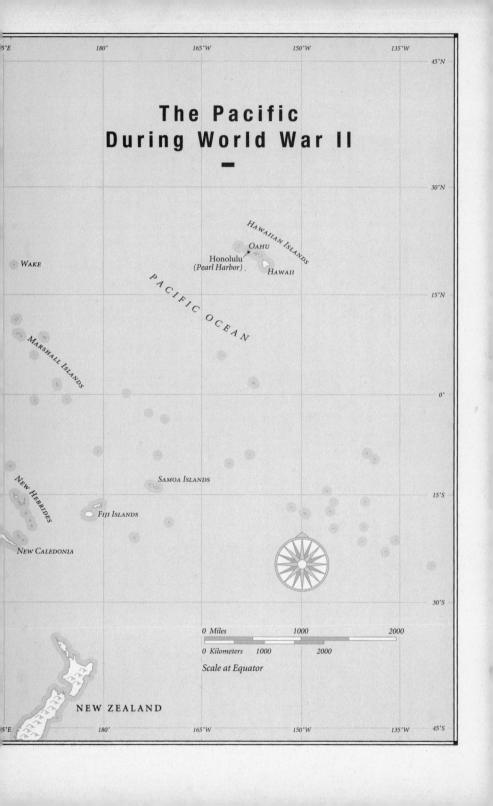

The Pacific
During World War II
—

Hawaiian Islands

WAKE

Honolulu
(Pearl Harbor)

OAHU

HAWAII

PACIFIC OCEAN

Marshall Islands

New Hebrides

Samoa Islands

Fiji Islands

New Caledonia

| 0 Miles | | 1000 | | 2000 |
| 0 Kilometers | 1000 | | 2000 | |

Scale at Equator

NEW ZEALAND

45°N

30°N

15°N

0°

15°S

30°S

45°S

5°E   180°   165°W   150°W   135°W

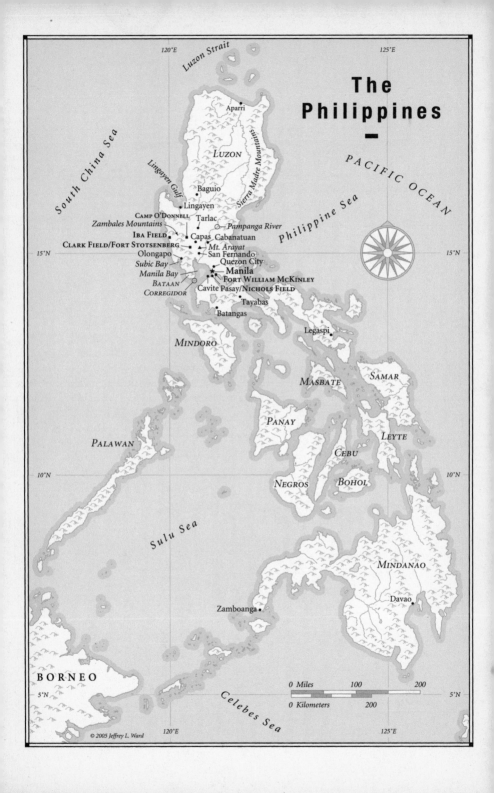

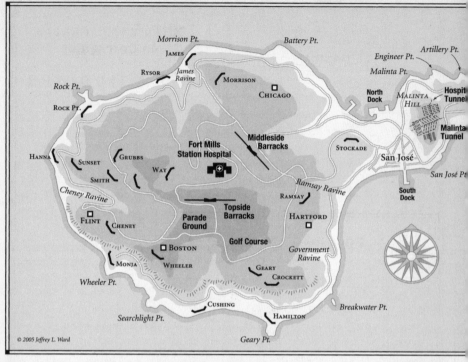

Morrison Pt.   Battery Pt.   Engineer Pt.   Artillery Pt.
JAMES   Malinta Pt.
RYSOR   James Ravine   MORRISON
Rock Pt.   North   MALINTA   Hospital
Rock Pt.   CHICAGO   Dock   HILL   Tunnel
HANNA   Malinta
         SUNSET   GRUBBS   Fort Mills   Middleside   Tunnel
         SMITH   WAY   Station Hospital Barracks
Cheney Ravine   STOCKADE   San José
                                                                San José Pt.
         FLINT   CHENEY   Parade   Topside   Ramsay Ravine   South
                                 Ground   Barracks   RAMSAY   Dock
                                           Golf Course HARTFORD
         BOSTON
         MONJA   WHEELER   Government
Wheeler Pt.   Ravine
                          GEARY
                          CROCKETT
                 CUSHING   Breakwater Pt.
Searchlight Pt.   HAMILTON
                 Geary Pt.

© 2005 Jeffrey L. Ward

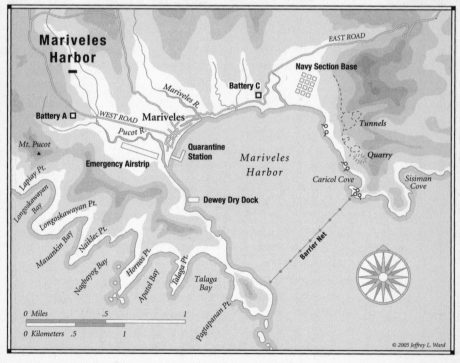

**Mariveles
Harbor**   EAST ROAD

                          Mariveles R.   Navy Section Base
                          Battery C
Battery A   WEST ROAD Mariveles   Tunnels
Mt. Pucot   Pucot R.   Quarry
                          Quarantine   Mariveles
Lapiay Pt.   Emergency Airstrip Station   Harbor   Caricol Cove   Sisiman
Longoskawayan   Cove
Bay   Barrier Net
    Longoskawayan Pt.   Dewey Dry Dock
Mauankin Bay   Naiklec Pt.
         Nagbayog Bay Hornos Pt.
                    Apatol Bay   Talaga Pt.
                          Talaga
                          Bay
                                   Pogtapanan Pt.

0 Miles   .5   1
0 Kilometers .5   1

© 2005 Jeffrey L. Ward

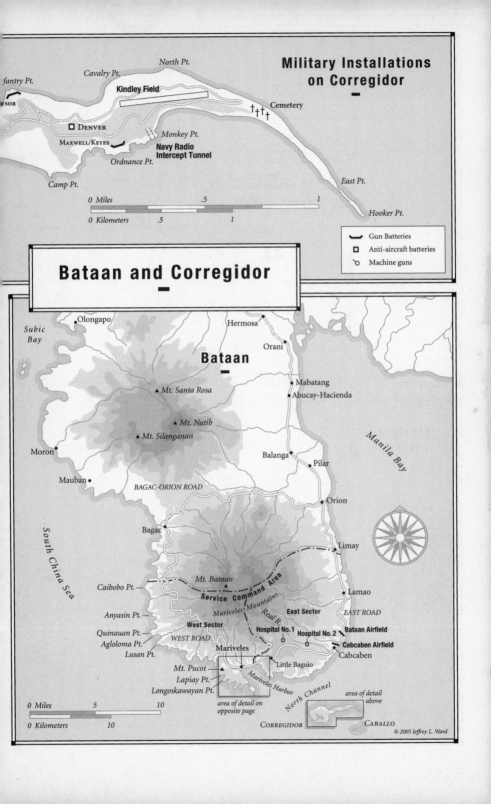

Military Installations on Corregidor

- _Infantry Pt._
- _Cavalry Pt._
- _North Pt._
- WSOR
- **Kindley Field**
- † † † **Cemetery**
- □ **DENVER**
- MAXWELL/KEYES
- _Monkey Pt._
- **Navy Radio Intercept Tunnel**
- _Ordnance Pt._
- _Camp Pt._
- _East Pt._
- _Hooker Pt._

| 0 Miles | | .5 | | 1 |
| 0 Kilometers | .5 | | 1 | |

Gun Batteries
□ Anti-aircraft batteries
o Machine guns

Bataan and Corregidor

- _Subic Bay_
- • Olongapo
- • Hermosa
- • Orani

Bataan

- ▲ _Mt. Santa Rosa_
- ▲ _Mt. Natib_
- ▲ _Mt. Silanganan_
- • _Mabatang_
- • _Abucay-Hacienda_
- • Moron
- • Mauban
- _BAGAC-ORION ROAD_
- Balanga
- • Pilar
- _Manila Bay_
- • Bagac
- • Orion
- _South China Sea_
- • Limay
- ▲ _Mt. Bataan_
- _Service Command Area_
- _Caibobo Pt._
- _Mariveles Mountains_
- _Real R._
- **East Sector**
- _EAST ROAD_
- • Lamao
- _Anyasin Pt._
- **West Sector**
- **Hospital No. 1** **Hospital No. 2**
- **Bataan Airfield**
- _Quinauan Pt._
- _WEST ROAD_
- **Cabcaben Airfield**
- _Agloloma Pt._
- _Lusan Pt._
- Mariveles
- Cabcaben
- _Mt. Pucot_
- • _Little Baguio_
- _Lapiay Pt._
- _Longoskawayan Pt._
- _Mariveles Harbor_
- _North Channel_

| 0 Miles | | 5 | | 10 |
| 0 Kilometers | | 10 | | |

area of detail on opposite page

area of detail above

CORREGIDOR

CABALLO

© 2005 Jeffrey L. Ward

CONTENTS

Prologue

GOVERNMENT RAVINE has fallen off the map. None of the Filipinos we meet on this tiny tropical island have heard of it. My father remembers its general location, but it has been nearly sixty years since he was on Corregidor, bivouacked with the U.S. 4th Marines on the night before he became a prisoner of the Japanese.

We step through four-foot-high *talahib* grass, mindful of the fact that we are in a natural habitat for pythons and vipers. We skid down a mud-slick embankment, grabbing onto eucalyptus saplings for support. I keep my eyes on exposed, gnarled roots, only to feel a dangling vine, as brown as twine, wrapped around my neck. The shade of the jungle canopy offers respite from the blistering sun. The trees are more mature, and we can make out remnants of an old dirt road at the top of a ridge that drops steeply to the sea. By his account, there should be a cave to the east where there was once a battalion aid station, but we have yet to find it. Perhaps he is mistaken after all.

They called it "the Rock." A formidable maritime fortress in the mouth of Manila Bay, Corregidor endured 300 air raids and one of the heaviest artillery bombardments of World War II during a grueling siege. The surrender of Corregidor by Lieutenant General Jonathan M. Wainwright on May 6, 1942, marked the chilling defeat of U.S. and Allied forces in the Philippines and the culmination of a series of lightning Japanese victories in the Pacific, from the attack on Pearl Harbor to the capture of Guam, Wake, Hong Kong, Malaya, Singapore, and the Dutch East Indies. With the fall of Corregidor, my father, one of roughly 12,000 men captured on the Rock, began his three-and-a-half-year odyssey as a prisoner of war.

We are in the Philippines to retrace a journey that began with hope and purpose in August 1941 and ended in the ashen ruins of Japan in September 1945. My father is eighty-six years of age and surprised by my interest. I am curious about a chapter of his life that in some ways is still being written. He comes to welcome my questions, a bridge between two men, two generations more than forty years apart, one of which has known war, one of which has not.

Like many former POWs, he has spoken little with his family about his wartime experiences. An Army Distinguished Unit Badge with Oak Leaf Cluster. An American Defense Service Medal with Base Clasp. An Asiatic-Pacific Area campaign medal with one bronze star. A Philippine Defense ribbon with one bronze star. A newspaper clipping from the *New York Herald Tribune* listing him as "missing." A photograph of the medical staff of the Kōbe Prisoner of War Hospital in Japan dated November 1944. These are the mementos of my father's war.

As children, my brother, sister, and I glimpsed these artifacts as rarely as we heard the tales behind them. Shards of memories came to light and were then tucked away, along with the navy uniform he stored in a government-issue footlocker that we rarely saw open. Only one incident can I recall with any clarity: my father and his buddies were once so hungry that they killed, skinned, and ate a cat. It appealed to a boy's delight in the grotesque, lent him a certain stature, and we inquired no further except to ask how cat tastes. "Gamey as hell" came the reply.

In retrospect it is odd but understandable that we grew up knowing so little about World War II, the most devastating war in human history. Fifty million lives were lost, 2.35 million Japanese died, 406,000 Americans were killed, and 78,976 Americans were listed as missing.

Between September 1940, when Congress enacted the Selective Service Act, and August 1945, 31 million American men registered for the draft and 16 million men and women served their country. The war mobilized civilian participation to an unprecedented degree. Nearly 2 million American women worked in defense factories; 59,000 women joined the Army Nurse Corps. Some 56,000 physicians volunteered for duty.

My father was not a combatant; he was a doctor, whose battles were fought on the frontline of disease. A lieutenant (junior grade) in the U.S. Navy Medical Corps, he was stationed on Bataan and then attached to the 4th Marines on Corregidor. As battalion surgeon in a campaign led by the army six years before the first Mobile Army Surgical Hospital (MASH) units came into being, his role was to help, not harm.

As if wars could ever be neat, clean, surgical operations, the war in the Pacific has been called a dirty war, a "war without mercy," as historian John Dower described it. Many American soldiers were instilled with racial stereotypes of the Japanese as treacherous, savage, subhuman. Roosevelt and Churchill themselves vowed to crush the "Barbarians of the Pacific." Such language bore a striking resemblance to the conception propagated by the Japanese of Westerners, who were, said the Japanese schoolbook *Cardinal Principles of the National Polity*, "intrinsically quite different from the so-called citizens of Occidental countries."

The Japanese viewed Americans in particular as soft, self-indulgent, and individualistic. The Japanese, by contrast, belonged to the genetically pure "Yamato Race," a tribe of "One Hundred Million" whose superiority lay in conformity. As *shidō minzoku,* the leading race, their goal, expressed as *hakkō ichiu,* or "Eight Corners of the World Under One Roof," was the subjugation of all other Asians and the replacement of Anglo-American imperialism with a new world order. Under Emperor Hirohito, this became the essence of their *kokutai,* or national polity.

U.S. and Filipino troops fighting on Bataan and Corregidor suffered horribly from hunger and disease. "They were expendable," to borrow the title of W. L. White's book about John Bulkeley and Motor Torpedo Boat (MTB) Squadron 3 published in 1944. Sacrificed on the altar of hubris, they were the casualties of an American military strategy known as War Plan Orange-3 that was doomed to failure. They were promised that "help is on the way" by General Douglas MacArthur while Roosevelt advocated a policy of "Europe First."

Japanese soldiers on Bataan confronted similarly harsh conditions, but they had reinforcements whereas the American and Filipino troops had none. They were indoctrinated with the code of *bushidō*—the way of the warrior—and the belief that there was no greater glory than to die in the service of the emperor.

The Pacific POW, said E. Bartlett Kerr, "underwent an experience unlike that of his millions of fellow veterans." Of the approximately 193,000 Allied prisoners of the Japanese in the Pacific, 36,260 were American.

POWs were systematically deprived of food and medicine. They were humiliated, beaten, starved, and in the worst instances tortured and executed. Their fate hinged on their own ingenuity, the "will to live," as one American doctor put it, the occasional kindness of camp guards and commandants, and sheer good luck. It was a war in which absolute power was punished absolutely.

Forty-two percent of the 25,580 U.S. Army and Navy personnel captured in the Philippines never returned. My father was one of the lucky ones. Like many prisoners of war, he could not have endured on his own. Fred Berley, George Ferguson, John Bookman, and my father, Murray Glusman, were a group—a team, as it were—of four navy doctors. From disparate backgrounds, they were dedicated to their professions, devoted to their patients, comrades in hardship and healing. All of them were decorated. As doctors, their perspective on war and captivity was unique, but none would valorize their experience. If they suffered under the Japanese, they also experienced moments of genuine compassion.

Three of them survived. One never made it home. The war defined them as young men, and while its imprint faded with time, it remained a palimpsest beneath the narrative of their lives. It colored their language, surfaced in their dreams, tempered their outlook, and sketched, however faintly, the world they created for their children. But they would rather bury their memories than exhume them.

"We did nothing extraordinary," my father said with characteristic understatement. "We lived in extraordinary times."

In *Civilization and Its Discontents* Freud wrote that one of the sins of contemporary education was its failure to prepare future generations "for the aggressiveness of which they are destined to become the objects."

This is the lesson I learned from my father and his buddies.

This is their story.

═══ 1 ═══

The Prettiest Girl in the World

HE WROTE TO HER almost every day, short letters, long letters, recollections, reminders, anecdotes and little jokes, dreams from the night before, and imaginings of their future, handwritten or hammered out on his new Hermes typewriter. It was November 1939, and he couldn't bear to leave her, nearly quit the damn navy when he saw Shanghai fade away.

They had met in Washington, D.C., in January of that year. He was in Naval Medical School, having earned the rank of assistant surgeon, lieutenant (junior grade); she had been living and teaching in Madison, Wisconsin. From the moment he first noticed her petal-white complexion, pert apple cheeks, and luxurious black hair, he couldn't stop looking at her, couldn't stop thinking about her. So when he was ordered that spring to report to the Asiatic Station once he had completed his postgraduate course of instruction, he slyly popped the question: "Do you think you can handle servants?" "Of course I can," she replied without equivocation.

A small-town schoolteacher from Wausau, Wisconsin, whose father was a conductor on the Northwestern Railroad, she may have come from a humble background, but she had an almost regal bearing born of self-confidence and the cool consciousness of her physical charms. She blossomed at Wausau's high school, where she enjoyed her popularity, planning parties, decorating for dances, serving on the student council, and playing the role of queen in the Waugonian Carnival. She even dated the captain of the football team, but she would not be wooed by either frivolousness or sport. She knew what the young doctor meant, and his intentions were earnest, in spite of a puckish demeanor and thick, bushy eyebrows that gave him a somewhat quizzical look.

George Theodore Ferguson and Lucille Ann Halada (pronounced "holiday") were married at St. Peter's Church by Father Urban Eberle in Chicago on May 20, 1939. His mother, unhappy with the prospect of losing her only son, refused to give the union her blessing. It was a small ceremony. The only Ferguson present was George's little sister, Jane, and the only Halada was Lucy's father, Roland. And it was a short ceremony, too, since they were on their way to San Francisco, where they would board the *President Garfield* for their trans-Pacific voyage. George looked dapper in his crisp navy whites. Lucy, as George called her—or Duchess when he teased her—wore a sleek black suit that defied fashion and tradition and made an indelible impression, even if it aroused in Jane that old superstition "bad luck."

He had little knowledge of Japan's war with China, its desperate need in the wake of the Depression to feed a growing population, acquire raw materials, and assuage the appetite of young militarists whose ethos would permeate all aspects of Japanese life, from the highest ranks of the Imperial Japanese Army down to kindergarten. Nor was he aware of Japan's historic animosity toward the United States. For George, like many American men, war was an abstraction, and military service a means to an end: it provided steady employment, paid for one's education, and paved the way to a prosperous future.

He was an optimist by nature, reared on the pioneer spirit of his hometown Kansas City, Missouri, that port of entry to the American West where the Missouri River bends north, the Big Blue River snakes south, and enterprising young men hit the overland trails. He was gifted with his hands, knew he could make things work, not just in theory but in practice. His childhood friend Jeanne Gier, a first cousin who had vowed as a little girl that one day *she* would marry him, marveled at his dexterity and determination. George once rigged a telephone line by stringing wire and tin cans through his neighbors' backyards on 53rd Street Terrace, and if the reception, both literal and figurative, was less than he had hoped for, it didn't deter him one whit from pursuing other engineering feats, like building a radio—from scratch. Another time his mother, Mary, came home to find her vacuum cleaner laid out piece by piece on the sidewalk in front of their house. She nearly burst into tears, but once he put it back together, she found that it worked even better than before.

He realized early that to fully understand how something functioned, you first had to take it apart, analyze the pieces to see how they fit together as parts of the whole. How else could you learn about transmission, suction, or locomotion? His skill came easily, and his curiosity sought ever greater challenges. The satisfaction he derived from his accomplishments gave him a sense of control that fostered not smugness but a belief in the possibility of doing good and the plausibility of a greater beneficence. A Catholic, he regularly attended mass on Sundays.

But some things were beyond one's control. After the crash of '29 his father, George, lost his job in the new field of time management. The

Fergusons lost their house, piled nearly everything they had in their car, and headed out for Detroit where George's uncle lived, only to have their car—and everything that remained in it—stolen. His father landed a job in Milwaukee as a beer salesman for Blatz's brewery but would wind up back in Kansas City before settling in Chicago. Money was a constant worry.

George was the first in the family to go to college, and he worked summers cleaning out beer vats at Blatz's to help pay for his tuition. From Marquette University he proceeded to the Naval Medical School in Washington, D.C., where orthopedics stoked his ambition. The field inspired him, the complicated way in which a simple gesture, like shaking someone's hand, for example, depends on the deviation of the radius and the ulna, while the tendons that come down from the inner aspect of the elbow and the volar move your fingers as the biceps and brachioradialis leverage your elbow. The names of the tendons themselves bespoke a malleable but lasting strength—*Flexor sublimis* and *Flexor profundus*. It was so beautifully worked out—the architecture of the body—the muscles and ligaments that give the human skeleton its shape and mobility, our stature and footing in this world. He was a man, you might say, who made an immediate impression and understood literally what sustains us, what moves us, what endows us with presence.

Lucy stole his heart. He couldn't say he really knew her; their courtship had been too brief for that. But he knew he loved her, he deferred to her, and he delighted in amusing her. Poised and as pretty as Greer Garson, she brought out the best in him, made him think the sky was the limit as they embarked on the greatest adventure of their lives.

Along with the service uniforms he had purchased in serge and elastique from Kassan-Stein's Custom Tailors in Washington, D.C., including a five-piece full-dress outfit, a blue raincoat, and a beaver overcoat, he packed a complete set of golf clubs, tennis and squash racquets, an 8mm Eastman movie camera, a Zeiss camera, and a small library of medical textbooks, Dorland's *Medical Dictionary* and Steindler's *Orthopedic Operations* among them.

The word was out: the Asiatic Station was a plum assignment. Work hours were short, nightclubs beckoned, the parties were lavish, and the liquor and women were cheap. The temptations were enough to entice any bachelor and sufficiently varied, with golf, horseback riding, hunting, and fishing, to satiate the officers who brought their wives along with them.

But the fact remained that Japan had been at war with China for the better part of a decade. In September 1931 Japan blamed the Chinese for blowing up the South Manchurian Railway, which the Japanese

Kwantung Army had sabotaged as a pretext to annex Manchuria. In January 1932 the Japanese attacked Chapei, the Chinese quarter of Shanghai, only to meet fierce resistance from the Nineteenth Route Army. In July 1937 the Kwantung Army staged another "incident" at the Marco Polo Bridge near Peking as an excuse to launch the second Sino-Japanese War. And in August Japanese forces again invaded Shanghai, this time emerging victorious and departing only after China agreed to the terms of their truce. By December 12 the Nationalist capital of Nanking had fallen to Japanese soldiers, who in an orgy of rape, mutilation, and mass murder killed an estimated 200,000 Chinese civilians. That same day Japanese Navy pilots bombed and sank the USS *Panay* above Nanking, the first Yangtze Patrol gunboat lost in eighty-three years of service.

The accounts of Japanese brutality in Nanking that reached American readers through Frank Tillman Durdin in *The New York Times*, Archibald Steele in the *Chicago Daily News*, and C. Yates McDaniels of AP, as well as in George Fitch's stills in *Life* magazine, were chilling. But it was the attack on the *Panay* up from Nanking that seized the public's attention. The sinking of the *Panay* on December 12, 1937, was a mistake, the Japanese averred after a howl of American protest, which quieted down once Japan forked over a $2.2 million indemnity. The incident hardened American resolve against Japan and American support of China. But the real concern was business. That was the purpose of a continued American military presence in Asia: to patrol the Yangtze River, the 3,500-mile lifeline to China's vast interior, where Standard Oil, Texaco, and Asiatic Petroleum had operations; to protect the U.S. Embassy in Peking and keep railroads open for American products; and to guard the International Settlement in Shanghai, a task assigned to the 1st and 2nd Battalions of the U.S. 4th Marine Regiment under the command of Colonel Samuel L. Howard.

George and Lucy sailed from San Francisco on June 11, 1939, and luxuriated in their three-week sojourn to Hawaii, Yokohama, and Manila. The staterooms on the *President Garfield* were comfortable, the meals elegantly served, and the drinks flowed—a concerted effort by American President Lines to make "travel Round the World" accessible "with continuous service on a clock-like schedule" for something less than a fortune. Hawaii was paradise, George wrote his sister Jane from the garden of the Royal Hawaiian Hotel in Honolulu, "with all kinds and colors of birds flying around. Just walked up Waikiki Beach to the Aquarium and this p.m. will go out to Palau which is an ancient battlefield." On July 1 they disembarked the *Garfield* in Manila and proceeded to Shanghai aboard the SS *Empress of Asia*.

They were dazzled by their entry into China. Shanghai teemed with activity. An elegant corniche known as the Bund curved around the Whangpoo River, anchored by the stately Customs House and distinguished by the neoclassical architecture of Shanghai's banks and foreign businesses. On the other side were gangplanks and catwalks leading up to the ships and small cruisers that plied the waters next to square-bowed junks with colorfully patched sails and sampans that floated like butterflies.

The vibrant clash of cultures couldn't have been more exotic. Streets bustled with cars, bicycles, peddlers, and pedestrians. Natives pushed wheelbarrows, pulled yellow rickshaws, or rode water buffalos bareback down Tibet Road. The sounds of hawking, talking, singing, and catcalling filled the air, which was pungent with the smell of raw fish, garlic, and charcoal smoke. In a Hongkew sukiyaki house you might hear half a dozen languages spoken at once—Russian, German, English, French, Italian, and Dutch in addition to Japanese and Chinese. But for all of its Asiatic accents, Shanghai was a city that catered to Western tastes. *The Shanghai Sunday Times* duly noted the arrival of George and Lucille Ferguson on its society page, with captioned cameo photographs of the newlywed couple.

Shanghai rises from the ancient mudflats of the Yangtze delta, its name meaning "above the sea." Since 1842, when the Treaty of Nanking terminated the Opium War, it had been open to the West and was divided into foreign enclaves, outside the old walled city, that were independent of Chinese law. The British dominated shipping, and in 1863 they consolidated their sector with the American concession to form the International Settlement.

The largest port in the Far East, Shanghai attracted merchants and traders, manufacturers and bankers, refugees and revolutionaries. It was the entrepôt of the Orient, its fleshpot, too, and in the 1920s and 1930s was a magnet for actors and playwrights, philosophers and poets from Charlie Chaplin to Noël Coward, from Bertrand Russell to W. H. Auden. Said Oxford aesthete Harold Acton: "Everywhere one jostled adventurers and rubbed shoulders with people who had no inkling how extraordinary they were: the extraordinary had become ordinary; the freakish commonplace."

Shanghai was hot, humid, and crawling with people, Acton wrote, like cicadas scurrying up a dunghill. Chinese laborers were mercilessly exploited in Shanghai's textile mills, three-quarters of which were foreign owned. Women and young girls toiled twelve hours a day, seven days a week, for less than $15 per month. In a city of 3 million Chinese residents in 1932, there were 50,000 licensed and 100,000 unlicensed prostitutes.

That same year 30,000 corpses were plucked from Shanghai's streets. By 1935 average life expectancy in China was twenty-eight years; in Shanghai it was even less. Foreigners could indulge in a sybaritic lifestyle built on the backs of cheap coolie labor, while the opium trade and prostitution flourished in parlors and backstreets. It was not uncommon to see bodies of Chinese floating down the Yangtze, victims of Japan's war with China.

Soochow Creek divides the city and flows southeast before emptying into the Whangpoo River, a branch of the Yangtze that elbows southwest. The Japanese occupied Yangtzepoo and Hongkew to the north, which they used as a base of operations for attacks against Chapei, headquarters of the Shanghai-Nanking defense area. The International Settlement stood to the south, while the old city hugged the near shore of the Whangpoo and bumped up against the French concession to the west.

By the late 1930s the Japanese represented the largest foreign contingent in Shanghai. Only 10,000 British and Americans inhabited the International Settlement, which the Chinese and Japanese regarded as neutral. But since the second Sino-Japanese War in 1937, the U.S. 4th Marine Regiment had taken a more active role to prevent the conflagration from spreading. Known as the China Marines, they had come to Shanghai in 1927 after Chiang Kai-shek, who aimed to free China from the tyranny of local warlords and foreign influence, marched into the city at the head of the Nationalist Army and routed the Chinese Communist Party.

The two-battalion regiment had an average strength of 1,200 officers and men who were responsible for the internal security of the International Settlement. They piled up sandbags, strung barbed wire across the bridges spanning Soochow Creek, and searched anyone crossing into their sector for arms and contraband. Their unofficial mascot became a mongrel pup that was picked up by B Company guards along the riverbank and named, fittingly, Soochow.

If things got hot for the leathernecks along Soochow Creek, they were even hotter after hours. Shanghai was a carnival of delights for young American men whose only previous contact with the opposite sex had been at church socials. "We was nineteen and pussy was ten cent," as Private James Carrington indelicately put it. "We were lovers instead of fighters," clarified Private Alton C. Halbrook, who drew $20.80 each month, belonged to a private club, had his own rickshaw, and partook of regular evening entertainment. "This town would ruin anybody in no time," the old China hand Joseph W. "Vinegar Joe" Stilwell famously said. "The babes that twitch around the hotels need attention so badly that it is hard not to give it to them."

The social hub for sailors and marines was the 4th Marine Club on

Bubbling Well Road, where men drank, dined, gambled, and ambled on to their next nighttime destination: The Majestic? Or the English men's club at the Palace Hotel, where they could puff on Havana cigars between sips of British ale and talk of current events?

The Chinese girls were simply irresistible. With dresses slit up to their thighs and silk blouses without bras they were more than willing to join a fellow on liberty for a meal or a drink. Many of the women in Shanghai—Chinese, Japanese, or Korean—lived with American, British, or French military men, often with more than one man at a time. Cecil Jesse Peart, a navy Pharmacist's Mate, shared a young Chinese woman with a shipmate of his until he saw his pal in the regimental hospital "giving the lab tech a little, narrow glass slide with a urethral smear on it." Their friendship continued, but not their common interest.

Sex was the lingua franca, and the talk was cheap. For the equivalent of one U.S. dollar you could purchase a bottle of Pinch scotch. Seven cents would get you a pint of vodka, and if you wanted, you could even buy a concubine. There was a brothel located near the regimental hospital on Gordon Road, which "made it rather handy for our medical staff," admitted Peart.

The officers preferred blondes, and the blondes were White Russian women who in their glittering beauty seemed to walk right off the silver screen. They haunted the Café de la Paix in the French concession and baited the men as slyly as Circe trying to snag Odysseus. Fluent in numerous languages, some tended the bar, while others worked the dance floor, where they encouraged smitten sailors to buy them watered-down drinks, dance for a dime a turn, and believe, for a moment, whispers of love.

Many of the White Russians were well educated and of noble birth, they said, having fled Russia after the 1917 revolution and migrated to China via Mongolia and Manchuria. They were "White" because they had remained loyal to the tsar instead of to Lenin. By 1934 an estimated 25,000 lived in the city, the second-largest foreign population after the Japanese. Many of them were also down on their luck and had children and parents to support.

The women worked as seamstresses, shopkeepers, hostesses, and harlots. While some toyed with the affections of drunken river rats, others sought the illusion of stability offered by a man in uniform and made every attempt to tie the knot at the Russian Orthodox church. The U.S. government frowned on such marriages and would recognize only ceremonies performed in the consulate.

Between nights on the town and fooling around, the lifestyle in Shanghai was so rich that the regiment had to order "conditioning hikes" for the marines, who walked around Shanghai carrying their weapons while trying not to gag on the stench of the honey-cart operators who dumped raw human waste into the sewers that lined their route. The marines lived like kings.

George and Lucy kept an apartment at the Cathay Mansions in the posh French concession, whose tree-lined boulevards evoked Haussmann's Paris. The rooms were furnished, the beds were made with Irish linen sheets, and the bathrooms were neatly tiled in black and white. From the rooftop garden you could see the river. They dined across the street at Le Cercle Sportif Français, known as the French Club, where evenings began at 10 P.M. but didn't hit full stride until 2 A.M. And on Sundays they liked to venture out of Shanghai for an afternoon of golf at the Columbia Country Club.

The important thing was neither the food nor the entertainment; it was being alone and being in love, and for five heavenly months they made plans for where they would live, the number of children they would have, the make and model of their car—a little Plymouth convertible or a coupe?—and the kind of medical practice George would set up. Shanghai was their honeymoon, a time of unbridled hope and misplaced certainty, and in the confluence of the two they strove to make every minute count.

George Ferguson reported for duty aboard the USS *Guam* in the very month that war broke out in Europe. On September 1, 1939, Germany invaded Poland, and two days later France and Britain declared war on Germany. By the end of September, the USSR had marched into Poland, Warsaw had fallen, and the German-Soviet Treaty of Friendship, Co-operation, and Demarcation had been signed.

The *Guam* was then one of five American gunboats that comprised the Yangtze Patrol and that navigated the ever-shifting waters of the "Long River," as the Chinese called it, from its mouth to Ipin, after which it was known as the "River of Golden Sand." The Yangtze Patrol represented the longest military operation in U.S. history, having been formed in 1854 shortly after Commodore Perry used the threat of force to open up Japan to trade. Vice Admiral William Glassford took over its command in May 1939.

The objective of the Yangtze Patrol (YangPat, for short) was simple: to ensure the safe passage of American merchant traffic and shield it from the growing menace of Chinese Communist bandits. The *Guam* was the smallest of the Yangtze gunboats, measuring only 159½ feet. She was a two-screw vessel with a shallow six-foot four-inch draft. Her size gave her an advantage over her sister ships on the Yangtze, where seasonal water levels could vary by as much as fifty to one hundred feet. Unlike the *Luzon*, *Mindanao*, *Oahu*, and *Tutuila*, the *Guam* could comfortably chug up to Chungking and make it as far as Pingshan during the summer, nearly 1,600 miles from the sea. She operated by coal-generated steam. Captain A. E. Harris was skipper, and under his command were four line officers, fifty-three sailors, and one doctor—George Ferguson.

By late November 1939 the *Guam* was toiling up the Yangtze, past Chinkiang, then Nanking, and on to Wuhu. She looked more like a Mississippi riverboat than a U.S. Navy warship; she even had her own bar. But her bridge was fortified, four armor-plated machine guns were mounted on the second deck, and two 3-inch guns were positioned aft and forward, beneath which was George's cabin. It was a small room, with a narrow mattress atop a chest of drawers, a bookshelf at its head, and a wooden dresser at a tight right angle. On top sat a squat steel safe with the ship's accounts in it, and George's Hermes typewriter. Shanghai may have disappeared in the distance, but Lucy was never far from his thoughts. If George posted a letter by 9 A.M., Lucy would have it the following day. Mail from the States took a good month and a half, by contrast. George would be upriver for three months at a time before he returned to Shanghai—and Lucy.

There was never enough time. Even when the *Guam* was back in Shanghai, George had to maintain his medical responsibilities. He'd leave their suite in the Cathay Mansions early in the morning, hail a cab down to the dock, and row out to the *Guam* in a gig, and if he had to remain on call through the evening, Lucy would join him in the ship's dining room. If not, they'd dine together at the Cathay Mansions or go out for dinner, a show, and a nightcap. George still had to be back on board by 8 A.M. the next morning.

Duty upriver was hardly strenuous. There were few medical cases for George except the monthly syphilis inspections, so he was assigned to Ship Service and then the Navy Club, checking inventories and auditing accounts. He quickly made friends with Ensign James O'Rourke, the Commissary Officer on the *Guam*. George and Jim fraternized like backyard buddies, popping in and out of each other's cabins without warning, swapping stories about Lucy and Betty—Jim's intended—and even writing to the other's girl and exaggerating their misdeeds.

If it weren't for the hundreds of patients George saw at Wuhu General Hospital, his professional life would have been "pretty dull," he admitted. In Wuhu he honed his skills performing gallbladder surgery, amputations, and enucleations and removing cysts and tumors. He even delivered his first Chinese baby. In some ways it was perfect practice for a young physician. He completed his rounds by noon, and then the day's recreations began.

After the fall of Nanking, Chiang Kai-shek moved upriver, and Hankow became the provisional capital of "Free China," 600 miles from Shanghai. Then, in light of the advancing Japanese Army, the Chinese abandoned Hankow and in October 1938 retreated even farther up the Yangtze to Chungking, 1,300 miles from the sea.

The Japanese installed a puppet government in Hankow, which temporized—even socialized—with the American and European colony there. Six hundred miles west of Shanghai at the junction of the Yangtze and Han Rivers, Hankow was an ancient Chinese city that Marco Polo had praised in his *Travels*. Dotted with pagodas and marble tombs, it was a major exporter of black leaf tea to Odessa as well as a center of Catholic and Protestant missionary activity. Like Shanghai, it was divided into foreign concessions, and the foreigners liked to play hard. Just outside the Standard Oil compound was a rifle range, a drill ground, and a baseball diamond. Hankow even had its own golf course—built on top of an old Chinese cemetery. "This was Kipling's east of Suez," said Lieutenant Kemp Tolley of the YangPat's *Tutuila*, "with a bang."

In Hankow, George enjoyed horseback riding three times a week, the links at the Hankow Race Club, drinks at Rosie's Tea Room—the only joint with air conditioning—and dinner at Jimmy's, followed by dancing at the International Club. There were tea parties, cocktail parties, bachelor parties, dinner parties, pool parties aboard the *Guam*, and movies on the pontoon boat that accompanied it, like *Rebecca of Sunnybrook Farm* with Shirley Temple, which was "*pretty* good," George admitted to Lucy, "but all the *pretty* girls remind me of you, doggone it."

Nocturnal adventures frequently led down Dump Street, where Russian cabarets and bars sparkled with White Russian girls. The entertainment was extravagant, exhilarating, and exhausting. All the ship's officers had their own rickshaw boys to transport them about town; a few had light motorcycles; and by the time they negotiated the 150-foot catwalks that stretched out to the pontoon boat beside the *Guam*, the sun might be just a few hours from rising. Then on Sunday, with hardly enough time to recover from a hangover, the ritual started all over again.

Sometimes the *Guam* seemed more like a pleasure boat than a gunboat, a comic blend of nineteenth-century English naval tradition and twentieth-century taste, say, Gilbert and Sullivan on the rocks. You could drink yourself into oblivion, but you had to wear a uniform with a high collar, a tie, regulation khaki shorts, and stockings in the sweltering heat. You could listen to Toscanini, bowl, even go duck hunting from the ship's deck, but you had to observe military protocol and forms of address.

George was a curious combination "of rascality and sobriety," Jim reported to Lucy. He socialized with women but kept a gentlemanly distance, was amused and aghast at the alcoholic consumption around him. "I've never seen so much drinking before," George admitted to Lucy. "They get up at ten A.M. Sunday to get their Mint Julep Club going and by noon they're all stewed. Three months in this place can easily make a wreck of you if you'd let it. I can hardly wait to get back to your love and kisses." Captain Harris was in his cups so often that George worried he'd develop "the shakes." George protested too much. He drank, too, but he did so in moderation, and on those occasions when he overimbibed, he confessed to Lucy the next morning with the abashed air of a guilty choirboy.

They drank because that was the old navy culture, culture turned into habit, and because of a slow-burning realization that the world around them was being realigned in ways that would soon turn their days in China into the memory of a glorious summer. The chessboard of humanity was being divided into Allied and Axis powers. The United States passed a revised Neutrality Act on November 4, 1939, but the Japanese could make their move on Shanghai, Hankow, or Chungking anytime.

Lucy, meanwhile, was hardly languishing on the vine in Shanghai. By December she had taken a job at the Shanghai American School and maintained a busy social calendar. Every time one of the YangPat gunboats came into port, there would be ship's parties, elegant affairs where officers wore black tie, sailors dressed in swank, open-necked uniforms and snuggled with admiring Chinese girlfriends. The women, Asian and American, were gorgeous in full-length gowns. Lucy's escorts were always officers, and if she didn't have an escort, she would simply go alone.

She loved George's letters. They were funny, effusive, flirtatious, and smart. She missed being held by him, sitting on his knee, being reassured by him when her family back home was giving her the "silent treatment." She missed his voice, his advice, that cockeyed look when he teased her. She loved him for seeing through the reserve that others mistook for haughtiness when it was little more than shyness. And when he told her, again and again, that she was "the prettiest girl in the world," she believed him.

But there were some things George couldn't reveal entirely to Lucy. He had attended Edgewood Arsenal, Maryland, where he had been trained in chemical warfare. He was also versed in the ship's code. On

December 14, 1939, "a group of Japanese bombers about 12 flew over the ship today and sounded pretty ominous," he wrote. Then a fight erupted with a Japanese sentry, which turned the wires "hot with code" the next morning, "and since your hubby is on the coding board . . . I was pretty busy."

The crew of the *Guam* did their best to brighten a darkening mood by decorating the ship for Christmas, placing a tree on deck and, after mass and communion, serving up a turkey dinner that was surpassed only by the fruitcake and hot mince pudding for dessert. It was the first Christmas George had ever seen without snow, the first he had ever spent away from home. New Year's marked George's birthday, as well as his first encounter with Lucy. "Walked through a door and there you were. And now the U.S.N. has separated us . . . but 'they can't stop me from loving you.' "

Her absence only stoked his imagination. He fantasized about spending the summer with her, speculated about the "lots of children" they would have—at first twins, then a gaggle of six. But duty came before love, and a part of him found his short tours on the Yangtze Patrol "nice because when I see you on the return it's about the best event in my life."

In 1939 the United States imposed economic sanctions on Japan and in January 1940 terminated the 1911 Treaty of Commerce and Navigation. The Japanese made patrolling the Yangtze more difficult than ever for the Americans. Dealing with the Chinese ("friendly 'masters,' " as Glassford called them) had been one thing, but placating the Japanese invaders of China ("bitter rivals") was another. Clashes with sentries and armed patrols increased. The Japanese demanded regular inspections, which tested the mettle of even the most seasoned navy officer. They insisted on escorting the gunboats upriver, allegedly to protect them from Chinese artillery fire from the riverbank. They destroyed American property, arrested and detained foreign nationals, buzzed and even bombed the YangPat boats.

That didn't stop the Japanese from showing another face entirely. Japanese officers drank like fish, and they enjoyed entertaining the Americans, proffering cigarettes, sake, warm champagne, and cheap scotch. But when Japanese officers began to strip to their undershirts and remove their suspenders, the Americans beat a hasty retreat—especially if there was a geisha in the house.

In April 1940 Germany invaded Norway and Denmark. By mid-May the British Strategic Air Offensive was launched against Germany's cities, and in early June, Italy declared war on France and Britain. George now followed the news closely.

The armistice France signed with Germany on June 22 neutralized its garrison in Shanghai. The future of Shanghai's International Settlement itself was in doubt: "Every day now the Japanese have sent a squadron of bombers out of Hankow and they fly low directly over the ship," George wrote to Lucy. But he still clung to the hope that they could have a home in the city. That same month George participated in a poison gas exercise, and the crew of the *Guam* watched Universal News reels about the evacuation of Nanking and the bombing of the *Panay* as if to remind themselves of Japan's deadly intentions. George also saw *Submarine Patrol*, the 1938 John Ford movie about an incompetent naval officer commanding an old submarine chaser and its motley crew. "Pretty good but not very humorous at this time," he opined.

Early July saw the beginning of the Battle of Britain and the evacuation of Hong Kong. George wrote somberly: "War news . . . It looks a great deal like the U.S. is going to be involved somewhere." The summer temperatures soared, and he chafed at Captain Harris's enforcement of the navy uniform.

Lucy escaped the heat by taking a trip to Japan with Mary Lingenselter, an Iowa girl who also taught at the Shanghai American School. They visited cosmopolitan Kōbe, stayed at the Imperial Hotel in Tōkyō designed by Frank Lloyd Wright, soaked in the natural hot springs in Miyanoshita, and took in the views of Mt. Fuji from the banks of Lake Kawaguchi, in the heart of Fuji National Park. The farther away Lucy was, the more George pined for her. He moved her photograph so that her image was the last he glimpsed before going to bed at night and the first he saw in the morning. "Lucy," he wrote in mid-August, "I love you so much I can't put it into words."

By late August 1940 the British withdrew their ground forces from Shanghai to defend Singapore, leaving the meager 4th Regiment, down to only 900 men, to safeguard the city's uneasy status quo. In September Japan joined Germany and Italy in the Tripartite Pact, and in October Admiral Thomas C. Hart, commander in chief of the U.S. Navy's Asiatic Fleet, moved his headquarters from Shanghai to Manila. The only fleet ships north of Philippine waters were the China gunboats and the occasional navy transport.

Then in November Hart ordered the evacuation of dependents of the Asiatic Fleet, some 2,000 women and children. Lucy sailed on the *Mariposa*, and their parting was tense. Was this what it had come to? To have gotten this far together only to be separated by the greatest distance? To leave one home for another that had never really been? They had no choice; it was an order. George feared "difficult situations arising" between the United States and Japan, and in preparation the gunners on the *Guam* began machine gun practice. "Do you remember our last picture together and the song at the Candlelight Club," he asked, " 'Wish Me Luck'?"

By February 1941 the Chinese were massing forces around Hankow, and the Japanese were withdrawing thousands of troops, it was bruited, downriver to Nanking. International tensions didn't stop George from having dinner one night with the Italian consul beside German and Japanese officers. The next morning Japanese planes threatened the *Guam* "as if they would give anything to let loose a few bursts of machine gun fire." That only confirmed the rumor he had heard that the Yangtze Patrol would serve as the spearhead of the Asiatic Fleet and "remain in Hankow as bait."

Instead, the *Guam* returned to Shanghai in early April as the Yangtze was being closed down to traffic. Three men were on nightly watch to guard against sabotage, even though "it would be the easiest thing in the world to have us projected into a Japanese conflict by doing some damage to one of our gunboats." Downstream a Japanese cruiser beamed her searchlight over the waterfront.

The changes in Shanghai were unmistakable. Some 20,000 to 25,000 Japanese ground troops could be mobilized around the city, which had turned into a base for Japanese Army, Navy, and Air operations. By contrast, the United States had only 800 marines ashore with attached naval personnel.

The *Guam*'s name had been changed as well. On April 5, 1941, she became the *Wake*, having relinquished her name to a large new cruiser that became part of Rear Admiral F. S. Low's Cruiser Division 16. War was inevitable, George believed. In a letter to Lucy he apologized for getting her tangled up with a navy doctor instead of with "a good old fashioned practitioner of medicine." On May 20, their second anniversary, he confessed that "more than half of these last two years I've spent trying to be content just thinking about you."

Soon his letters would be censored. His location could no longer be divulged, and he was told by an old school chum who worked for the *Daily Advertiser* in Tōkyō that the Japanese perusing his mail got a kick out of his comments on the general political situation. Mail from the States had slowed down considerably since the American President Lines ships had been pressed into service for the European theater.

In June 1941 German and Italian assets were frozen in the United States, Italy declared war on the USSR, and Germany invaded the USSR. President Roosevelt declared a national emergency. That same month the Japanese bombed Chungking, and the U.S. Embassy and the Standard Oil compound were damaged. "Maybe we'll have a war & maybe I'll get a bit more practice who can tell!" George joked in a diary entry of June 21. He was growing weary of the Yangtze Patrol, the mad dashes in and out of Shanghai at an admiral's whim, the tiresome inspections by the Japanese, the lack of medical cases that truly interested him. War would be a diversion, all right, so long as it was over by November 1941, when he and his friend Lieutenant Alfred Littlefield "Smitty" Smith, medical officer of the USS *Luzon*, were due to go home.

That summer George and Jim O'Rourke rented an apartment in Hankow while on leave—a furnished four-room penthouse atop the International Export Company, with a houseboy, a coolie, and a gardener—all for eighteen dollars apiece per month. The two men were as giddy as new college roommates. The irony wasn't lost on George: it should have been Lucy. "I really think if you were here I could learn to like Hankow," he wrote. But he knew he was "trying to visualize something that will never happen."

The Japanese had already invaded northern French Indochina with the acquiescence of the Vichy government in a brazen overture to "The New Order" in Asia. On July 24, they moved south to seize the ports of Saigon, Tourane, and Camranh Bay. President Roosevelt responded on July 26 by closing the Panama Canal to Japanese merchant traffic and freezing Japanese assets in the United States. The American, British, Chinese, and Dutch powers—the ABCD, as they were unofficially called—placed an embargo on what Japan needed most: oil.

George's summer vacation was bittersweet, an unacknowledged farewell to a world that was vanishing before his eyes. Bombers flew up to Chungking daily. Inflation reared its ugly head. Hankow was being drained of its foreign population. The Japanese outnumbered the Americans and British at the Race Club twenty to one. Captain Kenneth N. Lowman, the Fleet Surgeon, assured George that he would be returning to the States on time. George couldn't wait to meet Lucy in San Francisco, then begin his residency at the Great Lakes Naval Training Station. He began counting the days until Christmas. "Isn't there a song called 'All I Do Is Think of You'?" he asked.

George found his medical responsibilities superseded by military ones. Doctors, of course, were noncombatants, and the Hague Convention prohibited them from engaging in combat except in self-defense. In the field they were required by the 1929 Geneva Convention to wear a brassard that displayed a red percale cross on a white rectangle of cotton. Pinned to the left sleeve above the elbow, it was stamped on the inside with an identity card number, which was the same as that on the Geneva Convention identification card that doctors and corpsmen were supposed to carry.

"I can load a rifle in the dark, use a submachine gun, fire the Lewis machine guns of the ship, handle a riot gun with dexterity and a killing gleam, put on a gas mask in fifteen seconds, and the rescue breathing outfit in twenty, fire a .45 revolver or pistol with 'deadly accuracy' at 50 yards, use a Browning automatic rifle with the best of them and even use the Morse code a 'little,' " he wrote in exasperation to Lucy. "What a doctor."

Such measures weren't taken without reason. The security of the International Settlement was at stake, as well as the fate of hundreds of foreign nationals who remained in the Yangtze River valley. In early September Admiral Hart concurred with the recommendation of Colonel Howard of the 4th Marines and Admiral Glassford that the time had come to evacuate all naval forces in China. A unified Northern Command incorporating American and British interests was established, with Admiral Glassford at the helm. Plans were quickly formulated to take a last stand in Shanghai, or to withdraw up the Whangpoo into Free China. Then in November Admiral Hart ordered Glassford to withdraw all naval forces in North China to Manila.

Colonel Howard prepared to evacuate the two battalions of the 4th Regiment to the Olongapo Naval Station on Subic Bay in the Philippine Islands. They would embark on two American President Lines steamers, the *Madison* and the *Harrison*, which would arrive in Shanghai from Manila and Hong Kong respectively. The ships were refitted as transports and flew the Naval Reserve pennant. They were supplied with extra lifejackets and rafts for the marines and given procedures for radio communication with Admiral Hart's staff in Manila. On the journey north to Shanghai, officers on both the *Madison* and the *Harrison* noticed the ominous tide of Japanese troop ships and naval vessels heading south. The *Madison* and the *Harrison* would sail from Shanghai under submarine escort, transporting a regiment of some 800 men. Ammunition, field equipment, medical supplies, rations, motor transport, clothing, and household effects were loaded onto the *Harrison*, in that order of importance.

On the evening of November 26, the American Club hosted a farewell party for the marines. The next day, Thanksgiving back in the States, Colonel Donald Curtis's 2nd Battalion left Shanghai on the *Madison*. On the morning of the twenty-eighth Colonel Howard led the 1st Battalion and the last of the 4th Marines down to the President Lines dock on the Bund, followed by the regimental band and colors. Thousands of spectators turned out. A Scotsman in full kilt stepped onto the balcony of the Foreign YMCA playing his pipes in their honor. Near Jimmy's on Nanking Road a band of Americans dressed in restaurant whites joined the procession, adding a little American swing. "Outwardly we cheered, smiled, and waved," remembered one spectator, "but inside we knew we'd never see them again." As novelist J. G. Ballard later wrote in *Empire of the Sun*, "The 50-year-long party that had been Shanghai" had come to an end.

Meanwhile the flat-bottom river boats of the Yangtze Patrol were being readied for their first oceanic voyage. Naval supplies and medical stores were emptied from warehouses, packed, and loaded for transport. Spare propellers and parts were stashed on the gunboats. Communication equipment from the regimental radio station was stripped and installed in the building of the Consulate General. And if something couldn't be taken, like the radio tower, it was taken down and sold as scrap or destroyed.

Chinese workmen outfitted the *Luzon* and the *Oahu* with watertight window shutters and steel doors, raised the blower intakes, and secured the masts, funnels, and lifeboats. But their decks remained only a few feet above the water.

On November 24 the *Wake* left Hankow "like a Bat out of Hell," George wrote in his diary. Two Japanese ships escorted her, and she was back in Shanghai on November 28. She was to remain behind as the communications ship of the Consulate General.

As soon as the *Wake* pulled alongside the *Luzon* at 2:30 P.M., George received orders to take passage on the *President Harrison*, which was departing at three o'clock. Colonel Howard had already bid adieu to the crowds on the Bund. George barely had time to pack. He scrambled into a gig, headed down the Whangpoo, and clambered up the ship's ladder to make it on deck by 2:55. The last contingent of the 1st Battalion was already on board. Once at sea, they received their orders from Admiral Hart. The *President Harrison* would first unload the 4th Marines at Olongapo, where they were charged with the beach defense of Subic Bay under the command of Lieutenant Colonel Curtis Thurston Beecher. Then she would complete the final leg of her journey to Manila, sixty miles to the south.

Shortly after midnight on November 29 the last U.S. naval forces withdrew from Shanghai. By dawn the *Luzon*, carrying Admiral Glassford and George's friend, medical officer Lieutenant Alfred Littlefield Smith, had steamed past the Yangtze fairway buoys and was heading south in the China Sea, followed by the *Oahu*. The sea was calm and the weather was clear until the *Luzon* pulled out of the lee of the islands off Hangchow Bay. Then the wind picked up, and the waves began to surge. It was the season of the northeast monsoon.

To avoid the storm, the captain set a course south by southwest. That way the *Luzon* would pass through the Formosa Strait, taking advantage of the lee formed by Formosa's western shore and repairing to Hong Kong if necessary.

On the morning of December 1 a squadron of Japanese planes flying in perfect *V* formation appeared overhead at a mere 3,000 feet, then disappeared to the south, only to reappear in the north, a maneuver that was repeated throughout the day. The *Luzon* increased her speed from fifteen to seventeen knots. By the time she approached the northern tip of Formosa, the seas were high and the troughs long. Instead of taxing the steering engine and using too much rudder, the helmsmen learned to "let her yaw." The little ship rose up the waves, then slid down them, with a disconcertingly sharp roll. Lifelines enabled officers and crew to walk about the ship without worry—until Japanese men-of-war were spotted on the horizon.

One Japanese destroyer passed between the *Luzon* and the *Oahu* flying the international signal for "Stop." A little later another cautioned, "You are heading into danger," while a third insisted: "Head north immediately." A Japanese cruiser aimed its guns but withheld its fire. The American gunboats cavalierly answered by hoisting an "interrogatory" signal, indicating that the commands had not been understood or were being summarily ignored. Later that afternoon a Japanese merchant ship sped up astern of the *Luzon*, its searchlight flashing an unintelligible message.

The gunboats resumed their southerly course. The *Luzon* radioed Admiral Hart in Manila, who dispatched the minesweeper *Finch* and the submarine rescue vessel *Pigeon*, should the gunboats require assistance. But the rescue vessels themselves needed help. The *Pigeon* had not only damaged her rudder on the high seas, she had lost one of her anchors. The *Finch*, which had to tow the sister ship, had lost both anchors and limped toward the lee of Formosa for repairs.

Japanese aircraft and men-of-war shadowed the little fleet through December 2 and 3, but the gunboats faced another, more immediate danger. Once they were in the Formosa Strait, the seas turned choppy and they could no longer ride the waves. A northerly gale combined with a strong current blew up mountains of water. The gunboats soared to a peak, then lunged into a receding crest, pitching 28 to 30 degrees in a breathtaking three-second roll. A wall of green water slammed into the forecastle of the *Luzon* while the surging sea engulfed the stern, threatening to turn the ship broadside. The captain worked furiously to keep the swells behind him. He cut the speed and steered gingerly. The engine raced anyway, grinding, whining, a terrifying, inhuman sound of metal straining against metal that sent a shudder down the *Luzon*'s spine.

As the gunboats neared southern Formosa, a Japanese cruiser flying a Rear Admiral's flag approached the *Luzon*, sending an "Admiral to Admiral" signal. By searchlight it requested, "Please alter your course ten degrees to the left to clear our exercise area," and that was all. Glassford breathed a sigh of relief; he was happy to oblige.

The change in course oriented the *Luzon* and the *Oahu* directly toward Manila, but getting there was hell. Glassford now realized it would have been wiser to have avoided Formosa entirely. As he clung to a weather rail of the *Luzon*'s bridge deck just before dawn on December 4, he wondered if they would make it. Not the gunboats, which had performed valiantly, but the men themselves. At one point the *Luzon* rolled a heart-stopping 45 degrees to starboard, then 46 degrees to port. Smokestacks choked on water. Al Smith watched dishes that had been on a shelf protected by a side rail come sailing over the deck and smash into pieces. Waves lashed the *Luzon* with such force that her sides were indented between the ribs. The *Oahu* was in even worse shape. The ship's inclinometer recorded an almost unbelievable roll of 56 degrees to starboard and 50 degrees to port. The forward hold and the ship's officer and forward crew's compartments were flooded. For two nights the stalwarts of the Yangtze Patrol had gone without sleep and hot food. It was impossible to sit down without being jerked around violently by the ship's movements, much less rest.

And then, in an event as miraculous as the sunrise itself, they found themselves in the lee of Luzon, the largest island in the Philippines, where the water was as smooth as glass. By the evening of December 4 the *Luzon* and the *Oahu*, storm-battered but safe, arrived in Manila. Under clear skies the next day, the fifty-five-year-old Admiral Glassford lowered the two-star ComYangPat flag, and the Yangtze Patrol, after eighty-eight years of operation, was officially dissolved, its gunboats attached to the navy's Inshore Patrol.

The *President Harrison* had arrived in Manila on Tuesday, December 2. The journey was comparatively calm for George Ferguson and the 4th Marines, except for a reported strafing during the night. Machine guns had been strapped to topside rails, and blackout procedures were enforced. The men cheered when four American D-class submarines sent to escort them north of Formosa surfaced and displayed their colors. George was temporarily assigned to the Cañacao Naval Hospital, just south of the Cavite Navy Yard in the 16th Naval District. As he eagerly anticipated his orders for departure, he quartered at the Avenue Hotel in Manila.

On December 4 George heard the news he had been aching for: Fleet Surgeon Kenneth N. Lowman informed him that he would be leaving

Manila the following Monday via the *President Grant*. The long-awaited day had finally come. After more than two years as a Yangtze Patroller, George Ferguson was going home. Now he and Lucy could celebrate their first Christmas—and anniversary—together, fulfill the dreams they had shared in the letters they had written each other almost every day across an ocean of time. Now they could start a family.

The day was set, December 8. Back home, across the international dateline, it was Sunday, December 7, 1941.

2

Pearl of the Orient

FOUR MONTHS EARLIER, in August 1941, Lieutenant (j.g.) Murray Glusman watched crowds of well-wishers from the deck of the *President Garfield* as she prepared to sail from San Francisco. The air was filled with the shouts and cheers of families and friends. The young navy doctor looked elegant in a white suit offset by a dark necktie and complemented by white shoes, but he knew no one there. He threw a streamer of confetti toward the dock and watched it flutter into the bay to become, in a moment, no more than a bit of refuse.

The *President Garfield* now avoided Japan and skirted the Caroline and Mariana Islands north of Guam, which were under Japanese control. The ship was prohibited from radioing its position or announcing its arrival. But the cloak of secrecy made the nineteen-day journey to the Philippines no less pleasurable for its passengers—mostly military—with stops in Honolulu, Shanghai, Hong Kong, and finally Manila.

It was the most luxurious trip Murray had ever taken. Meals were sumptuous, movies were shown on deck, and there was gambling and of course drinking. He mixed with officers, socialized with civilians, and chatted with Lieutenant (j.g.) John Jacob Bookman, a fellow graduate of NYU's College of Medicine. He read in the reclining wooden chairs on the promenade, tried out his brand-new Graflex Speed Graphic camera, and gazed at the seabirds and flying fish skimming alongside the ship and the dolphins dancing in its wake. At night you could see the Southern Cross pinned to the dome of the sky. He was as far as he had ever been from home.

He loved the sea, the patterns of light on water, the pull of tides and currents, the smell of salt on skin. As a child in New York City, he had watched huge ocean liners—the *Franconia* and the *Mauretania*, the sister ship of the *Lusitania*—steam up Ambrose Channel and through the Narrows before they entered the Upper Bay of New York Harbor and tied up at their Hudson River berths on Manhattan's West Side. He imagined the vast distances they traveled, the distinguished guests and movie stars among the thousands of passengers they transported halfway across the world. Once he salvaged a naval history of the War of 1812 from a garbage can, took it home, and pored over it in the evenings, losing himself in the dramatic illustrations and stories about the sloops *Hornet*, *Wasp*, and other early American warships. And when he was a resident in neurology at Welfare Hospital on Welfare Island in the East River, he thrilled to the sight of PT (Patrol Craft Torpedo) boats darting up on practice runs from their base in the Brooklyn Navy Yard, where Lieutenant (j.g.) John Bulkeley commanded Submarine Chaser Division 2. One day a submarine nosed so close to Welfare Island, you could almost reach out and pet it. With its seemingly limitless horizons, the sea aroused in him a sense of mystery, challenge, and freedom.

His father, Lewis, had fled Odessa to avoid conscription in the Russo-Japanese War of 1904–5. His mother, Sophie, had emigrated to escape the poverty and pogroms in Kiev under Tsar Nicholas. They arrived in America as teenagers not speaking a word of English, met, married, and had three children. They settled at 335 East Houston Street, two of 1,562,000 Jews who emigrated to the United States between 1881 and 1910 and turned Manhattan's Lower East Side into the largest Jewish community in the world. "Little Israel," it was called.

The building on East Houston was a shtetl unto itself, with a butcher, grocer, furrier, hat maker, bootblack, bookkeeper, and even a few peddlers among its residents. The tenants were mostly Russian and Austro-Hungarian; a few Italians lived next door. Lewis learned enough English to finish first at the Brooklyn College of Pharmacy, then set up his own drugstore. An observant Jew, he kept a kosher household but still worked on Saturdays.

His life in America revolved around his business. He never seemed to enjoy the independence his long work hours had earned. A stern man with a quick temper, he denied himself almost any luxury. The atmosphere in the house was stultifying for his elder son, Sidney, and his youngest child, Estelle. She remembered Lewis hunched over a table at night, reviewing the day's accounts, a bare lightbulb overhead.

Houston Street was in the heart of the city's Tenth Ward, which in 1900 was the most crowded spot on earth. Eighty-two thousand people lived in a half-square mile, more than 700 people per acre. It was squalid, noisy, and cramped, with six-story walk-ups, basement apartments, windowless tenement rooms, and sweatshops. In 1914, the year Murray was born, a male garment worker earned about thirty-five cents an hour. At night the neighborhood came alive with dance halls.

The clash of Old World and New, sacred and profane, enfranchised and dispossessed, created fertile ground for political activism and artistic innovation. The sculptor Jacob Epstein, the painter Max Weber, the novelist Henry Roth, and songwriters Ira Gershwin and Irving Berlin all had their roots in New York City's Lower East Side. Home to the *Jewish Daily Forward* under Abraham Cahan, the largest Yiddish daily newspaper in the world, it was hearth to the fires of trade unionism, socialism, communism, and anarchism. Many of its denizens were first-generation Americans determined to make it—in business, law, medicine, and entertainment— and to do so on their own terms.

The store on the corner of East Houston Street sold patent medicines—elixirs and emollients, salves and solutions—and prescribed drugs that Lewis made by hand with a mortar and pestle, calibrated carefully and packaged individually. Large glass jars labeled in Latin held medicinal powders. Amber and cobalt bottles with green stoppers lined high wooden shelves that were reached by a sliding ladder. Pills were stored in small oak filing drawers until they were counted out onto a pill board and poured into bottles to fill prescriptions. Business transactions took place in a backroom, where a clerk by the name of Max Levine balanced accounts. Sophie spent much of her time at the front of the store, greeting friends and neighbors, exchanging gossip and news. The family rarely ate together, except for an occasional meal at Ratner's on Delancey Street, because work was Lewis's priority.

Patrons relied on Lewis for medical advice and first aid. He was the liaison to the nearest hospital in case of an emergency—a broken bone, for example—that he couldn't treat. The first recorded telephone exchange in America originated in a pharmacy, and since few of Lewis's neighbors had phones in the 1920s, they used the drugstore for incoming and outgoing calls. As a young boy, Murray collected nickel tips for delivering messages left by callers.

The pharmacy was part general store and part emergency room before hospitals had their own ER units. Pharmacists also had access to alcohol and engaged in bootlegging during Prohibition, a lucrative but risky business in Lewis's case since one of the most famous Prohibition "dicks" of the era, Izzy Einstein, lived just below him.

You could always tell when there was a serious accident in the neighborhood because a crowd would be milling in front of the pharmacy waiting for an ambulance to arrive from Bellevue Hospital, the first hospital in the nation to offer a municipal ambulance service. The ambulances were built on a Model T Ford chassis and had an open back, a fold-down seat on one side, and a gurney on the other. In their smart hospital uniforms with their Civil War, kepi-style hats, the interns cut an impressive figure. Quickly and authoritatively they moved through throngs of bystanders to attend the victim of a streetcar accident, a gunshot wound, or a cinder lodged in the eye. The pharmacist's son, Murray, had a ringside seat. That's what I want to be, he thought: a doctor.

Like his own father, he was fascinated by chemicals. He attended Townsend Harris Hall high school, which attracted some of the city's brightest young minds and where Jonas Salk was a student. He applied to Columbia College but at fifteen was considered too young, so he attended New York University instead, majoring in chemistry and fulfilling his pre-med requirements. In 1934 he entered the College of Medicine at New York University–Bellevue Medical Center and was awarded his M.D. in June 1938, by which time Germany had already annexed Austria.

Lewis adored Murray. He was the emblem of his success in America, and perhaps that knowledge gave Murray the confidence to pursue a lifestyle completely foreign to the one he encountered in his own home, yet without fear of losing his place in the family. He laughed at the mystical beliefs of his *zaide,* who accepted Kabbalist texts as truth and in a fury told Murray he would grow up to be a bum. He rejected his father's orthodoxy, dated non-Jewish girls, and became good friends in his residency with the Protestant chaplain, the Reverend H. W. van Couenhoven, affectionately known as Father Van. He was tickled by the slapstick humor of Laurel and Hardy and enjoyed listening to music, be it a Beethoven symphony or one of the popular songs of the day with curiously foreboding titles—"Smoke Gets in Your Eyes," "Deep Purple," or "Two Cigarettes in the Dark." He especially enjoyed hearing his girlfriend Laura sing.

They had fallen in love in the summer of '39 at Unity House, a resort in Pennsylvania's Pocono Mountains established by the International Ladies' Garment Workers Union. Murray had worked there as a waiter in high school when he was a member of the Young People's Socialist League, and he returned as the resident physician. Laura was on the entertainment staff. Unity House was a large adult camp that catered to Jewish singles and young marrieds. There was Lake Tamiment for rowing and canoeing, tennis courts and riding trails, and secluded Deer Lake for romantic walks in the woods. On top of Bushkill Mountain was Camp Tamiment, where Murray had also been a guest.

Tamiment was founded by the American Socialist Party and funded by the Rand School for Social Research. Its inspired cultural program attracted an extraordinary array of talent. Max Liebman directed The Tamiment Players and perfected the concept of the weekly Saturday-night musical revue. On a tip from composer-lyricist Sylvia Fine, he discovered a crazy redheaded comedian by the name of Daniel Kaminsky whom he signed in 1939 to play opposite Imogene Coca under the stage name of Danny Kaye. And he lured a brilliant nineteen-year-old dancer by the name of Jerome Rabinowitz to Tamiment, where he introduced his first choreographic work, *Death of a Loyalist*, under the name of Jerry Robyns, later known as Jerome Robbins. The songs, skits, and dances presented each week by The Tamiment Players became the basis of *The Straw Hat Review*, which was produced on Broadway at a cost of $8,000 in the autumn of 1939. As much as he loved Tamiment's Saturday-night revues Murray never missed an opportunity to hear Laura sing.

A coloratura soprano, she had a beautiful voice. "America's youngest opera singer," the *Philadelphia Ledger* announced the year before when listing her appearance as Olympia, the mechanical doll, in Offenbach's *Tales of Hoffmann*. "Baby Opera Star," said the caption above a photograph of the self-possessed nineteen-year-old with shoulder-length brown hair, a full mouth, dark eyes, and a gaze that coyly avoided the camera. She had studied piano with her father, the choir director of a local temple in the Bronx that was so dilatory in paying his salary that he declared himself an atheist. She majored in music at Hunter and took voice lessons from Henry Baron, who had performed at the Metropolitan Opera House. Once she began to audition, she changed her name from Reichman to Reade, her stage name.

Charming, vivacious, outgoing, and fastidious, Laura was the kind of woman to whom a man who was naturally reserved was instantly attracted; she made him feel different from the way others perceived him and from the way he thought of himself—bolder, more spontaneous, more fun, and more at ease. There was a warmth to her speaking voice and a resonance to her letters that was at once yielding and embracing. She lit up the room. She knew she'd landed a catch with Murray, and she made sure she was on her best behavior with him, wasn't too impetuous, and kept a lid on a mouth that could make a marine blush. Murray took her places she couldn't easily afford—restaurants, concerts, shows. He'd dated many women before, but he felt there was an unspoken understanding between them. Laura kept a photograph of Murray posed in front of Lake Tamiment wearing an open-collar short-sleeve shirt beneath a dark-colored sweater vest with his hands on his hips. He looked like he owned the world.

In the spring of 1940 American involvement in Europe seemed imminent. Some of the attending physicians at Welfare Hospital had fled Berlin and Vienna to escape Nazi persecution. Murray was young, healthy, built like a football player with wavy mahogany hair, and single. He had fashioned a life for himself that he loved, but he knew he was an ideal candidate: he could be of service.

He associated the army with the horrific trench warfare of the Great

War and reasoned that if you had to fight, if you had to go to war, you might as well live it up beforehand, and the way to live it up was in the navy. Either you survived a battle at sea, or you went down with your ship—a clean end to the story.

So in November 1940 he joined the Naval Reserve, and as an assistant surgeon with the rank of lieutenant (j.g.) he requested duty on a battleship. He was called up in June 1941 and reported to the Third Naval District in Brooklyn on July 7. Just one week prior he had been appointed Chief Resident in Neurology at Welfare Hospital. His professional career was stopped dead in its tracks; his plans for research in neuropsychiatry were put on hold. With a simple order from the chief of the Bureau of Navigation, Chester W. Nimitz, he found himself in a completely new hierarchy, and he was on the bottom rung of it.

Three months was standard training for men to become officers— "ninety-day wonders," they were called. Murray had three weeks. He learned about the Navy Regulations and Customs for Medical Corps officers through a fourteen-assignment correspondence course. He had been at the U.S. Naval Hospital in Brooklyn for such a brief time that the commanding officer, Captain G. E. Robertson, remarked in his Report on the Fitness of Officers: "This officer has been on duty at this hospital too short a period to form a true opinion of his ability." His only other training had been two months of ROTC at New York University in 1930. That didn't stop the U.S. Navy from giving him orders to sail for Manila on August 8, 1941.

His family said goodbye to him at Grand Central Station as he waited for the sleek Twentieth Century Limited that would take him to Chicago in a mere sixteen hours en route to San Francisco. Their farewell was emotional yet typically restrained. Murray tried to make light of the situation by giving his parents a fifth of bourbon as a parting gift. Lewis was proud of his son for becoming a doctor, proud that his adopted country had vowed to defeat Nazism. But he was also deeply worried. He decided not to open the bottle until he knew Murray was safe. The last thing Murray saw from his Pullman car window was his brother Sidney running alongside as the locomotive slowly gathered speed.

On a drizzly afternoon in September 1941 the *President Garfield* eased into Manila Bay. On her port side was Corregidor, the tadpole-shaped island that warned ships of its presence with a nineteenth-century Spanish lighthouse and massive coastal guns. On the starboard side you could see the mountains of Batangas Province. The *Garfield* slipped into her berth at Pier 7, and when John Bookman and Murray Glusman stepped off the gangway, they found themselves in a city that could have sprung from one of Somerset Maugham's tales of the South Seas.

The waterfront was bustling with Filipino laborers. The smell of copra was everywhere. Lieutenant Commander H. C. Brokenshire, an attending surgeon, greeted the two men. A corpsman drove them to Sangley Point, a hook-shaped peninsula on the southern end of Manila Bay that housed the U.S. Naval Hospital at Cañacao.

There was a reason Manila was called the Pearl of the Orient. A necklace of elegant houses encircled Manila Bay. Coconut palm trees swayed along the shoreline, and an equestrian trail ran nearby, beyond which rose dark green hills and mountains that turned purple in the haze. The sunsets were as beautiful as the undulating iridescence on the inside of an oyster shell. The jewel in the American commonwealth, Manila was a symbol of U.S. power in the Pacific, won after Commodore George Dewey's momentous naval victory over Spain in the war of 1898. At low tide you could see the rusting hulks of the Spanish Fleet off the Cavite Navy Yard.

Pier 7 was known as the "million-dollar pier," built in the 1920s on reclaimed land to accommodate luxury liners. Just beyond lay Dewey Boulevard, which boldly announced American interests. The Manila Hotel, where General Douglas MacArthur made his home in a sumptuous mahogany-paneled suite, overlooked the water. Across Luneta Park was the elegant Army-Navy Club, where you could sip drinks on the veranda for fifteen or twenty cents apiece as you watched the sun set or listen to old "sunshiners" at the bar tell tall tales once too often and impress junior officers with little except a capacious talent for alcoholic consumption. Due south was the Malacañang Palace, the residence of the president of the Commonwealth of the Philippines, Manuel L. Quezon. Stately and imposing, it was a dramatic contrast to the wood-frame dwellings that grew out of the landscape, and it conveyed wealth that was anything but common.

The streets of Manila were crowded with stalls that reeked of deep-fat frying. Vendors hawked their wares and cried *"Balut"*—duck eggs that were just ready to hatch before they were boiled in water and sold as a delicacy. Cab drivers swerved like madmen to avoid *caretelas,* the two-wheeled carriages pulled by *calesa* ponies. Donkeys and *carabao*—water buffalo—swayed beneath their burdens. Bicycles veered in front of brightly colored, red and yellow Pambusco buses. *Cascos*—cargo boats used as houseboats—bobbed along the Pasig River. In the old walled city of Intramuros, men stood in doorways smoking black cigars and women sat beside windows chewing betel nuts.

The ride to Cañacao gave the navy doctors their first glimpse of the rural Philippines. The natives lived in *nipa* huts, shacks built on stilts and made from bamboo with roofs of thatch. The floors were slatted so you could drop scraps down to the pigs and chickens below. The dwellings were more primitive than the worst tenement conditions John and Murray had ever seen in New York City. But it was hard not to respond to the friendliness of the Filipinos or admire the simplicity of a lifestyle that depended on the fish they caught and the rice they harvested for sustenance. The language they spoke was Tagalog, meaning "of the river."

Cañacao, which stood in a lush tropical setting on the west fork of Sangley Point, was under the command of Captain Robert G. Davis. The hospital had been built by the Spanish in 1871 and was originally managed by the Sisters of Charity. After the Spanish-American War it was operated by the U.S. Navy to support the naval base at Cavite, across Cañacao Bay on the east fork. The Pan American Clipper touched down just offshore and made weekly runs between Manila and San Francisco, moving passengers and mail. It was a five-day trip, weather permitting.

The army had its own facility near Intramuros. Sternberg General Hospital was named after the father of American bacteriology, George Miller Sternberg, who served as Surgeon General during the Spanish-American War. Colonel Percy J. Carroll was the hospital's commanding officer.

The Army Medical Department was established in 1818 to reform a grossly inadequate medical service that had changed little since the days of the American Revolution. The Navy Medical Department—the Bureau of Medicine and Surgery (BUMED)—was formed in 1842 to address the health problems seamen had faced since the so-called Quasi-War with France in 1798–1800. In the aftermath of the Spanish-American War, an Army Nurse Corps was created in 1901, and a Navy Nurse Corps followed suit in 1908. The marines comprised a separate service within the navy, while the Air Corps was literally the wing of the army.

BUMED was younger than the Army Medical Department, smaller, and clubbier. "The navy gets the gravy," the saying went. BUMED also had the advantage of being overseen by Rear Admiral Ross T. McIntire, Roosevelt's personal physician who reported to the Chief of Naval Operations.

Navy doctors were assisted by medical corpsmen who had undergone two months' training at the Medical Field Service School on the Marine Corps base in San Diego, California. You began as a Hospital Apprentice, 2nd Class—an "HA deuce"—advanced to Hospital Corpsman, made Pharmacist's Mate with the first stripe, and went on up to Chief Petty Officer if talent and opportunity allowed.

Corpsmen were responsible for evacuation of the wounded; they performed all nursing and first aid functions, swept floors, cleaned clinics, made beds, and disinfected heads. "The women did all the brainwork," quipped one corpsman. "Candy asses need not apply!" bragged another.

If rivalry was fostered between the army and the navy, the navy and the marines were as tight as ticks. Marines called navy corpsmen "Doc" out of respect and bought them drinks after hours; navy whites could often be seen in the company of marines in khakis or in greens.

In the field corpsmen carried canvas musette bags stenciled with a red cross above USN in black block letters. Standard-issue supplies were six gauze bandages; a diagnostic tag book and pencil; four tubes of tincture of iodine; one bottle of ammonia; two rubber tourniquets; an instrument case containing pins, scissors, and forceps; eight packages of sublimated gauze; one jackknife; one spool of adhesive plaster; and one roll of wire for splints. In the Philippines, corpsmen were also supplied with sodium chloride (salt) pills, halazone tablets (for water purification), sulfadiazine (an antibacterial agent for wounds), quinine sulfate, and morphine tartrate syrettes (for pain). Medical officers were armed with a hypodermic needle sterilizer, operating scissors and knives, forceps, silk braided sutures, a clinical thermometer, and an eye dressing and burn injury kit.

John Bookman remained at Cañacao until September 21, when he was transferred to the Navy Section Base at Mariveles, on the southern tip of the Bataan peninsula, thirty miles west of Manila. He had graduated from medical school in 1939, a year after Murray, but because he joined the Naval Reserve a few days earlier, he had seniority over him. John would become the medical officer in charge of the dispensary at Mariveles. He had made a pallid impression on Murray.

Murray, meanwhile, was ordered to report to the Cavite Navy Yard, where his work in the dispensary, Admiral Hart stated, was "required in the public interests." He would have preferred duty at sea, but being in the Philippines, he quickly realized, was an education in itself.

———

If you think of Luzon as a giant lobster claw with its grip around Manila Bay, the Bataan peninsula to the west becomes the pincer and the province of Cavite to the east is the crusher. Hot and dusty in the dry season, crowded with *nipa* shacks, Cavite played a pivotal role in the history of the Philippines. Cavite was the site of the old Spanish naval arsenal just eight miles south of Manila, and a seedbed of Filipino insurgency dating back to January 20, 1872, when rebels attempted to overthrow its small Spanish fort, San Felipe. Loyalist troops quelled the rebellion, and thirty to forty Cavitenos were swiftly executed. Three Filipino priests fighting for equal recognition—Burgos, Gómez, and Zamora—were unfairly implicated in the Cavite mutiny. The thorn in the side of the Spanish clergy, they were summarily tried, tortured, and garroted in public. Their execution stoked the flames of Filipino nationalism.

Twenty-five years later, the firebrand Emilio Aguinaldo spearheaded a revolution in Cavite and declared himself leader of his own republic, until he was persuaded by the Spanish to relinquish his claim for cash on condition that he leave the Philippines. Aguinaldo went into exile in Hong Kong, where he remained true to the revolutionary cause and purchased arms in support of it. He was in Singapore in April 1898 when he approached the American consul who cabled Commodore George Dewey back in Hong Kong. "I requested him to come," Dewey wrote in his autobiography, "as it was possible that he might have valuable information at a time when no source of information was to be neglected." War between the United States and Spain had been on the horizon since the U.S. battleship *Maine* was sunk in Havana harbor on February 15, 1898, at a cost of 260 lives. A native-led insurrection against the Spanish in the Philippines could bolster the American cause for intervention, just as Cuban patriots fighting for independence played into the hands of American expansionists. *Cavitismo,* as it came to be known, was the embodiment of the Filipino rebellious spirit.

Once Congress demanded Spain's withdrawal from Cuba and granted President McKinley the right to intervention, Spain declared war on the United States on April 24, 1898. The United States responded by declaring war on Spain the next day, retroactive to April 21. The first salvo was fired not at Cuba but 10,000 miles away, in the Philippines.

On May 1, 1898, just minutes after midnight, Commodore Dewey slipped into Manila Bay on the flagship USS *Olympia* to locate and engage the Spanish squadron. The *Baltimore, Raleigh, Petrel, Concord,* and *Boston* followed at a distance of 400 yards between ships. A tropical haze hung over the water in the early morning hours, but at 5:40 A.M. the enemy was spotted within 5,000 yards, just off Sangley Point. Dewey casually ordered his captain: "You may fire when you are ready, Gridley."

Eleven out of twelve warships in the Spanish battle line were sunk in just seven hours. Spain, which began colonial rule under Miguel López de Legazpi in 1565, suddenly lost the first Asian country appropriated by the West. The United States not only won its first important naval battle since the War of 1812, it made its first territorial conquest overseas. With Spain's defeat, Cuba was granted independence, while Guam, Puerto Rico, and the Philippines became U.S. possessions.

America gained one of the finest natural harbors in the Pacific, but it had not won the support of the Filipino people. Dewey unofficially supported insurgent operations against the Spanish in the Philippines, allowed Aguinaldo to take up quarters in Cavite, and even provided him with arms. Washington took a harder line. Meanwhile, Aguinaldo assumed control of Luzon and declared Filipino independence on June 12, 1898. He called for a constitutional convention, which drafted the first democratic constitution in Asia—only to have his plans undermined when Spain, which had surrendered its garrison in Manila to the United States, granted the United States sovereignty over the Philippines for a $20 million payment.

A reluctant imperialist, President McKinley had sampled the mood of the American public and declared that the Filipino people were "unfit for self-government." But McKinley was an ardent Christian who wanted to prove "that the mission of the United States" was one of "benevolent assimilation." At the time, Major General Elwell Stephen Otis commanded American troops in Luzon. In a draft proclamation McKinley cabled to Otis on December 26, 1898, before the Senate had ratified the Treaty of Paris, the president proposed annexation of the archipelago.

To Aguinaldo this meant war, and he rallied 30,000 troops against his new enemy. But once again the United States fired the first shot, this time to quell the so-called insurrection, which escalated into the full-blown Philippine-American War. It was a bloody, gruesome conflict. The Americans tortured their Filipino captives by forcing water down their throats and pouncing on their stomachs to elicit confessions. The Filipinos buried American prisoners of war alive and sprinkled trails of sugar toward their mouths so they could be devoured by ants. The Americans razed to the ground entire villages of men, women, and children, and it appears that they shot wounded prisoners.

Savagery was easy to justify against an enemy seen as subhuman. Rudyard Kipling's poem "The White Man's Burden," written in 1899 in response to the war, immortalized Western perceptions of Asians as "fluttered folk and wild . . . sullen peoples, half devil and half child."

Brigadier General Jacob Smith adopted that view with a vengeance in one of the most brutal campaigns waged by Americans in the Philippines. To retaliate for a surprise Filipino attack on the seventy-four-man garrison of Company C, 9th U.S. Infantry, at Balangiga on September 28, 1901, Smith allegedly ordered Major Littleton W. T. Waller to "kill and burn," to turn the island of Samar into "a howling wilderness." The objective was to eradicate guerrilla forces led by Vicente Lukban. No Filipino over ten years of age was to be spared. By year-end, more than 750 *insurrectos* had been captured or killed, and more than 1,600 homes were destroyed.

The "war of insurrection" outraged many Americans. At its peak, the United States committed 71,528 troops—nearly three-quarters of its army—to the distant archipelago. Filipinos were hired to assist in the battle against Aguinaldo's forces and then formed into the Philippine Scouts. By February 1901 the Philippine Scouts were an official unit of the U.S. Army.

That same month Mark Twain excoriated American imperialism in an essay that appeared in the *New York Sun* entitled "To the Person Sitting in Darkness." "There must be two Americas," Twain thundered. "One that sets the captive free, and one that takes a once-captive's new freedom away from him, and picks a quarrel with him with nothing to found it on; then kills him to get his land."

Aguinaldo was captured in 1901, the insurrection was declared over in 1902, though resistance continued for years. Dead were 20,000 Filipino soldiers and an estimated 200,000 civilians. With the U.S. victory, the forces of civilization had won over "the black chaos of savagery and barbarism," proclaimed President Theodore Roosevelt.

As if to atone for a war they initiated, the Americans began building a nation. They constructed roads and bridges, dug dams and artesian wells. They engineered sanitation and sewage systems, eradicated smallpox, introduced a five-day work week, and instituted American-style public school education with English as the language of instruction. The city's most illustrious buildings were intended to evoke the neoclassical ideal that inspired Daniel Burnham's architecture in Washington, D.C. The Army-Navy Club was erected in 1909, the Manila Hotel in 1912, and both were designed by Burnham's student William Parsons. William Howard Taft, the first civil governor of the Philippines, commissioned Burnham himself to design the summer capital at Baguio in the style of an Adirondack great camp, nestled in northern Luzon among verdant forests and cooled by mountain breezes.

By then relations between Americans and "our little brown brothers," as Taft dubbed them, were warm, though gross economic inequities persisted and America monopolized imports into the Philippines. The Filipinos accepted American institutions and benefited from their "can do" optimism and expertise. In 1935 the United States granted the Philippines "internal autonomy," and Manuel L. Quezon, who had fought as a nationalist guerrilla during the "insurrection" and surrendered to Major General Arthur MacArthur in 1900, became the first president of the commonwealth. As called for by the Tydings-McDuffie Act, the Philippines would achieve independence in 1946.

In the spring of 1934 Quezon approached MacArthur's son, Douglas, with the idea of becoming his national defense adviser. Douglas MacArthur had seen three tours of duty in the Philippines and was chief of staff of the U.S. Army. He had genuine affection for the mercurial Quezon. His enjoyment of the Filipino people, he said, exerted "a grip that has never relaxed." Nothing if not confident, he assured Quezon that under his guidance the Philippines would be able to defend itself by the time it gained independence. Roosevelt and Secretary of War George H. Dern approved the appointment, which MacArthur saw as a "fitting end" to his military career.

But the primary role of the Philippine Army, according to the U.S. Army's War Plans Division, was not defense but the suppression of armed insurrection. Due to the lack of resources, it "would be wholly ineffective, in itself, to protect the Philippine Islands against Japan." For that the Philippines would have to depend on the United States. It was a fact that caused Quezon, whose "first duty" was to the Filipino citizenry, great ambivalence in his personal relations with MacArthur and toward America's war strategy in the Philippines.

Since the Russo-Japanese War of 1904–5, the United States had regarded Japan as its only potential enemy in the Pacific. As early as 1906 Leonard Wood, who became governor general of the Philippines, predicted a Japanese attack on Hawaii as well as the Philippines. Manila was some 5,000 miles from Honolulu, but a mere 1,800 from Tōkyō, and Manila Bay was coveted as one of the most desirable natural harbors in the East.

Strategists argued that the Philippine Division, the primary U.S. Army unit in the islands (consisting of the Philippine Scouts and one American regiment), was no match for the Japanese. U.S. Army War College studies predicted that Manila could be held for only a few months in the event of a Japanese attack. Others argued that Manila Bay had no strategic significance since the Pacific Fleet couldn't possibly arrive in time to relieve the defenders. At best, the defense of the area would be part of a sacrificial delaying action.

In its war plans the Joint Army and Navy Board had assigned Japan the color orange, and the United States the color blue. The strategy to defeat Japan was referred to as War Plan Orange and called for the retreat of 43,000 troops to the Bataan peninsula in an attempt to stave off the enemy, hold Corregidor, and thereby protect Manila Bay. At the first shot the main components of the U.S. Asiatic Fleet were to withdraw behind the Malay barrier and engage Japanese shipping while awaiting the Pacific Fleet's westward advance from Pearl Harbor. But in spite of numerous revisions to the plan, the latest being War Plan Orange-3, the same conclusion emerged: the Philippines could not be defended. The Philippines relied on the United States for its defense, yet the United States had long written it off as indefensible. Europe, Roosevelt decided in January 1940, came first.

General MacArthur, however, considered WPO-3 defeatist. On July 27, 1941, he was named commander of the newly formed U.S. Army Forces in the Far East (USAFFE), which comprised 31,000 U.S. Army troops and 120,000 officers and enlisted men in the Philippine Army. The next month WPO-3 blossomed into the Rainbow Plan, which gave precedence to the war against Germany over the war in the Pacific theater. MacArthur nonetheless insisted that the Philippines could be defended. The "citadel type defense" of Manila Bay, envisioned in the Orange and Rainbow Plans, had to be changed to an all-out defense of the archipelago. A fleet of motor torpedo boats and the addition of B-17 bombers could protect the coast of Luzon, MacArthur claimed. The newly mobilized Philippine Army would make enemy infiltration "practically impossible" because it would hold the beaches "at all costs."

The War Department agreed and in November 1941 incorporated MacArthur's tactical ideas into the revised plan known as Rainbow 5. In a matter of weeks the granite-jawed general had managed to reverse decades of military thinking. He was convinced that the Japanese wouldn't attempt an invasion of the Philippines until April 1942, by which time the defending forces would have increased to 200,000 men.

Army Chief of Staff General George Catlett Marshall promised that U.S. troop strength in the Philippines would be doubled by the end of 1941. Hundreds of B-17 heavy bombers would arrive as soon as possible, vowed Secretary of War Henry Lewis Stimson, a former governor of the Philippines, to be followed by hundreds of pursuit planes and heavy guns in early 1942.

It was as if the army had single-handedly declared possible what the navy had long said was improbable. As Admiral Albert Winterhalter, commander in chief of the U.S. Asiatic Fleet, tersely expressed his opinion in a cable to the Office of Naval Operations in 1916:

```
BELIEVE SUCCESSFUL DEFENSE OF ALL PHILIPPINES
OR ANY PART IMPRACTICABLE, PROHIBITIVE COST
NEEDLESS SACRIFICE. COMMAND OF SEA ONLY
PROPER SECURITY. NAVY BASES UNDEFENDED
USELESS.
```

By September 1941, the Cavite Navy Yard was a beehive of activity. Commands in English and conversations in Tagalog were interrupted by the sounds of hammering, welding, drilling, and riveting. Engines whined, ensigns cursed, and dock hands hurried to tie up boats or undo lines for the vessels coming and going from the horseshoe-shaped pier.

The major port facility of the Asiatic Fleet since the autumn of 1940, the Navy Yard was built around old Fort San Felipe and occupied the eastern half of Cavite, whose name, derived from the Tagalog *kawit*, means "hook." At peak capacity, some 6,000 to 8,000 Filipinos and Americans worked there day and night. Their job was to repair and arm the boats in Lieutenant John Bulkeley's Motor Torpedo Boat (MTB) Squadron 3, as well as maintain and supply the six S-class submarines, the tenders and minesweepers, cruisers and destroyers of the Asiatic Fleet that were between patrols, escorts, or naval exercises in the southern islands.

Machine shops, storehouses, a foundry, a radio laboratory, and a receiving station lined Guadalupe Pier. The *Pillsbury* and the *Peary*, the latter an old four-stack destroyer that was the flagship of Destroyer Division 59, were moored at Central Wharf. The submarine tender *Otus* docked at the head of Machina Wharf, where two fleet-type submarines, the *Seadragon* and the *Sealion*, floated next to the minesweeper *Bittern*. A power plant, a joiner shop, a captain's quarters, a drafting room, and a submarine shop cornered Machina Wharf, at the tip of which was the destroyer receiving station and the dispensary.

Seven hundred tons of ammunition were stored at the center of the Navy Yard, which was protected by three antiaircraft batteries at Sangley Point (A), Caridad (B), and Binakayan (C), and was manned by the 1st Separate Marine Battalion at Cavite. The batteries were armed with four 3-inch dual-purpose (surface or air) guns of World War I vintage with a range of 15,000 feet, supported by water-cooled .50-caliber machine guns from Battery D. The high water level of Cavite meant that slit trenches could be dug to a depth of only two to three feet. An SCR-270B mobile air warning device on loan from the army and operated by the communications unit of the 1st Separate Marine Battalion was set up at Wawa Beach near Nasugbu, in Batangas Province, a hundred miles to the south. This was radar (an acronym for "radio detection and ranging"), and it was so secret that the mechanic who worked on the generator didn't even know what it was for. The 270B was designed for early air warning and could compute the distance and azimuth but not the altitude of an aircraft. It had a range of 196 miles, but there were only two other functioning units in the Philippines, one at Iba Field on Luzon's west coast, and another in Ilocos Norte, near the Cape Bojeador lighthouse on the north coast. The army's air warning system depended on primitive radar, visual surveillance, and "wooden ears" that could detect the rumble of aircraft from afar. Some were made by Native Americans in the 60th Coast Artillery Regiment on Corregidor; others were in northern Luzon. They were ingenious devices but limited in effectiveness by a range of only thirty miles and their inability to differentiate sounds.

Admiral Hart had a distant view of Cavite from the offices of the Asiatic Fleet in the Marsman Building on the Manila waterfront. The Japanese also closely watched Navy Yard activities and reported back to Tōkyō on arms shipments and troop arrivals. Thousands of Japanese had penetrated the fabric of Filipino life, dominating the photography business, operating service stations, and working as barbers and bartenders while they spied for their government. Nearly half the Japanese nationals in Manila, American counterintelligence estimated, were Japanese military reservists. Japanese military personnel had flown photoreconaissance missions in commercial airplanes over the Philippines. They had layouts of Malinta Tunnel on Corregidor and maps of coastal artillery positions, just as the Japanese before Pearl Harbor had obtained precise maps of military facilities down to the location of every U.S. battleship, submarine, seaplane tender, and torpedo net. The U.S. Navy extensively mined Subic Bay and Manila Bay, but from the air, the Cavite Navy Yard was an enemy aviator's dream.

Murray reported to Lieutenant Commander Hjalmer A. Erickson, Medical Officer of the Yard in charge of the dispensary.

"You and I have a lot in common," said Erickson, a Seventh-Day Adventist.

"We do?" the young lieutenant asked in surprise.

"Yes, we do."

"How so?"

"Well," he explained, "we observe the Sabbath just like Jews."

What a funny son of a bitch, Murray thought. Then again, the 16th Naval District had a reputation for funny sons of bitches. Rumor was the last commandant, Rear Admiral John M. Smeallie, had attempted seppuku by plunging a Moro dagger into his stomach and had to be invalided home. Rear Admiral Francis W. Rockwell took the distraught admiral's place.

The dispensary was a two-story wooden structure with a carpenter's shop on one side and a print shop on the other. Examination rooms were on the ground floor. The medical officers were housed in the bachelor officers' quarters above, which Murray shared with Erickson, Lieutenant (j.g.) Gordon K. Lambert, and Lieutenant (j.g.) Ferdinand V. "Fred" Berley. Erickson notwithstanding, it was a solid group of men, but it was Fred whom Murray found most interesting.

Fred had been transferred to Cavite on August 21, 1941, after serving at the regimental hospital in Shanghai. Slightly built but tough as nails, he was a former Golden Gloves champion with a bit of swagger. But he was affable, talkative, and always ready to offer advice—the kind of guy who knew the ropes before anyone else had even seen the rigging. Wasn't afraid to remind you of that fact, either. He loved to tell stories and often saw himself as a character in them. As if on cue, he'd narrow his eyes when the plot thickened, then open them wide in amazement as if hearing the denouement for the first time. He was disciplined, dedicated, well educated, and street smart.

A Chicagoan by birth, he was the eldest of three brothers whose father, Guy, had emigrated from Alta Monte, Italy, in 1898. A close-knit family, the Berleys lived on Chicago's West Side, a beautiful section of the city whose broad boulevards, open spaces, and natural attractions just beckoned to a young boy. A few blocks from where they lived was the vast Conservatory at Garfield Park, where you could see bananas, orchids, and palms growing in one of the eight exhibition halls. Walk west to lovely Columbus Park, and you could swim, play tennis, golf, explore the waterfalls, or just stroll along the streams that meandered through a meadow. Take the streetcar to the end of the line, and you'd be in the woods, which was where Fred spent much of his time as a Boy Scout, honing skills, learning how to be self-reliant and how to lead while still being part of a team.

His father worked long hours as an engineer for the Chicago Tunnel Company in the city's Loop. His uncle Sam encouraged the boys in sports—boxing, baseball, cycling, weightlifting. Fred bought a BB gun that he and his brother Guy used to target their kid brother, Alfred.

They'd set a bull's-eye on a pillow, set the pillow on Alfred's rear, and then fire away. "Some fun!" as Alfred described it. But Alfred worshiped his elder brother—a talented athlete, a gifted pianist, and captain of the high school fencing team. Fred excelled at whatever he put his mind to and had a knack for bringing home girls who, on Alfred's scorecard, were simply "knockouts."

Fred had wanted to be a naval officer for as long as he could remember. He wasn't so sure about medicine—that was his parents' idea. In 1930 he entered Northwestern University and joined the Naval Reserve Officer Training Corps. He graduated after four years with a commission as a line officer ensign, DVG (deck volunteer grade). His ambition was to be a naval aviator, but at five foot six he was too short to pass the physical. ROTC actually paid for a quarter of Northwestern Medical School, which was quite an incentive during the Depression, so medical school it was. There were cruises every summer in ROTC, and Fred found life aboard ship—slinging his own hammock, standing the various watches, firing the different guns, and engaging in battle practice, whether on a World War I submarine chaser or on the battleship USS *Arkansas*—fascinating.

In 1937, a year before graduating from Northwestern Medical School, the Medical Corps began examinations for navy internships. There were only twenty positions around the country. Fred placed fifteenth out of all the candidates and chose San Diego, where he did ob/gyn and pediatrics in civilian hospitals. There were only 731 medical officers in the navy at the time, so if you didn't know someone personally, chances were you knew about him through someone else.

Fred had first arrived in Manila in September 1939 on the *President Polk* and was assigned as medical officer of Destroyer Division 58, whose four ships, *Stewart*, *Barker*, *Parrott*, and *Bulmer*, roamed Philippine waters, engaged in torpedo practice near Mindanao, and maneuvered off southern China. Then he joined the regimental hospital of the 4th Marines in Shanghai.

In December 1940 he was given temporary duty for a week on the *Isabel*, the aging flagship of the Yangtze Patrol. Upriver he assisted the chief of surgery, a woman, at a hospital in Wuhu whose hallways were lined with patients. In those days a general surgeon did everything from brain surgery to orthopedics. They used cotton for sutures, which was new to Fred—he'd only worked with catgut and silk—and paper for sponges. Instruments were boiled, then placed in a Lysol solution and rinsed off with sterile water. The experience was invaluable and confirmed for him his professional goal.

He was tired of urology and, by the summer of '41, tired of Shanghai, which like an aging beauty had lost its charm. The regimental hospital needed to detach a junior medical officer, and Fred was happy to volunteer. Not until he was on board the *President Harrison* did he receive his orders to go to the 16th Naval District. He was ready for a change, even if Cavite was the last place on earth he would have chosen. What he wanted more than anything was to be a surgeon. He was dextrous and determined, and his mind was scalpel-sharp. He liked the precision that surgery demanded, the challenge, and the cool head it required when you were faced with unforeseen complications.

Murray admired Fred's forthrightness, but he was quieter by nature, less experienced in challenging authority, and less effective when doing so. It wasn't so much that he lacked self-confidence; sometimes he simply couldn't express himself in a way that best served his interests. Fred would call a spade a spade; Murray would wonder why a spade was a spade. He tended to think dialectically, so when he spoke, or questioned an assumption, there was often an ironic edge to what he said, which some found provoking. He didn't like showmen, had little tolerance for bluster, and his opinion showed. Sometimes he felt Fred's behavior bordered on braggadocio. For crying out loud, he'd brought along the Golden Gloves buckle he'd won as a kid, the teak chest he'd had custom made and monogrammed in Shanghai, even his little spaniel, Droog! But there was no denying it—Fred knew a lot, and not just about a few things, either. He could get away with saying what he thought because he was respectful, cooperative, and devoted to his work. He had a strong moral fiber and was a natural teacher, always willing to lend a helping hand. "A well trained medical officer who is interested in his profession," remarked Colonel Howard when he recommended Fred for a promotion in August 1941. "Personal and military character excellent." The new Fleet Surgeon had promised him, Fred wrote his parents, that "when our time comes to go home, we would go home on time and not any longer. So you can most definitely expect me to arrive around the first of March." Most definitely, indeed.

Duty at the dispensary consisted of routine physicals, vaccination checks on passengers from incoming boats and planes, and "short arm"—or venereal disease—inspections. Condoms were rarely used, as Fred discovered with the 4th Marines in Shanghai, so prophylaxis entailed irrigating the urethra with 10cc of Protargol (strong protein silver) in a glass V-shaped syringe. "The prevention of venereal disease is most important and must be faithfully and conscientiously carried out," urged Section 9 of the 1939 edition of *Handbook of the Hospital Corps, U.S. Navy*. "It is not agreeable duty, as the patients often are under the influence of liquor, foul-mouthed, and disorderly, but if venereal disease is prevented by the treatment it is worth all the effort expended."

In Chefoo, China, the U.S. Navy had virtually run a red-light district. Navy doctors examined all of the prostitutes in a two-square-block area for venereal disease, and whether voyeur or connoisseur, you had to surrender your liberty card to Shore Patrol in order to enter it. Then to get your liberty card back, you had to visit the venereal pro-phylactic station. Circumventing this process could result in losing your pay.

In Cavite, on- and off-base prophylactic stations were also estab-lished. The Marine Corps provost marshal was responsible for registering local prostitutes and bringing the "ladies" to the Navy Yard for inspec-tions twice weekly, Wednesdays and Saturdays. Venereal disease was a "persistent problem" in the native Filipino population, according to the Cavite health officer, Dr. Sanchez, and it reached almost epidemic pro-portions. For fifty dollars an enlisted man could buy or build a *nipa* hut and "shack up" with a barrio woman. Air Corps officers condoned such behavior: it helped control the incidence of infection and reduced the rate of alcoholism.

Navy corpsmen looked after the marines at the three antiaircraft bat-teries around Cavite, and the navy doctors made weekly visits to check on them. Every Wednesday Fred drove out to Battery C at Binakayan in a station wagon. Ernest J. "Ernie" Irvin, Pharmacist's Mate 2nd Class, hopped in for the ride back so he could stock up on sodium bicarbonate tablets, atropine, and first aid supplies from the dispensary.

The navy doctors conducted promotion exams for the marines and also had to be on hand at antiaircraft practice. One day 2nd Lieutenant Willard C. Holdredge of Battery C approached Murray: "Say doc, you wanna try to hit the target?"

At the edge of the tiny village of Binakayan, at the mouth of the Imus River, Battery C was so far off the beaten path that the navy could hardly keep track of it. Water-cooled machine guns were mounted on tripods in a turnip patch and trained on a target sleeve towed by a plane. The am-munition was painted different colors so you could identify which guns had scored a hit.

What the hell, Murray figured. He had never touched a machine gun in his life. His gunnery experience was confined to popping off kitchen mice as a kid with his Daisy air rifle. He took aim along with the other gunners, fired on command, and then ran over to the sleeve once it fell to the ground. It was clean except for one bullet hole—Murray's. These guys are going to be my protectors? he asked himself. I'm in deep trou-ble, he thought.

American soldiers in the Philippines worked "tropical hours"—from 6 A.M. to 1 P.M. Hours at the Navy Yard dispensary were also short, and the workload was light. Over at Sternberg the army doctors simply called it a day at noon.

It was a thoroughly enjoyable lifestyle for the medical officers, who shared a Chinese cook as well as a Filipino houseboy and whose monthly pay of $201.34 went a long way. The cook's salary was $15 to $20 a month, the houseboy $5 to $10, a *lavendera* or washerwoman cost $7.50 to $15. There were few automobiles in Cavite, so the men got around town in brightly colored *caretelas* or by bicycle.

On weekends Fred liked to play golf at the Wack-Wack Club outside Manila with Ernie Necker, the head of Mackay Radio, or he would hunt snipe in the rice paddies of Bataan with Fleet Surgeon Ken Lowman, who would then prepare a feast for the entire staff. Sometimes Murray would accompany them, not hunting but shooting the rural landscape with his new camera. He'd even brought along a blank album to keep a photographic record of his days in the Philippines.

For many Americans in the islands, news came via Don Bell's daily report at noon on KZRH ("The Voice of the Orient") while they tuned into KZRM and KZRF for the reigning hits—"My Heart Belongs to Daddy," "Chattanooga Choo Choo," and "The Boogie-Woogie Bugle Boy of Company B." The *Manila Daily Bulletin* ("The Exponent of Philippine Progress") catered to the American community and carried Associated Press, Reuters, United Press, and Bulletin Service newswires. You could even catch the UCLA-Stanford football game if you switched on the shortwave early in the morning.

Nights in Cavite the navy doctors would go out to dinner for Cantonese fried rice and sweet and sour pork, hit O. E. Hart's Dreamland cabaret (where a turn with a *bailarina* cost ten centavos), or take the *San Felipe* ferry to Manila. There they could see the latest Hollywood releases—Edward G. Robinson in *Tiger Shark*, Martha Raye and Dorothy Lamour in *Tropic Holiday*, Joan Davis and Jinx Falkenburg in *Two Latins from Manhattan*. Or they'd haunt the sleek Jai Alai Club with its four bars and four restaurants, drop in at the Alcazar, or stop by the Bamboo Hut. In their white double-breasted sharkskin jackets, black ties, and slacks, they made as sharp an impression on the Filipino girls as the White Russian women made on them.

Being on the other side of the world in an entirely new social context gave one license, many believed, to suspend the vows they had made to their wives and girlfriends back home. They saw it not as betrayal but as a natural consequence of time, place, and circumstance. Besides, the temptations were too great: a walk along the bay at sunset; a stroll through Intramuros in the evening; a furtive glance, a casual touch, an invitation to dance. Nights in the islands were hot, humid, and scented with the perfume of gardenia and night-blooming cereus. Filipino women smelled different, tasted different, their faces dabbed with rice powder, their hair gleaming with coconut oil, their lips tinted with *gumamela* petals. The loss of one love was often requited in the arms of another. But it was still difficult not to think of those you left behind.

The stream of luminaries passing through Manila, from the Russian foreign commissar Vyacheslav Molotov, to Kurusu Saburō, special assistant to the Japanese ambassador to the United States, to Clare Booth Luce, on assignment for *Life* to interview MacArthur, only fueled rumors of war. By late November 1941 most of the Asiatic Fleet had been ordered to southern Philippine waters, with the exception of Patrol Wing 10, the submarines and their tenders, the minesweepers, and two seagoing gunboats, the *Asheville* and the *Tulsa*.

On November 27, after diplomatic talks between Secretary of State Cordell Hull and Ambassador Nomura Kichisaburō collapsed, Admiral Hart, High Commissioner Francis B. Sayre, and MacArthur secretly convened in Manila. MacArthur had received a "final alert" from the War Department. "Hostile action possible at any moment," the cable warned. Admiral Harold Raynsford Stark, Chief of Naval Operations in Washington, informed Hart, "An aggressive move is expected by Japan in the next few days." The Philippines, the Malay Peninsula, and Borneo were cited as possible targets.

The Navy Yard was ordered to be in a "state of readiness." Battery C was put on five-minute notice. Machine gunners guarded the ammunition depot. A motorboat patrol swept the waterfront. Sand-filled barricades surrounded Fort San Felipe, air raid drills went into effect, trenches were dug where practicable, and inflammable oils and explosives were removed to Sunset Beach. The Navy Yard as well as Sangley Point were under partial blackout. The windows of Cañacao's operating rooms were shuttered so that surgery could continue as normal.

By December 4 a condition of "three-day readiness" was assumed. Total blackouts were now ordered, and antiaircraft batteries were authorized to fire on unidentified planes. Admiral Hart and Major General George F. Moore, commander of the Philippine Coast Artillery and the Harbor Defenses of Manila and Subic Bays, expected hostilities to break out at any moment.

At 0300 on Monday, December 8, 1941, Lieutenant Colonel William T. Clement, duty officer at the Asiatic Fleet headquarters, informed Admiral Hart of an urgent message intercepted by a radio operator: "AIR RAID ON PEARL HARBOR. THIS IS NO DRILL." Hart quickly notified all units of the Asiatic Fleet: "Japan started hostilities. Govern yourselves accordingly." Major General Richard K. Sutherland, USAFFE chief of staff, notified MacArthur and passed the news on to all commanders. Troops were ordered to take up their battle positions at once.

At 0530 Lieutenant Commander Erickson woke Fred Berley in the Bachelor Officers' Quarters of the Cavite Navy Yard. "Fred, we just got word. The Japs bombed Pearl Harbor."

"Good," Berley growled. "Now we can lick the sons of bitches." Then he rolled over and fell back asleep.

For the first few hours Manila was strangely calm. George Ferguson slept until 1100. He had spent his last night on the town carousing with Jim O'Rourke at the Bamboo Hut and the Jai Alai Club. Then he heard the news. "Japan attacks America," the radio reported again and again. "PEARL HARBOR BOMBED. WE ARE AT WAR WITH JAPAN," newspaper headlines screamed.

The Japanese had attacked Wake and Guam, bombed Hong Kong, seized the International Settlement in Shanghai, and captured the USS *Wake*. They bombed Camp John Hay in Baguio, and Fort Davao in Mindanao. Police patrolled the streets of Manila, armed with .45 revolvers and billy clubs, and began a sweep for Japanese aliens. At the Japanese News Agency men were toasting the emperor with shots of sake as Filipino Constabulary troops, dressed in fatigues and sporting Springfield and Enfield rifles, burst in. They rounded up suspects, including the American-born Arthur Komori, who worked for the U.S. Army in counterintelligence, and threw them all into Bilibid Prison or confined them to Japanese-owned establishments such as the Nippon Club on Taft Boulevard. Shopkeepers piled sandbags shoulder high in front of storefronts. MacArthur issued a message of calm and confidence to the Filipino people.

At Nielson Field on the outskirts of Manila, Major General Lewis H. Brereton, commander of the Far East Air Force (FEAF), had expected an attack as soon as the sun rose. Unable to see MacArthur, Brereton appealed to Sutherland, MacArthur's chief of staff, for permission to bomb Formosa, where Japanese Army pilots from the 11th Air Fleet were waiting for the fog to lift. But Brereton couldn't pinpoint a target. Sutherland told him to stand by. General Henry "Hap" Arnold, commander of the U.S. Army Air Forces, placed a transoceanic phone call to warn Brereton not to have his "entire air force destroyed" in the wake of Pearl Harbor. With reports coming into air force headquarters of enemy flights, Brereton ordered aloft planes of the Interceptor Command as well as unarmed bombers from Clark Field, sixty miles northwest of Manila. At 1010 a photoreconnaissance mission over southern Formosa was authorized, and shortly afterward Brereton received a phone call from MacArthur. They agreed to wait for recon's results, after which "the decision for offensive action" would be Brereton's. Brereton issued orders for two heavy bombardment squadrons from Clark Field to prepare for their mission against southern Formosa "at the latest daylight hour today that visibility will permit." By 1130 Brereton's B-17s were back at Clark Field being loaded with bombs while the P-40 fighter escorts were refueling.

Then at 1225, as officers were still having lunch and the ground crew strolled from the mess halls to the flight line, twenty-seven twin-engine Mitsubishi bombers flying at 22,000 to 25,000 feet—well beyond the range of antiaircraft fire—swarmed over Clark Field. Sakai Saburō and his squadron of Zero fighters had arrived just ahead of them:

> The sight which met us was unbelievable. Instead of encountering a swarm of American fighters diving at us in attack, we looked down and saw some sixty enemy bombers and fighters neatly parked along airfield runways . . . the Americans had made no attempt to disperse the planes and increase their safety.

Air raid sirens blared, men grabbed their helmets, donned their gas masks, and dove into trenches and drainage ditches as hundreds of bombs fell around them. Tons of explosives rained down on the administration and operations buildings, the barracks, hangars, and landing field. Fully gassed planes burst into fireballs, igniting the surrounding grass and trees. The earth seemed to leap to the sky as explosion followed explosion. Tracers streamed from antiaircraft positions manned by the 200th Coast Artillery, and two Japanese planes plunged like comets flaming out. But the pilots and their aircraft at Clark Field didn't stand a chance. A second wave of twenty-seven planes roared in for the kill, followed by a posse of thirty-four Zero fighters that riddled the Flying Fortresses and Curtiss P-40s parked wingtip to wingtip "on the ground! on the ground!" exclaimed Roosevelt when he heard the news.

Forty miles to the west, shortly after 1230, twelve American P-40s from the 3rd Pursuit Squadron were returning to Iba Airfield from a patrol over the South China Sea. Unaware of the debacle at Clark, they were puzzled by their inability to make radio contact with the base— when suddenly they heard a warning from Iba. An enemy air force was rapidly approaching from the west. But it was too late. Fifty-four Mitsubishi Type 1 bombers escorted by fifty Zero fighters intercepted them and reduced Iba field to ashes.

In little more than an hour, 80 men were killed and 150 were wounded. Clark and Iba airfields were left smoldering ruins. Eighteen B-17s, fifty-three P-40s, and three P-35s were destroyed. The strength of the Far East Air Force was cut in half.

Manila would be next, Admiral Hart's office was warned. Air raid sirens wailed throughout the city. George Ferguson tried to get over to Cañacao, but there wasn't a car, taxi, or *caretela* that wasn't being used by the army, navy, or evacuating civilians. The boat to Sangley Point had left without him. And there was no chance, he now knew, that he would be going back to the States.

He remembered his long days of boredom on the Yangtze River and his boyish enthusiasm at the prospect of hostilities breaking out, which he had seen, opportunistically, as a chance to gain more medical experience. "Damn it have 2½ years of this damn place behind and indefinite time ahead. Oh Hell!" he wrote in his diary. If his hopes of seeing Lucy were dashed, George didn't let anyone know. This was no time to feel sorry for himself. Besides, he had little doubt that his dreams would be realized; it was only a matter of when. He accepted his lot with a trace of resignation and a wink of self-knowledge. "Guess better not gripe too much," he concluded.

Few in the Philippines were privy to the full extent of the disaster at Pearl Harbor, just as it was impossible in the States to obtain accurate information from early news reports. A total of 2,403 servicemen and civilians had died, and another 1,178 were wounded. Eighteen warships were sunk or damaged, including the *Arizona, Oklahoma, West Virginia,* and *California,* and 188 planes were lost. It was "a date which will live in infamy," pronounced Roosevelt on December 8, 1941, as he asked Congress to approve a declaration of war against Japan.

"So far," the president acknowledged the next evening in his fireside chat, "the news has been all bad." It would only get worse, Murray thought. The "Pearl of the Orient" was about to lose its luster.

3

Red Sunset

ŌHASHI KAZUKO was a student at Atomi Women's College in Tōkyō when she heard the news of Japan's attack on Pearl Harbor. "Today, December 8, before dawn, the Imperial Army and Navy entered into a state of war with American and British forces in the western Pacific," read the first bulletin from Imperial General Headquarters (Daihonei), issued at six A.M. An hour later Radio Tōkyō began playing Meiji-era songs such as *"Gunkan-mōchi"* (the Warship March) and *"Battō-tai"* (The Drawn Sword Brigade). The city awakened to newspaper vendors ringing bells to hawk the morning extras.

Young women in Kazuko's dormitory gathered in a large hall, where the air crackled with excitement. Some shouted, while others literally wept with joy. Japan had proven her might. No longer would she have to submit to Western policies, demands, restrictions, or stereotypes. Japan had found a way out of her economic woes. Now she would be a world power. She would expand her sphere of influence just as the great colonial powers England, Holland, and France had done in India, Malaya, and Indochina. Just as America had done in the Philippines. Taiheiyō Sensō—the Pacific War—had begun.

Kazuko's father, Ōhashi Hyōjirō, was a gifted surgeon who taught at Ōsaka University Medical School. He had been called to active duty in 1937, having received "the red paper" (*akagami*) from the Office of the Draft (*chōheika*) in Wakayama. He was a practicing Buddhist but was invigorated by the spirit of militarism that swept through Japan in the 1930s and led to full-scale war with China. "Now I can be a man!" he exclaimed on learning of Pearl Harbor. Only five foot four with high cheekbones, a broad face, and a clipped mustache, he thrust an ancestral sword into his belt.

Miyazaki Shunya was the son of family friends and in junior high school at the time. He feared for his country's future: America was so big—how could Japan possibly prevail? He was relieved upon hearing of Japan's stunning success in the sneak attack. "Truly it is time for the one hundred million of us Japanese to dedicate all we have and sacrifice everything for our country's cause," said the prime minister, General Tōjō Hideki, in a radio address that afternoon. "As long as there remains under the policy of Eight Corners of the World Under One Roof this great spirit of loyalty and patriotism, we have nothing to fear in fighting America and Britain."

Japanese novelist Dazai Osamu put it more bluntly: he was "itching to beat the bestial, insensitive Americans to a pulp."

There was no way Japan could win a war against America, Fred Berley believed. The United States was the richest country in the world, her population was nearly twice that of Japan, and she was blessed with vast natural resources. In 1941 U.S. steel, aluminum, and motor vehicle production surpassed that of any other nation on earth and many of them combined.

But twenty years of disarmament and isolation had taken their toll. In 1939 the U.S. Army ranked eighteenth in size on a scale of the world's fighting forces, flanked by the armies of Portugal and Bulgaria. Japan boasted 2.4 million combat troops and another 3 million reserves, whereas combined American, British, and Dutch troops in East Asia amounted to a paltry 350,000. The Japanese Army had racked up five years of combat experience in China, while U.S. Army forces in the Philippines were run like an old boys' club, softened by a torpid lifestyle in the tropics. "The Philippine situation looks sound," MacArthur confidently told journalist John Hersey in mid-1941. In reality, it was anything but.

At the beginning of the war, the Japanese Army Air Service had better planes, the Japanese Navy had more surface ships, and the Japanese Army had guns of more recent manufacture, albeit from older models. The Zero fighter, introduced in 1940, outclassed any airplane in the U.S. Army and Navy air forces. The twin-engine Mitsubishi bomber known as the Type 96 "Nell" had a range of 2,300 miles, compared to the B-17 Flying Fortress, which was limited to 1,850. Japan's cruisers, unlike those in the U.S. Navy, were fortified with torpedo tubes, and the torpedoes themselves had far greater range. Japan had a superior 47mm antitank gun, its .25-caliber Arisaka rifle was lighter, quieter, and more easily assembled and concealed, and its light machine gun was more adaptable to jungle warfare. The Japanese had developed a versatile 50mm grenade launcher, erroneously referred to by the Americans as a "knee mortar," in addition to a portable 70mm gun capable of hurling an 8.8-pound shell a distance of two miles.

By contrast, the armament of Fil-American forces was a museum hall

of outmoded weaponry. Their 1898 Vickers-Maxim 2.95-inch pack howitzers were drawn by horse or mule; their 75mm guns were wooden-wheel
mounted; and the dual-purpose (surface or air) 3-inch guns used in the
three antiaircraft batteries around Cavite were vintage World War I. The
average American infantryman relied on the 1903 Springfield, a .30-
caliber bolt-action rifle with a five-round internal box magazine: it was
declared obsolete in 1918, even though it carried a more powerful punch
than the .25-caliber bolt-action Arisaka rifle and was modeled after the
same 1898 Mauser design.

The Philippine Army, conceded Major General Jonathan M.
"Skinny" Wainwright, commander of North Luzon Force, "lacked even
obsolete equipment." Infantrymen were poorly trained, practicing with
wooden weapons, and many had never fired a real gun before being
handed an M1917 Enfield rifle. Shoddy American-issue canvas shoes
were too narrow for Filipino feet, while *guinit* helmets made from var-
nished coconut turned their heads into flashing targets in the sunlight.

At 7,000 men strong, Philippine Army divisions were smaller than
their American and Japanese counterparts, and by December 1941,
there were only eight of them on Luzon, two of which were from the
Visayas. But not all had been fully mobilized, and only one out of three
regiments in each division had completed refresher training when hostilities broke out. For the defense of northern Luzon, Wainwright had a
paltry 28,000 troops at his disposal—not the 200,000 that MacArthur
claimed on paper—and they had to cover an area hundreds of square
miles in size.

The American-trained 45th and 57th Infantry Regiments of the
Philippine Scouts were issued Garand semiautomatic rifles and were
widely admired for their courage and professionalism, if not for their
equipment and supplies. First Lieutenant Mark Herbst, a doctor with
the 3rd Battalion, 57th Infantry, opened the case of medical instruments
he had been issued and discovered that they dated back to the 31st Infantry's 1918 Siberian expedition. Some medications were from 1917-
type medical chests and were so old they were useless. The 31st Infantry
had the distinction of being the only American infantry regiment in
the Philippines out of 22,000 U.S. Army troops in the Philippines. But
their reputation was more for bibulosity than for bravery; hence their
moniker, the "Thirsty-First." Conditioned by peacetime and supplied
with surplus equipment, Fil-American forces, remarked historian Richard Connaughton, were preparing to fight their "first land battle of the
Second World War with the weapons of the First."

Fred had seen Japanese naval power at its finest when he was medical
officer of Destroyer Division 58 and his ship, the *Parrott*, was ordered to

South China in February 1940. There in the harbor of Kulangsu, a jewel of an island, was the Japanese destroyer, *Harukaze*. "Spring Breeze" (as her name meant) was a real beauty compared with the old four-stackers of the U.S. Navy's Asiatic Fleet. Fred even had a chance to go on board when he and the *Parrott*'s skipper, Commander E. N. "Butch" Parker, were invited by the captain of the *Harukaze* to watch sword and bayonet exercises in celebration of the mythical anniversary of the founding of the Japanese Empire on February 11. Japanese battleships such as the *Yamato*, commissioned one week after Pearl Harbor, were the largest in the world, displacing 65,000 tons or more and bristling with 18-inch guns, compared with the 35,000-to-40,000-ton battleships armed with 16-inch guns in the Royal Navy and the U.S. Navy.

Still, the idea of Japan attacking the United States was unbelievable, even though the possibility had been discussed in American military circles since 1906. Fred would soon find out just how unprepared America was for war.

Prewar medical mobilization in the islands depended on the 12th Medical Regiment, the Philippine Scouts, and the Philippine Army. They engaged in maneuvers with the chief U.S. Army unit in the Philippines known as the Philippine Division, comprising the American 31st Infantry Regiment and the 45th and 57th Infantry Regiments. They surveyed Bataan for medical support of frontline troops and hospital sites in the rear. They schooled officers and enlisted men in field medicine, medical supply, and hospitalization, and they instructed regimental bandsmen, traditionally used as litter bearers, in first aid.

Once Rainbow 5 went into effect in November 1941, Sternberg was designated as the primary hospital in Manila with enough annexes throughout the city to accommodate 3,000 to 5,000 casualties in the event of hostilities. The complex, known as the Manila Hospital Center, came into being on December 8 under Colonel Percy J. Carroll, Sternberg's commanding officer. Eight annexes were quickly set up in the reconverted Jai Alai Club, Estado Mayor Barracks, the Spanish Club and Girls' Dormitory on Taft Avenue, Philippine Women's University, Santa Scholastica College, Fort William McKinley, Holy Ghost Convent and College in Quezon City, and De la Salle College. With the exception of Fort William McKinley, which already had an army station hospital, their staff and supply needs were enormous.

Twenty surgical teams were formed, primarily from army medical officers and enlisted men. Army, navy, and civilian nurses lent invaluable assistance. The Army Medical Corps and the Philippine Department scoured Manila to procure all available bandages, medicines, antimalarial drugs, and surgical equipment. Filipino Medical Corps and Dental Corps personnel were recruited from the Philippine Army Medical School at Camp Murphy in Manila to work as motor pool, assistant supply, and mess officers. Rizal Station served as the medical depot. Subdepots were established at Orion, Tarlac, Los Baños, and Cebu.

Captain Robert G. Davis, commanding officer of Cañacao, worried that the naval hospital's proximity to Cavite placed it in "great danger." A more immediate threat was the Sangley Point radio station, with its three 600-foot towers, any one of which, if hit, could fall onto the hospital. Sandbags were placed around Cañacao. Trenches and air raid shelters were dug in the Sangley Point area. Patients and medical and nursing staff were absorbed by Sternberg and the Estado Mayor annex a block away.

But the location of Sternberg raised similar concerns because it was directly across the street from Philippine Army Headquarters and was forced to observe blackout regulations each night. Estado Mayor, only recently vacated by a battalion of the 31st Infantry, was another desirable target. Nonetheless patients and staff from Fort William McKinley, one of five station hospitals in the Philippines including Fort Stotsenberg, Fort Mills on Corregidor, Camp John Hay in Baguio, and Fort Brent on Mindanao, would soon move into Estado Mayor for the simple reason that Fort McKinley itself was a likely target.

Technically noncombatants, the medical officers were issued World War I doughboy helmets, gas masks, sidearms and were told to be on the lookout for sabotage. Lieutenant (j.g.) Gordon K. Lambert was trained in industrial medicine and ordered to set up battle aid stations in the Navy Yard—where casualties could be sorted and first aid administered in areas protected from enemy fire. He placed Fred Berley in charge of the Navy Yard dispensary.

"Gordon, the dispensary won't last two minutes in a bombing raid," Fred said in no uncertain terms. "It's all wood, it's in the middle of the yard, the paint shop is on one side, and the printing shop is on the other."

Fred suggested an alternative: the old paint locker behind the dispensary, which was made of concrete blocks a foot square and was built below street level. There was a door on the side, a window to the left, and an arched ceiling, above which was the old brig. Lambert agreed, and Fred had it stocked with bandages, operating instruments, kerosene lamps, and flashlights. He enlisted forty-five stretcher bearers from the radio school, the band, and the receiving ship. After a cursory lesson in first aid, he told them to report to the old paint locker on the double anytime there was an air alert.

At 0300 on the morning of December 9, 1941, Captain Davis was awakened at Cañacao Hospital by the sounds of heavy bombing over Nichols Field, a mere six miles away. The sky was streaked with red and yellow tracer bullets, bursts of antiaircraft fire, and the blaze of burning hangars and planes. The submarine tender *Canopus* steamed away from the Navy Yard as a safety precaution and was ordered to the Port Area of Manila, where torpedoes and spare parts were unloaded and hastened to Corregidor, but the Japanese had other targets in mind.

Women employees were ordered to stay home, and civilians began to evacuate Cavite. Aviation gasoline and oil tanks were emptied and dispersed throughout Manila Bay. The navy began destroying secret nonessential documents.

George Ferguson was assigned to Cañacao, where he found "everyone still running around in gas mask helmets and brown uniforms." The staff was jumpy at the sound of the air raid alarms. "They're right though," he remarked in his diary. "Wish I had sent everything home."

That evening Fred Berley rode his bicycle to the movie house to catch *Abe Lincoln in Illinois*, starring Raymond Massey, Gene Lockhart, and Ruth Gordon. Around 2000, midway through the film, an air raid siren went off. Fred rushed to put on his gas mask, manned his station, and received his first casualty. A sailor from the *Sealion* had jumped for cover down a submarine hatch and torn a seven-inch gash in the lateral aspect of his right upper thigh, through the skin, the fascia, and the muscle itself. Fred sewed up the wound, then sent him to Cañacao once the all-clear sounded. No raid materialized. The rumble of bombs continued through the night.

Midmorning on December 10, Private First Class Irvin C. Scott, Jr., looked at the oscilloscope on the mobile SCR-270B unit at Wawa Beach near Nasugbu and spotted an ominous airplane formation approaching Manila Bay from the north. The duty radioman tried to reach Sangley Point but to no avail. He then made contact with Army Radio on Corregidor, but the Army Radio operators there hadn't heard of the SCR-270B and wouldn't believe the sighting.

The same finding raised an alarm at Far East Air Force interceptor headquarters at noon. Enemy planes were tracked forty-five minutes away. Brereton scrambled twenty P-40s and fifteen P-35s, but they were overwhelmed by fifty-two Zero fighter planes escorting eighty or so bombers.

At 1235 Fred Berley was waiting for a slice of apple pie in the Officers' Mess of the Cavite Navy Yard when a siren blared from the powerhouse. Fred and Murray grabbed their gas masks and sidearms and ran to the paint locker, where a group of workmen stood gazing over at

Sangley Point. Lambert and Lieutenant Commander C. T. Cross, a dentist, were fast on their heels. Ships, submarines, and seaplanes gunned their engines to get away from the Navy Yard as quickly as possible. Then twenty-seven planes from the Japanese Imperial Navy's 11th Air Fleet, flying southeast from Formosa, sailed over Manila at 21,000 feet.

It was a lovely day, the sky azure, flecked with clouds. "Look at those planes," Fred said as fifty-four Mitsubishi Zero fighters in two groups of twenty-seven approached Cavite at 23,000 feet. "I can see the bombs!"

They were oddly beautiful as they fluttered down like leaflets glinting in the sun. The first stick hit the water, causing waterspouts to erupt from the sea refracting rainbows of color.

"Get the hell inside!" Murray yelled.

The second stick hit Sangley Point, and then the bombers swept over Cavite, breaking into groups of nine. Within minutes they leveled the torpedo repair shop, the supply office and warehouses, the signal station, the commissary store and receiving station, the barracks and officers' quarters. Walls of flame leaped out of the earth, and plumes of thick, oily smoke boiled up into the sky. Then a bomb hit the brig above the old paint locker.

Jesus Christ, Murray thought, the war has just begun and I'm going to die.

He was strangely calm. He was in peak physical condition, at the beginning of his professional career, and here, now, none of it mattered: not school, college, or medical education; not family, friends, or Laura; not strength, willpower, hope, or prayer. Nameless, faceless, he was invisible to the Japanese, a target not for practice but to be destroyed.

A terrific concussion shook the structure, seeming to lift it right off the ground. Dust and debris blasted through the window. A palm tree rocketed up and plunged down into a crater. The din was earsplitting as bombs fell, buildings imploded, and ground defenses answered back.

The paint locker withstood the hit, but the brig was in flames. The earth vibrated from explosions. The power plant was ablaze, reducing water pressure to a trickle and rendering the firefighting equipment useless. Rear Admiral Francis W. Rockwell, commandant of the 16th Naval District, called Manila for help, worried that the fires would reach the ammunition dump.

Waves of Japanese bombers flew over Cavite with impunity, completely out of reach of the antiaircraft fire. With power-train fuses, the 3-inch guns had a vertical range of 17,000 feet and a horizontal reach of 6,000 yards. But Japanese fighters could fly up to 27,000 feet, and bombers as high as 26,000 feet. The ship and shore batteries fired anyway.

Out at Battery C, Corpsman Ernie Irvin watched an American P-40 pancake down into mud. Two PBYs—Catalina flying boats—took off from Sangley Point, luring a dive bomber from an enemy squadron over Nichols Field. Battery A opened fire, and the plane went screaming into Manila Bay, the only kill of the 1st Separate Battalion at Cavite.

A bomb rattled down into the engine-room hatch of the *Sealion*; another blew apart its conning tower, which slammed into the conning tower of the *Seadragon*, instantly decapitating the engineering officer. Inflammable liquid from the *Sealion* splashed onto the *Bittern*, setting her deck on fire. Shrapnel and incendiary bombs splattered Central Wharf. One bomb slammed into the *Peary* and shattered its foremast, killing eight of her crew. Erickson, whose first name, Hjalmer, means "one who loves the sea," was blown into the bay and emerged with a chunk of shrapnel lodged in his shoulder.

Out of fright, Filipinos ran from cover during the bombing and were shredded by shrapnel. Some were having lunch just outside the main gate of the Navy Yard. The wounded straggled to the porch of the Navy Yard dispensary, only to be decimated when it received a direct hit. Body parts hung from fences. One woman had her clothes blown off. Another civilian ran terror-stricken with his right pants leg shorn away, exposing bone from his midcalf to his buttocks. You could see the tendons and muscles as clearly as an illustration in *Gray's Anatomy*, but strangely enough there didn't seem to be any blood. Private Ted "Willie" Williams, a marine who worked in the Air Warning Service in Batangas, was driving a truck toward the bridge that separated Cavite from the barrio of Caridad when he stopped to pick him up. The injured man opened his mouth as if about to say something and then died before Williams's eyes.

Over at the garage near Fort San Felipe, a sailor ran with a baby drenched in blood calling "Medic! Medic!" One corpsman took the baby, while another promptly gave the sailor an injection. "Not me," he shouted, "the baby, you fool!" He was completely unaware that his left arm had been severed at the shoulder. The ground was strewn with dead and wounded. One headless corpse remained with collar and necktie perfectly intact.

Casualties began to pour into the paint locker. A Filipino workman's hand was dangling from his wrist; Fred amputated it instantly. But someone had forgotten fuel for the kerosene lamps, so the doctors and corpsmen worked in darkness, the wounds of their patients—burns, lacerations, fractures, and the cyanotic pallor of shock—illumined by the eerie glow of flashlight. The heat from the fires soon forced the men outside, where the sky was black with smoke.

High winds fanned the flames in the yard. Marines formed firefighting brigades with buckets of water, while Filipino fire companies tried to prevent the ammunition depot from igniting. Civilians combed neighborhood drugstores for medicine and gauze. The docks were lined with wounded. Murray helped evacuate patients to Cañacao by truck; then he and Lambert joined Fred down at Guadalupe Pier, commandeered a launch, and ferried more casualties over to the hospital. On the way they saw two marines sitting on a raft in the middle of the bay, strapped to two warheads they had salvaged from the torpedo warehouse. Murray couldn't believe what he was seeing. They were laughing and waving like ghouls in a Bosch painting, as if the carnage in Cavite were nothing but a bad dream.

Forty minutes later, when the bombing was finally over, Ernie Irvin jumped into a *banca*—an outrigger canoe—to see if the pilot in the P-40 was okay and found him bawling like a baby. He was out of gas, he said. He had seen one of his buddies blown up when he took off from Nichols Field, he explained. But there were no holes in his plane, he had plenty of ammo, and his guns weren't jammed. It's his story that's full of holes, Irvin thought.

At 1600 the cry went out: "The admiral says clear the yard!" Trucks couldn't keep up with the number of dead being transported from Cavite to the temporary morgue. The hospital's front lawn was covered with bodies. The boat landing behind it was pooled with blood. Inside, Cañacao was overflowing with hundreds of wounded. The lights were out, the elevator had died, patients lined the stairwells. After first aid was administered, civilians were transferred to local Filipino hospitals around Cavite, or to Philippine General in Manila. Some casualties were evacuated onto the *Maryanne*, J. Marsman's diesel yacht, and disembarked at the Army-Navy Club, where ambulances and buses were waiting to take patients and personnel to Sternberg. Lieutenant Commander James D. Boone ran beside a patient's stretcher to finish amputating a leg before he reached the evacuation boat.

The medical officer of the *Otus* burst into tears when he saw Berley. "Fred," he said, "I thought you had been killed." Berley had been right to challenge Lambert—changing the location of the main battle aid station had saved their lives. But one corpsman, Durward Allen Laney, who was assigned to Lieutenant (j.g.) Robert G. Herthneck of the Dental Corps, somehow hadn't gotten the message. Laney was killed instantly when the dispensary took a direct hit. Five corpsmen attached to Cañacao were missing and believed dead.

Murray was assigned to the receiving and shock wards at Cañacao. Fred helped triage the wounded. They cleaned and dressed lacerations, applied splints, injected morphine sulphate when necessary, and administered tetanus antitoxin.

The operating rooms on the top floor were working full blast under generator light. The mangled bodies of men, women, and children were "brought up to us and dumped like piles of human offal," said the chief of surgery, Lieutenant Commander Thomas Hirst Hayes, "all guts and brains and bones."

Fred asked Hayes if he could be of further assistance. They could use an extra hand, Hayes replied. Fred slipped on a surgical gown and, with Lieutenant Commander Carey Miller Smith, assistant chief of surgery, operated until the early hours of the morning.

In less than twelve hours, 285 patients passed through Smith's OR. The casualties were gruesome—severed limbs, facial lacerations, disfiguring burns, bodies ripped by shrapnel. Fred was soaked to the skin in blood, and the nurses could only rinse his gown and bring it back to him wet before he bloodied himself again. He slept in the crawl space under Cañacao as fires stole darkness from the night.

Some 300 bombs had fallen on Cavite, an area of just 50 acres. The *Sealion* was crippled; the *Seadragon* and *Bittern* were damaged; 233 Mark 14 torpedoes that carried 500-pound warheads were lost. Five hundred people were killed, including the first five U.S. submariners to die in the war; 400 more were wounded. The Navy Yard was ravaged, perforated by so many craters that from the air it looked as if Cavite itself should have sunk. Only Dreamland and the Marine Corps barracks were left standing.

MacArthur's wife, Jean, and their small son, Arthur, saw the inferno from the terrace of their sixth-floor apartment in the Manila Hotel. Admiral Hart, a veteran of the Spanish-American War and World War I, watched helplessly from the rooftop of the Marsman Building. The naval base was inoperable. The remnants of the Asiatic Fleet would steam south, with the exception of the submarines, the tender *Canopus*, some PBYs, and Bulkeley's MTB Squadron 3.

In the coda of destruction you could hear the lowing of cows and the howling of dogs deserted by their fleeing masters. Hundreds of canines feasted on human corpses before cannibalizing their own kind. The smell of scorched flesh, decaying bodies, and dead animals lingered in the air.

Murray and Gordon Lambert spent the night at the Caridad School Yard. In the morning they picked up Fred and headed for Manila. Cavite was still burning, and the Naval Ammunition Depot was expected to blow at any minute. Cañacao was marked with a white cross and escaped the bombing unscathed, but the radio towers made a natural next target. All patients had been evacuated to Manila, where naval personnel were divided into four surgical teams and assigned to the annexes in Colonel

Carroll's Manila Hospital Center. Each team had a dentist to assist in facial wounds.

The road to Manila was clogged with civilians bound for the hills. Whatever was left of their homes they stuffed onto *carabao* carts and into *caretelas*, strapped to packhorses and bicycles, baby carriages and wheelbarrows, or simply carried on their backs. Bloodied and dirty, the doctors received a change of clothes at the army supply depot and joined the Estado Mayor annex, where patients were being treated by the former Cañacao staff.

Hayes took one look at the junior medical officers and realized that they had little idea of what lay ahead. They were young, smart, enthusiastic, and altogether lacking in field experience. He hoped there would be enough time for some basic training "before too much was expected of them."

That evening Fleet Surgeon Lowman came to Estado Mayor with his driver and took Fred to the Army-Navy Club, where Ernie and Rose Necker were waiting. Lowman told him that Lieutenant Commander Ernest Marion Wade, the acting regimental surgeon, had requested that Berley rejoin the 4th Marines in Olongapo. If Fred didn't want to go, Wade would choose someone else. Fred was happy to oblige, but when he returned to Estado Mayor, he found Hayes in a fury. Berley's orders had come in. Where the hell had he been?

"With Captain Lowman, sir," Fred replied.

Hayes simmered down, but thereafter Fred thought, This is no friend of mine.

The Cañacao staff was on the move again. Erickson had made arrangements to establish a new naval hospital at Philippine Union College, a Seventh-Day Adventist school seven miles outside Manila in Balintawak. Why? To become some haven for refugees? Hayes resented the fact that the navy's prewar plan had been abandoned. The district medical officer, Captain Davis, was supposed to turn command of Cañacao's staff over to his executive, and that should have been Hayes. But it hadn't happened that way. Instead, circumstance and personal preferences had determined directives. Davis seemed more interested in sitting out the war "in the country," Hayes bristled, than coordinating activities with the army, to which the navy was attached for tactical purposes.

As a result, doctors were dispatched around Manila like ambulances racing to the latest emergency. Murray was sent to the annex at Holy Ghost Convent and College. Fred was transferred to Olongapo after the Japanese bombed the naval station and destroyed a fleet of PBYs at their moorings. George remained behind to help set up an aid station at the end of Cañacao Boulevard on Radio Road. There they could treat the antiaircraft batteries that had moved into the hospital and radio area, a 2,000-strong contingent of the Philippine Army and remnants of the 16th Naval District.

In the meantime the Provisional Military Police and detachments from the Filipino Fleet Reserve began to bury the dead at the Cavite Navy Yard. George, Lieutenant Commander R. C. Strong, and three corpsmen were on hand to help identify bodies.

It was a grisly task. Corpses were bloated beyond recognition. Eyeballs had exploded in sockets from the heat. Brain matter oozed out from fractured skulls. The stench was overpowering. Some men were sick; others wore gas masks. They drank liquor freely. Commander Strong wept. Of the 167 bodies he disposed of, George could identify only seven. They cremated a few by dousing them with kerosene; bomb craters became tombs for the rest. Laney's remains were never found. There was no chaplain present to recite from Genesis 3:19, "You are dust and unto dust you will return," only Commander Strong to offer a few words of solace before the makeshift graves were filled with dirt.

In two days the Japanese had eviscerated the U.S. Pacific Fleet's Hawaii base, crippled the Far East Air Force, scattered the Asiatic Fleet, and destroyed its base of operations. They had landed at Aparri on the north coast of Luzon and reconnoitered around Lingayen Gulf.

In two days the navy doctors witnessed death on a scale they couldn't possibly have imagined, realized how close they themselves had come to dying, and been sobered by the role chance played in their survival. Laney's fate could just as easily have been their own.

They were left with nothing except the clothes on their backs. Murray's camera equipment, Fred's memorabilia, their tuxedoes and bow ties, their sharkskin jackets, their medical texts and black bags, the signs of their accomplishments and potential, all were destroyed. Home was a memory now, without any artifact, just as the pictures Murray had taken in the Philippines, the furniture Fred had brought over from Shanghai, and the mementos of their lives in the Pacific had literally gone up in smoke.

They saw, finally, how quickly identities could be erased, how tenuous was the thread between existence and annihilation. Cavite, as Marine Corps Private James L. Kent put it, was a "red sunset."

4

Invisible Enemies

IN THE DENSELY FOLIATED FOOTHILLS of southern Bataan, Lieutenant (j.g.) John Jacob Bookman stalked a silent enemy. Small and elusive, it haunted the streams that flowed down the mountains of the peninsula's interior. It looked harmless enough, but it carried a parasite that made men tremble with cold, then rage with hellishly high fevers, until the cycle of violent chills and drenching sweats began all over again. Left untreated, the parasite could weaken the body's immune system and induce lethargy, delirium, coma, and finally, death. *Anopheles minimus flavirostris* was its name, a small, speckled mosquito that can ingest more blood than its own body weight, and it was the primary vector in the Philippines for *Plasmodium falciparum,* the most lethal cause of human malaria.

The parasite is introduced into the bloodstream by the female mosquito as she feeds on a human host. Then it becomes motile, migrates to the liver, divides into merozoites, and breaks through the cell membrane. In just seven days a few dozen malaria sporozoites can spawn tens of thousands of merozoites that surge into the bloodstream before the immune system has time to respond. In another week, when telltale symptoms begin to appear, the single-celled protozoa will have established a colony that numbers in the trillions, and those colonies can bring armies of men to their knees.

Malaria flourished in the swamps around Rome and ravaged German troops who tried, in the tenth and twelfth centuries, to conquer "The Queen of the World." The disease played a decisive role in the Siege of Mantua in 1796–97. During the American War Between the States it annually infected more than 50 percent of the Caucasian troops and 80 percent of the Negro soldiers in northern armies. In the first year of the Spanish-American War, malaria accounted for 90,461 hospital admissions, and in Macedonia in 1918 it afflicted nearly 100,000 French and more than 25,000 British troops. In the 1930s it was estimated that there were between one and two million cases of malaria in the Philippines "at all times."

Bataan's lowland rivers, its freshwater streams with undercut ledges, and its shady banks where one bathed, washed, and cooked were the ideal habitat for *Anopheles minimus*. The natives could vouch for it. On the flat eastern coastal plain, infection rates in the villages reached 50 percent or more.

Armed with Patrick Manson's *Tropical Diseases*, the nineteenth-century "Manual of the Diseases of the Warm Climates," John wondered why military strategists hadn't addressed the threat posed by malaria before. After all, War Plan Orange-3 had called for the withdrawal of 43,000 troops to Bataan as a delaying defensive action until naval reinforcements could arrive from the United States.

But how could Bataan be defended if the defenders themselves were laid low by disease? How could you fight two enemies at once? MacArthur himself had contracted malaria in 1904, when he supervised a survey of the military reservation at Mariveles. Didn't anyone in the army understand the extent of the malaria problem on Bataan?

The question surprised no one more than John Bookman himself, an Upper East Sider whose ambition was to practice internal medicine in New York City, not parasitology in the Philippines. He couldn't have been more out of place in this torrid tropical wilderness. But as foreign as it was to him, he managed to make a home out of it.

———

Tall and slender, with a hawkish nose and light blue eyes, John had a self-effacing demeanor that could be seen as an attempt to dissociate himself from an illustrious family history, or as a ploy to be remarkable by his very unremarkableness.

He grew up in a five-story building that his father, Samuel, had purchased at 48 East 82nd Street, between Park and Madison Avenues. The family of five had a staff of seven: a governess, nurse, cook, waitress, laundress, chambermaid, and chauffeur.

Samuel was a biochemist whose father, Jacob Bookman, had emigrated from Germany to America in 1841. Jacob had settled in Selma, Alabama, worked in textiles, and then made a fortune in real estate. He moved to New York City, sold properties to Andrew Carnegie, and became a member of Temple Emanu-El, the first Reform Jewish congregation in New York City, founded in 1845. Samuel managed his father's estate and also worked at Mount Sinai, where he established the first biochemistry laboratory in an American hospital. In 1917 he founded a clinic for diseases of metabolism, mainly diabetes. One of his pupils was Bela Schick, who invented the diphtheria immunity test that bears his name. Another colleague was Burrill B. Crohn, who described the intestinal infection known as Crohn's disease. Yet another was Arthur Koplik, who identified the blotchy red, white, and blue spots on the lining of the cheek that mark the beginning of measles.

Samuel Bookman was a part of America's medical elite, and his family enjoyed the privileges of German-Jewish aristocracy. His wife, Olga, modeled their home after the furnished period rooms she so admired in the Metropolitan Museum of Art down the street. Their daughters, Edith and Virginia, wore clothes fashioned by seamstresses. Debutante parties were thrown at the Ritz-Carlton Hotel. All of the children attended private schools, vacationed in Lake Placid, New York, and spent some summers in France, where the family kept an apartment in Paris overlooking the Place Vendôme and was chauffeured around the countryside in a 1924 custom Cadillac Landaulet. John's sisters were encouraged to mix in German-Jewish circles, where friendships were fickle and morals were lax, especially during Prohibition. Parties were frequent, quarts of champagne were stowed beneath banquet tables, and young debs frequently "came home with the milkman" or nonchalantly slipped the house keys to their boyfriends. Virginia wasn't like that; she simply eloped. She knew that permissiveness had its limits and that her parents were apt to frown upon her marriage to Sam Saffro, who was of Russian-Jewish descent and lived on the West Side.

John went to the prestigious Collegiate School for Boys, the second-oldest boys' school in the country, and in 1931 graduated from Storm King, a prep school in the Hudson River valley. He had been left back one grade, missed another due to illness, and would suffer repeated bouts of mononucleosis. He was premed at Brown University, worked at Cold Spring Harbor laboratory on Long Island during the summer, and after graduating from NYU's College of Medicine had a rotating internship at Lincoln Hospital in New York City until July 1, 1941.

In choosing a medical career, John was following in his father's footsteps—until he found himself in the steaming jungle of Bataan.

———————

Twenty-five miles long and twenty miles at its widest, the Bataan peninsula is punctuated by a series of volcanic peaks 3,000 to 5,000 feet in height, from Mt. Santa Rosa in the north to Mt. Bataan in the south. The rocky west coast plunges down to the China Sea, while the east coast eases into Manila Bay. The entire province of Bataan was formerly a military reservation, and each year Philippine Scout regiments would go there to build ammunition *bodegas* or bridges, or to stockpile artillery shells right out in the open. Military planners drew a main battle position for Fil-American forces across the northern part of the peninsula, from Mauban in the west to Mabatang in the east. A rear battle position was established that stretched from Bagac to Orion.

Towering monkey pod, mango, and acacia trees lined Bataan's ridges. *Talahib* and *cogon* grass grew waist high in its ravines. Stands of *talisay* offered cover and shade near open ground. The interior was so dense with *ipil-ipil* trees, bamboo thickets, and *molave* plants tangled with rattan vines that visibility was reduced to ten yards while the brightness of midday turned into twilight's gloom. Soaring *balete* rose from buttress roots that could shelter three or four people, but the natives feared they were haunted by evil spirits. You learned not to be surprised by the wild boars and wild chickens crashing through the underbrush in Mariveles. Occasionally you came across a five-to-eight-inch track in the dirt left by a python slithering down from the mountains in search of water.

The climate is brutal. In the dry season, the temperature averages 95 degrees during the day and 86 degrees at night, but it feels hotter because of the high humidity. In the rainy season, which begins in early June and lasts until November, monsoons fan across Manila Bay and over Luzon, flooding rivers, washing out roads and bridges, and leaving quagmires of mud. It is a striking landscape inhabited by a people who lived in abject poverty yet were remarkably friendly to their American "brothers." Dewey himself had fallen in love with Luzon, whose peaks, he wrote in his autobiography, reminded him of the Green Mountains of Vermont.

On the southern slopes of the Mariveles Mountains was "Little Baguio," where the quartermaster, construction, supply, and defense works engineers were stationed in the sector known as the Service Command Area. The Navy Section Base was carved out of the 100-square-mile Service Command Area, which fell under the aegis of General Allen C. McBride, MacArthur's deputy from the Philippine Department. As far back in the rear as you could go, the Section Base was still within the "ultimate defense area."

The Section Base hospital was a modest two-room clinic that had been slapped together with four-by-eight-foot sheets of plywood half an inch thick, nailed to two-by-four-inch wooden frames, and it was here that John worked as the medical officer. He was conscientious, resourceful, and affable. He made friends easily and quickly established his authority. If his thoroughness was a thorn in the side of MTB Squadron 3, he had won the respect of his peers.

At last John had emerged from his father's influence to become something very different from the man he was in New York City. Samuel was proud of him for it. He kept a picture of John at the Navy Section Base dressed in his whites and wearing a smile as wide as a sunflower.

Mariveles combines the beauty of the jungle with bluffs that drop down to the ocean, beyond which rise jagged pinnacles of rock. Two miles away, as if it had broken off from the tip of Bataan, lies the diminutive island of Corregidor, so close it seems as if you could skip a stone across the water and hit it.

The spur on the pincer of Bataan, Mariveles was once a strategic sentry at the easternmost point of Manila Bay. Under Spanish rule, ships sailing to Manila from Philippine and foreign ports had to stop off at a rambling, one-story concrete building so crews could be checked for cholera and smallpox. Mariveles became the site of the U.S. Public Health Quarantine Service Hospital. The old Quarantine Station, as it was now called, served as the administration building for the Section Base commander, who felt a special connection to Mariveles history because whenever he sat at his desk, he found himself staring at an erstwhile bidet fastened to the floor in front of it.

Legend has it that in the early seventeeth century a young friar from Bataan fell in love with a nun named Maria Velez. They fled from their orders by horse and *carabao,* only to be captured and turned over to the local magistrate, Corregidor, who sentenced them to eternal separation. Angered by the judge for assuming a divine role, a merciful God intervened. While he took pity on the young lovers, they had violated their vows, so he decreed they would stand as monuments to fidelity as well as divine justice. Maria Velez would lie for eternity atop the mountain on Bataan that bears her foreshortened name. The friar could gaze at her forever from across the channel, his frown fixed in stone on the isle of El Fraile. And the magistrate who came between them was frozen in time as the island of Corregidor, with two islets, representing the horse and *carabao*—Caballo and Carabao—behind him.

Mariveles was little more than an impoverished barrio near the finest natural harbor on the Bataan peninsula. For its Section Base, the navy had acquired 150 acres of land that were rich with rice paddies and mangroves and allowed the natives, for whom a mango tree amounted to an annual salary, to work as tenant farmers. Construction was undertaken by Pacific Naval Contractors, which was owned by Morrison, Knudsen of Boise, Idaho, the same firm that had built up Wake Island and Sangley Point. But the work on the base was never finished, which meant that it could never serve the purpose for which it was intended: a shallow-water port for the maintenance and repair of destroyers.

On December 8 MacArthur privately acknowledged to Sutherland the need to "remove immediately to Bataan." By December 10 the general was mapping a retreat for Fil-American forces, falling back on the very strategy he had criticized for being a "passive" defense: War Plan Orange-3. The logistical hurdles were enormous. There were 66,000 Filipino and 12,000 American troops in Luzon. Moreover, since WPO-3 had been suspended at MacArthur's insistence, 18,000 tons of supplies had been moved north to prepare for MacArthur's plan of holding the beaches, and additional supplies were sent south to support defense positions there.

When G-3, MacArthur's operations section, had proposed that Bataan be stocked as "a safety measure," MacArthur had adamantly refused. A troop withdrawal to Bataan was inevitable, but MacArthur had nonetheless demanded that Corregidor be supplied first.

Once Corregidor was stocked, the priorities for Bataan were clear: ammunition and food, matériel and fuel, and medical supplies, in that order. Fifteen thousand tons of ammunition and truckloads of tank replacement parts were already on the peninsula. The army procured huge amounts of canned meats and fruit from Armour, Swift, and Libby and stocks of polished rice from Chinese merchants. There were 2,295,000 pounds of canned salmon; 152,000 pounds of canned fruit and vegetables; 8,000 pounds of fresh beef; 100,000 dry rations; and large stores of clothing and equipment. By agreement with the oil companies, the army took over the distribution of commercial gasoline.

The quantities were prodigious, but given the number of meals that were necessary to sustain combat troops at an average daily intake of 4,000 calories, they were alarmingly low. Commonwealth regulations forbade the transfer of rice and sugar across provincial lines. With the fall of Luzon imminent, the government feared that the Philippine people wouldn't have enough food under Japanese occupation. Five thousand tons of rice sitting in the Cabanatuan Rice Central depot, in addition to 2,000 cases of canned fish, corned beef, and clothing in Tarlac, were off limits to the military. The rice alone could have fed the troops on Bataan for nearly a year.

There were enough field rations for only thirty days, enough rice for twenty. WPO-3 had anticipated a holding action on Bataan lasting up to six months, but for a considerably smaller force than actually moved to the peninsula. So there was another invisible enemy the men would face on Bataan: hunger. And hunger only made them more susceptible to disease.

Then there was the problem of time, for even under the best of conditions it was projected that supplying 43,000 men on Bataan, as called for by WPO-3, would take a minimum of two weeks. MacArthur didn't even broach the idea of retreat to President Quezon until December 12, the day Germany and Italy declared war on the United States, and he wouldn't officially implement it until the beach defense was tested on December 22. The delay would have disastrous consequences. Tons of supplies would be shipped from Manila to Bataan by boat, barge, lighter, and rail, but there was only one two-lane overland route, and tons more would be left behind.

———

John Bookman wasn't the first doctor to be concerned about the problem of malaria on Bataan. A malaria survey had been undertaken in the Philippines in the early 1920s at the instigation of the International Health Board and Governor General Leonard Wood. Attempts at malaria control were made at the major sugar mills and haciendas of Pambanlag, La Mitra, and Carmencita and in the municipalities of Florida Blanca and Porac. First applied in 1927 at Fort Stotsenberg in Manila with seemingly beneficial results, Paris green (copper arsetoarsenite) was the larvicide of choice. But rigorous studies weren't conducted until Henry L. Stimson became Governor General in 1928. His keen interest in the health and welfare of the Filipino population led to the creation of the Advisory Committee for Malaria Control.

From 1924 to 1929 the Philippine Health Service, in conjunction with the Rockefeller Foundation, commissioned field studies of malaria, but the data and reports obtained by the sanitary engineer, J. J. Mieldazis, were deemed inadequate. Victor Heiser, an associate director of the Rockefeller Foundation, then sought a doctor and scientist who was up to the challenge of malaria in the Philippines and the "outstanding problems" of bacillary dysentery, typhoid, and intestinal parasites. The man who filled that role and embarked on new, scientifically controlled studies was a young doctor then living in Owls Head, Maine, by the name of Paul Russell.

Russell arrived in Manila in January 1930 and began to study malaria in birds while keeping an eye on ways to reduce the cost of malaria control. He found that 1 percent of Paris green could be mixed with 99 percent charcoal and effectively eliminate mosquito larvae. He developed an automatic paddle-driver that could float on streams and evenly distribute the larvicide. And he experimented with fish (gambusia) as a means of naturally disposing of mosquito larvae.

But Russell's early findings didn't solve the larger issue of malaria control. Having visited thirty-six provinces over two and a half years in the Philippines, he proposed a new set of recommendations: treating streams breeding *Anopheles minimus* with Paris green; supplying local barrios with bed nets; making quinine "available to the people of malarial regions as freely as possible"; and removing the 50 percent duty on plasmochin, a compound developed by I. G. Farben in 1926 that was more effective than quinine but turned out to be highly toxic. The plan hinged on the revolutionary step of carrying out "anti-larval measures" at the local level under medical supervision instead of under a centralized Malaria Control Division, "because doctors in this part of the world will not get their feet muddy expect [sic] in cases of urgent personal necessity," he confided to Heiser. Even schoolboys who built fences, dug ditches, and planted vegetables as required by their curriculum, he argued, could engage in malaria control in their biology studies.

Russell visited Bataan in July 1931 with Major Rufus L. Holt of the U.S. Army Medical Research Board, as part of a general sanitary survey for a proposed army base south of Limay. Bataan was mostly jungle. There were "few foot trails, even fewer pack-trails, and no roads," as Colonel Richard C. Mallonée, adviser to the 21st Division of the Philippine Army, described it.

The problems Russell found on Bataan were numerous. Malaria as well as dysentery and typhoid—a scourge among Americans at the onset of the Spanish-American War—were common. The jungle on either side of the trail from Limay to Bagac was nearly impenetrable. Medical evacuation of the sick and wounded "would be extremely difficult," as would communication between army units. Sand fleas and mosquitoes plagued the lower elevations, while above 2,000 feet there were "myriads of leeches." The lumber company Cadwallader Gibson had had an extensive concession in Limay but folded up its operation in large part due to malaria, moving to Camarines Norte.

Malaria control in the 145-square-mile area selected for the line of resistance would involve treating 155 miles of streams with Paris green, 30,000 yards of irrigation ditches on either side of the peninsula, clearing stream banks, relocating an already infected native population, and spraying barrios. "Costly and time-consuming," Russell admitted, but malaria control was "absolutely essential to the continued operation of troops in this area."

That said, he came to the unsettling conclusion in April 1932 that "no *practical* control can be achieved anywhere in the islands in less than 10 years." Quinine bisulfate, derived from the bark of the cinchona tree, was effective for routine treatment, but "drugs alone," Russell warned, "will never control or materially reduce malaria in the Philippines."

Russell's pleas fell on deaf ears. In the decade since, the U.S. Army had made virtually no attempts at preventing malaria on Bataan. Quinine prophylaxis was favored over an antimosquito program. Back in 1917 when he was U.S. food administrator, Herbert Hoover saw an urgent need to "raise quinine" in the Philippines. Nothing was done, however, until four years later, when Governor General Wood, a Harvard-educated doctor who had watched a forest ranger in the Philippines die from the disease, procured the seeds of *Cinchona ledgeriana* from Java and turned them over to Arthur Fischer, director of the Philippines Bureau of Forestry. In six years Fischer was cultivating plants in Baguio. But Fischer found a more favorable climate for cinchona in the southern islands, and in 1927 he relocated the plantations to Mindanao. By 1936 Fischer was shipping bark to Manila, where he set up a factory that as of December 1941 was producing five and a half pounds of totaquinine daily.

Three months earlier Lieutenant Commander Thomas Hirst Hayes, who held the title of chief of sanitation for the Manila and Subic Bay areas as well as chief of surgery at Cañacao Hospital, attended a conference of visiting and resident medical officers. Hayes pointed to a circle he had drawn on a map of Bataan and said: "There lies our disease threat in this war." A survey conducted from September to December 1941 on Bataan uncovered malaria in all of the coastal villages. The disease would peak during the dry season from February to May. Thus far there was only one case of malaria among naval personnel in Mariveles.

As he collected mosquito larvae from the ponds and streams of Bataan looking for *Anopheles minimus,* John Bookman wondered what the health consequences of War Plan Orange-3 would be. Would there be enough quinine to treat infected troops and prevent others from falling ill? What would happen in the event of a malaria epidemic?

———————

Lieutenant Colonel Curtis Thurston Beecher "didn't exactly relish the idea of being shot at again." Beecher was well acquainted with war. He had served with the regiment in France during World War I. But in the wake of Pearl Harbor, there was a job to be done, which was to augment the marine guard at the Navy Section Base in Mariveles with the 1st Battalion, 4th Marines from Olongapo.

Because there were few facilities in Mariveles, the *Dewey* dry dock was hauled down from Olongapo. Submerged during the day to avoid enemy bombers, it was floated 200 yards off the beach on the western shore for the repair of PT boats and small craft. A barrier net was towed across the harbor entrance, moorings were put in for submarines and destroyers, and the surrounding waters were protected by a network of mines. Clockwise as you faced the harbor were the Quarantine Station, behind which was an emergency airstrip; the Section Base camp, positioned above Sisiman Cove, where Bulkeley's MTB Sqadron 3 made its home; and the *Canopus*, camouflaged in green and khaki to blend into the tropical foliage around Caracol Cove on the eastern shore. The *Maryanne*, now the flagship of the Inshore Patrol, escorted submarines through the minefields. Every time the Japanese tried to bomb the *Canopus* and missed, the crew treated itself to the newly killed fish that floated to the water's surface from the explosive impact.

Beecher knew it would be suicide to concentrate the marines in wooden barracks at the Section Base, so with the exception of a small guard, they hid in the hills behind Mariveles. The navy employed hundreds of Filipino workers, among whom were numerous fifth columnists. When lumber came in by the shipload, they would step up onto wooden pallets and proclaim the virtues of the Greater East Asia Co-Prosperity Sphere (Daitōa Kyōeiken), as Japan euphemistically called its military campaign to dominate Asia. The marine guard would just as quickly arrest the rabble-rousers and turn them over to the mayor of Mariveles, who was happy to help prosecute them.

By late 1941 war preparations at the Section Base reached a feverish pitch as the marines in Mariveles Harbor unloaded mounds of materials from Olongapo, Manila, and Cavite, including the furniture, iron bunks, and personal effects they had brought over from Shanghai. The days were long—ten to twelve hours, even on Sunday.

After hours there was little reward for all of their hard work except hitting Guzman's bar for a round of drinks, a game of duck pins, or billiards in the backroom. Or you might visit one of the *swali* shacks that seemed to spring up out of the ground like mushrooms after rain. As darkness fell, you could hear the sound of the jungle goblins back in the marine barracks—the lizards scurrying about on the canvas rooftops, the spiders the size of your fist fleeing into rolled-up tent flaps at the glare of a flashlight. The windows were screened, and the men slept under bed nets, or "mosquito bars." Which was a good thing, because it was at night, during the dry season between 2200 and 0300, that *Anopheles minimus*—"tiger mosquitoes," the troops called them—was most active in its search for human prey.

5

Exodus

RUMORS SPREAD like wildfire in Manila. The Americans had sunk the Japanese aircraft carriers that had launched the attack on Pearl Harbor! A thousand Japanese troops had stepped ashore at the mouth of the Pasig River! Germans wearing American uniforms had landed at Legaspi! A mirror tied to a tree at Clark Field had guided Japanese bombers to their target! A secret radio transmitter operated by a Japanese-American couple had been discovered at Cavite!

The truth was even stranger. President Quezon's gardener and masseur both turned out to be officers of the Imperial Japanese Army. One marine remembered sitting in Fuji's Bar, across the plaza in Cavite, on the night before Pearl Harbor, listening to the nickelodeon play Kate Smith's "God Bless America." Nurses at Sternberg reported missing menstrual cycles. Medical officers "suffered from nervous tension with anorexia (poor appetite), nausea and diarrhea," according to Sternberg's chief of medicine, Colonel James O. Gillespie. A patient at Cañacao was operated on and pronounced dead; when he arrived at the morgue door, he sat up and asked: "What ward are you taking me to?" A statement issued by Admiral Hart's office reported, erroneously, that all Cavite Navy Yard medical personnel had been killed when the dispensary was hit.

Manila was bombed regularly between noon and 0100. "You could set your watch" by the raids, said Captain John Wilkes, commander of Submarine Squadron 20. "We even advanced the lunch hour to eleven so we could eat before we dived into slit trenches."

But on the morning of December 19 George Ferguson and the men at his aid station on Cañacao Boulevard heard another rumor: reports of decreased activity "all over" the Philippines. Around noon he and Lieutenant (j.g.) Bernard W. Cohen, a navy doctor from Cañacao Hospital, ventured inside the triangle formed by the three radio towers at Sangley Point. Then, like clockwork, an air alarm sounded, followed by a flutter of bombs. A radio tower was knocked out instantly, the rear of a house was blasted to pieces, the power station received a direct hit, and 55-

gallon drums of aviation gasoline burst into flames. The roar of the fires drowned out the sound of planes and exploding bombs, one of which tore a hole in the road eighteen feet deep and twenty-three feet wide. The two doctors scurried like rats looking for shelter. They ran into a building that shook like a tambourine, with furniture dancing to its beat. George bolted out a side door after the first wave of planes passed and felt something hit him. His left knee was bleeding, and his right knee was knocked out laterally at a 45-degree angle. He hobbled down to a bomb shelter, where dozens of casualties began to stumble in. As best he could, he helped evacuate the wounded to Cañacao Hospital three blocks away, and from there they were ferried to Manila. A second alert sounded, and the two doctors ducked into the crawl space beneath the hospital. The hospital was supposed to be earthquake proof, but it heaved and groaned under the strain of bombs until it looked as if the overhead beams would cave in at any moment. When the all-clear sounded, there were thirteen dead—twelve of them marines—and forty wounded. Some had been incinerated in the fires. George suffered a small shrapnel wound in his left knee and a sprained right knee. It was nothing to worry about, he told himself, maybe a couple of torn ligaments.

The stress of war was beginning to show. Blackouts in Manila were frequent. Flares mysteriously brightened the skies, causing the trigger-happy Filipino soldiery, convinced they were the handiwork of fifth columnists, to cut loose at the source. Gasoline was rationed, headlight shields were mandatory. Businesses closed down, shops were boarded up, food was hoarded, and there was a run on the banks. Traffic—whether motorized, animal-drawn, bicycle, or pedestrian—was a nightmare.

George would have been okay, if it weren't for that ringing in his ears and a throbbing headache. Probably a concussion, he thought. After a sandwich and coffee for dinner, he downed five aspirin and slept on the hospital porch. That night a marine shot himself through the head. "Couldn't take it," George noted drily in his diary.

The next day Lieutenant Colonel John P. Adams, commander of the 1st Separate Battalion, was ordered to evacuate Cavite and position Batteries A and C around Mariveles. MacArthur formally requested command of the 4th Marines, and Admiral Hart, who considered the regiment the best available infantry in the Philippines, obliged. Henceforth Colonel Howard would report to MacArthur at USAFFE Headquarters. Excess naval personnel were to be attached to the 4th Marines, who were given the crucial role of beach defense on Corregidor. The marines and navy would continue to have their own medical support and supplies.

The admiral and the general had never gotten along well, even though

Hart had known MacArthur's family for four decades. Sixty-four years old, the diminutive Hart had been a close friend of MacArthur's older brother, Arthur, and was one of the few who dared to say, "Come on, Douglas. Sit down and let someone else talk." Hart outranked MacArthur; MacArthur wanted all U.S. naval forces in the Philippines under his command. MacArthur complained to Washington about the Asiatic Fleet's "inactivity" while the Japanese Navy demonstrated "complete freedom of action" in Philippine waters. Hart complained of MacArthur's inability to entertain anyone else's opinion except his own and admitted that "there has been very little get-together."

The Japanese didn't merely control the seas, they controlled the skies. Enemy planes passed daily over George's aid station. Antiaircraft fire crackled from the rear. Barge traffic on the Pasig River moved only at night. "Lord this business is nerve racking," George wrote. "If only we could see a few of our own planes around here it would help."

But the Far East Air Force had few planes left. Eighteen P-40s and fifty-two A-24s were en route to Manila via Brisbane in the seven-vessel *Pensacola* convoy, which also carried a field artillery brigade, ground elements of the 7th Heavy Bombardment Group, ammunition, bombs, and assorted vehicles and equipment, as well as 4,600 U.S. troops. When the planes were unloaded and assembled in Australia, however, they were found to be lacking key combat equipment. So the two fastest ships—the *Holbrook* and the *Bloemfontein*—sped out of Brisbane without the longed-for air support, but with the field artillery brigade and naval supplies that MacArthur and Hart so desperately needed.

On the morning of December 21 the submarine *Stingray* spotted the Japanese invasion fleet off of Lingayen Gulf. MacArthur ordered tanks to the north and Brereton's planes to the skies, then alerted beach defenders that landings were imminent. Hart sent four submarines to the Lingayen area to join the *Stingray.* But they failed spectacularly in their attempts to sink Japanese landing force vessels. The waters were shallow, there was no place to hide from enemy depth charges, and the Mark VI magnetic exploders, which Hart himself had helped develop back in 1929, were faulty. Torpedoes ran four feet beneath their targets and failed to detonate even when they hit them. Only *S-38*, commanded by Lieutenant Wreford "Moon" Chapple, made a successful kill, sinking the 5,445-ton troop transport *Hayō Maru.* Opposition from Brereton's reduced air force was even less effective. To compound the problem, MacArthur had expected the Japanese to land near the mouth of the Agno River, at the southern end of Lingayen Gulf, where Fil-American forces had emplaced the muscle of their artillery. Instead, some eighty-five enemy transports bearing the bulk of the enemy invasion force headed to points north forty miles away.

By December 22, 43,110 men from Lieutenant General Homma Masaharu's 14th Army and Lieutenant General Tsuchibashi Yūichi's 48th Division had landed in rough seas along a fifteen-mile stretch of the Lingayen Gulf coast virtually uncontested. Of them, 34,856 were actually ground troops. Their only opposition came from a Filipino battalion of the 11th Division near Bauang that, in spite of its brave defense, could do little to prevent the Japanese from establishing a beachhead. Homma would make Bauang his 14th Army Headquarters, by which time his troops were swarming down into central Luzon. Many infantrymen of the 48th Division rode bicycles. Manila was only 100 miles to the south.

"The enemy has landed scattered elements along the shores of Lingayen Gulf," MacArthur trumpeted over local radio in Manila on the evening of December 22. "My gallant divisions are holding ground and denying the foe the sacred soil of the Philippines. We have inflicted heavy casualties on his troops, and nowhere is his bridgehead secure. Tomorrow we will drive him into the sea."

Lingayen wasn't MacArthur's only problem. The next night, as if in answer to an idle boast, 7,000 troops mostly from Lieutenant General Morioka Susumu's 16th Division, began coming ashore at Lamon Bay, 200 miles to the southeast. The area was defended by the 1st Regular Division and the 51st Division of the Philippine Army, but resistance soon turned into a rout as forces fell out of position. A rope was now coiled around Manila's neck.

Homma's troops had been ashore at Lingayen for forty hours before MacArthur, on the evening of December 23, finally reverted to War Plan Orange-3. The rationale was that standing off the Japanese in the north would enable Major General Albert M. Jones's South Luzon Force to circumvent Manila and ease through the bottleneck of San Fernando by January 8 while Major General George M. Parker prepared Bataan's defenses. Engineers would dynamite the two bridges south of San Fernando at Calumpit that enabled Highway 3 and the main line of the Manila Railroad to cross the 500-foot-wide Pampanga River, thereby slamming the door shut in the face of the Japanese. Then North Luzon Force, under the command of Major General Jonathan Wainwright, would retreat to Bataan.

Wainwright took the news hard. The Philippine Scouts of the 26th Cavalry could fight valiantly, but the Philippine Army was a sorry spectacle. The 11th Division scattered after the Japanese made it to shore, as did two regiments of the 71st Division, when Homma's troops attacked them four miles south of the Baguio junction. MacArthur's forces to the northeast were completely cut off. His much-vaunted beach defense was in tatters. Admiral Hart was moving his headquarters to Java. General Brereton was secretly retreating to Australia. Wainwright knew it meant "the last ditch."

The Japanese had made a mockery of MacArthur's vow to defend Luzon's coastline "at all costs." Weeks had been lost when vital elements of WPO-3 could already have been in place. Now, at the eleventh hour, MacArthur was forced into a devil's bargain by trading a failed military strategy for one that would knowingly sacrifice the defenders of Bataan and Corregidor.

Back in Washington, the Arcadia Conference began, which established the Combined Chiefs of Staff Committee, composed of the U.S. Joint Chiefs of Staff and the British Chiefs of Staff to advise Roosevelt and Churchill on a coordinated military strategy. The Americans proposed British General Archibald Wavell as supreme commander of the combined American-British-Dutch-Australian command (ABDA) in the Southwest Pacific. Admiral Hart became Wavell's naval commander. But in a study submitted at the conference, U.S. Army planners concluded "with ruthless severity and some overstatement," thought Secretary of War Stimson, that the Philippines could not be reinforced. MacArthur's hope for an offensive from Australia to Mindanao was judged "an entirely unjustifiable diversion of forces from the principal theater—the Atlantic."

"Everybody knows the chances are against our getting relief to him," Stimson admitted in his diary, "but there is no use saying so beforehand."

———————

Masses of men and matériel began to fall back along five defensive positions from the Aguilar-Urdaneta line (south of Lingayen Gulf) to the Bamban-Sibul Springs line just north of Mt. Arayat. This was no textbook retreat, like those of McDowell's army in the Battle of Bull Run and General Lee at Gettysburg. It was a delaying action, and the Philippine Scouts fought for every inch of ground. Important tank and artillery movements rolled out at night to avoid the threat of enemy air attacks. The North Luzon engineers followed the retreating columns, demolishing bridges once they had crossed them. But a single act of the Japanese—bombing the bridges at Calumpit, thirty miles north of Manila—could bring the South Luzon Force withdrawal to a grinding halt. Homma, however, misread the migration, believing it to consist of scattered elements of the Philippine Army. So as the Japanese closed in on Manila, the Fil-American exodus continued into Bataan.

Simultaneous with the retreat of troops was the army's medical evacuation of Manila. Sternberg was deactivated in three phases. The first cadre of medical officers and nurses left Manila on December 22. Their destination was Limay, Bataan, where Hospital No. 1 was established east of the barrio as a frontline surgical facility near the Abucay-Hacienda line. The 1,000-bed hospital had been anticipated by WPO-3. Its components were already in storage at Camp Limay, a battalion post where a quartermaster depot stored food and gasoline for the defense reserve. Colonel James "Ducky" Duckworth was commanding officer. Lieutenant Commander Carey M. Smith of Cañacao Hospital was chief of surgery, assisted by navy nurse Ann Bernatitus.

But to call it a hospital is like calling a hut a hotel. Hospital No. 1 was a primitive facility in the wilds of Bataan. The structures were wood-framed, open to the elements, and roofed with *nipa*-thatch. Only the convalescent ward, medical supply, and storehouses were protected overhead—with galvanized steel. There was one X-ray machine, and pressure-cookers heated by Bunsen burners were used as sterilizers.

A second echelon departed on December 24 to install General Hospital No. 2, a convalescent facility in the rear at Kilometer 162.5 on the road from Manila. Colonel James O. Gillespie was commanding officer, and Lieutenant Colonel Jack Schwartz was surgeon. Situated on the south bank of the Real River, 1.25 miles west of Cabcaben, Hospital No. 2 was outfitted by the Engineer Corps with its own water-purification plant, equipment from the annex at Estado Major, provisions that the quartermaster was able to scrounge up in Manila, and small shipments from Cebu and Iloilo.

The medical supply depot was a mere half-mile away, but the speed of the evacuation, the confusion, and the congestion meant that crucial equipment was abandoned, looted, or lost. The irony is that some ninety regimental dispensaries were en route to the Philippines when war broke out.

The final group from Sternberg included 450 patients who were transported aboard the *Don Estaban* to Corregidor, where they were transferred to the army hospital in Malinta Tunnel. Colonel Carroll escorted the handicapped and severely wounded to Port Darwin, Australia, on the *Mactan*, an interisland ferry whose passengers included the last army nurse to leave Manila, Floramund Fellmuth. The eleven navy nurses from Cañacao were unaccountably left behind.

Meanwhile the evacuation of Olongapo was under way. Hayes, designated regimental surgeon of the 4th Marines, quickly assembled his team from navy medical staff. Hayes named Marion Wade battalion surgeon of Colonel "Red" Anderson's 2nd Battalion, while Wade relied on Lieutenant Benjamin Bruce Langdon and Fred Berley for support. After Olongapo was bombed, the station hospital was abandoned for a field unit buried so deep in the bamboo jungle that at midday it was shrouded in gloom. Hayes was determined to remove as much medical equipment as was possible from Olongapo and incorporate its medical personnel into the Navy Section Base.

Fred wasn't worried. On December 23, 1941, he wrote his parents:

> *Dear Folks:*
>
> *It looks as tho the war is going to delay my coming home for a while—but I don't think it will be too big a delay.*
>
> *I am well & happy and shall do my best to continue to stay that way—so don't worry—please. We are fighting for a most just cause and I am more than glad to be doing my small bit.*
>
> *My love to all.*
>
> *Your son,*
>
> *F. V. Berley*
>
> *U. S. 4th Marines, P.I.*

No big deal. The war wouldn't last six months.

The new medical detachment of the 4th Marines was nearly complete once George Ferguson joined John Bookman in Mariveles.

But back in Quezon City, Murray Glusman was told to remain at Holy Ghost Convent and College as part of a skeleton force to await the Japanese in Manila. He felt as if the axis of the world had just shifted, yet somehow he was expected to stay in place.

The flaws in the army's prewar plan for the Manila Hospital Center were now all too apparent. Valuable time, effort, and equipment had been wasted as medical teams hopscotched the city. With the Japanese advancing rapidly from Lingayen in the north and Lanon Bay in the southeast, the concept of stable warfare was no longer valid. Enemy strategy was determining daily movements in a situation where there was a conspicuous gap in the chain of command. The battle lines on Bataan had already been drawn. So what was the point of keeping navy personnel and equipment in Manila? Murray wondered. Shouldn't the medical staff be where they could be of some help?

The navy did its best to prevent the Japanese from seizing American supplies in Manila. More than 100 tons of supplies and field equipment were shipped from the Cañacao Naval Medical Supply Depot alone.

One complete battalion field unit was sent to Mariveles, where it was set up in an area behind the Navy Section Base known as Camp Dewey to treat an overflow of patients from the dispensary. Another partial battalion field unit was assigned to the 1st Separate Battalion in Mariveles and then moved to Corregidor.

But the dispersal of medical equipment throughout the eight annexes of the Manila Hospital Center made a complete evacuation impossible. Major Orion V. "Pete" Kempf, Sternberg's medical supply officer, worked day and night to move stocks by truck to the Philippine Medical Supply Depot near Hospital No. 1 on the Bataan-Mariveles road and by barge to Corregidor. Further efforts were hampered once Filipino crews abandoned the railroads and transportation by train screeched to a halt. As a result, substantial stores were left behind at Clark Field, at Fort McKinley, and at Fort Stotsenberg, which had been prematurely abandoned by American officers and fell prey to looting. Red Cross warehouses in Santa Ana and Santa Mesa were vandalized; depots at Tarlac and Los Baños were sacked. Rizal Stadium was stacked high with food and supplies that never made it to Bataan or Corregidor. What had miraculously survived the bombings of the Cavite Navy Yard and Sangley Point, but couldn't be removed on time to Mariveles and the Rock, now had to be destroyed.

On December 24 at his office in the Marsman Building, Admiral Hart informed Rear Admiral Rockwell that MacArthur was planning on declaring Manila an "Open City" on Christmas Day. Hart himself had just learned the news, which gave him twenty-four hours to remove all ships, submarines, and supplies from Manila. Under the Geneva Convention, military activity was prohibited in an "open city." The intention, as the proclamation stated, was "to spare the Metropolitan area from the possible ravages of attack, either by air or ground." The Japanese used it as an open invitation to step up bombing.

Since Hart was transferring headquarters south, Rockwell would assume command of all naval forces in the Philippines, which amounted to six PT boats, two submarine tenders, three minesweepers, three river gunboats, two district and two civilian tugs, and two converted yachts. Headquarters of the 16th Naval District would be relocated in one of the four navy tunnels on Corregidor. It was Rockwell's last meeting with Hart, and it was interrupted three times by air raids.

In a separate meeting Rockwell instructed Colonel Howard to mine the Olongapo Naval Station and incorporate the 1st Separate Battalion into the 4th Regiment. Before Olongapo was demolished, Fred Berley ventured into the abandoned PBY barracks, where in one of the lockers he found a few towels, a Gem razor, a toothbrush, and eighty pesos. He took down the locker owner's name and left him a note saying he'd return the money when he got back to the States.

There was no time to lose. The *Canopus* was hit that day, bomb fragments spattering its decks. The naval medical supply depot was demolished. Depth charges were placed in the forward torpedo room and conning tower of the *Sealion* to scuttle it. Manila's waterfront was about to go up in flames.

That same morning Hayes arrived in Mariveles with Lieutenant (j.g.) Robert G. Herthneck of the Dental Corps, and Pharmacist's Mate Jeremiah V. Crews. On his way in he met Lieutenant John Edward Nardini at his aid station in the Cabulog River valley, "a gentleman and a scholar." Then he went to the Section Base dispensary to introduce himself to John Bookman, "another excellent medical officer." They were in the midst of a conversation when an air raid siren sounded. Bookman and Hayes took cover in one of the tunnels under construction. Explosions rolled like thunder into the hills.

The Japanese had spotted the Free French freighter SS *Si Kiang* fifty yards offshore in Mariveles Harbor. Bound for Indochina, she had been intercepted and detained by the Americans. Colonel Otto Harwood, an army quartermaster officer, decided to seize her valuable cargo of gasoline, kerosene, and flour for the Camp Limay depot and requested a marine guard. Harwood had spent the past ten days dispersing stocks from Limay for the supply of troops along the East Road. The bulk of the work took place at night to avoid aerial detection, but the *Si Kiang* was unloaded in broad daylight. It was an invitation to disaster. Enemy planes plastered the ship with bombs before targeting the Section Base and moving on to Manila Bay installations. The fuel had already been salvaged, but five million pounds of flour were lost.

A PT boat sped out to the sinking vessel. Ambulances and litter parties rushed down to the dock. John Bookman and George Ferguson stood by to receive the wounded at the Camp Dewey aid station. It was the first bombing of Mariveles and their first medical emergency together. The two doctors worked coolly, quickly, professionally. George, who had years of experience over John, demonstrated keen judgment without ever being judgmental, without ever pulling rank. He was colorful, colloquial, and always made the best of a bad situation, and this one wasn't too bad. John liked him immediately. A few of the wounded were evacuated to Hospital No. 1 in Limay. Overflow patients from the Section Base were bedded down in Nardini's aid station. But it was clear that the Section Base dispensary would also have to be evacuated. In a broad, open meadow, it stood in the crosshairs of enemy bombers.

Hayes saw at first hand the smooth, well-oiled operation the junior medical officers ran in Mariveles, and it filled him with pride. The air raid was over by 1600, but the flames from the ship burned through the night, lighting the way for bombers along the East Road. "Just why they didn't come back that night and blow hell out of us is difficult to understand," Hayes later wrote. Eight marines from the 1st Battalion were on board the *Si Kiang.* Two were killed, and three were injured along with a dozen or so crew members. They were the first losses sustained by the 1st Battalion, the first men in his unit George had seen die.

As Hayes put it, "Life was a matter of staying under cover in the bamboo jungle, no canvas was permitted, the camps were constantly moving, bathing facilities were the stream beds, and one slept on the ground near a foxhole or some convenient ditch into which one could roll in the event of an air attack."

On Christmas Eve, MacArthur, President Quezon, High Commissioner Sayre, and their respective families and staffs evacuated Manila for Corregidor. Manila's gold, silver, paper money, and securities were packed into trunks, lockers, and whiskey crates to be deposited in the government vault in Corregidor's Government Ravine. Brigadier General Richard J. Marshall, USAFFE deputy chief of staff, was instructed to stay behind until the withdrawal of men and matériel was complete. Quezon ordered his executive secretary, Jorge Vargas, and his secretary of justice, José Laurel, to remain in Manila "to deal with the Japanese."

The Port Area was deserted. The *Sealion* exploded at midnight. Pillars of fire illuminated the sky in the absence of moonlight. The *Canopus* steamed toward Mariveles, "with great columns of smoke astern of us," said Captain E. L. Sackett, "as evidence that the army was scorching the earth as they prepared to withdraw into Bataan."

Manila awoke to "a strange Christmas Day," remarked the *Manila Bulletin*, "facing with fortitude the peril of enemy bombs and alien invasion, besieged with false rumor and seeking comfort in the 2,000-year-old observance of the birth of Christ." Bing Crosby's "Adeste Fidelis" was playing from the loudspeakers in Manila's City Hall tower when it was interrupted by the wail of an air raid siren. The bombing of the docks and harbor installations intensified.

The Sangley Point radio station, marine railway, and ammunition depot were detonated with depth charges and dynamite by the demolition detail of the 1st Separate Battalion at Cavite before they left for Mariveles.

The district naval intelligence officer, Lieutenant Mike Cheek, destroyed confidential documents and nonessential files. One million gallons of oil were sent up in flames. The city was ringed with fire. The last directive of Rear Admiral Rockwell, 16th Naval District commandant, to Captain Davis was "to maintain a naval hospital in the Manila area." But the army viewed Balintawak, where the Cañacao medical staff were in residence at Philippine Union College, as a potential battleground. So the naval hospital unit and its patients were moved again—the third time in as many weeks—to Santa Scholastica College. Murray's orders were changed as well.

Around noon Murray was dispatched by Colonel Carroll and Captain Davis to Philippine Union College. There he joined two medical officers, one dental officer, and fifteen corpsmen preparing to leave for Mariveles. But only one truck was available, so Murray and seven corpsmen returned to Manila, where he was instructed by Admiral Hart's office to leave by boat at 1600. No boat was available. He quartered his men in the White House Hotel.

Christmas carolers strolled through the streets, their songs punctuated by explosions. The gasoline and oil stores of Caltex, Mobil, and Shell were being jettisoned in the Pandacan district, sending flames hundreds of feet into the air. It was Murray's last night in the city, and he asked Galia, one of the White Russian women from Shanghai, if she would spend it with him. She was visibly nervous when they checked into the Manila Hotel. He had registered her as his wife. But it was a romantic evening, and from their bed they watched the nighttime sky streaked with mysterious red flares and intermittent gunfire. The war seemed far away, unreal, its sounds muffled by distance and desire. He would be gone in the morning, and he knew he would never see Galia again. She must have known the same, must have been used to it, too. But she wanted him to understand why she had been so uncomfortable at first. He was Jewish, and she hadn't ever thought she could marry a Jewish man.

In the early morning hours of December 26, Admiral Hart stole away from Manila Bay aboard the submarine *Shark*. A banner was strung across City Hall that declared Manila an "Open City" and implored "No Shooting." The newspapers carried the text of the proclamation and reported that Hong Kong had fallen. A column of smoke from the bombing of the waterfront eclipsed the sun. Every boat and *banca* in the Pasig River, it seemed, had been sunk. Masts of doomed ships poked through the water like so many dead branches. It was time to say goodbye.

From Manila the road to Bataan runs north on Route 3, swings southwest at San Fernando on Route 7, then goes down the coast on the East Road—the old National Road—past the steep zigzag below "Little Baguio," and on to Mariveles. When two vehicles met head on, you had to creep over to the shoulder or backtrack until you found a cutout to let the other pass. When an enemy plane flew overhead, you pulled under a tree, and dove into a trench or a foxhole if you could find one.

This was the main artery for thousands of Fil-American troops en route to positions and encampments, and for days it was choked with traffic—army jeeps, Bren gun carriers, Pambusco buses, cars, *caretelas,* and *carabao*-driven carts. The dust and fumes from tanks, trucks, trailers, and half-tracks were nearly asphyxiating to the foot soldiers and civilians. The dirt tracks leading back into the hills—*bundok,* the Filipinos called them, or boondocks, as the Americans interpreted them—were "black with people striving to reach their native villages before the murderous armies overwhelmed them," wrote AP correspondent Clark Lee.

Philippine Army soldiers held up two fingers to signal "V for Victory Joe." To which the wiseacres of the 192nd Tank Battalion replied, toward the end of the retreat: "V for vacate, Joe." Drivers lost their way, tempers frayed, engines overheated, fuel was depleted, and vehicles broke down. Philippine Army engineers stopped traffic and blew bridges, sometimes too soon, leaving marching men stranded on the wrong side of a river. Soldiers were separated from their units; units were separated from their food and supplies. Along the way the army could be seen digging in defensive positions and gun emplacements.

The Japanese had breached the second line of defense in northern Luzon. They had crossed the Agno River, bypassed the exhausted 26th Cavalry of the Philippine Scouts, and broken through Highway 3, which runs south of San Miguel down to San Fernando. They had forced the 11th Division of the Philippine Army back, elements of which had been cut off by the Lingayen landings. In southern Luzon two Japanese columns were moving west from Lamon Bay, grinding toward the capital city. The noose around Manila was tightening.

Murray and his corpsmen slipped through by truck. The corpsmen were armed to the teeth with pistols and daggers and looked more like a band of brigands than medical personnel. Hostile planes threatened the exodus, but their efforts were sporadic. When the men reached Mariveles, it was obvious something was wrong. The place was a ghost town. Where the hell was everybody? Murray wondered.

Suddenly the commanding officer of the Section Base, W. H. Harrington, came barreling up and bellowing at the top of his lungs: "Godammit! I told you guys to take cover when an air raid siren goes off, and the next one who doesn't, I'm going to shoot!"

Murray explained that they had just come from Manila, hadn't heard the alarm, and certainly would have taken cover if they had. They hid in the woods, and once the all-clear sounded, Harrington proudly showed off the Mariveles Harbor defenses. By accident, he fired a .50-caliber machine gun, which sent a stream of bullets skittering across the water.

Killing your own men, Murray thought. The idea was absurd.

6

Rendezvous

You never knew how you were going to react under fire. Some men were stoic, some hysterical. Some men saw a job to be done, some couldn't help but run. Some men soiled themselves, some kept a stiff upper lip. Some saw the air compress before their eyes, some tasted metal in their mouths. The bomb craters became graves, and the graves left gaping holes in the lives of loved ones back home that were never filled in, not really, not completely. As Chaplain William Thomas Cummings is alleged to have said in one of his field sermons on Bataan: "There are no atheists in foxholes."

George Ferguson would turn twenty-eight on New Year's Day. It was a time of reckoning, to be sure. Two and a half years in the navy, three weeks of war. Five hundred dead at Cavite, four hundred injured, one suicide. Fourteen dead at Sangley Point, seventeen wounded. Two and a half years of marriage, and not one Christmas or New Year's with Lucy. He was about to become a full lieutenant.

He keenly felt her absence, imagined the void he had created in her life, which had changed dramatically since she returned from Shanghai to the States. Going back to Wausau must have felt like walking into an old bedroom you hadn't slept in for years. Lucy decided to move in with a friend in Evanston, Illinois, where she taught first grade at Highland Park.

George couldn't complain. Life at the Section Base in Mariveles had been pretty good. The rooms were small, but the view was swell. There were showers, laundry service, even a hole in a nearby rock for a bomb shelter. Hell, the place was a palace compared to that pothole he had hidden out in near Cañacao. Like the rest of the marines concentrated in Mariveles, the doctors were already on rations of two meals a day. They supplemented their diet with crackers, hardtack, canned meat, and whatever provisions they could find. Unlike Fred, who had no Christmas meal during the arduous retreat from Olongapo, George enjoyed a little holiday ham and turkey in his supper. "What a Christmas but glad I'm alive," he penned in his diary. "Wounded all okay."

The Section Base was protected by Lieutenant William F. Hogaboom's Battery A, which surveilled harbor facilities from lookout points on Pucot and High Ridge. Up the East Road in a dried-out rice paddy surrounded by bushes was Willy Holdredge's Battery C, insulated with several thousand sandbags. A small mountain stream nearby was used for cooking, cleaning, and bathing.

To the southeast were seven tunnels that had been blasted out of a hillside with jackhammers and dynamite for a naval ammunition and mine depot, diesel oil and fuel storage, headquarters and personnel. Two more tunnels were excavated at the Mariveles airstrip. The tailings were dumped into rice paddies to lay a base foundation for the roads.

Mariveles was now the temporary headquarters of the 4th Marines. With the exceptions of Batteries A and C and the radar detachment of the 1st Separate Battalion, the regiment would move to Corregidor on the nights of December 27 and 28. Most of the marines were bivouacked in the bamboo jungle because of the danger of air raids. George replaced John Nardini as battalion surgeon of the 1st Separate Battalion—or "Desperate Bat," as he called them. He took command of the aid station in the Cabulog River valley, which relieved the Section Base dispensary of further care for them.

John and Murray would remain behind to oversee all medical activities in Mariveles, assisted by Lieutenant (j.g.) Bernard Cohen, who had arrived from Balintawak and set up shop at the Quarantine Station. Murray was amazed at the change that had come over John since he'd last seen him in Manila. Sociability had replaced shyness, and confidence had won out over insecurity. John seemed to know everyone at the Section Base, down to the mining engineers. His position as medical officer conferred a certain authority, but it was the manner in which he interacted with officers, enlisted men, staff, and Filipino laborers that earned him their respect. Every once in a while he could even get those cowboys in MTB Squadron 3, Captain John Bulkeley and Lieutenant Robert B. Kelly, to listen to him. What had initially appeared to Murray as a pale personality bloomed into full color. Murray couldn't have imagined such a profound transformation. He found himself far more at ease with John now that John seemed more comfortable with himself, more open to the idea of friendship. Perhaps what was most surprising was Murray's own surprise at how quickly people can change.

How fitting, then, that Fred should give John a nickname after meeting him at the Section Base dispensary. Their backgrounds and personalities—a whip-smart Chicago boy and a blue-blooded New

Yorker, a career officer and a reservist—couldn't have been more different. But there was nothing pretentious about John. He was good-natured, even-tempered, solid. Murray loved to speculate; John was more rational. Murray could be exasperating with his "on one hand, on the other hand, on the third hand" approach to a problem; John was more predictable, hence more reliable. Murray chafed at authority; John quietly accommodated it. As friends pin monikers on one another, so Fred did with John by calling him Jake. Which happened to be an abbreviation of John's middle name, in honor of his enterprising grandfather, Jacob Bookman. He thought of John as his closest friend.

On the night of December 28 Fred Berley went to Corregidor by barge with the 2nd Battalion. Hayes departed by ship with Bob Herthneck and Pharmacist's Mate Jeremiah V. Crews. Early moonrise bathed the bay in a gossamer mist. Deck lights were turned off, smoking was prohibited, and voices were hushed as the vessels slowly wove their way through the minefield in North Channel. The island loomed out of the darkness, rising to a head 393 feet high at Malinta Hill and tapering down to a tail at Hooker Point, its aura of mystery enhanced by stories of its might.

Three and a half miles long and one and a half miles at its widest, Corregidor's diminutive size and its strategic position as the sentinel of Manila Bay had made it a prized possesion over the centuries. Chinese pirates had once occupied the Rock, as did Moros and the Dutch, but it was the Spanish who reestablished Corregidor as a fort. Their occupancy ended abruptly on May 2, 1898, when two ships from Commodore Dewey's fleet, the *Raleigh* and the *Baltimore*, landed at Corregidor to demand its surrender before its coastal defenses fired a single shot. The island quickly passed into American hands. By November of that year it housed a convalescent hospital. Not until May 1908 did it become a U.S. garrison.

At the request of Washington, fortification of the island was begun in 1904 by the Manila Army Engineers. Eventually twenty-three heavy rifle and mortar batteries were installed around the "head" of the tadpole. The guns were huge, in some cases weighing up to ten tons apiece. Batteries Crockett, Wheeler, and Cheney boasted 12-inch "disappearing rifles" that hid behind concrete parapets 3 feet thick during loading and had a range of 17,000 yards. Battery Way held four mammoth mortars forged by Bethlehem Steel in 1890 and sunk in concrete pits. Battery Geary had eight mortars, including the later model M-1908. As antiquated as they looked, they could fire one round per minute with a range of 14,000 yards in any direction. Batteries Smith and Hearn could be elevated 30 degrees and drop a target 29,500 yards away. Antiaircraft batteries were armed with 3-inch guns, .50-caliber machine guns, and 60-inch Sperry searchlights. The 59th Coast Artillery Regiment had a separate searchlight battery.

The north shore of the Rock faces Bataan; the south shore is distanced from Cavite by a crescent of small satellite islands that were converted into fortresses as well. Closest to the Rock is Fort Hughes (Caballo), which brandished two 14-inch rifles at Batteries Woodruff and Gillespie, in addition to four deadly M-1912 mortars at Battery Craighill, whose range of 19,300 yards enabled them to reach either Bataan or Cavite. Next is El Fraile, known as Fort Drum, a craggy outpost that was leveled to the waterline, then rebuilt with walls 25 to 36 feet thick, and sported four casemated 6-inch guns on the sides of the hull, and two twin-gun 14-inch turrets on the bow. The 14-inch guns required shells that weighed 1,560 pounds each and 440 pounds of powder. With a little cabin, a sixty-foot fire control cage mast, and a searchlight to complete its nautical appearance, Fort Drum was known as the "concrete battleship." Farthest away and just 500 yards from the south shore of Cavite is Carabao Island. Renamed Fort Frank, the island juts vertically from the sea, flaunting two 14-inch disappearing rifles at Batteries Greer and Crofton, and eight M-1908 mortars at Battery Koehler.

As a result of the 1921 Washington Conference and the 1930 London Naval Treaty, fortification on Corregidor ground to a halt. But that didn't stop three diehard army generals from initiating construction of a simple "tunnel road" under Malinta Hill, allegedly for the convenience of the small Air Corps garrison at Kindley Field. Their plan was anything but simple, and it took seven years to complete. With old mining equipment and convict labor from Bilibid Prison in Manila, a sprawling underground complex was built that included a main east-west passage 825 feet long and 50 feet wide, with some fifty lateral tunnels about 150 feet long. Nicknamed "little San Francisco" for the electric trolley line that ran through its main tube and all the way down to the water's edge, Malinta Tunnel was a subterranean city that contained headquarters for General MacArthur and the USAFFE as well as General Moore's Harbor Defenses, repair shops, storage facilities, and a 1,000-bed army hospital at its northeast end. The quartermaster area branched off the south end and led to four adjoining navy tunnels—Affirm, Baker, Roger, and Queen, where the 16th Naval District had its headquarters. Near Monkey Point was a separate Navy Radio Intercept Tunnel, where ten officers and fifty-one enlisted men under the command of Lieutenant Rudolph J. Fabian operated a "Purple" machine and engaged in the highly secretive work of intercepting and decrypting Japanese radio traffic. On January 30, 1940, Station CAST, as it was called, provided Roosevelt with the first military intelligence of a Japanese naval buildup in the South China Sea.

Corregidor's armament, while old, was still formidable. The island was defended by Americans in the 59th and 60th Coast Artillery Regiments and by Filipinos in the 91st and 92nd Coast Artillery Regiments. The army boasted that it would take 100,000 Japanese to seize "the Gibraltar of the East." But Corregidor's defenses were designed to repel an attack from the sea, not from the air; only two batteries were operative when war broke out; and many of the island's guns were exposed to Bataan and Cavite.

The island was mapped into four sectors. Topside was the northwestern plateau, high above the sea. Middleside lay beneath it. Bottomside connected the tail to the head, sloping down to the North Dock, which was reserved for the army, and the South Dock, reserved for the navy. Above South Dock rose Barrio San José, which housed the families of Filipino servicemen before hostilities broke out and was formerly the seat of Corregidor's government during Spanish rule.

MacArthur moved into a cottage on Topside after his wife, Jean, complained of the odor in their Lateral No. 3 quarters, emanating from the laboratory of Leland D. Bartlett of the Philippine Division's 4th Separate Chemical Company. High Commissioner Sayre had a house near the Kindley Field airstrip. Quezon, racked with tuberculosis, preferred the openness of a large tent outside the mouth of Malinta Tunnel.

———

The Post Medical Inspector greeted Hayes at North Dock and offered to put him up for the night at his quarters on Topside. A trolley took Fred Berley to Middleside barracks, where the 60th Coast Artillery was billeted along with the newly arrived 4th Marines. A massive rectangle of steel-reinforced concrete three stories high with a ground level loggia, Middleside was much vaunted for being bombproof.

But by the light of day, Fred thought Corregidor looked more like a country club than a citadel. There was a parade ground, athletic field, golf course, and tennis court. Army officers at Fort Mills, as post headquarters was known, were dressed smartly in starched khakis, shirts, and ties. The Officers' Mess was located just outside Malinta Tunnel on a raised wooden platform and partly tented to shield the men from the sun. At night they kicked back, drank beer at the Officers' Club, and went to the Topside cinema for the latest feature or to San José to bet on a cockfight. When they weren't decoding top-secret Japanese messages, the boys from the Radio Intercept Tunnel liked to drive around Corregidor in a 1930 Packard touring car. Officers even had their own designated beach, protected by a shark net on the north shore, west of Infantry Point. A historic lighthouse built by the Spanish in 1853 lent a picturesque air to this oceanic idyll, sweetly scented with bougainvillea and hibiscus and lush with flame, frangipani, and fire trees. Corregidor was cooler than Bataan due to the gentle sea breezes—and blissfully free of mosquitoes.

Word on Bataan was that the Rock's 5-inch antiaircraft guns also kept enemy planes from straying any closer to the island during bombing runs to the mainland. When Fred discovered that there actually weren't any 5-inch antiaircraft guns on Corregidor, he thought, Oh boy. It's going to be Cavite all over again.

That morning, December 29, Hayes and Herthneck set up a temporary regimental medical headquarters—one field desk and a few folding canvas chairs—on the top floor of Middleside. In the early afternoon they had an appointment with the Post Medical Inspector at the old Fort Mills Station Hospital on Topside. In the meantime, they toured the island to get the lay of the land.

Space was at a premium on Corregidor: the Rock was packed with 9,000 men, stacks of ammunition, and numerous supply dumps. At the beginning of the war the station hospital—a 200-bed facility—was transferred to the north end of Malinta Tunnel, which was already being encroached upon by the staff and families of High Commissioner Sayre and President Quezon. There was no room for a separate navy hospital, Hayes realized after conferring with Beecher. Battalion aid stations would have to move near beach positions with the marines. All surgical cases would be handled by the one tunnel hospital. Lieutenant Colonel William Riney Craig, the commanding officer, begrudgingly allowed Hayes to maintain his field desk, two chests, and chairs near the receiving lateral for marine and navy casualties. This was the lofty Office of the Regimental Surgeon, 4th Marines. Hayes had dual responsibility as medical officer of the 16th Naval District, which meant providing medical supplies and services to naval personnel on Bataan, on the fortified islands, and on ships still in the Manila Bay area.

Shortly before noon Fred returned to Middleside after visiting his friend Bob Kelly of MTB Squadron 3, who had sped over from Bataan in a PT boat. Hayes had just concluded his meeting with Beecher and was on his way to the station hospital when an air warning alarm sounded at 1145. Within minutes forty bombers from the Japanese 5th Army's 5th Air Group appeared overhead with nineteen fighter escorts.

Fred strapped on his doughboy helmet and hit the deck in the same ground-floor room as Lieutenant Colonel Donald Curtis. He found himself in front of a door, exactly where he didn't want to be. But he couldn't move; the room was packed with 4th Marines. Hayes hurried back to Middleside, where he lay pressed up against a file cabinet. The bombers broke off into waves of nine, striking the island lengthwise with 200- and 500-pound bombs and strafing the AA batteries with machine gun fire.

The Far East Air Force couldn't spare a single P-40 to oppose them, but the guns at Fort Mills, Fort Hughes, and Battery C in Mariveles retaliated, expending more than 1,100 three-inch shells and blasting thirteen medium bombers out of the sky while the .50 calibers took credit for four dive bombers. Japanese pilots raised their altitude from 24,000 to 28,000 feet, which meant that by the time the batteries could reach them, the planes were so close they had already dropped their eggs. It seemed as if an entire regiment was pinned to the concrete deck.

"They knew we were there—apparently had waited for us to get bunched before visiting us," said Hayes. The old Fort Mills Station Hospital (which was shaped like a cross to distinguish it from Corregidor's other structures), the Officers' Club, and the Topside barracks were struck first. Then a 300-pound bomb scored a direct hit on Middleside a hundred feet to Fred's left, cascading through each floor like a stone dropping in water before it blew apart the room's walls and blasted out its doors and windows. The concussion was unbelievable. Hayes found himself clawing cement trying to disappear beneath it.

"I wasn't afraid," said Private 1st Class Ernest Bales of the 2nd Battalion. "I was scared shitless."

During the lull ammunition boxes stored outside crackled with fire until the word went around: "Here they come again." At 1300 the 11th Air Fleet took over from the army planes and continued the attack until 1415. At one point Hayes noticed a label on the cabinet drawer above him that read DEAD FILE. He tightened his helmet, rolled over to adjust his gun belt, and reached for the rabbit's foot he kept attached to it, only to discover that it was gone. Fred felt as if every bomb had his name on it.

The last group of bombers, twin-engine, twin-tail "Nells" from the Japanese Navy's 22nd Air Flotilla, swung into Mariveles Harbor and went after the *Canopus.* Amazingly, only one armor-piercing bomb hit the ship, whose camouflage was offset by the white gash of a cliffside rock quarry operated by the Atlantic Gulf and Pacific Company. The bomb penetrated the deck, blew open the magazines, and threatened to detonate the tender's ammunition. Smoke billowed from the burning vessel. Fire crews aimed hose streams down hatches. A rescue team ran belowdecks and into the engine room to extricate the wounded while Chaplain Francis Joseph McManus gave last rites to those fatally scalded by steam blasts. Fortunately a flood of water gushing from broken pipes prevented the rest of the powder from igniting. Soon the men on the *Canopus* put up their "Business as Usual" sign while the last submarines in the Asiatic Fleet prepared to leave Philippine waters. The *Canopus* would remain behind as a floating repair shop for the army and the few naval craft that remained in Manila Bay.

An estimated sixty tons of bombs were unleashed on Corregidor that day. Barrio San José, the cinema at Topside, a navy gasoline storage dump at the tail of the island, and the reservoir at Middleside—all were hit. The electric trolley line was destroyed, and almost every wooden structure was burned to the ground. Two of the five fatalities at Battery Boston "were blown clear into the trees," Chaplain John K. Borneman discovered. The Post Medical Inspector, whom Hayes and Herthneck had hoped to see, was killed instantly at the old station hospital. The raid left Fred shaking like a leaf.

The real target, as far as Lieutenant General Homma was concerned, was the "center of the American Far Eastern Army Command." Homma's attack was brazen, but his losses were high. In spite of his claim that Corregidor's batteries had been silenced, not one gun was permanently damaged, and most of the concrete structures remained intact.

Back in Mariveles, after treating casualties from the *Canopus*, Bernard Cohen gave George a shot of whiskey from a bottle he claimed the Japanese had dropped by mistake. "Well the Lord knows they are dropping everything they've got so it's not improbable that it did fall in his lap," George joked. "Glad it wasn't a bomb."

Like everyone else George had heard the rumors of the *Pensacola* convoy, "due in very soon," he believed. But the Japanese had already established bases in Borneo, and the ships that had set sail from Brisbane on December 28—the *Holbrook* and the *Bloemfontein*—couldn't possibly breach the enemy blockade. The supply line between Australia and the Philippines was severed. The longed-for reinforcements that had seemed to be just on the horizon disappeared beneath it. Nevertheless, Roosevelt assured MacArthur: "I give to the people of the Philippines my solemn pledge that their freedom will be redeemed. . . . The entire resources in men and materials of the United States must stand behind that pledge."

On the morning of January 2, George landed on the Rock with remnants of the 1st Separate Battalion, newly designated the 3rd Battalion, 4th Marines. Back on Bataan, Murray and Bernard Cohen took over the Cabulog River valley battalion aid station, which was close to a medical supply dump, reasonably well equipped, and able to accommodate up to thirty-five patients. The river flowed nearby, and the sounds of the bats and birds were oddly comforting at night.

The aid station was located over the hill from the Mariveles barrio and close to Battery C, which was fast gaining a reputation for its number of kills: "Death Valley," Corpsman Ernie Irvin dubbed it. But success was a double-edged sword. The Japanese were determined to silence the battery instead. In their Radio Manila broadcasts they referred to the area as "Mariveles Fortress." That day enemy planes returned for an encore.

There was a strange, muffled sound to the bombs that fell on Mariveles. The soil in southern Bataan is particularly loamy, and many bombs plunged several feet below ground before their fuses ignited. The resulting explosions were almost vertical, like geysers. This inhibited dispersion and helped protect man-made structures—to an extent.

The Japanese zeroed in on the barrio. Battery C roared into action, showering the aid station with shrapnel. Glusman and Cohen ran outside for cover, where they had their first lessons in field medicine. They treated casualties wherever they were out of the line of fire, be it a foxhole or a riverbed. They even performed an amputation in a ditch. With the abandonment of the Section Base dispensary and Cohen's sickbay at the old Quarantine Station, they were overwhelmed with wounded. The line of evacuation ran up the East Road to Hospital No. 2, just below Limay. Most cases could be removed within twenty-four hours, but ambulances were frequently strafed and easy targets for bombers.

The Japanese had destroyed the dispensaries at the Cavite Navy Yard, Olongapo, the Navy Section Base in Mariveles, and the old station hospital on Corregidor. Murray was beginning to feel as if he were being followed, as if a bull's-eye shadowed his every move, as if their aid station would be next. You couldn't help but be jittery—flinching at the sound of a jeep or truck backfiring, glancing over your shoulder or up at the sky, straining to hear the sound of approaching planes or the thunder of bombs in the distance. As one of the first American doctors in World War II to work behind the marines in action, he learned a chapter of navy medicine that was just being written. In the field, doctors and corpsmen were targets just like doughboys and leathernecks. There was one difference: they were defenseless.

= 7 =

Opening Salvos

THIRTY MILES ACROSS the water the people of Manila rose on the morning of January 2, 1942, to find Japanese soldiers entering their city. "They came up the boulevards in the predawn glow from the bay riding on bicycles and on tiny motorcycles," wrote *Life* photographer Carl Mydans. "They came without talk and in good order, the ridiculous pop-popping of their one-cylinder cycles sounding loud in the silent city." From their rooms in the Bay View Hotel, Mydans and his wife, Shelley, watched them lower the American flag in front of the High Commissioner's residence. Then the Japanese flag was raised in its place as a band played "*Kimigayo*," the national anthem. Radiant red on a field of white, it represented Amaterasu, the Sun Goddess and mythical progenitor of the mighty Yamato line.

The *Manila Bulletin* issued a free four-page extra with the headline ORDERLY OCCUPATION and that included a statement from the High Commissioner's Office:

> At this time it is our best judgement that businesses should open today, and this will be the most reassuring thing for the public. Excessive movement in the streets should be avoided, but the occupation forces should be presented with the fact of a city operating quietly and normally.

The scene was anything but normal. Pier 7 was in flames, fires burned out of control, and a "carnival of looting" went unchecked in the Port Area after the quartermaster threw open government warehouses to the public. Shiploads of provisions remained behind. Trucks, jitneys, ice wagons, bull carts, "even a police car" drove away with foodstuffs, furniture, beds, mattresses, appliances, lumber, bolts of wool and sharkskin, cigarettes, and rusted sheets of corrugated iron. A newspaper advertisement placed too late by I. A. Marquez & Co., "Architects & Builders in

Quezon City," shilled for a "Re-enforced Air Raid Shelter. From P500 up. We also sell Sandbags. Delivered anywhere in Manila or Suburbs." The men on Bataan and Corregidor could have used some. The Japanese were bombing them daily and assessed the damage the next morning with a high-wing monoplane known as Photo Joe or a twin-engine, twin-tail observation plane.

War Plan Orange-3 assumed that Japan would make a surprise attack on the Philippines, but the Japanese failed to anticipate an American withdrawal to Bataan, instead envisioning a battle for Manila. With Manila safely in Japanese hands, Imperial General Headquarters reasoned, Homma could ship out the crack 48th Division to Java. The 7,500-strong 65th Brigade would take its place. But the "Summer Brigade," under the command of Amherst-educated Lieutenant General Nara Akira, was an occupation force, not a fighting one. The men were older, ill trained, and underequipped for the battlefront. If MacArthur overestimated the number of enemy troops in Luzon, Homma's intelligence grossly underestimated the number of USAFFE forces on the peninsula.

By January 7, 80,000 American and Filipino soldiers were entrenched in defensive positions on Bataan, 50,000 of whom were on or near the main line of resistance. Wainwright was in charge of I Philippine Corps on the west side of the line. Parker commanded II Philippine Corps to the east. Fil-American forces had numerical superiority but were stretched over a wide area, whereas the Japanese could concentrate their strength, pick their targets, and outnumber USSAFE positions. Moreover, the Japanese controlled the air and sea.

The Battle for Bataan began in earnest on January 9 with an attack against the II Corps on the Abucay line. The 57th Infantry of the Philippine Scouts guarded the East Road, the untested 41st Division of the Philippine Army stood to the left, and Major General Albert M. Jones's 51st Division of the Philippine Army occupied the extreme west portion of the line from the slopes of Mt. Natib to Abucay-Hacienda five miles away from the town. Withering artillery fire from II Corps prevented Colonel Imai Takeo's 141st Infantry from making any gains on the East Road, though Colonel Takechi Susumu's 9th Infantry reached Album on the western side unopposed.

At almost the same time, the 5th Air Group under Colonel Hoshi Komatarō began a three-day campaign against I Corps artillery positions, airstrips on Bataan, and targets in the Mariveles area. The barrio was bombed again, and this time it was burned to the ground when a movie theater storing ammunition took a direct hit. The statue known as *The Cry of the Balintawak,* commemorating the Filipino rebellion against Spain in 1896, stood with its arms outstretched amid flattened buildings and palm trees with their fronds blown off.

At dawn on January 10 MacArthur and Sutherland left Corregidor by PT boat to bolster the troops on Bataan. They landed at Mariveles, drove up to Balanga on the east coast of Bataan in a Ford sedan to inspect Parker's II Corps senior officers, and then conferred with Wainwright along the Pilar-Bagac road.

"Where are your 155mm guns?" MacArthur asked Wainwright.

There were six of them, Wainwright replied, then suggested they walk over to two of the guns nearby.

"Jonathan," said MacArthur, "I don't want to *see* them. I want to *hear* them!"

It was MacArthur's only trip to Bataan once the fighting began, and the men in the field would never forgive him for it.

"Shit," said Ernie Irvin of Battery C. "We never saw the bastard!"

Murray was driving to the Section Base around 0800 on the morning of January 10 when he noticed a plane coming in low over the bay as if making an approach for a landing. Then he saw the "flaming asshole" on the wings of a Zero as the fighter locked in on him. Two other fighters began strafing the road and beaches. He jumped out of his car, whipped out his .45, and ran looking for a foxhole. But no foxhole was in sight. He dove into a creek bed that protected him on three sides. The odds were in his favor, he figured—until he saw all three planes bearing down on him at no more than 500 feet. They opened up their machine guns, and he fired back wildly. This wasn't war, he thought, it was blood sport, and it was only by a miracle that he escaped unhurt.

That same day Japanese planes dropped hundreds of leaflets over the very positions MacArthur had visited:

> *Sir: You are well aware that you are doomed. The end is near. The question is how long you will be able to resist. You have already cut rations by half. Your prestige and honor have been upheld. However, in order to avoid needless bloodshed and to save the remnants of your divisions, you are advised to surrender. Failing that, we will continue with inexorable force which will bring upon you only disaster.*
> *Yours Very Sincerely,*
> *General Homma Masaharu*
> *Japanese Expeditionary Force*

On January 11 the Japanese launched their first heavy infantry attack. Colonel Imai Takeo's eastern column, the 2nd Battalion, 141st Infantry, took aim at the juncture of the 41st Division and Colonel George S. Clarke's 57th Combat Team, Philippine Scouts. It was early evening, around 1900. There was a "weird" cast to the light that Clarke couldn't explain, though it didn't seem to come from tracers. Japanese artillery and mortar fire against the II Corps line was met with a blast of machine gun fire. And then the strangest thing happened. Japanese soldiers who seemed "crazed by dope" walked head-on into an artillery barrage. Each man carried a trench mortar, and many of them had light machine guns, and they kept on coming—for hours. The first wave shouted *Banzai* and deliberately set off land mines, blowing themelves up to clear the field for subsequent troops. Then another wave of men, again shouting *Banzai,* hurled themselves against a barbed-wire entanglement. Pinned in place, they were easy targets for Fil-American gunners, and that seemed to be the point. For they formed a human bridge over which the troops behind them could advance. In spite of stiff resistance, the Japanese managed to knock L Company of the Third Battalion, 57th Infantry, back to the reserve line; they even stole their foxholes. But the next morning the 21st Infantry of the 21st Division of the Philippine Army reclaimed the Abucay line.

In the meantime, hundreds of Japanese snipers had circumvented the main battle position. Members of an elite special service corps, they were expertly camouflaged with branches and leaves. As many as eight might hide in the bole of a tree; as many as 150 could be on the ground. They remained perfectly quiet, still as statues, until a target came into their line of fire. American officers were particularly prized. The Japanese used their language skills to entrap: "Kill me, Americano," they'd say to lure troops out into the open. Or one Japanese soldier would proclaim "Me surrender!" emerging from the brush with a rifle over his head. Then, as an American went forward to disarm him, others would spring up in a deadly ambush. The Japanese rattled Filipino soldiers by calling out in Tagalog, *"Ikaw ay mamatay,"* meaning "You are going to die." The words were terrifying in the darkness to a people who were naturally superstitious. You didn't know who was speaking, and you could only guess where they were. Sniper parties were formed to flush them out, and by the end of the next day most of the Japanese had been eliminated. Clarke was determined to "take as few prisoners as possible."

Hunger was a constant companion. Supplies were moved from the Camp Limay depot and a large dump near Little Baguio to distribution points so they would be accessible to the fighting and service units. But there simply wasn't enough food. Between the soldiers, sailors, airmen, marines, and some 26,000 Filipino refugees, there were 110,000 mouths to feed on Bataan and Corregidor. Half-rations were officially prescribed on Bataan on January 6, but it would be difficult to furnish a daily diet of even 2,000 calories. Other food sources were sought.

January was harvest season, and grain had been stacked in fields that were cultivated along Manila Bay, but much of it remained unthreshed. So the Corps of Engineers dismantled two rice mills at Orion and Balanga, and moved them to the Little Baguio dump; soon the mills were yielding 30,000 pounds of polished rice a day. The supply of *palay* (unhusked rice) lasted a month.

A quartermaster bakery was set up in early January and operated as long as there was flour. Fish traps were rigged along the coast and netted thousands of pounds of fresh seafood daily—until Japanese dive bombers destroyed them. For meat, the quartermaster and the Veterinary Corps rounded up *carabao* for slaughter. The carcasses were shipped to Corregidor for cold storage, then ferried back to Bataan at night for consumption. Many of the *carabao* were abandoned by Filipinos fleeing the Japanese. But many were also poached by hungry soldiers who saw the beasts of burden as a large steak on legs. *Carabao* were worked like oxen—the natives used them to pull plows through the rice fields. Their meat was tough and stringy, tasting "just like the mud it used to wallow in," according to one gourmand, but it was packed with protein. Poaching reached such proportions near the Navy Section Base that on January 15 Captain John H. S. Dessez, commanding officer of the U.S. Naval Reservation and all naval units on Mariveles, issued a warning concerning "Livestock, slaughter of."

```
    It is reported that indiscriminate slaughter
of livestock in the U.S. Naval Reservation and
adjacent areas is being conducted. This live-
stock is private property although it may appear
to be wild. This slaughter will be considered
looting and will be treated accordingly.
```

In early January MacArthur had sent a dire warning to the War Department regarding the food crisis: "If something is not done to meet the general situation which is developing the disastrous results will be monumental." The delay in implementing WPO-3 was already taking its toll.

Theft was not limited to what could be eaten. At Cabcaben the Army Quartermaster Corps had set up an unloading station for vessels that had made the run from Manila. The area was under guard, but during one air raid marauding marines stole provisions that they ended up sharing with the boys from the 192nd Tank Company. When Ted Williams spotted an unattended tractor trailer nearby with its keys still in the ignition, he swiftly commandeered it for the mobile 270B radar unit in his detachment that had been moved to Bataan from Batangas. Williams was also able to "requisition" drums of fuel for the 192nd Tank Company, and as a token of appreciation, the sergeant offered him a ride in a tank one night.

"It's a ball, Willie, you'll getta bang outta it!"

The twenty-year-old marine jumped at the opportunity. That evening, with two other tanks in tow, they turned onto a dirt road that led straight into the line of defense. It was hot inside, dusty, and difficult to breathe. After several miles the commander waved his hand, and the tanks rumbled off the shoulder and hid beneath the trees. They kept their engines idle for hours. In the moonlight, the road looked like a tunnel dug out of a forest of rattan and bamboo. Finally the tank commander nudged the driver. Japanese soldiers on single-speed bicycles were heading in their direction. He waited until they passed by. Then the driver punched the starter, and the tank roared into action, charging its prey. Five .30-caliber machine guns opened fire, mercilessly mowing down the unsuspecting riders and raking the underbrush for those who dove into it for cover. The tank thundered up the road dragging down and crushing to death anyone and anything in its path. The carnage of the night still clung to the tank's undercarriage and rollers when it returned to camp. It made Williams's stomach churn.

He knew the symptoms well. A pain in the small of the back. A throbbing headache. Chills that made you tremble so violently beneath a layer of blankets that your cot shook and your teeth chattered. You fell into a deep sleep, only to awaken drenched in sweat with a howling fever. Remission the next day, then the cycle began all over again. It was exhausting, debilitating, and there was no point staying in Mariveles.

Murray was too ill to treat himself; he could barely sit up in bed. But once a corpsman got him to Hospital No. 2, he found that the staff there didn't want to treat him either. As 2nd Lieutenant Leona Gastinger, an army nurse, described it: "If you went off into the wildest part of the jungle and brought along a bunch of bunk beds and set them up by a little stream and supplied yourself with a few pills, you'd have an idea of what Hospital Number Two was like."

Except there were no pills, at least for Murray. He knew what he had and the one thing he needed—quinine bisulfate. But he was told he had to wait for a white blood cell count. Nothing worse than an army nurse telling a navy doctor what he had to do. The problem was that the pathologist, Captain Harold Keschner, was so overwhelmed with cases, as Captain John R. Bumgarner acknowledged, that "he and his assistants couldn't possibly run malaria smears on all patients." The hell with that, Murray thought. He'd die if he stayed there. With the help of his corpsman, he returned to his aid station, scrounged up some quinine, and was back at work in a week, half the average stay for a malaria patient. A good thing, too. For the site of Hospital No. 2 alongside the Real River was a perfect breeding ground for mosquitoes.

As 1st Sergeant Houston Turner of Company B, 31st Infantry, said: "We had wounded and sick in the company that refused to go back to the hospital. . . . You were always better off with a buddy, because at least that way someone would take care of you." Ruth Straub, a nurse at Hospital No. 2, put it another way: "I guess we are all self-imposed prisoners-of-war," she wrote in her diary. "All we're doing is protecting our own lives."

Miraculously, John Bookman managed to escape malaria but not hospitalization. Murray had him admitted to Hospital No. 1 for acute, nonsuppurative cellulitis. The cellulitis cleared up after a few days, but John was nagged by edema. One of the consequences of malnutrition, edema causes an increase in the body's water content relative to the loss of tissue and is recognized by puffiness around the face and ankles, though it can also take more severe forms. Patients suffering from malaria, dysentery, anemia, and vitamin deficiencies were particularly prone to it.

Malaria aside, the Cabulog River valley grew too hot for comfort. Enemy air activity intensified, bombers overshot Battery C, and fighters sprayed the area with machine gun fire. Murray's aid station was in danger. He contacted Carey Smith and evacuated his patients to Hospital No. 1. Then he joined John and Bernard Cohen in the only place that was secure: underground.

Tunnel No. 4 was one of the nine storage tunnels in the Mariveles area. Unfinished, it also sheltered crew members of the *Canopus* who preferred ships to machine guns and would rather work at night and sleep during the day. A hundred feet long by ninety feet wide, it was sparsely outfitted with a small radio and telephone communications center, administrative offices, and a field kitchen. Down the center ran a narrow-gauge mine railroad, and overhead a string of bare lightbulbs. Steel double-deck bunk beds lined the chiseled walls. The water that dripped from overhanging rock was trapped and piped for showers, which were voluntary.

Beyond the beds was a small hospital in a lateral tunnel that John had improvised with a portable operating table, a wheeled stand for a glucose drip, scalpels, hemostats, scissors, and a white pan for bloodied instruments. The doctors worked there during the day and slept outside at night.

Necessity made strange bedfellows. During one raid an Army Air Corps lieutenant dashed in for cover and ran smack into John's arms.

"Hello," John said politely as he extricated himself from the stranger. "I'm John Bookman."

"And I'm David Hochman," came the abashed reply.

Hochman was another New Yorker, surgeon of the 16th Bombardment Squadron, a unit of the 27th Bomb Group. They had arrived in Manila in late November, though the fifty-two A-24s that would have given them wings—and were part of the *Pensacola* convoy—never made it to the Philippines. An air force without planes. A navy without ships. An army without food. They had much in common.

With Hayes stationed on Corregidor, the navy medical staff on Bataan reported to E. L. Sackett, captain of the *Canopus* and commander of naval forces in the Mariveles area. Sackett had cleverly listed the submarine tender, tilted its cargo booms, blackened the areas around its bomb holes, and ignited oily rags in smudge pots to shield her from the attention of Japanese bombers. From the sky the Old Lady looked like an abandoned hulk—but at night she was the belle of the ball, buzzing with activity as a machine shop, repair shop, and weapons forge. In spite of her bedraggled appearance, the *Canopus* offered the best accommodations around, with hot showers, cold drinking water, and refrigeration, which enabled her to serve what Sackett considered the greatest luxury, "real butter." First Lieutenant Carter Simpson of Battery C couldn't get over the elegant dinners in the ship's ward room, where officers were attended "by mess boys in white jackets!" he noted in his diary. To top it off, the *Canopus* stored barrels of ice cream mix that the galley gladly turned into chocolate sundaes for those who asked. Such amenities made her a natural attraction for army officers romancing nurses, marines ostensibly on business from Corregidor, and the boys from MTB Squadron 3. Crippled in her outward appearance, the *Canopus* was a floating pleasure dome for officers and their guests, far removed from the rugged life of the front.

Shortly after MacArthur's visit to Bataan, the Japanese sneaked around opposite sides of Mt. Silanganan in the Natib mountain massif, infiltrating Parker's left flank and Wainwright's right. II Corps fell back north of Abucay, rallied, then launched a counterattack on January 12, aided by the 21st Infantry. On January 16 Nara's 65th Brigade went after the 41st and 51st Divisions on the left side of II Corps. The 41st Division held despite the beating it took from the Japanese. But the Filipino captain of Company G in the 51st Division panicked and his troops scattered, as did the 53rd and 52nd Reserve Regiments. Machine guns and rifles, ammunition and equipment were abandoned, seized by the Japanese, and turned against the fleeing Philippine Army. Jones's 51st Division was in tatters. Wainwright's 31st Infantry was called in to reclaim the west flank of II Corps, and fierce fighting followed over the next five days.

The men were hungry, tired, and sick. Communications with corps headquarters frequently broke down. Some had been on the front lines for two weeks, averaging only three to four hours of sleep a night. There was no quinine for malaria prophylaxis, so if they were infected, they drank liquid quinine straight out of a shot glass. They had little water and food and resorted to eating raw sugarcane. Or they fingered the bodies of dead Japanese soldiers—for crackers, fish bouillon, and rice balls.

Army Chief of Staff Marshall had assured MacArthur that "the President [has] personally directed the Navy to make every effort to support you." MacArthur did his rhetorical best to invigorate American and Filipino forces. In a proclamation issued on January 15 he announced:

> Help is on the way. . . . Thousands of troops and hundreds of planes are being dispatched. The exact time of arrival of reinforcements is unknown. . . . No further retreat is possible. . . . If we fight we will win; if we retreat we will be destroyed.

West of Mt. Natib, the Japanese launched attacks on January 16 against Wainwright's I Corps, which was exposed on three sides—north, east, and from the South China Sea. Wainwright's men were thinly stretched, and on January 21 a Japanese battalion led by Lieutenant Colonel Nakanishi Hiroshi infiltrated the right flank of the Philippine Army's 1st Regular Division, gaining access to the West Road.

Acting on Sutherland's recommendation of January 22, MacArthur ordered a withdrawal to the Bagac-Orion line of defense. In the haste of retreat, the medical detachments lost valuable equipment as the line troops deserted them.

Hospital No. 1 was inundated with casualties. Enemy planes flew overhead almost hourly. In one twenty-four-hour period 182 major surgical operations were performed. Twelve hundred patients were treated in twenty-nine days. But the inexorable Japanese advance forced a relocation south, and on January 26, the facility moved to Little Baguio at Kilometer 155. The very next day the old hospital, clearly marked with red and white crosses, was leveled by Japanese pilots dropping incendiary bombs.

The Japanese knew what the emblems signified. The red cross had been formally adopted in the first Geneva Convention of 1864. Indeed

Japan, along with Britain, France, Italy, and the United States, was one of the first countries to join the International Federation of Red Cross and Red Crescent Societies in 1919.

Wainwright's front was twenty miles north of Mariveles. The coastline in between was notched like a jigsaw puzzle with coves and points that gave rise to steep cliffs crowned by thick vegetation. The jungle was so dense, you couldn't see more than two arms' lengths in front of you. The heat was unbearable—the hottest dry season ever on Bataan, some said. Exhaustion and dehydration were constant dangers, and the drone of insects an unnerving annoyance.

Parts of the West Road, which extended from Mauban in the north down to the peninsula's tip, ran perilously close to the sea. An amphibious attack could jeopardize the supply line of I Corps. But General Allen C. McBride's Service Command had few men to protect it, so on January 9 Rockwell directed Captain Dessez to create a naval battalion for ground combat. Dessez assigned Commander Francis J. Bridget of Patrol Wing 10, the ranking naval aviator in the Philippines, to organize the fighting force. Navy corpsmen provided medical support. The seriously injured would be removed to the only functioning aid station in the Service Command Area: Tunnel No. 4 where John, Murray, and Bernard Cohen were standing by.

Short and fiery, "Fidgety Frank" (as the army nicknamed Bridget) set up a command post near the old Quarantine Station and selected 150 of his own men from Air, Asiatic Fleet, 130 crewmen from the *Canopus*, roughly 120 marines from Batteries A and C, 120 general duty men from Cavite and Mariveles, and 80 men from the Cavite naval ammunition depot. Lieutenant Commander Henry "Hap" Goodall of the *Canopus* was second in command.

A motley crew it was, and Bridget turned to the marines to make soldiers out of the lot of them. In a two-day crash course they offered instruction in guns and grenades, weapons and tactics. The marines of course were outfitted for land operations; the navy men weren't. They used coffee to dye their whites, hoping it would turn them khaki, but instead they emerged a ghastly mustard yellow. They pilfered arms, cadged ammunition, and wrapped themselves in bandoliers like Pancho Villa's men. Some bluejackets could barely tell the difference between the muzzle of a rifle and its butt. Others admitted they had no idea how to load the damned things. There was one canteen for every third man, so the rest carried cans that doubled as pots. As yet no wire had been strung for field telephones, no radios were available, and most of the newly trained men were unversed in hand and arm signals. They spoke openly on patrols; some even smoked cigarettes. But what they lacked in experience they more than made up for with enthusiasm: they were hunting Japs.

So was Bulkeley's MTB Squadron 3, except that four men and one vessel had already been lost to the enemy. The squadron was also without Bob Kelly, who had commanded PT-34 and nearly lost his arm. Kelly suffered a gash in his hand nearly three inches long and an inch wide that left the tendons exposed. He had resisted John's attempts to treat it, and sepsis had set in. The hand blew up to the size of a catcher's mitt. John shipped the lieutenant off to the Malinta Tunnel hospital on Corregidor, where he was cooped up for two weeks and dropped thirty-five pounds.

"We need you," Bulkeley said to Kelly, bleary-eyed from exhaustion.

Kelly appealed to his doctor, who agreed to have him discharged if he promised to come back every other day for treatment.

On the night of January 22 Bulkeley and Kelly were charging up toward Subic Bay in PT-34 when they spotted a vessel lying low in the water. It signaled in dots and dashes; then, when it was twenty-five yards away, its light suddenly went out.

"Boat ahoy!" Bulkeley called out on his megaphone.

A blast of machine gun fire answered, and Bulkeley cut loose with his .50 calibers. Tracers illuminated the nocturnal seascape, revealing the steel-plated bow and stern of a landing barge with helmeted Japanese soldiers on board. The PT-34 circled it like a shark. Bulkeley and his men grabbed their automatic rifles and started pumping bullets into it. Another burst of machine gun fire whirred by, and Ensign Barron Chandler was "bleeding like a pig," shot in both ankles. Reynolds, the boat's cook, played Pharmacist's Mate and poured iodine onto the wounds, which Bulkeley wrapped in tourniquets. It was near dawn when the Japanese barge went under the waves.

PT-34 was heading back to Sisiman Cove when Bulkeley turned around and spotted another landing vessel. They raced toward it, opened fire at 300 yards, and approached within 50 feet. Bullets bounced off the barge's plated armor until a tracer hit the fuel tank and it burst into flames. Bulkeley pulled up alongside, lobbed in a few grenades, and then jumped into the sinking craft, tommy gun in hand. There were only three Japanese on board; one was dead; two were wounded, a captain and a private. The captain fell to his knees and pleaded, "Me surrender! Me surrender!"

Bulkeley hoisted them aboard PT-34, where they were placed under

armed guard. Staring at the American with the ragged beard and hol-
stered pistols at his sides, the captain feared he would be executed. But as
they sped back to Sisiman Cove, Bulkeley wiped the oil from his eyes
and examined his head wound. The private, who had been shot five
times, asked for a smoke, and one of the crewmen held a cigarette to his
mouth while he inhaled. Kelly couldn't get over it.

"Ten minutes before, we'd all been pumping steel, hating every Jap
in the world. Now we were sorry for these two, they were so abject,
sitting there on the deck—little half-pint guys—the youngest boy in
our crew looked like a full-grown man beside them. Our crew all came
up to take a look. People had been scared of these guys? It seemed
impossible!"

Two barges of Lieutenant Colonel Tsunehiro Nariyoshi's 2nd Battalion, 20th Infantry, had been lost. The survivors split into two groups.
One party of 300 men ended up along the coast at Lapiay, Longoskawayan, and Naiklec Points, bearing machine guns, mortars, and artillery. The remaining 600 soldiers landed seven miles to the north at
Quinauan Point. The front had come to the rear.

On the morning of January 23 marines from Battery A were standing
watch in a lookout tower on Mt. Pucot when they spotted an enemy
landing at Longoskawayan Point, a mere 2,000 yards from Mariveles. At
617 feet, Mt. Pucot was due west of Mariveles Harbor, and whoever
controlled it would control southern Bataan. They notified Commander
Bridget, who immediately ordered Holdredge and Hogaboom to con-
firm the reports, but he failed to inform either of the other's activities.

Platoon Sergeant Robert "Duke" Clement led a patrol of thirty-six
sailors to support Holdredge and Hogaboom. Lieutenant (j.g.) Hohn
"Swede" Janson was his backup. They scoured the shoreline between
Lapiay and Longoskawayan Points looking for signs of infiltration,
but by the time they got there, the coast was clear; there was no sign
of enemy activity. Clement led his men up a game trail at the end of
Longoskawayan Point, and at the top of it they stumbled upon a
Japanese command post. It was deserted except for two Japanese
cooks dressed in loincloths—*fundoshi*—who went scurrying off in the
opposite direction. Two cauldrons of rice were steaming on a fire. Stacks
of enemy rifles were theirs for the taking, as were maps, even a pair of
binoculars. They loaded up on arms and were planning their ambush
when two Japanese officers and two enlisted men appeared out of the
brush. Clement's men killed two of them instantly, but the other two got
away. Then Lieutenant Janson was shot in the middle of the forehead.

The bullet went clean through his skull and exited the parietal bone. Still conscious, he asked Clement which patrol was on the next ridge to Mt. Pucot.

"First Lieutenant William F. Hogaboom's," Clement replied.

"Hey, Hogey," Janson said. "We have found a Jap CP."

His voice was faint.

"Hey, Hogey," he whispered. "We have found a Jap CP."

Then, ever so quietly, "Hey, Hogey. We have found a Jap CP."

His voice faded into silence.

Clement had sent a runner back to Bridget's command post to request a stretcher and corpsman for Janson. A machine gun suddenly opened fire, shredding a young mahogany tree in front of his eyes. Clement pulled out his .45 and fired three times; the enemy gun went silent. The Japanese had been reconnoitering and digging in positions on the Mariveles side of the ridgeline. Unarmed Japanese protected by a covering guard fanned out over the ridge, scattering into a valley at the right. Clement's men picked off a few more of them, and a firefight ensued. When the shooting stopped, he saw blood spurting from his wrist. He placed a flat object against the wound, tightened his bandolier over it, and was able to stanch the bleeding. But fragments had also hit him in the arm and face.

The firing alerted Holdredge, as well as Hogaboom, who arrived with his platoon. Janson was in a coma. Hogaboom had a corpsman check on him first, then dress Clement's wounds. The bandages were white, which made him a more conspicuous target. Hogaboom himself had been hit. Soon four sailors arrived with a stretcher to evacuate Janson. The two marine patrols withdrew to a blocking position between Mariveles and Longoskawayan while Bridget gathered reinforcements at the Section Base. A diary found later on the corpse of a Japanese officer marveled at "the new type of suicide squads, which thrashed about in the jungle, wearing bright-colored uniforms and making plenty of noise. Whenever these apparitions reached an open space, they would attempt to draw Japanese fire by sitting down, talking loudly, and lighting cigarettes."

On January 25 Holdredge sent a patrol of twenty-two men out for reconnaissance on Longoskawayan Point. It was a Sunday morning, hot and clear. Private 1st Class Wilfred "Chick" Mensching of Gun 3 wore his khaki shirtsleeves rolled up to the elbow, someone else's khaki pants that were too big for him, leggings, high-top shoes, and a doughboy helmet. They were going down a small incline on Mt. Pucot when a Japanese machine gun nest opened fire. Mensching felt his left arm shake. He fell on the ground, covered in blood. He couldn't hear or see anything until he discovered Private 1st Class Stephen J. Treskon, also of Gun 3, bending over him. Treskon removed the belt from Mensching's trousers and tied a tourniquet onto his leg to stop the bleeding.

Holdredge's platoon had been hit hard. Private 1st Class Warren I. Carver of Battery C was killed. Six navy men from the *Canopus* lay dead. Eleven marines were wounded. Corpsman Ernie Irvin maintained a first aid station a hundred yards behind the lines. When Mensching was brought in, he was laid down next to another wounded marine, whom Irvin began to work on immediately.

"Take care of Mensching first," the wounded marine said. "He doesn't look like he's going to make it."

Mensching recognized the voice. It was Holdredge, who had been shot in the hip. Irvin flushed Mensching's leg wound with a bottle of io-dine, which burned like the devil.

"The hell I'm going to go," the nineteen-year-old Mensching insisted. "I'm going to make it."

The naval battalion needed help. Commander Bridget had already re-ceived two 81mm mortars from the 4th Marines on Corregidor and a machine gun platoon. The mortars, set up on a saddle northwest of Mt. Pucot, blasted Lapiay and Longoskawayan Points, forcing the Japa-nese to evacuate Lapiay.

That same day Bridget contacted USAFFE Headquarters in Malinta Tunnel. Longoskawayan Point was 12,000 yards from Battery Geary on Corregidor, which had eight 12-inch mortars with a 14,000-yard range and a 360-degree field of fire. The 670-pound antipersonnel shells had a bursting radius of 500 feet. Just after midnight on January 26, Battery Geary concentrated eight rounds on the enemy.

It was "the first firing by major caliber artillery guns at an enemy since the Civil War," noted Major General George F. Moore. Four rounds hit the shoreline; the other four were wide of the mark. The fires were so intense, it was impossible for Lieutenant Richard P. Fulmer to "spot" for accuracy and orientation. Over the next two days Geary fired another twenty-four rounds, and when the battery was on target, the ef-fects were shattering.

The descending shells sounded like boxcars in the sky. "Tōjō," the marines would holler, "count your men—we're going to take a few." Flames blackened the jungle floor, leaving Japanese positions completely exposed. Colonel Paul D. Bunker, who was in charge of Corregidor's Seaward Defense Command, supervised Geary's "shoot." Bunker wished "that we could see what that Langoskawayan [*sic*] Point looks like, after all our shelling—and we're wondering how anybody could be left alive on it." One wounded Japanese prisoner later told an interrogator for G-2, MacArthur's intelligence section:

> We were terrified. We could not know where the big shells or bombs were coming from; they seemed to be falling from the sky. Before I was wounded, my head was going round and round, and I did not know what to do. Some of my companions jumped off the cliff to escape the terrible fire.

But other Japanese soldiers were undaunted. They climbed into trees so they could shoot marines in the back. They burrowed into caves, where they were safe until they faced the deadly ingenuity of the naval battalion.

Hap Goodall of the *Canopus* had had the brilliant idea of equipping three motor launches with .50-caliber machines each and reinforcing them with boiler plate. "Mickey Mouse battleships," they were called, but the purpose for which they were suited was no laughing matter. The miniature fleet churned eight miles up the coast, took aim at the cliffs where the Japanese were holed up, and fired directly into the rocky orifices. The Japanese never stood a chance. It was as easy as shooting ducks in a barrel.

On the dawn of January 27, marine mortars and Filipino artillery pummeled Longoskawayan Point. But a disorganized attack by the naval battalion led to a Japanese counterattack, forcing the Americans to withdraw. Hogaboom knew they couldn't hold their ground without reinforcements. They were tired and hungry, and their ranks were stretched thin.

Corpsman Ernie Irvin was pressed into service to help hold the line. His chest crisscrossed with bandoliers of bullets, he carried five grenades in his first aid kit and stood guard at a trail leading up to a ridge, two hours on, two hours off. He had eaten only two sandwiches in four days and was so low on water, he joked, he didn't need toilet paper; he used a whisk broom. In the early morning hours of January 28, 500 men from the 2nd Battalion of 57th Infantry, Philippine Scouts, relieved the naval battalion.

The next day the Scouts, supported by Corregidor's 12-inch mortars, succeeded in regaining Longoskawayan Point. Even the minesweeper USS *Quail* joined the action, firing point-blank at Japanese soldiers from 1,300 yards offshore. Then the naval battalion's armored launches moved into position again for mopping-up operations. Three hundred

Japanese infantrymen were killed; another 600 died at Quinauan Point. An entire battalion, General Homma rued, was "lost without a trace." Combined losses for the naval battalion and the Philippine Scouts were 22 dead, and 53 wounded.

Three days later a Japanese flotilla of twelve barges attempted another landing to reinforce the beachhead at Quinauan Point. They were welcomed by a large-scale, coordinated attack from land, air, and sea. The 26th Cavalry mobilized to forestall a landing at Caibobo Point, and Battery D of the 88th Field Artillery and Battery E of the 301st lit into the Japanese. The army called in the last four P-40s in the Far East Air Force to bomb and strafe landing craft, while Bulkeley tore up the coast with two PT boats that nailed two barges.

His landing force reduced by half, Major Kimura Mitsuo's 1st Battalion, 20th Infantry, scurried ashore instead to the north of Quinauan Point, between Anyasin and Salaiim Points. But after twelve days of bloody fighting the Philippine Scouts forced hundreds of Japanese back to the edge of Quinauan Point. It was a fifty-to-sixty-foot drop to the sea. Then the Americans and Filipinos saw something that was as mesmerizing as it was sickening.

"Scores of Japs," as Captain William E. Dyess of the 21st Pursuit Squadron described it, ripped off their uniforms and leaped, shrieking, to the beach below. Machine gun fire raked the sand and surf for anything that moved, until the waves of the South China Sea were "stained with blood." One Filipino gunner "shrieked with laughter" whenever he scored a hit from the precipice above.

Other Japanese soldiers hid in the caves and crevices of the cliffs. Wainwright ordered a "proffer of honorable surrender," but the Japanese replied by firing on the troops who made the offer. MacArthur's headquarters had even provided a sound truck and two nisei—Richard Sakakida and Arthur Komori, both of whom had worked in counterintelligence in Manila—to make an appeal, but the response was the same. The Scouts themselves were hardly eager to take captives. When they reclaimed their own dead, they found bodies mutilated beyond recognition; others had clearly been tortured to death. Instead of having a sobering effect on American and Filipino troops, the grisly evidence only excited feelings of revenge.

"The old rules of war began to undergo a swift change in me," Wainwright admitted. "What had at first seemed a barbarous thought in the back of my mind now became less unsavory. I thought of General U. S. Grant's land mine at Petersburg and made up my mind."

Wainwright arranged for a small gunboat to shell the caves, and when that failed to dislodge the enemy, he sent in a platoon from the 71st Engineer Battalion of the Philippine Army to lower into them time-fused, 50-pound boxes of dynamite. But the tactic backfired, killing a Scout engineer. So the engineers lobbed dynamite grenades into a cave where fifty Japanese soldiers had retreated and "blew the place to pieces." Finally, white sheets were lowered over the cliffs to mark remaining Japanese positions, and Goodall's little armored fleet was given the signal to open fire. But after ten minutes of shelling, the "Mickey Mouse battleships" were dive-bombed by four Japanese planes. The navy gunners continued to blast away in spite of the 100-pound fragmentation bombs bursting around them, until one of their boats was hit. Three crew members were killed, and four were wounded, including Goodall himself. Goodall ordered the two remaining boats ashore, where the sailors improvised stretchers and evacuated the wounded on the West Road to Mariveles.

With the annihilation of Kimura's 1st Battalion, the Battle of the Points was over.

While the Battle of the Points was being waged on Bataan's west coast, the Battle of the Pockets, as it came to be known, raged along the reserve battle line. Now the main line of resistance, it stretched from Orion in the east to Bagac in the west.

On January 26 Colonel Yoshioka Yorimasa's 1,000-man force from the 3rd Battalion, 20th Infantry, blew a hole through the 1st Regular Division of the II Corps position. I Corps troops bottled Yoshioka's men into two defense perimeters—Big Pocket at Tuol and Little Pocket at Cotar—and after two weeks of fierce fighting, Scouts, Philippine Army troops, and tanks from Company A, 192nd Tank Battalion squeezed out the enemy positions.

A similar attack against I Corps succeeded and enabled the Japanese to establish "pockets" of resistance. Once the Japanese dug in, "we had to go up and practically breathe" in their faces, Wainwright remarked. The fighting was "fantastically improbable," as junior officers rode atop tank hoods and tossed grenades into foxholes. When the return fire was too hot, bow-hunting Igorot tribesmen and head-hunting Negritos from Brigadier General William E. Brougher's 11th Division volunteered to take their place and directed tank drivers by banging on one steel side or another with a wooden club. By February 17 the main line of resistance had been restored. "There was so much killing," remarked U.S. Army doctor Captain Ralph Emerson Hibbs, that "the jungle stank with the odor of the dead."

Between the Battle of the Points and the Battle of the Pockets, an entire Japanese regiment—Colonel Yoshioka's 20th Infantry—was decimated. As Lieutenant Malcolm M. Champlin, a former FBI agent from Baltimore and naval aide to Wainwright on Bataan, coolly described it: "When surrounded and asked by loudspeaker, both in Japanese and English, to surrender, the answer was '—You, Yank. Come and get us.' We did."

A mile away from Longoskawayan, the navy doctors in Mariveles experienced the Battle of the Points through the flesh-and-blood evidence of it. Shrapnel had not only ripped through Chick Mensching's leg, the doctors discovered, it had also perforated his pack, his shoulder, and it had lodged in his spine.

It was early in the morning when Mensching woke from surgery. More casualties had arrived. A Filipino woman was brought in dead, impaled by a fence post during another bombing raid on Mariveles. Mensching stayed in the tunnel hospital for three days until he was evacuated by ambulance to Hospital No. 1. He had developed gas gangrene caused by *Clostridium welchii,* an anaerobic bacterium that—like anthrax—lies dormant in the soil. The bacteria thrive in deep lacerations and puncture wounds where torn tissue prevents exposure to air.

"If you're going to cut my leg off, let me die," he told a surgeon who approached him with a bandage shears.

The field hospitals were plagued by gas gangrene. The bacteria penetrate muscle, where enzymes gorge on blood and tissue and create gas bubbles that cause limbs to swell up quickly. The swelling causes blood clots, cuts off circulation, and emits a nauseatingly sweet smell. At that stage, absent bacillus antitoxin, there was only one known cure: amputation. But Lieutenant Colonel Frank Adamo of Hospital No. 1 discovered that the bacteria could be killed by making an incision in the infected muscles longitudinally, debriding the dead tissue, cleansing the area with hydrogen peroxide, and leaving the wound open to the air.

"I'm just here to cut your bandages," the doctor replied. The hospital would treat his wounds, but they couldn't hold him against his will. By early February Mensching was back at Battery C, where Ernie Irvin saw him through to recovery.

The ragtag naval battalion had succeeded in thwarting a vastly superior Japanese force behind the lines. Army machine gun nests and light naval guns were now in place to deter further landings. Their job done, Bridget's men were detached from Bataan and sent to Corregidor to reinforce the 4th Marines' beach defense.

The navy doctors experienced only the consequences of the battle.

They could clean and disinfect wounds, suture lacerations, set fractured bones, remove shrapnel, and relieve pain with morphine, but the logic they operated by was deductive by necessity. They had little time to take medical histories; frequently casualties were in shock, and shock, whether pre- or postoperative, was a major cause of death. They treated effects without fully understanding causes, injuries without knowing the circumstances that had led to them. Did a shrapnel wound come from enemy or friendly fire? Was a bullet wound the result of holding the line or scattering in retreat? If they found shards of porcelain, they knew, as Duke Clement did firsthand, that they were from Nambu machine guns, which took porcelain bullets. But removed from the front, the navy doctors fought a different kind of war, one in a continuous present where the only constant was a steady influx of injuries and an increasing incidence of disease.

———

After the Battle of the Points, Japanese casualties were evacuated to Hospital No. 1. Major Alfred A. Weinstein was one of the army doctors who helped clean their wounds and operate on them. Then they were fed, issued linens and towels, and given "the same chow, cigarettes, and candy that our men got, no more, no less."

One Japanese soldier with a bullet wound in his upper arm fled the operating room, "wild-eyed with terror," as he was being strapped down for anesthesia. He was finally cornered and put to sleep. Asked why he had been so scared, an interpreter explained that "his officers have told him that the Americans torture and kill all prisoners."

After a while the Japanese prisoners of war learned enough English to talk with the hospital staff. They loved American baseball, were wild about Babe Ruth, and insisted that the Japanese would never bomb a hospital. They were grateful for their treatment at the hands of the Americans and could not understand why the United States and Japan were fighting. Of several dozen Japanese POWs, only two died.

Ironically, their treatment as POWs appears to have been more favorable than that accorded Japanese-Americans in the hysteria that swept across the United States in the aftermath of Pearl Harbor. "It is possible to test the loyalty of American citizens of Caucasian origin," declared California attorney general Earl Warren, "but not the loyalty of Japanese Americans." Decades of simmering resentment had boiled over into ugly racial stereotyping. Japanese-Americans were considered potential threats to Boeing Aircraft in Washington State, to defense plants in Los Angeles, and to transportation and communications facilities. Second-generation Japanese-Americans were the most dangerous, believed Secretary of War Henry Stimson. The fact that no evidence of sabotage had been discovered in the months since Pearl Harbor was merely confirmation, argued Colonel Karl R. Bendetsen, engineer of the evacuation program, "that such action will be taken." After all, said Lieutenant General John L. DeWitt, commander of the Western Defense Command, "a Jap is a Jap." On February 19, 1942, Roosevelt signed Executive Order 9066, authorizing the internment of all Japanese-Americans. Over the next eight months 111,999 "persons of Japanese ancestry" were forcibly relocated from California, Washington, and Oregon and placed "in the Zone of Interior in uninhabited areas where they can do no harm under guard," as Bendetsen described it. In ten spartan relocation camps they were held for an average of 900 days, their rights subject to military edict, whereas the rights of the Japanese prisoners of war in Hospital No. 1 on Bataan were respected by the medical staff and protected under the 1929 Geneva Convention Relative to the Treatment of Prisoners of War.

Admissions to Hospitals Nos. 1 and 2 were restricted to serious surgical or medical cases, those who were expected to be out of commission for more than twenty-one days, and "all psychoses and cases requiring mental observation." Medical evacuation procedure called for wounded soldiers to be carried or lifted by stretcher to a battalion aid station, which was typically 500 yards behind the line of combat. This was the first stage in the chain of evacuation that enabled a casualty to be transported to a hospital in the rear, if necessary. Treatment was limited to controlling hemorrhages, treating shock, applying splints, bandages, and tourniquets, closing chest wounds, and administering morphine. A mile behind each battalion aid station was a collecting station, where sometimes emergency care was given and sometimes the wounded were merely inspected. Five miles behind the collecting station was the division clearing station, where it was determined if a casualty could endure the trip to the evacuation hospital, or required emergency surgery in a field hospital, which was usually adjacent to a division clearing station.

But nothing was as usual on Bataan. At Hospital No. 1 the army used a navy doctor, Carey Smith, as its chief of surgery, and a dozen navy corpsmen from Mariveles. And for the first time in U.S. history, nurses—American and Filipino—worked just a few kilometers behind the lines. Many of them preferred wearing army men's shoes, army men's socks, and army men's coveralls—size 40—which were kindly provided by the Far East Air Force boys. Ann Bernatitus, the sole navy nurse on Bataan, described the scene at Hospital No. 1: "Wounded men would be waiting in lines of stretchers for us to get to them. Some amputations—maybe a leg, maybe a little one like a finger—abdominal operations, head cases, everything. People can get hit anyplace by a bomb. You'd be amazed about how little people complain, especially soldiers, and about how much punishment a human body can take." The most unusual patient to be admitted to Hospital No. 1 was surely a baby girl whose Chinese mother was married to an American serviceman. She was named Victoria Bataan, slept in a bamboo cradle, and was swaddled in clothes sent over by Corregidor's quartermaster.

From Hospital No. 2 the nurses could see dogfights and numerous bombings. The "angels of Bataan" were essential to the hospital organization, yet doctors and nurses alike were pushed beyond endurance. Personnel fell asleep outside to the sound of cicadas and monkeys chattering in the trees, iguanas skittering, and rats scurrying in the underbrush at night.

A shortage of fuel, a shortage of woolen blankets to treat shock, and a shortage of surgical equipment in the field made evacuation an arduous journey. As a result, medical installations were improvised closer to the front and took over responsibilities typically performed in the general hospitals. Accommodations were sought wherever there was shelter, be it a massive stone church (like the one at Abucay that doubled as a regimental aid and collecting station for the 57th Combat Team of the Philippine Scouts) or a clearing station carved out of the jungle (such as the 400-bed field hospitals for the 21st and 41st Medical Battalions of the Philippine Army). The policy of forward hospitalization evolved by necessity. As Colonel Wibb E. Cooper, surgeon, U.S. Forces in the Philippines, was well aware, it was "in direct violation of all standard medical tactics." Because if the front fell back, the forward medical installations would be overrun by enemy troops, as had happened in the Malayan campaign. For that reason the 12th Medical Battalion of the Philippine Scouts was transferred from II Corps to Luzon Force as an emergency evacuation force.

As one piece of doggerel put it, the situation was normal—all fucked up. Hence the word *Snafu*.

> If you hear a muffled chortle
>   Then look close above the portal
> There you'll see the sign immortal
> Snafu.
>
> Operation maps galore
>   Spread by G's upon the floor
> Prove what Sherman said of war
> Snafu.
>
> Couriers dash in and out
>   Chiefs of Sections madly shout

Not a person now can doubt
Snafu.

When in danger fear or doubt
     When the bombs fall all about
Run in circles, scream and shout
Snafu.

Japs have landed everywhere
     And their planes control the air
We can only stand and blare
Snafu.

Air support we sadly lack
     Day by day our lines fall back
But the troops will never crack
Snafu.

Anti-aircraft standing by
     Firing way into the sky
But the Japs just fly too high
Snafu.

Slopes of Natib are tabu
     Far too steep for me and you
But the hardy Japs came through
Snafu.

All day and through the night
     Troops would rather stand and fight
But they've seen the awful sight
Snafu.

Warning sirens ghastly wail
     Like a banshee in a gale
Turns the whole damn Army pale
Snafu.

Close the gap between the corps
     But the corps commander swore
Through that gap no Jap can pour
Snafu.

Rations have been cut in half
     Now our bread is mixed with chaff
But we still can force a laugh
Snafu.

Hang on still another day
　　Help is surely on the way
So we hold the Japs at bay
Snafu.

The aid station of the 2nd Battalion had been so close to the Abucay front that army doctor Captain Ralph Emerson Hibbs could hear the cries of the Japanese after each mortar explosion. At one point Major Moffit ordered a litter team across the line, and both bearers were wounded.

Hibbs was furious. "Damn it!" he admonished Moffit. "I wish no one would order my men forward for casualties without my approval. What do you want them to do, kill the Japs, advance the line, and at the same time pick up the wounded?"

There were twenty-eight men in Hibbs's medical detachment and, during the Abucay-Hacienda battle, a dozen or so in his aid station who were "tagging, applying tourniquets, compressing wounds to stop their bleeding, giving hypos and oral medications, washing and bandaging, fitting slings. . . . My hands were bloody all day." There were no IVs on the front, no plasma for transfusions. Those who could walk were given field tags that were hung around their necks with a brief description of their wounds and then advised to get their asses to the rear as quickly as possible. For the nonambulatory, litters were made from bamboo poles that were tied together with vines, and then a blanket was stretched between them. A collar was fashioned at one end so the litter could be dragged by *calesa* pony—the Bataan Ambulance Service, the men joked—or by hand.

Once casualties made it to Hospitals Nos. 1 and 2, they awaited treatment in open-air *nipa* and bamboo sheds, in litters on sawhorses, or on the ground. Most wounds were from shrapnel or small arms fire. Many were abdominal and inflicted by the 1905 Arisaka rifle (Model 38) or the 1937 Arisaka sniper's rifle (Model 97), both of which took a .255-caliber bullet. Later models used a heavier .303-caliber bullet that would have drastically increased the mortality rate. Remarkably, out of 15,000 admissions to Hospital No. 2, there were only 303 recorded deaths.

One thing the Americans on the front and in the rear understood well: they had encountered a foe unlike any other. Demeaned for their short stature, their nearsightedness, their thick, round glasses, and their comical buckteeth—in a word, for being "yellow"—the Japanese had proven themselves to be ruthless and fearless warriors. They were willing to fight to the death.

8

Never Surrender

BEFORE GOING INTO COMBAT, Japanese infantrymen were armed with a copy of the Field Service Code, or *Senjinkun*. A few pages in length, it was the modern soldier's handbook, published and distributed on January 8, 1941, by order of General Tōjō Hideki "so that those in the zone of combat may wholly abide to the Imperial Rescript to enhance the moral virtues of the Imperial Army."

The *Senjinkun* was prepared by the Ministry of the Army and codified by the inspector general of the Department of Education, Yamada Otsuzō. Yamada had solicited opinions of university professors in Tōkyō and Kyōto—even the poet Doi Bansui—in its composition. The *Senjinkun* was intended to prevent a recurrence of massacres such as the Rape of Nanking, but it served instead as a primer of Japanese militarism.

It was the foot soldier's duty, said the *Senjinkun*, "to spread *kōdō* [the Imperial Way] far and wide so that the enemy may look up in awe to the august virtues of His Majesty." The Imperial Way combined "valour tempered by benevolence" even though war demanded "a crushing blow" to the enemy. That meant calmly facing death, "rejoicing in the hope of living in the eternal cause of which you serve."

Bound by the honor of his name, a soldier should never "suffer the disgrace of becoming a prisoner." Privation was his lot, which depended on integrity, austerity, and the triumph of duty over desire. While a soldier was "always prepared to expose his corpse in the field," there was "nothing more to be regretted than to fall a victim to disease." Discipline, obedience, self-sacrifice, and cooperation were characterisitic of the soldier's spirit. But on the battlefield aggressiveness, determination, and perseverance came to the fore. "Always retain the spirit of attack and always maintain freedom of action," admonished the *Senjinkun*. "Never give up a position but rather die."

One stricture in the *Senjinkun* can be traced to the Sino-Japanese War of 1894–95. In September 1894 General Yamagata Aritomo arrived in Seoul and issued a "written appeal to the officers" that concluded: "Should it be desperate fighting, under no circumstances may you be captured alive. You should rather die bravely and without reluctance, and maintain the honor of the Japanese warriors."

Yamagata's directive appears to be the first that specifically prohibited Japanese soldiers and officers from becoming prisoners of war. It became known as *gyokusai* (a death of honorable annihilation), which means, literally, "the shattering of crystal."

Ritual suicide itself dated back to the early years of the shogunate, when samurai warriors committed seppuku on the death of a *daimyō*, or master. As Yamamoto Tsunetomo wrote in the *Hagakure* (*Book of the Samurai*):

> Meditation on inevitable death should be performed daily. Every day when one's body and mind are at peace, one should meditate upon being ripped apart by arrows, rifles, spears, and swords, being carried away by surging waves, being thrown into the midst of a great fire, being struck by lightning, being shaken to death by a great earthquake, falling from a thousand foot cliff, dying of disease, or committing seppuku at the death of one's master. And every day without fail one should consider himself as dead.

The *Hagakure* was used by Japanese militarists in the 1920s and 1930s to revive the tradition of the samurai warrior, elements of which were incorporated and deliberately distorted in the *Senjinkun*. But by the time the *Hagakure* appeared in the eighteenth century, seppuku had actually been long outlawed. Which was why the author, instead of killing himself after his *daimyō* Nabeshima Mitsushige died in 1700, as had been the custom, became a Buddhist priest instead.

Historically the emperor was removed from politics. For centuries martial matters were handled by the samurai, often in spite of the wishes of the imperial family. By the early nineteenth century the power of the shogunate was substantially diminished. Japan had no navy; she had no adequate coastal defenses; she saw the Indian subcontinent subjugated by European maritime powers, and an unequal treaty system imposed on China. After U.S. Navy Commodore Matthew C. Perry and his four "black ships" appeared in Edo Bay in 1853, Japan had little recourse but to acquiesce in trade with the West in a treaty negotiated by the American consul, Townsend Harris. Her humiliation at the hands of the *bakufu*, the shogun's government in Edo, led to calls for a stronger state.

In 1868 the imperial institution was restored in the person of the fifteen-year-old Meiji emperor. But it was Japan's ministers who ruled, and "Rich country, strong military" (*fukoku kyohei*) became the slogan of the day. Japan learned from her adversaries, turning to the West for lessons in parliamentary government, finance, education, and technology, while justifying the restoration of the emperor system with the heft of its mythical past.

In the *Nihon Shoki*, one of the earliest surviving records of Japan, Jimmu was the first emperor, who promised in 660 B.C. to "extend the line of the Imperial descendants and foster rightmindedness."

The capital was to be expanded "so as to embrace all of the six cardinal points [of the compass] and the eight cords may be covered so as to form a roof." This was the policy known as *hakkō ichiu*, meaning "Eight Corners of the World Under One Roof," and it was the first expression of Japanese polity, popularly referred to during the Meiji period as *kokutai*.

The early Japanese believed in Shintō, or "the way of the gods," which was distinct from Buddhism, a Chinese import. The gods were *kami*—natural phenomena, mythological creatures, or real men who inspired awe. Emperors were "distant *kami*," worthy of reverence by the common people, wrote Norinaga Motoori, a celebrated student of Shintō in the late eighteenth century.

In 1889 the divine status of the emperor was formalized by the Imperial Constitution, which declared the sovereign "sacred and inviolate." It also gave him "the supreme commmand of the Army and Navy," with the powers to declare war and peace and to conclude treaties. But in reality the emperor's role was largely symbolic, a source of national unity reinforced by Shintōism, which became Japan's "national faith."

Seven years earlier the emperor had presented Army Minister Ōyama Iwao with the Imperial Rescript for Military Men (*Gunjin Chokuyu*), which stated in its first article that the primary responsibility of the military was to the country. The military man's loyalty to his nation was "heavier than the mountains," but death was "lighter than a feather." Japanese militarists believed that they alone understood the "imperial will" and intentionally misinterpreted this directive as a call for blind faith in the emperor instead of loyalty to the state. With the military independent of political control, the soldier became its puppet.

In the four decades after Matthew Perry's four armed ships entered Edo Bay, Japan remained the "hungry guest" at the table of nations, suffering under an inequitable treaty system. She was smaller than the state of Texas, strapped for raw materials, and saddled with the demands of a growing population. Japan was at a crossroads: expansion or collapse. After adopting the European model of colonialism in Asia and the Western Pacific, Japan emerged as the only non-Western empire in modern history.

Japan's prize for defeating China in the Sino-Japanese War of 1894–95 was Formosa and the Pescadores. With her victory in the Russo-Japanese War of 1904–5, she won world power status. Peace with the Russians was formalized in the Treaty of Portsmouth, which was deftly negotiated by President Theodore Roosevelt and Secretary of War William Howard Taft. Japan was granted the Liaotung Peninsula in Manchuria, southern Sakhalin, and dominance over Korea in exchange for American control of the Philippines. In addition to controlling the South Manchurian Railway, she claimed the best naval base at Port Arthur and one of the most coveted ice-free ports in northeast Asia at Dairen. Such victories "naturally paved the way," wrote Kase Toshikazu, "for the gradual ascendance of the military."

Coupled with the economic success of the *issei* (immigrant generation) in California and an influx of Japanese who fell on hard times in a postwar depression, they also stoked fears in the United States of the "Yellow Peril." In October 1906, the Oriental Exclusion League arm-twisted the San Francisco Board of Education into removing all Japanese students and transferring them to a segregated school for the Chinese.

Anti-American rioting erupted in Japan. Roosevelt intervened to reverse the school board's decision, and ultimately persuaded Tōkyō to restrict immigration to the United States. But there was simmering resentment in Japan over the Portsmouth Treaty, which gave the Japanese only limited control over Manchuria. Meanwhile, exclusionist fervor boiled over into rioting in the United States in the spring of 1907, and the press fanned a "war scare."

Privately Roosevelt admitted in a letter to his son that Japan's victory over Russia played into American interests. The United States could now curb both Russian and Japanese expansion in Asia, if necessary. While the president refused to believe that yellow journalism and nativist prejudice could provoke hostilities between nations, relations between America and Japan were tense enough by 1907 for strategists at the Naval War College to formulate the Orange Plan, which envisioned war with the empire.

Japan developed her own defense plans. A key feature of her strategy was to add eight battleships and eight cruisers to her fleet, and to protect herself with an ever-expanding ring of buffers and new bases. In 1910 Japan formally annexed Korea and renamed the country Chōsen; its capital, Seoul, became Keijō. In 1914 Japan seized the German South Sea islands—the Marianas, Carolines, and Marshalls. By 1921 almost half of Japan's budget was allocated to the military, much of it spent on naval armaments. The five-power disarmament treaty that evolved from the Washington Conference of 1921 was negotiated by America and

Japan allegedly to equalize naval strength in the western Pacific for a period of fifteen years. In reality, the United States sought to restrain Japan's advances into China. Economically, Japan could not sustain an arms race and had little choice but to submit to arms limitations. The Washington Conference granted the United States parity with Great Britain in terms of capital ship tonnage and 40 percent superiority over Japan to account for distance and refueling. But a "nonfortification clause" prohibited further improvement of naval bases or seacoast defenses belonging to the United States, Great Britain, France, and Japan west of Midway Island. The London Treaty of 1930 placed additional limitations on the numbers and types of cruisers that could be built by the United States, Great Britain, and Japan.

On the heels of the Harding administration's austerity and Hoover's budget cuts during the Depression, the effect in America was a reduction in naval personnel and combat strength. The trend would be reversed only when a former assistant secretary of the navy, Franklin Delano Roosevelt, assumed the presidency, but not before he trimmed an already meager 140,000-man army.

In Japan, militarists who had harbored resentment since the Washington Conference assumed control of foreign policy. In 1931 the Japanese sabotaged the South Manchurian Railway at Liutiaoko outside of Mukden, blamed the Chinese, and their Kwantung Army occupied Manchuria, a territory historically disputed by China, Japan, and Russia. Manchukuo (as it was renamed) was the booty, a puppet state of some 34 million financed with the profits of an opium cartel and "ruled" by the charismatic twenty-seven-year-old emperor Henry P'u Yi, though it was the Kwantung Army that pulled the strings. Said Nishi Haruhiko, deputy foreign minister at the time, "The Ministry could do nothing but give in gradually to the pressures of the military."

Six years before the Russo-Japanese War began, Nitobe Inazō published in English *Bushidō: The Soul of Japan*. A Quaker who worked on behalf of the League of Nations, Nitobe glorified the samurai code, but he was a champion of peace. He translated *bushidō*—the way of the warrior—as chivalry, and chivalry was the "leaven among the masses" that would prevent Japan from sliding into the morass of Western materialism. It was, he wrote, "a flower no less indigenous to Japan than its emblem, the cherry blossom." *Bushidō* was the most widely read book of the Meiji era outside Japan. Theodore Roosevelt was so impressed with it that he purchased sixty copies for his friends.

Nitobe saw himself as a "bridge of transpacific understanding." But he vowed never again to set foot in the United States until the repeal of the 1924 Immigration Restriction Act, which was designed to limit the numbers of Italians, Poles, and Russian Jews entering America and that closed the door entirely on the Japanese.

By then Japan depended on the United States for a full 45 percent of its export market, 60 percent of which was in raw silk. Its fortunes were so closely linked to its rival across the Pacific that it was said, "When America sneezes, Japan comes down with the flu." Japanese silk reelers zealously watched U.S. Steel stock prices as indicators of broader market moves on Wall Street. But the introduction of rayon followed by the Depression delivered twin blows to Japan's economy, from which she would not recover prior to the Pacific War.

After the invasion of Manchuria, Nitobe broke his vow and decided to return to the United States in an attempt to explain Japanese policy. Before embarking, he confessed: "I left on each of my earlier trips to America full of hope and optimism. This time there is little hope." His American friends vilified him as an apologist for pan-Asianism, while in Japan he was branded a traitor for criticizing the militarists. Far from being a stabilizing influence, *bushido* was the tinder that fueled ultranationalism in Japan.

In 1933 Japan withdrew from the League of Nations, and in 1937 she launched a war in North China after the so-called Marco Polo Bridge incident, twenty miles south of Peking. Her colonial conquests lent credence to the belief fostered by militarists: Japan had a divine destiny. And that destiny, embodied in the person of Emperor Hirohito, was to unify the world through *kōdō,* the Imperial Way.

9

"Help is on the way"

HOMMA MASAHARU was behind schedule. The fifty-four-year-old lieutenant general perplexed the Japanese High Command. Of aristocratic lineage, he towered over his countrymen at five foot ten, looked distinctly Eurasian, and had a penchant for poetry, drama, and star-crossed romances.

Homma was indisputably brilliant, but he was also a notoriously poor judge of character. Having graduated from the Army Staff College with honors, he was fluent in English, and in 1918 was assigned to the headquarters of General Herbert Plumer, commander of the Second Army of the British Expeditionary Force in France. He returned to England in 1920, where he was attached to the Aldershot Regiment. In the meantime he married Tamura Toshiko, whose mother had been a geisha in Akasaka and whose father was General Tamura. When Homma learned that his wife had become a prostitute in his absence, he attempted suicide, and then, instead of divorcing her, he tried unsuccessfully to woo her back. In 1922 Homma was designated the Japanese Resident Officer in India, attached to the British East Indian Army. He was back in Japan by December 1925 as a major with the Imperial Army Headquarters staff. Then he fell in love and married Takata Fujika, a geisha who was fifteen years his junior. In 1927 Homma was chosen as personal aide-de-camp to Prince Chichibu, a younger brother of Hirohito. Three years later he was a full colonel, the military attaché to the Japanese Embassy in London, and by 1933 an appointee to the Japanese commission at the Geneva Disarmament Conference, which sought to counterbalance French and German interests.

By 1935 Homma was a major general in charge of the 32nd Brigade in Wakayama, and two years later he took over the Army Propaganda Department, a branch of the General Staff. He glorified the war against China, which he felt was necessary if Asia was to free itself of European domination, but he remained ardently pro-British, which was tantamount to being pro-American. Many Japanese considered Homma a pacifist, more suited to civilian than army life. He was opposed to Tōjō, the pro-German candidate for minister of war who had been chief of secret police in Manchuria. Once Tōjō became head of the army as well as prime minister, Homma's views were immediately suspect, as were those of nearly all of the more liberal-minded Japanese officers. After Nanking fell, Homma declared: "Unless peace is achieved immediately it will be disastrous." Homma had been led to believe he would be made Deputy Chief of the General Staff once the position became vacant. Instead, he was removed from any policy-making positions. In July 1938 Homma was transferred to China, where he served as commander of the 27th Division and then the Tientsin Defense Army, responsible for quelling domestic unrest. Given Japan's deteriorating relations with Britain, Homma closed the Japanese concession in Tientsin, and in December 1940 he was sent to Formosa to take charge of the Formosa Army. He remained there until November 1941, when he was appointed commander of the 14th Army, whose unit code name was *Watari,* meaning "to cross."

"A paper genius," Homma was a superb strategist brazen enough to question the objectives of his superiors. But until Bataan he lacked real combat experience. Homma grew increasingly aloof from his troops while investing more authority in his staff officers, daring to take them at their word. It was Homma's Achilles' heel.

Army Chief of Staff Sugiyama Gen had ordered Homma to conquer the Philippines by the end of January, a mere fifty days. The plan was aggressive and necessarily so: the war in China was bleeding the Japanese Army of troops. The 65th Brigade was to plow down the Bataan peninsula in two columns, on the east and west coasts, then make a final push toward Mariveles. As the 14th Army operation order read, the objective was simple: "annihilation of the enemy."

The Japanese, boasted Tōjō, had conquered Hong Kong in eighteen days, Manila in twenty-six, and Singapore ("the greatest disaster and capitulation in British history," lamented Churchill) in seventy. With the invasion of Borneo, they won access to rich oil fields; in Kuching, Malaya, to petroleum; in Ipoh, to tin and rubber. "Japan is no longer a have-not nation," crowed the Japanese Planning Agency. To celebrate their victories, the Japanese held lantern parades in Tōkyō, drunk with joy. But twice in one week, on January 13 and January 20, the emperor pressed Sugiyama to accelerate the offensive in Luzon. And here was Homma, mired in the backwater of Bataan.

His intelligence officer had underestimated enemy troop and matériel strength, the 65th Brigade was untrained, and the American and Filipino forces had proven far more resilient than anticipated.

Homma's idea of a seaborne assault on Longoskawayan to make an end run on Mariveles was a disaster. Japanese aircraft, supporting the second landing, couldn't even find the 57th Infantry on the ground. Air-dropped supplies often fell into the hands of American and Filipino troops.

While Major Kimura saw the destruction of an entire battalion at Longoskawayan as a "glorious death," simple arithmetic told a different tale. Fourteenth Army losses would mount to 2,700 dead and more than 4,000 wounded. On February 13 Homma pulled his forces back to blocking positions and regrouped. The poet-general appealed to Imperial General Headquarters in Tōkyō for replacements and reinforcements. Only then could he launch a final offensive on Bataan. An unsettling lull fell over the front as Homma—and the Fil-American forces anticipating his next move—waited.

In early February 1942 Washington decided to evacuate MacArthur from Corregidor to Australia. Quezon was so dispirited that on February 8 he sent a blistering letter to Roosevelt via Army Chief of Staff George Marshall.

My people entered the war with the confidence that the United States would bring such assistance to us as would make it possible to sustain the conflict with some chance of success. All our soldiers in the field were animated by the belief that help would be forthcoming. This help has not and evidently will not be realized. Our people have suffered death, misery, devastation. After two months of war not the slightest assistance has been forthcoming from the United States. Aid and succour have been dispatched to other warring nations such as England, Ireland, Australia, the N.E.I. and perhaps others, but not only has nothing come here, but apparently no effort has been made to bring anything here. The American Fleet and the British Fleet, the two most powerful navies in the world, have apparently adopted an attitude which precludes any effort to reach these islands with assistance.

As a result, while enjoying security itself, the United States has in effect condemned the sixteen millions of Filipinos to practical destruction in order to effect a certain delay. You have promised redemption, but what we need is immediate assistance and protection. We are concerned with what is to transpire during the next few months and years as well as with our ultimate destiny. There is not the slightest doubt in our minds that victory will rest with the United States, but the question before us now is: Shall we further sacrifice our country and our people in a hopeless fight? I voice the unanimous opinion of my War Cabinet and I am sure the unanimous opinion of all Filipinos that under the circumstances we should take steps to preserve the Philippines and the Filipinos from further destruction.

Quezon proposed that the Philippines be granted their independence immediately so the islands could be declared neutral, American and Japanese forces could be withdrawn, and the Philippine Army could be disbanded. He would, he said, make the same offer to the Japanese publicly if the United States accepted his proposition.

In an accompanying letter, MacArthur wrote that High Commissioner Sayre approved of Quezon's idea; then he gave his own assessment of the situation:

The troops have sustained practically 50% casualties from their original strength. Divisions are reduced to the size of regiments, regiments to battalions, battalions to companies. Some units have entirely disappeared. The men have been in constant action and are badly battle worn. Their spirit is good but they are capable now of nothing but fighting in place in a fixed position. All our supplies are scant and the command has been on half rations for the past month. . . .

You must be prepared at any time to figure on the complete destruction of this command.

Roosevelt rejected Quezon's proposition outright. He sympathized with the plight of the Filipino people but chided Quezon for his naïveté in believing Tōjō's claim that Japan would respect the independence of the Philippines.

I have only to refer you to the present condition of Korea, Manchukuo, North China, Indo-China, and all other countries which have fallen under the brutal sway of the Japanese government, to point out the hollow duplicity of such an announcement. The present sufferings of the Filipino people, cruel as they may be, are infinitely less than the sufferings and permanent enslavement which will inevitably follow acceptance of Japanese promises.

In a secret radiogram of February 10 Roosevelt reminded MacArthur: "It is mandatory that there be established once and for all in the minds of all peoples complete evidence that the American determination and indomitable will to win carries on down to the last unit." MacArthur could arrange for the capitulation of Filipino troops, if and when it was necessary. He could also facilitate the evacuation of Quezon, his family, and his War Cabinet. But the Americans could not relent "so long as there remains any possibility of resistance." Roosevelt's line could have been borrowed from the *Senjinkun*, which stated simply: "Do not give up under any circumstances."

His imperatives were at odds with his priorities. By Washington's Birthday the Japanese had conquered Java and Sumatra, invaded Timor, and bombed Darwin, Australia. Roosevelt used his fireside chat of February 23, 1942, to dispel rumors, shore up morale after a string of Allied military defeats, and defend his administration's war strategy. He hailed MacArthur and his men for their defense of the Philippines, which has "magnificently exceeded the previous estimates of endurance," but concluded after all that it would be "a hopeless operation" to send the Pacific Fleet to relieve them so long as island bases remained under Japanese control. Roosevelt dared to say what Stimson would not after the Arcadia Conferences.

Quezon put on a brave public face. "I urge every Filipino to be of good cheer, to have faith in the patriotism and valor of our soldiers in the field, but above all, to trust America," he broadcast from Corregidor on February 28. "America is too great and too powerful to be vanquished in this conflict. I know she will not fail us."

Privately, he excoriated American policy in a blast of Spanish invective aimed at MacArthur's chief of intelligence (G-2), Colonel Charles A. Willoughby, who was fluent in the language:

> I cannot stand this constant reference to England, to Europe. . . . I am here and my people are here under the heels of a conqueror. Where are the planes that this *sinverguenza* [creep] is boasting of? *Qué demonio*—how typically American to write in anguish at the fate of a distant cousin while a daughter is being raped in the back room.

———

While the ground war came to a halt on the front, aerial attacks continued against the rear and tested the mettle of the marines who remained in Mariveles. The Japanese bombed Battery C "six, eight, and sometimes ten times daily," 1st Lieutenant Carter Simpson noted in his diary. One late-afternoon raid turned the area around the Section Base into a moonscape with fifteen craters thirty-five feet in diameter. It took hours to control the fires in order to protect food and ammunition. But remarkably little damage was done to matériel, and since the majority of the bombs fell in flat open spaces, there were relatively few injuries.

From the safety of Tunnel No. 4, the navy doctors treated marines manning Battery C and crew members of the *Canopus*. You could breathe easier after sundown, though no fires were allowed outside. On most nights, artillery flashes shattered the darkness. The muffled sounds of warfare were the background music to sleep.

At the same time, another war was being waged against the twin enemies of hunger and disease. When fodder ran out for the 26th Cavalry, Wainwright sacrificed his prize jumper Joseph Conrad, who became fodder for his own men. "We ate the 26th Cavalry right out of the saddle," bragged Private Lewis Elliott of the 60th Coast Artillery. Horses along with army pack mules, pigs, and cattle from Cavite were short-term staples in a diet in which anything was fair game.

The only real chance of relief came from boats running the Japanese blockade or air shipments from Australia. On moonless evenings two 400-ton motor vessels, the *Bohol II* and the *Kolambugan*, succeeded in making two trips each through the mine fields between Corregidor and Looc Cove, south of Manila Bay. With food procured by American agents in Cavite and Batangas, they added some 1,600 tons to Bataan's stocks. But by mid-February the voyage was too hazardous, and the operation ceased.

In the southern Philippines the quartermaster depot in Cebu City had huge stores of food, clothing, medicine, and gasoline to support Brigadier General William F. Sharp's Visayan-Mindanao Force. Additonal supplies were culled from surrounding provinces. The 1,000-ton *Legaspi* made two runs to Corregidor before it was shelled by the Japanese and abandoned. The *Prinscesa* succeeded in delivering 700 tons of food, and *Elcano* 1,100 tons. But after ten ships were sunk by the Japanese or scuttled by their crews at an estimated loss of 7,000 tons of food and supplies, blockade-running to Corregidor came to an end.

Air deliveries were made from Australia to Mindanao and the Visayas, not Luzon. Medical supply officer Colonel George S. Littell and Major John D. Blair combed Melbourne and Sydney for quantities of quinine, morphine, anesthesia, and vitamins to be sent to the islands, but their resources were strained after ten air shipments. Colonel Percy J. Carroll of the newly formed Office of the Chief Surgeon was furious when he learned that pilots encountering mechanical difficulties would rather dump their medical supplies than sacrifice cartons of cigarettes. Except for a few additional shipments via submarine, Bataan and Corregidor were effectively sealed off from the rest of the world.

UP correspondent Frank Hewlett summed up the mood of the men on Bataan in a few lines that served as their unofficial anthem:

> We're the battling bastards of Bataan,
> No mama, no papa, no Uncle Sam,
> No aunts, no uncles, no cousins, no nieces,
> No pills, no planes or artillery pieces,
> And nobody gives a damn.

Bob Kelly had a tentative date with his girlfriend, Peggy, an army nurse in the Malinta Tunnel hospital, for March 15. She was going to call him on the eleventh on the Signal Corps field telephone around 0600 for confirmation. But her hours had been changed, and she couldn't reach him until 1430.

The fifteenth was out, he told her.

Would the sixteenth be any better? she asked.

Couldn't make it on the sixteenth either, he said.

"Nothing would be any better," he added.

And then he said goodbye.

She asked where he was going, but he couldn't tell her.

She asked if he was coming back, and he couldn't tell her that, either.

She knew, then, that it really was goodbye and said, quietly, "But it's been awfully nice, hasn't it?"

That evening, under the cloak of darkness, MacArthur, his staff, family, and their Chinese amah, Ah Cheu, were spirited away from Corregidor. Four boats from MTB Squadron 3 made up the little flotilla, led by Lieutenant John Bulkeley in PT-41. Bob Kelly's PT-34 brought up the rear. Their swashbuckling manner and audacious assaults on the Japanese had earned the approbation of even MacArthur. "My pirates," he called them. The retinue included fifteen army and two navy officers, among them Sutherland, Marshall, and Rockwell, whose position as Commandant of the 16th Naval District was assumed by the commander of the Inshore Patrol, Captain Kenneth M. Hoeffel. General Tōjō, the cook's pet monkey, kept little Arthur MacArthur company.

It was a white-knuckle journey down Mindoro Strait. Waves fifteen to twenty feet high crashed over the decks, reefs lurked in waters unfamiliar to the crew, and the Japanese preyed on the coast by air, land, and sea, searching for signs of enemy infiltration. MacArthur was violently seasick, his wife, Jean, was ill, and the cold salt spray left them chilled to the bone.

Asked by a sailor if he wanted to be helped belowdecks, one ailing general draped over a torpedo tube on Kelly's boat moaned: "Let me die."

When Rockwell saw Kelly sighting with his fingers as they passed an island, he inquired:

"Don't you have a pelorus?"

Kelly didn't; neither did Bulkeley.

"How in hell do you navigate?" Rockwell demanded.

"By guess and by God, sir," the handsome lieutenant replied with a smile.

Finally, after thirty-five hours of battling the elements and playing cat-and-mouse with the Japanese, MTB Squadron 3 arrived safely at Cagayan de Oro, on the north coast of Mindanao. MacArthur was so grateful, he awarded the officers and crew the Silver Star "for gallantry and fortitude in the face of heavy odds."

Brigadier General William F. Sharp accompanied the entourage to Del Monte Field, but there were no planes available for the next leg of the journey. When a decrepit B-17 finally showed up, MacArthur refused to fly in it. Four days later the general and his party took two B-17s to Darwin, Australia. But since Darwin was being bombed, they landed forty miles to the south at Batchelor Field. They'd barely touched down when a report came in of Japanese planes heading their way, so they hastily departed for Alice Springs aboard a C-47 transport. The next day, March 18, the MacArthurs embarked on a train bound for Adelaide, where the general was greeted at the station by reporters hankering for a headline:

> The President of the United States ordered me to break through the Japanese lines and proceed from Corregidor to Australia for the purpose, as I understand it, of organizing the American offensive against Japan, a primary object of which is the relief of the Philippines. I came through, and I shall return.

On the way to Melbourne MacArthur was joined by Brigadier General Richard J. Marshall, USAFFE deputy chief of staff, who advised him of Australia's combat strength: 25,364 Americans, none of whom were infantrymen; no tanks; fewer than 250 combat-ready aircraft; and only one remaining regular division of the Australian Army, whose forces were sapped by campaigns in the Middle East. In other words, there were 7,000 trained Australians to defend an entire continent. MacArthur was stunned by the news. "God have mercy on us!" he exclaimed.

Before he left Corregidor, MacArthur wanted Wainwright "to make it known throughout all elements of your command that I'm leaving over my repeated protests." Wainwright assured him he would. While most understood "what the score was" and realized the disastrous effect that MacArthur's capture would have had on morale, morale was shaken nonetheless. Humor was the antidote. Songs and snipes, jokes and jibes were already in circulation.

One lyric was composed by Lieutenant Henry G. Lee to the melody of "The Battle Hymn of the Republic."

> Dugout Doug MacArthur lies ashaking on the Rock
> Safe from all the bombers and from any sudden shock
> Dugout Doug is eating of the best food on Bataan
> And his troops go starving on.
>
> Dugout Doug's not timid, he's just cautious, not afraid
> He's protecting carefully the stars that Franklin made
> Four-star generals are rare as good food on Bataan
> And his troops go starving on.
>
> We've fought the war the hard way since they said the fight was on
> All the way from Lingayen to the hills of old Bataan
> And we'll continue fighting after Dugout Doug is gone
> And still go starving on.

Then there was the story about a soldier on Bataan who boasted to his new acquaintance, "I've been in General MacArthur's mess," which earned a Groucho Marx retort, "I was in a mess with him also."

For one regiment on Bataan, MacArthur's name was literally in the can. "I am going to the latrine," the men said whenever nature called, "but I shall return."

The open disdain extended from the lowliest private up through the officers' ranks. Nailed to a tree at Army Headquarters on Bataan was a calendar showing a quaint sailing ship in a languid breeze, below which was scribbled: "We told you so. Help *is* on the way."

Murray and John never saw MacArthur on Bataan. Fred and George never saw him on Corregidor. One day in February 1942 Seaman 1st Class Darwin F. "John" Kidd, who had worked as Admiral Hart's assistant in the Marsman Building in Manila, was leaving the south end of Malinta Tunnel and heading for the Radio Intercept Tunnel when an air raid alarm went off. He was walking around the sandbags at the exit when a rather tall individual came tearing in, knocked him over, didn't slow down, and didn't look back.

"Watch where you're going!" Kidd shouted.

A colonel helped him to his feet.

"Who in the hell was that son of a bitch?" Kidd sputtered.

"You don't know who that was?" the kindly colonel asked.

"Absolutely not," maintained Kidd.

"That's General MacArthur."

Private 1st Class Richard T. Winter of the 59th Coast Artillery maintained that Lee's ditty was a far cry from the truth. On one occasion Winter watched MacArthur walk out of Malinta Tunnel, pack his corncob pipe with tobacco, and light up in the middle of a bombing raid. On another occasion Captain Roland G. "Roly" Ames of Corregidor's Battery Chicago saw MacArthur refuse to take cover. AP correspondent Clark Lee claimed that during the December 29 raid on Corregidor MacArthur was "standing in front of his house . . . even when the bombs hit near him, and the planes came low and close." He had, after all, proven his valor during World War I as commander of the 84th Brigade in the Aisne-Marne offensive, which won him his second Croix de Guerre and the title Commander of France's Legion of Honor. But to the men on Bataan there was more bluster to MacArthur than bravery; more grandstanding than greatness; hence the sobriquet "Dugout Doug." That perception was reinforced by MacArthur's nighttime escape to Australia, and it certainly wasn't lost on the Japanese, who proclaimed in the *Japan Times and Advertiser* in Tōkyō that MacArthur had "fled from his post."

The fact that Roosevelt choreographed MacArthur's departure because he valued his "military genius," as Roosevelt's doctor Ross McIntire described it, was little known either in the Philippines or in the United States. But once Roosevelt awarded MacArthur the Medal of Honor on March 25, MacArthur's legendary stature was secure.

"His utter disregard of personal danger under heavy fire and aerial bombardment, his calm judgment in each crisis, inspired his troops, galvanized the spirit of resistance of the Filipino people, and confirmed the faith of the American people in their armed forces," the citation concluded. The citation was written by Army Chief of Staff General George C. Marshall. But it was based largely on Sutherland's copy, and in all likelihood burnished with MacArthur's gift for self-promotion, though lacking the general's signature grandiloquence.

MacArthur was made a hero in spite of what one historian has called "the greatest twin U.S. military disasters in history." General Brereton took the blame for the destruction of the Far East Air Force. Admiral Hart—who resigned on February 13 as the ABDA naval commander— was criticized for the inaction of the Asiatic Fleet. Yet control of the skies was lost as a result of MacArthur's inaction. Marshall was indefatigable in his attempts to cover up for MacArthur despite MacArthur's failure to defend the Philippines, though "the assumption," as Air Corps chief General Henry H. "Hap" Arnold remarked, had always been that the Japanese "would hit the Philippines first." In the absence of military victories, as Roosevelt was keenly aware, what America needed most was hope.

Streets, bridges, buildings, parks, flowers, and baby boys were named in honor of the great man. There was a dance named the MacArthur Glide. The National Father's Day Committee judged him the "Number One Father for 1942." The Blackfoot Indians of Montana even saw fit to adopt him as Mo-Kahki-Peta, or Chief Wise Eagle. Naturally there was a movie about MacArthur, *America's First Soldier.*

Several weeks earlier, in a display of distinctly unheroic behavior, MacArthur had recommended to the War Department that citations be given to all units on Bataan and Corregidor—except the navy and marines. What better way to offend Corregidor's defenders? Rear Admiral Rockwell suggested that perhaps this was an oversight. Sutherland assured him it was not. The marines and the navy, MacArthur felt, had had their moment of glory in World War I. The leathernecks shot back in verse:

> Mine eyes have seen MacArthur
> With a Bible on his knee,
> He is pounding out communiques
> For guys like you and me,
> And while possibly a rumor now,
> Someday 'twill be a fact,
> That the Lord will hear a deep voice
> Say, "Move over God, it's Mac."

Indeed, of the 142 communiqués issued from Corregidor between December 8, 1941, and March 11, 1942, one name was paramount: MacArthur.

In the meantime, without consulting MacArthur, the War Department promoted Wainwright to lieutenant general in charge of the newly designated U.S. Forces in the Philippines (USFIP), which included the remains of the naval forces in the Philippine Islands. Wainwright appointed Major General Edward P. King, Jr., commander of Luzon Force and turned over to him his old headquarters—a trailer parked just north of Mariveles. "Skinny" Wainwright was enormously popular with his men and regularly visited the front on Bataan, often in the line of fire. On assuming his new command on Corregidor, he rectified MacArthur's slight by giving credit where credit was due: to the marines as well as to the navy.

Lieutenant General Homma was well aware of the change in command. On March 19 hundreds of beer cans trailing red and white streamers were air-dropped over Bataan and Corregidor carrying the message:

> *Your Excellency,*
>   *We have the honor to address you in accordance with the humanitarian principle of Bushidō, the code of the Japanese warrior. . . .*
>   *You have already fought to the best of your ability. What dishonor is there in avoiding needless bloodshed? What disgrace is there in following the defenders of Hong Kong, Singapore, and the Netherlands East Indies in the acceptance of honorable defeat?*
>   *Your duty has been performed. Accept our sincere advice and save the lives of those officers and men under your command. The International Law will be strictly adhered to by the Imperial Japanese Forces and your Excellency and those under your command will be treated accordingly.*
>   *If a reply to this advisory is not received from Your Excellency through special messenger by noon, March 22, 1942, we shall consider ourselves at liberty to take any action whatsoever.*

Wainwright did not take the liberty of replying.

By the time MacArthur evacuated Corregidor in mid-March 1942, daily rations on Bataan were one-half to one-third of those on Corregidor. In late March they were reduced from 2,000 to 1,000 calories and stripped of vitamins A, B, and C, when 1,500 calories was considered the bare minimum for subsistence. Flour ran out. Fresh or canned meat was reduced from six ounces a day to 1.22 ounces—usually corned beef—though efforts were made to provide six ounces of fresh meat every third day. Coffee, tea, sugar, and butter vanished in rapid succession.

When white rice was exhausted, the men turned to musty red rice, and when the meat ration disappeared, they hunted deer, monkey, lizard, iguana, quail, wild pig, and dog. *Calesa* pony, mule, horse, and *carabao* were the most popular items on the new menu, in that order. Monkey ranked last. Tough as tires, it felt "like eating your little brother," said Private Alton C. Halbrook, a truck driver in the 4th Marines. They picked mangoes, bananas, coconuts, and papayas, then in desperation turned to the *nami,* a tuber that was poisonous unless properly prepared. They went fishing for sea bass and shark with dynamite: pack a condensed milk can with TNT, insert a blasting cap with a 3-inch fuse, ignite, and toss. They washed down their chow with water from artesian wells or from 55-gallon storage drums that tasted of gasoline, and when the supply dried up, they drank from *carabao* wallows, mountain pools, and streams contaminated by waste. There was a "favored" distribution list, according to Brigadier General Allen C. McBride of the Service Command Area, for those most in need. But as food grew ever more scarce, ration trucks were hijacked, dumps were raided, and the occasional shipments from Corregidor were pillaged.

Soldiers were shedding not just a few pounds but ten, twenty, even thirty pounds. They were weak and quickly tired. They suffered tachycardia and palpitations with minimal exertion. Some experienced hallucinations; others fainted on chow lines. The combat efficiency of I Corps was reduced to 45 percent and of II Corps to 20 percent. As Colonel Harry A. Skerry said of a battalion of the 71st Infantry: "From the standpoint of trained, well-fed troops . . . it was an utter nightmare." Unless food stocks were replenished, Wainwright warned General Marshall on March 28, the men on Bataan would starve.

The lack of food was one problem. The lack of quinine, as Murray discovered early on at Hospital No. 2, was another.

When war broke out, the Philippine Department Medical Supply Depot had enough quinine sulfate for thirty days of prophylaxis, at the prescribed rate of 10 grains (.650 gram) of quinine per man each day. Standard treatment was 2 grams of quinine daily for five days, followed by .030 gram of plasmochin napthoate three times daily for five to seven days. Atabrine could be substituted for quinine, but the supply of atabrine and plasmochin was itself limited, and the dosage was imperfectly understood. Moreover, men on atabrine complained of nausea, upset stomach, and diarrhea, and to add insult to illness, their skin turned yellow. When the supply of quinine tablets was depleted, powdered quinine sulfate was administered instead. Brown, bitter, and insoluble, you had to spoon it down before you gulped your chow. The taste was so unpleasant that quinine roll calls were mandatory.

A dearth of mosquito bars and nets, combined with inadequate quinine stocks, led to an epidemic of malaria on Bataan. The disease cut a swath through the ranks of Bataan's defenders. Filipino civilians behind the lines were "a reservoir for malaria," noted one army colonel. Filipino Brigadier General Vicente Lim of the valiant 41st Division, which had launched the first attack against the Japanese in Abucay, suffered from malaria and estimated that a third of his troops were dying from that disease and dysentery. "We have no medicines to give them," he told

Colonel Carlos P. Romulo, who broadcast dispatches to the Filipino people over the Voice of Freedom from Malinta Tunnel, and periodically visited Bataan.

By early March, 60 percent of the medical personnel at Hospital No. 2 were laid low with malaria, and hundreds of malarial patients sought admission each day. Ward No. 2 handled mostly malaria and dysentery cases, but the army doctor in charge of it, Captain John R. Bumgarner, was nearly incapacitated by the disease.

Indeed, the man who had introduced cinchona to the Philippines, Colonel Arthur Fischer, was himself recovering from malaria on Bataan. A hundred thousand kilograms of bark were available in Mindanao, and Wainwright arranged to have Fischer flown there to gear up an extraction project. But Japanese forces prevented Fischer from carrying out the plan. He was evacuated to Australia with seeds in hand to establish plantations in South America, where the cinchona tree had originally been discovered in the mid-seventeenth century.

"It is my candid and conservative opinion," wrote Colonel Cooper on March 10, 1942, "that if we do not secure a sufficient supply of quinine for our troops from front to rear . . . all other supplies we may get with the exception of rations, will be of little or no value." Finally, one million tablets of quinine arrived by air from the medical depot in Cebu, but it was too little and too late.

By late March hospital admissions on Bataan for malaria cases climbed to 1,000 cases per day. The disease had taken root, and though its symptoms might go into remission, without proper treatment they were bound to recur. Chick Mensching, wounded at Longoskawayan Point, suffered an astounding thirty-eight bouts of benign tertian malaria. What was needed to treat the most serious cases—cerebral malaria foremost among them—was quinine dihydrochloride and distilled water for intravenous injection.

Compounding the malaria problem were the enteric diseases that resulted from drinking unboiled water, bathing downstream, and inadequately cleaned mess gear. This was a particular problem for native Filipinos, who had only recently been introduced to single bore-hole toilets. Impetigo, hookworm, ringworm, roundworm, and scabies were also common. Bluebottle flies swarmed over straddle trenches—and food. The men ate with one hand while waving away flies with the other. Cross-infections were inevitable.

Sanitary conditions at the Filipino refugee camps were even worse, remarked Lieutenant Walter H. Waterous of Hospital No. 2, "the most deplorable I have ever seen and the death rate in them was appalling." One camp was one and a half miles below the Real River from Hospital

No. 2; another was on the other side of Mariveles. A separate medical facility was established in a ravine north of the Mariveles airstrip by the surgeon of the Philippine Army. Called the Philippine Army General Hospital, it was staffed entirely by Filipinos and treated Filipino refugees and Philippine Army personnel with the most rudimentary equipment and supplies.

Soon the two general hospitals groaned under a patient load of 7,000, more than three times their combined capacity. "Patients are being admitted in droves, all medical cases," wrote Ruth Straub, one of five army nurses transferred from Corregidor to help relieve the workload at Hospital No. 2. "Had to clear another section of the jungle for beds. Casualties of the day's bombing are still coming in, and the operating room staff has been called back to work."

Film ran out for the sole X-ray machine on Bataan at Hospital No. 1. Lister bags were a scarcity; chlorine stocks were drained. Gauze, bandages, and cotton were in short supply. Infected plasma led to hepatitis, and the lack of blood, said John Bumgarner, meant that "officers and enlisted men were constantly being canvassed to find more donors, and some of the staff gave two to three units in a relatively short period of time." When the bacillus antitoxin for gas gangrene was exhausted, the number of amputations mounted in spite of Adamo's innovative treatment. "Time and a good vascular surgeon could have saved many extremities," admitted Bumgarner.

The sick lay in army cots out in the open. Only the most serious cases had the benefit of tents or half-shelters. The scene looked like a Civil War battlefield, except that overhead was a canopy of acacia, bamboo, and mahogany trees.

The men faced their plight bravely. There were few behavioral disturbances among them. Hospital No. 2 had a separate ward for psychiatric observation, but the number of cases, given the constant exposure to daily bombing and shelling, was surprisingly small. There was no place to retreat, nowhere to hide.

On March 25 Colonel Gillespie of Hospital No. 2 was invited on an inspection tour of Philippine Army General Hospital. He knew the area well from the time he had served as surgeon of the USAFFE Advance Echelon on Signal Hill, and he was uncomfortable with how easily Japanese planes swooped in from the sea, flew parallel to the road, and targeted the antiaircraft battery. He politely declined. The day of the visit, the hospital was bombed, and Colonel Victoriano Luna, its commanding officer, was killed.

Both Hospitals Nos. 1 and 2 were identified with red and white crosses, but the former was boxed in by an ammunition dump to the left, a motor pool on the right, and the 200th Coast Artillery behind it. It was too enticing a target to resist.

In the early morning hours of March 30, two Japanese twin-engine bombers locked onto the hospital compound and let loose with incendiary and demolition bombs. Army doctor Major Alfred A. Weinstein was startled from his sleep by "the roar of exploding bombs and a pungent odor of smoke." Bleeding from a small head wound, he stumbled outside into a drainage ditch, where he felt his "chest heaving with terror." Carey Smith was hugging the floor of Ward No. 1 when a bomb exploded between the nurses' quarters and the OR thirty feet away. The left wing of the officers' quarters was completely destroyed. The hospital headquarters, the Officers' Mess, and the main operating room were shattered with fragments. Twenty-three were killed, among them two corpsmen, Private 1st Class Fred Lang and Sergeant Spielhoffer; seventy-eight were injured. That same day the Japanese broadcast an apology in English over KZRH in Manila. "We regret the unfortunate bombing of Hospital #1. It was a mistake." Duckworth thought the bombing was accidental: Weinstein was convinced it was deliberate.

The lull in ground combat brought relief nonetheless. Hospital No. 1 managed to host two afternoon tea dances for the doctors and nurses in the Officers' Mess, and it arranged a swimming party at Sisiman Cove, where guests watched Japanese planes bomb Corregidor. "Romances flourished with an intensity unknown in peacetime," observed Weinstein. Three nurses were married on Bataan, in spite of military regulations forbidding it.

Captain Dyess of the Bamboo Fleet, as the remaining P-40s on Bataan were called, helped throw a party for the nurses of Hospital No. 2 in a *nipa* hut decorated with Japanese trophies. Over a door mounted with *carabao* antlers was a placard that read:

THE DYSENTERY CROSS
Awarded to the Quartermaster by
THE MEN OF BATAAN FIELD

A piano was salvaged from a bombed-out village, canned pineapple juice and crackers were served, and soon there was dancing on the bamboo floor. "It had been so long since we had seen white women," Dyess confessed, "we were shy and awkward."

The self-published broadside *Jungle Journal* boosted spirits and kept the rumors flying with stories worthy of a stateside tabloid. There was the one about the B-19 that dropped a bomb on Mt. Fuji "and now there's 2 inches lava [*sic*] all over Japan." Another reported a tidal wave the U.S. Navy caused as it sped toward the empire.

Japanese propaganda leaflets dropped over Bataan were traded "like baseball cards," recalled army doctor Captain Paul Ashton. "Don't Wait to Die," began one of them. "Feel soft against me and . . . rest your warm hand on my breast." With their drawings of buxom beauties, platters of bountiful food, and seductive appeals for surrender, they appealed to the basest of instincts. Japanese-controlled KZRH repeatedly aired the song, "Waiting for the Ships That Never Came In," while Filipinos were urged in Tagalog to kill American officers and cross over to "freedom and safety." American attempts to lure the Japanese on Bataan to lay down their arms were no less crude. "It is cherry blossom time back in your homeland. . . . You ought to be home with your families and loved ones. . . . Come and surrender . . . and your shipment back home will be guaranteed," read one message written by the nisei Richard Sakakida.

Diversions were short-lived. The cumulative effects of disease and malnutrition had already sapped the strength—if not the will—of Fil-American forces on Bataan. The few remaining pilots in the Bamboo Fleet were issued extra rations on March 27 so they wouldn't lose consciousness during combat missions. Some of the frontline troops were lucky enough to receive double portions of rice and flour from Corregidor for Wainwright's last stand. As the service company commander of the 31st Infantry summed up the situation: "Hunger and disease were greater enemies than the Japanese." They were enemies the Japanese faced, too.

———————

Wada Kinsuke was a medic assigned to Colonel Takechi Susumu's 9th Infantry. He had trained for three months at the army hospital in Kyōto, where he learned anatomy and first aid. Japanese field equipment was more sophisticated than the Americans might have imagined, but actual treatments were not.

The standard-issue leather musette bag was packed with a surgical pocket case, needle and sutures, syringe, camphor solution, alcohol, medicated soap, opium tablets, bandages and gauze, stethoscope, morphine solution, rubber catheter, mercuric chloride tablets, and tincture of iodine. There was aspirin for headaches and fever, and quinine in limited quanties for malaria, which was later replaced with atabrine. Patent medicines, as well as vitamins B and C, were used extensively. Many of the other drugs had already been discarded by American and European counterparts, and some preventives were entirely useless. Field instrument cases included a sterilizer, nickel-plated carbon steel instruments as opposed to stainless steel, and antiquated blood transfusion kits. Plasma was unavailable.

On paper, two or three medical officers were assigned to each battalion, and each platoon in forward areas had one medic who accompanied troops into combat and doubled as a litter bearer to help carry the wounded back to dressing stations. Medics were responsible primarily for minor ailments and water purification. Medical officers administered treatment, intervened in outbreaks of infectious diseases, and cooperated closely with company COs. They carried their personal swords and were given army pistols so they could kill themselves if captured. They were also issued Red Cross brassards, which they tended not to wear.

Japanese aid stations were primitive. Field hospitals were one and a quarter miles behind the lines, and their organization was flexible enough that they could be broken into smaller units that functioned independently. Unlike Allied patients, Japanese wounded did not receive postoperative care. Standard daily rations for Japanese troops were 62 ounces and consisted of boiled rice, pickled plums or white radishes (*daikon*), bean paste soup, some vegetables, and occasionally fish and meat. But by January 1942, the Japanese 14th Army was scraping the bottom of its rice bowl, and by mid-February rations dived to a mere 23 ounces, which was still slightly better than what was doled out to the Fil-American forces.

There was little food up in the mountains, though, and hardly any meat. For water, Japanese troops sometimes slashed tree trunks to tap the moisture inside. Once Wada came across a beautiful stream in a valley. Three platoons of men made a run for it. They guzzled the cool liquid and were soon doubled over with diarrhea. Wada was sick for two weeks.

The 14th Army began its campaign on Bataan with only a month's supply of quinine, so malaria prophylaxis was restricted to frontline troops. By mid-March the little quinine that remained was reserved for treatment only. Initially Wada had plenty of the febrifuge. He had a mosquito net, too, but he refused to use it because of the heat. Soon he came down with malaria. Almost all of the soldiers, it seemed, suffered from dysentery. Wada believed that dysentery could be cured with "will and spirit," but not even "will and spirit" could vanquish malaria.

The medics had no support. Wada found it impossible to evacuate the wounded through the jungle back to a dressing station. He watched many men die, deprived of any medication whatsoever. They were starving on the frontlines, and after the first assault on Bataan, they were near exhaustion.

The Japanese 14th Army surgeon, Lieutenant Colonel Horiguchi Shusuke, estimated that 10,000 to 12,000 Japanese were sick with malaria, dysentery, and beriberi by February 1942, leaving only 3,000 effective fighting men. The mortality rate from malaria was high; some units were reduced to 10 percent combat efficiency. Japanese hospitals on Bataan couldn't keep pace with battle casualties, much less medical cases.

One February night, as Colonel Takechi began withdrawing the 9th Infantry from the bamboo thicket just beyond the intersection of Trail 2 and the main line of resistance, Wada's entire platoon was eliminated. It was hard being alone, hard knowing that you owed your life to "the spirits of the dead."

On March 27 MacArthur was joined in Australia by Manuel Quezon, who declared in a proclamation aired on Corregidor over the Voice of Freedom: "I call upon every Filipino to keep his courage and fortitude and to have faith in the ultimate victory of our cause." Once Quezon reached America, where he would retire to a sanatorium in Saranac Lake, New York, he privately denounced MacArthur for his failure to defend the Philippines and reinforce Australia.

By April, MacArthur had established General Headquarters, Southwest Pacific Area Command (GHQ/SWPA) in a tall bank building in Melbourne at 121 Collins Street. He was now responsible for Australia, the Bismarck Archipelago, the Solomon Islands, New Guinea, and the Netherlands East Indies (not including Sumatra), with military authority over the U.S. Army, Navy, and elements of the Army Air Force. East of Melbourne was the vast Pacific Ocean Area (POA), which fell under the command of Admiral Chester W. Nimitz, over whom MacArthur had seniority.

MacArthur had sworn that help was on the way to the Philippines, but none of the efforts to reinforce the islands—submarines from Hawaii, aircraft from Australia, or the plans that included planes loaded with supplies from China and a surprise attack on Japanese naval forces by American B-17s—provided the relief he had promised. The fate of the garrison seemed clear once the silver reserves of the Philippine Commonwealth were dumped into Manila Bay in March 1942. Nearly $16 million in pesos was removed from the government vault, packed in whiskey crates, taken by truck to South Dock, loaded on lighters, and sunk between Corregidor and Fort Hughes. It was great fun at first, said Lieutenant (j.g.) Kenneth R. Wheeler, who volunteered for the job, but the task soon grew arduous. Entire barges were scuttled with boxes of silver on board. The message was obvious: money could be recovered, men were expendable.

Back home, the U.S. government sent a different message to the families and loved ones of those in the field. Laura Reade anxiously awaited news of Murray's whereabouts. A few days before Homma launched his final assault on Bataan, she received the following letter:

March 27, 1942

My dear Miss Reade:

You are advised that the Bureau has just received a report dated March 17, 1942, in which Lieutenant (junior grade) Murry [sic] Glusman, United States Naval Reserve, was reported as being alive and well.

You may be assured that we are very glad to furnish this good news and hope that it will be a source of joy to you.

Sincerely yours,

RANDALL JACOBS,

Chief of Bureau [of Navigation]

Alive, yes, but things were far from well. By April 1 Murray and John were seeing increasing numbers of stragglers from the front in Mariveles. They asked for food and medical care and told stories of having nothing to eat except "a little rice and a dab of salmon." Morale was bad, they said. Artillery fire approached nearer by the day. The lines were falling back, they were being breached, and the breaches couldn't be closed. The troops were ravaged by malaria, dysentery, and food deficiency diseases. By April 1 Luzon Force was on its last legs, reported Major General King's surgeon, Lieutenant Colonel Harold W. Glattley.

"Help is on the way," John scrawled in his Bataan diary. "What crap."

10

"Wherever I am . . . I still love you"

IN THE EARLY MONTHS OF 1942, the medical officers on Corregidor were in a far more advantageous position than their buddies on Bataan. Two weeks before the implementation of War Plan Orange-3 in late December 1941, Colonel Chester H. Elmes, the post quartermaster, transferred 25,800 tons of food from the Manila Quartermaster Depot to Malinta Tunnel. The "defense reserve" was sufficient to feed 10,000 men for 180 days—there were only 9,000 men on Corregidor and the satellite islands at the time. But little of Corregidor's surplus made it to the embattled Bataan peninsula. In fact, the reverse was true. On January 24, 1942, MacArthur ordered Major General Moore to increase subsistence reserves for the harbor forts—which meant valuable food stocks on Bataan were actually removed to Corregidor.

Officers and men were still on half rations, but the walls of Malinta Tunnel were piled high with crates of food, medical supplies, and ammunition. There were some who wanted to have their cake and eat it, too. On March 18 a truck on its way to antiaircraft batteries on Corregidor was stopped by military police, bulging at the seams with bacon, sausage, ham, raisins, canned peas, potatoes, corn, and peaches. Troops on Bataan could only dream about such luxuries. There were enough rations on Corregidor to last 20,000 men until July 1, 1942—if the Rock could hold out that long.

With the Japanese blockade of Philippine waters, mail to the United States slowed to a trickle. Lucy Ferguson received only three letters in three months from George while he was stationed on Corregidor, and they left via submarine.

It was midwinter in Evanston, Illinois, and bitterly cold. Her heart skipped a beat when she opened an envelope postmarked February 5, 1942, and stamped "Passed by Naval Censor."

Dearest Lucy:

Here I am again with apologies (as usual) for not being able to write sooner. Also for breaking up our plans for a X-mas celebration but it seems that there is a little job that must be performed before returning. . . .

At one time I thought I was on my way back, in fact I even had passage on a President Ship with orders to report to Pensacola for training in aviation medicine. How does this latter strike you? Don't say it, I think I know and was going to make arrangements to have it remedied. All of the rest of the gang got away, at least on the way and out of the area, with the exception of yours truly, and the two other gunboat medicos.

I certainly hope that I can allay your fears for my safety because we all feel safe and confident of returning. There were only two occasions when I had any doubts about the above and that was when we were still uninitiated in the art of avoiding little Japanese messages of death from the sky. After a short apprenticeship in this sort of thing one gets to know the best methods for self preservation and believe me we all have it down pat. . . .

Here is some news for you. I made Lieut. about a month ago and am wearing the two stripes around but this doesn't mean much except for the additional salary that it conveys. Practically everyone around here has been given a promotion of some sort and an ensign or jg is a curiosity.

Hope that you haven't disposed of the car and that you will keep it in good running order as it will soon become very valuable to us on our trip "around" the USA. You know I hate to have to buy a pursuit plane or a tank to make that trip although some day they will be cheaper than automobiles and thicker than flies.

By the way will you keep tab [sic] on the latest in men's clothing because that will be the second item on my list when I return (you will be the first). At present I have two snappy khaki outfits and usual accessories such as tin hat, gas mask, canteen, rain coat etc. Am afraid that all the little trinkets and presents and film that I wanted to bring you have been lost although there is a slight chance that they can be recovered.

Will you please get in touch with Mother and Dad in Chicago? I believe that Dad is still working for Marshall-Jackson Co. on Clark Street. Give them my love and say that everything is fine and I am getting fat on this war. Tell Jane that I expect her to be famous for something or other by the time I return.

Well Darling I guess You [sic] made a mistake marrying a Navy

*MD but I want you to know that wherever I am sent and however
long I am kept out here I still love you with all my heart. Some day we
will get a chance to use that furniture purchased in Shanghai and our
lives will start over. Just another honeymoon. Remember!*

> *All my love,*
> *George T. Ferguson*

George had arrived on Corregidor on January 2, 1942, and painted
the rosiest picture for Lucy. He had slept in fourteen different places
since December 8, was irritable from numerous bombings, and soon
found the 1st Battalion aid station surrounded by bomb craters "all
within fifty yards" of one another. Some mornings he spent most of his
time ducking for cover into Malinta Tunnel, where the echo of bombs
reverberated against its cavernous walls. But what good would it do to let
Lucy know? She'd get the point through his humor. Tell her any more,
and she'd only worry. Besides, if you could imagine the future being a
whole lot worse, the present didn't look half bad. He shared his darker
thoughts with his diary.

Fred had also been promoted to full lieutenant, but his letter to his
parents was far less sanguine.

Feb. 5, 1942

Dear Mom & Pop,

*I hope that things are going along well at home and I would sure
like to hear from you all—a letter might possibly reach me if you
address me in care of the Commandant 16th Naval District via Post
Master San Francisco, Calif.*

*There is nothing that I can tell you except that I am well, safe &
sound.*

*I miss you all as much as you undoubtedly miss me, but at the
same time I am glad that I am able to do my bit for the thing we are
fighting for. Words cannot describe the inhuman, barbaric, hateful
menace we are fighting—nor should the world ever forget their treacherous & malicious type of cunningness [sic]—nor shall it rest until we
drive them so deep that they may never rise again. Sorry to sound so
bitter but I am sure that I am far from alone in my sentiments.*

> *My love to you all,*
> *Your son*
> *Fred*

The December 29 bombing was the worst. By early January 1942, 4,000
to 5,000 people had crowded into Malinta Tunnel, where an early warning

system announced the approach of enemy planes with flashing red lights as sirens wailed outside.

Malinta was safe from bombing and artillery fire, but its operations were still vulnerable. Power and cold-storage plants were exposed, as were electrical, water, and sewage lines, which were knocked out in the air raids on Corregidor between December 29 and January 6. The tunnel was ventilated with electric blowers, but you couldn't help feeling oppressed by its cave-like atmosphere. The air smelled of sweat, stale food, the blood of the wounded, and the sharp scent of eye-watering disinfectant the sanitary squad used to mop the cement floors twice a day. Respiratory ailments flourished. Dampness caused skin to break out in boils known as Guam blisters. Lack of privacy and minimal contact with the outside world strained even the most seasoned relationships. The absence of daylight, the strange "bluish glow" of fluorescent bulbs, and the sense of confinement made some feel as if they were living in a prison.

As one wag described tunnel life in the *Navy Evening Gopher*, a news sheet produced by Lieutenant Warwick Scott of Rockwell's staff:

> Tunnels, dust, heat, and flies
> Everyone telling little white lies
> Bombs, and craters, rotten roads
> Army trucks shrapneled carrying loads. . . .
>
> Bottomside, sandbags, cold stores, gas
> Gopher, coding room, Sunday mass
> And now that we've learned to love this Rock
> Let's return to Manila, from old North Dock
>
> The sooner the better is what I say
> Let's pack our grips and—ANCHORS AWEIGH!!!

———————

The 4th Marines were the only infantry unit on Corregidor. Colonel Beecher's 1st Battalion occupied the East Sector, which extended one and a half to two miles from Malinta Hill all the way to Hooker Point—the tail of the tadpole. The terrain was rugged at the center, exposed, and a mere 800 to 1,000 yards at its widest. John Nardini was Battalion Surgeon until he was called for emergency medical assistance at Hospital No. 2 on Bataan and replaced by the Assistant Battalion Surgeon, George Ferguson. The aid station was at the highest point on Malinta Trail, about 200 yards east of the lateral entrance to the army hospital in Malinta Tunnel.

Lieutenant Herman R. Anderson's 2nd Battalion was tasked with the West Sector and tended by Battalion Surgeon Marion Wade and Assistant Battalion Surgeon Fred Berley. And Lieutenant Colonel John P. Adams's 3rd Battalion was responsible for the Middle Sector, cared for by Battalion Surgeon Lieutenant George R. Hogshire and Assistant Battalion Surgeon Lieutenant (j.g.) Edward F. Ritter, Jr.

The Office of the Regimental Surgeon, occupied by Thomas Hirst Hayes in Malinta Tunnel, had lines of communication radiating out to the battalion aid stations, each of which was manned by a Battalion Surgeon, a dental officer, and five corpsmen. Beyond the battalion aid stations were sub-aid stations, each staffed with an Assistant Battalion Surgeon and two corpsmen. And beyond the sub-aid stations were the company aid men who were closest to the defense line. If evacuation were necessary, corpsmen would tag patients and notify the battalion aid station by telephone or runner. The wounded would then be carried by stretcher to designated points along Corregidor's roads, where they would be retrieved by ambulance—in the case of the 1st Battalion, a one-and-a-half-ton Chevrolet truck. That was the organization of the medical department of the 4th Marines on Corregidor, which operated as a unit of the army hospital in Malinta Tunnel.

Few preparations had been made for a beach defense before the 4th Marines arrived on Corregidor in December 1941. They quickly began clearing underbrush, digging trenches, installing machine gun and mortar emplacements, filling sandbags, setting tank traps, land mines, sea mines, placing cable barriers in the North and South Dock inlets, and stringing barbed wire entanglements across ravines and the nearly 4,000 yards of beaches where a possible landing could take place.

More than twenty miles of barbed wire was spooled out in the East Sector alone. An estimated two miles of tunnels had been constructed since hostilities began. In the first series of air raids on Corregidor, shallow tunnels collapsed and bombproof shelters became death traps instead. Colonel Lloyd E. Mielenz, the engineer in charge of fortification of harbor defenses, reconfigured bomb shelter design and directed that no new tunnels were to be built unless they were buttressed overhead by fifty feet of rock. The antiaircraft batteries had their own tunnels for protection of crews and ammunition, as did many other units, which used them for headquarters and aid stations like termites on a log about to be tossed to the flames. Concrete splinter-proof roofs helped protect coast artillery men, but the batteries were constant targets of enemy fire and provided a steady stream of casualties to the navy doctors in the field.

George used a cave for shelter. At night he slept outside on a canvas cot. Some of the island's creatures were curious enough to visit.

15th Feb. Sunday
   Woke up other day and small lizard in bed and me [sic]. *Cat mewing during night rqd. rock before he withdrew. Must have been a British cat. Animal about 2½ feet high and light skin approached the bed and slight movement on my part scared him away. Rat makes nightly trip across bough of tree overhead and is outlined clearly by the moon. That covers the nightly escapades of local animals. Monkeys, deer, gecko, multi-colored birds and flies complete the picture.*

Two miles of additional tunnels would be blasted, shoveled, scooped, and scraped out of the Rock. Most men were grateful for the cover they provided. The problem was that some came to depend on it, whether there was an air raid or not.

Many officers, including Colonel Wibb E. Cooper, chief surgeon, USAFFE, wouldn't come out of Malinta Tunnel even when there was an all-clear. The syndrome became known as "tunnelitis," and those who suffered from it were denigrated as "tunnel rats." The generals, joked the gunners of the seacoast and antiaircraft batteries, deserved the "DTS Medal" for "Distinguished Tunnel Service." In spite of its humorous name, tunnelitis combined symptoms of agoraphobia and, for those who had been exposed to bombardment, shell shock.

Fred had a particularly bad case of it. After the December 29 bombing of Middleside barracks, the 2nd Battalion moved into James Ravine, on the northwestern coast of Corregidor. Headquarters was located in a bombproof dugout, and the aid station was in a tight space near the entrance. There was no room for hospitalization, so those requiring medical care were treated in bivouac areas. Fred had become so jittery that he ran for cover at the sound of a truck engine revving up, and during one air raid he was promptly chewed out by Colonel Anderson.

"Walk! Don't run!" Anderson shouted at him.

Fred couldn't help himself. It was the damnedest thing. The tunnel seemed to beckon to him. But he quickly got over his tunnelitis once he joined E Company out at Wheeler Point, on the southwestern side of the island. The area was wooded, it was a steep drop to the sea, and 200 yards down South Road was a spring that gushed water, which the men used as a shower. Fred was in charge of the battalion sub-aid station. Away from the siren call of the tunnel, he now felt safe. He ventured freely outside and during air raids simply jumped into a foxhole. A tunnel protected you physically, but if you relied on it psychologically, he now understood, it could exacerbate your fears to an almost paralyzing degree.

Next to Wheeler Point was Battery Monja, consisting of two 155mm guns—one of them dug into the cliffside. They were operated by the Philippine Scouts, and Fred built latrines off to the side of their little camp, sanitizing them by setting them afire with ammunition. Once a week he drove to Malinta Tunnel to report to Hayes and stock up on medical supplies. But he never saw the regimental surgeon himself outside the tunnel.

On February 17 several hundred men from the crew of the *Canopus*, the Cavite Naval Ammunition Depot, Battery A, and the Philippine Army and Air Corps—many of whom had fought in the Battle of the Points— were detached from duty on Bataan and transferred to Corregidor. One Filipino doctor by the name of Gomez and two corpsmen manned an auxiliary aid station in the 1st Battalion sector. A graduate of the Philippine School of Medicine in Manila, Gomez told George about a mysterious fever on Bataan that seemed to respond to quinine and aspirin. The disease, of course, was malaria, but there were others who suffered from enigmatic fevers that defied diagnosis.

George estimated that 35 percent of the new arrivals from Bataan developed malaria regardless of quinine prophylaxis and some 50 percent of them were ill with acute gastroenteritis. He suspected bacillary dysentery, which is transmitted by flies in contact with human feces, and implemented a rigid sanitary program in an attempt to control it. But the dysentery patients were released too early from the Malinta Tunnel Hospital, and the malaria patients were denied admission altogether. Just as malaria seemed under control, an epidemic of follicular tonsillitis broke out, and then George himself was struck with amoebic dysentery.

An acute infection, bacterial dysentery is triggered by shigella organisms that lodge in the lower intestine. The culprit is the parasite *Entamoeba histolytica,* ingested in its cyst form. Poor sanitation and overcrowding facilitate its spread. Flies are a common vector as they light on food. You may feel tired, spike a fever, be seized with sudden abdominal pain. There is an intense urge to defecate. Feces may be laced with mucus, pus, and blood, until your bowels secrete nothing but a thin stream of water. Dehydration, delirium, and, in rare cases, death may ensue. The symptoms of amoebic dysentery resemble bacillary dysentery, though the former can lead to severe blood loss and affect any organ. Most commonly it attacks the liver, causing acute peritonitis, which can be fatal. Sulfa drugs were used to control bacillary dysentery. Amoebic dysentery was treated with emetine, which the United States had sent to Japan after the Tōkyō earthquake of 1923. In the absence of drugs, men were put on a diet of rice gruel and given a combination of charcoal, magnesium sulfate, and warm tea enemas.

A constant concern for the defenders was nutrition. The 4th Marines were down to 30.49 ounces of food per day, which included 8 ounces of meat, 7 of flour, 4 of vegetables, 3 of milk, and 2 of rice. It was a veritable feast compared to rations on Bataan, but the reduced diet exacted a toll. The sick took longer to recover. Wounds required more time to heal. The symptoms of food deficiency diseases were beginning to appear.

Fred was constantly hungry. He marveled at the Filipino enlisted men who found food that he couldn't even see. They dug up wild *camotes,* a kind of sweet potato, and never lacked fresh fish, which they nabbed with bamboo spears. Fred tried his hand at the new sport. He put on a pair of bamboo goggles with lenses fashioned from soda bottle glass and glued into frames with sap. Then he slipped into the South Channel, spear in hand. In contrast to the Officers' Beach, where George went for afternoon dips, the waters here were unprotected. Fred made sure a marine accompanied him in case any sharks got curious. But his Boy Scout experience proved for naught. He didn't catch a thing, though he was caught buck naked a couple of times during bombing raids.

The bombs bursting on Corregidor varied in size from 100 to 1,000 pounds—small antipersonnel bombs, large high explosives, and fragmentation bombs that contained just about everything except the kitchen sink: nuts, bolts, scrap metal, even pieces of concrete. The planes that delivered them, usually Mitsubishi Type 100 medium bombers code-named "Sally," flew out of range of Corregidor's 3-inch guns, which could fire only up to 8,300 yards with Scovil Mark III powder train fuses at a maximum elevation of 80 degrees.

Frequently the tropical glare, the smoke, and the haze from fires prevented the sighting of aircraft until they were on their "way in" at about 45 degrees. Once Batteries Boston and Chicago obtained 2,700 rounds of mechanical fused ammunition from the *Seadragon*, which slipped into Corregidor's waters on the night of February 4, gunners were able to raise their ceiling to 9,100 yards at close range and "Give 'em hell." But 50 percent of enemy aircraft remained out of reach.

At first the Japanese pursued area bombing; then they began picking their targets. Interior portions of the island were pocked with craters. Military installations on the perimeter were still largely intact, including the power and cold-storage plant just west of the North Dock.

There was a lull in bombing activity from January 15 until March 23, but all was not quiet on the Rock. Photo Joe teased machine gunners by flying just out of reach at Battery Point, and on February 6 the Japanese began to shell the fortified islands with 155mm guns from the Kondō Detachment in Cavite Province. In mid-March the volume of the assault was turned up when 240mm howitzers from the Hayakawa Detachment joined the band.

One morning while Fred was having porridge for breakfast, a shell exploded a hundred yards from E Company. Any closer, he thought, and it would have been all over. At night they watched firefights as the Japanese shore batteries between Sapang and Ternate, south of Manila, opened up on Forts Drum and Frank. At least when you were bombed, you could see the planes beforehand. Experienced gunners like Roly Ames could tell where the bombs would land by the sound they made falling. There was no such warning with artillery fire, Fred learned. By the time you heard the whistle of a shell, it was too late.

George was in a hot spot. The East Sector was being shelled morning and night. "I wonder what it's like to be free of all fear of bombs, shells, invasion, lizards, ants and monkeys," he wrote in his diary. His tone was one of childlike curiosity, as if fear were no longer an occasional occurrence, but a state of being, as natural as the weather and as all-encompassing. Yet at its heart was a new fear, one that was rarely articulated at this stage of the siege, even if it was on the minds of almost everyone in its midst: What would happen if the Japanese took the Rock?

10 March 1942. Here we sit and listen to daily taunting by William Winter [of KGEI, San Francisco] *and others. All being directed at Japan and flaunting their failure in PI. Hell! If they so desired they could shoot 200,000 troops in here and finish our proud chortling.*

That was just what the Japanese wanted, and on March 24 they resumed the bombing of Corregidor in seven air raids over fourteen hours. For the first time heavy bombers were deployed and nighttime raids were inaugurated. Planes swept in over the island from the southeast, targeting Kindley Field, Middleside, and Topside. Battery Chicago was slapped twice, the No. 1 gun of Battery Wheeler was knocked out, an ammunition dump on Morrison Hill exploded, the cold-storage plant was disabled, and the house that Wainwright had inherited from MacArthur and just vacated for the security of Malinta Tunnel was destroyed. It was "the largest air raid so far carried in the Philippines," the Japanese boasted in the press. In the last week of March alone, Corregidor weathered sixty-four high-altitude aerial attacks.

One day Wainwright visited Battery Monja, and the Japanese welcomed him with an air raid. Wainwright, his aide, Fred Berley, and others took refuge in the plotting room of the battery's casemate. Walking stick in hand, Wainwright kept on talking about the great camouflage those "yellow-bellied bastards" had. Then, all at once, he turned to his aide and said, "Let's go."

"Well, general," his aide said, "the All-Clear hasn't sounded yet."

"I don't give a damn," the general replied. "Let's go."

And off they went.

The batteries on Corregidor had radios, and the men would gather around them at 1800 to listen to the world news. Battery M made a point of telephoning the news to men in the field to dispel the wild rumors that circulated. William Winter's claims on KGEI had a dispiriting effect on the Rock's defenders, who knew of the Japanese victories in Malaya, Singapore, Java, Sumatra, and Burma.

When Winter goaded the Japanese from the safety of his San Francisco studio, "I dare you to bomb Corregidor!" one 4th Marine responded: "I wish I had that SOB in my foxhole."

March 30 saw an unexpected morale booster on Corregidor, as George recorded in his diary.

31 March 1942. Six days of intense bombing and shelling and few deaths and fewer injuries. Japanese have lost about 10 planes and 50 men and have done no damage to Corregidor. Yesterday afternoon was extremely exciting and rejuvenating. Two motored silver Jap Bombers came over at about 5 p.m. & were fired on by AA Bat "Denver." Both were hit and one had wing blown off. It was a most beautiful sight to see it spin into a 90 degree dive and plunge into the bay about 300 yds. from USS Mindanao. . . . The other plane exploded in mid-air and there was nothing left but a few fluttering pieces. Bombs were dropped in bay and hit nothing. The whole island gave vent to a chorus of cheers and yells and I am now hoarse.

For a brief shining moment, Homma's ultimatum seemed like an idle boast. Fred was among those who cheered. But he remembered what Lieutenant Commander William E. "Pete" Ferrall, skipper of the *Seadragon*, had said when he arrived on the Rock on February 4: no fleet could possibly come to the aid of the embattled garrison. The *Seadragon* left the following day with the navy's code-breaking equipment—the Red and Purple machines—and the CAST staff. A hundred bags of outgoing mail were also taken on board, among them

George's letter to Lucy and Fred's note to his parents. There was no incoming mail.

The men on Corregidor may have been more fortunate than those on Bataan, but most of them had come to the same conclusion as Fred Berley: this war was going to last a helluva lot longer than six months.

11

"We are not barbarians"

COMBAT IS A SPARK for creative expression. Wars show men and women in extreme situations, forced to make instantaneous life-and-death decisions with consequences that ultimately define character. The defenders of Bataan would boast no aesthetic achievement comparable to Henri Barbusse's *Under Fire,* Ernst Jünger's *Storm of Steel,* John Dos Passos's *Three Soldiers,* or Erich Maria Remarque's *All Quiet on the Western Front.* But they had their own scribes and scribblers, bards and balladeers. They kept diaries and journals, composed songs and penned doggerel, and jotted thoughts on notepads, in composition books, or like John Bookman, in ledgers sawn in half. Their artists were Private Benjamin Charles Steele, an aircraft dispatcher attached to the 19th Bomb Group, and Lieutenant Colonel Eugene C. Jacobs of the Army Medical Corps. Their poets were Captain Calvin Ellsworth Chunn of the 45th Infantry, Philippine Scouts, and Lieutenant Henry G. Lee of the 31st Infantry, Philippine Division, whose eloquent words in "Fighting On" touched the hearts of Fil-American forces on the front in the hours before the final assault:

> I see no gleam of victory alluring
> No chance of splendid booty or of gain
> If I endure—I must go on enduring.
> And my reward for bearing pain—is pain.
> Yet, though the thrill, the zest, the hope are gone.
> Something within me keeps me fighting on.

In late February and March Japanese reinforcements streamed into the Philippines to bolster the badly beaten 65th Brigade and the 16th Division. Lieutenant General Kitano Kenzō's 4th Division added 11,000 men from Shanghai; Major General Nagano Kameichirō's 21st Division, another 4,000 originally intended for duty in Indo-China. The 1st Artillery Headquarters (led by Lieutenant General Kitajima Kishio) arrived from Hong Kong, and two heavy bombardment regiments flew in from Malaya. Homma's artillery strength on Bataan was now more than doubled. He had long-range 240mm howitzers, ammunition, gas masks, food, bandages, quinine, and chlorine for water purification. The Japanese Army even had a division of prostitutes on Bataan. Derisively called "Shock Absorbers" by Fil-American troops, many of the "comfort girls" were of Korean origin.

The men and matériel were now in place for a coordinated assault against the main line of resistance. Homma's inspiration to attack, he said, "came from a San Francisco broadcast which stated 'this is the darkest hour since Pearl Harbor' and indicated a lack of food and medicines." His intelligence was correct. Three clearing stations stood in the path of his advance, forcing the 12th Medical Battalion to evacuate thousands of patients to the rear. It was "total chaos," said Colonel Cooper. The roads were jammed, one convoy was caught in the crossfire, and the patient census of Hospitals Nos. 1 and 2 swelled to 2,700 and 6,000 respectively. Once Mt. Samat was bagged, the Japanese would crash through the Mt. Limay line and drive down the East Road, if necessary, while the west flank made its feint. Mariveles was the destination; Corregidor was the prize.

For Christians, April 3 was Good Friday. For the Japanese, it was the anniversary of the death of Emperor Jimmu, the first imperial ruler, and they honored his spirit by launching a brutal artillery assault against the most vulnerable sector of II Corps—on the extreme left—to the accompaniment of a sustained aerial bombardment. "There is no reason why this attack should not succeed," Homma wrote in his operational diary the night before. He estimated a Japanese victory within a month.

One hundred and fifty pieces of artillery—guns, howitzers, mortars—mercilessly pounded American and Filipino positions, as Major General Mikami Kizo's 22nd Air Brigade dropped more than sixty tons of bombs on the American line to smooth the ride for Japanese armor and infantry. Communications were cut, cane fields and bamboo copses crackled in the flames, and thick smoke and dust blanketed the battlefield. Hundreds were cremated as fires leaped over clearings to feed on the jungle beyond. Then General Nara's tanks punched a hole through the battered 41st Division, many of whose troops fled to the rear in fright. Some 3,000 casualties staggered into Hospital No. 2 that day.

The offensive was relentless. The 41st Division withdrew, and by April 4 the Japanese had pushed the 21st Division back to a reserve line on the northwest slopes of Mt. Samat. Each advance was preceded by a barrage of artillery and air attacks, and the targets were not always troop concentrations or artillery positions.

"Every vehicle that tried to move was bombed," said Sergeant Abie Abraham of the 31st Infantry. "Every wire-laying detail, infantry, troop, and every individual moving in the open was subject to these spot bombings."

On the morning of Easter Sunday, a bomb landed at the entrance to Hospital No. 1, blowing up an ammunition truck passing by. The concussion hurled nurse Juanita Redmond to the floor. Corpsmen dashed out into the yard with litters, but the men in the ammunition truck had been killed instantly. The planes roared back. Nurses and corpsmen tried frantically "to cut the traction ropes so that the patients could roll out of bed if necessary, broken bones and all." Some became hysterical and shrieked in pain; others were petrified with fright, refusing to move.

Lieutenant (j.g.) Claud Mahlon Fraleigh of the Navy Dental Corps was assisting Carey Smith in an operation when a second wave of planes came over the hospital. Smith was furious and refused to leave the OR. "Damn it," he said, "if they get me, they're going to get me on my duty." Then a raft of 500-pound bombs hit the mess and the doctors' and nurses' quarters, and a 1,000-pound bomb crashed through the wards. "I heard myself gasping," recalled nurse Juanita Redmond. "My eyes were being gouged out of their sockets, my whole body was swollen and torn apart by the violent pressure. This is the end, I thought." Corrugated tin roofs flew off of buildings, bamboo sheds were blown apart, and iron beds bent "like paper matches." Army nurse Hattie Brantley dashed into the orthopedic ward for help and found that Chaplain William Cummings had climbed onto a desk and was reciting, as blood streamed down his arm and chest from a shrapnel wound, the Lord's Prayer.

Ten bombs in all fell on the hospital, killing 73 men and wounding 117. Smith, Fraleigh, Bernatitus, and Brantley were all unharmed. The wounded were evacuated to Hospital No. 2. This time the Japanese didn't bother to apologize.

The American line had been broken, and two Philippine Army divisions were decimated. Later that day the Right Wing of the 4th Division under Colonel Satō Gempachi seized Mt. Samat and planted the Rising Sun on its summit. A desperate counterattack the next day failed, by which time another division of the Philippine Army had been routed, and the Japanese penetrated 7,000 yards south of the main line of resistance.

American and Filipino combat troops were so weakened by malnutrition that some could barely move out of their foxholes, much less fight.

Full rations were finally ordered for them on April 7, and food stores that had been transferred from Bataan to augment Corregidor's reserves were now shipped back, but it was too late. That night, the Japanese 16th Division prepared for the final push to Mariveles. And that night Major General King returned in tears from a meeting with Lieutenant General Wainwright on Corregidor.

"We didn't know how in the hell Bataan held up," said Seaman 1st Class Austen Andrews, who watched the fighting on the peninsula from the gunboat USS *Oahu,* out in Manila Bay. Thousands of rounds of shells fell per hour. "At night you could see the artillery duels with the tracers going back and forth. We were right even with the line and I'd never seen such fire power."

"The worst day was April 8," remarked Private 1st Class Wilburn Snyder of the 3rd Battalion Medics, 31st Infantry. "The Jap bombers came over in waves. Then they'd send in the fighters to strafe us. . . . I lived through everything else, but I never felt I'd live through this." They also dropped leaflets over Bataan that mocked: "Your U.S. convoy is due in the Philippines on April 15 but you won't be alive to see it. Ha! Ha!"

The fighting was vicious and losses were heavy on both sides. But rifles were useless against dive bombers. The Japanese succeeded beyond even Homma's dreams. One line after another buckled beneath their advance—at the Mamala River, the Alangan River—until Wainwright carried out MacArthur's order and directed King to stage "a sudden surprise attack" with maximum tank and artillery strength against the Japanese at Olongapo. King realized the order was impossible to execute. II Corps was a shambles. The U.S. 31st Infantry had been reduced to 160 men, the 26th Cavalry to 300, the 57th Infantry to 500. American and Filipino soldiers were spent, starving, and scared, and many, like the Philippine Constabulary troops east of the 31st Infantry, simply ran away. Yet MacArthur had forbidden Wainwright to capitulate "under any circumstances."

"Already our hospital, which is filled to capacity and directly in the line of hostile approach, is within range of enemy light artillery," said King on the evening of April 8. "We have no further means of organized resistance." With 75,500 men still under his command, as many as 100,000 Filipino civilians at risk, and no resources to resist, King made the "ignominious decision" to surrender. He did not bother to inform Wainwright. "Because I do not want him to be compelled," he told his staff at midnight, "to assume any part of the responsibility." As if nature herself were rising up in revolt, an earthquake rattled Bataan. The Radio Intercept Tunnel on Corregidor wriggled "like a snake," said Lieutenant Commander T. C. Parker.

When Wainwright heard of King's decision four hours later in Ma-linta Tunnel from a night duty officer, he shouted, "Tell him not to do it!" But it was too late. King had already sent Colonel Everett C. Williams, white flag of truce in hand, to arrange for a meeting with Homma Masaharu. Thousands of troops on Bataan began to emerge from the jungle "like small spring freshets pouring into creeks which in turn poured into a river," said one observer. The river was the East Road, which led to Mariveles, and it was flooded with soldiers frantically trying to flee to Corregidor.

The hospitals on Bataan and their 8,700 sick and wounded were de-fenseless. General King ordered Carey Smith and Frank Adamo to Cor-regidor. Colonel Duckworth sent as many nurses and corpsmen as he could spare. The nurses of Hospital No. 1 boarded Pambusco buses for the agonizingly slow ride to the harbor. Trucks, jeeps, command cars, and ambulances were crammed with men who seemed aged beyond their years, haggard and dirty in the unearthly glow of forest fires that blazed wherever bombs fell. They fled from hunger, disease, and above all fear of the Japanese. They could only hope to find a way—a boat, a barge, a *banca*—to cross the North Channel to Corregidor.

Mariveles was mayhem. The Japanese were convinced it was the site of Luzon Force headquarters, said aide-de-camp Major Achille C. Tis-delle, Jr., "because General King had had his engineers continually repair small buildings there for that purpose." HQ was actually "hidden in the woods." Mariveles paid dearly for the deception. It had been bombed daily in the last week in March and was targeted again in early April; then the Japanese initiated nighttime "nuisance raids." Navy oil caches were hit. Telephone, power, and water lines were smashed. Antiaircraft fire was an open invitation for retribution. On April 6, ominous news from the front had reached Mariveles. Then on April 8 came word that the army's eastern flank was retreating toward the harbor.

Earlier that day Captain Kenneth M. Hoeffel, commandant of the 16th Naval District, informed E. L. Sackett, captain of the *Canopus* and commander of naval forces in the Mariveles area, that no navy or army forces would be evacuated to the Rock. Corregidor was crowded beyond capacity. But at 2230 that night Hoeffel reported that Wainwright had agreed to accept one Philippine Scout regiment and all naval forces in Mariveles to augment the 4th Marines on beach defenses. Officers and men from the Philippine Army and Philippine Army Air Corps joined the evacuation, which had to take place immediately, before Japanese tanks rolled into Mariveles and dawn's light turned navy forces into de-fenseless targets for Japanese planes.

Hoeffel ordered the "demolition of everything remaining that might be of military value to the enemy." That included arms, provisions, personal effects, fuel, stores, ships, and more than 5,000 tons of ammunition and bombs in the ordnance depot and the three active supply points on Bataan. The *Dewey* dry dock was harnessed with ten 155mm projectiles, the *Bittern* was packed with 200 pounds of dynamite, the *Canopus* moved into twelve to fourteen fathoms of water, where she sank after her torpedo locker and forward magazine flood valves were opened. At 0100 on April 9 the two tunnels at the Mariveles airfield were blown; the rock crusher and its power plant went at 0300, as did Tunnels Nos. 6 and 7, which had been used by base force personnel. But Tunnels Nos. 1, 2, and 3 stowed ammunition, gasoline, diesel oil, and dynamite and were too close to the docks to be blown safely, while Tunnel No. 4 served as headquarters. They were timed for simultaneous demolition at 0415 after the evacuation of key personnel.

John and Murray were detached from duty in Mariveles and ordered to report to Colonel Howard, commanding officer of the 4th Marines on Corregidor. "Transportation other than government is not involved in the execution of these orders and none is authorized," the order stated. The problem was finding transportation of any kind.

Soldiers, civilians, and refugees swarmed toward Mariveles, desperate to escape from Bataan. Officers abandoned their units even under the threat of court-martial. Thousands more were on the way, walking, running, fleeing from their homes, their infantry positions, begging for a ride as shells from Corregidor's artillery careened overhead. But there weren't enough vehicles, there weren't enough vessels, and there wasn't enough time.

Boys from the Philippine Army walked single file, without their guns, dejected and as ragged and aimless as hobos.

"Where ya going, Joe?" Ernie Irvin of Battery C asked.

"I'm go to the probince to see my companion," one after the other said.

They sat down on the Mariveles airstrip, where Japanese planes strafed them "like shooting fish in a barrel," said Irvin.

Ammunition dumps in the hills were ignited, fuel was torched, and army trucks were set on fire or pushed into Manila Bay. The ground shook from heavy detonations as combat battalions destroyed their equipment. Batteries disabled their antiaircraft guns. Soldiers smashed their rifles with sledgehammers.

Throughout the night Battery Hearn fired from Corregidor to delay the enemy advance southward toward Mariveles. Colored flares etched crazy patterns on the sky, as white-hot metal from exploding shells streamed down like shooting stars. "You could have read a newspaper by the lurid glare," said Captain Dyess.

The nurses from Hospital No. 1 bunched together at the dock as Japanese artillery retaliated. Behind them the nurses of Hospital No. 2 were trapped in a riptide of traffic that seemed to be moving in several directions at once and then went slack when an ammunition dump was blown along the East Road. Men hurried to the waterfront, carrying whatever arms, food, and fuel they could salvage from the storage tunnels.

Murray hurried down to the wharf with four patients under his care. John scrambled to find passage. They missed the *Manapla*, which departed from the base force dock at 0345 with 175 passengers, but squeezed on board the *San Felipe*, which left ten minutes later with 225 passengers. Others were not so lucky. They jumped into tugs or onto barges, *bancas*, or makeshift rafts; or like Karl "Otis" King and his buddy Isaac C. Williams of the 4th Marines, they swam across the shark-infested bay. Juanita Redmond watched "sick at heart" as several were killed in the water by artillery fire.

Meanwhile Seaman 1st Class John Kidd had been sent on the navy detail that was ordered to seal the entrance of the ammunition storage tunnel midway between the Section Base perimeter and Sisiman Cove. The dynamite was unstable. Nitroglycerine oozed over their hands as they gingerly set down boxes of explosives in a pile for fuse placement. They rolled the fuse out from the tunnel entrance—and found that it reached only halfway down the slope to their motor launch. They lit the fuse and bolted. The intention was to cave in the mouth of the tunnel, but the blast detonated the dynamite in the rear, causing an earth-shattering explosion. A burst of orange flame enveloped the mountain. The concussion knocked the men flat. Carey Smith was on his way to Mariveles from Little Baguio when the detonation blew him out of his car. The mountainside trembled, triggering a landslide and disgorging boulders the size of small houses.

Huge rocks were hurled half a mile out into the harbor, sinking small craft, killing four men, injuring nine others, and scattering body parts—including a human head—an extraordinary distance through the air. A motor launch and a motor boat from the *Canopus* were struck, and one of them sank instantly. Murray and John watched from the deck of the *San Felipe* as it slowly threaded its way toward Corregidor through waters laced with minefields.

Bataan looked as if it had erupted. It was an apocalyptic end, and the strange thing, Murray thought, was that it was beautiful. He was far enough away to see it abstractly—the exploding shells, the bursting bombs, the multicolored flares, the sky streaked with white-hot metal, the fire on the mountain—far enough to realize that another part of his life had gone up in flames.

At 0500 on April 9 John and Murray arrived safely at Corregidor's North Dock. A few hours later the Japanese threw down the welcome mat and greeted them with an air raid. Three more bombing attacks would follow while Topside came under artillery fire from Cavite. The officers and crew of the USS *Luzon*, were forced to abandon ship in South Bay and take up positions at Battery Gillespie on Fort Hughes. George's friend, Medical Officer Lieutenant Alfred Littlefield Smith was among them. By then the Americans on Bataan had already raised the white flag of surrender.

At 0900 Major General King was escorted by the Japanese to the experimental farm station at Lamao, where he was met by Colonel Nakayama Motoo, Homma's senior operations officer. Nakayama was taken aback that it was King, not the commander of U.S. Forces in the Philippines, who was offering to formally surrender, but King told him he was unable to communicate with Wainwright. Nakayama would not even look at King, who sat across from him at a long table.

"My forces are no longer fighting units. I want to stop further bloodshed," said King.

"Surrender must be unconditional," insisted Nakayama.

"Will our troops be well treated?"

"We are not barbarians," Nakayama replied.

Homma had anticipated capturing 40,000 men, not 75,500. Filipinos accounted for roughly 64,000 of them, Americans for 11,500. Japan's Dōmei News Service gloated that the Americans and Filipinos had "begged for a halt in hostilities after six days of fierce Japanese assault." Indeed, the fall of Bataan marked the single greatest military defeat in U.S. history. But Lieutenant Colonel Harold K. Johnson of the 57th Infantry Regiment saw a different reason for it. "It wasn't the enemy that licked us; it was disease and absence of food that really licked us." The magnitude of the capitulation and the condition of their captives took even the conquerors by surprise.

———

In late March Homma had approved a two-phase plan for the removal of Fil-American prisoners from Bataan. Colonel Takatsu Toshimitsu was to assemble all prisoners in Balanga, the capital of Bataan Province, nineteen miles away from Mariveles. Because that leg of the journey was expected to take a day or less, no provisions were made for food or water. Transportation officer Major General Kawane Yoshikata would lead the second stage north to San Fernando and all the way to Camp O'Donnell in central Luzon. "Rest areas, sanitary facilities, water stations, kitchens, food stores, and other supply depots were to be stationed at short intervals along the route," wrote Richard Mallonée. "Hospitals were to be set up in Balanga, Lubao, and, if one arrived from Japan in time, at Orani."

But the Japanese were caught short in their preparations because they projected the surrender of Fil-American forces in a month, not a week; they underestimated their number by two-thirds; and they failed to take into account the debilitated condition of their captives. Kawane had only 200 trucks at his disposal for 64,000 Filipinos, 11,500 Americans, 6,000 civilian employees, and as many as 26,000 refugees. Thousands upon thousands of men were sick, hungry, and exhausted. Many of them were too weak to walk and had no food or water left to drink. They were "patients rather than prisoners," remarked the former Luzon Force surgeon Colonel Harold W. Glattley. Homma claimed that Colonel Nakayama had said nothing about the health of the American and Filipino soldiers after his meeting with Major General King. "I thought it was no worse than our own troops," he maintained.

"There were far more Americans and Filipinos than we estimated," admitted Hitome Junsuke, a propaganda officer whose unit in Manila prepared the leaflets that were dropped over Bataan. "And we weren't prepared for them in any way."

By the afternoon of April 9, Japanese soldiers were converging upon Mariveles on horses, on bicycles, and on foot, in tanks, staff cars, and trucks—Fords, Chevrolets, and GMCs, to the astonishment of the Americans. It was fiendishly hot. The scene made Sergeant Ralph Levenberg of the 17th Pursuit Squadron think of the exodus of the Jews from Egypt. Privates were mixed in with officers, artillerymen with infantry, the U.S. Army with the Philippine Scouts—"just a jumbled mass of humanity," said Captain Mark Wohlfeld of the 27th Bombardment Group. Only later, at Limay and Orion, were Filipinos separated from Americans, and civilians from military, in groups of one hundred and columns of four. Colonel Ernest B. Miller "marveled at how it was possible even to have stood up for one week" against the well-oiled Japanese war machine he saw amassed on Bataan.

One division staff officer phoned Colonel Imai Takeo of the 141st Infantry with the order to "kill all prisoners and those offering to surrender." Imai refused to comply unless he saw the written command from Army Headquarters. The order was never produced, and in the meantime Imai proceeded to set more than a thousand prisoners free.

But other Japanese officers were shown an order, supposedly bearing Homma's seal but apparently forged by Colonel Tsuji Masanobu and his friends. Tsuji had been specially sent from Singapore—where he helped instigate the slaughter of 5,000 Chinese—to hasten the fall of Bataan. The captives should be executed, he argued, the Americans as Caucasian colonialists and the Filipinos for betraying their Asian brothers.

The killings began in Mariveles, where the Japanese used twenty-five Filipino soldiers for bayonet practice. The East Road would be stained with blood, littered with bodies—bloated, blackened, crawling with maggots and green flies. Private Blair Robinett of Company C, 803rd Engineers watched a Japanese soldier toss one American, "uneasy on his feet," into the path of an oncoming tank column. One after another the tanks rolled over the corpse, until there was nothing left except the shadow of a uniform pressed into the dust. "Now we knew," said Robinett, "if there had been any doubts before, we were in for a bad time." Ted Williams had watched in horror as Americans in the 192nd Tank Company did the same thing to the Japanese—except their victims had been soldiers on bicycles, not captives on foot.

Armed with bayonet-tipped rifles and brandishing swords, the Japanese goaded, prodded, slapped, pushed, and horse-whipped their quarry on the grueling sixty-five-mile march from Mariveles to San Fernando. Troops from Luzon Force captured inland trickled down trails to swell the rising tide of men. Artesian wells ran close to the coastal road, but "you didn't dare stop to get water," said Sergeant Charles Cook of the 27th Bombardment Group. "They'd bayonet you if you tried." Major Bert Bank went five days without being allowed any water at all and subsisted on a single rice ball "about the size of a fifty-cent piece."

The Japanese looted personal items, stole what remained of C-rations, and lifted canteens. One captive who refused to relinquish his ring had his entire finger lopped off with it. Men chewed sugarcane, gnawed raw turnips, and to slake their thirst they sucked moisture out of banana leaves. Stragglers were clubbed, shot, or eviscerated. Those who could still stand were forced to bury their ailing buddies alive. "If you fell," said Staff Sergeant Harold Feiner of the 17th Ordnance Company, Provisional Tank Group, "bingo, you were dead."

The roadside was strewn with corpses, some of them headless, some of them castrated with their genitals shoved into their mouths. When Filipino civilians in Lubao began tossing rice, candy, casava cakes, and cigarettes to the weary procession, "the Jap guards went into a frenzy," said Captain Dyess, "slugging, beating, and jabbing bayonets indiscriminately." At night the men were cooped up in barbed-wire enclosures, warehouses, and cockfight pits. Dysentery ran rampant, but the Japanese refused to let the Americans dig latrines. There was little sympathy for the sick and wounded.

The Japanese would be roused to murderous rage whenever the impulse seized them. In a ravine near the Pantingan River, Filipino officers and noncoms from the 91st, 71st, and 2nd Regular Divisions were rounded up, bound with phone wire, tied together, and then forced to listen to a speech through an interpreter: "Dear friends, pardon us. If you surrendered early, we will not kill you. But we suffered heavy casualties. So just pardon us. If you have any last wish before we kill you, just tell us." The Japanese drew their swords and bayonets, and for the next two hours slaughtered 300 to 400 Filipinos from behind.

Those who survived the march to San Fernando were gathered into groups of 115 and packed into steel boxcars for the sweltering twenty-five-mile trip by narrow-gauge railway to Capas. From there they trudged another eight miles west to O'Donnell, where they were confined as "captives." It was a designation, asserted camp commandant Captain Tsuneyoshi Yoshio, that was beneath even the dignity of prisoners of war.

Between 5,000 and 10,000 Filipinos perished on the journey to O'Donnell. Up to 1,100 American lives were lost on the way. In total, more Fil-Americans died on the march from Mariveles than during the entire defense of Bataan. Homma's men made a sham of *bushidō*. The principles of *kōdō,* so loftily expressed in the *Senjinkun* as "valour tempered by benevolence," lay trampled on the battlefield of Bataan.

Imperious, victorious, the Japanese would prove to the Americans their superiority as a race, and demonstrate to the Filipinos, whom they were allegedly liberating, their indomitability as a power.

12

"I go to meet the Japanese commander"

THEY ESCAPED the fall of Bataan by just hours. Weary but relieved, Murray and John walked into Malinta Tunnel to receive their orders from Regimental Surgeon Thomas Hirst Hayes. The remaining eighty-eight army nurses from Hospital No. 2, "every last one of them with her chin up in the air," said Wainwright, reached the Rock later that morning. They had fled Bataan only to land in the center of a bull's-eye.

Corregidor struck them as a wonder. The Malinta Tunnel hospital had electric lights, running water, clean sheets, and white-enameled bedside tables. There was food, medicine, showers, flush latrines, and an operating room with sterilizers. Connected to the northeast end of Malinta, the main hospital tunnel had fourteen laterals, about eight feet wide and with arched ceilings ten feet high. These served as wards for "Surgical," "Respiratory," "Dental," and "Dispensary," as well as a mess area and separate sleeping quarters for doctors and nurses. Thin metal partitions draped in sheets were all that separated the laterals from the steady flow of tunnel traffic. Several small radios were tuned to KGEI in San Francisco and to the Voice of Freedom, broadcast from a makeshift studio nearby.

"Bataan has fallen!" announced Philippine Army Lieutenant Normando Ildefonso Reyes over the air, reading a speech written by Lieutenant Salvador P. Lopez.

> Filipino and American troops of this war-ravaged, bloodstained peninsula have laid down their arms. . . . Besieged on land and blockaded from the sea, cut off from all sources of help, these intrepid fighters have borne all that human endurance could bear. . . . But what sustained them through all these months of incessant battle was a force more than physical. It was the thought of their native land and all that is most dear to them, the thought of freedom and dignity, and pride in these most priceless of human prerogatives.

Hospital staff numbered 100, and with the notable exceptions of Carey Smith, Ann Bernatitus, and the navy corpsmen, it was all army. By contrast, Hayes had only a team of four in Malinta Tunnel: Regimental Dentist Bob Herthneck, Pharmacist Crews, and two corpsmen. The rest of his men—doctors and corpsmen alike—were in the field. Cooperation between the army and navy medical organizations evolved out of necessity rather than goodwill, which overrode, for the most part, traditional rivalries.

"Probably never before have two branches of the service been so intimately related," Hayes enthused in his notes. "The Army furnished the majority of care to all services behind the lines in [sic] Corregidor; the Navy furnished the majority of care to all services in the field. Both services present and acting in *both* areas." But the navy was never entirely accepted into the army fold. Hayes complained that he was denied officer accommodations even though they were available.

Malinta was crowded to overflowing with army units. During bombing raids men slept in relays throughout the day and night on portable cots or atop packing cases. Some hid in its labyrinthine spaces to avoid reporting to any command. Morale was so low after the fall of Bataan that Wainwright, himself tormented by the loss, issued a statement affirming that Corregidor could and would be held. "If the Japanese can take the Rock," he said, "they will find me here no matter what orders I receive."

Corregidor needed all the help it could get. The navy personnel, Philippine Scouts, and Constabulary forces who had been evacuated from Mariveles were pressed into a new unit called the Provisional 4th Tactical Battalion, under the command of Major Francis H. "Joe" Williams. They would augment the Regimental Reserve, which included Major Max W. Schaeffer's Headquarters and Service Company. John Bookman was designated Battalion Surgeon of the new 4th Tactical Battalion, which was bivouacked east of Geary Point along a trail that ran to Government Ravine.

The marine beach defense was also bolstered wherever and whenever possible. George watched the 1st Battalion grow from 700 to 1,200 after absorbing Philippine Army, Philippine Air Corps, and U.S. Army elements. Not only did his workload increase, but his responsibilities extended to army units in the East Sector as the tactical situation demanded. Murray was appointed assistant surgeon of the 1st Battalion, and George greeted his colleague with a bar of chocolate in the midst of an air raid.

"Thanks, pal," Murray said, on first meeting George. "When's breakfast?"

"That's it," George replied. "And dinner's after dark because the Nips spend all day trying to blow out our galley."

Murray took to George at once. He liked his forthrightness, his jocular tone, and he appreciated his willingness to share. *We're hungry, we have no support, and we're getting our asses shot off,* he said in so many words. But he said it like a boy laying down the rules of the neighborhood for the new kid on the block while speaking in the gang's code. George was almost exactly a year older than Murray, though their birthdays—falling on New Year's Day and New Year's Eve, respectively—were merely a day apart.

The chocolate bars came from D-rations, which were issued on Corregidor in February and formulated to compensate for a missing meal. Highly concentrated four-ounce cakes, they were supposed to be supplemented by a rice ration. First Battalion troops and attached personnel used to go to mess at the Officers' Beach, but artillery fire forced the galley to be relocated to a blocked-off road that was defiladed from Bataan, about 200 yards from the east entrance of Malinta Tunnel. Water was hauled by truck in empty 155mm, 8-inch, and 12-inch powder cans, the lines having been shattered by hostile fire. You couldn't eat, you couldn't drink, you couldn't wash your clothes because you couldn't set them out to dry without becoming a target. The chalk *V* emblazoned on helmets stood for Victim, some joked, not Victory.

Then there was the word *Nip.* Unlike *Jap,* a derogatory term in use since McCauley's *With Perry* was published in 1854, *Nip* was of recent coinage, as if an animal had just been discovered that needed a name for classification. And the species, as represented by caricatures in American military manuals and mainstream media, was subhuman. The Japanese had their own oral language before they borrowed Chinese (*kanji*) characters, and *Nippon* was the Japanese pronunciation of the character the Chinese read as *Jih-pen,* which they conferred upon the country of "sun-origin." *Nip* became accepted jargon in the American press not in spite of its negative overtones, but because of them. "Chief Tomas picked up three Nip pilots forced down in his territory," reported *Time* magazine on January 5, 1942, in the first recorded use of the word in the United States. *Nip* served as both noun and adjective, its truncated form resonant with meaning, as in *nip in the bud,* to cut something down to size or eradicate it before it takes root; *nip* as in "to steal" or "seize"; and *nip* as in the bite of an animal—a horse, say, or a donkey, dog, or monkey. Crafty, dangerous, stripped of their humanity, *Nips* were abstractions, easy to hate and easier to kill.

You couldn't escape the bombing and shelling on Corregidor, not even in Malinta Tunnel. The walls shook, the lights swayed and flickered, and particles loosened from the vaulted ceiling. The ventilating fans went off to prevent smoke from spreading into the laterals, and the air became suffocatingly close. A hush descended during the sudden blackouts, when doctors worked by flashlight. The muffled sounds of destruction conjured the darkest scenarios. You couldn't tell day from night, dawn from dusk. You lost your perspective because you literally couldn't see.

George had no such problem—he saw more than he wanted to. The marines were nearly three-quarters finished digging a tunnel for his sick bay, "blasting, mucking, shoveling, and shoring" twenty-four hours a day. Scoured out of a cliff, it was only large enough to accommodate twelve patients in addition to medical personnel and equipment. The tunnel faced north, protected from the Japanese artillery massed on Cavite but shielded from Bataan only by camouflage at its entrance.

On Murray's first day on the Rock, two waves of bombers pounced on 1st Battalion positions from Infantry Point up to the auxiliary aid station, while Japanese artillery fired from Bataan and Cavite. "Couple casualties and air compressor hit and lot of us going to chow were caught right in middle of it," George jotted in his diary. "We were just lucky."

They were, though the three earthquake tremors that shook Corregidor at 1343 on April 9, 1942, were enough to make anyone wonder how much longer their luck would hold out.

That afternoon a column of Japanese tanks heading for Mariveles entered the compound of Hospital No. 1. At 1335 Colonel Duckworth, the commanding officer, surrendered to Major General Matsuii, field commander of the Imperial Japanese Army forces. Hospital No. 1 had 1,800 patients, 33 of whom were wounded Japanese POWs. They were confined to a separate ward and entrusted to Captain Black of the U.S. Public Health Service. Apparently one of Matsuii's officers was related to a prisoner, but he was satisfied that the Japanese had been well cared for by the Americans. Once Hospital No. 1 was surrounded with sixteen tanks, Matsuii allowed Duckworth and his skeletal staff to resume their work.

The surrender at Hospital No. 2 was more ominous. At 2000 two Japanese officers and twenty enlisted men summoned the *ichiban,* meaning "number-one man," Colonel James O. Gillespie. After a lengthy interview they issued orders for an enforced blackout, restricted movement and use of the Real River, and claimed possession of all hospital property. "Anyone caught violating this rule will be shooted," announced the Japanese interpreter. A guard was posted, ward doctors were issued passwords, and then the Japanese, in spite of repeated protests by the Americans to the second-ranking medical officer of the Japanese Army, Major Sekiguchi Hisashi, surrounded the hospital area with twenty-three artillery pieces. Battery personnel moved into the laundry, the mess, even three of the hospital wards. Several nights later a Filipino woman with a three-month-old baby and a three-year-old son was dragged from her bed in a tent adjacent to Ward 6 and raped repeatedly by a drunken Japanese sergeant and his cohort.

The Americans had raised Red Cross guidons and white flags to protect Hospital No. 2, but the Japanese were intent on using "our wounded," said Major Stephen M. Mellnik of Corregidor's Coast Artillery Corps, "to make ramparts around their guns." The Allies were now in the line of their own fire. Battery commanders on the Rock were given orders not to target the area and soon had coordinates of the hospital compound in hand. But commands were then issued to knock out any enemy guns that could be positively identified within the perimeter. On April 22 one shell overshot its target, killing five Americans and wounding fourteen.

The day after the Japanese entered Hospital No. 2, Sekiguchi ordered the release of all Filipino doctors, dentists, and corpsmen. Those who wanted to remain behind were driven out at bayonet point. Their Filipino patients were evacuated at once, supposedly so they could go home. But many of them had recently undergone surgery for amputations, abdominal wounds, and fractures. Others were suffering from malaria, dysentery, and malnutrition. A few were completely blind; still others had bloody dressings on their wounds. Lieutenant Walter Waterous estimated some 2,000 wounded were discharged from Hospital No. 2. No transportation was provided. Weeks later, the bodies of hundreds of Filipino patients—who either died or were killed by the Japanese—were visible along the East Road. Waterous's Filipino colleagues believed that as many as 50 percent had perished.

Japanese soldiers who marched past the hospital in the direction of Mariveles "appeared tired, but all were in excellent physical condition," Colonel Cooper later wrote, "and their state of nutrition and muscular development was in marked contrast to the pale and emaciated bodies of our personnel and sick." The patients at Hospital No. 2 were suffering from edema and peripheral neuritis, and their wounds and fractures were healing slowly due to malnutrition. The Japanese were unmoved by their plight. Within forty-eight hours of their arrival, Sekiguchi's men had looted the food stocks at Hospital No. 2, "and what remained of the medicine," said Waterous. When the American doctors asked for an increase in sustenance, the Japanese replied that the transportation simply wasn't available, in spite of the fact that the Japanese had no problem in providing for their troops in the hospital area from several tons of American foodstuffs they seized six and a half kilometers away. Despite repeated requests from American doctors for increased sustenance, the Japanese refused to turn over a single sack of white rice. "We got nothing," said Colonel Gillespie, "except one issue of fly-blown fish that was discarded as unfit for human consumption."

In little more than a month Hospital No. 2 would be disbanded. A medical detachment and 550 patients were bused to a warehouse adjacent to Hospital No. 1 at Little Baguio, while 750 ambulatory patients and a minimal staff remained behind. "Many of us turned our backs, with mixed emotions, on Hospital No. 2 forever," wrote Colonel Duckworth in his last official report. "That this small group in less than three and a half months had built and operated hospital facilities for 16,000 patients is, we believe, a truly remarkable event."

Murray's stay with the 1st Battalion on Corregidor lasted exactly one day and night. On April 10 he was designated Assistant Battalion Surgeon, 4th Tactical Battalion, responsible for the 13 officers and 300 enlisted men who comprised the Headquarters and Service Company. He had one corpsman, Pharmacist's Mate Cecil Jesse Peart, to help him. Many of the men in H&S had administrative and regimental supply responsibilities, but they were needed now as reinforcements. Before the fall of Bataan, Schaeffer had assembled them each afternoon in their bivouac area, where they were instructed in weaponry and infantry tactics.

The area, known as Government Ravine, was on the southwest side of the island. A part of the Government Reservation, it was wedged between Battery Ramsay to the north and Batteries Geary and Crockett to the south. But it appeared only on maps of Corregidor classified as "SECRET." The Japanese knew exactly where it was, though. Government Reservation, after all, housed the Philippine Treasury.

The 4th Tactical Battalion was positioned to the west of H&S. By the time they began training, the Japanese had already stepped up their bombardment—which meant that the troops of the Regimental Reserve, along with the medical officers and corpsmen who tended them, spent much of each day huddled in foxholes on the trail that ran from Government Reservation to Geary Point. Lulls were used for target practice, field drills, and resupply. At night the men listened eagerly as army veterans of Bataan shared their knowledge of Japanese battle tactics. They were quick learners. They had to be.

Murray soon knew what George meant about mealtimes on the Rock. His galley was hit three times in just as many days, and his medical supply dumps might as well have been targets on a string. From

Cavite, the Japanese could see troop concentrations in the area, truck activity on Government Road (which snaked around the reservation), and the water tank to the northeast. Murray had that strange sensation again of being watched. The Japanese were just warming up.

Major General Moore, commander of the Philippine Coast Artillery and the Harbor Defenses of Manila and Subic Bays, described the first day of action on Corregidor after the fall of Bataan:

0800—On the morning of 10 April, for the first time, an enemy observation balloon was seen rising from the vicinity of Lamao, concurrent with a bombing attack on Topside.

0835—Second string of bombs landed at Middleside.

0850—Shells from Cavite shore fell near Ordnance Point.

0950—Fort Frank under fire.

0952—Four flights of three each bombed Topside and Morrison Hill.

0958—Two bombers again hit Topside.

1056—Enemy shelled Corregidor from south mainland (Cavite shore).

1115—Bombs dropped at Bottomside and Morrison Hill.

1127—Two heavy bombers hit Morrison Hill.

1144—Four heavy bombers hit between Morrison Hill and Middleside.

1313—Nine heavy bombers, in flights of three, dropped bombs along south shore roads.

Immediately after King's capitulation, the Japanese began making preparations for their final offensive. They started by moving 250 field pieces, ranging from 75mm guns to 240mm howitzers, to the south face of Mt. Mariveles and along the southeastern coast of Bataan. Ravines and wooded slopes afforded natural protection to Japanese batteries. Corregidor's defenders, without observation planes or balloons and without counterbattery equipment, had difficulty spotting them. By contrast, the Japanese could always call in Photo Joe or the observation balloon, Peeping Tom, to assess damage and readjust their sights accordingly.

By mid-April, the Japanese had amassed more than 400 guns on Bataan, many of them 240mm howitzers. For every shell fired from Corregidor, the Japanese returned four. They plotted almost every flash emanating from the Rock, computed firing data, mapped and targeted on their topographic charts every battery they spotted, and systematically eliminated those batteries. They had detailed information on harbor defenses as well as supply and communication lines. But they were oddly uninformed regarding Malinta Tunnel, convinced that it was connected under water to the tunnel network in Mariveles.

The Japanese preferred mortars and howitzers for weapons. Light and medium mortars are portable, and while their shorter barrel restricts their range, their elevation (usually from 40 to 80 degrees) makes them more useful than a cannon for hitting targets on rugged terrain. The howitzers were also more suitable for hilly, forested topography and, at a size of 240mm (9.2 inches), capable of inflicting tremendous damage. The steeper trajectory of both guns meant that the shells penetrated the ground more deeply, and the explosions sent splinters flying in all directions.

Homma had bragged that he could bag Corregidor in a week, and April 25 was initially slated as the day of invasion. But two factors delayed it: a lack of landing barges and an outbreak of malaria. Small craft were obtained from Lingayen, Nasugbu, and Olongapo. Bound for Cavite, where they were armed and outfitted with bulletproof iron plates, they were forced to sneak through the North Channel at night while Japanese artillery blasted Corregidor as a diversionary tactic. Amphibious exercises were then conducted at Orani on Bataan, but the regiment that was scheduled to land on the first night—the 61st Regiment of the 4th Division—showed up with only 250 out of 3,000 men. The reason was simple: malaria. The disease that had nearly brought the Americans to their knees on Bataan now threatened to subdue the Japanese.

Just before Bataan's fall, 15,500 Japanese troops were in hospitals. Once the Japanese occupied southern Bataan, the number surged to 30,600, some 28,000 of whom were malaria patients. The 4th Division was hit especially hard. Homma had requested quinine from Saigon and Tōkyō "nine or ten times," but an air shipment of 300,000 tablets did not arrive until month's end.

The 14th Army field order for the invasion of Corregidor was finally published on April 28, but it was not released to the troops until May 2. May 5 was designated "X Day."

———————

What a change of heart, George wrote in his diary:

> *Yes, Bataan fell but what of it. . . . For a few days it appeared that a surrender of Corregidor was in order but now we are going to defend the fortified islands and really are in a good position to do so. Already we have had help from Southern based Flying Fortresses in bombings at Cebu, Davao and Manila. Planes, hangars, ships and installations have been hit severely. An entirely new attitude has been developed*

here, and now defense and extermination of a few thousand Japanese looks easy.

Hope flared on Corregidor. On April 13 a lone B-17 on its way back from a bombing mission over Nichols Field flew east of the Rock, and the pilot, Frank Bostram, waggled his wings in greeting. The men were dazzled by what they saw. The day before, ten B-25s had arrived at Del Monte Field in Mindanao, along with three B-17s. A gang of P-40s and P-35s went on to strafe a Japanese fighter squadron based in Davao. Could this be the help that had been promised for so long?

In a direct plea, Wainwright had proposed to MacArthur on March 27 that bombers based in Australia stage a surprise attack against Japanese naval forces guarding the route to Corregidor. The tactic was to divert them from eight blockade runners from Cebu and Iloilo that were loaded with food, medicine, and ammunition. But the aircraft were late, the six pursuit planes on Mindanao that were to escort the convoy were bruised from action, and Cebu was invaded on April 10. Before Cebu fell, the ships and their cargo were destroyed. George was jubilant about a plan that was stillborn.

By April 14 the Japanese succeeded in destroying or crippling Corregidor's North Shore batteries. In some areas beach defense had no contact with Malinta Tunnel, which meant orders were being given without eyes, and reinforcements could not be summoned when needed. Soon the island was encircled with Japanese artillery—from Cabcaben, Mariveles, Batangas, and Cavite.

As the pace of the bombardment increased, "life on Corregidor took on a faster, more intense tempo," said hospital assistant Maude R. Williams.

The smallest and most simple pleasures became sought after and treasured as they became increasingly rare and dangerous—an uninterrupted cigarette, a cold shower, a stolen biscuit, a good night's sleep in the open air.

There was a heightened feeling that life was to be lived from day to day.

Symbols were cherished. On April 18, a shell fragment from a 240mm battery on Bataan struck Corregidor's flagpole, a mainmast from a Spanish ship sunk in the Battle of Manila Bay and erected in 1898. The flag slid down toward the ground as if in resignation. But before she touched the earth, Captain Brewster G. Gallup, Technical

Sergeant Ezra Smith, and a Philippine civilian, Honorio Punongbayen, ran to repair the halyard and raised the flag as shells burst around them. Wainwright awarded the three men the Silver Star for gallantry. What none of them realized was that Japanese pilots as well as gunners on Bataan had aligned the 100-foot-high flagpole into coincidence with the crosshairs of their telescopes.

That same day Lieutenant Colonel James H. Doolittle and a squadron of B-25s took off from the carrier USS *Hornet* and penetrated Japanese airspace uncontested by the army and navy. They bombed Kōbe, Nagoya, Yokohama, and targeted Tōkyō at noon. Fifteen of the sixteen planes crash-landed in China, though there were only nine fatalities from the mission. For American spirits at home and for the troops abroad, the effect was galvanizing, like a "shot of adrenaline," said the nurses on Corregidor. Nothing was more sacred to the Japanese than their homeland, and the Americans had invaded it with impunity. Of the captured fliers, three were executed and five were sentenced to life imprisonment. In revenge for the raid and to seize local airfields to prevent another, the Japanese went on a rampage in China that claimed an estimated 250,000 lives.

The Doolittle raid was a harbinger. "We never for a moment doubted that we would win the war," said John. But winning would cost the Allies dearly.

On April 22 an observer on Fort Frank spotted what looked like "invasion barges" southwest of Longoskawayan Point. Battery Geary didn't take it kindly. As Colonel Bunker wrote in his diary, "We hope we raised hell with them and spoiled their projected trip."

Then on April 24 intelligence reports indicated a possible Japanese landing force assembling on Bataan's east coast. That afternoon Geary provoked a fantastic artillery duel with an enemy howitzer. A massive 240mm gun as solid as a tank, the howitzer quickly turned its wrath on Battery Crockett. Crockett was helpless; she faced away from Bataan. The rear of the battery was protected by a barrier of oil drums filled with earth, but a 400-pound projectile pierced her defenses. The blasts were blinding. Steel fragments ricocheted off of concrete walls, while a fire raged in the battery's lower passages. Captain Lester I. Fox, a surgeon with the 59th Coast Artillery, was tending the wounded when a shell detonated and broke his leg. He was hopping around on the other leg helping to organize a fire crew when another shell landed and blew off his right elbow, blinded him in his right eye, and left him with several fractured ribs. One gunner was killed, several more were injured, and Crockett's No. 1 gun was neutralized. The explosions threatened Battery Hamilton, above which was an ammunition dump.

Fort Drum fired in retaliation. Salvo after salvo sailed over Government Ravine. Murray's corpsman, Cecil Peart, tried to evacuate a casualty at the height of the barrage but it was too dangerous to evacuate him to the Malinta Tunnel hospital. At 1751 Fort Drum finally silenced the enemy howitzer. Then Geary came under siege from a smaller gun.

Minutes later Major James V. Bradley, Jr., of the 2nd Battalion took a call at his Wheeler Point Command Post from a runner at Geary Point. An American soldier named Henriques had been seriously wounded at Battery Crockett and removed to Battery Hamilton. It was a spinal injury, but Lieutenant Napoleon Magpanty had few supplies with which to treat him. Could a doctor be sent?

"No, we can't do that now," Bradley said. "The road is being shelled, and it's littered with fragments."

Typically company aid men or corpsmen are responsible for evacuation, but on Corregidor battalion surgeons removed the wounded as the situation demanded.

"I'll go and get him," Fred Berley volunteered.

Meanwhile Japanese aircraft flew into the fray and scored a direct hit on the ammunition dump between Crockett and Hamilton, causing a huge conflagration. Seventy-five-millimeter antiaircraft shells exploded uncontrollably as clouds of dust and smoke tongued the sky.

Fred jumped into a truck and headed out for Battery Hamilton with Navy Chief Quartermaster George R. Williams and Private First Class Charles F. Jonaitis. The South Shore road was swept by enemy fire and studded with shrapnel from the burning dump. All personnel had been warned to clear the area for fear that Crockett's magazine would blow, but Berley, Williams, and Jonaitis were able to remove Henriques safely to the E Company aid station. Shells continued to ignite even after the firing had stopped. Once the all-clear sounded, Henriques was taken to the Malinta Tunnel hospital.

"I don't know what came over me," Fred said afterward. "I just felt we had to go out and get him."

———

"You would hear the cars long before they reached the tunnel," wrote AP correspondent Clark Lee on Corregidor:

The urgency of their horns, blowing all the way down the hill from Topside and then up the slope from Bottomside, told you they were bringing dead and those about to die and those who would be better off dead. The MPs would make the cars slow down as they drove into the big tunnel and they would stop at the hospital tunnel and blood would be dripping from the cars or the trucks. Then the stretcher bearers would gently lift out the bloody remnants of what had been an American soldier or a Filipino worker a few minutes before. They would lift out carefully the eighteen-year-old American boy who would never again remember his name, or his mother's name, or anything else, but would just look at you blankly when you spoke to him.

On the night of April 24 the U.S. engineer launch *Night Hawk,* under the command of First Lieutenant James Seater, went on a reconnaissance mission up the east coast of Bataan with volunteers from the 59th and 60th Coastal Artillery. Off Lamao they spotted a small boat with two Japanese men in it, whom they quickly took prisoner. The *Night Hawk* resumed her patrol north toward Limay when she was hailed by a larger ship flying the Japanese flag. The *Night Hawk*'s gunners answered with a fierce fusillade of cannon and machine gun fire, killing most of the crew and torching the ship.

As the *Night Hawk* began to tow its quarry, Japanese boats raced out from the shore. The *Night Hawk* cut loose and sped back to Corregidor. The two prisoners, meanwhile, tried to escape by jumping overboard, but the Americans shot them dead in the water.

The next day enemy dive bombers targeted shipping in the South Channel, Corregidor's roving guns opened up on 250 Japanese near Barrio San José on Bataan, and Geary lambasted an enemy dump. A string of bombs fell on Fort Hughes, and the Japanese lobbed shells from Bataan and Cavite, one of which landed in Geary's pit, causing serious injury. Engineer Point came under heavy fire, and then that ammunition dump was struck as well.

Due north of George's position, Engineer Point was "a hellish place" to reach, as George put it. He scrambled down with Pharmacist's Mate Donald Edmond Bansley and Private First Class Graham H. Andrews. George treated one casualty for burns on the feet, lacerations to the scalp, and multiple abrasions. They were searching for more wounded when they noticed a case of grenades on fire a mere five feet away. They dove into a dugout just before the ammunition dump began to detonate. Between explosions Andrews scrambled down around the bluff and reported two more wounded, one of whom was severely burned. High tide made it nearly impossible to get around the point, unless you swam or were lowered by rope. But if they did that, they'd be completely exposed. They waited until dark to retrieve them. "Wet, oily, slick rocks through smouldering ruins of explosions dump and into Hospital lateral," George wrote in his diary entry for April 25. "Days [*sic*] work done."

As intense as the aerial activity was over Corregidor, it usually stopped in the evening. After a day of being cooped up in Malinta Tunnel, there was nothing like going outside for a breath of fresh air, a cigarette, and a little small talk—maybe a romantic stroll beneath the stars with one of the army nurses on "Lover's Lane," the stretch of road that ran down to the beach from the tunnel entrance. Sometimes a voice broke into song, "The Yellow Rose of Texas" or "Home on the Range," and inspired a sing-along. But on the evening of April 25, it was the Japanese who began to serenade Corregidor, shelling Topside at 1831 and Morrison and Grubbs at 1922.

Suddenly at 2158 a 240mm shell crashed near the west entrance of Malinta Tunnel. Bystanders ran for cover, but the concussion slammed shut the ten-foot-high reinforced entrance gate. A second shell careened into the crowd. Arms and legs were wrenched from bodies; shrapnel tore into flesh. One army nurse, Helen Cassiani, watched in horror as a severed head rolled by her feet. Corpsmen ran to the scene from the hospital lateral, pried open the iron rails, and extricated the wounded.

Said Juanita Redmond:

We worked all that night, and I wish I could forget those endless, harrowing hours. Hours of giving injections, anesthetizing, ripping off clothes, stitching gaping wounds, of amputations, sterilizing instruments, bandaging, settling the treated patients in their beds, covering the wounded that we could not save. . . .

I had still not grown accustomed to seeing people torn and bleeding and dying in numbers like these. When *one* patient dies, it is agonizing enough; when you are faced by such mass suffering and death, something cracks inside you—you can't ever be quite the same again.

The tragedy could easily have been prevented. The presumption that it was safe to be even a few feet outside Malinta Tunnel for a even a few moments irked George.

Net result 14 dead and 68 injured, many severely. More casualties than several days of intensive shelling have produced. People have been warned but that wasn't sufficient. Too many come out for air, sit near entrance and then hope to scramble in if necessary. It won't work and Japs know it.

Ten days earlier forty Philippine Army men had been buried alive in Morrison Hill when a burst of mortar fire triggered a landslide that sealed the entrance to their tunnel behind Battery James like a crypt.

During one air raid Murray's dugout collapsed, and half the hill that supported it was carried away in the blast. Some marines made sure they had shovels in their tunnels and a three-inch piece of pipe protruding from them for air.

Another time Murray dove into a culvert where he had gone to treat a casualty just a few days before. By the time he reached him, the man had bled to death. Shrapnel had ricocheted off of a tree and whizzed through the narrow opening between the sandbagged entrance and the culvert's top, striking him in the head. As Murray listened to the bombs explode around him, he figured the odds of that happening again were in his favor. But if the Japanese could spot tunnel entrances, only the deepest recesses were secure. The problem, as Wainwright realized, was that you couldn't fight a land battle from underground.

It seemed as if no one was listening to the pleas of the men and women on Corregidor, but on April 26 Wainwright received a radio message from one man who understood the situation well: the governor of Malta. In one month the bombs dropped on the strategic British naval base in the central Mediterranean exceeded the entire blitz on England in 1940 and amounted to thirteen times the tonnage dropped on Coventry by the Luftwaffe on the night of November 14, 1940. General William Dobbie knew whereof he spoke. In April 1942 Malta suffered on average 190 enemy air attacks each day, but the base still held:

People of Malta send their warm greetings to the gallant defenders of Corregidor. They have watched with profound admiration the magnificent fight you have put up which has been a great inspiration to us all. You are giving untold assistance to the Allied cause.

God grant you may soon reap the fruits of victory.

Wainwright replied:

The officers and enlisted men on Corregidor deeply appreciate the sentiments expressed in your message. In our efforts to contribute to the common cause of freedom for which the Philippine and American troops are now fighting we are inspired and encouraged by the historic stand which has been made by the gallant defenders of Malta.

With God's help, both our peoples shall soon join hands across the seas in celebrating the return of freedom to the democratic nations of the world.

God's help was more like Job's luck.

The morning of April 29 was warm and clear, a beautiful dawn for Emperor Hirohito's forty-first birthday. The Japanese celebrated by launching a massive assault against Corregidor waged by Colonel Inoue's 4th Field Artillery Regiment and Colonel Koike's 22nd Field Artillery Regiment. "While the enemy artillery is being annihilated," read the 14th Army Operations orders, "vital installments shall be burned and destroyed. Enemy camp sites will be unexpectedly harrassed and terrorized, paralyzing the enemy."

At 0730 three dive bombers struck Malinta Hill, "the anchor of beach defense" at the eastern end of the island. Artillery gunners on Bataan blasted Bottomside, Peeping Tom checked their aim, and the festivities began. Both the North and South Docks were hit, both portals of Malinta Tunnel were shelled, and Middleside Barracks was bombed. Two ammunition dumps near Topside exploded, fires burned fiercely in the stockade, and plumes of smoke snaked thousands of feet into the air. The tunnels quivered; sandbags were set on fire. Trees burst into smoldering embers, while tents and clothing crumpled like autumn leaves.

Andrews brought in two casualties to George's aid station. Another man with an abdominal shrapnel wound had to be evacuated to the Malinta Tunnel hospital. Meanwhile Pharmacist's Mate Bansley and Lieutenant (j.g.) William L. Strangman of the Dental Corps retrieved an injury from Engineer Point.

The bombers came in waves, at 0730, 0755, 0923, and 0957. Artillery mauled Malinta Hill, 10,000 shells rained down on Corregidor, coming so quickly they sounded like machine gun fire. Numerous batteries responded—on enemy guns, observation towers, Cabcaben Road, truck columns on the Cavite shoreline—but it was difficult to gauge their effectiveness due to the breakdown in communications. George kept notes during much of the barrage:

Another intensive bombardment started at approx 10 AM and is continuing now. . . . Dive bombers still worrying hell out of all hands. So far we haven't had very many casualties and how [sic] my fingers crossed. Well the rest of this day should be interesting to say nothing about exciting.

It was both. Cheney and James Ravines were soon under fire, and later that afternoon eight bombers ripped into the head of Ramsey Ravine, one load fell on the parapet of Battery Way, and a refrain was played for Middleside. By day's end 106 tons had been dropped on Corregidor in eighty-three sorties. One hundred 240mm shells were concentrated on Battery Way alone. The Japanese knocked out several of Battery Geary's mortars, blasted three 75mm beach defense guns that faced Bataan off of Malinta Hill, and destroyed a four-barrelled 1.1-inch pom-pom gun. When a 240mm shell hurtled down a nearby ventilation shaft, igniting a generator gas tank, fire swept through a searchlight tunnel incinerating the platoon commander and four of his men. Happy birthday, indeed.

Morale had taken a beating on the Rock. Japanese bombers flying between 25,000 and 30,000 feet were out of range of the antiaircraft guns, artillery men suffered shell shock, and all some could do was "duck down in their gunpits," as Lieutenant Colonel E. L. Barr of Battery M put it. The problem for the defenders was that many of Corregidor's guns couldn't bear north. Fort Drum fired over Murray's aid station, and a Philippine Scout battery piped in from Barrio San José, but to little effect.

The roar of the Rock turned into a distressing diminuendo as observation stations were hit, plotting rooms were damaged, and power plants were knocked out. Seventy-five-millimeter beach defense guns stayed out of the action for fear of disclosing their positions before a landing. The fact that many of Corregidor's guns weren't firing back made the troops even more jittery.

The only respite from enemy artillery—if respite it was—came from air raids. "During the day we lived like moles burrowing in the ground," remarked Colonel Beecher, "and came out only at night." Rats frequented dugouts, ants ate the rat bait, and the dugouts themselves grew moldy. Then Japanese artillery started harassing the garrison after dark. George learned subconsciously to roll out of his cot in his sleep. "I guess my life saving reflex is well developed," he wrote in his diary. "Here's hoping I outgrow this after the war."

Rations left men hankering for more, water was restricted to one canteen per day, and reserve stocks in Malinta Tunnel were so low that showers had been prohibited since April 15. Bottles crashed to the floor in the hospital laterals during bombardments, and a new expression gained currency: "Pardon me, Colonel, that last Jap round bounced the phone right off my desk." Cordite fumes seeped into the ventilation shafts, and the dust was so thick that nurses covered patients' faces—and their own—with wet gauze. Fifty feet underground Malinta's residents were thrown off their feet by the force of concussions.

Some men preferred to be anywhere but Malinta Tunnel. Lieutenant (j.g.) Charles B. Brook of the 4th Tactical Battalion found it so depressing, it made him think of trench warfare in World War I. During one particularly heavy artillery attack, he stepped into an ammunition storage tunnel for cover. "You'll never get wounded in here," cracked one old sergeant.

On April 17 Wainwright had requested a navy seaplane to replenish Corregidor's medicine chest and to remove nurses, civilian women, and older American officers. He radioed MacArthur in Australia, who agreed to send the only two PBYs at his disposal. MacArthur asked that a staff officer, Colonel Stuart Wood, and several cryptographers be removed as well. They were joined by two Philippine Army lietuenants, one of whom was Salvador P. Lopez, author of the "Bataan Has Fallen" speech. At 2300 on the night of April 29 two Catalina flying boats landed in the mineswept waters between Corregidor and Caballo Island "like the messengers from another world that they were," said Wainwright. The moon was full, and once medicine and mechanical fuses for the 3-inch antiaircraft ammunition were unloaded, twenty American nurses were boarded, including Lieutenant Juanita Redmond, who kissed Wainwright in gratitude before the planes departed for Lake Lanao, Mindanao, en route to Australia. They left just in time. The assault on Corregidor was about to reach new heights.

Batteries Way and Geary were impeding Homma's progress, and he personally ordered their destruction. On May 1 enemy bombers hammered both entrances of Malinta Tunnel and sealed Battery Chicago's fate. On May 2 the Japanese drew a bead on the Geary-Crockett locus with 240mm howitzers, right where John and Murray had aid stations. For five hellish hours Corregidor was pounded with 3,600 shells. Explosion followed explosion at the rate of twelve shells per minute or one shell every five seconds. There were enough shells to fill, Wainwright and Moore calculated, 600 trucks.

Traveling nearly at the speed of sound, they caused terrific concussions on impact. The noise on the Rock was deafening. Wainwright himself had his hearing damaged one morning. He was lighting one of MacArthur's cigars—a Tobaccolero—after breakfast, when a 240mm shell plowed into the bulwark that protected the end of Malinta Tunnel. "My head suddenly felt as if someone had rammed a red-hot pipe through one ear and out the other."

Pain occurs in the ear at 140 decibels. At 185 decibels, the tympanic membrane can burst, and at 200 lungs might rupture. The blast from a 240mm shell measures 200 decibels or more, a volume at which neural activity is disturbed, equilibrium is thrown off, and the body literally vibrates with the acoustic assault on the eardrum. Speech was lost in the roar of explosions, thought was impaired, and people moved as if in a state of suspended animation. The sound of artillery was an unforeseen weapon in the siege of Corregidor, disorienting and debilitating, and impossible to escape from in the field.

By the late afternoon of May 2 a brisk westerly wind fanned the flames on the Rock. Shovels and wet sacks were the only extinguishers available because the fire department refused to leave Malinta Tunnel in the midst of the barrage. Many of the roads were impassable anyway because of shell and bomb craters. Even disabled guns such as Denver Battery were shelled again as pit crews huddled helplessly and the wounded awaited aid.

Denver lay on an exposed ridge west of Kindley Field. This was George's territory, but evacuation was technically a corpsman's responsibility. He knew that any movement could draw enemy fire. A choice had to be made, a risk had to be weighed, but in the heat of the moment thought merged into action with the speed of instinct. He jumped into an ambulance—but the damn thing wouldn't start. So he drove an Army Command car on the enfiladed North Road and brought his casualties back through the east end of Malinta because a fire had broken out in front of the hospital itself.

While Corregidor was under attack from Bataan, Fort Hughes was being shellacked from Cavite. Fort Drum and Fort Frank opened up counterbatteries in angry reply. Then at 1627 an earth-shattering explosion rocked Topside. A 240mm shell breached Battery Geary's ammunition magazine, which held 1,600 sixty-two-pound powder charges. The impact was cataclysmic. Some men were convinced it was an earthquake, others the end of the world. Murray's aid station quivered. He thought the entire island was going to explode. A 13-ton mortar was catapulted into the sky and landed on the golf course 150 yards away. Fred watched in awe as a six-ton fragment of reinforced concrete, "as big as your living room," careened through the air and severed a tree trunk four feet in diameter before crashing into a ravine.

John, just a few hundred yards below Geary, rushed to the shattered battery, where Major Williams and Captain Austin C. Shofner were the first marines on the scene. The smoke was nearly impenetrable, but the shelling had stopped. The Japanese knew at once that they had scored a bull's-eye. Fortunately Geary's commanding officer, Captain Thomas W. Davis III, and pit officer 1st Lieutenant Harry C. Minsker had had the foresight to empty the magazines of one of the inoperative gun pits before their men were forced under cover. Of the sixty-man pit crew, six were dead, and another six were wounded. Captain Calvin E. Chunn of the 4th Battalion was one of the injured, suffering cuts and lesions "when an enemy shell exploded within a few feet of him on Geary trail,"

John noted. Williams and Shofner were badly burned trying to rescue survivors. Four men remained trapped behind a concrete wall.

Murray imagined the Japanese dancing with joy. By day's end, only one of Corregidor's mortars—Battery Way—could counter the might of Japanese howitzers on Bataan. A garrison of approximately 12,000 men stood against an enemy force of 250,000. Ordnance repairmen couldn't get a leg up on the damage to the Rock's guns. Beach defense installations had been pulverized, landing areas on the north shore of Kindley Field were softened, and telephone lines were down. The casualty rate among the 1st Battalion was low, but losses among senior officers ran high.

Hundreds of men had been killed on Corregidor, hundreds more had been wounded, and thousands suffered from respiratory complaints, malaria, jaundice, and acute gastroenteritis. Some gunners experienced weakened vision from vitamin A deficiency, which they tried to remedy with boric acid and cod liver oil. With the increased patient load, Malinta Tunnel hospital expanded into three additional laterals. Among the injuries were abdominal perforations from bomb fragments and shrapnel; wounds to the feet and buttocks from men trying to protect heads and torsos as they hit the deck; and numerous fractures as well as tendon and joint injuries.

Surprisingly there were few psychiatric cases. Shelling produced more neuroses than bombing because of the element of shock, but aside from several suicides, psychotic episodes were rare. The reason, Cooper speculated, was that "there was no zone of interior to which the individual could be sent, and everyone knew that. Another factor may have been that there was no letup." That didn't stop malingerers from blowing off big toes or inflicting tibial and tarsal injuries in an attempt to avoid a foot soldier's duty.

The island was warped by the force of firepower. Murray felt like a fox in the forest watching the trees disappear around him. Once so heavily wooded you could hardly see the sky, Government Ravine was now largely shorn of its vegetation. Even tropical wildlife displayed the hallmarks of fear. During one air raid, a monkey scampered into Malinta Tunnel, frightening the humans by its evident distress. Parts of the North Road had been blown into the sea. Entire cliffsides collapsed under bombardment. What had first appeared to Berley as a posh country club was leveled into a landscape of skeletal buildings and smoking ruins. The Japanese were literally grinding down the Rock.

"There was dust a foot thick" on the ground, said Sergeant Louis E. Duncan, and it was so heavy in the air that it blinded Corregidor's spotters. Corregidor looked "more like the Mojave Desert," added Brigadier

General Lewis C. Beebe, "than a densely populated tropical island," except that it was littered with shell fragments and debris. Almost anywhere you walked, there was a bomb crater within twenty-five yards.

The following day, May 3, Wainwright reported to MacArthur: "Situation here is fast becoming desperate. . . . The island is practically denuded of vegetation and trees leaving no cover and all structures are leveled to the ground. Communications and utilities are almost impossible of maintenance. Casualties since April 9 approximate 600."

By now, several thousand Filipino laborers had crowded into Malinta Tunnel. "They relieved themselves where they stood," dropped their trash around them, and refused to leave, according to MacArthur's finance officer, Colonel John R. "Jack" Vance. Sometimes the dead lay on stretchers in the hospital laterals "awaiting a lull in the bombardment for burial."

Conditions in the field, George noted in his diary, were far worse.

3rd May 1942 Sunday.
It is now 1100 and artillery has pounded in constantly for 4 hours. One heavy bombing raid and here we sit in our hole dirty, unshaven, trying to subdue peristaltic wave and urinating in a gasoline tin. . . . I would like to have a recorder here to send this all back for re-broadcast to U.S. defense workers, pacifists, Army, Navy and Marine Commanders, Congressmen, etc. Corregidor still stands but who can claim any credit especially since no attack has been made on any of the fortified islands directly. Bombers and artillery will not take an island even if every man was killed. So here we are wondering just what the hell is in the Japanese mind and more important the American mind.

What was in the Japanese mind was a carefully planned two-pronged attack beginning with the East Sector, which was held by the 1st Battalion, 4th Marines. On the first night 2,400 men from Colonel Satō Gempachi's 61st Infantry Regiment—the Left Flank Force—would initiate the invasion by landing on the tail of the tadpole and capturing Kindley Field. They would be reinforced by infantry from the 23rd Independent Engineer Battalion and the 1st Battalion of the 4th Engineer Regiment and tanks from the 7th Tank Regiment. An arsenal of firepower would come courtesy of the 1st Company, Independent Mortar Battalion, the 51st Mountain Gun Regiment, and the 3rd Mortar Battalion. Lieutenant General Kitajima Kishio's 14th Army artillery was charged with knocking out Corregidor's big guns and enemy ships in the bay, while the 16th Division would execute a feint attack against El Fraile and Carabao Islands.

The next night the Right Flank Force would land in the West Sector of Corregidor between Morrison and Battery Points, then converge with the Left Flank Force to seize Topside. Led by the 4th Division's Major General Taniguchi Kureo, it consisted of the 37th Infantry, a battalion of the 8th Infantry, and an element of the 7th Tank Regiment. "The vital points of enemy positions will be overwhelmingly crushed," read the 14th Army orders, "and the enemy troops especially the ones concealed in wooded areas will be exterminated. The final attack support will be as vigorous as the opening fire."

At 2130 on the night of May 3, the *Spearfish* paid a last visit to Corregidor. The submarine slipped past a Japanese minesweeper and destroyer, then surfaced outside the South Channel minefield. She winked her conning tower light, and a small boat approached from the Rock, but its twenty-five passengers took skipper Jim Dempsey by surprise. Thirteen of them were women—army nurses, an officer's wife, and the sole navy nurse on Corregidor, Ann Bernatitus. Twelve officers followed, including Commander E. L. Sackett of the *Canopus* and Wainwright's ailing assistant chief of staff (G-3), Colonel Pete Irwin. Footlockers full of records, rosters, and the last outgoing mail were hoisted on board. By 2230 the *Spearfish* was 200 feet under the sea, stealing its way toward Fremantle, Australia. Fifty-four army and twenty-six Filipino nurses remained behind.

Prior to her departure, Ann Bernatitus asked Ernie Irvin, who had been pulled off beach defense in Government Ravine to work in the Malinta Tunnel hospital, if he wanted to write a letter to his mother back in Louisiana. She'd mail it for him from Australia.

"No," said Irvin, a kid who came from a broken Cajun family and had helped support his mom since he was twelve. "It might give her false hope."

He had seen what the Japanese had done in China. "They chopped off more heads than you could shake a stick at." He figured they'd wipe out the Americans on Corregidor and then rumble on to their next rampage.

"Why don't you just go and eat a frozen Milky Way and think of me when you eat it?" he said in farewell.

By May 4 the situation on Corregidor was dire. Thunderous artillery issued from Bataan. Planes dive-bombed the East Sector, while Topside was still under fire. The Air Warning lines were severed, and the Inshore Patrol was immobilized. Fifteen invasion barges were spotted being towed from north to south in the early afternoon, but they were out of range of Corregidor's guns.

"With morale at present level," Wainwright wrote in a secret message to Army Chief of Staff General George C. Marshall, "I estimate that we have something less than an even chance to beat off an assault."

The Japanese directed their fire at mobile guns, searchlights, and the area between North and Cavalry Points on the northeast shore. In a ferocious assault that began at 1500, shells rained down on the Rock with such frequency that "it sounded," said Murray, "like one continuous explosion." Scattered artillery fire continued throughout the evening, and searchlights were on the alert, but the only one to reach Corregidor's shores that night was a Filipino civilian in a fishing boat. He carried a simple message from Philippine intelligence on Bataan:

Expect enemy landing on the night of 5/6 May.

A Philippine Army officer in Manila radioed Wainwright that "extensive landing maneuvers" had just been practiced near Cavite, and "thousands of bamboo ladders" were being made to scale the cliffs of Corregidor. Antitank barricades were improvised in Malinta Tunnel from concrete pillars attached to the trolley rails.

On the morning of May 5, Colonel Howard, commander of the 4th Marines, called a conference of his senior officers to consider the probability of an assault. Sergeant Edward D. Dennis, the only enlisted man present, had studied Japanese tactics in China and cautioned that the Japanese favored nighttime landings one hour before the moon was at its height. The Japanese had timed the invasions of Singapore and Hong Kong for moonrise, and on the night of May 5 moonrise was at midnight. Colonel Howard decided to stick to the regiment's orders and let the men sleep until an hour before dawn. "Damn that full moon," Major General Moore exclaimed. "They'll probably come tonight."

Some of the Rock's defenders, George noted, had already abandoned their positions.

5th May Tuesday 1942. For two days we have been under heavy concentrated artillery fire and 2 or 3 X a day 5 diver bombers work us over. I hate to say it but the morale is about the lowest it ever has been and a fairly large number of men have refused to stay in their positions. Can't very well blame them when they practically have their guns blown out of their hands. Artillery barrage in certain areas makes it suicide to even stay there. . . . When I say that I mean 5 to 15 shells in air all the time. . . . Well to sum [sic] the situation.

Things don't look very pleasant. Guns out, morale gone, positions not manned, unrestricted air activity, water hard to obtain and one meal a day.

In one extraordinary twenty-four-hour period an estimated 16,000 shells fell over Corregidor, an island of 1,732 acres only slightly larger than New York City's Central Park. Most of the shells were 150mm caliber, and many of them were fired from gun emplacements around Hospital No. 2 on Bataan. The Japanese were using 6,000 American and Filipino patients as human shields.

At 1447 the Rock recorded its 300th air raid. By early evening the Japanese opened up with a withering attack on the fortified islands and a furious concentration on James Ravine, the North Shore, and the 1st Battalion sector. Beach defense guns were blown apart, searchlights were shattered, and land mines erupted. Fort Drum and Fort Frank lobbed 14-inch shells onto enemy boat concentrations off Cabcaben. By 2100 the marines had manned what was left of Corregidor's beach defenses.

It was a grueling day but by 2200 enemy fire had quieted down. George had just stepped out of his aid station to make his bed for the night when he saw a brace of Japanese motor boats off the North Shore and a hail of tracer machine gun fire. Enemy artillery made it impossible to stay outside. A barrage of shells fell at the mouth of Malinta Tunnel and the entrance to the hospital lateral.

Wainwright was lounging in his Lateral No. 10 quarters when he sat up from his chair and said to Brigadier General Beebe: "I don't like the sound of that, Lew."

Nighttime artillery attacks were unusual because the Japanese couldn't check for accuracy and didn't like to waste their ammunition.

Wainwright listened for a few minutes before leaving to confer with Moore and added: "I'm afraid we're in for it."

The intent of the attack was clear: keep the reinforcements in and the casualties out. The invasion of Corregidor was on.

At 2230 a message went out to the beach defenses commander: *"Prepare for probable landing attack."*

Ten minutes later an intense line of fire was laid down along the northeast shore below Kindley Field. The tail of the tadpole was in flames. Then Colonel Beecher received a report of a small flotilla of barges approaching the area between North Point and Infantry Point. Searchlights glared at the intruders, only to be quickly smashed by enemy artillery. Streams of phosphorous shells poured into the sky as Philippine Scouts lacerated the Japanese with 75mm guns from undisclosed positions near North Point while marines opened up with

M-1916 37s and beach defense machine guns. On Kindley Field, a platoon of Mobile Battery under Lieutenant Thomas A. Hackett pumped hellfire from antiaircraft guns. The Japanese huddled at the center of their landing craft or tried desperately to swim for shore. Many of them drowned. Within minutes Satō's badly wounded Left Flank Force narrowed in on a strip of coastline between Cavalry Point and North Point. The water was stained with blood and oil.

The stragglers who made it to the beach were corralled by terror and confusion. From the cliffs of Corregidor the defenders hurled grenades, slid twenty-five-pound fragmentation bombs, and threw rifle and small arms fire at soldiers, who dropped like Kewpie dolls. Some begged for mercy, claiming they were Filipinos, but their pleas were met with laughter and lead. It was a massacre, yet the Japanese would not be stopped. They stepped over their own dead as they had on Bataan, regrouped, countered with deadly 50mm grenade launchers, and readied for hand-to-hand combat. By 2315 what was left of the Left Flank Force of the reinforced 1st Battalion, 61st Infantry, had landed. Now they were moving inland.

Ten minutes after the 1st Battalion came ashore, ten landing craft carrying 785 men from the reinforced 2nd Battalion were swept east of North Point. Miscalculating the currents in the North Channel, boats from the 1st Sea Operation Unit found themselves directly in the crosshairs of the Rock's defensive positions. Battery Way, which had been plastered by a counterbattery in Cabcaben, roared into action under the command of Major William Massello, Jr., and Captain Frederick A. Miller, using Battery Erie's 100-man crew. Antiaircraft guns lowered their sights to blaze away at sea-level targets. Battery Craighill on Fort Hughes harassed the invaders with mortar fire. To a Japanese eyewitness in Cabcaben, it was "a spectacle that confounded the imagination, surpassing in grim horror anything we had ever seen before." Marines hidden in the bluffs riveted barges with .50-caliber machine gun fire and zeroed in on the beaches as if they were "shooting ducks in a rain barrel," said Private First Class David L. Johnson. Platoon Sergeant William "Tex" Haynes turned into a one-man, two-gun battery, spraying the enemy with .30-caliber machine gun and rifle fire until he was blown apart by a grenade. Eight out of the ten landing craft were sunk, but some Japanese had crept ashore near North Point and gained a foothold along the north edge of Kindley Field.

Shortly before midnight Colonel Howard called in his reinforcements, and Schaeffer's Headquarters and Service Company emerged from their foxholes in Government Ravine. A tank trap protected them from artillery fire as they crossed Bottomside and filed into Malinta Tunnel, where they were handed arms and ammunition. Murray was left behind to join John and the 4th Tactical Battalion, which was still in bivouac to the west. He climbed uphill and headed over toward Geary Point as the moon rose. Alone in the dark, armed only with a service revolver, it was all too easy to mistake the rustle of bamboo for a footfall, a passing shadow for the Japanese.

At 0020 a Marine Corps runner ran into Malinta, breathless, to report that enemy troops—"probably 600"—were now on the east end of Corregidor. A battle line was drawn across the top of a ridge beneath Water Tank Hill to prevent the Japanese from advancing on the tunnel, a mere 750 yards away.

At 0100 Joe Williams's 4th Tactical Battalion, John and Murray among them, gingerly walked the shell-pocked South Road, their progress impeded by the bombardment of the South Dock before they hastened into Malinta. The shelling was so fierce in the 1st Battalion sector that George couldn't make a move outside his dugout.

> *Well, we opened a bottle of Champagne and toasted each other [and]*
> *made a white red cross flag and sat tight. It was absolutely impossible*
> *for us to get out or people to get in.*

Malinta was filled to capacity, its entrance was clogged with "tunnel rats." The blowers were off, the heat was unbearable, and fumes from the diesel generator infused the air. The remaining nurses were instructed to destroy all records and keep gas masks and helmets at the ready.

By then one part of Satō's 1st Battalion had cut across the tail of Corregidor to seize Monkey Point on the southeast shore. The other part was heading west toward Malinta Hill. Within half an hour the Japanese had reached the high ground of Denver Battery, which gave them a commanding position over the approach to the beaches and stood 1,000 yards from the tunnel entrance. They were advancing to the water tanks when they ran into a furious counterattack led by Marine Captain Noel O. Castle of Company D. Castle was killed in the action, but his men had momentarily pushed the Japanese back. Marines who gathered from various companies to keep the enemy in check were rushed by soldiers screaming *"Banzai! Banzai!"* before they again forced a retreat.

At 0200 the two companies of Schaeffer's Headquarters and Service Company began moving out of Malinta to stage a counterattack against Denver Battery. Lieutenant Hogaboom's Company P was in the lead and ravaged by enemy machine gun fire coming from the base of one of the stone water towers on Water Tank Hill. By the time Company O left, flares were rising over the Japanese position, the signal for an artillery attack from Bataan. Company commander Captain Robert Chambers, Jr., and Quartermaster Clerk Frank W. Ferguson scrambled into bomb craters for shelter. When Schaeffer arrived on the scene, he organized scattered elements of the Regimental Reserve into isolated counterattacks. But they were unable to uproot the Japanese from their positions in Denver Battery.

From the army hospital the doctors knew how quickly the situation was deteriorating from the hundreds of wounded who streamed into Malinta, on foot, on litters, filling the laterals to overflowing. They knew it as surely as Wainwright did when MacArthur reinstated War Plan Orange-3 on Bataan. There was one difference: there would be no retreat this time. Corregidor was the last stand.

At 0400 General Wainwright received a radiogram from President Roosevelt:

YOU AND YOUR DEVOTED FOLLOWERS HAVE BECOME
THE LIVING SYMBOLS OF OUR WAR AIMS AND THE
GUARANTEE OF VICTORY.

At 0430 Colonel Howard played his final hand and ordered the 4th Tactical Battalion to reinforce the 1st Battalion. The 2nd and 3rd Battalions remained in place in the Middle and West Sectors in the event of further landings. Infantry was coopted from the 59th Coast Artillery, antiaircraft artillerymen, and any navy men from the intercept tunnel without specific assignments. Corregidor's last remaining reinforcements consisted of 500 marines, sailors, and soldiers "untrained in infantry tactics," remarked Colonel Beecher, "but brave and determined." Williams led his men in platoon column from Malinta, but before the last of them had even made it out of the tunnel, they were decimated by enemy fire. Many of them were "wiped out," Wainwright said, "in front of our eyes."

In the chaos of the night, the Japanese infiltrated marine positions, while some Americans found themselves behind enemy lines. The fighting was brutal, the battle lines at times no more than fifteen to twenty yards apart. Contact among battalions, companies, and platoons was sporadic at best. Runners were the only means of communication.

"Joe, what in the hell did you bring me?" Schaeffer asked once Williams caught up with him.

"I have my whole battalion here," Williams replied, "or what's left of them. Where is your unit? And what position do you want my battalion in?"

Schaeffer was unnerved. "Joe, I don't know! . . . I don't know where in hell my noncoms are. I think they're all dead!"

"Dammit now, you relax. I'll take over this situation," Williams responded.

At 0600 Williams ordered a counterattack to regain ground around Denver Battery. Forward elements of the Japanese were less than 500 yards from the east entrance of Malinta. Williams was "a tiger," a welter-weight boxing champion who seemed absolutely fearless.

But Japanese resistance was formidable. Schaeffer was pinned down in his position by machine gun fire and nearly hysterical from a grenade blast that he thought had blinded him. Williams had him evacuated to the Malinta Tunnel Hospital, where Murray examined him. There was no damage to his eyes. Schaeffer had panicked, that was all. He would be okay if he could only calm down.

The machine gun nest at the base of one of the water tanks was thwarting the marine advance. Two old leathernecks, Sergeant Major Thomas F. Sweeney and Quartermaster Sergeant John H. Haskins, im-provised a relay offense. Sweeney clambered to the top of the old stone tank to lob grenades below while Haskins resupplied him. Fearless and efficient, the two marines eradicated the sniper, but Haskins was killed while laddering up, and Sweeney was fatally wounded soon after taking out another machine gun.

At dawn the Japanese who were holed up in Battery Denver sus-pected that Frank Ferguson and Corporal Alvin E. Stewart of the 803rd Engineers were leading an outflanking maneuver. Satō's men had antici-pated the move and began retreating toward the rear. The Americans opened fire, picking off twenty enemy soldiers before Ferguson was shot twice in the face.

Unbeknownst to Williams, another enemy flotilla had approached Bottomside at 0440. Batteries Way and Stockade fired on the landing craft and were joined by Fort Drum, which had been pounding the Cab-caben docks on Bataan. Barges were blown apart, and small boats cap-sized. Half the landing craft were sunk. A curtain of smoke hung over the wreckage. The Americans were convinced that they had thwarted a third assault. "My God," Lieutenant General Homma exclaimed when he learned of the unexpected reverses, "I have failed miserably on the as-sault." The Americans were mistaken, but so was Homma Masaharu.

The counterattacks were heroic. Williams fought valiantly "every-where along the line, organizing and directing our attack, always in the thick of it, seeming to bear a charmed life," said Navy Lieutenant Charles B. Brook. While Williams hit Denver Battery from the east, 1st

Lieutenant Mason F. Chronister led a platoon of volunteers from the Radio Intercept Tunnel and the 60th Coast Artillery from the west. Then they ran into Japanese reinforcements from the newly arrived 3rd Battalion, 61st Infantry.

At daybreak, the Japanese Army Air Service resumed the bombing of Corregidor and artillery attacks intensified, but the lines below Water Tank Hill were too tightly drawn for fire to bear down on them. The Japanese themselves were so low on ammunition that they fought bayonet to bayonet to hold on to Denver Battery. The tide was turning. The Japanese set up a mortar battery on North Point and a machine gun on Cavalry Point, but after heavy fighting, Williams's men succeeded in silencing both. The path seemed clear for the remnants of the 4th Battalion to hook up with the remnants of the 1st.

Then Lieutenant Otis E. Saalman of the 4th Battalion staff saw a terrifying sight: two Japanese Chi Ha tanks and one M3 Stuart tank captured on Bataan had just landed on Corregidor and were clawing up from the beach.

––––––––––––

Casualties on Corregidor had mounted steadily, but there were few corpsmen in the field. The 1,000-yard run from the mouth of Malinta to the Denver Battery line had turned into a graveyard. Infantrymen volunteered as litter bearers, some of them quickly realizing that it was safer to spend a little time in the hospital lateral than to remain on the front. Murray was sympathetic, but it meant soldiers were abandoning their posts.

The wounds resulted not simply from bombings or artillery fire but from light machine guns, rifles, and grenades. Entry wounds tended to be smaller than exit wounds. Bullet wounds were cleaner than shell fragments. Small arms fire had an effect similar to high-explosive fragments. Shell bursts at close range caused massive tissue destruction that could shred the intestine, detach the liver, spleen, or kidney from the peritoneal cavity, and cause instant death. The destructive force of the firepower exceeded anything the army and navy doctors had ever seen in civilian surgery.

Lieutenant Brook had often wondered what it would be like to wage battle with a bayonet. When he heard the word "Charge!" at the base of Calvary Hill, he found himself cursing, screaming at the Japanese until he "felt a small explosion." His leg was shattered, and he knew at once, "I'm going home." An army officer tied a tourniquet around his leg, and Brook was "lugged" to the hospital on a piece of sheet metal. Bystanders looked on in horror at his wound. The chaplain told him he'd be taken straight to the operating room, and the limb was amputated without anesthesia. He could feel the cold of the steel knife as it cut through his leg.

Captain Chunn of the 4th Battalion replaced Lieutenant Bethel B. Otter after Otter was killed trying to destroy an enemy nest near the water towers. Chunn had already been wounded when Battery Geary took a direct hit on May 2, but now he was wounded again while charging the Japanese as they were trying to emplace a 75mm mountain gun.

One soldier Murray saw in the OR had a basal skull fracture from being shot in the head. "I don't want to die! I don't want to die!" he pleaded. But he was dying, and you tried to put his words out of your mind because they spoke just as easily for you. There was nothing to be done except hope that he passed away peacefully and painlessly. He died before Murray's eyes.

That morning an urgent call came into Malinta from the Radio Intercept Tunnel out at Monkey Point. The aid station had forty casualties but only a Chief Pharmacist's Mate and a Pharmacist's Mate 3rd Class to tend them. Could regimental headquarters send over a medical officer? Hayes gave Murray, the junior medical officer, his orders.

Murray knew where the fighting was. Monkey Point had been taken by the Japanese at 0100. The Radio Intercept Tunnel was well behind enemy lines.

"I can't go through Japanese lines, sir," Murray said.

"That's an order," Hayes admonished.

Murray could have obeyed, and he should have obeyed as an officer of the U.S. Navy. But it would have been suicide to do so.

"I'll go see Major Schaeffer," he replied, and he did.

"Sir," he addressed Major Schaeffer, "I have an order to take an ambulance out to the Radio Intercept Tunnel. Is the road clear?"

Schaeffer could hardly believe his ears.

"What the hell do you think we were trying to do out there?" Schaeffer barked. "The road's cut. It's impossible to get through."

Murray went back to Hayes and related his exchange with Schaeffer. Hayes was adamant.

The commander's firmness only strengthened the young lieutenant's resolve.

"Who issued this order?" he dared to ask.

"Colonel Cooper," Hayes replied, though he was unaccustomed to answering to a man nearly twenty years his junior.

"Then I'll go see Colonel Cooper," Murray declared.

When Murray found Colonel Cooper, chief surgeon, U.S. Forces in the Philippines, he described the situation.

Cooper spoke to him as if he were teaching a child how to cross the street. "Look," he said pointing to the air warning alarm. "See that light over there? That light is red, which means you can't go out of the tunnel. When that light changes to green, you can go."

This is the blind leading the blind, Murray thought. Since the fall of Bataan, he had been bivouacked in Government Ravine with the Headquarters and Service Company, who regularly got the shit shelled out of them. He'd never seen Hayes outside Malinta Tunnel. Cooper hadn't shown much of his face, either—Berley and Nardini could attest to that. Didn't they understand what was happening? The Regimental Reserve was in shreds. There wasn't going to be an all-clear.

The marines were helpless. There were no antitank guns on the Rock—they'd all been destroyed when Bataan fell. Their automatic weapons fire pinged off of armored carapaces glinting in the sunlight as Japanese tanks began to wipe out pockets of resistance. The 1st and 4th Battalions fell back to the shell-blasted trenches of their final defense line in front of Malinta. Enemy artillery fire from Bataan redoubled. The line couldn't hold. The Japanese slipped through both flanks and made a pincerlike movement for the tunnel itself.

By 1000 Wainwright had reached his decision. "It was the terror that is vested in a tank that was the deciding factor," he later wrote. "I thought of the havoc that even one of these could wreak if it nosed into the tunnel, where lay our helpless wounded and their brave nurses."

Between April 29 and May 6, more than 200,000 rounds of Japanese artillery had been fired at Corregidor. Six to eight hundred men lay dead; 1,000 more were wounded. Most of the officers in the Headquarters and Service Company had been killed, and the Inshore Patrol had virtually been wiped out.

The toll on the Japanese was even higher. Two-thirds of their landing barges had been sunk, and half of the men in them had drowned. Hayes estimated that 4,000 Japanese had died during the invasion.

Soon the Rock began sending its final dispatches.

From the Radio Intercept Tunnel, Captain Kenneth M. Hoeffel, commandant of the 16th Naval District, proclaimed: "One hundred and seventy-three officers and twenty-three hundred and seventeen men of the Navy reaffirm their loyalty and devotion to country, families and friends." The transmission was picked up by the radioman on the *Spearfish,* still on its journey to Australia with the last evacuees from Corregidor.

The Rock's defenders were given another message: "EXECUTE PONTIAC," the code phrase for surrender. At 1040 Major General Moore issued orders to destroy matériel in excess of .80 caliber and disable all other artillery equipment. Firing pins were pulled from rifles and tossed into the water. Top secret maps, files, and records were shredded. In Lateral No. 3 Colonel Vance and his assistants were busily cutting up more than two million Philippine pesos with shears.

Out at Wheeler Point the 2nd Battalion was frustrated by not having an opportunity to engage the Japanese. Fred Berley insisted on keeping his .45 service revolver and his Springfield rifle just in case.

"You can't have that," Major Bradley told him. "Put your Red Cross brassard on."

Fred tried to argue with him: "Look, at least I can defend myself a little bit."

Bradley was adamant.

Fred hid his weapons behind a wall in his aid station tunnel, and then they waited.

No one knew what to expect from the Japanese. A sanctuary during the siege, Malinta could become a catacomb on capitulation. The tunnel had been designed to be gas proof, but the requisite equipment hadn't arrived in time. Leland D. Bartlett was the canary in the mineshaft. He had trained Philippine Scouts in chemical warfare and was posted as a "gas sentry" at the tunnel's south entrance. Corpsman Ernie Irvin was terrified the Japanese would roll into Malinta with tanks and flamethrowers.

From the depths of Malinta twenty-two-year-old Corporal Irving Strobing, an army radio operator from Brooklyn, tapped out a plaintive farewell:

```
THEY ARE NOT NEAR YET. WE ARE WAITING FOR
GOD ONLY KNOWS WHAT. HOW ABOUT A CHOCOLATE
SODA? . . . WE MAY HAVE TO GIVE UP BY NOON,
WE DON'T KNOW YET. THEY ARE THROWING MEN AND
SHELLS AT US AND WE MAY NOT BE ABLE TO STAND
IT. THEY HAVE BEEN SHELLING US FASTER THAN
YOU CAN COUNT. . . .
    I KNOW NOW HOW A MOUSE FEELS. CAUGHT IN A
TRAP WAITING FOR GUYS TO COME ALONG FINISH IT
UP. GOT A TREAT. CAN PINEAPPLE. OPENING IT
WITH SIGNAL CORPS KNIFE.
    MY NAME IRVING STROBING. GET THIS TO MY
MOTHER. MRS. MINNIE STROBING, 605 BARBEY
STREET, BROOKLYN, N.Y. THEY ARE TO GET ALONG
O.K. GET IN TOUCH WITH THEM AS SOON AS
POSSIBLE. MESSAGE. MY LOVE TO PA, JOE, SUE,
MAC, GARRY, JOY, HOPE THEY BE THERE WHEN I
```

```
COME HOME. TELL JOE WHEREVER HE IS TO GIVE
'EM HELL FOR US. MY LOVE TO YOU ALL. GOD
BLESS YOU AND KEEP YOU. SIGN MY NAME AND TELL
MOTHER HOW YOU HEARD FROM ME.
    STAND BY. . . .
```

Wainwright chose midday on May 6 as the time of surrender so the Japanese would be in control of their prisoners by dark. He had heard reports of the rape and carnage that had accompanied the fall of Singapore. Brigadier General Beebe had already prepared a surrender message addressed to Lieutenant General Homma, which he broadcast in English over the Voice of Freedom four times, beginning at 1030. A nisei sergeant who had translated the text read it in Japanese, but the shelling continued unabated. Then Wainwright addressed President Roosevelt.

> With broken heart and head bowed in sadness but not in shame
> I report to Your Excellency that today I must arrange terms for the
> surrender of the fortified islands of Manila Bay. . . .
> With profound regret and with continued pride in my gallant
> troops I go to meet the Japanese commander. . . .
> Goodbye, Mr. President.

At 1200 General Wainwright ordered Colonel Bunker to lower the Stars and Stripes on Topside and run up the white flag of surrender. The guns of Corregidor were silent. As "Taps" played and the national and regimental colors burned, the Japanese dive-bombed the Rock. Colonel Bunker, Lieutenant Fulmer, Major General Moore, and Private Malone stood at attention. "My God," said Colonel Howard, "and I had to be the first marine officer ever to surrender a regiment."

The Japanese continued to fire on Corregidor with artillery that encircled Hospital No. 2, even though the white flag was visible from Bataan.

Later that afternoon Wainwright was escorted to Cabcaben aboard a Japanese tank barge, but his attempt to negotiate the surrender of the four fortified islands was rebuffed by Homma.

"No surrender will be considered unless it includes all United States and Philippine troops in the Philippine Islands," Homma snapped through his interpreter, and stalked off from the meeting.

There were 40,000 men in the southern islands of Mindanao and the Visayas under the command of Major General William F. Sharp. Wainwright would have to assume command of the Visayan-Mindanao Force and order Sharp, "by virtue of authority vested in me by the President," to surrender.

Wainwright felt he had no choice. When he returned to Corregidor that evening he found that the Japanese had surrounded the east entrance of Malinta, and they commanded the area from the west entrance to Morrison Hill and beyond. Another complement of enemy troops had arrived at Bottomside that afternoon, and by nightfall an attack was being planned against Topside. The blood of the entire garrison would be on his hands, his aide, Major Thomas Dooley, cautioned. Wainwright proceeded to Barrio San José, where Colonel Satō Gempachi, commander of the Corregidor invasion force, had his headquarters. Just before midnight, "a tremendous artillery bombardment" showered the west end of the island. At 2400, Lieutenant General Jonathan M. Wainwright tendered the unconditional surrender of all troops in the islands. The Philippines had fallen.

The men on Corregidor were stunned. Surrender was something most had never expected, few had ever witnessed, and none had ever prepared for. Was it true the Japanese didn't take prisoners? Did they kill their captives the same way the Japanese had killed themselves at Longoskawayan Point for fear of being captured?

George Ferguson sat down and wept at the news, he was "just so disappointed in the good old U.S.A." Fred Berley, tough as nails, fought back tears. John Bookman wondered what could possibly come next, while Murray Glusman felt relief—relief that the bombing and shelling, after twenty-seven days, had finally ceased.

13

Limbo

TIRED, HUNGRY, DEMORALIZED, and defeated, the men on Corregidor became symbols of fearlessness and fortitude, loyalty and endurance. If Bataan was "a minor epic in the sweeping panorama of world tragedy," Hanson W. Baldwin eloquently remarked in *The New York Times* on April 10, 1942, Corregidor stood as a shining affirmation of the nation's "unconquerable soul." Undersecretary of War Robert P. Patterson compared the "gallant effort" of the 8,000 Americans and nearly 5,000 Filipinos to the defense of Charleston in the Revolutionary War.

But to their parents, they were not symbols, they were sons; to their wives, they were husbands; to their girlfriends, they were lovers; to their sisters, they were brothers; and they were missing.

```
MAY 8, 1942
MR. LEWIS GLUSMAN
167 RIDGE STREET
NEW YORK, NEW YORK


   THE NAVY DEPARTMENT EXCEEDINGLY REGRETS TO
ADVISE YOU THAT ACCORDING TO THE RECORDS OF
THIS DEPARTMENT YOUR SON LIEUTENANT JUNIOR
GRADE MURRAY GLUSMAN UNITED STATES NAVAL
RESERVE WAS PERFORMING HIS DUTY IN THE
SERVICE OF HIS COUNTRY IN THE MANILA BAY AREA
WHEN THAT STATION CAPITULATED X HE WILL BE
CARRIED ON THE RECORDS OF THE NAVY DEPARTMENT
AS MISSING PENDING FURTHER INFORMATION X NO
REPORT OF HIS DEATH OR INJURY HAS BEEN
RECEIVED AND HE MAY BE A PRISONER OF WAR X IT
WILL PROBABLY BE SEVERAL MONTHS BEFORE
DEFINITE OFFICIAL INFORMATION CAN BE EXPECTED
CONCERNING HIS STATUS X SINCERE SYMPATHY IS
```

```
EXTENDED TO YOU IN YOUR ANXIETY AND YOU ARE
ASSURED THAT ANY REPORT RECEIVED WILL BE
COMMUNICATED TO YOU PROMPTLY X
```

```
                    REAR ADMIRAL RANDALL JACOBS
               CHIEF OF THE BUREAU OF NAVIGATION
```

The identical cable was sent to Samuel and Olga Bookman, Guy and Victoria Berley, George and Mary Ferguson, and to Lucy Ferguson with one exception: "husband" was substituted for "son."

The men were all part of the navy's fourth casualty list, which covered the period from April 16 to May 10, 1942. To rub salt in the wound, the War Department asked the public to refrain from requesting further information. "To comply" with such requests, Undersecretary of War Patterson explained, "is humanly impossible at a time when military communications are strained to the utmost."

The press couldn't resist an opportunity to pander to sentiment and national pride. The *New York Post* staged a photograph of Murray Glusman's family for a maudlin article that began: "They died or are missing, these New York boys, in the line of duty." The *New York Journal-American* ran a snapshot of John Bookman smiling in his navy whites. Fred Berley's dashing photograph appeared in the *Chicago Daily Tribune*, while George Ferguson's story was featured in the local newspaper in Evanston, Illinois.

By then the idea of sacrifice in the name of patriotism was taking root in American soil. On April 27, 1942, Roosevelt introduced an economic initiative to raise revenues and conserve materials through bond sales, increased taxation, wage and price controls, and food and fuel rationing. If American soldiers, airmen, sailors, and marines were willing to fight for their country, the president explained in a fireside chat, another kind of sacrifice—of money and material goods—would have to be made on the home front. The dividend would be victory, a theme cleverly exploited by Secretary of Treasury Henry Morganthau, Jr., in his war bond drives and the 5 percent "Victory Tax" surcharge. Americans warmly embraced the notion of giving up something to safeguard their freedom.

But what did it mean—"missing"? It was seeing someone in your mind and not being able to hold him. It was looking at a photograph and wondering if that person was dead or alive. It was talking out loud, only to be answered by silence. It was reading the last letter you'd received over and over again. What it meant was not knowing, a state of uncertainty that was in some ways more difficult to accept than death itself, because you couldn't go forward, you could only gaze back. You were in limbo.

George's last correspondence with Lucy was postmarked April 8, 1942, the day before Bataan fell, and revealed not a hint of trouble:

Dearest Lucy:
Here is the third in the series and three months have elapsed since my last birthday. Eating pretty well and still going strong but would surely like to be going back to meet you in that city called San Francisco. Perhaps it will be sooner than we expect. . . .
   Still hear KGEI and the commentator William Winter every evening at 6 PM and it all sounds pretty good especially the part where WW says "And you shall have planes, tanks, guns." Well we are waiting; more than that the men are fighting and doing a damn good job of it too. . . .
   Give my regards to your folks and help them in any way you care to. It would be interesting to know what the Red Cross has got you all doing to help out. I read an article somewhere that the school teachers had been requested to donate a few hours of their time to the cause. And Please [sic] remember I love you with all my heart and have hopes of a very pleasant future.

And then by hand he added the word "Soon" at the end of his type-written letter, forgetting to close it with a period.

For those on the home front, the lack of specific information concerning the missing was compounded by the lack of reliable news on the war in the Pacific. Reports were often inaccurate, contradictory, or out of date. H. Ford Wilkins's front-page *New York Times* article on December 9, 1941, about the bombing of Manila caused alarm for anyone with relatives in the Philippine capital, but the next day the headline claimed "LUZON INVASION 'IN HAND' OUR FORCES SAY." A subhead reported "Cavite Pounded From Air," but the article devoted not even a full sentence to the destruction of the Navy Yard. "Fires were seen at the Cavite naval base and at Nichols Field," Wilkins wrote, as if he were relying on secondhand sources and hadn't witnessed them himself.

The wire services provided some of the best reporting—Clark Lee's dispatches for AP, Frank Hewlett's for UP, and Curtis Hindson's for Reuters. Twenty-four-year-old John Hersey cabled dispatches from Bataan to *Time*. Carl Mydans sent back gripping photographs in black and white, as did newlywed Melville Jacoby, who with his wife, Annalee, filed stories for *Time* as well as *Life*. But whether their stories appeared in glossy magazines or daily newspapers, you wouldn't learn much about the navy men on Bataan from any reporter in the Philippines.

In fact, one could glean more about the destruction of the Cavite

Navy Yard from Japanese communiqués posted in *The New York Times* than from the paper of record itself—until, that is, Bataan fell, and the *Times* ran a story on April 11 under the headline "NAVY ROLE A HEROIC CHAPTER":

> Washington, April 10—Sailors and marines played an important part in the gallant defense of Bataan Peninsula, but most of their accomplishments have been secret up to now because of the lack of facilities to communicate their story to the Navy Department.

Their accomplishments were secret because the Navy Department had apparently chosen to keep them that way. News of the attack on the Asiatic Fleet just two days after Pearl Harbor had been more than the public—and the navy—could bear. Families, friends, and loved ones didn't officially learn of the destruction of the Cavite Navy Yard until four months after the event. Even then it was difficult for anyone to comprehend the extent of the carnage until Melville Jacoby's harrowing photographic record appeared in *Life* magazine on April 13, 1942. In the meantime people depended on what the available sources could print, but the sources themselves were drying up.

Two days after Manila was declared an "open city," the offices of the *Manila Herald* were bombed by the Japanese. Carl and Shelley Mydans were captured on January 2, 1942, and confined to the civilian internment camp established by the Japanese in the Royal and Pontifical University of Santo Tomás. H. Ford Wilkins, city editor of the *Manila Daily Bulletin*, A.V.H. Hartendorp, editor of *Philippine Magazine*, and D. T. Boguslav of the *Manila Tribune* (which became the occupation newspaper) were also taken captive. When Clark Lee heard the rumor that KZRH radio announcer Don Bell, whose real name was C. Beliel, had been caught by the Japanese in Manila, tortured, and killed, he decided to leave Corregidor with the Jacobys aboard the *Princesa de Cebu* on February 22. Carlos Romulo, who headed the Voice of Freedom, left Corregidor a day before the men on Bataan lost theirs, though the broadcasts continued without him.

The news slowed, the letters ceased, and then came the cables from the Bureau of Navigation identifying the missing. What it meant, as Murray's younger sister Estelle put it simply, was that "life stopped for the family."

By 1700 on the afternoon of May 7 the captured officers were assembled in Malinta Tunnel. American and Filipino enlisted men were gathered around its west entrance under a blazing sun. As tired and weary as they were, they rose to their feet when they saw the Japanese escorting

Wainwright and his staff outside. The general looked to the right, then turned to the left, his head slightly bowed. Private Everett D. Reamer, who had served as a rifleman with Battery F of the 60th Coast Artillery, could see tears on Wainwright's cheeks. The Japanese forced the enlisted men back to the tunnel entrance and ordered them to raise their hands for a propaganda photograph. A guard flung the dogtags off of Reamer's neck with the tip of his bayonet. He didn't dare pick them up.

Wainwright was on his way to KZRH's studio in Manila to broadcast the surrender message he had written to General Sharp, to Colonel John P. Horan in the mountain provinces of northern Luzon, and to Colonel Guillermo Nakar of the Philippine Constabulary in the Cagayan Valley. It was almost midnight by the time he delivered his address. His voice was uncharacteristically husky and laden with emotion. The transmission was picked up by commercial radio in San Francisco, retransmitted to the War Department, and analyzed by the psychological warfare branch of Army Intelligence as well as Wainwright's family and friends. They were convinced that the voice was not Wainwright's.

No American or Filipino wanted to believe that the entire archipelago had fallen to the Japanese. In Santo Tomás, internees hoped USAFFE commanders elsewhere in the Philippines would disregard the order or that it would be countermanded by MacArthur. But MacArthur no longer had communication with Corregidor. Sharp abided by Wainwright's orders, though thousands of Filipinos left their units in northern, central, and southern Luzon to join American-led guerrilla operations or organize their own. Wainwright and his staff were confined to the University Club at the corner of Dewey Boulevard and South Avenue in Manila. He never saw Corregidor again.

The Japanese interrogated captured American officers throughout the day at their bario San José headquarters. They wanted to know about the rumored tunnel between Bataan and Corregidor, the whereabouts of the Philippine bullion, and the two-year cache of food they had heard about on American radio reports.

"How many airplanes are there on Corregidor?" they asked Major General Moore's operations officer, Colonel William C. Braly.

"If you can find one, you're smarter than we were," he quipped.

The aftermath of battle was gruesome by the light of day. Burial details were organized for the Americans and Filipinos killed in action at shoreline defenses and inland positions. Corpses were piled like sandbags outside Malinta Tunnel, coal-black from decay, bloated to three times their normal size from the tropical heat until they split open like overripe fruit. The stench of putrefying flesh was nauseating. Some were burned at the tunnel's east entrance. Others were removed to Kindley Field, where they were stacked into huge funeral pyres, doused with gasoline, and ignited.

Traditionally the Japanese sent home the ashes of fallen soldiers (*eirei* or "heroic spirits"). One American work detail was organized and ordered to chop off the hands of the dead so they could be returned to the families of the deceased. Leland Bartlett asked his chemical department "to clean up the battlefield and to disinfect the grounds" with chlorinated lime. Meanwhile, he gathered "all the quinine, all the sulfathiazole, all the narcotics" he could from the aid stations.

On the evening of May 7 another request for medical assistance was relayed from the Radio Intercept Tunnel. "Japanese treated us very well in the hospital tunnel and made no effort to hinder us at all," noted George. But it wasn't until 2200 that Murray was able to take an ambulance out to Monkey Point.

On the way there a Japanese soldier stopped him and politely removed his gold wristwatch.

"Thank you," he said in English.

It would have been foolish for Murray to resist. What he wanted to say was, "Take your goddamned hands off of me, you son of a bitch." But it was dark, he was unarmed, and all too easily he could have been another dead American by the side of the road. The watch—a gold Wyler-Incaflex—had been a present from his buddy Charlie Lipsky, and while he regretted its loss, more troubling was his inability to defend himself, being robbed of his authority, stripped of his choice.

"You're welcome," Murray replied.

The casualties in the Radio Intercept Tunnel had been well tended and bedded down by corpsmen Daniel MacDougall and Robert Clark Crawford. Murray tagged them, rendered assistance where necessary, and arranged for their evacuation.

The next day a long line began to snake east from Malinta Tunnel down to the 92nd Garage Area, an old army seaplane station converted into the motor pool of the 92nd Coast Artillery Regiment on the island's South Shore. The Japanese set up a "registration center" where the captives provided name, rank, and serial number. Each man was assigned a number that was painted on the back of his shirt or trousers. Filipinos were separated from Americans, and officers from enlisted men.

Then roughly 12,000 American soldiers, sailors, marines, Philippine Army troops, and civilians from the fortified islands were concentrated in an area 1,500 feet long by 500 feet wide: the concrete apron that enabled seaplanes to land on Corregidor. A sprawling mass of humanity lay broiling in the sun. Temperatures were in the high 90s. Some 800 cases remained in the Malinta Tunnel hospital, but even ambulatory patients were forced to assemble in the 92nd Garage. Men were so cramped for space, they could hardly turn around. For the first three days there was no shelter and little food. Water was stored beneath the concrete seaplane ramp and could be hoisted up by rope and bucket. Shell holes were used for human waste. Flies crawled over bodies and into ears, noses, and mouths while men slept.

Soon order was forged from chaos. Officers and enlisted men were organized into groups of 1,000 under the command of an American colonel, with sub-groups of 100 each. Filipinos were separated from the Americans "by an imaginary line." You were required to salute your captors if you still wore your hat, or bow from the waist if not. Anyone who left the compound unescorted by a Japanese guard, it was threatened, would be shot.

Alton Halbrook saw the consequences of disobeying the Japanese. His friend Jack Kirkland was a big strapping fellow with a handlebar mustache and an eagle tattoo on his chest that spread from shoulder to shoulder. The kind of guy who didn't take orders lightly. Kirkland refused to bow. When several Japanese soldiers approached him for his infraction, he lashed out at them. They struggled with him until they were able to tie his hands behind his back. Then they beat him until Kirkland seemed to get the message. But the Japanese weren't through with him. With his arms still pinned to his back they strung him up by his thumbs and hung him from an A-frame high enough so his feet were just touching the ground. By the time they let him down, Kirkland couldn't move his limbs. The Japanese worked him over again, and all Kirkland could do was charge blindly like a bull. They beat him nearly into unconsciousness. Finally they let him go, but not before breaking both of his arms between the elbow and wrist.

"This was the example that they set for us," said Halbrook. "This guy was a tough Marine. He was the meanest mother going, and they broke him."

Another American soldier was in agony from two broken legs and a mutilated arm. He had refused medical treatment from the Japanese, and attempted, unsuccessfully, to shoot himself. He begged Private John R. Brown, Battery A, 60th Coast Artillery, to end his misery. Brown obliged, and the Japanese soon escorted him down to the beach along with another man from the 803rd Engineers accused of insubordination. The reports of a submachine gun followed. They were never seen again.

The Japanese took what they pleased—watches, wallets, money rolls, college rings, wedding bands, fountain pens, pencils, eyeglasses, even forks from mess kits. Officially the practice was forbidden, but in the first few hours after the surrender, Japanese officers made a point of staying outside the Radio Intercept Tunnel while their enlisted men tried to steal everything of value in it. All of the captives were shaken down, not once but repeatedly. Some Japanese soldiers were literally up to their elbows in wristwatches, and "numerous scuffles" broke out between them over their prized possessions. Aside from watches, they delighted in fountain pens, and to the Americans they seemed just "queer for boots."

They just as quickly raided the Quartermaster lateral, leaving the food they didn't want. They loved sweets, but they couldn't stomach tomatoes, corned beef, or abalone. The Americans were forbidden to take anything without the guards' permission.

Compared to the conduct of the Japanese at the fall of Singapore, in which soldiers from the Malay Brigade seized the Alexandra Hospital and bayoneted to death patients and Royal Army Medical Corps personnel, the occupation of Corregidor was orderly. As one American remarked, "They dreaded coming onto Corregidor as much as we dreaded seeing them." Some had actually served as assault troops in Hong Kong and Singapore. When they entered the headquarters of the 16th Naval District in Tunnel Queen, armed with bayonets and grenades only to encounter no resistance, they became "almost jovial," said Lieutenant Commander Melvyn H. McCoy. But you could never predict their behavior. They had met no resistance at the Alexandra Hospital in Singapore, either, and they turned it into a bloodbath.

The Japanese initiated work details, forcing prisoners to remove food stocks from Malinta Tunnel, dismantle radio transmitters, reconstruct gun positions, repair the island's roads, rebuild the airstrip, and retrieve brass shells that were then shipped back to Japan for scrap. On one detail Corporal Robert E. Haney was collecting shrapnel when he saw something glisten in the red earth: a small human hand dried almost to transparency.

As George described the activities of May 10:

We raked a lot of small branches together for burning and unknowingly raked a lot of unexploded small arms ammunition in too. Some commotion for a few minutes much to the amusement of the Japanese sentry and consternation of Commanding Colonel. Well anyway started the clean up drive.

That same day, the Japanese reenacted the invasion of Corregidor for a propaganda newsreel. They ordered the Americans to fall into two lines with their hands raised while soldiers shouted *"Banzai!"* and bayonets glittered in the sunlight. The newly captured looked authentic enough, "exhausted, dirty and ragged," said 2nd Class Petty Officer

Frank Hoeffer, a former cook for the *Oahu*, except that they were laughing, "which probably didn't look so good on the screen in Tokyo."

The men scavenged for food, clothing, cooking utensils, and firewood. They slipped into Malinta Tunnel, where they stole preserved peaches, and Vienna sausage, and played catch with the canned abalone that the Japanese wouldn't touch. Soon thousands of shelter-halves were pitched side by side in the 92nd Garage like butterflies in the sand. Planks, boards, corrugated iron, and rags were used as shade against the sun. Latrines were dug in the hillsides. Philippine pesos were used as toilet paper. The Americans bathed on their section of beach, but upstream the Filipinos used theirs as an open latrine, causing a stream of sewage to run down the shoreline and leading to an outbreak of diarrhea and dysentery. A system was devised for distributing rations, which the Japanese finally began to supply. Water was chlorinated and doled out from an old well until it could be piped in. There was one spigot for nearly 12,000 men.

They peeled off in twos, threes, or fours. Better to have a buddy stand in line for hours to fill a canteen while you guarded the few things the Japanese hadn't stolen from you. Better to have somebody watch your back as you nosed around for food. Better to have someone who would share his food with you if you came up empty-handed.

Powerless against the Japanese, they now fought a daily battle that brought out the best and worst in human nature. Rank and the privileges it conferred were fast becoming quaint appurtenances. Street-smarts and intuition often triumphed over reason. The victorious won not by vanquishing a common enemy. They won, simply, by circumventing death. The game was survival, and the rules changed during the course of its play. The men had stepped into a limbo of morality, and limbo, of course, was the first circle in Dante's hell.

———

Major Bradley had been in no hurry to leave his position at Wheeler Point on the morning of May 6. A sheer wall of rock separated him from the Japanese above, their guns raised, shouting *"Banzai!"* Enemy planes flew low overhead.

"Let them come and find us," he said to Fred. But the men of the 2nd Battalion were without food, and as the day wore on and the fighting subsided, Bradley agreed to use a white sheet as a flag and march to Bottomside. The Japanese stopped them, shook them down, then allowed them to proceed. Fred managed to hide a watch and a ring in his shoes.

The marines were being steered to the 92nd Garage Area, and Fred began to follow them. A Japanese soldier, seeing his Red Cross brassard, pointed a bayonet at his stomach and motioned toward Malinta. Fred marched to the hospital tunnel.

There he found George, and together they made a campsite near the tunnel entrance, complete with firepit. But it was Murray and John who had a larder of food. The junior medical officers had lifted flour, corned beef, canned fruit, and canned vegetables from an unfinished lateral, almost from under a Japanese sentry's nose.

"You know," said Fred, "I'm a pretty good cook."

Murray remembered the meals Fred had prepared in the Bachelor Officers' Quarters in Cavite after coming back from a day's hunting with Ken Lowman in Bataan. He remembered that he was a damn fine surgeon. And he would never forget that he had saved his life by getting him assigned to the battle aid station in the old paint locker instead of in the Cavite Navy Yard dispensary.

"Should we let him in?" he teasingly asked John.

"Of course we should," John replied.

It was only natural that the four navy doctors should become a team and that the friendship among them would rise from common bonds. George and Fred were midwesterners, Catholic, and had two years' seniority because of their tours in the Far East. John and Murray were New Yorkers, Jewish, graduates of NYU's College of Medicine who saw themselves not as career naval officers but as civilians in the navy. There were differences in upbringing, outlook, and temperament, but their wartime experience—Cavite, Bataan, Corregidor—united them. They had seen men die in the field and in hospital, and in the interests of self-preservation they subscibed to a single ethos: "All for one, one for all." They even had an adopted father, Carey Smith, who at the ripe old age of forty-three had seniority over all of them.

They worked together and ate together, at night they slept together, and they took turns stealing food. None of them had ever stolen before—it would have been inconceivable back home. But they were as far from home as possible, in a situation more foreign than any they could have imagined. Besides, they reasoned, they were merely taking what was rightfully theirs. They knew where the guards were stationed, and they saw how to sneak around them. So they alternated shifts. Murray and John went foraging the first night; Fred and George went the next. They ferreted out food in the darkness, stuffed it into pillow cases, and divided their spoils.

On one occasion, Hayes caught Murray with a stack of flapjacks he had made with flour and a little mineral oil on a hot plate.

"Would you like some?" he asked the regimental surgeon.

Officers and gentlemen didn't comport themselves that way, Hayes replied. He had seen how quickly discipline had broken down after the surrender, how enlisted men ignored authority and officers relinquished it.

Officers and gentlemen, Murray thought, also weren't supposed to be wasting away. He and his buddies had no interest in abdicating their responsibilities as navy medical officers, but they couldn't carry them out if they went hungry. So the hell with protocol, so long as the Japanese didn't catch them. They'd take their chances and risk the consequences.

Down at the 92nd Garage Area they set up an aid station with a rotating service and were joined by some army doctors. There was a line twenty-four hours a day. Men crumpled from heat stroke, their bodies broke out in Guam blisters, and tropical ulcers chewed at their flesh. Malaria resurfaced, and the inequitable distribution of rations led to more cases of malnutrition. The doctors had no medicine for diarrhea and practically no bandages to change dressings. About the only thing they did have was argerol, a mild antiseptic used to treat venereal disease.

After a few days Fred approached Sergeant John David Provoo, who served as an interpreter for the Japanese, and asked to be taken back to Malinta Tunnel. He demanded to see the commanding officer and insisted that the Japanese provide some medication, which they did: aspirin, sulfanilamide, bismuth, and Mercurochrome.

With a little medicine, the navy doctors, said Colonel Cooper, "performed almost impossible feats . . . in their efforts to keep alive the thousands who were suffering from prostration, dysentery, and malnutrition." Stretcher cases were carried up the hill to the Malinta Tunnel hospital. Two of the doctors became the latest admissions: Murray was hospitalized with fever, and George had another bout of amoebic dysentery.

When the rains came, the heat lifted over Corregidor and spirits rose at once. The skies opened like giant sluices, and a chorus of Irving Berlin's "God Bless America" rose spontaneously from the huddled masses in the 92nd Garage Area. But then misfortune assumed another shape.

Colonel Beecher described the scene on the night of May 22, after he returned from a day of interrogations by Japanese officials:

It was like plunging into a swimming pool. We slid and slipped down to the road in the Stygian darkness, cursing our luck and getting soaked to the skin. We found the camp a morass; as many as could had taken shelter in the wrecked buildings of the 92nd Garage; our pitiful shelters of blankets and shelter halves afforded no protection—we and our few salvaged possessions were drenched.

All night long we stood or sat in misery, wet and cold. With dawn the rain ceased and a bright sun revived our drooping spirits. A rumor had been circulated through the camp during the night

that we were to move the next morning. About 8:00 o'clock the rumor was proved correct, we were ordered to leave the area by 9:00
that morning.

Saturday, May 23, was a soggy, gray morning. Hayes ordered Fred
and John to the 92nd Garage with a group of twenty-five corpsmen,
where they took their place at the end of a long line of POWs. By 0900 a
column began marching up a steep hillside path on the way to the South
Dock. The sky soon cleared, and by afternoon the sun beat down relentlessly as they waited for hours in an old rock quarry. The prisoners were
under guard, and launches shuttled them in groups of forty out to three
Japanese naval transports that had anchored in San José Bay. The loading
continued until darkness began to fall, when inexplicably the Japanese
ordered the medical contingent back to Malinta Tunnel. By then nearly
12,000 men had been packed onto three vermin-infested vessels 5,000
to 8,000 tons in size.

It was raining up on deck but stifling in the hold. The men spent the
night "in the most suffocating condition imaginable," said Major
Stephen Mellnik. There was no food, no medical care, and no relief for
the dysentery patients. On the morning of the twenty-fourth they sailed
across Manila Bay and dropped anchor south of Manila, several miles off
Parañaque. Landing barges went out to meet them, gangways and Jacob's
ladders were lowered, and the captives were crowded into the boats in
groups of roughly 100. But the barges stopped short of the Manila
shoreline in about four feet of water. Men tied their shoes around their
necks, held their belongings over their heads, and slogged the rest of the
way through the surf.

Once on land, they were paraded north on Dewey Boulevard toward
Manila in columns of 4 and groups of 1,000. They were wet, and their
feet blistered horribly. It was a calculated attempt to publicly humiliate
those captured on Corregidor. The invincible Japanese had liberated the
poor Filipinos from the arrogant Americans. They kept their prisoners in
line with mounted cavalrymen and soldiers, who prodded stragglers with
bayonets or whacked them with rifle butts. The Filipino citizenry were
not so easily cowed. Some flashed V for Victory signs; others sneaked the
bedraggled men food, cigarettes, and candy, at the risk of being slapped
or beaten. Garden hoses were stretched across Dewey Boulevard at the
Admiral Apartments so a lucky few could could rehydrate themselves, after which they continued on past Intramuros, east around the Metropolitan Theatre, across Quezon Bridge, and onto Quezon Boulevard
before entering Bilibid Prison.

May Harries, an American on a sick pass from Santo Tomás Internment Camp, watched the procession:

> From twelve o'clock that noon until six I watched what the Jap
> newspapers called the "March of Humiliation"; watched my coun-
> trymen, ragged and barefoot, weary and defeated. . . . But it was
> mistaken propaganda on the part of the Japs, for the Filipinos
> watched with sympathy and tears for the defeated . . . not cheers
> for the victors.

Back on Corregidor, Fred and John had no idea where the others had
been taken, and no idea why they had been held back. The uncertainty
was unnerving. There were rumors that they were moving to Topside,
being transferred to Manila, even repatriated to the United States!

"Absolutely impossible to discover our destiny," wrote George, who
was tired of being cooped up in Malinta Tunnel.

31st May 1942
I would give anything to get established in some sort of a normal life
again but guess this mass living is compulsory. It really gets annoying
to have every smallest action witnessed and even questioned by a
few. . . . Allowed no one to go outside tunnel from 6 PM to 10 PM.
Got slapped by an officer on 29th for not snapping to attention faster.

They were also wearying of the daily diet, which had fallen under
2,000 calories. The "seconds racket" had become increasingly difficult.
Corned beef hash and rice were the bulk of the day's chow. George was
delighted by the arrival of cracked wheat, which came in sacks emblazoned with a Red Cross and the words "a gift of the American people."
The sacks must have been intended for China before they were seized by
the Japanese in Manila. Rich in thiamin and niacin, the cereal was teem-
ing with weevils, but the men wolfed it down in a thin porridge for
breakfast and sometimes for dinner as well. Fred thought it was fine so
long as you ate it in the dark. Consider the bugs protein, he told himself.
Roast it, and you could brew coffee. It was amazing how quickly tea and
canned tomatoes could seem like haute cuisine.

Captain Burton C. Thompson of the U.S. Army Veterinary Corps,
whom Fred knew from his periodic inspections out at Wheeler Point,
was mess officer at the Malinta Tunnel hospital. Thompson stockpiled
food to distribute to the wounded. One afternoon, Private Halbrook
found several cases of peaches and brought them out of the tunnel. That

evening Sergeant John David Provoo asked a navy corpsman if Thompson could get him some dessert for the Japanese officers.

Provoo was a former G-2 clerk for the army in Manila. He had lived with a Japanese family in California, became fluent in the language, and in 1940 visited Japan to be ordained a Buddhist priest. Provoo had once been considered for counterintelligence in the Philippines, but the Army Counter Intelligence Corps rejected him on grounds of suspected homosexuality and sympathizing with the Japanese. After the surrender, Provoo shaved his head and took to wearing a kimono.

Thompson told the corpsman that Provoo could go to hell. As Fred was sitting down to his evening meal in the hospital mess, he saw two Japanese soldiers march past him. Within minutes they returned with rifles fixed and bayonets pointed at Thompson's back. He was quickly tried, sentenced, and tied up by the hands and feet. Corporal Everett R. Waldrum drove a Japanese corporal and several soldiers out to Monkey Point, where Thompson was shot five times in the head. The next morning Halbrook went out to the execution site with the Japanese officer of the day to bury Thompson. By the time Halbrook returned to Topside, the Japanese had already broken into Thompson's footlocker. The officer grinned as he stepped into Thompson's boots while wearing his own shoes. Afterward Hayes called the navy doctors in for a conference to stress the importance of caution in dealing with the Japanese. But Hayes was missing a crucial point: Thompson had been betrayed by an American.

On June 25 the army nurses and some 200 patients in the Malinta Tunnel hospital were moved to Topside. The old Fort Mills Station Hospital was in the process of being restored. Its roof was blown off and its walls were blown out, but the center of the cross was partly intact. Shell holes had been repaired, and more than a dozen unexploded shells had been removed. Fred was ordered to transfer medical equipment and supplies from the Malinta Tunnel hospital.

Life at Topside was a pleasant break for the medical staff, "1,000 percent better than that damn tunnel," noted George. "I don't see how the Army Medical Corps stood it for 6 mos. Glad I'm in the Navy Medical Corps and lived outside."

Colonel Cooper agreed. "A holiday atmosphere prevailed. We had an 'it's good to be alive' air about us." They had a radio as well, and a pledge from the Japanese commandant that no soldiers would be allowed to enter the hospital without prior authorization. Anna Williams, an army nurse, helped decorate the compound with fresh-cut gardenias. On one visit the Japanese commandant made the extraordinary gesture of presenting the staff with "a large iced cake of which he was very proud, some small cakes and some beer."

As well-intentioned as he may have been, the level of medical knowledge among his doctors quickly raised eyebrows. After the fall of Corregidor, the Japanese had set up a whorehouse in Middleside. One Japanese doctor demanded a vaginal speculum so he could examine the "comfort women" for venereal disease. None was to be found, though some joker turned up a nasal speculum from a veterinary medical kit intended for a horse—to the Japanese doctor's delight and the amusement of the Americans.

Their holiday at Topside was short-lived. One week later Colonel Cooper was ordered to evacuate the old Fort Mills Station Hospital. Almost the entire navy contingent—fifteen medical officers, five dental officers, one pharmacist, forty-seven corpsmen, and two chaplains—and all of the American and Filipino Army nurses were to be transferred to Manila. Hayes summoned the navy doctors.

"All right, now who's the junior medical officer here?" Hayes asked.

He knows damn well who the junior medical officer is, Murray thought. Was then, am now, always will be, at least in this group. Hayes's name took on another meaning entirely. Murray began to feel like the perennial freshman whose fraternity hadn't quite finished "hazing" him, as if the command to go behind enemy lines at Monkey Point hadn't been test enough.

"I am," he said.

Murray was ordered to remain at the station hospital on ward duty, along with Army Captain Thomas Hewlett and navy corpsman Loren E. Stamp. They were responsible for the 200 men who were held in a camp down at Bottomside and were used for salvage and work details. George, Fred, and John were to secure as much medical equipment as possible and arrange for the transfer of 280 patients to Manila.

On July 2 the 7,000-ton *Lima Maru* anchored in the North Channel off Bottomside. Fred enlisted a group of Filipinos to help move medical equipment out onto a small boat, then carry it—an X-ray machine, an operating table, an autoclave, instruments, water sterilizers, and a complete dental outfit—up an old plank used as a gangway. Nonambulatory patients were taken aboard by stretcher. Once in the forward hold, Fred could tell immediately what the vessel had been used for: cavalry. It was hot, stank of manure, and then men were packed in "like sardines," said George. They spent a restless night on the *Lima Maru*. George finally fell asleep up on the steel deck, curled around a capstan.

In the morning fifty-seven American army nurses and thirty-one Filipina nurses along with seven Filipina women boarded the *Lima Maru*, bringing the total number of passengers, including refugees, Chinese cooks, and others, to 1,277. It was early afternoon by the time the ship pulled into Pier 3 in Manila. Some of the nurses had been given tea and rice cakes during the voyage by "a nice Jap," as army nurse Madeline Ullom put it. Otherwise the only food they were issued since leaving Corregidor was a can of salmon apiece.

The city was eerily quiet. All but the smallest shops were closed. The American nurses were taken by bus to Santo Tomás Internment Camp. The nonambulatory patients and the Filipina nurses were driven to nearby Bilibid Prison, where the women were separated from the men by a fourteen-foot-high wall. Those who could walk followed on foot.

It was strange to see Japanese flags flying over familiar landmarks such as the High Commissioner's residence, where General Homma now had his headquarters. Occasionally a Filipino flashed a V for Victory sign or tried to slip one of the men some food. At 1500 they arrived at Bilibid, "a sweaty, tired and squalid gang," said Hayes. George felt like he had stepped into "a dirty filthy mess of humanity."

To their families, friends, and loved ones, their whereabouts may have been unknown, their status in limbo. But to the Japanese they were *horyo*—prisoners of war.

14

Horyo

As THEY FILED THROUGH the massive iron gates of Bilibid, they carried with them their personal belongings, the medical supplies they could manage, and the images conjured up by prison: of a one-room jail, a municipal cell block, a state penitentiary. Fleeting notions assembled from a glimpse of Rikers Island, the Chicago jail, or the U.S. Federal Penitentiary in Leavenworth, Kansas. Pictures of suffering from Sunday school sermons, stained-glass windows, Dumas, Dostoevsky, and Malraux. They carried with them their individual visions of hell as surely as schoolboys were haunted, Wordsworth wrote, by "shades of the prison-house." But nothing could have prepared them for Bilibid.

Bilibid looked like something out of the late eighteenth century, a decrepit version of the all-seeing Panopticon that the English utilitarian philosopher Jeremy Bentham had envisioned as a model prison. The name means "to wind round, to coil up," or "to be bound" in Tagalog. The original structure was built under Spanish sovereignty in 1865 and housed Filipino criminals as well as political prisoners. The rebel leader Emilio Aguinaldo had been held there in chains. In the early twentieth century the Americans reconfigured Bilibid as a radial prison, and by 1924 Ramon Victorio, director of the Bureau of Prisons in the Philippines, could assert in a lecture before the American Prison Congress in Salt Lake City: "I sincerely believe that the standard of civilization and culture of a people is measured not only by the sum total of its material wealth but also by the character of its penitentiary institutions." Bilibid, he said with pride, was "one of the best public edifices" in Manila. It had survived seismological shocks and weathered floods. It also occupied seventeen acres of prime real estate in the heart of the city. By 1939 most of Bilibid's inmates were transferred to New Bilibid Prison in Muntinglupa, and the old facility fell into ill repair.

Like the spokes in a wheel, eighteen one-story buildings roughly 20 feet by 120 feet radiated out from a low central guard tower, creating a circle of surveillance. Nine of the buildings were occupied by the Americans and used as hospital wards. The windows were open, barred, and shaded with hinged shutters. In the so-called outer compound was the Old Back Building, an unfinished three-story structure without plumbing that served as a holding pen for POWs in transit. Bilibid was enclosed with a whitewashed brick wall fourteen feet high, capped with an 1,800-volt electrified wire. Sentries were posted at each corner. The effect of the Panopticon's design, as Bentham had written, was "to induce in the inmate a state of conscious and permanent visibility that assures the automatic functioning of power."

Captain Robert G. Davis, director of the old Cañacao Naval Hospital unit, no doubt intended to carry out the last order he received from Rear Admiral Rockwell, before headquarters of the 16th Naval District was moved to Corregidor on December 21, 1941. But maintaining a naval hospital in the Manila area proved to be more pipe dream than possibility. Since their capture in Manila on January 2, 1942, Davis and his staff could do little at Santa Scholastica as Japanese guards as well as doctors systematically stripped the hospital annex of quinine, cots, tables, chairs, clocks, cars, and trucks. Over the next few months detachments of doctors, corpsmen, and patients were transferred to the POW camp at Pasay Elementary School in Rizal. By May 9 the evacuation of Santa Scholastica was nearly complete.

Five hundred men were crowded into an eighteen-room schoolhouse in Pasay that had a one-room dispensary. After the Japanese robbed Davis of the icebox he used to refrigerate vaccines, he tried keeping them cool by burying them in the ground. The problem was the heat. One evening the temperature hovered around 100 degrees an hour after sunset.

When some 300 POWs from Camp O'Donnell landed at Davis's doorstep on May 23 suffering from malaria and beriberi, "weary, undernourished . . . some abused," they found a hospital unit without equipment and doctors with only meager amounts of medicine. "The Japanese suggested that if any patients were near death we might help them along," Davis smoldered. "Think of that for humanity."

One week later the Cañacao group was transferred to Bilibid, where 8,000 POWs from Corregidor had been funneled into a facility with a maximum capacity of 5,200. Most of the men captured on the Rock were shipped out to the prison camp at Cabanatuan in central Luzon within a few days. The sick remained behind in Bilibid. Their care, said Captain Kusamoto, director of the hospital, would fall to the navy doctors.

The top brass were dispatched to a POW officers' camp in Tarlac, eighty-five miles north of Manila, en route to Karenko in Formosa.

Davis departed Bilibid on June 3. Wainwright would soon follow and be reunited with Generals Moore, King, Parker, Jones, and Beebe. "Anything," said Davis with a sigh of relief, "will be better than Bilibid." Before leaving, he appointed Commander Lea B. Sartin chief medical officer. Commander Maurice Joses was executive officer, and navy corpsman Edward F. Haase, who spoke Japanese, served as camp interpreter.

Prison conditions at Bilibid were appalling. Guards shouted commands and waved bayonets for men to fall in line in groups of fifty. They stole whatever "souvenirs" hadn't already been filched from them on the Rock. Dinner was a tin of watery rice. POWs were pressed into quarters where they slept on concrete floors. Plumbing and electrical fixtures had been ripped out, the roofs leaked, and the windows were unscreened. There was one shower, one three-quarter-inch pipe that supplied water, and a ninety-foot-long latrine that pulsed with maggots and oozed into an open cesspool 200 feet from the galley. In the dry season it stank like a city zoo, and in the rainy season the grounds flooded with two to three feet of water. The old chapel was used as a temporary infectious diseases ward, but it had no water or toilets. Dysentery cases lay covered with Guam blisters. Bilibid was more like a charnel house than a prison. The Japanese euphemistically called it an "accommodating place."

Sartin's men could have despaired when they saw patients splayed on cell block floors, too weak to move, lying in their own excrement. They could have been overwhelmed by the masses of men, many of them malnourished, who slept outside without beds or blankets and with only a foot of space between them. Instead, they turned this field of misery into a functioning hospital.

The navy corpsmen got to work quickly, tearing their undershirts into washrags, cleaning, scrubbing, and disinfecting. Electricity was installed, commodes with flush tanks were built, and showers were erected. They covered the cesspool, drained it into the city sewer system, and fabricated a Japanese-style straddle trench as a *benjo* (toilet). They constructed a wood-fired incinerator as diagrammed in the *Handbook of the Hospital Corps* so they could dispose of waste and reduce the swarms of flies. They even concocted a primitive refrigeration device they called a "coolator"—a wooden frame draped in gunny sacking that was kept wet to help preserve meat for the camp soup. With materials from existing structures, they built examination and dressing tables, benches, and wooden platforms for beds.

The hospital was located in the lower half of Bilibid. Separate facilities were designated for a surgical ward, a dispensary and outpatient service, a pharmacy, as well as a dental ward, a dressing room, and an X-ray room. The infectious diseases unit was situated in the upper-right corner of the compound, near the cemetery. Officers had quarters distinct from hospital corpsmen; there was even a separate Sick Officers' Quarters. A commissary was set up behind Building 4 under the supervision of Navy Pay Clerk C. A. Hanson. Coffee, sugar, peanuts, tobacco, canned salmon, sardines, bananas, and mongo beans were made available by a Japanese merchant named Uemura. Prisoners could draw against accounts, and a 10 percent "profit" was charged to all sales for the benefit of the Indigent Sick Fund. Bilibid's patient census would average 700.

Sartin now had his hospital organization in place, but it was like a house without furniture, a medicine chest minus pills. The army medical officers and corpsmen who arrived from Hospital No. 1 on Bataan on June 19 had been told by the Japanese that they were being transferred to "a first-class, well-equipped" medical center. They left a modestly stocked facility behind, only to walk into the shell of one with hundreds of patients suffering from malaria, dysentery, and diarrhea or recovering from wounds, fractures, and amputations. They had little in the way of medicine or supplies.

The second wave of navy doctors and corpsmen who arrived from Corregidor on July 2 were a blessing. George, Fred, and John brought urgently needed drugs and dressings. The equipment they assiduously loaded onto the *Lisbon Maru* was stacked outside Bilibid's gates, awaiting inspection. But some of the most important medicines—quinine sulfate for malaria, emetine hydrochloride, carbarsone, and bismuth for dysentery—remained in short supply. And there was one crucial item that was absent entirely: a microscope.

In spite of the hard work Sartin's men had put into Bilibid over the previous month, it was a shock to the new arrivals from Corregidor. "Here are piled and crowded into dingy barred prison barracks all the wrecks and human flotsam and jetsam of Bataan and Corregidor," wrote Hayes. But sanitation was greatly improved, the hospital galley functioned smoothly, and once the operating room was outfitted with equipment from Corregidor, the navy doctors were ready for their assignments.

Hayes was made chief of surgery. Fred was assigned to the Sick Officers' Quarters, George fit right in with orthopedics, and John worked in the infectious diseases ward. What amazed the men was the comparatively small number of casualties resulting from the defense of Corregidor. The incidence of medical cases was another matter. The responsibilities that the navy doctors had assumed were daunting, but unlike other POWs who were assigned to work details, they had the chance to practice the profession for which they had been trained, a goal toward which they could work, a purpose to their days. Sartin requested scrolls of supplies on a weekly basis, and on a weekly basis his requests were denied. But you couldn't focus on what was missing. You made do with what you had, even if what you had was rarely enough. The one thing you couldn't afford to lose was hope.

Bilibid became the primary POW hospital in the Philippines and a transit facility for prisoners en route to other camps in the archipelago or in the Japanese Home Islands. There were a total of 30 POW camps in the Philippines and 170 in Japan. Officially, it was known as the United States Naval Hospital Unit, Bilibid Prison, P.I., until the Japanese decided that the reference to the United States was inappropriate and renamed it the Bilibid Hospital for Military Prison Camps of the P.I. Senior medical officers acted as camp administrators, and the chief medical officer served as the liaison with the Japanese. That was Sartin, the "Old Man," the moniker traditionally given the commanding officer of navy ships and stations.

Small, thin, in his early fifties, with a paternal manner that some mistook as meekness, Sartin lost no time in presenting Nogi Naraji with a copy of the 1929 Geneva Convention Relative to the Treatment of Prisoners of War.

Nogi was a captain in the Medical Corps of the Imperial Japanese Army. Broad shouldered and smooth complexioned, he was more Mandarin-looking than Japanese. He was just thirty years old in August 1942, when he assumed the position of staff medical officer of the War Prisoner Headquarters, located in Manila's University Club.

Nogi was ultimately responsible for medical supply and medical care at Bilibid, Cabanatuan, Pasay Elementary School, Baguio, Los Baños, and later Davao and Santo Tomás. He took his orders first from Major General Morimoto Iichirō of the 14th Army, commandant of the prisoner of war camps in the Philippines, and then from Lieutenant General Kou Shiyoku. His colleague, 1st Lieutenant Momota, was in charge of food, clothing, and daily necessities.

Immaculately dressed in an open-necked white shirt beneath a tropical-weight khaki jacket and matching khaki pants tucked into high black boots, Nogi had an obvious fondness for Western culture. He was nearly fluent in English and had read Marx, Tolstoy, Ibsen, and Gorky. Several of the POW doctors with whom Nogi interacted, army as well as navy, found him initially compassionate and responsive to their needs.

Captain Kusamoto, whom Nogi relieved as director of the hospital at Bilibid Prison, had been anything but. On an inspection tour, Kusamoto asked Chief Machinist George B. Gooding, the American camp warden, if Commander Sartin was the senior American officer. Indeed he was, said Gooding of Cañacao's former chief of medicine. Whereupon

Kusamoto turned to Sartin and said: "All right, you are responsible for the prison, and if anyone escapes, your head comes off."

The 1929 Geneva Convention Relative to the Treatment of Prisoners of War was derived from the Geneva Convention of 1864 for the Amelioration of the Condition of the Wounded and Sick of Armies in the Field. The Geneva Convention was revised in the aftermath of World War I as an international covenant to guarantee food, clothing, shelter, proper sanitation, and humane treatment for prisoners of war. Most countries and their dependencies signed the Geneva Convention; not all of them ratified it.

According to the Geneva Convention, a belligerent power's first obligation was to create a prisoner of war bureau that could quickly advise families of the whereabouts and addresses of their relatives. In Japan, this was known as the Horyo Jōhōkyoku, or Prisoner of War Information Bureau, which was established between December 1941 and March 1942 under General Uemura Seitaro as part of the Military Affairs Bureau of the Ministry of War in Tōkyō. For the approximately 324,000 Allied POWs and civilian internees held in Japan and Japanese-occupied territories, the Horyo Jōhōkyoku had a staff of twenty-six, including office boys. The Horyo Jōhōkyoku was in charge of maintaining records of individual POWs. Imperial GHQ was ultimately responsible for POW camp operations.

The Geneva Convention stipulated that prisoners were "subject to the laws, regulations, and orders in force in the armies of the detaining power." But the "detaining power" was expressly forbidden to use prisoners in work that was directly related to "war operations" or that was "unhealthful or dangerous." Attempted escape—even if repeated—was considered a disciplinary crime, and as such, the most severe punishment could not exceed thirty days. In the event of a judicial proceeding, the "detaining power" was obligated to inform the representative of the "protecting power" immediately. Should a trial result in a death penalty sentence, the "protecting power" was to be notified of the charges and the "circumstances of the offense" at least three months in advance of the execution of the sentence. Switzerland became the protecting power for the United States in Japan. The International Committee of the Red Cross functioned as "a service agency" that acted "for the benefit of prisoners."

Japan had its own regulations for the treatment of prisoners of war dating back to February 1904, when Army Instruction No. 22 was issued during the Russo-Japanese War. This was to accommodate terms of the Laws and Customs of War on Land of 1899, a precursor to the Hague

Convention. Article 2 unequivocally stated that "prisoners of war shall be treated with a spirit of goodwill and shall never be subjected to cruelties or humiliation." The rules were revised in 1905, 1909, 1914, and on December 23, 1941, "to meet the requirements of the present war."

By and large Japan's treatment of some 79,367 POWs during the Russo-Japanese War was humane, efficient, and with the help of the Japan Red Cross Society, particularly responsive to the sick and wounded. This stood in marked contrast to the brutality exercised by the Americans toward Filipino civilians during the Philippine-American War and to the fate of Boer refugees under the British, who were consigned by Lord Milner, high commissioner for South Africa, to the world's first concentration camps during the Boer War.

Prisoners of the Japanese were required "to conform to the discipline and regulations of the Imperial Army." The Japanese, in turn, were expected to respect the dignity of the captured officer, his health, and his well-being. Individual army commanders had considerable discretionary powers. POWs were allowed to keep their personal belongings, or they could be "held in deposit" and returned on the cessation of hostilities. Enemy officers were even permitted "to carry their own swords." Article 11 was unusually accommodating. The sick and wounded could be returned or exchanged so long as they swore on oath "not to take part in combat during the remainder of the same war."

While POWs were never to be subjected to "cruelties or humiliation," punishments were harsh. Article 6 stipulated that escapees could be stopped "by armed force and if necessary killed or wounded." The Japanese prescribed a separate standard of court-martial for POWs, whereas the Geneva Convention insisted that the process conform to the prevailing military practice. There was no due process, just as in the Meiji constitution there was no guarantee of basic human rights.

During World War I Japan captured 4,269 Germans in Tsingtao, China; they may have been treated well, but Japan's policy toward prisoners of war was about to undergo a profound change. In March 1920 Russian partisans demanded that the Japanese garrison in Nikolaevsk, at the mouth of the Amur River, disarm. The Japanese attacked instead. On orders from their brigade, the Japanese then laid down their weapons, only to be imprisoned and massacred within months. This marked a turning point in Japanese attitudes toward surrender. By 1941 the doctrine of "no surrender" was codified in the *Senjinkun*. If a Japanese soldier would choose death over capture, how could he be expected to respect enemy prisoners of war? Human life, as Japan made clear in its neocolonial exploits in Korea, Formosa, and China—indeed, within the ranks of its own military—was cheap.

Japan was a party to the Fourth Hague Convention of 1907, the Versailles Treaty (whose Article 171 prohibited the use of poison gas), and the Red Cross Convention of 1929. Although it signed the 1929 Geneva Convention, it refused to ratify it. Whether this was because the "no surrender" doctrine prevented the Japanese from becoming POWs themselves and therefore placed a unilateral obligation on Japan; or because the Geneva Convention called for unmonitored meetings between POWs and representatives of a neutral power, which were considered potential security risks; or because Japan recognized that its standard of living was so far below that of the United States and England that there would be an unbridgeable gap between the subsistence provided to POWs by the "detaining power" compared to that of the "protecting power," remains unclear.

But disdain for international law and the humane treatment of prisoners of war emanated from no less an authority than the emperor himself. Japan was in gross violation of both the Fourth Hague Convention and the Versailles Treaty before World War II even began. Hirohito failed to condemn the barbarities committed by the Imperial Japanese Army in the Rape of Nanking. He authorized the use of poison gas in July 1937 for mopping-up operations in the Peking-Tientsin area, and he approved the North China Area Army's annihilation tactics referred to as *sankō sakusen* ("burn all, kill all, steal all") against Chinese Communist guerrillas. He stood by as the Japanese Navy Air Force indiscriminately bombed Chungking in May 1938, causing 5,000 noncombatant deaths, and he sanctioned the use of bacteriological weapons by Unit 731 of the Kwantung Army against China in 1940.

In December 1941 the Swiss legation in Tōkyō representing the United States, the Argentine chargé d'affaires speaking for the British Commonwealth, and the Swiss legation on behalf of South Africa began to pressure the Japanese government to abide by the articles of the Geneva Convention. On February 4, 1942, Foreign Minister Tōgō Shigenori advised the Allies that "first: Japan is strictly observing the Geneva Red Cross Convention as a signatory state; second: although not bound by the Convention relative [to the] treatment of prisoners of war, Japan will apply *mutatis mutandis* provisions of that Convention to American prisoners of war in its power." Less than a month later, the POW Maintenance Regulation was issued, which stated that prisoners of the Japanese were to receive rations comparable to those given Japanese officers and enlisted men, which amounted to 420 grams of rice per day and 640 grams for heavy labor. Supply and enforcement were separate matters.

Army Minister Tōjō Hideki was far less sympathetic to the plight of

POWs even though he knew of the atrocities committed against Fil-American captives after the fall of Bataan. In late April 1942 Tōjō chaired a meeting of War Department section chiefs to address the POW issue. Lieutenant General Murakami Mikio, head of the Prisoner of War Information Bureau, urged that the Geneva Convention be observed. Tōjō disagreed. If the Greater East Asian War was intended to liberate Asia, he argued, Japan's superiority must also be impressed upon the newly emancipated. Not only were "all prisoners of war to engage in forced labor"—officers and enlisted men alike—but their humiliation would be carried out in full public view. Insubordination or attempted escapes were punishable by death. Instructions to this effect were formulated in early May 1942 and emphasized repeatedly by Tōjō in his discussions with camp officers in Japan, Korea, Formosa, and Southeast Asia.

In early August 1942, the very month that Homma Masaharu was relieved of his command of the 14th Army and recalled to Tōkyō, it was General Murakami's turn to chair a conference on the POW question. Some fifty camp commandants were in attendance. The fair treatment of prisoners of war, he countered, would enhance Japan's reputation abroad. POWs were to be separated by nationality, they would be paid, they would be able to wear insignia designating rank, and they would work once they swore their obedience. These instructions were issued on August 15, but they didn't go into effect until a full year later. Many commandants felt no obligation to comply.

Meanwhile, alarmed at the number of POW deaths during the building of the Siam-Burma Railway (which began in July 1942), Murakami sent an order to all commandants to ensure improved treatment of prisoners of war. Murakami's jurisdiction extended to Japan, Korea, Manchuria, Formosa, and occupied China, which were considered war zones, not Southeast Asia. Compliance remained a problem. Elsewhere, camp commanders were required to submit detailed monthly reports. But in some cases an entire year elapsed before the Horyo Jōhōkyoku in Tōkyō finally received them.

In the Philippines, however, captives of the Japanese were officially granted POW status as of August 1942. Under the terms of the Geneva Convention, this entitled them to monthly pay commensurate with their rank—minus a few deductions. A first lieutenant received 85 pesos in Japanese occupation currency—printed in English—less 60 pesos for room and board, minus 5 pesos for "compulsory savings deposit" for a net total of 20 pesos in cash each month. Perhaps Nogi said it best when he told Sartin that Bilibid Prison would indeed operate in accordance with the articles of the Geneva Convention—"as interpreted by the Imperial Japanese Army."

Captivity did not put an end to interservice rivalry. The army proposed that Bilibid have a joint army-navy command. Sartin rejected the idea. Five army medical officers, two army chaplains, and two enlisted men were already on Bilibid's staff. The old Cañacao group numbered more than 100, they'd worked well together as a unit for six months, and Sartin felt that navy corpsmen were in general better trained than their army counterparts. "The best possible care," he believed, was assured by "continuity of team work." Besides, there were disturbing reports that the army corpsmen who had arrived at Bilibid from Hospital No. 2 on May 27 were selling medicine at black market prices. "The Army doctors condone this action," Carter Simpson noted in his diary entry of that date. "In a case like this a court martial is too good."

The army, Hayes bitterly recalled, had treated the navy men like dirt on the Rock: "We will never forget we were denied quarters with Army officers and were made to sleep in the toilet." Colonel James Duckworth was the embodiment of Hayes's grievance. He arrived at Bilibid like an English viceroy in India, with a valet, an administrative assistant, and twenty pieces of luggage in tow. The navy doctors from Bataan and Corregidor would also never forget that the old Cañacao group had—Rockwell's order notwithstanding—sat out the war and were in far better physical condition as a result. Still, it was good to be back in the navy fold.

A partition ran down the center of Cell Block No. 3, which separated the junior from the senior officers, and it was there that George, Fred, and John had their quarters. Gordon Lambert, who had come to Bilibid from Pasay with the Cañacao unit on May 30, 1942, was already at home there and had built a wooden bunk for Fred about a foot or so off the ground, on top of which lay a thin mattress that could be rolled back so the bed could double as a table. Gordon briefed Fred on life at Bilibid, which was as different from the situation on Corregidor as Santa Scholastica College was from Pasay Elementary School. George was delighted that Father Cummings was in the same cell block with him.

Like Pavlov's dogs, the men learned the day's routine by the ringing of bells. At 0630 seven bells announced reveille. Ten minutes later six bells meant *tenko*—the Japanese roll call—and at 0730 two bells signaled breakfast. One bell at 0830 heralded the beginning of work, two bells at 1200 spelled lunch, one bell at 1400 indicated the end of the rest period, and one bell at 1700 marked the end of the work day—but not the end of the bells. Supper was served at 1730, to the tune of one bell, followed by six bells at 1830 for evening *bangō* (count-off) at 1840. Finally four bells at 2100 turned off the lights, and an encore of three bells at 2200 warned that no one was allowed outside except authorized personnel. If, by that time, you weren't suffering from tinnitus, you were allowed to go to bed. Or as Hayes put it in a rare moment of levity, "To sweat and boil and stew and then perhaps—to sleep."

The Japanese were obsessed with *bangō*, which could eat up to four hours out of your day if there was a miscount. They busied themselves with paperwork and affected to abide by regulations with barely a pause before punishing those who violated them. They periodically posted rules, but what other guidelines did the POWs have? There was nothing in the officers' training that prepared them for imprisonment, and nothing in the *Handbook of the Hospital Corps*. Fred and John, like many prisoners, refused to speak Japanese in protest, but they made sure they understood their orders: *Ki o tsuke!* (attention). *Keirei!* (salute). *Atsumare!* (line up). *Mae susume!* (quick march). *Tomare!* (halt). *Yasume!* (at ease). Misinterpretations triggered violent repercussions. The message was clear: keep your nose clean, your ass covered, when a guard walks by, bow at the waist or risk getting whacked in the face.

Men were dying almost daily at Bilibid—of dysentery, malaria, and beriberi. With the cemetery beneath the north wall often under three feet of water, ID tags for the deceased were preserved in small glass bottles. The most pressing problem was malnutrition. There were three meals daily: "Rice, rice, and more rice," as George put it. The rice itself was "in poor condition," noted Pharmacist Clarence Shearer, formerly in charge of the naval medical supply depot at Cañacao, "dirty, moldy and full of weevils and worms." It was peppered with rat droppings, cooked in five-gallon gasoline cans over an open-pit fire, and ladled out in canteen-cup servings as *lugao*, a watery gruel with the consistency of oatmeal. Occasionally *lugao* was supplemented with a thin soup flavored with small pieces of meat, vegetables—usually *kangkong*, a weed from the mudflats of the Pasig River that was used as filler in swine swill—or fish. Once the Japanese brought into the POW galley the skeleton of a large tuna. Sartin took the carcass to the Japanese quartermaster to suggest that a mistake had been made. There was no error, he was told; of such stuff was delicious broth made. The POWs buried the bones instead.

In June alone Sartin appealed three times to Captain Kusamoto for "proper diets for the sick." Eggplant and tomatoes were delivered rotten and swarming with maggots. "There is so much that could be done for these very sick and injured patients if only supplies, equipment and food were available," lamented Shearer. Between them, George, Fred, and John had smuggled enough corned beef, tomatoes, evaporated and condensed milk, Vienna sausage, and flour from Corregidor in July to get by in Bilibid for a month. After that they relied on the pesos Fred had "borrowed" in Olongapo and the pittance that remained of their monthly pay to purchase eggs, papayas, bananas, evaporated milk, lemons, limes, and occasionally even meat when the prison commissary stocked them.

"You are unfortunate in being the prisoners of a country whose living standards are so very much lower than yours," Hayes was warned by an American-educated Japanese officer on Corregidor. "You will consider yourselves ill-treated when they think you are being treated swell."

News of the war reached the navy doctors from a steady influx of patients—POWs who had been captured on Bataan, imprisoned in O'Donnell, Cabanatuan, Pasay, Lipa, or Palawan, or assigned to work details in the Port Area, at Clark and Nielson Fields, and in Batangas. They heard of the horrific march prisoners had been forced to make from Mariveles to San Fernando. They learned of the hellish work detail in Tayabas Province, where POWs, tormented by clouds of mosquitoes and clusters of leeches, tried to hack a road out of nearly impenetrable jungle.

Tayabas, wrote Paul Russell in his survey of the Philippines in 1931, was one of the most malarious regions in the entire archipelago. The prisoners spent their nights along a polluted river southeast of Manila near Lamon Bay and were ravaged by the disease. Six weeks after the project began, 150 out of 235 POWs were dead. Those who survived were brought back to Bilibid caked in feces, exhausted, dehydrated, and deformed by starvation "as though they were little old men," said Captain Paul Ashton, an army doctor who was so sick in Tayabas that his friends didn't think he would recover.

Corporal Paul W. Reuter of the 19th Bomb Group was another survivor who arrived in Bilibid on July 1 swollen to the waist with wet beriberi, "covered with scabies," and suffering from dengue, pellagra, scurvy, and jaundice. Then he developed anemia. Lieutenant Commander George P. Hogshire coated him with sulfur paste for scabies and gave him atabrine for jaundice. Since there was no plasma with which to treat the anemia, he found another POW willing to donate blood for five cents per cubic centimeter.

On July 10 thirty-three more patients from the Tayabas road detail arrived at Bilibid in horrific shape, all of them malnourished. George found it difficult to contain his anger:

This afternoon at about 4:30 I saw something to make one's blood boil and go emotionally berserk. Should have been a movie made of the scene and circulated to every US city and then I'll bet you couldn't stop the current until —— wiped out to the man. Three loads of prisoners came in from the south . . . where a road is under

*construction. Every one of them to the man was a living skeleton and
just about able to drag themselves along. Some couldn't do that but
collapsed upon sliding off the truck. All but one was a dysentery case.*

Words couldn't express his outrage, and if they could, to whom would
he address them? Who, if he cried out, would hear him? The suffering of
others shook George to the very core of his being. The indifference to human life contravened his strict sense of morality as a Catholic and ran
counter to the values he upheld as a practitioner of medicine. Language
failed him, and the ellipsis in his diary entry was a haunting reminder of
the effect so much suffering had on him. "He always got on with people,"
said his first cousin Jeanne Gier. "He didn't care if he was talking to a five-
year-old or a twenty-five-year-old." And here he was in Bilibid consumed
with animosity, hating the Japanese as blindly as they hated him.

Things were worse at Cabanatuan, said Father Theodore Buttenbruck, a German padre from Christ the King Church in Manila, who
gave a sermon at Bilibid on July 19. Thirty to forty POWs were dying
daily. "At this rate," George quipped in his diary, "a few years will deplete
the Americans in these here parts. Thank you again Uncle Sam." Most of
the prisoners in Cabanatuan had been transferred from Camp O'Donnell after it was shut down in late May 1942. More than 2,000 of
the 9,300 American POWs at O'Donnell and 27,000 Filipinos had
died there before the 14th Army relieved Captain Tsuneyoshi, the camp
commandant, of his command. Homma Masaharu hadn't bothered to
pay a single visit to O'Donnell—much less to any POW camp in the
Philippines—though Major General Kawane had advised him of the
camp's excessive mortality rate.

John escaped malaria on Bataan, but in August 1942 at Bilibid he
came down with dengue fever, a highly infectious disease caused by a fla-
vivirus transmitted by the aedes mosquito. Also known as dandy or
breakbone fever, for the extreme joint pain experienced during the onset
of the illness, dengue is common in the tropics. You might wake up in
the morning feeling just fine and in no time at all experience such extreme pain—in the fingers, toes, or limbs—that you can't finish getting
dressed. A sudden chill comes on. Your head and eyes begin to ache. Dis-
coloration appears in your face, your pulse rate increases, and your temperature spikes. Finally, a rash may break out on your hands, wrists,
elbows, knees, and the soles of your feet. Dengue is not fatal, but there
are few prophylactic measures that can prevent it, other than isolation.
Once the disease runs its course, joint and muscle pain may persist. Relapses are not uncommon. Bedrest is the typical recommendation. John's

illness was a sobering reminder that diseases don't discriminate among their victims. Indeed, dengue was in danger of becoming an epidemic at Bilibid. Fred suffered from dengue and was "down to skin and bones," according to Hayes, who had had five bouts with it himself. But the Japanese appeared to be unfamiliar with the disease, Sartin learned after he and Nogi attended a conference on malaria at the Manila Hotel.

Sartin continued to press the Japanese authorities for more drugs. He also appealed to Morimoto to allow the POWs to purchase food and supplies from Manila. Camp Warden Gooding had already established a brisk black market in foodstuffs, as a result of his friendship with Sergeant Tokonaya at Pasay. A mango, which sold for five centavos on the street, cost a peso inside Bilibid, the equivalent of fifty cents. Men clamored to pay the inflated prices if they had the money. If they didn't, they were out of luck—and out of food. Soon two corpsmen, Richard H. Mayberry and "Tommie" Thompson, built a crude galley from bricks and scrap lumber. This was the "diet kitchen" where, under the supervision of navy dental officer Lieutenant (j.g.) Stanley W. Smith, special meals were prepared for patients suffering from extreme nutritional deficiencies.

The Japanese patrolled Bilibid day and night, but visitors were adept at smuggling items into it. Nancy Belle Norton, an American schoolteacher in Manila, made regular stops in a *calesa* that concealed fresh fruit, baked goods, and native sugar. She also acted as a courier for news and mail. Lieutenant Walter H. Waterous, an army reservist who had a successful ophthalmological practice in Manila before the war, was allowed to receive Filipino technicians who brought in thousands of frames and Bausch & Lomb lenses for the POWs as well as their jailers. His associate, Maxima Villanueva, wrangled an MP pass that gave her regular access to Bilibid. In addition to fixing spectacles for the Japanese, almost all of whom wore glasses, she managed to smuggle in nearly 180,000 pesos over a two-and-a-half-year period. The guards themselves were another source of contraband—if the money was at hand—as were Filipino sweethearts.

Ralph Hibbs, the army doctor from Hospital No. 1 on Bataan, would tie a letter to a rock and throw it over the prison wall to his girlfriend, Pilar Campos. The daughter of the president of the Bank of the Philippine Islands, Pilar was a ringleader of the Filipino underground and regularly sneaked in food and medicine. Father Buttenbruck proved he was a man who practiced what he preached and delivered to Bilibid's medical staff a much-needed microscope. Fortunately, Fred still had the pesos he had "borrowed" from Olongapo. He shared the food he purchased from the commissary with George and John. Other POWs pilfered rice and sugar from work details and concealed their booty in pants legs and shoes.

So the men began to *quan,* a catchall word reputedly invented by Master Sergeant Tabaniag of the 45th Infantry, Philippine Scouts, and derived from the Tagalog word *kuwan.* The POWs used it as a noun, verb, and adjective to refer to one thing: food. *Quan* meant a small group of men cooking a meal over an open fire. *Quan* meant to scrounge, swap, or save anything edible. *Quan* meant, simply, delicious, and you could use it interchangeably in one sentence, as in: "Whatcha quanning in that quan, Joe? Smells very quan. Howse about sharing some quan with me?"

The navy doctors shared their *quan* with one another, whether they had a little or a lot. As George wrote in his diary:

> *27th August Thursday 1942. Yesterday the food situation improved when the store opened up & plenty of bananas, eggs, & even got 6 thin pork chops from a Filipino MO. So last nite we really splurged & two fried eggs, pies, 7 pancakes, sugar, butter, and rice.*

But their bounty was short-lived. By the fall of 1942 "the ravages of poor diet and lack of vitamins," Sartin wrote, were all too apparent. Firewood, stripped from dilapidated buildings, was a scarcity, and before long open fires were forbidden. Without adequate food, recuperating patients slid into relapse, while those in fair health fought a battle against time.

An increasing number of men had lesions on their hands and shins and suffered from sore mouths. The symptoms were consistent with pellagra—*mal de la rosa,* the Spanish called it when they identified the disease in the early eighteenth century. A red rash appears first; then the body literally tries to shed its skin, breaking out into blisters that crust over and slough off. The gastrointestinal tract can become so inflamed that swallowing water and eating food is agony. The "scourge of the American South" in the early twentieth century, pellagra was long thought to be germ-borne, until Dr. Joseph Goldberger, a surgeon in the U.S. Public Health Service, discovered its cause: a lack of niacin, normally derived from protein in meat, fish, and vegetables.

Xerophthalmia and optical neuritis also began to appear in "alarming numbers," along with hideous corneal ulcers caused by a lack of vitamin A. Left untreated, they clouded vision, distorted perception, and as Al Smith and Ted Williams discovered firsthand, could lead to permanent impairment.

But of all the vitamin-deficiency diseases, beriberi was the most serious, and virtually all of the POWs suffered from it in one form or another. Up until the late nineteenth century beriberi, like pellagra, was believed to be germ-borne, but the cause was again nutritional. In the Philippines, when rice was milled, the outer layer of the grain—or pericarp—was half-removed. The pericarp is rich in essential vitamin B_1, the absence of which can disrupt the metabolism, causing peripheral nerve damage and enlargement of the heart. Fatigue, irritability, and memory loss are early symptoms, which in "dry berberi" are followed by searing pain in the legs, feet, and toes. Sweating, grotesque swelling, and warm skin characterize "wet beriberi," which literally floods the body's interstitial spaces and can culminate in cardiac arrest.

Bilibid had been a major center for the experimental study of beriberi at the turn of the century. But as long as POWs were forced to endure a rice-heavy diet, they could only watch the slow, painful deformation of their bodies—the shrunken muscles, palsied limbs, swollen ankles, and distended bellies—that terminated for many of them in death.

═══ 15 ═══

"The last thin tie"

MURRAY'S CURSE was a blessing in disguise. The sole navy doctor left on Corregidor, he and Army Captain Thomas "Tommy" Hewlett looked after a salvage detail of some 200 POWs under the command of Lieutenant Colonel Lewis S. Kirkpatrick. Hewlett was an orthopedist by training, in charge of surgery. Murray took over internal medicine. They were assisted by twenty-four navy corpsmen.

Murray and Tommy got along well. They were relieved by their new responsibilities and the complete lack of oversight. No Commander Hayes or Colonel Cooper to tell them what to do now. As officers they had complete freedom of movement on the Rock. They shared private quarters in the old Fort Mills Station Hospital and enjoyed beds with mattresses, intermittent electricity, and occasionally running water. There was even a Hallicrafter radio they could tune in, to follow the war's progress on KGEI.

All of the medical equipment on Corregidor had been removed to Bilibid, so Hewlett fashioned an operating table from a dining room table, which he covered with a bedsheet. Then he made a steam sterilizer from a metal boiler. The mess hall became the OR, where Hewlett conducted more than forty major surgical procedures. Murray performed his first appendectomy and assisted Hewlett in several hernia operations. He also served as Hewlett's anesthesiologist, using the open drop-ether technique. It was a primitive method of sedation: ether was dropped onto a gauze-covered wire mask, which was placed over the nose and mouth; the ether was inhaled and diffused from the lung aveolar spaces into the bloodstream and tissue cells. Twelve drops the first minute, twenty-four the second, forty-eight the third, and ninety-six the fourth, until the patient was out.

There was food on Corregidor, but not enough. The Japanese allowed the Americans to go fishing with dynamite, using Brightwork polish cans—army staples—packed with TNT and fitted with caps and fuses. On behalf of his patients, Murray appealed for more food to the Japanese medical officer, who in turn spoke to the Japanese quartermaster. To his surprise, the ration was increased with corned beef, sardines, and flour from Malinta Tunnel. They were well stocked the next week, when Murray decided to try his luck again. Poker-faced, he appealed to the same Japanese medical officer, who again spoke to the same Japanese quartermaster. The ruse worked: another case of sardines, corned beef, and more flour. Earlier on Corregidor Murray had resorted to stealing food with John; now he had learned the art of the bluff. He excused his behavior on the grounds of necessity. In a world where the old rules no longer held, pragmatism won over principle, unscrupulousness over honesty.

The Japanese set up a store near Bottomside that sold canned milk, corned beef, peanuts, bananas, and sugar—goods that they had appropriated from Malinta Tunnel—but black market prices made them almost unaffordable. The real reason for the commissary was to try to recover some of the fifteen million silver pesos that the Americans had dumped between Corregidor and Fort Hughes before the surrender and that were mysteriously finding their way back into circulation. Twenty tons of gold bullion and silver from the Philippine treasury had already been removed by the submarine *Trout* in early February 1942.

"Say doc," a navy diver asked Murray one day, "do you think you can get this black stuff off these coins?"

The pesos were coal-black from sitting in salt water. Back in May, Captain Takeuchi of the Japanese Army Engineers had launched a salvage operation using local Filipino divers. They relied on an old, manually operated oxygen pump designed for a maximum depth of 90 feet. But the Filipinos were inexperienced, and the silver, scattered over a large area, lay 120 feet beneath the sea. Two of the divers succumbed to the bends; another died underwater when his helmet was accidentally pulled off. The remaining Filipinos refused to dive anymore. Only eighteen boxes of silver had been recovered.

In June the Japanese recruited six POWs from Cabanatuan who had been navy divers on the USS *Pigeon.* They retrieved equipment from the *Canopus,* reconstructed from memory a decompression chart, and figured out how to raise, using a three-sixteenths-inch recovery cable, boxes of the precious metal that weighed 300 pounds apiece. They also figured out how to sabotage the operation.

At first the American divers pried open the wooden boxes on the ocean floor with a marlin spike and stuffed the pesos into their underwear and tennis shoes. Then they developed a system. While a crate of silver was being hoisted up on one side of the barge, a ten-tug pull on the air hose signaled that a stash of coins stuffed into denim sacks cut from dungaree legs or old gas mask bags was ready to be hauled up on the opposite side. Boatswain's Mate 1st Class Robert C. Sheats of the USS *Canopus* would go into the water, ostensibly to make sure that the air hose was free of the recovery cable, and attach a weighted line to the purloined treasure. As the deck hands struggled to bring the crate on board, a screen of divers would hover over the contraband as it was pulled up on the other side, dump the loot into a bucket, and cover it with diving gear. At day's end the men divvied up their gains. They even managed to scavenge from Malinta Tunnel some muriatic acid, an electric grinder, and a wire brush to clean their loot.

Murray had a better solution. He simply dipped the pesos in nitric acid—then, after brushing them with Japanese tooth powder, they gleamed like newly minted coins. He thought of it as his contribution to devaluing Japanese occupation currency, which was barely worth the paper it was printed on. The motor pool became a clandestine silver exchange, where 50 pesos could buy 100 dollars, personal checks accepted. Little more than 2 million pesos was ever recovered by the Japanese on Corregidor, most of it thanks to a group of Moros who were experienced pearl divers from the Sulu Archipelago.

Murray had become a thief, a gambler, and now, literally, a money launderer. If only his father had known. But the real value of his work was in caring for the patients in the old Fort Mills Station Hospital from the 200-man work detail on Corregidor. Not one man was lost during the postsurrender period when he was on the Rock. The medical decisions that were made were his and Tommy Hewlett's alone.

Back in New York City, Lewis Glusman had already written to the New York Life Insurance Company to inquire about his son's policy. At a time when Murray, in captivity, was so proud to be a doctor, proud to have gotten out from under Hayes's shadow, his father was expecting, any day, to receive news of his death.

The chief of surgery at Bilibid, Thomas Hirst Hayes, was one difficult son of a bitch. He was smart, erudite, disciplined, and demanding, quick to judge others but perhaps hardest on himself. A native of Philadelphia, Hayes was married and had a young son, Thomas Jr., nicknamed Barnacle because he weighed on his mother like the shells on the hull of a ship. "Just a country boy at heart," he signed a photograph of himself. Far from it—he was a complicated man, talented and troubled. With seventeen years' experience as a navy officer under his belt, his sometimes holier-than-thou demeanor rubbed the junior officers raw with resentment. "Terrible Tommy," they called him for his temper, which blew over as quickly as a summer rainstorm.

Hayes liked to read a book a week, take notes, and then reread the same books the next year, take notes, and compare the changes in his interpretations. At Bilibid he kept a diary that remains one of the most detailed records of POW life in the Philippines. For his son he made a photographic album of his prewar tour in the islands. He was an artist who, on the evacuation of Cañacao, left an unfinished painting "still on the board" of the very scene where Dewey and Admiral Topete y Cervera "fought it out in 1898." He even tried his hand at writing short stories in Spanish.

In spite of an intense friendship with Dental Corps officer Bob Herthneck, "my closest comrade," Hayes thought of himself as very much alone. In prison he came to expect the worst of humanity, and not surprisingly, he found it. "Emaciated carcasses look up with staring eyeballs sunk deep in bony sockets," he wrote on arriving at Bilibid. "The conglomerate horror of it all beats upon my sensibilities as an outrageous defiance against all the principles of civilization, and dispels any delusion I may have of human progress." He deplored the profiteering that was permitted by Camp Warden Gooding. He castigated the Americans for their arrogance and provinciality. And he railed against "the stuffed shirt, high and mighty Army boys" who patronized Colonel Manuel G. Olympia, chief of the medical service, Philippine Army. Hayes was anti-Semitic, homophobic, and harbored homicidal rage toward the Japanese. On seeing POWs walking "like Haitian zombies" from the Tayabas detail, he declared:

> At no one other moment have I hated with the intensity of that moment. . . . I swore and vowed that I would never be satisfied nor content on earth until every vestige of Nippon was destroyed—until I have personally known the feel of ramming a bayonet into their guts, starving them, looting them of all they hold dear. . . . If my hunger for their blood is abnormal, they have made me so.

He was also struck with a sense of foreboding. "I knew when I left for the Asiatic just one year ago that this present plight, or death or both was in my immediate future," he confided to his diary. He feared that he would be among the last Americans to leave the Philippines, by which time "we will be bombing our own Americans wherever we bomb."

"Old Hazy," as the junior medical officers also dubbed him, seemed to live behind a veil of contempt. If their basic training was on the battlefield, they had a recruit's dislike of their commanding officer, and their esprit de corps was the stronger for it. What they couldn't see beneath the badgering, the bluster, and the denigrating comments was that Hayes had enormous respect for many of them.

Before leaving Corregidor, Hayes compiled fourteen detailed narrative histories of the Navy Medical, Dental, and Hospital Corps personnel on duty with the 4th Marines in the Philippines. Fred suspected he had lost favor with Hayes because of his friendship with Fleet Surgeon Ken Lowman. But in his "Report on Medical Tactics," Hayes lauded John for his work at Camp Dewey and the Section Base Hospital in Mariveles. He praised George for his perseverance on Corregidor during hostile activity that was "heroic, modest and served as an inspiration to every officer and man serving under him." And he admired Murray, whose Medical Corps education amounted to less than twelve weeks by correspondence course but whose sound judgment, steadfast performance, and "conduct under fire" were "worthy of the best traditions of our Service." "It was inspiring to see," Hayes wrote, "the cool competency and willingness of the youngsters, many of whom were having their first taste of blood and fire, and they did splendidly. I have been proud of them ever since."

Hayes was a stickler for protocol, a firm believer in discipline who insisted that doctors in the Medical Corps "must be *officers*." But he had sense enough to adapt medical tactics to a situation whose handbook was yet to be written. Having lived in the tropics for years, he knew that "a Mayo Clinic isn't necessary for excellent results." At Bilibid, ingenuity and improvisation were a means to that end.

"Osler has said that the physician who cannot successfully treat malarial fever," John wrote in his medical notes, "should not be practicing medicine. Insofar as this refers to only the fever of malaria this is true. Insofar as it refers to malaria itself it is not true."

The standard course of treatment for malaria couldn't be carried out in the majority of cases due to a lack of quinine. But what John noticed at Bilibid was that even those patients who had completed six months of quinine therapy, in addition to courses of atabrine, suffered relapses as early as three weeks later. The reason, he thought, was malnutrition, which lowered the body's resistance. But it wasn't only food and quinine that were in short supply at Bilibid.

Lacking emetine, the doctors administered ground charcoal to dysentery patients because it absorbs intestinal gases. To avert an epidemic, Radio Electrician Earl G. Schweizer, who replaced Gooding as camp warden in October 1942, designed a self-flushing latrine. To reduce the spread of infection, a fly-trapping contest was implemented—two beers for each can of flies caught. To treat scurvy, they rounded up limes, which seafarers of yore had found to be an effective remedy for vitamin C deficiency. To combat beriberi, they cultivated mongo beans in tins and jars and then steamed them like lentils. And to fight vitamin B deficiency, they doled out half-canteen cups of yeast, which the San Miguel Brewery in Manila provided for Bilibid's "diet kitchen."

Due to the shortage of gauze, bandages were washed and reused. Due to the shortage of paper, the doctors wrote their patient notes on the reverse side of Chinese immigration certificates dating back to the 1920s. Due to the shortage of soap, they simply rinsed their clothes in water. But there was no shortage of patients, and the doctors themselves were riddled with illness. As Hayes wrote with Dostoevskian disdain: "We are all sick." In September 1942, 37 percent of all hospital admissions were doctors and corpsmen.

Most of the old Cañacao Naval Hospital staff still had their khaki uniforms, tatters of their group identity. Tunics were cut from shirts, shorts were tailored from pants, and once shoes wore out they were replaced with *bakyas*—native clogs carved from scraps of wood and secured with cloth or leather straps across the instep. Santo Tomás, the civilian internment camp, made a special donation of clothes to the hospital. Those on work parties in the Port Area, or Pandacan, or at Fort McKinley simply wore the Japanese-issue loincloth, or *fundoshi*.

The men reused coffee grounds until the brew was a pale shadow of itself. When coffee ran out, they baked banana skins and crumbled them in hot water for a cup of joe. If they had soap, it doubled as toothpaste. For cigarettes they substituted bitter black cheroots, and for toilet paper they were given a sheet apiece each day. They honed their razors on shards of glass and made sure their mess-kit spoons lasted for years.

Ingenuity and improvisation were woven into the social fabric of Bilibid as well, a patchwork of interests, desires, and wide-ranging abilities. Fred loved to bake and seemed to whip up ingredients out of thin air. He presented Carey Smith with a cake on his birthday, then played fiddle while John and George serenaded their "adopted father." Corpsman Johnson drew up a menu with a variety of dishes "à la Bilibid." Signed by the "Chief Chef, Chief Dish & Bottle Washer, and Chief Bookkeeping & Purchasing Agent," it was embossed with the "Bilibid Seal," which showed a man in profile thumbing his nose above two crossed keys on a mock escutcheon, beneath which unfurled a banner that read: "SNAFU."

The POWs had access to a circulating library that was housed between Buildings No. 1 and No. 2, and a medical library on the second floor of Building No. 18. The Philippine Red Cross provided books as well as athletic equipment.

Volleyball and baseball were favorite pastimes, as was deck tennis, the net for which was made from hemp. In the evenings the men read or listened to recordings such as "My Prayer," "Always Forever," and "Sunrise Serenade" on a Victrola that had been smuggled into camp. They played cards, placed bets as to when they would return to the States, and shared war stories. John patiently tried to explain to George the "finer points" of bridge. Lieutenant Max Pohlman, a devilishly handsome doctor from Los Angeles County Hospital and the self-proclaimed "King of the Auto Courts," regaled the men with tales of nubile nurses and other amatory adventures.

Saturday nights the POWs put on a "camp show" with music, songs, and magic acts organized by Lieutenant Commander Clyde L. Welsh, chief of general medicine, and approved beforehand by the Japanese. Lieutenant Commander Cecil Charles Welch, chief of outpatient service, made a hobby of collecting favorite recipes from the men—for steak and stews, fried chicken and mashed potatoes, pumpkin pie and apple crumb cake. At night, they dreamed about food—rarely about sex. Hayes admitted that he was afraid of his dreams. "They break up my steeled defense against thought, memories, hopes and fears."

His fears were justified. The punishment for sending a note outside Bilibid was burning it and eating its ashes. The punishment for talking back to a guard was a beating, being forced to squat on your heels for hours, or both. When Corporal Robert C. Barnbrook attempted escape on September 26, 1942, he was sentenced to two and a half years in the military prison on the other side of the compound, but he died of beriberi before he completed his term. When two army colonels and the navy supply officer from Mariveles were caught after an attempted escape from Cabanatuan, Hayes heard, they were tortured and executed. Rumor had it that Lieutenant (j.g.) Bernard Cohen, whom John and Murray had worked with in Mariveles, succeeded in escaping from the Penal Colony in Davao and made it safely to Australia.

Fortunately Nogi seemed a decent fellow. He looked the other way as Nancy Belle Norton slipped food, medicine, and clothing into camp on a regular basis until she herself was imprisoned. He let Hayes go outside Bilibid on an excursion to the Port Area, where "a miserable lot" of POWs from Cabanatuan were boarding a Japanese merchant ship—destined for Japan. Afterward he took him out to dinner. Hayes was convinced that the war with Japan was essentially racial in nature, and in spite of his antipathy toward the Japanese people as a whole, he found Nogi singularly well intentioned.

Nogi refused to believe either the Japanese or the American reports of the war's progress. But George pinned his hopes on both news and rumor, some of which emanated from a radio set the POWs concealed in Bilibid. The Battle of Coral Sea in May 1942, followed by a decisive American victory at Midway in June and a bloody campaign for Guadalcanal launched in August, surely signaled an aggressive Allied counteroffensive The war would be over in a month, KGEI reported in early September. Two days later George exclaimed, "November seems to be the promised time now & we are planning our first few days of release. Wow!!!" But by November he could only admit, "Well, another month has gone by rapidly and still waiting for Yanks & Tanks." Then there was the strange rumor that Hayes had heard about a Japanese transport ship loaded with 1,800 British POWs captured in Singapore. Bound for Japan, it had been torpedoed and sunk by American submarines.

Time waiting was well spent by the POW doctors. Nearly 500 operations were performed by the surgical service in the first six months at Bilibid, noted Lieutenant A. M. Barrett, who worked with Fred and Hjalmer Erickson in the Sick Officers' Quarters—appendectomies and amputations, orthopedic repairs and rib resections, gastroenterostomies and hemorrhoidectomies, anal fistulas and circumcisions. Only one patient died, and he had been moribund on admission.

POWs flowed into Bilibid from Clark Field, where they suffered from malnutrition and food deficiency diseases, and from Cabanatuan, where the army doctors had no emetine or carbarsone and the prison population was decimated by amoebic dysentery. Others were quarantined in Bilibid for typhoid fever.

Pellagra continued to proliferate. Dengue accounted for more than a third of hospital admissions in September 1942. But it was dysentery that remained an "outstanding" problem in Bilibid, indeed throughout the Philippines.

In June 1942 Ted Williams was on a work detail at Clark Field when he discovered two large bottles of bismuth and paregoric in the dispensary. He turned them over to an army captain for future use, and soon Williams himself contracted amoebic dysentery. He was kept at Clark and isolated from the other POWs until he was hauled back to Bilibid in a flatbed truck. By then he was so weak he couldn't stand up and had to be carried to the infectious diseases ward on a stretcher. "Do you know why you're here?" Dr. Welsh asked him. "Because I'm going to die," Williams whispered.

There were no beds or mattresses in the infectious diseases ward because with dysentery you lose complete control of your bowels. Men lay on a bare concrete floor. A large tub was filled with water and creosote for washing soiled clothing. If you lived, you got your clothing back; if you died, it was recycled to another POW. Williams was given the native remedy of ground charcoal, which had little effect, he thought, except to turn his feces black. Paregoric, an opium derivative that tastes like licorice, helped relieve abdominal pain. But he also needed bismuth, and the army captain from the Clark Field detail refused to give him any. Eventually the amoebic dysentery cleared up, and then Williams developed bacillary dysentery, which Lieutenant Commander E. M. Wade treated successfully with plasma he was able to obtain from Nogi.

Williams survived by becoming a "dog robber," army parlance for an enlisted man working for an officer. He was paid in extra food—clean rice, sugar, mongo beans, and mangoes—which didn't save his sight but in all likelihood saved his life.

Thirteen men died in Bilibid in June 1942, thirty-three in July, and twenty-one in August. Dysentery ranked as the leading cause of death, followed by malaria. The Japanese permitted religious services on Sunday, and in early October Chaplains Cummings and Perry O. Wilcox gave a memorial for all those who had perished since the outbreak of war. Nogi attended, and afterward the Japanese High Command presented the POW hospital personnel with cookies, candy, and four bananas apiece. The Americans expressed their gratitude in "a letter of appreciation," but the irony wasn't lost on them. The Japanese showed more respect for the dead than for the dying.

———

Murray arrived at Bilibid on December 10, 1942, the first anniversary of the Cavite bombing. Far from losing weight, he'd actually gained a few pounds on Corregidor. Sometimes being the low man on the totem pole had its benefits. Sometimes, he now realized, you had to think counterintuitively. Being with the senior medical officers was not necessarily the best option.

He was glad to be reunited with the gang, but Murray found prison conditions wanting compared to life on the Rock. Bilibid's death rate had leveled off, but the food ration was abysmal. Eighty percent of the hospital patients suffered from one kind of nutritional deficiency or another. When Sartin appealed to Nogi to request more medicine from the International Committee of the Red Cross in Geneva, he was informed that the POWs couldn't have what the Japanese didn't have.

The senior Japanese medical officer, Colonel Ishii, evidently agreed that rations at Bilibid were insufficient for malnutrition patients. Ishii recommended that each man receive 100 grams of canned meat daily. But the Japanese also claimed that their own troops were virtually immune to vitamin-deficiency diseases. "Had we been obliged to subsist only on what the Japs have given us," noted Hayes, "there isn't one of us who would be able to carry on and work today."

On December 23 a Christmas miracle arrived at Bilibid in the form of British Red Cross parcels from Geneva. "Really increased the morale," George wrote, "and you should see the smiling faces this P.M." Less than two weeks later American Red Cross boxes arrived via the *Gripsholm,* which brought a total of 445 tons of supplies for POWs and internees in United Nations countries. It was the best possible present from home:

American Red Cross
STANDARD PACKAGE NO. 8
for
PRISONER OF WAR

FOOD

Evaporated milk, irradiated	1 14½ oz. can
Lunch biscuit (hard-tack)	1 8 oz. package
Cheese	1 8 oz. package
Instant cocoa	1 8 oz. tin
Sardines	1 15 oz. tin
Oleomargarine (Vitamin A)	1 lb. tin
Corned beef	1 12 oz. tin
Sweet chocolate	2 5½ oz. bars
Sugar, granulated	1 2 oz. package
Powdered orange concentrate	2 3½ oz. packages (Vitamin C)
Soup (dehydrated)	2 2½ oz. packages
Prunes	1 16 oz. package
Instant coffee	1 4 oz. tin
Cigarettes	2 20's
Smoking tobacco	1 2¼ oz. package

The packages weighed eleven pounds apiece and had to be divided between two men. The POWs pawed through them like squirrels, sniffing, hoarding, devouring. Lifesavers for some, they were currency for others. The corned beef had an almost immediate effect on edema and skin ulcers. On the other hand, it was odd to see chaplains, of all people, trading cigarettes for food, which to the doctors was tantamount to a criminal offense. One sailor died from stomach distension after ingesting the contents of an entire Red Cross parcel in one sitting. The Japanese were amazed to see foodstuffs packed in tin cans and foil, which had disappeared from daily life in Japan, so dire was the military's need for scrap metal.

Along with the Red Cross parcels came a supply of medicine at Bilibid, but not all of the items in the Red Cross parcels ended up in the right hands. One POW stole packs of cigarettes, which he then sold to a Filipino *calesa* driver for one and a half pesos apiece; the driver resold them on the black market for a tidy profit. The ruse was unraveled when the *calesa* driver was discovered one day with 300 pesos in his pockets. Sartin took responsibility and was publicly reprimanded by Nogi. The 300 pesos were deposited in the Indigent Sick Fund. "A public act," Sartin observed, "to cover up the far more extensive theft being carried out by the Japanese themselves." Manila was flooded with goods the Japanese had purloined from Red Cross packages.

In the meantime the Japanese issued every POW a box of matches, a cake of soap, and formatted postcards so the men could write home. The design was the brainchild of a Japanese graduate of Columbia University. Beneath the Imperial Japanese Army letterhead was a series of statements with multiple choice options or a one-line space for fill-in-the-blank answers. The purpose was to dictate the information a POW could divulge and limit the text of messages to facilitate translation and censorship.

IMPERIAL JAPANESE ARMY

1. I am interned at _____
2. My health is—excellent; good; fair; poor.
3. I am—injured; sick in hospital; under treatment; not under treatment.
4. I am—improving; not improving; better; well.
5. Please see that _____
_____ is taken care of.
6. (Re: Family): _____
7. Please give my best regards to _____

Even with such restrictions, the idea of writing home was as liberating as the glimpse of life beyond Bilibid that George and John caught one day from the third floor of the inner compound. But only fifteen letters had come into Bilibid. One of them was for George, and it was from Lucy. "Boy, oh Boy what a thrill, she didn't say much but it was all good. Dated June 5th was opened 2x. Passed it around for a few to read." And what they read made them think of their own sweethearts and families, of what they'd left and what they'd lost, of farewells and homecomings. "Very few people (only one other M.D.) got a letter," George noted, "and this is hard to understand."

The reason was twofold. The whereabouts of many POWs captured in early 1942 was a mystery to U.S. authorities because the Japanese still hadn't released their names or camp locations. Late in 1942 Japan issued instructions on how to address mail to POWs even if their particular camp was unknown. Mail received by the Japanese Red Cross Society was simply forwarded to the Horyo Jōhōkyoku, which was quickly overwhelmed. Soon a mail distribution center was established in Tōkyō and operated by POWs from Ōmori Main Camp, but it was shut down after a year for fear that prisoners were harvesting too much information from it. As a result, the responsibility for processing reverted to the Horyo Jōhōkyoku, which was unable to cope with the enormous task of first translating and then censoring mail. Many letters simply sat in sacks throughout the Philippines and Japan and remained undelivered and unread. While POWs wondered why there was no word from home, their loved ones felt as if they had poured their hearts out into an ominous silence.

Laura Reade hadn't heard from Murray in more than a year and a half. In January 1942 the Navy Department wrote to her that he was "alive and well," but in March his exact whereabouts were "not available at this time." On May 18 he was classified as "missing in action," a designation he would carry until June 1943. Murray became a thought, a memory, a rent in the fabric of everyday life. But how do you overcome the pain of absence? Do you confront it or bypass it, dwell on it or move forward? How can you still love someone if you only think of them in the past tense?

"My boy," Max Pohlman told him with a wink, "you are missing the best years of your life."

Murray didn't need to be reminded.

––––––––––

Bilibid was a village behind walls, with shops (a pharmacy, a tailor, a commissary), a hospital, a library, a church, magistrates (senior officers), commoners (enlisted men), town meetings, a rumor mill, ritual observances, thieves, moralists, ministers, chroniclers, and even a brig within a prison for those who broke laws determined by the Japanese.

A choir made up of POWs sang carols on Christmas Eve, and Protestant and Catholic services were performed in the chapel just before midnight. "Why can't everyone just be a Catholic?" George wondered out loud, to the amusement of Murray and John. "It's such a fine religion." He knew they were both Jewish. Even their dogtags were imprinted with a *J*.

At one point the Japanese ordered Lieutenant Commander Cecil Charles Welch to compile a list of POWs by religion, and he dutifully asked each prisoner his faith. To Welch's inquiry, Murray boasted: "My family's been Jewish for thousands of years and I see no reason to change now." John was just as adamant. It was a foolish taunt in spite of the Jewish presence in East Asia. Jews emigrating from Russia or fleeing Germany had found refuge in Shanghai and Japanese-occupied Harbin. Kōbe's well-established community dated back to the nineteenth century, when Jews arrived not as refugees but as traders. But since the Anti-Comintern Pact of 1936, Nazis had been infiltrating Japan, and anti-Semitism was on the rise. In some cases the Kempeitai, Japan's Gestapo, identified Jews and arrested and imprisoned them as suspected Communists or spies. Neither Murray nor John was an observant Jew—science, in their opinion, gave the lie to religion. Their claim was an assertion more of identity under threat than of genuine conviction. Welch wisely reported their religion as Christian to avoid any possible repercussions.

The doctors at Bilibid had their individual specialties, but they quickly gained familiarity with a range of diseases that were almost numbing in their consistency. Their remarks to their patients were cool, clinical, and precise, betraying no emotion as they recorded the symptoms and recommended treatment for one POW after another suffering from cross-infections. And they could only speculate on the cause of death when bodies of POWs were delivered from Pasay, then hastily buried by the Japanese.

There was one case, however, that Fred would never forget. Corporal Lloyd D. Adams had been bitten on the face and leg by a rabid dog when he was on a work party at Balanga. He was placed in Bilibid's isolation ward and given a course of rabies vaccine provided by the Japanese, but it did little to stop the virus from multiplying in the brain and surging through the efferent nerves to the salivary glands. Adams went insane. He salivated uncontrollably and developed hydrophobia. His spasms—triggered by the most innocuous stimuli—became so violent that the disease seemed to have seized his body, to speak and act for it in a bizarre parody of human behavior. Ted Williams could barely see from xerophthalmia, but at night and at *bangō* he could hear the most horrible screaming. The spectacle induced in Fred a sense of awe in the face of the incurable.

Doctors quickly learn to separate the personal from the professional, but some relationships at Bilibid blossomed into friendships. Corporal Donald E. Meyer, who had been stationed at Nichols Field with the 693rd Aviation Ordnance, suffered a depressed skull fracture and a dislocated hip on Corregidor. When he arrived at Bilibid in October 1942, Carey Smith and Lieutenant E. R. Nelson tended his hip fracture first. Later Nelson and George Ferguson operated successfully on his skull.

Meyer recovered beautifully. "I knew he would be a friend to me always," he said of George.

Some cases, however, were medical mysteries. Murray was intrigued by patients complaining of "painful feet." Their extremities felt as if they were on fire, they said. Their fingers tingled, and the discomfort in their toes was so intense that some of them couldn't walk. Was it neurological in origin, psychological, or nutritional? he wondered. Was it dry beriberi? Murray began to experiment by administering 20 milligrams of thiamin each day. Nogi was so concerned about the "sore foot syndrome" that he appointed Hayes the head of a "commission" to study the disease, and together they visited Philippine General Hospital and the Institute of Hygiene in Manila. The incidence of "painful feet" decreased as the daily diet was supplemented with meat, mongo beans, and black-eyed peas from the Indigent Sick Fund. But what exactly caused it?

Less of a mystery were the malingerers. Captain Arthur Wermuth of the 57th Infantry, Philippine Scouts, was a legend on Bataan for his guerrilla attacks against the Japanese. Oddly enough, "One-Man Army" Wermuth always had a temperature when he came in to see Fred, and Fred couldn't understand why—until he caught Wermuth dipping the thermometer into a cup of hot water when his back was turned.

Avoiding work, pilfering supplies, profiting from the misery of others—what levels wouldn't some of the POWs stoop to? Hayes wondered. Disease affected the human body, and it threatened the body politic as well. When the plague struck Periclean Athens during the Peloponnesian War, according to Thucydides, the state descended into "unprecedented lawlessness." "In the midst of affliction and misery," Boccaccio wrote of fourteenth-century Florence during the Black Death, "even the revered authority of laws, divine and human, had all but lapsed and dissolved." At Bilibid, with so little for so many, temptations were hard to resist, especially since the threat of punishment—at the hands of the Americans—had lost its sting. They were already in jail, a separate social unit within an enemy hierarchy in an occupied country. Was survival compatible with morality? Hayes speculated. Was the veneer of civilization really so thin? "The inner man is little more than a beast," Hayes concluded with Hobbesian gloom after just a month and a half inside Bilibid.

Sartin was neither tough enough on POWs when they violated camp regulations, nor would he stand up to the Japanese. He was uncomfortable with authority, but his position demanded that he exercise it because the Japanese, Murray observed, had a time-honored respect for "place." The emphasis on hierarchy in Japanese society dated back to feudal times. In the military it translated into rank, and in civil society, status. As Hayes put it, "If we act as a hospital we will *be* a hospital in the eyes of the Japanese, and we will get more and be able to do more as a result."

———————

In January 1943 the Japanese began showing propaganda newsreels that extolled the nation's expeditionary successes. One of them was *Toyo no Gaika,* or *Victory Song in the Orient.* Produced by the Ministry of War, it was a black-and-white film that blamed American jazz and movies for their corrupting influence on the Filipino people and used several hundred POW officers and enlisted men from Cabanatuan as extras in sequences depicting the fall of Bataan and Corregidor. The final scene showed General Homma on horseback reviewing his troops at the victory parade in Manila and closed with the anthem of the Japanese Navy, *"Umi Yukaba,"* or "Across the Sea":

> Across the sea, water-drenched corpses;
> Across the mountains, grass-covered corpses.
> We shall die by the side of our lord,
> We shall not look back.

Impervious to the message of his country's propaganda, Nogi then let the POWs watch a feature that was pure Hollywood: Laurel and Hardy's *Fra Diavolo.* The entire camp turned out—stretcher patients, men hobbling from "painful feet," those who were confined to the back wards, even the Japanese. Boy, did it feel good to laugh at Stan and Ollie's slapstick antics, grown men hardened by the experience of war and captivity guffawing like little kids, laughing until tears came to their eyes. It was the first in a string of American movies shown that included the Marx Brothers' *Room Service* and *Boys Town* with Mickey Rooney and Spencer Tracy—but not before the Japanese dutifully played newsreels celebrating their victories at Pearl Harbor and Singapore.

For their own amusement, the navy doctors formed the Papaya Club. Members were required to grow a mustache and a Van Dyke, and you couldn't shave it off without permission of the group. The penalty was a twenty-centavo papaya to each member, or another twenty-centavo food item if papayas weren't in season. Max Pohlman ended up looking like Trotsky—and getting fined. Hjalmer Erickson, Hayes thought, bore an uncanny resemblance to Hitler. Fred already had a mustache. And poor Murray was so fair-haired that he had to use the magnifying end of a hand-held mirror to see any whiskers at all.

In February 1943 Bilibid's medical staff began offering courses of instruction to inmates, from math and astronomy to English and engineering. For a brief period Bilibid was an open university within prison walls. It was one way for the doctors to keep as up to date as possible in their respective fields while sharing their knowledge with their fellow POWs. Hayes joked that he was "majoring in Spanish, minoring in Japanese, taking a few hours of 'domestic Science' (lab course only), and a course in 'Applied Economics.' " For class flower he voted for *kangkong*, and for mascot, a rabid dog.

Murray taught chemistry, using Smith's *Inorganic Chemistry* as a text. When he wasn't brushing up on anatomy and neurology, he devoured Wells, Tolstoy, and Dreiser. He dismissed Hemingway's *The Sun Also Rises* as "terrible, pointless stuff," but Erskine Caldwell struck a chord, not for the quality of his prose but for his earthy realism. It was Caldwell who said: "I suppose there is plenty to eat somewhere if you can find it; the cat always does."

The Japanese, for their part, held language classes for POWs and instructed them in calisthenics. Murray had studied Hebrew as a child, he spoke Yiddish with his parents, and he understood German. Unlike Fred and John, he had no reservations about learning Japanese; he saw what a useful tool it could be. Yakushiji Kunizo, the camp interpreter, later solicited written accounts from those who had marched from Mariveles to San Fernando. Should the POWs tell the truth? Wouldn't the Japanese lose face? Was it a ruse that would result in reprisals against the Americans? Camp Warden Schweizer asked Yakushiji point-blank. Yakushiji replied that Tōkyō wanted to know the truth, Geneva was involved, and POWs could submit their reports anonymously. As Hayes recorded in his diary:

> *Schweizer informed Yakashisi* [sic] *in that case he would get reports that would mark that march as the most bestial atrocity-filled incident of all military history. Yakashisi admitted he expected so. The result was, the accounts submitted contained every atrocity imaginable, shootings, bayonetting, burying alive, beatings, denial of food and water, plundering and robbing, denial of medicine and medical care of the sick.*

Shortly afterward Tōkyō's intentions were cast into doubt. POWs were prohibited from teaching any more classes. The Japanese feared they had ulterior motives.

In March 1943, food deficiency cases decreased, and in April not one death was recorded in Bilibid. Adequate quinine, atabrine, and plasmochin led to "a noticeable decrease in the incidence of malaria," John wrote. But there was a disturbing development on April 15. A draft of POWs from Pasay arrived "in hellish shape from hard labor, starvation, very little water," said Hayes. "From this group we learn the Japs are mad as hell about losing Guadalcanal and have read of our tanks actually rolling over them and raising hell. Pasay is without doubt a reprisal camp of the worst order." And the most horrific kind of revenge, as far as Hayes was concerned, was medical experimentation. Japanese doctors were using American POWs as guinea pigs.

That didn't stop the Japanese from honoring the enemy's dead. In May, Memorial Day services were held at Bilibid's burial plot just inside the north wall, where in a pauper's graveyard the POWs made every attempt to uphold military decorum. The old Cañacao staff broke out their navy whites; corpsmen shined officers' shoes, polished their medals, and brushed off their insignia. Senior American officers attended, as did Captain Nogi Naraji and 2nd Lieutenant K. Urabe. Major General Morimoto sent flowers. Other POWs wore the ragged remains of uniforms or whatever tattered clothes they could cobble together.

A six-piece camp orchestra opened with "One Sweetly Solemn Thought," which was followed by sixty seconds of silence. Chaplain Cummings read the roll call of Bilibid dead; Chaplain Wilcox recited Scripture. Flanked by navy and army corpsmen standing stiffly at attention, Sartin solemnly placed a floral wreath on the graves as the band struck up "My Buddy." After a prayer by Chaplain Wilcox and a rendition of "Tenting Tonight," the ceremony concluded with "Taps." The cornetist, Pharmacist's Mate Barnard R. Bell, had only one leg. A fitting example, Murray thought, of "the wounded playing for the dead."

By then the rainy season had begun, "a welcome relief mostly from the dust," noted John, "not so much the heat." But it also coincided with a reduction in food, which consisted mostly of "very thin camote soup and rice." The stream of goods that had flowed into Bilibid through the underground was reduced to a trickle because the food supply was now under occupation control, leaving no place for merchant middlemen.

In peacetime the diet recommended by the Board of Nutritional Research at the University of the Philippines was a mere 2,600 calories daily for the average Filipino adult male. Low in protein, low in calcium, low in the vitamins and minerals derived from fresh fruit and vegetables, it was completely lacking in eggs, cheese, and milk. The Filipino diet was overly reliant on cereals, and in the rainy season, it depended heavily on the camote. For the POWs, soon even the camote disappeared, and they found themselves eating the greens from the top of the camote vine—and rice.

Meat was an anomaly in the Japanese diet. Buddhist practices proscribed it. Francis Xavier, known as "the Apostle of the Indies," made the ability to survive on a frugal diet a precondition for sixteenth-century Christian missionaries. Some missionaries, however, tried to introduce the Western practice of eating beef and horsemeat, which the chief minister Hideyoshi outlawed in his anti-Christian edicts. When Townsend Harris arrived in Japan and asked for milk, the story goes, he was told, "Cow's milk is for calves to drink." Not until 1872 did an emperor taste meat for the first time.

Canned meat had been used in Japanese military rations since the Satsuma Rebellion in 1877. The Japanese Navy in particular recognized its importance in preventing beriberi, while an 1889 study conducted by army physician Mori Ōgai, one of the most important writers of the Meiji period, favored a rice-based diet over a Western one. Corned beef became popular after the Tōkyō earthquake of 1923, but by 1935 meat was still only a small part of the typical Japanese diet, the average daily consumption amounting to a mere 6.1 grams.

Before the war the average daily caloric intake in Japan was 2,175, which was even lower than that recommended in the Philippines and 30 percent less than the 3,148 calories consumed in the United States. Ninety-five percent of the Japanese diet derived from vegetable foods, and it was lighter in protein than the average daily American diet by 25 grams. Physically the Japanese were considerably smaller than Americans, and the population had a greater percentage of children. So even if the POWs were receiving as much food as Japanese civilians, their diet was woefully inadequate.

Manileños were subject to severe rationing during the Japanese occupation. Rice and bread were available, but after the first two years, sugar, fuel, and shoes would vanish. Like the Fil-American troops during the Battle of Bataan, civilians resorted to eating dogs, cats, rats, snakes and bats. The much-vaunted Co-Prosperity Sphere, Hayes quipped, had turned into the "No Prosperity Sphere." Matches, toilet paper, and soap were hard to come by "at any price." The typical method of lighting your pipe was to "stand in the sun and fire it through your lens," which was easier said than done when the monsoons came. In general, the treatment of POWs at all the camps began to deteriorate, which meant they had to be more self-reliant than ever.

Murray decided to put his background in chemistry to use by trying to convert starch into sugar. "Most of the people in the pharmacy thought I was nuts," he confessed. But he succeeded in producing "a pretty fair glucose syrup" with a slight caramel flavor. Now if only he could get his hands on some malt and rice starch, his experiment would produce "Beer!"

Fred suffered the next "brainstorm"—raising chickens. On July 6, 1943, the men bought a native rooster for three pesos, and two yellow and white hens for four pesos apiece. By 2100 that evening Murray could report, "They still haven't been stolen. Maybe that's a good omen." It was, but it was a month before they started laying small, soft-shelled eggs. The yellow hen was a mean little pecker and had to be tied up. The white hen, like a true Bilibid denizen, came down with conjunctivitis.

A less auspicious omen was when Nogi brought half a dozen adult pigs into Bilibid from Cabanatuan—not for the Americans but for the Japanese. The POWs built a pig pen, and a Japanese boy was named "Keeper of the Pigs." But in a few months the porkers were anything but fat, dropping off one by one from cholera.

———

"I can hear the bang-bang, knock-knock of the box-maker, making crude coffins" for those waiting to die, Hayes wrote in July 1942. One year later his dear friend Bob Herthneck was dead. He had been in Lipa, where an airfield was being built, and returned to Bilibid suffering from paralysis of the soft palate and uvula. Herthneck was isolated in John Bookman's ward, where he died within twenty-four hours from what appeared to be basilar polio. The virus is highly contagious, and the navy corpsmen who were with him were also placed in quarantine. It was "a shock to us all," Murray wrote in his diary. Herthneck was a fellow New Yorker, and his death was the first among the navy medical personnel, but it would not be the last. "My one shipmate," Hayes grieved. "I feel very much alone."

In a note to Lucy, George described his own health as "excellent," but it was difficult to tell what that meant. On newly formatted postcards, POWs were now permitted to write up to fifty words apiece but were prohibited from referring to illness or malnutrition.

> Two letters from you have made me very happy. Working in Japanese
> established hospital. Have been on both orthopedic and medical
> services. Interested in orthopedic residency at Madison under Burns. If
> you feel the way I do apply for me mentioning Nelson. All my love to
> you and our folks.
> George T. Ferguson

Lewis and Sophie Glusman hadn't heard a word from Murray since Cavite was bombed on December 10, 1941; nor had Laura Reade. She had tried on at least three occasions since February 1942 to learn of his whereabouts. On June 8, 1943, she received a disconcerting letter from the navy:

Dear Miss Reade:

As you are aware, more than a year has elapsed since your friend, Lieut. (junior grade) Murray Glusman, U.S. Naval Reserve, was officially placed in the status of missing in action. According to the last information received he was serving with the Naval Forces in the Sixteenth Naval District during May 1942.

Although many of the personnel serving in Corregidor at the time of its capitulation have been reported as captured by the enemy, the list of prisoners submitted by the Japanese through the medium of the International Red Cross so far failed to include the name of your friend.

The Secretary of the Navy has given careful consideration to the circumstances surrounding the disappearance of your friend. On the basis of data on record, and in the absence of acceptable proof of death, the Secretary has directed that your friend be continued in a missing in action status until circumstances arise to indicate that such status should be changed. . . .

The Navy Department fully appreciates your anxiety and assures you that it will notify you promptly of any report it receives concerning your friend.

> *Sincerely yours,*
> *Randall Jacobs*
> *Rear Admiral, U.S. Navy*
> *Chief of Naval Personnel*

Two weeks later Murray's sister, Estelle, was playing Rachmaninoff's Prelude in C-sharp Minor on the piano when a letter arrived from the Navy Department for Mr. and Mrs. Lewis Glusman. The only one home, she opened the envelope and carefully read the contents.

```
The Bureau is glad to inform you of the
following, quoted from a report, "US/801,"
furnished by the Prisoner of War Information
Bureau, from official Japanese sources, via
Geneva, listing prisoners of war in the Philip-
pine Islands: "TOKYO CABLES FOLLOWING POW ALL
NAVY PHILIPPINES, LIEUTENANT M GLUSMAN." It is
considered that reference is made to Lieutenant
Murray Glusman, United States Naval Reserve,
and that he is now a prisoner of war.
```

Estelle called Aunt Dora, her mother's sister, to share the good news. When her parents returned, she handed them the letter without speak-

ing. Lewis and Sophie wept after reading it. They had no idea if Murray
was sick or wounded, well treated or abused.

"But he's alive," Estelle said.

"He's alive," Estelle repeated, as if to make sure it was really true.

It was the first time she had seen her father cry, tears of joy comming-
ling with sorrow because they were so utterly powerless to help their
son. Lewis was not a man of hope. An orphan who had been raised and
ill treated by his elder brother, he had struggled to get a foothold in
America, learn a new language, negotiate a new culture, and reach a
modicum of success. He had aspirations and expectations, but Murray
embodied his hope, and for too long hope was missing from Lewis's life.

Then out of the blue came a postcard dated July 14:

> *Am doctor prison hospital now 14 mos. Treatment, health good. How
> you? Some getting mail. Not me. Keep writing via Red Cross. How Sid,
> Essie, Charlie, Ziff? Tell Charlie regards Laura. . . . Love, Murray.*

He sounded good, didn't he? He sounded fine, just like Murray. Fine
with malaria, dysentery, and dengue. Fine with beriberi, pellagra, and
edema. They had no way of knowing, of course, how he really was, no way
of knowing where he was. Actually, many relatives of POWs had glimpsed
Bilibid without even realizing it: on December 14, 1941, *The New York
Times* ran an aerial photograph of Manila with the caption "Capital of
the Philippines." The focus of the picture, which apparently eluded the
Times, was the unmistakable Panopticon design of the municipal jail.

The very month that Murray was identified as a prisoner of war,
Samuel and Olga Bookman read an article aptly entitled "You'll Never
Know!" in *The New Yorker*. A "Reporter At Large" piece, it profiled navy
nurse Ann Bernatitus, who spoke to journalist Mark Murphy at the National Naval Medical Center in Bethesda, Maryland, after her return
from Australia. The Bookmans had no inkling of the connection between Bernatitus and their son. But the circumstances of the story were
so close to John's that it was almost as if he were hiding behind it.

Bernatitus described her wartime ordeal with a restraint born from
experience: her work with Carey Smith at Hospital No. 1 on Bataan, the
evacuation of Mariveles, the siege of Corregidor (which "would tremble
and shiver and shake until you wondered if you were getting it from the
bottom"), and her escape to Australia by submarine. Little did Samuel
and Olga realize that Carey was the "adopted father" in the family
formed by George, Fred, Murray, and John. Little did they know what a
changed man John had become, down to his nickname, Jake.

The story ended on a somber note:

"I would kind of like to go back to the Philippines someday. Maybe things will be different when *we* are not retreating. Maybe it's just my curiosity. . . . A lot of people we left behind we won't find when we get back out there. A lot of people—"

Her voice suddenly sounded odd. She twisted in her chair, and took a handkerchief from a pocket in her dress, and turned her face away from me. "Oh, nuts!" she said into the handkerchief.

On August 13, 1943, Murray wrote in his diary:

> *Bookman reminded me that 2 yrs. ago today we left San Francisco aboard the Garfield. We wonder when we'll be back there.*
> *I thought of the letter I wrote Laura describing the moment we left. . . . And the feeling of sadness & loneliness that engulfed me when I saw that thin strand of paper break as the ship slowly pulled away from the pier was not because of a prophetic vision of the present misery . . . but because actually I saw the last thin tie that bound me to the life I had known & loved just flutter to the pier & into the bay to become no more than a bit of refuse.*

In August the earth was flooded and spirits were dampened. The guards at Bilibid had become more vigilant, punitive, and there was the threat that the commissary would be discontinued. Sixty percent of the rice consumed in the Philippines was imported from Saigon, but the Japanese controlled distribution and sales, which left little for the Filipino people. With inflation soaring, basic foodstuffs were unaffordable for the average Manileño, and even less accessible to the average POW. There were reports that the Japanese were digging foxholes around Manila. An increase in dysentery corresponded to the decline in morale. Some POWs, like Captain Robert Chambers, Jr., were lucky enough to receive radiograms from home via Geneva.

In September 1943 Nogi reorganized Bilibid's POW camp administration. He had been humiliated the previous June, when Private Sanford Jack Blau was caught selling Red Cross items on the outside, using a Japanese guard as an intermediary. Sartin didn't notify Nogi of the incident until four days later. Blau was sentenced to twenty days in the brig, and Nogi was so furious with Sartin that he publicly chastised him for "his negligence in his official duty." Bad enough that Manileños were openly contemptuous of the Japanese.

Nogi replaced Sartin with Hayes as senior medical officer of Bilibid, and Marion Wade took over Maurice Joses's role as executive officer. In a statement Nogi read to Bilibid's medical staff, he praised Sartin for his stewardship but reprimanded him again for "the number of cases of infringement of the rule [*sic*] and regulations" over the past fourteen months. Nogi urged the new administration to abide by the following points, translated into broken English by Yakushiji:

1. Strict observance of the rule and regulation [*sic*] of Japanese Army. The executive officers are responsible for the supervision of all inmates to observe the rule and regulation.
2. Saturate among the inmates that it is the vice to hold such an idea of "Sponge on others," "Eat off from others and give no return."
3. Keep your morale high.
4. To those who are assigned as a new member of the organization, exert your sincere effort for the accomplishment of new task.
5. To those who are drafted to No. 1 Camp, I am so grateful for our effort exerted for the consummation of the function of this hospital.

With a patient census of 611 by late September, there were more doctors and corpsmen than necessary in Bilibid. Hayes was ordered to cut his staff in half. He asked Nogi if Sartin and Joses could stay behind, but Nogi refused. Then George, Fred, John, and Murray could also go, Hayes decided, as well as Stan Smith and corpsmen Richard Bolster, Bernard Hildebrand, and Ernie Irvin.

The foursome said goodbye to Carey Smith and Max Pohlman, to Marion Wade and Gordon Lambert, their friends from Cañacao, Cavite, Bataan, and Corregidor. On October 2, 1943, they were among 150 doctors, medics, and patients who were transferred sixty miles north of Manila to Cabanatuan POW Camp No. 1. But they left more than their friends behind at Bilibid—they shed their identities as doctors. For at Cabanatuan they were to assume a new role: not as medical officers, but as slave laborers.

═══ **16** ═══

The Good Doctor

SUNDAY AFTERNOONS were holidays for Ōhashi Hyōjirō and his family in Ōsaka. The esteemed surgeon who was so fortified by the news of Pearl Harbor played the *shakuhachi,* or bamboo flute, to relax. His younger daughter, Kazuko, practiced piano. His wife, Yukako, and elder daughter, Yasuko, and son, Hisamichi, sang popular songs from the Meiji Restoration.

Dr. Ōhashi was a professor of surgery in the Ōsaka Imperial University Medical Department. He lectured every day, except Sunday, when he performed surgery in the mornings. Some of his patients were casualties from the war in China, and sometimes he came home from the operating room with what appeared to be flecks of blood on his face. Their house stood on Matsuyama Street in front of Ōsaka Castle, which had been reconstructed in 1931 on the foundation of the sixteenth-century citadel. It was a spacious home, and like many Japanese doctors, he maintained a small clinic on the second floor that could accommodate six beds, and which he tended in the evenings. Hyōjirō and Yukako reserved another room for themselves. They loved to dance and rehearsed to a large collection of records. He even sewed his own pair of dancing shoes.

His father hailed from Hidaka in Wakayama Prefecture, in south-central Honshū, where he harvested rice and soy and amassed extensive landholdings. Hyōjirō grew up during the Taishō era, the period following the emperor Meiji's death in 1912, when Japan emerged as a great power with imperialist ambitions yet embraced Western culture. It was a time when popular representation in government was offset by the curtailment of civil liberties, when Tōkyō, as historian Ian Buruma put it, could be likened to Weimar Berlin.

He had met Yukako at a New Year's party in 1921. She was pretty, outgoing, and optimistic, the daughter of a wealthy Tōkyō family that had operated a money exchange business since the Tokugawa shogunate. She was admired for her complexion and kept it the palest white by using a cleanser made from bush warbler droppings and milk. In the light of Yukako's elegant urbanity, Hyōjirō seemed somewhat shy and provincial, but he quickly adapted to the tastes of her class. They were married in November 1922 and were planning on living in Tōkyō when the earthquake of 1923 forced them to take refuge in Ōsaka.

Hyōjirō became a skilled swordsman and talented calligrapher as well as a respected surgeon. Periodically he retreated to an inn in Nishinomiya so he could write haiku in solitude. He was particularly interested in religion and history. When Kazuko was a little girl, he used to tell her stories of the Battle of Tsushima, in which the Japanese decimated the Baltic squadron of the Russian fleet during the Russo-Japanese War. His knowledge of the West derived in part from his medical student days, when he had been a protégé of the German professor Fritz Hartel. Later, when he began to practice English with his son, Hisamichi, he spoke with a German accent. He became an ardent fan of American movies starring Charlie Chaplin, Harold Lloyd, and Rudolph Valentino that were hugely popular in Japan until the mid-1930s. Someday, he vowed, he would visit the United States. But would he be able to eat rice there? he wondered.

In 1943 Hyōjirō was scheduled to depart on a hospital ship heading south, but he developed a fever and a subordinate went in his place. After leaving port, the ship was hit by a torpedo and sunk. Hyōjirō remained in Ōsaka, pressed into service as a POW camp medical officer. The city famous for its tenth-century Temman-gu shrine, dedicated to the patron saint of learning, had become, by the mid-twentieth century, a monument to military production and the incarceration of prisoners of the Japanese.

The four navy doctors left Bilibid at 0400, stuffed themselves with food they had purchased from a Filipino vendor at the Tutuban station, and were herded onto a train: sixty-six POWs per boxcar, windowless, airless, so crowded it was impossible to move, much less sit down. They left as conditions were deteriorating rapidly at Bilibid, "mostly closing down on outside contacts," said John, "limiting money, and limiting spending at the store." It took eight hours to go by narrow-gauge railroad a mere sixty miles north of Manila. The "*Carabao* Railway Express," the POWs called it. Once they arrived in Cabanatuan City, the capital of Nueva Ecija Province, they were transferred onto trucks and hauled four miles northeast to POW Camp No. 1, Military Prisoner of War Camp of the Philippine Islands, otherwise known as Cabanatuan.

Cabanatuan sat on a vast, treeless plain that soaked up the sun like a giant clay pan in the heart of Luzon's rice-growing country. To the west rose the Caraballo Mountains, out of which flowed the Pampanga River, one tributary snaking east. The Sierra Madres curled down from the northeast, while the volcanic peak of Mt. Arayat marked the horizon to the south. The air shimmered with waves of heat. Natives tilled the earth with *carabao*-drawn plows and harvested rice by hand. They moved through the landscape as if in slow motion. When the rains came, Cabanatuan turned into a sea of mud.

"The place looks like a glorified hobo camp," John wrote in his diary. But instead of tents and cardboard shacks, dozens of one-story *nipa*-roof buildings with *sawali* sides were laid out into a large rectangle surrounded by three rows of perimeter fences up to ten feet in height. The Japanese posted armed soldiers in four-story guard towers that were interspersed with pillboxes at the camp's midpoints and corners.

The navy doctors had heard stories of life at Cabanatuan from their patients in Bilibid, and they weren't pretty. The Japanese had seized Cabanatuan City on December 29, 1941, terrorized the Filipinos, and established Cabanatuan at Camp Pangatian, formerly a barracks of the Philippine Army, and before that, a U.S. Department of Agriculture station.

Cabanatuan originally consisted of three facilities. Cabanatuan No. 3 was situated fifteen miles from the city and received the first group of POWs from Corregidor, via Bilibid, on May 27, 1942. By May 30 the prison census had swelled to 6,000. On May 31, another 1,500 POWs arrived at Camp No. 2, which was nine miles from town. The water supply there proved inadequate, and on June 3 the men were moved to Camp No. 3. In the meantime, prisoners from Camp O'Donnell straggled into Camp No. 1, pushing its population to 7,000. When two large drafts departed Camp No. 3 in October 1942, the remaining POWs merged into Camp No. 1, which was thereafter the only POW facility operating in Cabanatuan.

Main Street divided the camp into two parts, the northeast corner of which was occupied by POWs. The center of the American sector was called Times Square, bounded by Fifth Avenue—where the dispensary, chapel, library, and shoe and tailor shops were situated—and Broadway. The camp's westernmost side would house the hospital facilities, opposite the "Jap Area," as one map described it.

The barracks were open and raised off the ground, with two center planks as walkways. Each *bahay* (Tagalog for house) had been built to accommodate forty Filipino soldiers, but the Japanese jammed as many as 128 POWs inside them. The walls were hung with two tiers of wooden bays for sleeping. The lower bay was one and a half feet high; the upper bay was only three feet higher. As a rule, four men slept in each bay. Few of the new arrivals had mattresses, so they spread shelter halves or blankets over the bamboo slats. Width-wise each man had only a foot of space. You knew the boundaries of your area intimately, invisible property lines that you guarded zealously. You slept on your side and lay like a spoon to avoid breathing in another man's face. If you were five foot ten or taller, your feet dangled over the walkway. And if you had to go to the bathroom at night, you climbed over a mass of bodies and bumbled through the darkness to the saddle trench outside. Flashlights, lanterns, and candles were prohibited. There was no water in the *bahays,* except what was rationed for cooking, so you bathed in the rain; later, barrels of water were hoisted up on stilts and operated as lever-controlled showers.

The Americans organized Cabanatuan according to service branches. There were two groups of army personnel, and one of marine and navy men. Until September 1942 Colonel Boudreau was commanding officer, and Colonel James Gillespie was medical director. On August 31 both men were transferred to Karenko, the officers' camp in Formosa, and were replaced by "the mad marine," Lieutenant Colonel Curtis Beecher, and Lieutenant Colonel William Riney Craig, respectively. Lieutenant Colonel Jack Schwartz and then Lieutenant Colonel Gaskill handled dispensary services. Colonel Mori was the Japanese commandant until November 11, 1942, when he was replaced by Major Iwanaka, who in turn was succeeded by Major Takasaki on July 8, 1944. The Japanese medical officer in charge was 2nd Lieutenant Konishi Shoji until Suehiro Satoro took his place.

Camp conditions, said Captain William E. Dyess, "while better than those at O'Donnell, were nevertheless terrible." In the early months, the average daily diet "rarely reached 1,000 calories," according to Lieutenant Colonel Eugene Jacobs, the former regimental surgeon of the Philippine Army at Camp John Hay who was chief of the medical service at Cabanatuan. Polished rice and *kangkong* were the staples, with white or yellow corn as a substitute for the green swamp weed. Fuel to run the well-pump engine was insufficient, and at one point there were only three spigots for 9,000 men. Overflowing pit latrines that swarmed with flies and mosquitoes caused an outbreak of dysentery of near-epidemic proportions. There was no quinine to treat malaria or antitoxin for diphtheria.

The sight of the "battling bastards" who were transferred from Camp O'Donnell brought tears to Colonel Gillespie's eyes:

Inching their way along the road came a ragged formation of dirty, unkempt, unshaven, half-naked forms, pale, bloated, lifeless. They staggered and stumbled, some plodded, others uncertain of their balance and strength lay down only to be urged by attendants who in many instances were only slightly more able than those they were assisting. Limbs grotesquely swollen to double their normal size. Faces devoid of expression, form or life. Aged incredibly beyond their years. Barefeet on the stony road. Remnants of gunny sacks as loin cloths. Some stark naked. Bloodshot eyes and cracked lips. Smeared with excreta from their bowels. Thus they came . . . to the end of the road, the strong, young and alert men of the 31st U.S. Infantry, the Air Corps, Artillery and supporting services.

The hospital—with an operating room, surgical ward, clinic, mess, dysentery unit, and morgue—was set up under Gillespie's direction. Operations were performed for emergencies only; there was no elective surgery. The operating table was cut from scrap lumber, and the OR was without lights or running water. There was no post-op care. Either you returned to your *bahay*, or you lay on a bare floor. Next to the clinic was a commissary, run by Lieutenant Colonel Harold K. Johnson, where orders were filled by Tomás de Guzman and a Japanese *mestiza*, both of whom were pro-American. In all, 250 medical officers and corpsmen worked in the hospital, which opened in June 1942 with a patient census of more than 1,500.

Thirty wards designed to hold forty men apiece would be used to accommodate as many as one hundred patients each. When the buildings were originally numbered, the dysentery unit was skipped, so it became known as the Zero Ward. Isolated from other cases, the patients in Zero Ward were a study in collective misery: naked, skeletal, sprawled on a wooden floor. They were covered in feces and coated with vomit; their bodies twitched with bluebottle flies. They had no blankets, and initially there was no water for them unless it was collected from rooftops or ditches. Brooms were made from *cogon* grass and, later, soiled clothing. The stench was unbearable. Some couldn't make it to the latrines, 50 to 100 yards away; others died in the grass or expired beneath the barracks. Zero Ward took on another meaning entirely, remarked army doctor John Bumgarner: those who were admitted to it had virtually zero chance of surviving. The Japanese wouldn't set foot in it for a month. Bilibid looked like a university medical center by comparison.

In June 1942 Colonel Gillespie requested 750,000 five-grain tablets of quinine to treat 1,600 cases of recurrent malaria. By early August the Japanese had issued only 25,000 three-grain tablets, which had been salvaged from the Dutch East Indies. Doctors and corpsmen turned to native and natural medicines to treat other maladies. To control diarrhea, they combined charcoal from the mess-hall stoves and cornstarch with guava leaf tea. They advised dysentery patients to lie on their right sides so as not to upset the sigmoid colon. They cultivated soybean sprouts, which were rich in vitamin C, to combat scurvy. They fermented rice to produce vitamin B$_1$ and applied mud poultices to Guam blisters. They made dental fillings from silver pesos and false teeth from *carabao* teeth. There were even two POWs who shared one set of dentures, taking turns to eat. One doctor had found that alcoholic extracts of grass helped improve the coats of his pet rabbits back in Arizona; Paul Ashton used the concoction on patients suffering from scurvy and corneal ulcers, and "in every case" he noticed "marked improvement." To reduce the spread of dysentery, the Japanese ordered every man to catch fifty flies per day, and soon flies became currency. Loren E. Stamp, Pharmacist's Mate 2nd Class, charged twenty flies for a haircut or a shave. Perhaps the most important innovation came from Major Emmet C. Lentz, who was trained in military medicine. Lentz designed a ten-hole latrine and a self-irrigating septic system with water supplied by a bucket detail. To Ralph Hibbs, it was the eighth wonder of the world, "the Taj Mahal of Cabanatuan."

Fifteen hundred men—nearly all of whom were survivors of Bataan—died in the first three months at Cabanatuan from June to August 1942. Some of the POWs who succumbed to gastrointestinal diseases were subjected to autopsies by the Japanese, a process that began, bizarrely, with removal of the testicles. The final insult was to conceal the cause of death. If a man entered the hospital with hemorrhoids and contracted diphtheria, the Japanese listed the initial diagnosis as the reason for his demise, thereby completely distorting the medical picture.

John Nardini, who had arrived in June 1942 from Hospital No. 2 on Bataan and was one of the few navy doctors with a medical role at Cabanatuan, saw the worst of it. In the absence of medicine, all the doctors could do was instill hope, a will to live. "A kindly word and easy handling will do as much good as medicine," said army doctor Jack Schwartz, whose weight would drop to ninety pounds.

In the early months at Cabanatuan, a slow, steady stream of burial parties began arriving at the morgue each day just after breakfast. The bodies lay on wooden-frame pallets covered in *sawali*. It took four men to carry one corpse to the horseshoe-shaped cemetery three-quarters of a mile away. They buried the deceased in a hole they had dug the day before, and then they dug another hole for the next day's detail. Four men who were themselves ill, emaciated, struggling through the 100-degree heat to shoulder the burden of a lost buddy, staring into the abyss that awaited them. It was a parade of the dead, said John Bumgarner. During the torrential rains of summer, the odor of decomposing flesh hung over Cabanatuan like a cloud. "Pits were always full of water, and I have seen prisoners who . . . found it necessary to push arms, legs and heads down to keep them from floating long enough to cover them with earth," remarked Walter Waterous, chief of the EENT ward. Roving dogs tore at the exposed flesh. In the early months at Cabanatuan, the chaplains were prohibited from holding religious services; nor would the Japanese let them attend an interment.

Some prisoners appeared to choose their own deaths. One POW asked Captain Cecil M. Sanders to carry him outside.

"Why?" Sanders queried.

"I don't want to die in this stinking *bahay*," he replied. "I want to get out in the air."

Sanders refused. The man crawled outside and died.

Then there was the old soldier who announced, "I'm going to die tonight."

He held on to Sanders, who told him at 0300, "You'd better hurry up if you want to die tonight. The night's pretty short." He was dead at dawn.

Men gave up psychologically before yielding physically. The youngest POWs, between eighteen and twenty-two, fared the worst, perhaps due to inexperience and shock at their circumstances. Next came the forty-five-to-fifty-five-year-old group. Those between twenty-three and thirty-three years old had the best chances for survival.

Quanning boosted morale, reinforced group identification, and helped men get over "*bahay* fever"—irritability due to extreme overcrowding. Religious belief had minimal import as a survival factor. But placebos, which the Japanese culled from raids on Filipino drugstores, had a positive effect. Nardini stocked Dr. Carter's Pink Pills for Pale People and Lydia Pinkham's Vegetable Compound as part of his personal dispensary. The idea of medicine, the belief that something might help you and that someone cared enough to try, was a palliative in itself. "Self-pity," as Private 1st Class Ernest Bales remarked, would "put you in your grave."

As on Bataan and Corregidor, there were an unusually low number of psychiatric cases (which flared up as conditions deteriorated), and only two reported suicides. But as Gillespie wrote in his notes on Cabanatuan, composed while he was a captive in Formosa:

> Men generally degenerated; finer qualities of honor, fortitude, honesty and fair play disappeared. There was petty squabbling over trifles. Some stole, others secured additional food through fraud and cheating. Many engaged in mindless criticism and disrespect for those in positions of responsibility. Some of the officers were little or no better than the worst of the men. Under normal conditions most

of these individuals would not have been classed as psychopaths, but they evidently had a potential for inadequate behavior under the conditions of stress and privation, which was strikingly in contrast with that large body of men who conducted themselves with dignity, fortitude, honor and forbearance, through the long periods of captivity.

Doctors faced their own moral and ethical dilemmas. If you're responsible for 100 sick men, half of whom have their lives at stake, but you have only ten sulfa and ten quinine pills a day to give them, whom do you treat? A certain amount of triage was inevitable, though it wasn't publicly discussed among medical staff or chaplains. Nardini made the decisions himself. He chose those who were trying hardest to survive, those who understood that they had to adapt to conditions beyond their control yet never gave up hope of going home.

———————

The Japanese made POWs at Cabanatuan sign a declaration that was printed both in English and Japanese to the effect: "I swear that I will not attempt to escape or assist others to escape, under penalty of being shot." They forced the Americans to guard themselves, which was a violation of international law. In spite of the fact that Cabanatuan was fenced, isolated, surveilled twenty-four hours a day, and miles from the nearest barrio, forest, or stream, some prisoners found freedom a temptation too sweet to resist.

Around September 1, 1942, three POWs—Lieutenant Colonel Biggs and Breitung and Navy Lieutenant Gilbert, a mining engineer John knew from the Section Base in Mariveles—were caught in a drainage ditch trying to sneak under the fence. The Japanese stripped them down to their undershorts, tied them with wire to an entrance post, and beat them at every changing of the guard. Filipinos who passed by on the road were forced to bow to the Japanese and then club the POWs. A typhoon struck, the first of the season. After forty-eight hours without food or water, the escapees were driven off in a truck toward a small schoolhouse, where two were reputedly shot and one was beheaded.

One night Beecher was called to the main gate, where a Japanese doctor and adjutant told him through an interpreter that a prisoner had been shot while trying to escape. They wanted Beecher to see the body, which was lying in the middle of the main road, bordering the hospital area. He had scaled the fence, the interpreter explained. But the corpse was emaciated, and the grass alongside the road was trampled down, as if a body had been dragged out of camp to its present location. Beecher learned later that the POW was a psychiatric patient who had wandered out of his ward undetected, only to meet his death.

In April 1943 two POWs, Stobaugh and Kelly, successfully broke out of Cabanatuan and sent a note back via the underground postal service urging their pals to join them. The Japanese were furious and soon made Private John B. Trujillo of the 200th Coastal Artillery Corps an object lesson.

Trujillo was a perimeter guard who traded regularly over the fence with one of the Japanese sentries, who was eager to acquire watches and fountain pens, cigarette cases and jewelry. But one day the Japanese officer of the day appeared unexpectedly, and since barter was prohibited between prisoners and their guards, the sentry viciously turned on the American, held him at bayonet point, and claimed he had just attempted to escape. Trujillo was quickly tried and, over Beecher's objections, convicted and sentenced to death. First he was belted, clubbed, and kicked in the head. Then his hands were tied with barbed wire behind his back, and "three distinct sounds crashed through the silence of the plains as he paid the crime of being patriotic. A coup de grâce revolver shot followed a few sounds later," Calvin Chunn recorded in his notebook. POWs working the farm watched the scene in horror. Executions became public spectacles.

As Henry G. Lee wrote in a poem entitled "An Execution":

> Red in the western sun, before he died
> We saw his glinting hair; his arms were tied.
> There by his lonely form, ugly and grim,
> We saw an open grave, waiting for him.
> We watched him from our fence, in silent throng,
> Each with the fervent prayer, "God make him strong."
> They offered him a smoke; he'd not have that,
> Then at his captors' feet coldly he spat.
> He faced the leaden hail, his eyes were bare;
> We saw the tropic rays glint in his hair.
> What matter why he stood facing the gun?
> We saw a nation's pride there in the sun.

"Escape impossible," Colonel Mori had told the entire stockade. The POWs were divided into ten-man "shooting squads." If one man escaped, he warned, the other nine in this squad would be executed in retaliation. The atmosphere was charged with a slow, steady undercurrent of fear.

By the time the four navy doctors arrived at Cabanatuan in October 1943, the prison population was roughly 4,400, 1,500 of whom were in the hospital. The death rate had dropped to just one or two men a day. Barracks No. 32 became their new home, and as soon as Murray stepped into it, he saw that they had visitors: the place was crawling with bed-bugs and lice.

The camp was divided into three groups—Camp Supply, Camp Library, and Camp Utilities. In early 1943, Major Iwanaka, then the camp commandant, had determined the number of medical personnel who could work in the hospital and dispensary, and both were run by the army. With the hospital census reduced, the navy doctors and corpsmen from Bilibid had only a small medical role to play. Except for John Nardini, Bruce Langdon, and the senior officers—Sartin, Joses, and Hjalmer Erickson—they were consigned, like the enlisted men, to manual labor.

If a man could walk, the Japanese reasoned, he could work, and if he couldn't walk, his food ration was cut. This was known as the "No work, no eat" policy. But protest one violation, and you were apt to be subjected to another. Beecher and Schwartz were "slapped around" for voicing their objections.

The POWs' work ranged from farming to chopping wood, digging ditches, moving buildings, repairing roads, cutting hay and bamboo, "beautifying" the cemetery, and constructing an airfield, which violated Article 31 of the Geneva Convention forbidding work that bore a "direct relation with war operations." There were light and heavy equipment operators, cowboys who raised Brahma cattle for Japanese consumption, and truckers known as Kings, because they lived like royalty and were a regular source of news and contraband from Manila. When fuel for trucks became scarce, the Japanese formed a *carabao* caravan between camp and Cabanatuan City, whose jockeys were called "coxswains." Some enlisted men worked as dog robbers for the Japanese in exchange for food and tobacco. The least desirable job of all was the "honey detail," whose unfortunate handlers had to empty Japanese latrines and spread human waste on fields as fertilizer or "night soil." There was even a movie detail, whose stand-ins engaged in mock battles on Bataan for the Japanese propaganda film *Ano Hata o Ute*, known under the English pre-production title as *Tear Down the Stars and Stripes*. Directed by Abe Yutaka, a University of Southern California graduate who had lived in Hollywood for fourteen years, it was released in Manila in February 1944 as *The Dawn of Freedom*.

Each work party had a boss, or *honsho*. A Japanese sergeant named Nakatsui supervised the truck detail and was unusually solicitous. The farm boss, Ihara Kazutane, nicknamed "Air Raid," was notorious for his brutality. Beecher was careful to warn POWs of the consequences of their behavior:

> Do not oppose, insult, or offend the Japanese. Control your temper. Avoid all profanity in your official dealings. Bear in mind Article 60 of Camp Rules and Regulations: "For any violations of Regulations the death penalty may be inflicted." These words are unconditional. They mean just what they say; do not doubt them, do not test them; put your shoulder to the wheel and do your best.

John refused to speak Japanese but he could recite *bangō* in his sleep. Each morning the daily count-off began at 0615. *Ichi, ni, san, shi, go, roku, shichi, hachi, kū, jū.* Miss your turn, and you'd be whacked by a guard's "vitamin stick." If the count fell short, the guards made you start all over again. You'd already eaten *lugao* for breakfast, and by 0700 you were on your way to work. *Lugao* at noon, and you were back at work from 1330 until 1730. Finally, supper was served at 1800, and it was *lugao* once more. You were grateful, as much as you'd come to detest it. How many bowls had it been? Hundreds? Thousands? You'd say *arigatō* to express your thanks, even if the rice was milled, shorn of its vitamin-rich polishings. Occasionally it was supplemented with bits of *carabao* the size of hickory nuts.

George, John, and Murray all worked on the farm. So did Fred, until he was allowed to join the wood-chopping detail. The farm was the worst of them all. Rakes were made from wire and bamboo, hoes were cut from 55-gallon oil drums, and "things get done in the old coolie fashion," as John described it. A 200-acre plot had been cleared and cultivated northeast of the camp, and as many as 2,600 POWs toiled on it at a time. Many men wore nothing but *fundoshi.* They were barefoot, which was intended to deter escapes and also turned them into open portals for hookworm. And they were completely unprotected from a blistering sun. Murray was fortunate in having held on to his pith helmet.

They walked down a road along the edge of a field carrying five-gallon gasoline cans, turned right, and at a pile of fertilizer had the cans filled by a shovel crew; then they turned right again, walked down the opposite side of the field and into the furrows, slipping and sliding in the mud, until they reached the holes into which they dumped the fertilizer, and the routine began all over again. Their expressions were blank, their actions rote. Talking was forbidden, so they sang to themselves, cursed under their breath, counted silently, or fell into rhythms, ruts, and imaginary designs. Occasionally a solitary figure stopped to slap or brush off the red ants that feasted on arms and legs; otherwise the only stationary figures were the Japanese guards who stood at the four corners of the field armed with rifles, watching over the men until a white flag was hoisted up the pole on the guard tower and one of them shouted, in broken English, "Take a break." The rest period, *yasumi,* was fifteen minutes in midmorning and midafternoon. The men sat down on the roadside and took long swigs from their canteens, which had been lying in the sun since morning and were now filled with water hot enough for shaving. No one cared, because that was all they had, and before long they broke out some tobacco, rolled cigarettes with toilet paper, or lit up the native smokes sold in camp that they called "Awful Awfuls," because God were they awful and to Murray tasted about as good as hot tar. At least it was something—better than nothing—to break the mindlessness of work, the monotony of their lives.

The farm was planted with corn and *camote,* okra and eggplant, peppers and squash. From sowing to harvest, the work never stopped. The POWs irrigated the vegetables with water that they carried a distance of 500 yards in five-gallon cans. They weeded by hand. They cleared anthills that rose as high as five feet and were infested with cobras. They harvested the crop and in four-man teams hauled it back to camp on litters made from four-by-eight-foot wooden panels that weighed up to 600 pounds apiece or more. The produce was eaten by the Japanese in camp, shipped to headquarters in Manila, or sold at market in Cabanatuan City. Steal a *camote,* the guards said, and you'd be beaten with a pick handle or shot. Drop from heat stroke or illness, and there was no telling what would follow.

Private Walter R. Connell of the 34th Pursuit Squadron was one of those who had escaped from the farm, the Japanese claimed. Filipinos in a barrio two and a half miles to the east had turned him in, they said. His front skull was crushed, his right jaw was broken, he was bayoneted in the chest, right hip, and leg, and one eye was gouged out. He had gone to work that day with a temperature of 103 degrees. The Americans suspected that he had simply collapsed and was beaten to death for his crime.

In late October 1943 Murray received a radiogram from home. It was his first correspondence from his parents in nearly two years, and on November 1 he was allowed to write a fifty-word card in reply:

Was overjoyed to receive your radiogram & hear family well. Keep writing, wiring. Is Sid living at home? How are Ziff, Charlie, Irving?

Regards Dr. Edwin Zabriskie of Welfare Hosp. Tell him intend to study
neurosurgery when I return, will ask for his help & recommendation.
Hoping for reunion soon.
      Love,
      Murray Glusman

Of course you couldn't speak your mind. You couldn't say that the camp was running out of medicine; that the "Cabanatuan Shuffle" wasn't a new dance but was the characteristic gait of men suffering from beriberi peripheral neuritis; or that some men couldn't say what was on their minds anyway because they suffered dementia from the long-term effects of starvation, a condition the POWs called "rice brain." You couldn't write that others were so far gone, they looked like pathological exhibits in a museum of the grotesque, blown up to twice their size by wet beriberi, their eyesight occluded, their testicles as big as grapefruits due to a lack of vitamin C; or that the lines on their fingernails were growing transversely from malnutrition; that teenagers were suffering from "rice belly," with shrunken thoraxes and distended stomachs, their cheeks hollow, their eyes sunken, their chests concave, making them look like little old men. The procession of pathetic human beings tore at the hearts of the navy doctors, augmented their sense of powerlessness, and made them feel as if they had failed miserably in their mission.

In time the POWs were allowed to cultivate garden plots beside their barracks and wards. The Japanese provided some varieties of seed; others were pocketed from the farm detail. The men grew eggplant, okra, corn, radishes, peppers, papaya, banana, and soybeans, using implements fashioned from scrap metal, rusted pipe, and wood.

The wood-chopping detail was supervised by Lieutenant Frank Davis, navigator of the *Canopus*, and Fred was lucky to be assigned to it. Fifty to a hundred POWs were sent ten miles away to cut down trees, debranch them, chop them into three-and-a-half-foot logs, and then load them onto trucks. The wood was used for fuel to keep the kitchen fires going at Cabanatuan. Food was cooked in 25- and 50-gallon cauldrons, or *kawas,* on stone fire boxes in open sheds. The burned rice stuck at the bottom of the pots was prized for its taste.

The woodcutters worked in pairs, and it felt good to be out in the open, shielded from the sun. One Japanese noncom was especially accommodating and even let the POWs go for a swim in the Pampanga River on their way back to camp. On at least one occasion a guard shot a *carabao* so a little meat would be served with the next bowl of rice.

Fred's love of the outdoors, his Boy Scout upbringing, and his navy training had taught him a handful of skills. But he was amazed nonetheless by the ingenuity of the POWs at Cabanatuan, whose talents seemed to blossom like flowers in a junkyard. There were men on his detail who carved beautiful ax handles and intricately detailed cigarette holders, statues, and figurines. One prisoner made a violin from hardwood, another a guitar using sheet metal. Fred himself carved a pipe, using a handmade drill to bore a hole through the stem.

With scrap lumber, bamboo poles, and a little whitewash, Captain Ingerset and Sergeant Abie Abraham built the Carabao Café and Greasy Spoon Annex. Corporal Holliman and Private First Class Greenley designed a miniature nine-hole golf course alongside their barracks and whittled wooden golf clubs and balls until irons were smuggled in from Manila. Sergeant John Katz, a clerk on Corregidor, conducted the camp orchestra, culled from the former 4th Marine band. Called the Cabanatuan Cats, they performed every Wednesday with a repertoire that ranged from Gershwin's *Rhapsody in Blue* to "The Yellow Rose of Texas," and ballads such as "Mood Indigo," "Tenderly," and "In My Solitude." Saturdays were reserved for the Cabanatuan Mighty Art Players, who staged Shakespeare's *Othello*, Dickens's *A Christmas Carol*, and Thornton Wilder's *Our Town*. Lieutenant Colonel Ovid O. "Zero" Wilson, meanwhile, organized a weekly talent show known as the Little Theater Group. Audiences of 3,000 to 4,000 men gathered in a semicircle around the stage were common. Lieutenant Colonel D. S. Babcock started a camp library that eventually was stacked with the works of Shakespeare, Bertrand Russell, and Winston Churchill, as well as games and magazines such as *Life*, *Look*, *Saturday Evening Post*, *Ladies' Home Journal*, and *Mademoiselle*—many of which were supplied by the International Committee of the Red Cross and were slowly released by Japanese censors. The most popular periodical turned out to be not a glossy but a seed catalog from Australia with pictures of vegetables and fruits that made mouths water. Chaplain L. F. Zimmerman followed Babcock's lead with a hospital library for medical texts and journals. Some of the books came from Camp O'Donnell; many others were brought back from a medical conference in Manila that staff doctors were allowed to attend in November 1942. There was even a team of bookbinders who made glue from *lugao*, paper, and boards from Red Cross boxes, and string from cloth remnants. When the books became too shopworn to read, their pages were used to roll cigarettes—or finally as toilet paper. And of course there were movies, Edgar Bergen's *Look Who's Laughing* being one of the first films the navy doctors saw after arriving at Cabanatuan.

Personal items were zealously guarded. Paper was at a premium, initially scrounged from tin can labels. Then the camp received elementary school notebooks, in which the men wrote poems, songs, or recipes or kept diaries that they hid from the Japanese. If they needed a razor, they broke off the tip of their mess-kit knife, and if they were without a toothbrush, they used the split end of a twig.

They were just as industrious when it came to *quanning*. If you used a glass bottle like a rolling pin, you could crush rice into flour for making flapjacks, pies, or cakes. Substitute coconut fuel oil for vegetable oil, Red Cross ascorbic acid for baking soda, Eno's Fruit Salts for baking powder, and Japanese-issue shoe cream for pan grease. For a touch of peppermint in banana custard pie, Japanese tooth powder did the trick. Cornmeal for corn bread and "Indian pudding" relieved the tedium of a rice-based cuisine. The problem was finding enough fuel. Wood was filched from barracks, benches, tables, chairs, even latrine seat covers to feed the flames. Eventually Major Iwanaka banned individual outdoor fires, and *quan* kitchens were established instead.

Within three months of sowing seeds, the prisoners' garden plots began to yield beans, okra, eggplant, tomatoes, garlic, onions, and squash. The men eagerly consumed the vegetables, then experimented by making sourmash, mixing starch into a five-gallon demijohn filled with bananas, burned rice, *camotes,* sugarcane, ginger, and taro root. It tasted as bad as it sounds.

The outer perimeter of a garden could extend no farther than ten feet from the inner fence. One POW, Lieutenant Robert Huffcutt, a representative of the State Department in the U.S. High Commissioner's Office, knocked over a basket of eggplants, which rolled across the boundary. When he went to retrieve them, he was shot by 1st Lieutenant Toshino Junsaburō—"Liver Lips"—who fired two more rounds as Huffcutt lay dead on the ground.

There was a schedule of activities after work. Monday: lecture; Tuesday: *carabao* sing; Wednesday: lecture; Thursday: Captain Lawler's quiz program; Friday: *carabao* crap game; Saturday: jazz band, theater, or glee club; Sunday: religious services, which were held in mess halls or outside in a grove of papaya trees before chapels were built. There was no rabbi for the Jewish POWs, so Master Sergeant Aaron Kliatchko, a Russian immigrant who resided in the Philippines and had been trained as a cantor, held services on Friday evenings and over the High Holy Days.

After dark the men played acey-deucey, chess, checkers, Monopoly, pinochle, backgammon, and poker. Dice were made from *carabao* horn, the dots drilled out by dentists. The players talked, joked, and reminisced. They tore each other down, set each other up, even got down on all fours to conduct that classic medical experiment: Was it really true that passing gas could turn a match flame blue? But of all the games they played, none held their attention more than bridge.

Fred had received a deck of cards in a package from his parents, which led to a running game with George, John, and Murray. Bridge had become hugely popular at home and abroad and proved the perfect pastime for military men. A 1916 British recruiting poster featured three rather elegant men readying themselves for a game of bridge in the trenches above the caption: "Will You Make a Fourth?" The game's reputation spread around the world by ocean liner in the 1930s and won fierce devotees in the highest ranks of service. High Commissioner Sayre never played during peacetime, but he warmed to the game while on Corregidor. President Quezon was a well-known high-stakes player whose regular partner, Manuel Roxas, was now working for the Japanese puppet government in Manila and doubling as a spy. With its seemingly limitless number of individual hands and full deals, and its element of ambiguity, bluff, and double bluff, bridge was the playful metaphor for life and war—at once sublime, serendipitous, and subversive—and life *at* war.

The doctors sharpened their wits and honed their banter on the game. They teased and deceived while plotting the next move. Bridge took their minds off the day's work and gave them something to look forward to. It was their intellectual nourishment, and each man had his place at the table. But the game had to end sometime, and the loser, they agreed, would pick up the tab for their first big blowout back in San Francisco. "So far," John noted on November 17, 1943, "George is it." The question hanging over all of them was when they would make it home. As John admitted, "May '42 made prediction of war over by April '44—revision to be made. Now can't see it over that early but think it more likely as summer '45. A long time." Carey Smith put a bittersweet spin on their prospects when he sang:

> We'll be free in '43
> No more war in '44
> Hardly a man alive in '45.

They dreamed about home just as they fantasized about food. They pored over the few housekeeping magazines in camp and planned and designed the houses they would live in once the war was over. Food fueled the libido, while a lack thereof suppressed even talk about sex. A few POWs—one of whom was a marine, much to Fred's amusement—offered sexual favors, usually in exchange for food.

Wish fulfillment fed rumors, and the rumors ran wild. POWs would be exchanged for the Japanese interned in the United States! No, they were going to be transferred to a neutral country in South America! The Japanese had granted the Philippines independence! The officers from Bataan were to be knighted by the king of England! The sick and disabled could go home! Tōjō had resigned! Germany had surrendered! FDR had promised the Pacific war would be over by the end of '43! The rumors could be ridiculous, incredible, or just plausible enough to raise hopes, which then came crashing down and reinforced one's sense of isolation as fiction begrudgingly gave way to reality.

The guards at Cabanatuan were "meaner'n skunks," as Fred put it. Their hazing was constant. They beat prisoners on the head and shoulders with cudgels. They slapped them regularly in the face. "Air Raid" Ihara fully lived up to his reputation: you had to duck and cover if the little son of a bitch was on the horizon. Another guard on the farm used to taunt prisoners with a defanged cobra that was leashed to a walking stick. A common form of torture was to place a two-by-four behind a POW's knees and force him to squat, which cut off circulation in the legs and caused excruciating pain. "Cabanatuan," said John, "was the worst in terms of personal bodily abuse." Many of the guards were Formosan—"Taiwans," they were called—brutalized by the Japanese and denied the right to speak their own language. They were used only in rear areas, where they could be closely watched by their Japanese superiors.

The behavior of the guards reflected, in part, the culture of cruelty in the Imperial Japanese Army. Discipline was enforced with *bentatsu,* or corporal punishment, which was justified as an "act of love" by the officers on behalf of enlisted men.

"The discipline was terrible," said Kawasaki Masaichi, a sergeant who served in China from 1939 to 1943. "We were beaten every night. Why? I don't understand why. Just so we could be hit. We were far beyond reason."

Novelist Hanama Tasaki, who had served as a private in China, recounted a standing joke in the army:

The Lieutenant slapped the Sub-Lieutenant; the Sub-Lieutenant slapped the Sergeant; the Sergeant slapped the Corporal; the Corporal slapped the Private First Class; the Private First Class slapped the Private; the Private slapped the Private-Second-Grade; the Private-Second-Grade, who had nobody to slap, went into the stable and kicked the horse.

A slap in the face was the equivalent of a verbal reprimand, after which a Japanese soldier was required to thank his superior, *arigatō go-zaimasu*, for giving him his just deserts. Then he quickly regained his footing, as if nothing had happened. On one occasion, however, a Japanese noncom beat a "Taiwan" to death. There were no repercussions whatsoever.

But the violence that Allied POWs encountered at the hands of the Japanese was a shock. Indeed, the first English visitors to Japan had been horrified, in the early seventeenth century, by the violence of everyday life in the Orient (at a time when public beheadings and disembowelments were still common in London). The samurai used to slash corpses "until the wretched body was chopped into mincemeat." One Jesuit observer, Joao Rodrigues, remarked that "the delight and pleasure which they feel in cutting up bodies is astonishing."

Before World War II the average Japanese had had little or no contact whatsoever with Caucasians. With their "red" hair and blue eyes, Americans and Englishmen were the embodiment of the Japanese goblins of folklore. The Japanese found their strong body odor and tomentose torsos as repugnant as their mixed racial heritage. They were *ijin*, "strange people," or *ketō*, "hairy barbarians," inferiors who would forever be on the wrong side of the Japanese racial divide.

But being on the right side of the racial divide could be even worse. Filipinos found slapping particularly degrading, though it was a minor insult compared to the horrors they suffered at the hands of the Japanese. On the march from Mariveles to San Fernando, five to ten times as many Filipinos died as did Americans.

What threw the POWs off most was not simply the viciousness of the Japanese but their unpredictability—the accusations, outbursts, and ensuing repercussions. They had rules upon rules, which they made, remade, and disobeyed. They even changed the calendar. In March 1943 they declared Fridays, not Sundays, were rest days. Then they changed their minds, so Sundays were Sundays again. Violence against POWs was triggered by language problems, cultural differences, racial animosity, and the desire for revenge. Seemingly random, it collectively amounted to the systematic abuse of thousands of Allied prisoners of war, even though the guards, whether Japanese or Formosan, were required to memorize the *Senjinkun*.

The violence against POWs on Bataan was not unusual but became the norm, as if the war were still being waged, one side impervious to the other's surrender. *Gyokusai*, or "glorious self-annihilation," was predicated on destruction of the enemy in battle. The Allies themselves adopted a "take no prisoners" policy. But killing soldiers on a battlefield is one thing; killing unarmed prisoners of war who are being rounded up or are being held inside a concentration camp is another. There was nothing to fear physically from the Allied POWs, just as there was nothing to fear from the estimated 20,000 to 80,000 Chinese women who were raped and the estimated 260,000 noncombatants who were slaughtered during the Rape of Nanking. Or the British nurses who were raped during the Japanese invasion of Hong Kong in 1941 on "Black Christmas," or the doctors, patients, and POWs who were murdered, some of them bayoneted to death in their beds. Or the Australian nurses who were shipwrecked on Banka Island, Sumatra, in February 1942 and machine-gunned from behind as they stood in the waters off Radjik Beach.

In northern Luzon Igorots traditionally engaged in head-hunting. The Japanese did as well though they didn't have to look far: they beheaded POWs, and in New Guinea they devoured them. In one notorious incident on Noemfoor, they slaughtered Formosan laborers for food under the direction of Captain Sugahara, who also served as mess officer. They even cannibalized their own dead when they were starving. The practice was strictly forbidden by the Imperial Japanese Army, but as historian Tanaka Yuki has remarked, "Cannibalism was a systematic and organized military strategy, committed by whole squads or by specific soldiers working within the context of a larger squad."

John Dower pointed out that the Allies themselves were guilty of mutilating the bodies of fallen Japanese soldiers by removing ears, teeth, and heads as war trophies. Along with the mail, U.S. censors discovered, fingers were sent home as souvenirs. One infamous photograph published in *Life* magazine as "Picture of the Week" showed a pretty blonde posed with a skull that her fiancé had shipped her from the Pacific. The Allies executed would-be prisoners of war on Bougainville in the Solomon Islands and slaughtered "hundreds and possibly thousands of Japanese survivors" of a transport ship sunk by the USS *Wahoo* off the north coast of New Guinea. On Bataan, said Private James Kent, thirty-five Japanese were turned over to the Philippine Constabulary—and shot. But such incidents were unusual, just as capturing a Japanese soldier—who usually fought to the death or committed suicide—was itself an exception. "This is explained by the fact that in close work in thick cover (jungle) the man who fires first is the one who will ordinarily walk away," Major James C. Blanning of the 26th Cavalry noted in his diary. "The policy was when in doubt—shoot." When Japanese soldiers surrendered to American forces, in general, the treatment accorded them was humane. Dr. Marcel

Junod, chief delegate of the International Committee of the Red Cross in the Far East, found the care administered by American and Allied armies to the Japanese POWs he visited to be exemplary.

Many Japanese POW camp guards were disabled or retired soldiers. Others were civilians, with a rank below private. They asserted their authority over POWs by beating them; they effectively cannibalized prisoners by denying them drugs and sustenance so they were consumed by disease or perished from malnutrition. Colonel Irvin E. Alexander, who had marched from Mariveles to San Fernando and was transferred from O'Donnell to Cabanatuan, described some POWs there as "so emaciated that their skins hung on them like translucent parchment." It was as if the Japanese wanted to erase their identities from the notebooks of history. No sulfa drugs or quinine were received in Cabanatuan until late 1942. By year end more than 2,500 POWs had died, chiefly from dysentery and malaria.

There were exceptions to this picture, of course. Diphtheria broke out at Bilibid in September 1942, and Ralph Hibbs grew furious when Nogi refused to administer antitoxin. One hundred men died as a result. The disease had emerged two months earlier at Cabanatuan, where there were 350 cases and 125 deaths. Three days after the first diagnosis at Cabanatuan, Colonel Gillespie presented a plan to the Japanese medical staff for treatment and prevention, but it fell on deaf ears. Walter Waterous feared an epidemic after diphtheria antitoxin obtained through Philippine Red Cross channels dried up. He bypassed Colonel Gillespie entirely and went directly to 2nd Lieutenant Konishi Shoji. Konishi reported to Nogi and had warmed up to Waterous after being entertained in Manila by one of his friends, Manila Hotel steward Fred Malvier. Konishi let Waterous visit Bilibid, where, accompanied by Sartin, he made his case before Nogi.

"All right, you go with me," Nogi replied.

Nogi escorted Waterous to the medical depot along the Pasig River, where Lieutenant Colonel Pete Kempf had amassed medical supplies for the Japanese, and within thirty minutes Waterous had 3 million units of the lifesaving antitoxin, which he then divided with Sartin for his patients in Bilibid. Nogi let Waterous spend two days in Manila. During that time he allowed him to go back to his optometrist's office at the former American Chamber of Commerce on Calle David with eighty pairs of POW glasses that were in need of repair. There Waterous treated Nogi to ice cream and was visited by some of his old Manila friends, including Fred Malvier, who broke out a bottle of booze to toast their unexpected reunion. Waterous was permitted a second office visit, ostensibly to pick up the repaired glasses, and another celebration ensued. On leaving,

Nogi warned Waterous to be careful: the Japanese military police, the dreaded Kempeitai, were watching.

Thanks to the antitoxin, diphtheria was contained at Cabanatuan, and not a moment too soon. One POW, Sergeant Clarence M. Graham of the 60th Coast Artillery, was fading into and out of consciousness at Zero Ward and was about to be placed onto a litter when he heard a man say: "I think this guy must still be alive. He hasn't started to rot yet."

Another voice added, "Could be. I'll give him some water."

Graham was paralyzed. His hands, arms, and legs refused to move. His throat was constricted so he couldn't speak. But he could hear and see, and he feared he was going to drown because he couldn't swallow.

"Yah! He is still alive. He bubbles," came the gratified response.

"Let's get him out of here."

Graham was taken to a doctor and injected with antitoxin; with some extra food the chaplains brought, he soon began to recover. While diphtheria was common in Japan and the Japanese had produced their own antitoxin for treatment, they were unfamiliar with the toxoid that was used for immunization in the United States and that successfully prevented epidemics.

Between the lines of camp regulations and behind the guards' backs, the prisoners became expert at undermining the authority of their captors. Sometimes anything seemed possible, so long as you didn't get caught and cause the Japanese to "lose face."

They smuggled in shoes, sugar, vegetables, limes, *calamensi* syrup, and currency from the market stalls outside Cabanatuan, many of which were fronts set up by Horacio "Mut" Manaloto. Mut's principal agent was Tomás de Guzman, a schoolteacher in Manila whose wife, Agustina, was a doctor who donated stocks of her own medicine. They received money from the Chaplain's Aid Assocation, which used Lulu Reyes, a socialite, as a cover and Father Buttenbruck as a go-between. They accepted donations from priests in the Malate Convent and items from Masons that were concealed in the hollow bamboo frames of *carabao* carts returning to camp from Cabanatuan City. And they welcomed assistance from Anthony H. Escoda of the *Manila Daily Bulletin* and the *New York Herald Tribune*. Tony and his wife, Josefa, were affiliated with the Volunteer Social Aid Committee, whose members included Ralph Hibbs's girlfriend, Pilar Campos, and socialites Helen Benitez and Betty Wright.

Women were often the ringleaders of smuggling operations and employed other women as their agents. The Philippine Women's Federation set up a canteen a mile down the road from Cabanatuan that was ostensibly for the Japanese but that stored food and medicine until it could be smuggled into camp. A Philippine Red Cross nurse by the name of Angelina Castro plied her charms on one of Cabanatuan's medical officers, a reputed morphine addict by the name of Dr. Tamura. She was allowed to work at Cabanatuan and to enter and leave at will. Pilar Campos ingratiated herself with the officers and guards of Cabanatuan and regularly sent in parcels for Ralph Hibbs and other prisoners. Peggy Doolin, a Canadian, assumed a Lithuanian identity as "Rosana Utinsky," alias "Miss U." A twenty-two-year-old Igorot by the name of Naomi Flores, codenamed "Looter," served as her go-between. Outside the gates of Cabanatuan, Looter posed as a peanut vendor. Buy a bag of peanuts for a peso, and you'd get ten pesos in change. As a hawker, she made contact with Lieutenant Colonel Mack when he was on the farm detail, and Mack, alias "Liver," became her point man. Looter worked hand in hand with Lieutenant Colonel Harold K. Johnson, who was the purchasing officer at the Cabanatuan commissary and even took orders for items from other POWs, which Miss U filled and delivered to the camp.

Claire Phillips, also known as Dorothy Clara Fuentes, was another vital source of information and contraband. Known as "High Pockets" for the valuables she stuffed into her bra, she had married a U.S. Army sergeant who died on Bataan. High Pockets ran a Manila nightclub called Tsubaki (the Japanese word for camellia) that was patronized by Japanese officers. She used their confessions and indiscretions for intelligence purposes. She managed to slip more than 10,000 quinine tablets into Cabanatuan. "The medicines and foodstuffs provided through the underground," said Johnson, "were invaluable in saving the lives of many American prisoners." But there were entire segments of the camp population that never benefited from this underground pipeline, and the navy doctors were among them.

Smuggling was dangerous work, and those who engaged in it risked their lives. To travel from Manila to Cabanatuan, Filipinos were forced to ride atop boxcars, or between them, or even on the cowcatcher, which could rattle the nerves of almost any courier. Japanese guards regularly harassed them.

Inside Cabanatuan Lieutenant Homer T. Hutchinson, Corps of Engineers, assembled a shortwave radio from components that filtered into camp. From copper, acid stolen from a Japanese truck's battery, and zinc buttons removed from trouser flies, Hutch made a radio battery, which he stored in a Red Cross tin, and concealed a one-tube receiver in the false bottom of a canteen. He hid earphones in a pillow at night and, pretending to be asleep, picked up broadcasts from around the world, including KGEI. He even had a backup radio plugged into a chapel altar. But Hutch wanted to make sure that no one could ever finger him, so he played dumb as a stump. He wouldn't disseminate the news until the Japanese sent out a work party, or a new contingent of POWs arrived. Hours later he'd drop into conversation "I heard a good rumor"—about the latest naval engagement or American landing. And "nobody," said Al Smith, "knew where the rumor came from." As a result, bragged Alfred Weinstein, "We were never more than a week behind the news."

There was no end to the resourcefulness of the prisoners. Using snares made from pins and corn kernels as bait, they raided the goose pond on the Japanese side of the camp until half of the flock was hooked and cooked. Frank Davis bribed the *honsho* on the wood-chopping detail to let him bring back into camp food and fruit, chickens, and tobacco from the Filipino vendors on the outside. The supervisor of the *carabao* detail, a man named Fred Treatt, used a canteen with a false bottom as a letter pouch. Major Howard Cavender, formerly general manager of the Manila Hotel, was another conduit on the underground postal route. Major Wade Cothran, a businessman in the Philippines before the war started, organized a check-cashing operation that carried a 10 percent service charge. Donations went into a Camp Welfare Fund managed by Lieutenant Dwight Edison. Ted Lowen, an American who ran the Alcazar nightclub in Manila before the war, supervised a construction detail in camp. He shamelessly bribed the Japanese—watches for noncoms, rings for the guards—which enabled him to import "tons of food and hundreds of thousands of pesos" in 1943, estimated Weinstein.

The purchasing power of POWs was supplemented by their pay, and by pesos that had been expertly counterfeited by the Chinese in Manila. But more than just counterfeit cash was circulating in Cabanatuan. One ingenious POW fabricated sulfathiazole pills by mixing rice flour with cornstarch, stamping out tablets with the hollow brass jacket of a .30-06 cartridge, imprinting them with a *W* that looked like the Winthrop Pharmaceuticals logo, and baking them. He sold the placebos for a dollar a pop to Japanese guards, an estimated 50 percent of whom suffered from *baidoku,* or venereal disease, and continued to suffer from it in spite of their purchases. POWs at Bilibid also trafficked in counterfeit drugs, until the Japanese finally analyzed some of the tablets and broke up the racket.

By late 1943 the Japanese were clamping down on clandestine operations. They arrested and interrogated Naomi Flores three times and once tortured her for a week in Fort Santiago. They imprisoned Miss U, beat her, tortured her, and placed her in solitary confinement over a thirty-two-day period, releasing her only after she signed a document that read

in part: "Since I have been in Fort Santiago for questioning, I have received courteous treatment from all officers and sentries and been provided with good food." They exposed Colonel Mack, whom they
brutally interrogated and also threw into solitary. And eventually they
caught Guzman, who wound up in the Mandaluyong Psychopathic
Hospital. The Japanese prevented Father Buttenbruck from visiting Cabanatuan and the Escodas from bringing in supplies. Fred Treatt, Jack
Schwartz, Lieutenant Colonels Edward C. Mack and Alfred C. Oliver Jr.,
the camp's senior chaplain, would be incarcerated in the Japanese guardhouse for their role in the distribution of mail and money. Prices escalated as goods became scarce and the value of the peso plunged. Father
Buttenbruck was later executed, Pilar Campos was murdered, and the
Escodas were imprisoned, tortured, and killed.

Barracks inspections were common, and sometimes guards rifled
through personal belongings three or four times, searching for unauthorized books, literature, or maps. They took whatever they wanted. The
POWs frequently had advance warning and buried their contraband beforehand. One prisoner was doing just that after the sun went down
when a Japanese sentry called out, facetiously, *"Yasume!"* (at ease).

If some POWs managed to circumvent the Japanese, others were
willing to exploit any situation out of blind self-interest. There were
those who faked the symptoms of "painful feet" to avoid work details,
only to be discovered later in the day playing volleyball. Sergeant Jack C.
Wheeler felt the spirit move him after guzzling two bottles of Protestant
sacramental wine by himself. Warrant Officer C. A. Price was caught
selling sulfa drugs to Filipinos in Cabanatuan City. Still other prisoners
committed perhaps the most heinous of crimes, stealing food from fellow POWs. To turn against a comrade was only to augment the power of
the Japanese when the goal, instead, was to diminish it.

So the men verbally emasculated the guards, cut them down to size,
and dehumanized them by reducing them to nominal jokes. The popular American image of the Japanese—in publications ranging from the
venerable *New York Times, Collier's*, and *Time* to the Marine Corps's
Leatherneck—devolved into gorillas, baboons, and monkeys. To the
POWs the Japanese were "dwarfs," "midgets," "squinties," and "little yellow bastards." In his notebooks Calvin Chunn couldn't even bring himself to capitalize the word *jap*.

There was "Little Speedo," who was all business in front of officers
and noncoms, but as easygoing as could be when he was out of their
sight, and a notorious thief. His larger counterpart, "Big Speedo," had
been a Tōkyō policeman and was generally well liked until he casually
shot a deranged Filipino boy in the head for having sneaked under the

fence. "Air Raid" Ihara once whacked a line of 100 POWs in formation, knocking half of them down from behind, and he executed Major Charles F. Harrison for concealing seeds in the hollow heel of his shoe. There was Koshinaga, whose speech was so garbled he was dubbed "Donald Duck." Told he was named after a famous Hollywood movie star, he was flattered by the notion until he saw his namesake one day in a Disney cartoon at Cabanatuan. One guard was known simply as "Dumb-Shit." Insult and imprecation, the name reflected with deadly accuracy the way so many POWs were made to feel about themselves, as if their lives were an embarrassing hindrance, an offensive obstruction, no more than human waste.

The biggest morale boosters were Red Cross packages, which first arrived in Cabanatuan on November 28, 1942. The Japanese cut rations correspondingly. They removed the newspapers that were included in the parcels and went so far as to replace the standard-issue Old Gold cigarettes boasting "Freedom is our heritage" with Chesterfields. It didn't much matter to the men. The smell of tobacco smoke was intoxicating, "redolent of heaven and home," Murray wrote wistfully, "and I suppose the two are synonymous anyway."

The sudden increase in daily caloric intake coincided with a decrease in malaria and enteric diseases, though George was still subject to attacks of amoebic dysentery. But another disease was now visible in 10 percent of Cabanatuan's 5,000-strong prison population, Ralph Hibbs noted: gynecomastia. Grown men developed breasts the size of adolescent girls' and in some cases could even express milk. It was humiliating to the prisoners suffering from it, and Hibbs could only speculate that it was caused by an endocrine imbalance and inadequate vitamin intake.

Along with Red Cross supplies came medicines, and guards continuously harassed the POW doctors for treatment. Japanese headquarters strictly forbade the practice, but the officers ignored it. Gonorrhea was such a persistent problem among the Japanese that sulfathiazole tablets, which the Americans had only in limited quantities, were at a premium, whether real or counterfeit. Drugs became dollars, or pesos, or food. Instead of taking the medications prescribed for them, some POWs sold it. One prisoner was found dead from malaria, with dozens of quinine tablets in his possession.

As the black market dried up, the daily diet became one of subsistence. Meat disappeared. Granulated fish—which some said was really intended as fertilizer—was issued in its place and sprinkled by the spoonful over the rice ration, which fell to 300 grams daily. Inflation increased to such an extent that commissary expenditures soared to two

times the payroll receipts. Some items, such as duck eggs, literally quin-
tupled in price.

The men scoured Cabanatuan. They rooted through Japanese
garbage cans and made soup from the scraps. They hid frogs in canteens
and roasted them on sticks. Two men were so desperate that they cut up
corncobs into small pieces, ate them, and were found dead the next day.

As 1943 came to a close, the prisoners in Cabanatuan could tell the
war in the Pacific was turning against the Japanese. The signs were clear:
the lack of food, a shortage of gas that necessitated a daily *carabao* cart
train between the camp and Cabanatuan City, and articles in the
English-language *Nippon Times* and *Japan Times and Advertiser* that the
Japanese allowed into camp once a month. According to such accounts,
the Japanese were always fighting bravely, but their triumphs were in the
face of greater odds, and it struck Colonel Irvin Alexander that the authors who recounted the heroics of the Japanese military "would not object to resting in Tōkyō permanently, permitting others to gain all the
glory of defeating the Americans."

Christmas 1943 "was celebrated as beautifully at Cabanatuan as in
the finest church in the world," said 1st Lieutenant John M. Wright, Jr.,
of the Coast Artillery Corps. On Christmas Eve the glee club serenaded
the camp, and thousands of men turned out for midnight mass, which
was organized by Chaplain Thomas J. Scecina. The International Committee of the Red Cross sent a holiday radiogram extending "their most
cordial wishes for 1944" and affirming that "its associates all over
Switzerland and its delegates throughout the wide world are thinking
with deep affection of war prisoners, civilian internees, and their families." Major Paul Wing secretly photographed one of the ceremonies at
Cabanatuan and processed the negative with chemicals smuggled into
the camp, though there was no paper on which to print it.

To others, the Christmas cheer rang hollow; the singing sounded like
a dirge. The Japanese had begun a new campaign of harassment. There
had been no meat for nearly a month, John noted in his diary entry for
December 25. By mid-January singing, movies, and band practice would
be eliminated from camp activities. Then talking and smoking were prohibited after 1900.

John was tormented by a sense of stasis, of life going on without him,
of a career that lay dead in its tracks. After work details at Cabanatuan, he
had taken to repairing watches. He enjoyed the precision and concentration it required, adjusting the balance spring and escapement, fine-tuning
amplitude, calculating the daily rate, fixing time so it could move once
again. If only he could turn the clock back and start all over, or wind it
forward to the future so being a prisoner of war was in the past.

Seeing John at work made Murray think of the gold Wyler-Incaflex wristwatch that Charlie Lipsky had given him and that had been stolen on Corregidor. Stealing time, that was what the Japanese were doing. Murray was determined to keep up his contacts back home and stake a claim for himself by mail, even if it was from prison camp in the Philippines. But when would they return, and how? At what point would the Americans try to liberate the islands? And what would happen to the prisoners of the Japanese? The navy doctors had more questions than answers, but they felt certain of one thing: they would still be POWs next Christmas, whether they were in Luzon or Japan.

On February 7, 1944, Murray returned from burial detail and learned that a 200-man medical detachment was leaving Cabanatuan. Colonel Craig called a meeting at 1900:

> We have arranged the personnel into four groups. Of course you will realize it was a difficult job. Some of the people who wish to be together may have been separated—but we did our best. Perhaps some of you may have been able to do better—but we did our best. The casual medical officers here have been available for work detail—but that was no fault of ours—we had nothing to do with it—we did our best—we did our best.

Murray was incensed. Colonel Craig's explanation was bumbling self-exculpation. "I don't know how many years of post-grad. training the Col. had," he seethed in his diary, "but apparently his specialty was the inane." While a few army doctors and medics were included in the detail—Al Weinstein, John Bumgarner, and Major James Bahrenburg among them—the message couldn't have been clearer. Almost the entire navy medical group at Cabanatuan—doctors, dentists, and corpsmen—was being shipped out "for parts unknown."

As early as September 1942 the Japanese had begun transferring POWs from Luzon to Japan to augment a workforce that was being drained by the Imperial Japanese Army. Prisoners were used as slave laborers by some of Japan's largest corporations, and in jobs that aided the war effort—among them Hitachi Shipbuilding and Kawasaki Heavy Industries, Mitsubishi Chemical, and Mitsui Mining. They became coal and copper miners, stevedores and railyard workers, machinists and mill workers. They were loaded onto unmarked merchant vessels, or *shōsen,* built by some of the very companies they would soon be working for.

Rumors circulated of POW transports being sunk by American planes or torpedoed by American submarines. Hayes had heard them at

Bilibid. Weinstein had heard them at Cabanatuan. George got wind of them as well. But after his initial anger at Colonel Craig, Murray reasoned that the decision might work to his advantage after all, rumors notwithstanding. The Americans were bound to retake the Philippines, in which case Luzon would be at the center of a monumental battle. There was no point being in the bull's-eye again if they could avoid it. It was better to leave now. Or were they merely leaving one target for another, as they had so often?

The medical detachment was divided into four groups that would set up POW hospitals in Kyūshū, Ōsaka, Tōkyō, and Hokkaidō. For Fred, John, and Murray, there was one problem: George couldn't go with them. The Japanese were terrified of infectious disease, and George was still in the grip of amoebic dysentery. Anyone suffering from a parasitic illness had to be left behind. They tested the POWs by ramming a glass rod up their rectums. The men were forced to drop their trousers and place their hands on their knees or touch their toes. Then an eight-inch glass probe with a knob at the end was inserted anally, twisted, withdrawn, and a culture was taken for disease-causing organisms. The Japanese recorded 1,500 cases of amoebic dysentery at Cabanatuan in early 1944. But the test itself was notoriously unreliable.

Murray urged George to swap smears with someone who was healthy and who would rather remain in Cabanatuan. One of Craig's corpsmen, John Cook, claimed that a 4th Marine had substituted dog feces for his dysentery test courtesy of Soochow, the mongrel mascot of the regiment who survived the fall of Corregidor. Fred worried that George would get caught. But they couldn't break up the group, Murray argued. Not now. He knew it wasn't ethical, but expediency overruled what was right, and what had worked for them so far was staying together and pooling their resources, even if it meant betraying the very principles they had been trained to uphold. Hadn't Fred's pesos, which he had pocketed in Olongapo, kept them going during hard times at Bilibid? Hadn't stomach pangs quickly diminished any qualms John and Murray had had about stealing food from Malinta Tunnel? All for one and one for all meant not leaving anyone behind. *Quanning* wasn't just about sharing food or money; it was about friendship. Together they'd known fear, hunger, fatigue, ill health, and hope. Besides, they had that long-running bridge game, and it would be a shame to interrupt it now. If they could steal food that the Japanese had stolen from them, they could just as easily deal the Japanese someone else's shit in the interests of group survival. Or maybe, Murray reconsidered, he should stay on Luzon, too? Fake the diagnosis in order to be left behind?

George convinced him otherwise. He wasn't worried—he'd had

amoebic dysentery since Corregidor. He'd been sick as a dog in Bilibid, and as a doctor he'd spoon-fed charcoal to men who were melting away from the disease that would eventually kill them. But he'd be fine, he insisted. He'd catch up with them later. They'd have that blowout in San Francisco after all.

As the time for their departure drew nearer, their bridge game got longer and longer. They played in their barracks until it was too dark to see; then they moved their table outside to continue under the stars. On their last evening in Cabanatuan, George finally drew away from Murray, leaving him the low scorer. They'd finish the game in Japan, or on their way home.

At 0400 on the morning of February 26, 1944, the four navy doctors marched toward the main gate of Cabanatuan. George gave Fred a hand with his gear. They had just learned that the Americans had hit the atoll of Truk, where the Japanese Combined Fleet was based in the Caroline Islands. The fleet had been out to sea, but in mid-February American carrier planes destroyed 250 to 275 enemy aircraft and more than 200,000 tons of shipping. Operation Hailstone was the deadliest blow to Japanese mercantile power yet, and it neutralized Japan's air power in the southeastern Pacific. The Yanks were less than 1,800 miles away.

George said goodbye to his buddies and watched from behind the fence at Cabanatuan as they were loaded onto trucks by Japanese soldiers armed with rifles and bayonets. He knew that he could have gone with them. But as he headed back to his barracks, he felt certain that he had made the correct choice. He had done what was right.

=== 17 ===

"The Japanese will pay"

GUY AND VICTORIA BERLEY couldn't have missed the news on the morning of January 28, 1944. The headline of the *Chicago Daily Tribune* blared: "JAP ATROCITIES REVEALED." The subhead read: "Hero Relates Horror After Bataan Fall." The story was based on the reports of three USFIP officers—Captain William E. Dyess, Major Stephen M. Mellnik, and Lieutenant Commander Melvyn H. McCoy—who had escaped from the Davao Penal Colony on Mindanao. The actual account of the "Bataan Death March" (as the press dubbed the trek from Mariveles to San Fernando) began to appear the following Sunday in 100 associated newspapers around the country with an estimated daily readership of 40 million.

In *The New York Times* Samuel and Olga Bookman read the official text of the joint army-navy report on Japanese atrocities in the Philippines. They learned of the beatings, the beheadings, the torture, and the refusal on the part of the Japanese to offer food, water, or medicine to their prisoners.

The story opened the eyes of many Americans for the first time to the horrors suffered by Allied POWs in the Far East. It was followed the next month by a feature in *Life* magazine by Dyess and Mellnik, as told to Lieutenant Welbourn Kelley, which was then expanded into book form as *The Dyess Story*.

Dyess, Mellnik, and McCoy had actually escaped Davao ten months earlier, on March 27, 1943. In July 1943 they had met with General MacArthur in Brisbane, Australia. On hearing their descriptions of prison life at O'Donnell, Cabanatuan, and Davao, the general "tightened his lips," said Dyess, and vowed: "The Japanese will pay for that humiliation and suffering." But their story was hushed up for fear of reprisals against POWs and to avoid jeopardizing the mission of the exchange ship *Gripsholm*, which in September 1943 had set out with 140,000 Red Cross food packages intended for the prisoners of the Japanese.

In his first address of 1943 President Roosevelt had declared: "The period of our defensive attrition in the Pacific is drawing to a close. Now our aim is to force the Japanese to fight. Last year, we stopped them. This year, we intend to advance."

On May 8, 1943, the "Strategic Plan for the Defeat of Japan" was adopted by the Joint Chiefs of Staff. A multiphase campaign code-named Cartwheel, it envisioned a two-pronged offensive by MacArthur and Nimitz through the central Pacific. Four stages of operations would follow: the liberation of the Philippines; an advance to the China coast with the recapture of Hong Kong; the bombing of Japan from bases in China; and finally, the invasion of the Home Islands.

The plan was presented in Washington, D.C., at the Trident conference attended by Roosevelt, Churchill, and the Combined Chiefs. It was revised in August 1943 at the Quadrant conference in Quebec, which decided that strongholds such as Rabaul would be "neutralized rather than captured." A quiet port town in the Australian-mandated territory of New Britain, Rabaul had been seized by Japan in February 1942 and stood as its single most important air base in the Southwest Pacific. Thereafter Nimitz's offensive would have precedence over MacArthur's, with the aim of securing the Gilbert and Marshall Islands, Ponape and Truk in the Carolines, and possibly the Palaus as well as the Marianas by the end of 1944.

By late November 1943, at the Eureka conference in Teheran, the plan was revised yet again. Once Germany was defeated, Stalin pledged, the USSR would throw its weight behind the war against Japan, and "by our common front we shall win." There was little reason for the United States to continue to support Chiang Kai-shek, Roosevelt decided, in spite of his promises to the generalissimo just days earlier at the Sextant conference in Cairo. Instead of depending on China for air strikes against Japan, the United States could establish bases on Guam, Tinian, and Saipan for the newly developed four-engine B-29 Superfort.

Meanwhile America had launched its Victory Program, the single largest armaments campaign in U.S. history. The objective was to achieve not superiority but supremacy "in any theater of the world war," the president told Congress in January 1942. B-17s, B-24s, and B-29s would roll out of assembly plants. Factories turned out tanks, trucks, antiaircraft guns, rifles, and munitions. Naval and merchant vessels slid off of dry docks and into the sea. The numbers were impressive. For 1942–43 the goals were 185,000 aircraft, 120,000 tanks, 55,000 antiaircraft guns, and 16 million tons of merchant shipping. Wartime production as a percentage of the gross national product soared from 2 percent in 1939 to

40 percent in 1943. Military procurement surged from $3.6 billion in 1940 to $93.4 billion in 1944, when armaments production peaked. The 96,318 military and naval aircraft manufactured in the United States that year exceeded the combined total produced by Britain, Germany, and Japan.

In Japan, wartime spending surpassed even that of America as a percentage of the GNP by 1944, but Japanese productivity was outdistanced by that of the Americans. In the first sixteen months since Pearl Harbor, the GNP in Japan was nearly stagnant; output was increased through restrictions on consumer expenditures and nonwar investment. Japan's imports of strategic materials—coal, iron, bauxite, steel, and raw rubber—began to plummet as her merchant shipping capacity was literally sunk. In 1937 Japan purchased 80 to 90 percent of her aviation fuel from the United States, but after 1939 the importation of high-octane gasoline was restricted.

The Axis powers were up against an industrial behemoth that was producing, by 1944, 40 percent of the world's arms. The Office of Scientific Research and Development, headed by Dr. Vannevar Bush, had $1 billion earmarked for improvements in radar, sonar, the mass production of blood plasma, DDT, and penicillin and for funding the top-secret Manhattan Project. Nowhere would America's technological and military might be more devastatingly deployed than in the Pacific.

Increasing U.S. productivity depended on raising revenues and conserving resources. Through eight loan drives, the War Finance Committees ("Enlist for Victory . . . Buy Victory Bonds") sold an unprecedented $185.7 billion in securities to more than 85 million Americans. Housing for defense workers was subsidized, and food and gasoline were rationed. Women joined the ranks of factory workers, the Red Cross, and the uniformed services such as the WAVES (Women Accepted for Volunteer Emergency Service), WACs (Women's Army Corps), or as Lucy Ferguson did, the USO (United Services Organization).

Millions of Americans volunteered for civilian defense activities, seeded Victory Gardens, collected tin cans, razor blades, and used clothing for salvage campaigns; they were even urged to "Save Waste Fats for Explosives!" Companies and corporations donated advertising space to shill for war bonds, while advertisers managed to tie in almost any product to the war effort with slogans that ranged from the expected to the ridiculous: Plymouth ("U.S.A.'s Strength Is Power to Produce"), Westinghouse ("To Provide for the Common Defense, to Promote the General Welfare"), B. F. Goodrich tires ("In War or Peace First in Rubber"), Parke, Davis ("The little black bag that will help win the war"), Bell System ("A United Nation"), Western Electric ("End of an Enemy"), Alligator raincoats ("Smart America Defends Itself Against Rain!"), G&W blended whiskey ("Symbols of Leadership"), Vaseline Hair Tonic ("Ever try to comb a sailor's hair?"), Victory Free-Swing Suspenders by Paris ("No Metal Can Touch You"), and Dr. West's Miracle-Tuft Toothbrush ("America has a job to do . . . keep fit!").

Hollywood went to war by cranking out movies about the Flying Tigers, Wake Island, Guadalcanal, Navy Seabees, and the Doolittle raid. In 1943 alone no fewer than three movies about Bataan were released— *So Proudly We Hail!* and *Cry "Havoc"* (both of which were about the army nurses), as well as *Bataan*.

"Why aren't there any supplies?" asks one of the nurses in *So Proudly We Hail!* "I'll tell you why. It's our own fault. . . . Because we believed we were the world. That the United States of America was the whole world. Those outlandish places—Bataan, Corregidor, Mindanao—those aren't American names. No—they're just American graveyards."

Some of the most distinguished films were the combat documentaries—Leland Hayward's *Marines on Tarawa*, John Ford's *The Battle of Midway*, John Huston's *Report from the Aleutians and San Pietro*, William Wyler's *Memphis Belle,* and Louis De Rochemont's *Fighting Lady.* Army Chief of Staff George C. Marshall even enlisted Frank Capra to direct war orientation films for U.S. troops. Of the seven movies made under the collective title *Why We Fight*, only one of them, *The Battle of China* (1944), was about the war in Asia.

Families of Pacific POWs tried to keep abreast of the news by reading books, magazines, and newspaper articles. In 1942, Alfred A. Knopf published John Hersey's first book, *Men on Bataan*, based on his dispatches to *Time*. In 1943 Viking brought out Clark Lee's *They Call It Pacific*. Lucy Ferguson saved a copy of William L. White's story in *Collier's* magazine about John Bulkeley's MTB Squadron 3 that was excerpted from his book *They Were Expendable* and made into a movie filmed in the Florida Everglades starring Robert Montgomery and John Wayne, playing characters based on John Bulkeley and Bob Kelly.

The accounts were often sensational, with headlines such as "DEATH WAS PART OF OUR LIFE," inaccurate, and out of date. But it was hard to be critical of the information at hand when reliable information—about a son, lover, husband, brother—was so scarce. So if you feared the worst, you hoped for the best and read between the lines for consolation. You sought out news from any source, wrote to the parents of other POWs, wove a network of connections to catch a tip or two, and you prayed. Never regular worshipers before the war, the Bookmans began going to Temple Emmanu-El to pray for John's safe return. They contacted Lewis and Sophie Glusman and visited the Russian-Jewish couple in their austere apartment on the Lower East Side. Worlds apart socially, they suddenly had much in common. They were not alone. Their sons were two of 126 Pacific POWs from New York state.

Sometimes you refused to believe what you heard. The Bookmans were friends of Frank Weil, a founding partner of the New York City law firm Weil, Gotshal. Weil told Samuel he had received a report of John's death. Weil was president of the National Jewish Welfare Board, which had drawn up guidelines for the burial of Jewish sailors and soldiers in accordance with Jewish custom, and he maintained contact with the Chaplains Division. The Chaplains Division was on the distribution list of memoranda issued by the Bureau of Naval Personnel, but Samuel had received no corroborating information from it.

It was the news no parent could accept. How could he not have felt as if the very ground on which he stood were about to collapse beneath his feet? Samuel contacted the Navy Department immediately and Weil's information proved, blessedly, incorrect. John Bookman, previously reported missing in action as of May 6, 1942, was alive and a prisoner of war.

The Japanese were determined to slash Allied air and naval power by mounting sustained air attacks against the Solomons and New Guinea. Conceived by Admiral Yamamoto Isoroku, Operation 1 was launched by the Japanese Navy Air Force on April 7, 1943, against American forces on Guadalcanal. Allied air defenses inflicted heavy losses, but Yamamoto, lured by exaggerated reports of the plan's success, targeted Papuan bases next. On April 18 Yamamoto was on his way to southern Bougainville to congratulate his pilots for their bravery. But three days earlier U.S. Navy code-breakers had deciphered a message with his exact itinerary, which enabled American P-38s from Guadalcanal to intercept his plane, killing the architect of Pearl Harbor.

The Allied counteroffensive was accelerated in June 1943 as MacArthur and Admiral William F. "Bull" Halsey's forces moved against Japanese bases in the Solomons, attacking weakly defended islands and skipping more heavily armed garrisons. On November 23, the United States scored its first major victory in the central Pacific when the 2nd Marine Division, using newly introduced LVTs (landing vehicles, tracked), took the fortified island of Tarawa, one of the Gilbert Islands, after a vicious three-day fight at a cost of 1,009 American lives.

In January 1944 Rabaul was neutralized, and then in February Vice Admiral Marc A. Mitscher's Task Force 58 overwhelmed Truk, the Imperial Navy's own "Gibraltar of the Pacific." Later that month Admiral Nimitz ordered carrier-based airplanes to launch strikes against the Marianas, 1,000 miles away. Tōjō was right when he warned the Diet in December 1943 that "the real war is just beginning."

On February 26, 1944, the 200 POWs from Cabanatuan boarded a wood-burning train in Cabanatuan City and shuffled sixty miles down to Manila. After two years of Japanese occupation, the "Pearl of the Orient" looked like a piece of discarded costume jewelry. Storefronts were boarded up. Businesses were closed. Pedicycles and *calesa* carts took the place of cars and trucks. Except for an occasional Japanese Army vehicle flying the flag of the Rising Sun, dusty Azcarraga Street was bereft of motorized traffic.

They thought they had said goodbye to Bilibid forever, only to find themselves confined for two weeks in the Old Back Building. Nearby were hundreds of POW graves. The new Japanese commanding officer had cut rations by a third. Fifty percent of Bilibid's patients were now suffering from food-deficiency diseases. Al Smith and Ted Williams were almost completely blind. The Japanese issued "winter clothing" to the POWs from Cabanatuan culled from the old U.S. Navy uniforms stored in Cañacao. Fred was handed Captain Davis's jacket and overcoat. They then let the men purchase as much food as they could afford from the poorly stocked commissary.

The *Manila Tribune* was smuggled into Bilibid daily, and POWs on work details at the Pandacan oil refinery had access to a shortwave radio set. On February 21, 1944, the Philippines declared a national emergency. Guerrilla activity was widespread in the provinces, banditry was common, and civil unrest was exacerbated by severe shortages of food and clothing. The Japanese had implemented air raid drills, and foxholes were being dug around the capital. "Can 'Yanks and tanks' be far behind?" Hayes wondered.

The news was encouraging to the POWs except for one story: an unmarked Japanese merchant ship carrying Allied prisoners had been torpedoed and sunk west of Corregidor.

Before America entered the war, the International Committee of the Red Cross had appealed to the Allied and Axis powers to ensure the safety of prisoner-of-war transport ships. In February 1942, when significant numbers of Allied and Axis prisoners were in transit in the Mediterranean and Pacific theaters and casualties began to mount, the ICRC renewed its plea. In July 1940 a German U-boat had attacked the *Arandora Star* as it was on its way from Britain to Canada carrying 712 Italian internees and 478 German internees. More than 600 lives were lost. On August 8, 1942, an Italian vessel, *Nino Bixio*, was sunk by an

Allied submarine while sailing from Benghazi to Italy. Thirty-seven of the 201 Australian POWs on board perished. One month later the British passenger ship *Laconia* was transporting 800 Italian POWs when it was torpedoed in the South Atlantic by a German U-boat.

The ICRC proposed that such ships be marked for immediate identification, that they have adequate lifesaving equipment on board, and that their cargo be restricted to prisoners of war only, not to soldiers or arms. Transport by sea, the agency recommended, was a last resort to be undertaken only if no other option was available. Britain balked; the vessels would become easy targets. Germany countered that hospital ships, protected under international law, could be used in their place. The Allies suspected they would serve, instead, as a cover for troops and matériel. The Italians shared the Allies' suspicions. The Japanese maintained a position of stony silence.

In November 1942 the Combined Chiefs of Staff issued a directive pertaining to operations in the Mediterranean: "In view of the extreme importance of attacking enemy shipping and of the relatively small number of casualties to prisoners of war so caused, no prohibition should be placed at present" that would preclude attacking enemy ships. Seven weeks earlier more than 842 Allied POWs had been lost in the East China Sea when the USS *Grouper* torpedoed the *Lisbon Maru* while it was on its way from Hong Kong to Shanghai. As far as the Combined Chiefs were concerned, the plight of POWs in the Pacific wasn't even a consideration. Submarine warfare would continue as it had since Pearl Harbor, when Admiral Harold Stark, Chief of Naval Operations in Washington, issued the order: "Execute Unrestricted Air and Submarine Warfare against Japan." The objective was twofold: to destroy the Imperial Japanese Navy and to liquidate the merchant fleet in order to sever Japan's lifelines for raw materials. The strategic advantage was deemed more important than the prospect of Allied POW deaths. With no sea lanes to protect them from becoming targets of the U.S. Navy's air force, fleet submarines cruising at a depth of 125 feet or less were themselves at risk, even though they were armed with a radar set—the SJ—designed specifically to detect aircraft.

Japanese ship movements, both merchant and navy, were followed by the Fleet Radio Unit, Pacific, in Pearl Harbor (FRUPAC) and in Melbourne, Australia (FRUMEL). FRUMEL comprised the old CAST codebreaking unit from Corregidor. As the U.S. Navy's cryptological units, they intercepted, decrypted, and processed coded radio messages from the Japanese Navy. The top-secret intelligence they gathered was known as ULTRA, which referred also to enciphered Axis army communications that had been broken into by cryptanalysts. ULTRA was instrumental in revealing Admiral Yamamoto's objectives at Midway in June 1942, and it had enabled South Pacific cryptanalysts to decipher the admiral's ill-fated flight plan to southern Bougainville on April 18, 1943.

U.S. Navy cryptanalysts had penetrated the main Japanese naval operational code, JN-25, more than a year before Pearl Harbor. The Ship Movement Code (SM) was a primary source of information on ship loadings, army units by name, designation, the order of battle, and the number of troops at a given moment. The merchant or *"maru"* code was "a lower level code" and easier to break and read than JN-25. Frequently, messages were intercepted from a Japanese "port director" who would route a ship or convoy and advise the port of arrival.

"The Japanese were meticulous about giving noontime positions of merchant ships," said Donald Showers, who was deputy chief of the estimate section of FRUPAC in 1944. "You could plot that and figure out exactly where a ship was going to be every twenty-four hours. They were good navigators, and this was very reliable information for submarines. If we knew submarines were operating in assigned patrol areas, we'd convey latitude and longitude so they could intercept the ship or convoy."

Admiral Nimitz's headquarters in Pearl Harbor received the information on a regular basis. The operations officer for Rear Admiral Charles A. Lockwood, Jr., commander of the Submarines Pacific Fleet (ComSub-Pac) visited FRUPAC's offices daily to sift through their reports. Time-sensitive material could be conveyed to fleets at sea in an hour or less, if the ship had a cryptological system that could intercept and decipher FRUPAC's messages.

To prevent ULTRA data from being intercepted by friendly surface vessels, naval cryptographers devised a special code that only submariners could "copy" and that only the submarine communications officer could decode. Only the captain, executive officer, and those with high-security clearance were allowed to read such messages, which were then burned. Not even submarine skippers knew the real source of ULTRA intelligence.

The Australia-based submarines in Perth (ComSubSoWestPac), and later Brisbane, answered not to Nimitz, but ultimately to Mac-Arthur. And if MacArthur disagreed with a piece of intelligence, noted Showers, "he chose to ignore it." In spite of the divided command structure, "ULTRA tip-off messages," according to William Tuohy, "led to almost half the sinkings of Japanese ships claimed by submarines."

The Japan-Truk shipping lanes and the narrow Luzon Strait, where

Japanese convoy routes converged, became favorite targets of American submariners. Inspired by the success of German U-boats who attacked Atlantic convoys with concentrated force, ComSubPac began to experiment with three-boat "wolf packs" in September 1943, as opposed to the "lone wolf" patrols that were conducted in the Central Pacific in the previous twelve months. The results were impressive. In February 1944 American submarines attacked fifty-four Japanese merchant vessels exceeding 500 tons apiece, sending 256,797 tons of shipping to the bottom of the sea.

On February 25, the day before the medical contingent departed Cabanatuan for Manila, a Japanese convoy was targeted by two U.S. submarines, the USS *Raton* and the USS *Rasher*. The ships were on their way from Java to Ambon. On intelligence from ULTRA, Lieutenant Commander Willard R. Laughon of the *Rasher* opened fire on the 6,500-ton *Tango Maru* with four torpedoes, three of which exploded on impact. Then she prowled an hour and a half before ambushing the *Ryūsei Maru*. It was a spectacular kill; the vessel sank in just six minutes. Laughon radioed Lieutenant Commander James W. Davis of the *Raton* to apologize for "hogging the show." The *Ryūsei Maru* was carrying 4,998 Japanese soldiers. What Laughon didn't realize was that the *Tango Maru* had 3,500 POWs on board, 3,000 of whom died.

It was into these waters that the POW doctors and corpsmen were headed on March 5, 1944.

They marched from Azcarraga Street to Quezon Boulevard, past Quiapo Church, then over Quezon Bridge and into the Old City. In the distance they could see the Army-Navy Club and the Manila Hotel, memories of another lifetime. Tied up at battle-scarred Pier 7 was an unmarked, rusty old freighter, the 5,000-ton *Kenwa Maru*. Japanese civilians stood on line in front of them. What a difference, John Bumgarner thought, from the fanfare that had greeted him on his arrival in Manila three years earlier. The Japanese handed out a full page of "Regulations for Prisoners" that began with a list of offenses punishable "with immediate death" ranging from disobedience to the unpardonable act of using more than two blankets, to attempted escape. Prepared by the "Commander of the Prisoner Escort, Navy of the Great Japanese Empire," it concluded in roughly translated English:

> Navy of the Great Japanese Empire will not try to punish you all with death. Those obeying all the rules and regulations, and believing the action and purpose of the Japanese Navy, cooperating with

Japan in constructing the "New Order of the Great Asia" which lend to the world's peace will be well treated.

The civilians walked up the gangplank, then down into the forward hold. The 200 POWs followed, prodded by Japanese guards into the aft hold. With only passengers as cargo, the *Kenwa Maru* rode high in the water. The ship moved out into the North Channel near Corregidor, where it anchored before leaving that night. The sky was so clear you could see the Southern Cross.

The hold was an open quadrangle flanked on either side by two double-tiered bays. There was no fresh air unless the hatch was open. The POWs were given a pint of water daily and a honey bucket in which to urinate. Food was lowered through the hatch by pail. They were allowed topside only fifteen minutes each day for exercise. The *benjo* hung from the deck rail with a metal scupper that ran down the side of the ship, but to use it you first had to salute the armed guard, request permission, and then wait until permission was granted. Ernie Irvin volunteered to flush the *benjo*. Perhaps, he thought, he could sneak in a little bath with the saltwater hose when no one was looking. The hold was infested with vermin. On more than one occasion John Bumgarner was startled awake by rats running across his face and chest.

Eleven vessels were in the convoy. To evade submarines, the captain of the *Kenwa Maru* steered a defensive zigzag course. He had reason to be concerned, so did his passengers. The *Kenwa Maru*'s route was being tracked.

A radio message intercepted that day by the United States from the Japanese Army Air Service and translated by the Army Security Agency back in Arlington, Virginia, conveniently identified the ship, its ports of embarkation and destination, and the passengers on board:

```
Msg Manila to Tokyo. In accordance with RIKU A
MITSU Message [Army Top Secret] #114, the 200
medical personnel prisoners who are to be
transferred to Japan embarked on the KENWA
MARU. They are scheduled to debark at Moji.

Message addressed to: Ass't Chief of Staff,
Prisoner Office.
```

The next day the United States intercepted another message, this time from Japanese Water Transport, which disclosed the number and

names of the ships in convoy. "MATA" was the Japanese abbreviation for
ships traveling from Manila to Takao.

```
Msg Manila to Hiroshima. Mata #10 Convoy 11
ships: Kenwa, Kooho, Soorachi, Ogura #1 and
Tachibana Marus; Navy ships, Sandiego,
*Taketsu, *Nichitetsu Maru and 2 Unident Marus;
privately owned ship *Sonyasu Maru.--naval
Karukaya [Translator's note: a naval escort
ship].
```

The seas turned rough, and many POWs sickened from the roll of
the ship. To add to their unease, the *Kenwa Maru* made occasional stops
for sonar checks on Allied submarine activity. The men wondered what
the Japanese would do if they were torpedoed, whether there were
enough lifeboats, and how far they were from land. Some men prayed.
Fred had the crazy thought that he could swim to Formosa and escape.
They pushed such thoughts aside by playing bridge, poker, and craps.
They even staged a variety show.

Then one night the POWs heard the sound they were all dreading: a
submarine alarm. The Japanese rushed to batten down the hatches. They
turned off the lights. The men below heard frantic activity up on the
deck as they waited, listening, invisible. "I was seized with an almost
panic state," said Bumgarner. "For what seemed an eternity, we were in
pitch darkness and heard the sound of many depth charges."

Only one POW had a view of the action topside: corpsman Ernie
Irvin. Through the cracks in the *benjo,* he swore he saw a cruiser sink
stern first. The Japanese claimed it was all a drill, but the next morning
Irvin counted the ships in the convoy and found one was missing. But
the only American submarine remotely near MATA No. 10 convoy in
the first two weeks of March 1944 was the *Lapon,* which on March 9
torpedoed the *Toyokuni Maru,* a 5,792-ton cargo ship, and the 5,396-
ton *Nichirei Maru,* far west of the northern tip of Luzon and halfway to
Hainan. No other American submarines were even close. What Ernie
Irvin saw was fear.

The skies turned gray. Major James Bahrenburg, a trained pediatri-
cian, was called into the forward hold to attend to Japanese children who
had fallen ill. John Bumgarner accompanied him. Living conditions
were no better for the Japanese civilians, he realized.

Finally on March 12, after six days at sea, the *Kenwa Maru* pulled
into Takao Harbor, Formosa, a hundred miles east of southern China.
American intelligence intercepted the news:

Mesg Takao to Hiroshima. Tachibana, Ogura #1,
Sorachi, *Koho and *Kenwa Marus arrrived safely
from Manila, 12 Mar/1200.

Takao was the principal port on Formosa's southern coast, and the site of a major Japanese naval base. While the *Kenwa Maru* anchored there for two days, scores of Korean women helped load 200-pound sacks of raw sugar into small lighters. The bags were hoisted on board the *Kenwa Maru* by grappling hooks, and then the women lowered them into the hold below the POWs, where they stacked them neatly against the ship's ribs.

The sugar was unrefined, and the Japanese planned on converting it, through a process of fermentation, into airplane fuel. But sugar it was, and its sweetness beckoned to the hungry POWs. They crawled down the sea ladder, and like children opening presents before their parents have awakened on Christmas Day, they carefully slit open the sacks with their mess-kit knives. Then they stuffed their Klim dried milk cans and gas mask bags, pants pockets and socks, with sugar. They added sugar to tea, sugar to rice, sugar to the burned scrapings at the bottom of the soup cauldron, which tasted, as Ernie Irvin said, just like popcorn. Or they ate it as they found it: raw.

"The sugar ship," as some POWs called it, resumed its journey on March 15, passing through the Formosa Strait and then heading north into the East China Sea, where it ran into a typhoon. Before long the POWs could make out Okinawa to the east. The ship continued on a northeasterly course up the west coast of Kyūshū, passed Nagasaki and Fukuoka, and finally threaded its way through the narrow Strait of Shimonoseki. After nearly a month at sea, the *Kenwa Maru* arrived at the port of Moji on March 25. They had made it safely to Japan.

Moji was a major rail terminus at the northern tip of Kyūshū, connected by the recently completed Kammon Tunnel to Shimonoseki on the island of Honshū. The quaint train station, with its pagoda-style eaves, was one of the oldest in the country and made for an attractive port of entry against the backdrop of Mt. Yahazu. But the prisoners were not there for sightseeing. A former YMCA building near the docks served as the main barracks of Fukuoka No. 4, which housed American, British, and Dutch Indonesian POWs who worked as stevedores or on the railroad.

Customs officers frisked the men disembarking from the *Kenwa Maru* but failed to find any incriminating evidence. Nor did they notice that the *Kenwa Maru*'s cargo had mysteriously diminished in size during transit. The POWs were removed to Fukuoka No. 4, where they had their first bath in two and a half years. They were coated with dirt, and easing down into the warm water of the communal tub felt luxuriously good. After they were cleaned up—or as clean as they could be—each of the four groups was assigned to a Japanese officer.

Alfred Weinstein was sent to Shinagawa, which was part of Ōmori Main Camp, the sole hospital facility for POWs in Tōkyō as well as for many camps in northern Honshū. Lieutenant Nosu Shōichi ushered the men in his charge onto a coal-burning locomotive: Fred, John, Murray, Stan Smith, and corpsmen Ernie Irvin, Bernard Hildebrand, Bud Flood, Richard Wallace, and Bernard Stradley along with the forty-one others in his group. The train headed north from Moji, rattled through the Kammon Tunnel, and chugged up through Honshū, but its windows were shuttered so the POWs couldn't see where they were going. They were handed a boxed lunch (*bentō*) of pickled white radish (*daikon*), sea-weed, a little fish, and rice. They ate with chopsticks and the fare turned out to be far better than anything they'd been given on the *Kenwa Maru*.

A bath, a decent meal—so far so good. But there was something more than a little odd about Lieutenant Nosu. His head sloped to his brow, his ears protruded, and he walked with a pronounced limp in his left leg, but it wasn't any of those things; it was the way he spoke. Nosu had little English, yet he insisted on interrogating each doctor himself, and in a most exaggerated fashion: "I, Dr. Nosu, speak English poorly, understand very well. I opulate [operate], and I teach you doctors; you no good I send you to the mountains. I speak Deutschland, go to Deutsch-land medical school; English, American schools no good! Deutschland medical schools, number one. I teach you!"

Nosu was medical officer of the Ōsaka area POW camps, but he sounded like an idiot. Murray tried engaging him in German, but Nosu's German was even worse than his English. Did Nosu know anything about medicine? Murray wondered. As doctors, did the Americans and Japanese speak the same language?

18

Bridge over Hell

IN THE MID-SIXTEENTH CENTURY Portuguese castaways were washed up on Tanegashima's shores, Lusitanian ships began trading in Kyūshū, and in 1549 Saint Francis Xavier and two Spanish Jesuits introduced Catholicism to Japan. In 1600 a Dutch vessel piloted by the Englishman William Adams was blown off course and landed on the shores of Bungo.

Tokugawa Ieyasu, the first Tokugawa shogun, allowed Holland to open a trading post at Hirado and permitted the British to establish a factory there in 1613. But by 1616 Christian missionaries were expelled, free residence for Westerners came to an end, and trade was restricted to the ports of Hirado and Nagasaki. The English, convinced that neither a manufacturing nor an export business with Japan would ever be profitable, departed voluntarily in 1623. In 1630 Shogun Iemitsu issued the Edict of Kan'ei, which prohibited the import of books that propagated Christianity. From 1640 until Commodore Perry sailed into Edo Bay in 1853, Japan was a country closed (*sakoku*) largely to Western influence. Of the early Occidental visitors, only the Dutch, who managed to persuade the Japanese that Holland was not a Christian country, were allowed to remain, though they would be removed to the artificial island of Deshima in Nagasaki harbor, where the Portuguese had previously been confined.

During the *sakoku* period, inevitably, Japanese interpreters of the Dutch had the most contact with European ideas. An interpreter corps in Nagasaki stimulated Dutch learning, or *rangaku*. Its scholars—*rangakusha*—were steeped in neo-Confucianism and concentrated on those areas that had the most practical applications in Japan: astronomy, to better understand the agricultural cycle, and medicine.

The interpreters did more than merely interpret speech and translate books from the Dutch that were not specifically banned under the Edict of Kan'ei. They were keen observers who accompanied Dutch doctors into the homes of the ill, where they studied symptoms and watched

Dutch physicians prescribe treatment and practice surgery. Classical Chinese medicine, by contrast, was based on theories of balance and cosmology, the yin/yang polarity, and the cycle of Five Elements known as *wu-hsing*. The interpreters learned chemistry and physics, botany and zoology, pharmacopoeia and mineralogy as those fields were understood in mid-seventeenth-century Holland and Germany. They absorbed the work of Casper Schamberger, Willem Hoffman, Andries Cleijer, the German physician Engelbert Kaempfer, and Ten Rhijne, who was employed by the Dutch East India Company in Deshima. The lessons they learned enabled them to adapt the principles of European medicine to East Asian tradition. In so doing, they became cultural intermediaries between the West and the Orient. Their contributions, notably *Kaitai Shinsho,* the Japanese translation of an eighteenth-century anatomical text by German physician Johann Adam Kulmus, heralded the era of modern Japanese medicine and a science based on empirical observation. The interpreters became doctors.

––––––––

The journey from Moji took more than twelve hours. At one transfer station the POWs watched as numerous white boxes were being unloaded from a train: ashes, they surmised, of Japanese war dead. Nosu was furious. He screamed at Navy Lieutenant J. R. "Jack" George for disrespect as guards hustled the Americans away.

On March 26, 1944, the men entered Subcamp No. 13-B in the Ōsaka Prisoner of War Camp Area. Otherwise known as Tsumori, it sat opposite the Kizugawa Cement Factory on the Kizugawa River in an industrial landscape dominated by docks and shipyards.

The camp consisted of five wooden barracks 150 to 200 feet long and 30 to 40 feet wide. The barracks had bays on both sides and a walkway that ran down the middle. Officers had a separate office in the corner, which doubled as a two-man berth. The "drab-looking buildings," said Stan Smith, were "built on the soot-covered, cinder-strewn ground." Tsumori was a study in gray: gray sea, gray sky, gray earth. There had been frequent snow and sleet that month.

"Put your gear over here, fellows, and the commanding officer will be here in a jiffy to speak to you."

His accent was flawless, and his dress could have been mistaken for POW fatigues. Lieutenant Jack George put out his hand in greeting, but the American-educated Fujimoto Haruki quickly rebuffed him. He was an interpreter at Tsumori, and fraternizing with POWs, he curtly reminded them, was prohibited.

The new arrivals were shaken down by guards, who discovered the sweet lucre they had pocketed from the *Kenwa Maru.* "They took away all our medicines, some food, playing cards, books, games, and many personal and Red Cross items recently received," John noted in his diary. "A dreary, dirty, depressing camp."

It was strange, too, without George. They felt diminished not only in ability but potential. He was the one man among them who had the kind of life they wished they had waiting for them back home. They missed his sly humor and that quizzical expression even when he was deadly earnest. They missed the way he saw the human body as a beautiful mechanism made up of intricate parts, each with a specific bearing on the whole.They missed his letters from Lucy and his unquestioning faith. If Carey Smith was their adopted father, Fred now assumed the role of eldest brother, sharp and incisive. Murray was the youngest and in some ways most unpredictable. And John was the fulcrum upon which both of them depended. They had lost their fourth, and his absence brought them closer together.

Ōsaka, the second-largest city in Japan, was the country's commercial and industrial heart. Perched on Ōsaka Bay and defined by the Yodo River, it was a major exporter to the East and import customer of the United States, China, and India. Legend has it that in the seventh century B.C. the first emperor, Jimmu, subdued cave-dwellers called Tsuchigumo (Earth Spiders) in Naniwa (Ōsaka) before pacifying all of Yamato and founding the seat of his empire. The city was celebrated for its doll theater (*ningyō-shibai*), which evolved in the mid-seventeenth century, and it was home to the prolific playwright Chikamatsu Monzaemon, widely regarded as "Japan's Shakespeare."

In 1940 Ōsaka's population stood at 3.25 million, a figure that would shrink by nearly a third due to conscription and the war industry. The city became a major supplier of wartime ships, electrical equipment, machinery, and tools. Her arsenal alone provided 20 percent of the ordnance required by the Imperial Japanese Army. Nearly one-quarter of her half-million work force toiled in the manufacture of airplane parts.

The Ōsaka Prisoner of War Camp Area was under the command of Colonel Murata Sōtarō, who was based at Ōsaka No. 1 Headquarters Camp. Army Air Force doctor Lieutenant David Hochman, who had bumped into John on Bataan, was among the first Americans to arrive there on November 11, 1942, after a thirty-two-day voyage aboard the *Tottori Maru*.

Hochman reported to Nosu and found his behavior nothing short of bizarre. Nosu once applied a stethoscope to a patient's knee to diagnose beriberi. He did a chest examination while his stethoscope was pressed to a patient's earlobe. He diagnosed diarrhea and dysentery by listening to a patient's abdomen. He appeared to be completely ignorant of sulfa drugs, plasma, and the arsenical Mapharsen. He insisted on sending to work in the shipyards POWs who were too sick to be ambulatory. And he repeatedly stole drugs from the headquarters camp, which deprived seriously ill patients in the subcamps of desperately needed medicine. Hochman suspected that Nosu wasn't a doctor at all. Or if he was, he was the kind who stood on street corners peddling patent medicines.

By contrast, the fifty-three-year-old Murata, to whom Nosu reported, struck Hochman as an affable man. He was a widower whose three young children lived with their maternal grandmother in Kyōto. But his responsibilities extended over more than twenty-two camps holding thousands of Allied prisoners and allowed him to visit his family only once a month.

Others saw him as a clean-shaven, bullet-headed colonel with steel spectacles, clipped mustache, and the swagger of a Prussian officer. He warned prisoners that if they did not do their best for the empire, they would probably never see their loved ones again: "Our people will not forget that you shot at our brothers and sons. . . . For this you must pay your toll very heavily."

Ōsaka No. 1 Headquarters Camp provided medicine, clothing, and books for all POWs in central Japan—or at least it was supposed to. Subordinates such as Nosu appeared to wield enormous influence in day-to-day operations, but it was Murata who was ultimately accountable for the welfare of the POWs under his jurisdiction. As Kobayashi Kazuo, an interpreter in the Ōsaka-area camps, put it: "Nosu couldn't do anything without the permission of Colonel Murata."

Tsumori's camp commander, Lieutenant Habe Toshitarō, insisted on a rigorous military regimen, with frequent drills and inspections. POWs were awakened for *tenko* (roll call) in the middle of the night. The doctors had no medicine at Tsumori, but the Japanese did. Murata regaled the navy doctors with stories of the wonderful new hospital that was being built for them in Kōbe, but his words meant little to Tsumori's inmates, whose health, John wrote, "had been none too good."

The winter of 1943–44 had been hard on them. Charcoal pits were recessed in the barracks room floors for heat, but charcoal itself was rare. Down by the docks men shivered with cold, trying to keep warm by lighting fires in 55-gallon oil drums, which they fed with scavenged wood. When wood grew scarce, they filched fuel in any way they could, in one instance lifting an entire gangplank from a trawler tied up at a dock. Many suffered frostbite in their fingers, toes, and limbs. Red Cross parcels were withheld; mail was never delivered. One of the American doctors designated a special latrine for diarrhea cases, but it soon made no difference because everyone had diarrhea.

They were cold, they were hungry, and they were expected to work as welders, riggers, and riveters in the Fujinagata and Namura shipyards. POWs hauled rocks to fill in the boat basin, unloaded pig iron from lighters in Ōsaka Bay, toiled on destroyers, transports, and corvettes. Some were so weak they couldn't lift the logs that were used to ease vessels off of dry docks.

The poor food situation only hastened their decline. Rice, or barley and millet, was served three times a day. Greens and root vegetables, called *slum*, were added at suppertime, along with a ladle of *daikon* soup. To help control the runs, the men requested permission to bake bread from the last rice ration. One POW forged a key to a storehouse and managed to bring back some grub for his buddies. The Japanese thought a rat had gotten into their foodstuffs.

At Tsumori the navy doctors and corpsmen interacted with prisoners of other nationalities for the first time. They met Englishmen who had been captured at the fall of Singapore, Australians who had survived the siege of Rabaul, and Dutch POWs who had surrendered in the East Indies. There were also American civilians who had worked for Pacific Naval Contractors on Wake before Wake was attacked on December 11, 1941. They had come to Tsumori by way of a camp in Kiangwan, north of Shanghai.

Fred, John, and Murray refused to work in the shipyards. Not only was it hazardous, it was clearly related to war operations and hence prohibited under the terms of the Geneva Convention. They'd learned their lesson at Cabanatuan: they'd do what they were trained for and practice medicine, they asserted. No, they wouldn't, the Japanese informed them. The doctors would work as sanitation men, sweeping the streets, cleaning out the *benjo*, and fertilizing the soil with their own shit. The Japanese made them pay for what they perceived as their pride, Murray thought. They rubbed their noses in it to remind them of their place. The humiliation was deliberate, persistent, and public, a constant debriding that tested one's sense of self-worth.

Stan Smith and another navy dental officer, Lieutenant (j.g.) Wade H. Morgan, Jr., were allowed to practice dentistry once a week. The Japanese were among their patients. They supplied a little zinc oxide and some eugenol, and the dentists cooked up a local anesthetic, working gingerly when they heard the cry *"Itai! Itai!"* meaning "It hurts! It hurts!" Often they had no anesthesia at all.

Down in the shipyards the enlisted men enjoyed generally good relations with Japanese civilian workers. The Japanese shared news of the war's progress, but their accounts relied on the local press, whose stories had to conform to the Provisional Law for Control of Speech,

Publications, Assembly, and Association, and were scripted by Imperial General Headquarters. News of the Japanese defeat at Midway was suppressed, military losses were valorized, and authors of journalistic exposés were rewarded by prosecution and conviction.

For more accurate news POWs turned to secret shortwave radios. A Dutchman hid one, while a marine from Tientsin had another that was able to pick up broadcasts from Chiang Kai-shek in China. Seaman 2nd Class Richard L. Hotchkiss from Wake concealed a third set, until a fellow POW snitched on him.

Punishments at Tsumori were severe. B.H.J. Boerboom, one of the old-timers, was captured by a Japanese Army unit at Bandoeng, Java, on March 8, 1942, and was imprisoned at Tjilatjap, Batavia, and in Singapore. He had been in Tsumori since December 5, 1943, and had seen two incidents he was unlikely to forget.

Two Americans, Andrews and Cooley, had been caught stealing bread. They were beaten, thrown into the brig, and forced to stand at attention through the night. The first day of their confinement they were given no food or water. The second day they were allowed only two cups of rice and salty water and were permitted to use the latrine twice. One time, instead of going to the latrine, Andrews made a break for a washbasin to drink from the tap. The guard beat him on the head with a bamboo club. Andrews put up his arms in self-defense, which infuriated his captor. Three other guards—Shiozumi, Kashiwangi, and Kino— joined in the attack. They broke Andrews's arm, dislocated his shoulder, and four weeks later forced him to go back to work.

On another occasion Boerboom accompanied a doctor to examine a Dutch POW who lay unconscious in his barracks. Kino maintained the prisoner wasn't ill, he was just lazy. Kino went into the barracks with Kashiwangi, his fellow guard, and tried to make the man stand. When that proved impossible, Kino slapped him in the face. The guards left laughing. Two hours later the POW was dead.

The cold of March 1944 was impossible to shake. The temperature inside the barracks ranged from freezing to 45 degrees. The prisoners' clothing was cotton, as were their blankets, and they were so cold, Corporal Frank Gross admitted, they'd "double up at night with another guy" on their *tatami* mats. Nosu had the notion that in the mornings the POWs should throw open the windows and doors and vigorously massage their torsos with a towel to "make them strong and prevent pneumonia." The only thing that kept them warm, said John, was a hot bath, Japanese style. But baths were infrequent. When Samuel Silverman, a civilian worker from Wake Island, was asked his rank, he joked that he

Lieutenant (j.g.) George T. Ferguson, MC, USN, medical officer of the Yangtze Patrol boat USS *Guam,* 1939.

Lucille Ferguson holding a photograph of her husband, George.

Lucille Ferguson *(third row, far left, seated)* catches a show in Shanghai while George is upriver.

Lieutenant (j.g.) Ferdinand V. Berley, MC, USN *(left)*, medical officer of the Asiatic Fleet's Destroyer Division 58, with Lieutenant Commander E. N. "Butch" Parker of the USS *Parrott,* out on the town in Tsingtao, 1939.

RIGHT: Lieutenant (j.g.) John Jacob Bookman, MC, USNR, in New York City, 1941.

Lieutenant (j.g.) Murray Glusman, MC, USNR, en route to the Philippines on the *President Garfield,* August 1941.

Laura Reade, née Reichmann, was America's "Baby Opera Star," said the *Philadelphia Ledger* of the seventeen-year-old coloratura soprano.

The Japanese attack on the Cavite Navy Yard, home of the U.S. Navy's Asiatic Fleet in the Philippines, two days after Pearl Harbor, December 10, 1941 (across the international dateline).

ABOVE: The remains of the Cavite Navy Yard, as photographed on March 5, 1945.

Mariveles, Bataan, after a Japanese bombing raid. The statue in the foreground is *The Cry of the Balintawak,* commemorating the first Filipino revolution against Spain in 1896.

American-trained Filipino scouts emerge from the jungle of Bataan.

Melville Jacoby

On March 30, 1942, the Japanese bombed Hospital No. 1 on Bataan in spite of the red cross emblazoned on its rooftoop.

The Japanese celebrate victory on Mt. Limay, Bataan, in April 1942.

A captured Japanese war photograph shows Japanese soldiers firing a howitzer.

An aerial view of Corregidor, separated from the southern tip of Bataan by the North Channel and from the island of Caballo by the South Channel.

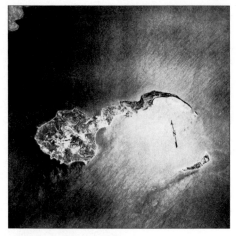

Corregidor's defenses were old but still formidable, designed to repel an attack from the sea, not the air.

The U.S. Army boasted it would take 100,000 Japanese to seize "the Gibraltar of the East," but 12-inch mortars on Corregidor in fixed-gun emplacements were vulnerable to bombing and shelling.

On December 25, 1941, the headquarters of the U.S. Army Forces in the Far East (USAFFE) was established on Corregidor deep inside Malinta Tunnel.

A sailor stands guard at the sandbagged entrance to the Navy Radio Intercept Tunnel on Corregidor, where code-breakers engaged in top-secret work, intercepting and decrypting radio traffic from the Imperial Japanese Navy.

General Douglas MacArthur and the ailing President Manuel Quezon of the Philippines in Quezon's tent on Corregidor.

Americans and Filipinos raise their hands in surrender on Corregidor for a Japanese 14th Army photograph taken outside Malinta Tunnel on May 7, 1942.

HERALD TRIBUN

Men From the

Lieutenant Murray Glusman
Missing

The New York Herald Tribune ran the names and photographs of New Yorkers listed as missing, according to the Navy's fourth casualty list, which covered the period from April 16 to May 10, 1942.

For the approximately 324,000 Allied POWs and civilian internees held in Japan and Japanese-occupied territories, the Horyo Jōhōkyoku (Prisoner of War Information Bureau) in Tōkyō had a staff of only twenty-six, including office boys.

An aerial photograph of Bilibid Prison in Manila. The dotted line in the center marks the wall that separated the prisoners' area from the Japanese quarters. Numbered areas are as follows: (1) staff quarters, (2) the diet kitchen, (3) the guard house.

A prewar postcard of Bilibid Prison.

A POW postcard, limited to fifty words, sent by Fred Berley to his parents from Bilibid Prison.

IMPERIAL JAPANESE ARMY

1. I am interned at—Philippine Military Prison Camp No. 3
2. My health is—excellent; good; fair; poor.
3. Message (50 words limit)
Working in Hospital. Everything alright.Received Red Cross Bo
last Xmas,much appreciated.Have received no letters although
others have.Perhaps not written properly.Take good care of my
household effects.Save newspapers and magazines.Notify frien
Hope everyone well at home.Don't worry; love to all,

Signature

American soldiers, sailors, and marines abandoned by the Japanese in Bilibid Prison on February 3, 1945, as American troops fought to liberate Manila.

Freed from Bilibid, Captain Fred G. Nasr of the U.S. Army Dental Corps holds three jars—one of rice, one of corn, and one (on the right) containing soybeans—representing more than the one-day ration for prisoners of the Japanese.

Thin to the point of emaciation from malnutrition and illness, liberated U.S. prisoners of war are photographed in Bilibid by Navy photographers on February 8, 1945.

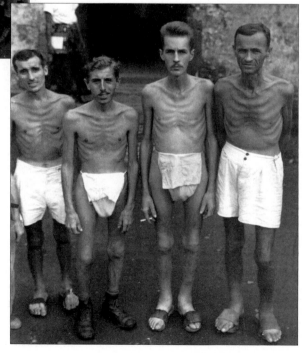

At Cabanatuan in 1942, Jim Neary, a West Pointer, stands in front of barracks beside a surface well and garden, where okra, eggplant, and pigweed were grown and devoured by POWs.

Christmas 1943 "was celebrated as beautifully at Cabanatuan as in the finest church in the world," said 1st Lieutenant John M. Wright Jr. This photograph was taken by Major Paul Wing. The negative was secretly processed with chemicals smuggled into the POW camp.

The Allied POW medical staff of the Kōbe POW Hospital in front of Ward No. 2, November 1944.

MEDICAL STAFF—KOBE PRISONER OF WAR HOSPITAL—Taken 28-11-1944
Back row:–E. N. Gonie, Lt. N.E.I. Med. (Pharm.), L. Indorf, Lt. N.E.I. Med. (Dent.),
I. J. Bookman, Lt. M.C. U.S.N.R. (Physician); M. Glusman, Lt. M.C. U.S.N.R.
(Neuro-Psychiatry), S. N. Smith, Lt. D.C. U.S.N. (Denist)
Front row:–F. V. Berley, Lt. M.C. U.S.N. (A Surgeon & Gen. Duties), J. A. Page,
Sur./Lt. Com. R.N. (Surgeon), H. Ohashi, Lt. Japan (Director), J. F. Akeroyd,
Hon. Major A.A.M.C. A.I.F. Physician

The Ōhashi family sits for a formal portrait in Ōsaka. *Front:* Hyōjirō *(left)* and Yukako. *Rear (left to right):* Yasuko, Kazuko, and Hisamichi.

A rare photograph of the *Arisan Maru.* Named after a mountain in Formosa, the 6,866-ton vessel first sailed out of the Mitsui Tamanao shipyards in Okayama Prefecture in June 1944.

Dressed in military garb, Japanese schoolchildren in Kōbe salute their teacher.

Japanese schoolboys practicing *kendō* ("the way of the sword").

Japanese schoolchildren donning cotton masks for fire-raid protection.

American propaganda leaflets were dropped over Japanese cities to warn civilians of impending B-29 incendiary attacks. "Japanese Citizens!" read one pamphlet. "You can absolutely not escape. There is no place you can hide, and resistance only means terrifying death. Demand the cessation of this hopeless resistance, that is the only path to saving your country."

A strike photograph of the June 5, 1945, B-29 raid on Kōbe, Japan.

Japanese civilians flee from the destruction of Kōbe caused by American B-29 fire raids.

The remains of Kōbe after three B-29 raids.

レンゴウグンノホリョヘ

ALLIED PRISONERS

The JAPANESE Government has surrendered. You will be evacuated by ALLIED NATIONS forces as soon as possible.

Until that time your present supplies will be augmented by air-drop of U.S. food, clothing and medicines. The first drop of these items will arrive within one (1) or two (2) hours.

Clothing will be dropped in standard packs for units of 50 or 500 men. Bundle markings, contents and allowances per man are as follows:

BUNDLE MARKINGS   BUNDLE MARKINGS

50 MAN PACK	500 MAN PACK	CONTENTS	ALLOWANCES PER MAN	50 MAN PACK	500 MAN PACK	CONTENTS	ALLOWANCES PER MAN
A	3	Drawers	2	B	10	Laces, shoe	1
A	1-2	Undershirt	2	A	11	Kit, sewing	1
B	22	Socks (pr)	2	C	31	Soap, toilet	1
A	4-6	Shirt	1	C	4-6	Razor	1
A	7-9	Trousers	1	C	4-6	Blades, razor	10
C	23-30	Jacket, field	1	C	10	Brush, tooth	1
A	10	Belt, web, waist	1	B	31	Paste, tooth	1
A	11	Capt, H.B.T.	1	C	10	Comb	1
B	12-21	Shoes (pr)	1	B	32	Shaving cream	1
A	1-2	Handkerchiefs	3	C	12-21	Powder(insecticide)	1
C	32-34	Towel	1				

There will be instructions with the food and medicine for their use and distribution.

CAUTION

DO NOT OVEREAT OR OVERMEDICATE   FOLLOW DIRECTIONS

INSTRUCTIONS FOR FEEDING 100 MEN

To feed 100 men for the first three (3) days, the following blocks (individual bundles dropped) will be assembled:

3 Blocks No. 1
(Each Contains)

2 Cases, Soup, Can
1 Cases Fruit Juice
1 Case Accessory Pack

1 Block No. 5
(Each Contains)

1 Case Soup, Dehd
1 Case Veg Puree
1 Case Bouillon
1 Case Hosp Supplies
1 Case Vitamin Tablets

1 Block No. 3
(Each Contains)

1 Case Candy
1 Case Gum
1 Case Cigarettes
1 Case Matches

3 Blocks No. 2
(Each Contains)

3 Cases "C" Rations
1 Case Hosp Supplies
2 Cases Fruit

1 Block No. 7
(Each Contains)

1 Case Nescafe
1 Sack Sugar
1 Case Milk
1 Case Cocoa

1 Block No. 10
(Each Contains)

3 Cases Fruit
2 Cases Juice

A flier dropped over POW camps in Japan by B-29s, announcing Japan's surrender on August 15, 1945, and identifying essential items in accompanying canisters. A cautionary note advises: "Do not overeat or overmedicate. . . . Follow directions."

The Japanese delegation aboard the USS *Missouri* in Tōkyō Bay, for the signing of the surrender, September 2, 1945. To Kase Toshikazu, a member of the Foreign Office, it was "the torture of the pillory."

General Douglas MacArthur, Supreme Commander of the Allied Powers, signing the surrender treaty aboard the USS *Missouri* in Tōkyō Bay, September 2, 1945. Lieutenant General Arthur E. Percival stands behind to the left and Lieutenant General Jonathan M. "Skinny" Wainwright to the right.

Recovered American Military Personnel (RAMPs) leave Yokohama Railroad Station with an honor guard flanking them on both sides, September 16, 1945. They were the last ex–prisoners of war who arrived from Ōsaka Prison Camp, where they voluntarily effected an orderly evacuation.

was the rankest man in the Pacific. If they were lucky, they smuggled in "skid soap" from the shipyard in a rag, a sock, or below the waist, because soap of any kind was at a premium. But there was so little fuel, lamented Colonel Murata, that his own family could afford to bathe only twice a month. Once the hospital in Kōbe was completed, he promised, the POWs would be taking their ablutions every week.

Tsukioka Yoshio used to watch them. He was a teenager whose father was in charge of the crematorium down the street from Tsumori. You weren't supposed to look into the camp; it was surrounded by a high wooden fence, beyond which was an electrified wire. But Yoshio couldn't resist peeking when the prisoners bathed in the large steel-bottomed tub that was warmed by a wood fire.

Every morning he saw the men march in rows of four down to the dockyard. They looked exhausted, emaciated. One day Yoshio took one of his grandfather's cigarettes and tossed it onto the street for a POW, who hastily picked it up. On another occasion Yoshio saw the Kempeitai arrive at Tsumori. They dragged a POW out of the camp and led him away in tears.

Many POWs succumbed during the winter. When a buddy died, he was carried on a litter or cart to the funeral home of Tsukioka-san. A chaplain always presided over the ceremony, and during one procession Yoshio counted as many as thirty men. He watched them pray over the body, heard them mutter "Amen." After the cremation the ashes were deposited in a small white box that found its final resting place in Juganji Temple, a pagoda located then on Tanimachi Avenue in Chuo Ward, Ōsaka.

Like other residents of Ōsaka and Kōbe, Yoshio's family suffered from the cold and a shortage of food. The war with China placed tremendous demands on the domestic food supply. In 1939, the year the "Rising Sun *bentō*" was popularized, thistle and pokeweed were recommended as rice substitutes to be served alongside locust croquettes. Rationing began in Japan's major cities on April 1, 1940, when Admiral Yonai Mitsumasa's "no-rice cabinet" ordered people to sell their gold to the government. "No meat days" were mandated twice monthly, pork was prohibited in Tōkyō, and fruit and vegetable distribution was regulated.

The Basic Necessities Control Ordinance of 1941 restricted goods for civilians, though senior army officers and bureaucrats never seemed to be lacking, due to their connections and black market contacts. By early 1942 Japan was already experiencing serious food shortages. The nutritional standard recommended by the Ministry of Health and Welfare for an adult Japanese male engaged in "medium-hard labor" fell from 2,400 calories a day to below 2,000. Military rations were roughly twice those for civilians.

With the armed forces consuming so much oil, and oil imports sagging to all-time lows in 1944, gas stations on the Home Islands went out of business. Women and high school students dug pine roots to extract oil, which was mixed in with gasoline for aircraft fuel. Cars, trucks, and trains were powered by charcoal-burning engines. But coal and charcoal themselves were in such short supply that businesses such as Tōkyō's posh Imperial Hotel were forced to regulate hot water use, while citizens economized by bathing infrequently, often without soap.

As early as 1943 U.S. steel production surpassed Japan's by "a ratio of one hundred to less than one," complained Matsumae Shigeyoshi, director of the Engineering Bureau in the Ministry of Communications. "At our present rate of production continuing the war will reduce Japan to a miserable ruin, however strong our faith in ultimate Japanese triumph may be." To augment dwindling scrap metal stocks, Japanese civilians donated buttons, nails, Buddhist temple gongs, pots, and pans; they even stole manhole covers to help the war effort. A popular story during the siege of Corregidor was that the Japanese had used Singer Sewing Machine parts in their shrapnel-laden bombs. After the island's capitulation, they dismantled some of its guns and shipped them home for scrap. To conserve energy, officials were recommending in 1944 that families unscrew one bulb from the lamps in their houses and designated 2200 as the time for lights-out. Sweet potatoes were fermented and used as a rice substitute for making sake and later were sown by millions of families to generate synthetic fuel for Japanese bombers. And to save leather and rubber, civilians wore wooden clogs instead of shoes or sneakers.

Extravagance, associated with Western values, was shunned in a spiritual mobilization campaign that dated back to 1938. Billboards proclaimed, "Luxury Is the Enemy." Women shed dresses and kimonos for peasant pantaloons known as *monpe*. Cosmetics and permanent waves were prohibited. Books and magazines were purged of "dangerous thoughts." Antiwar sympathizers were banned, as were authors of romances and even comic strips. Foreign films disappeared from movie houses, American jazz and popular music vanished from the airwaves, foreign words were excised from the Japanese language, and signs written in Roman letters were removed from public spaces. In baseball, a sport beloved in Japan, umpires had to learn the calls in their own language for the first time: *yoshi hitotsu* (strike one), *dame* (ball), and *hike* (you're out). Foreign residents were rounded up and held in internment camps.

Freedom of speech and assembly had been curtailed since 1941 in accordance with the National Defense Security Law and the Provisional Law for Control of Speech, Publications, and Assembly. Habeas corpus was skirted by the amended Peace Preservation Law.

Restaurants, kabuki theaters, and geisha houses were shut down under the Outline of Decisive War Emergency Measures, approved by the cabinet in February 1944. "People's bars"—government taverns with restricted amounts of liquor and cheap sake—took the place of neighborhood watering holes.

Women shouldered the burden of civil defense. Neighborhood associations—*tonari gumi*—comprising fifteen to thirty households each, were under the control of the Home Ministry to organize air raid drills, firefighting, food rationing, and labor services. Members dug trenches, made shelters beneath their houses, sewed cotton masks, and set up water-bucket relays. With the threat of air raids, they assisted the Home and Welfare Ministries by checking area residents for their blood types.

As of 1943, university, technical, and high school students were no longer exempt from military conscription. Boys as young as fifteen were drafted, while girls were pressured to become nurses, and the minimum age for cadet volunteers was lowered to fourteen. By 1944 millions of Japanese pupils above the age of ten were mobilized for war work in factories and fields. In Kōbe third- and fourth-year students, fifteen to sixteen years of age, toiled at Mitsubishi Heavy and Electric in some of the very same industries that exploited POW laborers. Schoolgirls helped assemble *Shidenkai* fighter planes, Japan's most sophisticated aircraft. The elderly were compelled to work simply to make ends meet.

Children were expected to bow at the *hoanden,* a small shrine at the entrance of every Japanese school that housed photographs of the emperor and empress, known as the "imperial likenesses." From the sixth edition of the national history textbook published in 1944, they were instilled with the idea of emperor worship. Japan was a divine land, and the sun goddess would protect it through a mystical union of man and nature. For years the curriculum for middle schools and above had included military training conducted by active duty officers, but now the rhetoric took on an even more imperialist—and racist—bent. At one school in Tōkyō children shouted, "Annihilate America and England! One, two, three, four," to the rhythm of their daily calisthenics.

Japanese propaganda flooded the airwaves and newspapers. Imperial General Headquarters regularly fed the press, and Dōmei, the official wire service, obliged by putting the best slant on war news. Radio broadcasts boasted of soldiers who "met honorable death rather than the dishonor of surrender" and celebrated the *banzai* charge on Attu in the

Aleutian Islands that sacrificed 1,000 Japanese lives in May 1943. Military marches and patriotic songs filled air time, to instill a martial spirit in the listening masses.

Political dissent was rare and readily suppressed. There was no antiwar movement, Ienaga Saburō remarked, because the government was in total control of the instruments of power. Even when the Left was still active, before Pearl Harbor, few dissidents emigrated west to protest Japan's expansionist polices in Asia. The *kokutai*, or national polity, predominated over the will of the people. As Tōjō Hideki remarked, "Truly it is time for the 100 million of us Japanese to dedicate all we have and sacrifice everything for our country's cause."

In spite of the hardships his family endured, Yoshio felt sorry for the prisoners of war.

———

On April 8, 1944, Fred and John were ordered to Lieutenant Habe Toshitarō's office and told to strip down to the waist. A Japanese doctor looked them over "as you would look at cattle," Fred recalled. Habe then instructed them to get their gear. Neither had any idea of their destination as they said goodbye to Murray. Nor did they know if they would ever see one another again. The group of four was in splinters, each man on his own.

Under armed guard, John was taken sixty miles south of Ōsaka to Wakayama POW Camp. Ringed by the Kii Mountains and overlooking Wakahura Bay, Wakayama is perched on the largest peninsula in Japan. According to Japanese legend, Wakayama rose from sacred ground. Its sixteenth-century castle became the seat of power for the shogunate's rule in western Japan. A temperate climate sustains farming, foresting, cultivating vegetables, flowers, and fruit—persimmons and plums, *hassaku* and *mikan* oranges. The Kuroshio current, off Wakayama, abounds with tuna, cutlass, and spiny lobster, but the fish supply in Japan declined by 60 percent due to a wartime labor shortage.

It was a small camp, composed of 395 POWs who had been captured in Hong Kong, all of them British except for three Australians. They lived in seven wooden barracks surrounded by a ten-foot-high fence. A quarter mile away was Wakayama Iron Works, a branch of the Sumitomo Steel Industrial Company.

Under 1st Lieutenant Kuranishi Taijirō, POW officers and enlisted men were divided into three eight-hour work shifts. The labor was arduous and dangerous. Production was low due to the shortage of raw materials, but the prisoners tended the blast furnace and manufactured steel pipe and bomb casings. There was a one-hour break for meals but no designated rest times. Breakfast and lunch were soup and rice; supper was simply rice. Meat and vegetables would disappear entirely. The POWs were doled out a small portion of fish once a week, if they received any at all.

When prisoners first arrived in November 1943, they were dressed in short-sleeve shirts and tropical-weight shorts. Nearly a month elapsed before they were issued cotton army fatigues, overcoats, and canvas and rubber split-toed *tabi*. During that time eleven men died of pneumonia. Another was killed when a load of slag that he was preparing to dump toppled over and crushed him to death.

The kitchens at Wakayama were unscreened. The latrines were open pits. When an epidemic of diarrhea broke out, John requested tar, oil, and lime to fly-proof them, but his request was denied.

There was a four-room dispensary for the POWs at Wakayama, but no permanent medical care. A Japanese doctor made infrequent trips from Ōsaka. Between visits a Japanese medical corpsman by the name of Okazaki Isojirō stole Red Cross medicines as they came into camp. John could tell; he managed to obtain a passkey to Okazaki's office where supplies were stored. Each night John held sick call and gave Okazaki a list of those too ill to work the next day. Invariably, sick POWs were forced to go to work anyway. Quotas had to be met. Wakayama Iron Works housed a large industrial hospital and was forced to provide medicine and food to POWs if they were to be productive as laborers. John wanted to use its facilities for surgical cases, but he was refused access.

Shiki Haruko was seventeen years old when she was put to work at the mill. The civilians were isolated from the POWs, but one day she saw a line of prisoners walking to the plant with guards at either end. "They were thin, exhausted," she said, and roped together to prevent escapes. POWs who died were cremated on a hill south of Wakayama. The ashes of civilians were deposited in Gokurakuji Temple, but those of the prisoners at Wakayama were never found.

The POW camp was a block from the beach in Wakayama and just across the street from Kasuga Shrine. But John and the other prisoners had little chance to partake of nature's bounty on the lovely Kii Peninsula, where elementary schoolchildren as young as seven-year-old Nakamura Ryūichirō were taught the expression *Ki chiku bei ei*, which means "devil-animal-American-British." Still, Wakayama was a holiday at the shore compared to Fred's experience in Ōsaka.

It was a bizarre location for a so-called POW hospital, a latter-day coliseum for the condemned. Ichioka was located beneath the concrete grandstand of a stadium at the Ichioka Athletic Field, not far from Ōsaka No. 1 Headquarters Camp. The hospital was established on October 19,

1942, for casualties of the *Lisbon Maru*, which had been torpedoed on September 27, 1942, by an American submarine, the USS *Grouper*, while on its way from Hong Kong to Shanghai. Of the 1,816 POWs aboard, there were 974 survivors, many of whom suffered from pneumonia, dysentery, and diphtheria contracted during the journey.

Ichioka was shaped like an attic space with a roof that met the floor on one side. A stone walkway fifty meters long divided the six sick bays that accommodated on average 100 patients. Wooden bays were placed eighteen inches above the floor, perpendicular to the walls, so patients lay on straw mattresses with their feet pointing toward the center. There were no windows, and there was no ventilation. Many of the sick were too weak to bathe at the wash trough. They lay curled up beneath wood fiber blankets, infested with lice, their hips covered with bedsores. These weren't humans, Fred thought; they were scarecrows.

The POWs at Ichioka were predominantly American, English, and Australian. Two British Army regiments were represented, the Royal Scots and the Middlesex, who had served with the China Fleet in Hong Kong. The Australians came mostly from C Force, having surrendered in Singapore. There were also Canadians and Javanese, along with a half-dozen lascars, Chinese, and a Swede—merchant seamen who had been captured by a German surface raider in the Pacific. Together they had sailed from Singapore on November 28, 1942, aboard the *Kamakura Maru* and arrived in Nagasaki on the anniversary of Pearl Harbor.

At first, Surgeon-Lieutenant Charles Anthony Jackson, a Royal Navy volunteer reserve, was the sole POW physician at Ichioka. Three naval sick berth attendants and three men from the Royal Army Medical Corps assisted him. A big, bewhiskered man with a reassuring bedside manner, Jackson had been a Harley Street surgeon back in London. Jack Hughieson, a Royal Navy telegraphist whom Jackson enlisted to help set up the hospital at Ichioka, described his initial impression:

> Our first reaction to the conditions we found was one of complete disbelief. The stench, as we entered the tight, enclosed space, was so bad, breathing was extremely difficult, and most of us suffered periods of vomiting. Mountains of rotten clothing, canvas sacking in a pulp condition, and soggy cardboard lay all around mixed with human excrement. Rats were everywhere, that scattered with our every move.
>
> Although one or two shovels were made available, most of us were forced to move this filth with our bare hands, and bury it in holes outside the confinement, in the surrounding grounds; which, when fenced in was to become our parade ground. If the Japanese

Military really wanted to tell us what they thought of us POWs, this camp said it all.

Ichioka filled up with patients from POW camps in Kōbe and Ōsaka who were too ill to work. Others had just disembarked from transport ships or died on the trucks conveying them to the hospital. The dead were piled up at one end of the camp. Rats feasted on corpses. Empty soy bean barrels were used as coffins. The Japanese insisted that two bodies fit into one barrel, which meant that POWs had to dislocate the bones of the deceased or break them to squeeze them in. Then the barrels were hauled outside the camp, doused with kerosene, and set afire.

One of Hughieson's jobs was down at a warehouse near the Ōsaka docks, shoveling rice from huge piles into sacks that he loaded onto Japanese Army transport trucks. Only when he finished was he allowed to sweep up the spillage, which included cigarette butts, matchsticks, and rat droppings. These became POW rations.

Jackson was livid, and when he asked the Japanese for an explanation, they answered him with a beating. In the meantime the men soaked the rice overnight so it would be clean before they cooked it, and they supplemented their diet by stealing fish heads at a dockside market. They had a watery bowl of rice for breakfast; a thin vegetable soup with three tiny finger rolls for lunch; and a small bowl of rice and barley porridge for dinner. When the Red Cross sent cough medicine to the camp, the POWs used it to flavor their rice and soup. They made tea by bringing water in an American canteen to a boil. Once the beverage was brewed, they removed the tea leaves so they could be dried and smoked. Nothing was wasted, and if you didn't have any tea, you simply drank hot water.

Medical supplies were furnished monthly by the Ōsaka Military Hospital, but the stocks of magnesium sulfate, kaolin, and atropine were limited. The Japanese at Ichioka didn't just rifle Red Cross parcels, they stole them outright. Some drugs could be purchased illegally from the guards, but there was no anesthesia. For surgery, Jackson used a razor as a scalpel and a hacksaw blade for amputations, sterilizing them first in the water that had been boiled for rice. He turned to his corpsmen to hold down patients during operations. Once Jackson resorted to using his own nail clippers to amputate the toes of a POW who had developed gangrene as a result of "painful feet."

From November 1942 until July 1943, 2nd Lieutenant Nishiura Kazuhiko was the Japanese medical officer in charge of Ichioka, and he took every opportunity to tell Jackson that the sooner his patients died, the better. The purpose of Ichioka was to weed out the sick patients from the healthy ones, so the commandants in the Ōsaka work camps could boast a better percentage of POWs toiling on the emperor's behalf. Sergeant Major Okano Kihichirō, by contrast, treated the POWs kindly, even if, as Jackson said, he "would not put himself to any great inconvenience to ensure justice."

Jackson was utterly unafraid of the Japanese and intervened regularly on his patients' behalf. The sick received one-third of the rations allotted to working POWs, which were "inadequate to maintain life," he alleged in October 1943. First Lieutenant Matsuyama Susumu, who succeeded Nishiura, asked the patients in one of the mess halls if anyone was hungry. Some of them were so weak they could barely make it from their beds to the table. They all raised their hands. At which point Matsuyama demanded that the men fall in, and the guards—Katō Masayoshi and Nayakayama Tarōkichi—began to thrash them, Jackson included, with belts, bamboo poles, and clogs. The Americans were singled out for especially harsh treatment. Tech Sergeant Sam Chasinov of the Coast Artillery Corps was beaten unconscious. Jackson revived him with an injection of vita-camphor, and when he came to, he was beaten again. The Japanese then ordered two English patients to finish eating all of the food. The men became violently ill; one went into a seizure. The rampage lasted two hours, after which the patients were drilled for another hour in Japanese Army commands. Within three weeks "four of the victims had died of their illnesses, which were undoubtedly aggravated by the experience," Jackson stated.

The guards—among them Bandō Bunhachi, a *gunzoku*, or civilian attached to the Japanese Army, and Katō Masayoshi, nicknamed "North and South" for his wandering eyes—were easily provoked. Katō drilled the men relentlessly to call them to attention (*Ki o tsuke!*) or to get them to bow *(keirei)*, or just to drill into them that he was the "big man." He made the POWs do *tenko* numerous times, sometimes during the night, and often to the accompaniment of slapping and kicking.

The beatings were most severe after the guards' monthly ration of sake. One night not just one guard but all of them came for *tenko*, wooden clogs in their hands or leather belts wrapped around their fists. The belts were the worst because of the lashing you'd get from the metal tongue. They also tried to kick the men in the testicles, which meant your shins and knees took the brunt of the blows in self-defense. The last thing you could do was go down; otherwise they'd be on you like a pack of dogs. As much as there was talk of striking back, "you took a bashing if you wanted to get home," as simple as that, said Roland "Dixie" Dean, a frontline artillery man in the Australian army who became a "piss tin and bedpan orderly," as he put it, by default.

In April 1944 the guards set up a race for the lascars and Chinese POWs. One of them, nicknamed "Lofty," filled a large bowl to overflowing with rice while the seventeen smaller ones were allotted just a few grains. Katō escorted the men to the far end of the hall and explained the rules. The first man to the table won the entire bowl of rice; the rest would go hungry. The POWs immediately began to jostle for position, fights broke out, and the guards restored order by whacking them with bamboo poles. Lofty blew his whistle, and the race began. The men surged down a narrow corridor, sick POWs were trampled underfoot; others were knocked into the concrete columns that supported the roof. When the winner claimed his trophy, he was thrown to the ground, the rice scattered onto the floor, and the men scurried for the remains—to the delight of the two guards.

The heat under the stadium's grandstand was unbearable during the summers. POWs quickly became dehydrated. Living conditions were no better for the Japanese, but at least they could cool off outdoors in the shade. The guards seized upon an idea to reduce the temperature inside. They gave buckets and bedpans to a group of fifty POWs, who stacked them by the faucets at the center of the stadium track. Then they formed the men into a chain that extended to the top of the bleachers. The Japanese carefully delineated their roofline from that of the prisoners. The buckets and bedpans were filled with water, the POWs passed them from man to man, dumped them on the concrete steps above the Japanese quarters, and then threw them back down to a "catcher" in the field, where they were refilled and the process began all over again.

One empty bucket fell short of its "catcher" and splintered on the concrete steps. The guards were furious and systematically beat every man in line. Work continued into the late afternoon. Finally a guard known as "Slap Happy Larry" ordered the POWs to "quick-march" out the main gate. A crowd of Japanese women and children gathered from the neighborhood to watch the barefoot prisoners in their *fundoshi*. Slap Happy Larry decided to put on a show for his audience and began beating the men so violently with a bamboo pole that some lost control of their bowels. He berated the POWs for carelessly breaking one of the emperor's wooden tubs. John Quinn of the Royal Marines remembered hearing applause from the spectators. For nights to come, the prisoners slept on their stomachs—their backs and shoulders raw from their wounds.

One day Lofty lined up six lascars in a corridor opposite six Chinese POWs and ordered them to hit one another in the face. The men reluctantly exchanged punches until Lofty gave a more vigorous lesson in how the sport should be played. Soon, a melee broke out, which the

Japanese ended after twenty minutes. The game was called *taiko binta*, and it was foisted upon Japanese recruits in basic training.

Time now for round two. Six Americans stood opposite six British POWs. The Allies had already decided that they wouldn't indulge the Japanese. They remained perfectly still, arms at their sides. Lofty was furious. Katō returned with two loaded rifles and threatened to shoot the POWs.

"Fuck the bastards," one of the Americans said. "We'd just as well be dead as put up with this bullshit. Fuck them."

"There we stood," said Quinn, "twelve pathetic, emaciated humans, ravaged and two and a half years into our period of starvation and degradation, and a sorry sight we must have looked. But twelve glorious and valiant people."

Occasionally the POWs engaged in more than passive resistance. Vengeance sometimes won out over suffering. When Japanese guards asked the Australian corpsmen for injections to treat their syphilis, "we always made sure the needle was dipped into the sputum tin of one of the TB patients before it was used," confessed Dixie Dean. Jackson would have nothing to do with the practice.

Nosu was known as the "Mad Butcher" of Ichioka, and his behavior struck the navy doctors as nothing short of bizarre. To cure diarrhea and dysentery he placed punks on the abdomens of patients, who were held down until the embers burned out, leaving scars the size of smallpox vaccination marks. He encouraged POWs experiencing "painful feet" to soak them in buckets of ice water or even snow, which often resulted in frostbite and required amputation. But there was another experimental procedure the Japanese performed that had even more serious repercussions.

It was May 9, 1943. The weather had warmed up, and a group of patients was sitting outside in the sun picking lice off of their undergarments. Second Lieutenant Nishiura Kazuhiko, the Japanese medical officer, strode by in high, black polished boots with a "cheese knife"—his samurai sword—swinging at his side. Four guards accompanied him. He told Jackson of his plans. The "painful feet" patients, he determined after reading a German medical text, were suffering from primary erythromelalgia, an unusual vasodilation disorder characterized by burning feet or hands. But the cause of primary erythromelalgia is unknown. Nishiura decided to treat it surgically. In an attempt to decrease or eliminate the pain caused by the syndrome, he would divide the sympathetic nerves in the abdomen. The procedure, called a sympathectomy, was a difficult and potentially dangerous operation.

Jackson was vehemently opposed to the idea—and was beaten unconscious for airing his opinion. Nishiura proceeded to select eight men, among them Simon S. McCloud, Staff Sergeant Carl E. Western of the U.S. Army Quartermaster Corps, H. Gay of the Royal Navy, and John Kidd, the feisty yeoman who had been knocked down by MacArthur as the general dashed into Malinta Tunnel during an air raid on Corregidor. Kidd was so bloated from wet beriberi that he could barely sit. His legs had swollen to twice their normal size. His abdomen was distended from edema, and his feet and toes were excruciatingly sensitive.

The patients were loaded into the rear of a dump truck and driven half an hour away to the Ōsaka Military Hospital. The first to be operated on was McCloud. After nearly an hour and forty-five minutes, it was Kidd's turn. He entered the OR, where he saw McCloud lying on the floor, surrounded by bloody gauze. The steel operating table was filthy. The doctor wore soiled cotton gloves. He injected Kidd with a spinal anesthetic—and hit a nerve that gave him a jolt like an electric shock and caused his legs to shoot straight out in front of him. An assistant held Kidd's feet while the doctor continued with the injection, then made the first incision in Kidd's abdomen. A geyser of fluid shot out of Kidd's saturated tissue where ordinarily there would be fat. Kidd was turned on his back, and the doctor made a seven-inch incision. After thirty minutes Kidd began to regain consciousness. He tried to get up and was punched over the left eye and slammed back down onto the operating table. Then he was given an intramuscular injection and a sheet was tied across his chest so he couldn't move. Kidd drifted in and out of a twilight state. He heard voices speaking quickly and then felt searing pain as the skin around the wound was grabbed roughly and closed. When the operation was over, Kidd was hoisted into the dump truck and hauled back to Ichioka, where he lay on the straw-covered floor.

There was no medication for postoperative pain or infection, and soon Kidd spiked a fever. At the end of the first week Jackson began removing Kidd's stitches. When he reached the next-to-last suture, the incision burst open. Blood and pus streamed out of Kidd's body and onto the mat beneath him. The stench was horrific. There was a gaping hole in his belly. Corpsmen irrigated the site with ordinary tap water and each day drained nearly a Klim container full of discharge. But the wound would not heal. Kidd's peritoneum was in danger of being torn from the walls of the abdomen.

Jackson was so concerned about the buildup of fluids that he inserted a six-inch probe into Kidd's right side. The probe disappeared. "The stitches have rotted, and the muscle is like a rubber band being cut and retracted," he told Kidd. "The infection has reached all the way around to the center of your back, where the fluid is being gathered." Jackson retrieved the probe with a dental forceps and applied a butterfly bandage, but the incision refused to close.

Sixteen days after the operation, Jackson came to a decision. "Kiddie," he began in his clipped English accent, "we're going to have to sew you up. Otherwise, you're going to die."

"Well, okay," Kidd replied in a flat Texas drawl.

"So we have three problems," Jackson continued.

"What's that?" Kidd said, more of a challenge than a question.

"One, we don't have anything to do it with, except the kind of needle you sew your clothes with. We have some cotton thread. We have some shirt buttons. We'll use those to suture you up."

Kidd nodded, waiting.

"The second problem," Jackson said, and paused, "is that you're going to have to help."

"What can *I* do?" Kidd asked.

"You're going to have to suck in your stomach so the needle doesn't perforate the stomach wall and spread the infection inside your abdomen. Otherwise you will die."

No argument there, Kidd thought. "Okay," he replied.

"And the third problem . . ." Here Jackson took a long pause. "We have no anesthetic."

Had Jackson been back in England, he would have used absorbent chromic catgut sutures to close the peritoneum and muscle layers and, for abdominal incisions, deep tension sutures made from either unabsorbent black silk, silkworm gut, linen thread, or wire. For deep tissue he would have asked his nurse for an eyed, round-bodied needle, and for the skin an eyed cutting-pointed needle. But that would have been in a British hospital. At Ichioka, Jackson had no surgical equipment, no anesthesia, no pain-killer. Just a needle, some thread, and a few buttons.

Jackson tempered the needle by heating it in the galley fires to put a suitable curve into it. He pushed the needle through Kidd's skin, working from the inside out, extracting it with a forceps. Then he looped the thread through the two eyeholes of a button. It was a painful, laborious procedure, a test of will and endurance on the part of the patient, and a triumph of resourcefulness and resolution on the part of his doctor. By the time Jackson was finished, Kidd's abdomen was as neatly buttoned together as a custom-made vest from a Savile Row tailor.

For months afterward Kidd was known as "Buttons," and he remained inactive for half a year. He had to learn how to walk all over again. Eventually he was flexible enough to be able to sit down on the ground outside the Ichioka stadium, find a patch of clover, and start eating clumps of it. His weight by then had dropped to eighty pounds.

Kidd was lucky. The post-op complications experienced by Nishiura's patients were many. Western lost the use of his legs. McCloud's feet had to be amputated. Gay suffered a burst abdomen and died within a week.

Gay was not the first POW to die in Ichioka at the hands of a Japanese doctor. In 1942 two American POWs who had tried to escape were escorted to army regional headquarters. The camp commandant and Sergeant Sawamura Masatoshi were ordered to "deal with them suitably." "Suitably" meant killing them, which a Japanese Army doctor did by injecting them with potassium cyanide. It was the ultimate perversion of a medical doctor's role.

The Japanese suspected Jackson of keeping detailed medical records. Moreover, he had been performing unauthorized autopsies and questioned the official cause of death listed for several POWs. They searched his gear, went through his office, and removed all papers pertaining to POW diet, caloric intake, and malnutrition. He was beaten by Nosu, then taken to Ōsaka No. 1 Headquarters Camp, where he was made to stand at attention for twenty-four hours and was cross-examined. He returned to Ichioka badly bruised. On March 24, 1944, Jackson and a Dutch medical officer named Irens were transferred to Kamioka, a lead mining camp in Ōsaka. The Japanese wanted no more trouble from the POW doctors.

The next day Major Okano appointed Major John Finch Akeroyd, an Australian doctor who had been interned at Taisho, an Ōsaka subcamp, senior medical officer of Ichioka. When Fred Berley arrived on April 8, he became the ranking American medical officer, and a new Japanese commandant was soon assigned to Ichioka: Ōhashi Hyōjirō.

Akeroyd was a large, imposing, mustachioed man, with an accent so thick that Fred had difficulty understanding him. Garrulous and generous, he was built like a rugby forward and had served as regimental medical officer with the 2/22nd Battalion before being taken prisoner on Rabaul. He had a wife, Barbara, and a young daughter, Margaret, who couldn't remember what he looked like, it had been so long since she'd seen him.

Akeroyd smoked heavily and coughed constantly. Fred slept next to him beneath the lowest part of the hospital's roofline. He could hear Akeroyd hacking away through the night and wondered if it was something more than smoker's cough. The ward was riddled with tuberculosis.

When Murray arrived at the stadium camp in June 1944, he was greeted warmly by Fred but he was horrified by conditions at Ichioka. Only one word could describe it: hellhole. What else would you call a so-called hospital where doctors beat patients and staff alike, where the quartermaster stole food from POWs who were so hungry they rooted around in the dirt like animals, where men begged to be taken back to their old camps because they believed they were in Ichioka not to get well but to die? On onionskin paper he kept a partial record of the medical experimentation at the camp and its disastrous consequences:

> *It is important to note that the condition these patients were suffering from was a "new condition" ("Painful Feet")—a disease due to inadequate nutrition & starvation. Treatment for this condition was simply improving the diet. Beyond this no effective form of treatment was known.*
>
> *The abdominal sympathectomies performed by Lt. Nishiura were formidable operations—require extreme caution & delicacy even by the most skillful surgeons. The value of these operations for this condition was highly questionable even on theoretical grounds. In effect Lt. Nishiura was using these patients as guinea pigs.*
>
> *The operation on Gay—without consent, & over the objection of Dr. Jackson—which resulted directly in Gay's death—constitutes even in its most favorable light manslaughter.*

These were not state-sponsored medical experiments, such as the extensive sterilization and castration operations performed by Nazi doctors in Auschwitz. Nor could they be justified on military grounds, as was the wide-scale testing of typhus sera in other German concentration camps. They were ad hoc experiments motivated by ignorance, sadism, and revenge.

The beatings at Ichioka were frequent, and how a man handled them could mean the difference between life and death. The worst part, Murray felt, was not the physical pain but the humiliation of not being able to strike back. You had to suppress your rage, swallow your pride, stare straight ahead, and keep your arms at your sides. You didn't speak. You didn't move. You tried your damnedest not to betray a flicker of emotion. You were forced into not reacting, and by doing so, you no longer registered pain, no longer acknowledged authority. Your fate was in someone else's hands but you controlled the situation by entering a zone where psychologically the enemy had ceased to exist. You learned not to feel.

The stories Fred told Murray were chilling. Once a week the POWs at Ichioka were supposed to be issued fish or meat. On May 8 Fred saw a delivery of fish at the camp, but little of it surfaced at mealtime. Fred asked James Kelleher, the chief cook and formerly a leading stoker for the Royal Navy, why it wasn't on the table.

"The Japs took it," Kelleher explained.

Katō filched about twenty fish for the guards and their families, leaving few for the prisoners.

Kelleher and Quinn, who also worked in the kitchen, protested the theft, first to Bandō and then to quartermaster Kitamura Shozo. But Kitamura, known as "The Snake," stole food regularly from the camp. Bandō was enraged with Kelleher for going over his head, and once Kitamura left, he struck the two cooks repeatedly about the face. Then he made them stand with their hands outstretched in front of Akeroyd and Berley's offices, haranguing and slapping them every few minutes.

Fred was furious. Akeroyd thought a protest would be of no avail.

"Well, I think the ward officer should know about it," Fred said.

"I'm telling you, there's nothing we can do," Akeroyd insisted.

"If you won't go, I will," Fred admonished.

Akeroyd went ahead and reported the incident to Major Okano, who was seated with a Japanese medical officer on his left and Katō on his right. The medical officer promptly sent for Bandō and dressed him down. Kelleher and Quinn were released immediately. The medical officer was none other than Ōhashi Hyōjirō.

Tenko was scheduled for 2000, but it was later than usual that evening. Ōhashi had gone for the night. Fred, Akeroyd, and 2nd Lieutenant Evert Manuel Gonie, a Javanese pharmacist with the Royal Dutch East Indian Army, stood before the morgue. Ambulatory patients were positioned in front of each hospital bay to report the number of bedridden men in them as Katō checked the muster. Akeroyd saluted, but Katō refused to acknowledge him. Then Bandō came around from behind and began hitting Akeroyd in the face. He screamed at the top of his lungs as he went down the row of prisoners, striking each one in turn. Katō unfastened his belt and worked Akeroyd over until Bandō returned and started down the aisle of prisoners again. Now Kitamura joined the fray along with Nakayama Giichi, who struck the men with his belt, jumping on top of a table so he could whip them in the face, ten lashes per man. They slapped, punched, and kicked the POWs, using bare hands, scabbards, and rubber-soled shoes. Sometimes three Japanese ganged up on one prisoner, as they did with Gonie. Next Katō stalked the sick bays, pulling men to their feet who he thought should be upright and pounding them mercilessly. One of them, Private Wade of the Royal Scots, had a rheumatic heart; another, an American lieutenant named Dupree, suffered from gangrenous feet. Akeroyd tried to intervene, only to be thrashed again by Bandō, who shouted as he went from bay to bay, "All men die, *jōtō* [good]! All men die!" The beating lasted ninety minutes, at the end of which Katō hustled Fred, Akeroyd, Gonie, and the Australian medic Sergeant R. A. Wickens into his office, where they were made to stand at attention before the beating resumed.

"Now you see you speak to doctor—no good!" Katō shouted.

There would be no mention of the incident to Dr. Ōhashi; the POWs had learned their lesson. Some of them were beaten so severely, they couldn't see. Hughieson wasn't sure that Fred would make it. But in time, his swelling went down, his cuts healed, and his bruises paled, though the memory of "the great fish incident," as it was called, would never fade.

Dr. Ōhashi, Fred learned, was a highly regarded surgeon in Ōsaka. The fact that he had listened to Akeroyd's complaint and acted on it immediately struck Fred as exceptional. Ōhashi was a protégé of Fritz Hartel, a native of Saxony who had lectured on surgery and clinical medicine in Ōsaka. He had earned his medical degree in 1928 from the prestigious Ōsaka Prefectural Medical College. His thesis, on leukocytosis, was written in German.

Ōhashi was eager to know more about Western medicine and he also wanted to improve his English. Fred, who for so long resisted speaking Japanese, spent an hour each afternoon tutoring him. And as it had been for the Nagasaki interpreters more than 300 years before, language was the bridge to cultural understanding.

Fred persuaded Ōhashi to personally examine some of the other patients at Ichioka. Ōhashi was shocked by their condition. He sat down on a chair and between clenched teeth emitted a long "Sssaaaahhh." Within days he hosted a veritable banquet, with more food than Fred had seen since the war began. Shortly afterward he confirmed the rumor: they would be moving to the new hospital in Kōbe, and Ōhashi would be its commandant.

A new POW medical staff was drawn from the doctors and corpsmen in Ichioka and the surrounding camps. In June 1944 Lieutenant Commander John Allison Page of the Royal Navy Volunteer Reserve arrived in Ichioka. Page had been captured at St. Teresa's Hospital in Kowloon, imprisoned at Amagasaki Subcamp near Ōsaka, and was named surgeon and principal medical officer. "The Royal Navy blokes welcomed him as they would have the Archangel Gabriel," said Dixie Dean. Akeroyd would be the sole Australian medical officer, while Ōhashi let Fred select two other doctors and one dentist for the American contingent. It was an easy decision. John was called in from Wakayama so he could rejoin Fred, Murray, and Stan Smith. Together with Louis Indorf, a physician from Timor, the Javanese pharmacist Gonie, and twenty corpsmen and cooks, the new Kōbe POW medical staff would care for the sick among the 6,000 POWs in fourteen Ōsaka-area camps. Unfortunately Akeroyd himself became a patient.

On July 3, 1944, Ōhashi took the unusual step of escorting Akeroyd and Fred to the Ōsaka Military Hospital for fluoroscopies. He also arranged for an X-ray of Akeroyd's chest, at a time when most hospitals in Japan had no X-ray film whatsoever. Sure enough, Akeroyd had a tubercular lesion on his left lung about an inch and a half in diameter and filled with fluid. Page and Fred operated on him on a kitchen table back in their office at Ichioka. John handled his post-op care, but Akeroyd's health remained poor. Fred figured the only reason he didn't catch the disease himself was because of the resistance he had developed as a result of a small tubercle on his lung that dated back to his sophomore year in college. As it was, he didn't think he would survive another three months in Ichioka.

Fortunately, Ōhashi Hyōjirō proved a man of his word. In just a matter of days Fred, John, and Murray saw the last of the stadium camp. On July 10, 1944, the newly designated Hospital No. 30, otherwise known as the Kōbe POW Hospital, opened its doors to the Allied prisoners of the Japanese.

=== 19 ===

Bad Timing and Good Luck

KŌBE IS BEAUTIFUL. Across the bay from Ōsaka, it nestles against the Rokkō Mountains, whose foreshortened peaks lend it the air of a bonsai garden. Originally a fishing village, Kōbe sprang up from Hyōgo Harbor, which was opened to foreign trade in January 1867, the year the shogun tendered his resignation as the Lord Chief Executive of the feudal government and a month before the emperor Meiji acceded to the throne. In 1868 the strip of fields to the east that included Hashiudo, Futatsuchaya, and Kōbe was staked out for foreign settlement. In 1880 the area was incorporated as the City of Kōbe, and in 1892 Hyōgo and Kōbe Harbors were combined into the Port of Kōbe. The main rail line from Shimonoseki would link Kōbe to Tōkyō.

Kōbe, said a municipal guide published in 1929, was "the vestibule of the country," boasting some thirty foreign consulates and residents from more than forty countries. Vibrant and cosmopolitan, Kōbe was the sixth-largest city in Japan, with a population that stood at 976,234 in 1940. You could hike in the hills in the morning and go for a swim in the afternoon, then shop in the elegant Moto-machi district or catch a Hollywood film in Shinkaichi. The talkies came to Japan that year, and Clara Bow, Jean Harlow, and Mary Pickford were immensely popular. Japanese girls were quick to copy their hairstyles. Japanese men wore the round, horn-rimmed *roido* spectacles made fashionable by the comic Harold Lloyd. Jazz was another American import that appealed to Japanese taste, thanks to Horiuchi Keizō, an MIT engineering student who joined the NHK (the Japan Broadcasting Corporation). And then there was baseball. With its own English-language newspaper and an "American pier" where foreign ships were berthed, Kōbe was Japan's most Westernized municipality.

But Kōbe was also a center of heavy industry, which was concentrated along the coastline in an east-west direction. Even before the war, signs were posted throughout the city in English and Japanese: NO PHOTO-

GRAPHING AND NO SKETCHING. Nippon Airplane and Kawanishi Aircraft, Japan's fourth-largest producer of combat aircraft, had plants in Kōbe. The Kawasaki Shipbuilding Yards constructed the 1915 battleship *Haruna* and produced 2,000-ton submarines, cruisers, and the aircraft carrier *Zuikaku* for the Japanese Navy. Mitsubishi Heavy Industries manufactured diesel engines, ship turbines, locomotives, and merchant vessels. Kōbe Steel turned out tanks, marine engines, and finished ordnance. A major source of military production, Kōbe was Japan's most important international port.

The hospital occupied the dormitory of a former American mission school in a quiet, hillside location in Kumouchi, Kōbe. Modest in size, three two-story wood-shingle buildings connected by covered walkways served as wards that could accommodate up to 200 patients. The ground floor of a separate administrative building housed an office, laboratory, and pharmacy, as well as dental, X-ray, and operating rooms. Upstairs were quarters for the doctors and corpsmen. Equipment was Japanese and American and included two small sterilizers and a charcoal-heated autoclave. There was ether and chloroform for anesthesia, morphine for pain, and a pharmacy stocked with medicine for a variety of ailments. From an article in the *Mainichi* (Daily) *Shimbun* the doctors learned of a new miracle drug called penicillin that refrigerated store ships were delivering to Pacific bases, though none was available to them in Kōbe. Still, the new hospital was a godsend after that hellhole Ichioka. There was a communal bath, a vegetable garden, and just beyond the fence, a creek that ran down the east side of the compound. The International YMCA donated books, religious services were tolerated, and POWs were permitted to write home once every four months.

A hospital canteen was open for business twice weekly and sold *ocha* (tea). The men received two meals daily and relished the *daikon* that appeared in their diet or, when the large white radish was unavailable, *miso-shiru*. By July 1944 Tōkyō had reduced the official rice ration for POWs to 390 grams, or 610 grams for heavy labor. At the Kōbe POW Hospital, the Swiss legation erroneously claimed that prisoners were receiving 3,000 calories a day, the same quantity and quality of food as the camp guards, when in fact they were receiving far less.

The POWs who worked as stevedores for Mitsui, Takahama, and Kōbe-go were held in a former warehouse of the Butterfield-Swires Company down by the waterfront. There were British prisoners from Hong Kong, and Australians who arrived in the Kōbe-Ōsaka area in 1943, survivors of J Force. Captain C. R. Boyce was the Australian medical officer in charge, and while he considered the Australians "pampered" in terms of medical treatment, he began referring more serious cases to the Kōbe POW Hospital.

Page requested that the hospital be marked with Red Cross insignia. The Japanese refused, just as Britain had refused to identify its ships for fear of attack by German U-boats. A Red Cross would only invite bombing by the Americans, Page was told, "because they always hit them."

Between them, Page and Fred performed nearly 100 operations at Kōbe, setting fractures, suturing lacerations, removing tumors, and draining abscesses. Patients recuperated on mattresses on the floor or on *tatami*-covered platforms before they were returned to work at Kōbe House and Ōsaka, Yodogawa and Sakurajima, Tsumori and Hirohata, Umeda and Tanagawa. John oversaw the tuberculosis ward, where he was assisted by corpsmen Ernie Irvin and Bud Flood, who were transferred from Ichioka and helped operate the X-ray machine. Murray worked in neurology and psychiatry.

The navy doctors were able to refresh their knowledge, refine their skills, and share notes, diagnoses, and observations. They had a language in common, and an experience tempered by blood, fire, and penury. In the heat of the moment, in plenty's absence, their resourcefulness was nothing short of inspiring. They studied the diseases that confronted them, even drafted papers for publication. For the first time since Bilibid, they were able to work together as a medical team. They were happy to assume old roles in a new place because doing good fostered hope.

In reality the Kōbe POW Hospital was a pet project of Colonel Murata Sōtarō, commander of the Ōsaka Prisoner of War Camp Area. It was a propaganda ploy to help convince world opinion, through the auspices of the International Committee of the Red Cross, that Japan was treating its prisoners of war well. The timing was hardly coincidental. On June 6, 1944, American, British, and Canadian troops stormed the beaches of Normandy in Operation Overlord. That same month, Admiral Toyoda Soemu, commander in chief of the Japanese Combined Fleet, vowed to vanquish the U.S. fleet if the Americans invaded Saipan. His bid led to the biggest carrier engagement of the entire war. The Battle of the Philippine Sea dealt a devastating blow to Japanese naval and air power. Two Japanese aircraft carriers, the *Taiho* and the *Shokaku,* were sunk in the first day alone, while radar-directed American fighters destroyed nearly 300 enemy aircraft in what was later referred to as "The Great Marianas Turkey Shoot." The Allies were winning stunning, nearly simultaneous victories in the European and Pacific theaters. The capture of Saipan followed on July 9 and forced Tōjō's resignation. One day later the hospital at Kōbe welcomed Allied POWs. As a Japanese propaganda pamphlet entitled "Victory on the March" explained next to a photograph of POWs being examined by a Japanese man purporting to be a doctor: "The sick are given full medical care and attention in the prisoners [sic] camps in Japan. Everything is done to assure their health."

The stevedores at Kōbe House had access to the English-language *Japan Times* and the *Mainichi Shimbun*. John Quinn, having married a Chinese woman in Hong Kong, was pressed into service as a translator because he could read *kanji*, the Chinese-derived characters that the Japanese used in their writing. The seriousness of Japan's situation was brought home when the men saw air raid shelters being dug along city streets while they were on their way to work in factories, and the antiaircraft positions being erected and sandbagged around Kōbe's harbor. Before long there were almost daily air raid drills. The hospital prepared two bomb shelters for the Japanese and one for the POWs. Two small reservoirs were filled with water in case of fire.

On August 18 the Swiss ICRC delegate, Heinrich C. "Harry" Angst, visited the Kōbe POW Hospital, and Colonel Murata made sure he was there to greet him. Murata praised the facility's "most suitable" location, the "mild climate, protection from harsh winds and an abundance of sunshine," as well as the thoroughly up-to-date equipment that rivaled "any first-class hospital in Japan." A cablegram Angst sent to Washington, D.C., via Geneva on September 18, 1944, quoted Fred Berley as expressing "SATISFACTION GRATITUDE FOR FINE HOSPITAL WHICH GREAT HELP FOR BOTH PATIENTS DOCTORS TREATMENT SATISFACTORY BEST HOSPITAL HE SAW SINCE POW STOP." But in his formal report, Angst naïvely gave the last word to Murata, who spoke as if one calculated good deed could absolve him of the crimes committed throughout the Ōsaka-area camps under his control: "Col. Murata affirms that in treating POW patients at the hospital he and the Japanese hospital staff are governed by principles of humanity and international justice." His subordinate Dr. Nosu put it another way. He informed the POW medical staff that, quite simply, no one was to die. "I command!"

Three days before Harry Angst's visit to Kōbe, an article in the *Ōsaka Mainichi* took a rather different view:

Difficulty grows: Americans are epicurean wild beasts. No nation on earth lives as much on meat as the Americans. This has deprived them of what should be the adequate quota of human decency. They have degenerated to such a depth that the resentment one would usually feel against a human being would be a luxury when applied to Americans. Since indignation towards the Americans would be sheer waste of sentiment, mankind owes it to itself to exterminate them with the same positive zeal as a civilized community would manifest in eradicating obnoxious insects.

The "principles of humanity and international justice" of which Colonel Murata grandiloquently spoke were hardly in evidence at Kōbe House. Or at the Kawasaki Branch Camp, where POWs toiled for Kawasaki Heavy Industries. Or at Ōsaka No. 1 Headquarters Camp, where they unloaded cargo for Sumitomo, the Ōsaka Ko Warehouse Company, and army contractors Kitamura and Heiki, or sweated it out in the steel mills of Ōsaka Tekko and Ōsaka Seio, which manufactured tank parts and built destroyers and cruisers.

Private Everett D. Reamer of the Coast Artillery Corps used to watch the Japanese staff enter the locked storehouse at the rear of his barracks in Ōsaka No. 1 Headquarters Camp and brazenly steal Red Cross food parcels. Reamer and five other POWs in *rokuban*, or Room No. 6, decided to stake their claim. He had been captured on Corregidor, imprisoned in Cabanatuan, and by August 1944 had lost almost forty pounds. The Red Cross parcels were intended for the POWs, so why should they be kept from the table? Besides, some of the fellows from Wake and Guam were already taking their fair share.

The men drew straws to determine who would lead the heist. Reamer came up short, followed by Private Louis C. Bradsher, also of the CAC. Because the headquarters camp was in a designated military zone, camp regulations required that at the end of each day a POW had to stand guard at night to make sure that only one man went to the *benjo* at a time. Bradsher would act both as guard and as Reamer's lookout.

On the night of August 10, Bradsher slipped by the *benjo*, switched off the light in the security area, unlocked the storeroom door with a key that had been forged in the foundry, and returned to his post. Reamer then grabbed three Red Cross parcels and hid them in the *benjo*, which was concealed by a thin wooden stall. Almost instantly Reamer heard the sound of hobnailed boots. The light must have been the tip-off. He crawled over into the next stall, knowing full well that if he was discovered, he'd be shot on the spot. The guards, meanwhile, were in a huddle by the storeroom, which gave Reamer the opportunity he was waiting for. He sneaked around them, continued on his way back to his barracks room, and squirreled up to the top level of the bay he shared with Mike Christle of the 4th Marines, where he lay perfectly still. The guards were hot on his heels. They beat up Bradsher, interrogated the other POWs in the barracks, and searched the bays but found nothing incriminating.

The next morning the Japanese cut off rations. There would be no food until the guilty party was found. That night Reamer confessed to Chief Boatswain's Mate Philip Earl Sanders, who was the American commander of the camp. Sanders listened sympathetically and said he would appeal to the Japanese for clemency. But Sanders himself was benefiting from the Red Cross parcels that the Japanese broke into, because they shared some of their booty with him. Sanders decided to turn Reamer and Bradsher in.

On August 14, 1944, while they were lined up for work, Reamer and Bradsher were taken to Colonel Murata's office. They were beaten, interrogated, tied to a bench so water could be pumped into their lungs, and questioned again. When that tactic failed to elicit a confession, they were forced to hold an office chair over their heads by the hind legs until they faltered and were slapped with a bamboo stick across the arms and back. Then they were made to stand at attention at the main gate twenty-four hours a day without food or water. They urinated down their legs, they defecated into their trousers, and they quickly dehydrated. Reamer's ankles swelled beyond recognition, and soon his mind and body went numb. On the evening of August 20, just as *tenko* was being conducted, nineteen-year-old Private Reamer collapsed.

Two British POWs rushed to his aid and took Reamer as well as Bradsher into their barracks for the night. "We're not going to let you kill them," the Britishers told the Japanese. They gave them food and water, but the next morning the guards came back for the two men. The Japanese placed them at the main gate for all to see, and at night confined them to a brig opposite the guardhouse that was so small, you could sleep on the floor only in a sitting position. Reamer and Bradsher were held there for nearly a month, subsisting on a small bowl of rice and a cupful of water twice daily.

A typhoon hit Ōsaka on the night of September 17, and by the next morning the camp was flooded. The guards tied the prisoners' hands behind their backs, strung their own shoes around their necks, and escorted the Americans to army headquarters in Ōsaka.

At 1300 Reamer and Bradsher were taken into a courtroom, where they stood before three Japanese Army officers, who served as judges, on the bench. They were asked through an interpreter to explain what had happened. One judge asked Reamer who he thought was going to win the war.

You bastards won't, he wanted to say, but reason won out over rashness. "It's only natural that as an American I think we're going to win the war," he explained.

Reamer and Bradsher were sentenced to one year solitary confinement.

"What do you think about that?" Reamer was asked.

"I don't think it's fair," he said, "because we only attempted to take what was ours to begin with."

After being handcuffed and hooded, they were escorted to a train. Reamer imagined his own execution, wondering if he was going to be shot or beheaded. Finally they arrived at Ōsaka Sakai Prison, where they exchanged their clothes for lightweight prison fatigues and were locked into their respective cells.

The room measured five by seven feet. A small barred window about three feet wide and eighteen inches high was situated in the cell door just above eye level, so the Japanese could see you without being seen. No books were allowed—not even a Bible. No exercise was permitted. You couldn't even stand up during the day. There was no running water, no heat, not a chair to sit on nor a bed for rest. A wooden pail was used as a toilet. A bare lightbulb burned continuously overhead. Food was pushed through a trapdoor, and at night you slept on the floor. Reamer recited the Twenty-third Psalm daily for strength. When the cell door closed behind him that first time, the teenager from Elizabethtown, Ohio, known to the Japanese as Prisoner No. 1589, wondered: "What now? Will this be the end for me?"

Dr. Ōhashi was intrigued by the American doctors. They seemed so knowledgeable, and their skills were so far beyond what he had encountered in Japan. But while their comparative experience and levels of expertise differed greatly, there was a common basis to their knowledge— up to a point.

In 1870, two years after the ascension of the emperor Meiji, the German system of medical education was adopted in Japan by cabinet decree. Pathological anatomy had been a weakness in Japanese medicine until students began to learn at the hands of European physicians. The emperor Meiji had lost six of his seven children in infancy to meningitis and appointed Hashimoto Tsutatsune, who had studied with a Dutch physician in Nagasaki, chief medical officer of his palace. Hashimoto went on to become medical officer of the Army Ministry and later surgeon general of the Japanese Army. By the late nineteenth century the faculty of Tōkyō's Imperial University Medical School was predominantly German. Japanese medical students continued to flock to Germany for instruction up until World War I.

At the same time, the German model of medical education was also the inspiration for sweeping reforms in American universities, whose medical graduates, lamented Charles Eliot Norton of Harvard, were so ill prepared it was "horrible to contemplate." Germany was preeminent in the laboratory sciences and in research, which were virtually nonexistent in pre–Civil War America when medicine was taught largely by apprenticeship. The medical school of Johns Hopkins University, founded in 1893, provided the new template. As in Japan, instruction was largely didactic. Lectures and rote memorization were emphasized at the expense of clinical and laboratory work. While the method of teaching changed in the United States in 1910, it remained the same in Japan throughout the prewar years.

Hopkins made a four-year college degree mandatory for admission. The medical curriculum comprised two years of laboratory science, followed by a two-year hospital internship and then a residency for specialization. In Japan the Doctor of Science degree was conferred upon almost every medical school graduate who simply completed two years of basic science, two years of clinical medicine, and an elective course of postgraduate study and research. There was no written examination comparable to the state medical boards in the U.S. in order to qualify for a medical license.

Before World War II the majority of Japanese doctors were graduates of *senmon gakkō*—second-class medical schools that often lacked a hospital affiliation for clinical experience. They were allowed to concoct their own prescriptions, sell medicine to their patients, and set up their own ten-bed hospitals. Pharmacists could prescribe and dispense drugs over the counter. Second-class doctors tended to work in rural areas; first-class doctors, such as Ōhashi, practiced in cities.

Despite a less rigorous approach to medical education, Japan claimed major scientific contributions to medical science. Kitasato Shibasaburō, a physician and bacteriologist, discovered the plague bacillus and helped Emil von Behring develop the tetanus antitoxin in 1892. In 1897 Shiga Kiyoshi discovered the dysentery bacillus, which was designated *shigella* in his honor. In the Russo-Japanese War, the Japanese Army medical service, noted Hans Zinnsser, was the first to demonstrate that typhoid fever in troops was preventable. In 1940 Shiga was still active at the acclaimed Kitasato Institute in Tōkyō, where Rockefeller Foundation funds helped build the new School of Hygiene that was run by Japanese professors trained at Harvard and Johns Hopkins.

But the same government that promulgated regulations for the study of medicine along secular European lines continued to allow doctors to engage in traditional Chinese medicine. *Kanpō,* as it was called, derived from the teachings of Buddhist priests and had been practiced in Japan since the sixth century A.D. What was mysterious or primitive by Western standards was a time-honored tradition in Chinese medicine. With little understanding of Asian culture, prisoners of the Japanese were apt to view *okyū* (moxibustion), *hari* (acupuncture), or performing surgery without anesthesia when novocaine hydrochloride was standard issue in American and British medical kits as ineffective at best and sadistic at worst. Just as some POWs were indignant about being given roots to eat when they were handed *daikon*, the white radish that is a staple of the Japanese diet.

Shintōism, the state religion that glorified the emperor at the expense of the individual (as it was interpreted in the first half of the twentieth century in Japan), complicated the ways in which Japanese medicine was practiced during the war and was frequently at odds with the principles of the Hippocratic oath. If it was better to die by committing seppuku than to surrender, then when the wounded, disabled, or diseased stood in the way of a military objective, the Japanese argued, it was better for them to succumb to the hand of a doctor. As one Division 17 operation order (marked "Military Most Secret," dated 12 January–18 February 1944) put it: "Arrangements to send the wounded and sick to the rear are being made, but if this causes too obvious an obstruction to the efficient execution of the withdrawal, unavoidable instances when wounded and sick must be disposed of are to be expected."

Japanese doctors were allowed to carry swords and pistols. Corpsmen brandished rifles with bayonets. They rarely wore Red Cross brassards and in some instances were called in as reinforcements for frontline troops. Forward-area hospitals were usually camouflaged, while troop transport ships were sometimes disguised as hospital ships carrying arms, ammunition, and combat personnel who were bandaged like patients.

Not only did Japanese doctors dispose of their own wounded and assist in suicides when soldiers were deemed useless to the emperor, they killed POWs who posed no threat to military objectives or internal security. At Khandok a live vivisection was performed on an unwounded African POW as if he were a surgical patient in some medical school's theater of the damned. As one witness described it, "The man was tied to a tree outside the Hikari Kikan Office. A Japanese doctor and four medical students stood around him. They first removed the fingernails; then, cutting open his chest, removed his heart on which the doctor gave a practical demonstration."

But government-sponsored medical experimentation on prisoners of war was another matter entirely. In Mukden, Manchuria, Japan's Unit 731 harvested POWs from the nearby Hoten camp and injected them with deadly pathogens as part of a bacteriological research program to develop biological weapons. The Japanese had used typhoid and cholera as biological weapons against China in 1940, and in March 1942 preparations were under way to release 1,000 kilograms of plague-infested fleas on Bataan, a plan that was abandoned when Bataan fell on April 9, 1942. Here, as in Nazi Germany, medical science was perverted in the interests of the state. What those interests were and how they were interpreted varied wildly from practitioner to practitioner as *bushidō*—the way of the warrior—came into contact with and often violated Western medical ethics.

As a doctor, Ōhashi was an exception. He was a devout Buddhist who prayed before performing his operations. He subscribed to the prevailing military ethos in believing that it was better to die by one's sword than face the ignominy of surrender. But he also knew that the Allied POWs felt no shame in being captives. They were proud as Americans, Englishmen, Australians, and Dutchmen. He prized their medical learning and felt no compunction about helping them treat their patients. He even assisted Fred Berley in a hernia operation. The esteemed surgeon from Ōsaka viewed the POW doctors not as his peers—he looked up to them as his superiors and acted, as Fred said, like a gentleman.

The medical picture at Kōbe differed considerably from what the American navy doctors had encountered in the Philippines. Recurrence of malaria was rare among those who had come to Japan, John noted, just as it had been for newly arrived British POWs from Thailand.

The incidence of tuberculosis, however, was high. The disease haunted Japan, its symptoms first described in a tenth-century medical text. By the late nineteenth century the death rate for *haibyō*, as it was known, was three times that of dysentery, the second most dangerous acute infectious disease. In 1940, Japan had the third-highest incidence of tuberculosis out of forty-seven countries, attributed in part to dietary deficiencies in protein and calcium, poor sanitation, and overcrowding. During the war tuberculosis became the leading cause of death among Japanese civilians, surpassing even the number of lives lost as a result of military action.

The technique Fred Berley used on tubercular patients was one he had learned during his internship in San Diego, though it originated in Europe in the late nineteenth century: artificial pneumothorax. Armed with only a syringe, a bit of tubing, and some sterilized bottles, he carefully drained the pleural cavity of liquid and replaced it with air to collapse the diseased lung in an attempt to contain the toxins produced by the tubercle bacillus. It was a painful procedure and a risky one without benefit of a fluoroscope or X-ray. But by listening carefully to the chest with a stethoscope, he was able to pinpoint the best place to insert the syringe. The treatment reduced coughing and fever and ultimately saved the lives, he believed, of several of his tubercular patients, including the ailing Akeroyd.

The most challenging surgery for Page and Berley involved a POW from the officers' camp in Zentsūji. A wing commander in the Royal Air Force, he sported a large malignant tumor on the parotid gland—the largest of the three salivary glands, which lies on the side of the face and extends from the earlobe to the jaw. Cancer had spread to the bone. To perform the procedure, the doctors first had to brush up on *Gray's Anatomy*, a copy of which they borrowed from Nosu. They operated beneath the brain, working gingerly when they encountered severe bleeding. John was dexterous in administering a mixture of chloroform and ether throughout the course of the five-to-six-hour surgery. The tumor was removed along with half of the maxilla, but a certain royal arrogance remained.

Initially the patient had to be fed a liquid diet through a nasal-gastric tube. Much of the staff donated their Red Cross powdered milk ration for his nourishment. In a few days he recovered sufficiently to sit up and eat.

"You know I should be eating in the Officers' Mess," he said to Dixie Dean, who had been charged with his care.

"What Officers' Mess?" Dean asked, incredulous. "There is no Officers' Mess here."

"Well, where do the doctors eat?" he inquired.

"Downstairs someplace. I don't really know," Dean replied. "Anyway," he continued, "you are a patient and you eat with the other patients. In this prisoner of war hospital all patients are equal, no ranks, and it doesn't matter if they are black, white, or bloody brindle, they all get the same treatment. They all get the same care, and they all get the same tucker. We have had American officers as patients, and they were happy with our treatment, no complaints. Major John Akeroyd, the RMO of the 2/22nd Battalion, is downstairs. He has TB, is happy to be treated as a patient, and was until recently one of our doctors. Perhaps you think that the doctors get an extra spoonful of rice. I don't think so, but if they do, bloody good luck to them, because with their help we may get home."

It was a brazen statement on Dean's part, but he couldn't help himself. What he really wanted to say was, You bloody, arrogant, upstart bastard.

The next day Page asked Dean if he had had a run-in with his patient, and Dean admittted he had.

"He can rest assured he will not be eating with the doctors," Page replied, and a few days later the lieutenant colonel returned to Zentsūji.

Beriberi was a significant nutritional disease in prewar Japan as a result of a thiamin-deficient diet that caused thousands of deaths annually. But unlike tuberculosis, beriberi actually declined during the war years due to government regulations that required rice to be undermilled, which preserved valuable thiamin in the pericarp—so long as rice was available. For POWs already suffering from it, wet beriberi remained a serious problem.

Diarrhea, another symptom of beriberi, was a common affliction in the camps. John drafted a paper on it at Kōbe and found that its causes varied, from amoebic and bacillary dysentery to pellagra, food substitutions such as soybean roughage, and any drop in the average daily caloric intake below 1,900. In extreme cases of starvation, diarrhea resisted treatment entirely.

But far and away the most perplexing complaint was "painful feet," also known as "burning feet," "electric feet," "hot feet," or even "happy feet" because of the hopping movements POWs made to avoid prolonged contact with the ground. The doctors at Kōbe set up a study group and prepared a handwritten paper on the subject.

The symptoms were well documented: a severe burning sensation in the soles of the feet, redness and slight swelling, followed by shooting pains. Depression, weight loss, forgetfulness, and circulatory impairment appeared in later stages. The discomfort was worst at night and during wet weather. The disease interfered with sleep, curtailed one's appetite, and could be so intolerable that during the winters in Japan patients plunged their feet into barrels of cold water or directly into the snow. Fourth Marine James Fraser developed gangrene as a result and watched his feet turn the color of eggplant from the big toe to the smallest, until the flesh peeled away and he self-amputated all ten digits with a nail clipper.

"Painful feet" wasn't a "new condition," as Murray believed. Symptoms of the disease had been described in European military campaigns in the late eighteenth and early nineteenth centuries, and in 1854 a near epidemic broke out during the Crimean War.

At Bilibid, the American doctors recorded 300 cases of "painful feet" out of a patient census of 800. In Soerabaya, Java, according to Louis Indorf, there were 500 cases out of 3,500 POWs from October 1942 to January 1943. In Hong Kong, Page estimated 2,000 cases out of approximately 7,000 POWs from May to December 1942. "Painful feet" appeared among POWs in the Far East during the first three to five months of captivity and afflicted Americans, British, Canadians, Australians, Dutch, Javanese, and Filipinos alike. There was a marked decline in incidence at the end of 1942 and the beginning of 1943, and the

Kōbe doctors could not point to any new cases in Japan. But "there were quite a lot of old cases which relapsed or became aggravated" during the prisoners' first winter in Japan.

What could the cause be? the navy doctors wondered.

It was well known that the POW diet was deficient in protein, fat, and elements of the vitamin B complex, which contributed to the prevalence of beriberi, while a lack of riboflavin and nicotinic acid caused skin lesions. Some victims of "painful feet" displayed lesions; many did not. Moreover, there were some who suffered similar vitamin deficiencies but did not present the symptoms of "painful feet."

Could toxicity in old and musty rice be a factor? Not necessarily, because in one officers' camp in Hong Kong a similarly poor-quality rice was provided without producing the same effect.

The vascular changes in the lower extremities suggested Raynaud's disease or erythromelalgia, which Kinosita Ryōjun, a pathologist at Ōsaka University, had seen in Japanese soldiers returning to Japan from the South Pacific.

The clinical picture for sufferers of "painful feet" was complicated by the fact that many POWs also had other diseases, such as pellagra or beriberi neuritis. Without controlled observation, laboratory analysis, or diagnostic aids, the doctors could only speculate—and experiment.

They tried administering vitamins A, C, and D—to little effect. They tried nitroglycerin and histamine—with indifferent results. Quinine seemed to provide some relief, but why, they couldn't say. So, concluding that "painful feet" was in all likelihood caused by a vitamin B deficiency, they fell back on an age-old home remedy: plenty of bedrest and a balanced diet.

———

As mysterious as ancient Chinese medical techniques were to the Allied POW doctors and their patients, one American therapy left the Japanese medical staff at Kōbe awestruck. The case involved a young American POW from Tennessee who was blind, and a British POW whose toes had been amputated as a result of "painful feet." The blind man managed to get around the hospital at Kōbe by towing on a little cart his buddy who served as the eyes behind him.

"Turn left," his friend would call out like a carriage driver. "Turn right." And the American would obey like a well-trained pony.

It was a pathetic sight, and a touching one, Murray thought. The men teamed up out of necessity to compensate for their respective infirmities. One had to get food for the other; the other had to show him where the food was before he could even get it. They were best friends out of need, two halves of one man.

Intrigued, Murray decided to examine the blind man's eyes. His patient had no corneal opacities, so he asked for an ophthalmoscope to examine the retina. The Japanese provided him with a reflecting ophthalmoscope of the kind that came into use in Europe and America a generation after Dr. Richard Libreich's invention in 1855. An antique, but serviceable—if you stood about three feet away from your subject. And what Murray saw took him by surprise. The retina was intact. The optic nerve appeared to be perfectly healthy, and the optic reflexes were normal. There were no signs of xerophthalmia. In fact, he could find no neurological or ophthalmological basis for the man's blindness. Then why couldn't he see?

In World War I German soldiers suffering from war neuroses in the field were typically treated with electric shock. Neurotics were considered malingerers whose symptoms were a result of the conflict between the instinct for self-preservation and a sense of duty. The doses were so high that men actually died during treatment; others committed suicide afterward. Given the choice, some soldiers decided the front didn't look so bad after all. In his "Memorandum on the Electrical Treatment of War Neurotics," written in 1920 for a special commission of the Austrian military, Freud suggested that psychoanalysis might be a more effective remedy for war neuroses than electric shock therapy.

A neurologist and also a bit of a dreamer, Murray was naturally drawn to psychoanalysis. He had read Charcot, the nineteenth-century French neurologist whose pioneering work on hysteria Freud had translated into German. And he had read the cornerstone of psychoanalytic theory, *Studies on Hysteria*, in which Freud and his co-author Josef Breuer argued that "hysterics suffer mainly from reminiscences." By hypnotizing their patients, Freud and Breuer were able to bring the memory of a traumatic event to light, at which point "each individual symptom immediately and permanently disappeared." Murray decided to try their technique on the blind American POW.

Slowly, calmly, he coaxed his subject into a trance. He asked him to describe in his own words the traumatic event, then firmly suggested that he would be able to see when he woke up. The result was not instantaneous, as Freud and Breuer had reported in their case histories. But after several sessions, Murray achieved his goal. On awakening to consciousness, his patient reclaimed his sight.

The Japanese were dumbfounded. The corpsmen were amazed. He'd been as blind as a bat, had had that faraway gaze that blind men have, couldn't even light a cigarette by himself—and now he could see? It seemed nothing short of a miracle, but it was not without its consequences. The Tennessean quickly abandoned his British buddy, who would now have to fend for himself on the chow line, having been discarded like an old appliance that has outgrown its usefulnesss.

Hysterical paralysis was a more common condition at Kōbe. One evening in the fall of 1944 a truckload of twelve to sixteen men arrived at the gate. Some of the POWs had been working on the Siam-Burma Railway. They had been removed to Saigon, and then transported from Singapore to Japan by freighter. For days on end they were kept down in the hold until their convoy, which included the *Kachidoki Maru* and the *Rakuyō Maru*, came under Allied submarine attack. Six hundred and fifty-six of the POWs who survived were taken to Japan aboard the 20,000-ton "whale factory" vessel *Kibibi Maru*.

Dixie Dean watched as Murray separated the healthy arrivals from the infirm. But it was obvious to Dean who was ill—they all were. They stank to high heaven, were filthy dirty, and couldn't lift one foot in front of the other. And there was the doc, saying, "He can walk." To which John Quinn replied: "And he can kiss my arse." Quinn proceeded to carry the prisoners to the hospital. The corpsmen bathed the men, fed them, and put them to bed. They were exhausted and malnourished, but Murray saw by their gait, by the paralysis they affected, that in some of the cases their physical symptoms merely mimicked illness; they were not caused by it. One by one he hypnotized them, and soon enough, like the blind marine from Tennessee, they were able to see and walk normally out of the hospital.

The question remained: what was the trauma that triggered their visual and motor hysteria? A beating, a torpedo attack, watching men die on land and at sea. Sometimes there was no sole causative factor except the general predicament of being a prisoner of war. Blindness or paralysis was an unconscious defense against the rigors of reality—and the prospect of more work details.

Some ethical dilemmas at Kōbe had life-or-death consequences but were quietly resolved. The doctors administered local and general anesthesia, depending on the operation, and morphine for post-op pain, though the opium derivative was restricted.

One patient suffered from secondary syphilis, with a wound in his left buttock "large enough to put a fist into," said Dixie Dean. He lay in a semicomatose state, his misery relieved only by morphine. One day the doctor stopped by on his afternoon rounds and asked Bud Flood the time of the last dose. The corpsman from Akron, Ohio, told him, and the doctor replied: "Give him another dose, now." Flood nodded, then looked at Dean, who looked back at him. The next dose would be lethal.

Flood went to the medical cabinet, prepared the injection, and approached the patient's bed. "I cannot do it, it will kill him," he said.

"Yes, I know, so hand me the syringe," Dean replied.

There was hardly enough flesh on the patient's arm to give him a proper injection, but Dean found a spot and injected the morphine. Twenty minutes later the patient was dead.

"Murder or euthanasia?" Dean wondered.

"Whatever name we give it, it was justified, it was necessary," he said afterward. It was only a matter of time, he rationalized, before syphilis would kill him, and the morphine could be used to relieve the suffering of other patients. He suspected that word would spread quickly around the hospital, but no one ever said a thing to him about it.

The American doctors were bound by common interest and mutual respect that warmed into lasting friendship. If POWs functioned as members of families, clans, and tribes, which were themselves defined by service organization, ultimately their identity was determined by nationality. Occasionally international tensions broke the surface calm. The Americans found the British patronizing, and Page in particular.

"It's *dyōōk*," Page corrected Murray's pronunciation during a conversation about the Duke of Windsor, "not *dōōk*."

"Well, I say duke," Murray answered testily, "because I come from New York, not *Nyōō* York."

Akeroyd told Dean he thought Tom McCready was a very solid bloke. When McCready heard the comment, he thought it meant he was "as thick as two planks." Dean assured him, "If he had meant otherwise, he would have said 'The man is a dill,' or 'He's a useless bastard.' "

The Aussies couldn't understand how the Yanks could curse each other to high hell and never come to blows. They themselves were regarded as the worst thieves, though the Royal Army Medical Corps had so many sticky fingers, the British doctors joked, that RAMC stood for Rob All My Comrades. At least everyone could agree about the Dutch. Contrary to their reputation for cleanliness in seventeenth-century Europe, they were judged the most foul-smelling because they bathed the least. Indian POWs kept themselves apart from American, British, and Australian POWs, though at Ichioka there had been flashes of racial animosity.

Such incidents were few and far between at the Kōbe POW Hospital. There was little time to nurse historical grudges when patients were dying of tuberculosis, pneumonia, and beriberi.

In September 1944 Guy and Victoria Berley received a handwritten letter from Mrs. Neva H. Newman of San Gabriel, California, who had picked up a shortwave broadcast from Radio Tōkyō at 2115 Pacific War Time on the fourth. She copied the message verbatim: *"I am in good health. Busy working in beautiful new hospital for Prisoners of War located on scenic site. Happily received your package and letters from home. Love Ferd."* Mrs. Newman added: *"I pray that soon your loved son may be reunited with you."*

Lewis and Sophie Glusman received a similar surprise at their home on Ridge Street. A West Coast ham radio operator intercepted a broadcast, relayed the text of it to the Army Service Forces, provost marshal general, POW Division, who then contacted the family: "Am in good health," it began. "Working as a neuro-psy . . . Hospital established for Osaka P.O.W. camp. Pleasant surroundings. Received your package and several letters. Love to all, Murray."

The broadcasts were the idea of a Japanese-born American named Kazumaro "Buddy" Uno, who had been on Bataan at the time of the invasion of Corregidor. With the blessing of the Imperial Japanese Army, Uno drew up a staff of American, English, and Australian POWs from radio, journalism, and nightclub entertainment. Their task was to read messages solicited from POWs in the Far East that were then transmitted overseas from Radio Tōkyō's downtown studios. Mixed in with these ostensible public service announcements was a fair dose of Japanese propaganda.

"This is *Humanity Calls*," began the program after an opening jingle, "bringing you messages from your missing men in Japanese prison camps. We know that when you hear these messages, you will help us by relaying them to those for whom they were intended."

The Japanese considered *Humanity Calls* so successful that it was followed later by a full half-hour segment, *The Postman Calls*. Reviews in the States were mixed. The *Prisoners of War Bulletin* advised listeners that the U.S. government could not vouch for the authenticity of any Axis broadcasts (the majority of which later turned out to be accurate). At Kōbe, recording equipment was actually brought into the hospital camp so POWs could tape their own messages, although the topics were preselected and there was a 150-word limit apiece.

In spite of its best intentions, the *Prisoners of War Bulletin* played an unwitting role in abetting Japanese propaganda efforts. Published by the American Red Cross, provided information on American POWs and civilian internees in the Pacific and European theaters. Such information, however, was tightly controlled by Axis powers and derived from visits made to a select number of camps by delegates from the International Committee of the Red Cross and the Swiss, Swedish, and Vatican legations. Between 1942 and 1945, the Japanese permitted slightly more than half of the sixty-five visits to POW camps requested by the protecting powers. No ICRC representative, for example, was ever allowed into Ichioka. That would merely have confirmed the reports of brutality and inhumane treatment of prisoners of war that began to appear in the American press ever since the *Chicago Tribune* broke the news of the Bataan Death March. As Dr. Marcel Junod, chief delegate of the ICRC in the Far East, later remarked: "In Germany particularly we were perfectly free to talk to the prisoners. With the Japanese it was entirely different."

The first of its kind in Japan, the Kōbe POW Hospital would show the Japanese in a different light. The November 1944 issue of the *Prisoners of War Bulletin* dutifully reported Harry Angst's August visit to the camp, stating: "Although the caloric value was stated to be 3,000 neither eggs, milk, fat margarine, cheese, sweets, coffee, nor canned foods were given to the prisoners. . . . food was the main problem."

The figure was an exaggeration. Three thousand calories was a third more than the average diet in prewar Japan. Even at Colonel Murata's "shop window," as Page called it, the sick received less food than the "heavy workers" down at the docks—about 2,000 calories daily. Fish and meat were supplied twice monthly "in ridiculously minimal quantities" of eleven to fifteen pounds per 150 men, Page quipped. Doctors and patients alike were on reduced rations because the higher command insisted, as Ōhashi explained to Fred, that they weren't contributing to Japan's war effort. Barley and millet seed replaced rice, supplemented by squash and occasionally dried fish heads. Soybeans were undercooked because of the lack of fuel and quickly passed through the digestive tract. Fred countered that the sooner patients had more food, the sooner they'd recover and be able to return to their work camps. The Allied medical staff tried to redress the imbalance by once again redistributing rations, but they were only partly successful.

By contrast, the POWs at Kōbe House were in robust condition. The reason was simple: they were stealing food from the ships that arrived in Kōbe Harbor, from the godowns along the waterfront, and from the Yoshihara vegetable oil processing plant, where some of them worked, about ten miles to the east. They forged keys so they could loot at their leisure the gigantic Mitsubishi warehouse that housed army supplies. Some of the companies they worked for provided meals. Occasionally Fred was able to cart some food and supplies back to the hospital—a little extra barley, some charcoal for the braziers they used to heat their upstairs quarters. He kept up the pressure on Ōhashi, and before long, miso and seaweed were added to their diet.

Jack Hughieson took matters into his own hands and became adept at snaring birds, using the vomit from patients as bait. Some of the bedridden were so sick that they had to be force-fed, an opportune moment for a corpsman to steal, though no such incidents were reported at the hospital. There were cases, however, where patients stole food from one another once their appetite returned. Fights broke out in the wards, which lasted but a short time due to the weakened condition of most of the men.

In October 1944, Ōhashi informed the medical staff of the Kōbe POW Hospital that a very important inspection was to take place. It must have been special, Stan Smith thought, because of the secrecy that surrounded it. More telling were the sides of beef the quartermaster delivered to the galley. When the Swiss delegate from the ICRC, Dr. Erwin Bernath, and the Swedish delegate, Per Bjoerstedt, arrived at the hospital on October 4, 1944, they conferred with Colonel Murata and Dr. Ōhashi at length. The conversations Bernath and Bjoerstedt had with Page, Fred, Murray, and Stan Smith were more limited in scope and were closely monitored by Japanese translators.

The ICRC representatives failed to note that one of the American corpsmen, Bernard Stradley, was nowhere to be seen because his face was black and blue from a beating Katō had given him the previous day. As for the feast of beef, it was "hurriedly removed," Smith said, "almost before the gate had closed" on the ICRC delegates. If such visits were staged at Murata's instigation, Page worried that the most urgent medical cases in the Ōsaka-area POW camps weren't even being sent to Kōbe. That way the colonel could boast of the hospital's impressively low mortality rate.

In the coming months prisoners in Kōbe received a flurry of mail. On several occasions the Japanese allowed POWs to pen hundred-word letters home. Bernath had passed along Murray's request to send his best wishes to his parents, which reached Lewis and Sophie in the form of a letter from Lieutenant Commander H. B. Atkinson, the officer in charge of the Casualty Notification and Processing Section. The missive didn't quite express the warmth a son might feel for his parents, but it was welcome nonetheless: "The Navy Department joins in your pleasure over this favorable indication of your son's welfare. . . . You may be assured that any further information received will be furnished you promptly." "Promptly" usually meant three to four months.

Packages from home were manna from heaven, a sign that you hadn't been forgotten, that someone was not only thinking of you but thinking of what you needed and what you might want. They were answers to wishes, responses to questions, hugs to kisses that immediately lifted the spirits of those who received them and aroused the admiration—and envy—of fellow POWs. It was odd that Murray hadn't heard from Laura in such a long time but not entirely unusual. Ernie Irvin had yet to receive a single letter from his family, much less a package.

In late December 1944, Ōhashi took another extraordinary step when he escorted the POW medical staff into downtown Kōbe for a little Christmas shopping. The mood on the streets was hardly festive. Restaurants were closed. Entertainment was restricted. The geisha houses were empty of women because they had been assigned to work details. Fish and beef were rationed about once a month now, *daikon* once a week. A Kōbe city circular recommended eating pumpkin leaves and stalks. The dregs of soybean milk were added to rice. For years rayon had been used as a cotton substitute in civilian clothing; then even rayon was diverted to the war effort. Rough fiber from wild plants was harvested for the manufacture of work clothes and school uniforms, but some children were too hungry to go to school. There was nothing for the POWs to buy, so Ōhashi shepherded them to a friend's house, where they were treated to persimmons. Being outside the hospital and in the city of Kōbe, tasting the air of freedom, was gift enough.

The Japanese allowed the POWs to send holiday greetings back to the States via Radio Tōkyō. POWs exchanged their own greetings among themselves. The "Boys of the Royal Navy at Kōbe Hospital" gave the "Boys of the American Navy at Kōbe Hospital" a handmade card cheerily acknowledging their maritime rivalry:

> There's talk about the two great lands
> Who has the greatest Navy
> And each one tells the other
> They always get the gravy
> But today's the day we all forget
> To snap at one another
> And hands across the ocean lads
> As brother should meet brother.

The Australians presented the Americans with a Christmas card designed by medic R. A. Wickens showing their respective flags crisscrossed above hands clasped in solidarity. Wickens composed a song for the occasion, "Waiting, Only Waiting," that concluded:

> We will tell of our dreams where we sailed the seas
> And we came back home elating,

And we met those dear, with a hearty cheer, but we wake
To find we're just waiting;
Waiting, only waiting
And every hour debating
The times we've had together
While waiting for the day.

Ōhashi found a piano in Kōbe that some White Russians put up for sale, and he let the POWs purchase it with their pay. They placed it in a hallway and organized a little holiday show for piano, concertina, and harmonica, with John Quinn on vocals. Then the Japanese camp commandant joined them on his flute.

Jan 1, 1945

Hello Murray,
    Season's Greetings. Happiest Possible Birthday. Received your message. We're all well, hopeful. Regards from my wife and the four Ziffs. Spiritual handshake across world.
    Charlie

Good old Charlie. The years unreeled at the thought of him. Charlie standing outside the building on East Houston Street, whistling for Murray to come outside and play. Charlie and Murray dressed in knickers, argyle sweaters, and caps as they hitchhiked up to Lake George, where they purchased an eighteen-foot canoe for a dollar per foot and camped out on Turtle Island, just across from Bolton Landing in the southern Adirondacks. Charlie and Murray ogling the girls at Coney Island, strolling down the esplanade to the sound of hawkers, calliopes, laughter, and thrill-seekers, the air sticky sweet with the smell of cotton candy, or sharp with the salt scent of the sea. Charlie, who was exempted from the service on medical grounds, had married his sweetheart, Anne, and was about to start a family.

For the POWs at Kōbe, there was always enough hope. They might not have enough food or medicine, but hope was never in short supply. And there was a lot to be hopeful for, as Charlie knew well.

"M'ARTHUR INVADES CENTRAL PHILIPPINES," headlined *The New York Times* on October 20, 1944. "FOOTHOLD TO SPLIT ISLANDS FIRMLY HELD; ROOSEVELT PROMISES JAPAN A LESSON NOW."

The invasion of Leyte Gulf was launched with an armada of awesome strength. Two hundred thousand troops from General Walter Krueger's Sixth Army were transported by Vice Admiral Thomas C. Kinkaid's Seventh Fleet to landing beaches on the east coast of Leyte in the central Philippines. A total of 738 Allied ships and amphibious vessels were involved in the operation, and more than 1,000 planes. U.S. naval forces outnumbered and outclassed the Japanese in every category—large carriers, small carriers, aircraft, battleships, cruisers, and destroyers. But the Japanese were setting a trap. In the SHO-GŌ (Victory Operation) plan, Admiral Toyoda hoped to lure Admiral Halsey's larger Third Fleet to the northeast of Luzon with Vice Admiral Ozawa Jisaburō's decoy force. Meanwhile, Vice Admiral Shima Kiyohide's weaker Second Strike Force would boil down the west coast of Luzon and slip into the Surigao Strait, as Vice Admiral Kurita Takeo's powerful Central Force penetrated the San Bernadino Strait to lock the American landing forces and the Seventh Fleet that guarded them in a deadly pincer movement. The Battle for Leyte Gulf, MacArthur had told the Joint Chiefs of Staff, would enable his forces to invade Luzon on December 20.

On the afternoon of October 20 MacArthur waded ashore at Leyte Island's newly won Red Beach dressed in crisp khakis, a braided hat, and signature sunglasses. It was the moment he had been waiting for since his nighttime escape from the Rock. By his side was Sergio Osmeña, who had assumed the presidency of the commonwealth after Quezon died the previous August. Speaking into a Signal Corps microphone, MacArthur announced: "People of the Philippines, I have returned! By the grace of Almighty God, our forces stand again on Philippine soil. . . . Rally to me! Let the indomitable spirit of Bataan and Corregidor lead on."

Yes, Charlie Lipsky had reason to be hopeful. And truth be told, in an official Japanese photograph of the Kōbe POW medical staff taken in late November, the men looked reasonably healthy. There was Fred Berley in Captain Davis's uniform, John Page in his, and Murray Glusman sporting a white navy cap, flanked by a slightly off-kilter John Akeroyd in an Australian slouch hat. Behind them stood the Javanese pharmacist Evert Manuel Gonie, Louis Indorf of the Royal Dutch East Indian Army, and gangly John Bookman. They were pale, somewhat drawn, and sunken-cheeked, particularly Stan Smith, off to the far right. But they were alert before the camera while Ōhashi stood squarely in front them, the stolid Japanese commandant in service dress, incongruously wearing a field cap, as if trying to convince the Japanese authorities that his sympathies were more martial than medical. The propaganda photograph doubled as a family portrait of a group of men from wildly disparate backgrounds bound by circumstance, bad timing, and good luck.

There was only one person missing: George Ferguson.

20

"Action Taken: None"

LIFE AT CABANATUAN had gone from bad to worse. "Many are the lessons to be gained from having experienced and seen our fellow men stripped of that thin veneer of convention, custom, and culture," Carter Simpson wrote in his diary on March 8, 1944, just a few days after the draft of 200 medical personnel departed the Philippines for Japan on the *Kenwa Maru.* "Few of us will come through this unchanged."

All of the POWs were losing weight. By early May daily rations had plunged to 1,700 calories at Cabanatuan. Most men had dropped twenty pounds since January. Riney Craig, Cabanatuan's medical director, had shed twenty-five. The POWs were not alone. Thousands of civilians died from malnutrition in 1944, when the food supply hit an all-time low in the Philippines. For Manileños, the typical daily diet consisted of little more than rice gruel, small portions of *camote* or cassava, even smaller amounts of dried fish (*tuyo, tinapa,* or *daing*), and *kangkong* leaves. Fresh meat and fresh fruit were rarities; beriberi, xerophthalmia, avitaminosis, and anemia were common.

Japanese quartermaster depots, meanwhile, were stocked with Red Cross supplies from the *Teia Maru,* which had rendezvoused with the *Gripsholm* at the port of Mormugao, India, in mid-October 1943 and delivered parcels in Shanghai and Yokohama. On November 6 the *Teia Maru* finally arrived in Manila, where it was unloaded by POWs from Bilibid. Japanese officers could be seen smoking Camel and Lucky Strike cigarettes. Japanese hospitals in the Philippines were soon flush with Johnson and Lily gauze bandages and absorbent cotton. As G-2 noted at Southwest Pacific Area Command (SWPA) headquarters in Australia: "Evidence is accumulating from distinct sources to demonstrate that little of the Red Cross supplies dispatched on the *Gripsholm* reached the intended destination." Also included with the ship's relief supplies were 3,403 bags of next-of-kin packages and mail for POWs and civilian internees in the Far East.

George would put conditions only in the very best light for Lucy. He was in comparatively good health. He was working now on the wood detail and, like Fred, benefited from the fresh air and exercise. In a fifty-word postcard dated May 6, 1944, he described his health as "excellent":

Dearest Lucy—your package well selected and greatly enjoyed during last month. Still eager concerning orthopedic residency at Wisconsin General Hospital or any place you would like. Please write family and give my love. Camp receiving books, letters now and I'm anxiously awaiting picture from you. All my love.
George T. Ferguson

In mid-May the skies darkened, and then came the rains. Rations were cut again after Memorial Day to 300 grams of rice and 50 grams of vegetables. Prices on some commissary items had risen 100-fold. What you earned from working seventeen days on the farm would buy you a single egg. "We are now approaching rock bottom," Simpson declared. "Starvation is no longer just an expression." The food that men could scrounge from their gardens or the vitamin pills they had hoarded from Red Cross medicines they received in 1943 were all that kept some of them alive. By August the diet slimmed down to 1,600 calories. Men were hungry, said Craig, "all the time." Morale hit an all-time low, and POWs resorted to one of the few options they had left: theft.

The Japanese were equally suspicious of their behavior. To prevent escapes, they forbade POWs from wearing shoes on work details. The Japanese forced medical personnel to work on the revetments at the Cabanatuan airfield to defend it against an aerial assault by the Americans.

For months huge drafts of POWs had left Manila for Japan. They came from all over the Philippines—Baguio and Bataan, Pas Piñas and Pasay, Clark Field and Palawan. The *Taikoku Maru* departed on March 24, 1944, with 308 men, followed by the *Canadian Inventor* on July 4 with 1,100, the *Nissyo Maru* on July 17 with 1,600, and the *Noto Maru* on August 27 with 1,135 men. The Japanese were emptying the Philippines of all able-bodied prisoners.

At Cabanatuan the enlisted men went first, leaving officers behind to perform their tasks—working on the farm, on the wood detail, in the galleys. By early September, the population of Cabanatuan was down to roughly 4,000 POWs. Then Japanese doctors began to examine those POWs listed by the American doctors as permanently disabled—men suffering from heart disease, hernias, impaired vision—and most of them, as Colonel Beecher remarked, were "now pronounced fit for duty and available for transfer."

"So long, see you later," George Ferguson waved to Al Smith as he was leaving Cabanatuan. It was cloudy, thundering at noon on September 3, 1944, when George was trucked out of the camp along with 211 other POWs. Among them were twenty doctors, two chaplains, and thanks to Hutch Hutchinson, the partial components of a shortwave radio. At 1700 they found themselves in Manila's Bilibid Prison, where they stayed in the Old Back Building. For George, it was a step back in time, but conditions at Bilibid had deteriorated greatly since he had been there with Fred, John, and Murray, even beyond what they had been at Cabanatuan.

Heavy rains flooded the Bilibid courtyard, backed up the sewage, and caused an outbreak of amoebic dysentery. The resistance to disease was so low that a mere scrape on the heel could lead to infection. As at Cabanatuan, the average daily caloric intake dipped below 1,600. Coconuts were the main source of nutrition. The Japanese pillaged American Red Cross parcels to such an extent, Hayes noted, that it "looks like we are feeding more Japanese than Americans." Even the pigs were starving. Air raid drills and blackouts were in effect. Sentries stood guard with fixed bayonets. Shelters and foxholes were dug for the Japanese. The roofs of buildings were marked with Red Crosses. Antiaircraft batteries were set up along the Luneta and began test-firing. The message to the POWs was clear, as Hayes wrote in his diary one day before George rejoined Bilibid's medical staff: "The siege of the Philippines is on."

> *Japanese air force in Luzon must be neutralized at least, and the shipping assailed. . . . We are sitting right on the target. The Japanese know that too and are taking advantage of it, in hopes that our presence here will protect them. We do not believe that this will deter our forces from doing what is necessary for the cause of an American Victory, and all of us are hoping that is the way they feel. . . .*
>   *Come on Yanks! Give us hell!*

At 0930 on September 21, 1944, American carrier-based airplanes from Admiral Halsey's Third Fleet swarmed out of a cloudbank over Manila as they headed east and southwest on bombing missions over Zablan, Nielson, and Nichols Fields. Internees at Santo Tomás huddled in the lobby of the main building, smiling and crying at the sight of the planes from U.S. Navy Task Force 38. "They are here!" one of them said. Up at Cabanatuan, thousands of POWs burst into cheers, and one of them began to sing, in a deep, resonant voice: "Mine eyes have seen the glory—"

The next day at 1545 the skies southwest of Bilibid Prison turned "black with planes," Hayes wrote in his diary. Japanese antiaircraft guns fired back, but the guards and POWs alike thought it *testo* until shrapnel and spent shells began to rain down as the bombers headed for the Port Area and the Pandacan oil district. The raid lasted two hours, during which five runs were made by 80 to 150 planes. Buildings were struck around Bilibid, one dud landed in a POW's bed, and a bullet bisected a shutter at a forty-five-degree angle, taking a piece of a prisoner's jaw with it.

"The Yanks have come!" Hayes exclaimed. The stage was being set for the Battle for Leyte Gulf, the springboard for the liberation of Luzon.

Some POWs weren't willing to wait. In the spring of 1944 Jimmy Carrington, the rowdy 4th Marine with the loopy grin who had had a ball on a dime back in Shanghai, decided he couldn't take it anymore. He'd worked until his clothes rotted off down at Palawan, where POWs were building an airfield for the Japanese near Puerto Princesa in preparation for the invasion of Australia. When he arrived in Bilibid with malaria, his buddy, Private 1st Class Joseph E. Dupont, a 4th Marine and a fellow Louisianan known as "Frenchy," didn't even recognize him. He'd shaved his head and grown a Fu Manchu mustache, and was as brown as a berry. He wanted to look like a Chinaman, he said. He'd also dropped below 100 pounds, but that wasn't part of his disguise; he'd picked up a parasite on a work detail at Nichols Field.

Carrington had thought it would be easy to escape from Palawan Barracks; a couple of the boys had already fled the coop. Getting off the island was the hard part. Bilibid was another matter. The Japanese were convinced it was escape-proof, hadn't even bothered forming POWs into "shooting squads." A prisoner would have to be crazy to try to escape. Manila was swarming with occupation troops.

Carrington was undeterred. He broached the idea to Ray D. Parker, a marine from Cedarville, Washington, who was game. Parker had already seen the way out: a gap between the central guard tower and the top of the prison wall that separated the POW compound from the military prison. It was just wide enough for a man to wriggle through on his side, using his elbows as leverage. Then all you had to worry about was hitting the 1,800-volt wire. Carrington had saved a pair of pants and a shirt for the occasion. He borrowed a knife from another buddy. If he was caught, he decided, he'd rush the Japanese so he'd be shot on the spot. Jimmy Carrington wouldn't be tortured anymore. He was at the end of his rope. Life was so hard; death would be the easy part.

At 2030 on April 15, Frenchy Dupont was sitting outside in an audience of POWs watching Ginger Rogers and Jimmy Stewart in *Vivacious Lady* projected onto a simple white sheet when suddenly a siren pierced the night. Red lights started flashing from the top of Bilibid's wall. Guards charged the crowd, rifles in hand, screaming, "Inside! Inside!" Many of the POWs were invalids on stretchers, and many, said Hayes, "were trampled in the wild chaos of the night."

The POWs were locked into their barracks. A Japanese officer with two sentries did a head count; the head count was repeated two more times. Then finally, at midnight, the barracks lights were turned off and the men were allowed to go to bed. The Japanese told the POWs nothing about what had happened, but *bango* revealed they were a man short.

The next morning the Japanese informed the camp that a marine corporal had attempted escape and that he was dead. The story was only partly true.

Parker had hit the wire. Jimmy Carrington could smell the smoke from his burning shirt. The shock knocked Parker back into the POW side of the compound, where Lieutenant Commander Marion Wade immediately cut the juice. When Parker tried to climb the fence again, he was pounced on by a gang of guards, and the rampage began. The Japanese beat Parker viciously. Wade and Camp Warden Earl G. Schweizer were caught in the melee. But Carrington had made it over onto the side of the military prison. He jumped another wall and then slipped out through the main gate onto Azcarraga Street and down España, where he flagged a *caretela*. The Filipino driver, Moses Gonzalez, concealed him in his carriage, then hid him in his own home for several days. Carrington, Gonzalez, and his wife shared the same bed. Gonzalez wouldn't even tell his mother about their new house guest. If the Japanese found out, they'd slaughter the entire family.

Gonzalez was associated with a Filipino resistance group called Marking's Guerrillas after Colonel Marcos Agustin, a former boxer and cab driver. Carrington wanted to join an American unit. He was led to the heart of Bulacan Province, where deep in the jungle, Lieutenant Edwin Price Ramsey of the East Central Luzon Guerrilla Area (ECLGA) had his headquarters camp. Ramsey found Carrington "an able, amiable soldier who adapted easily to guerrilla tactics." He made Carrington raise his right hand, swore him into the ECLGA, and commissioned him as a lieutenant, responsible for headquarters security forces.

When the Japanese Army occupied Manila on January 2, 1942, the military administration quickly ordered Jorge Vargas to assume the chairmanship of a reconstructed Filipino government that was responsible to the Japanese, not to the Filipino people. The Japanese even chose its name: the Philippine Executive Commission. As President Quezon's executive secretary, Vargas was one of the most powerful men in the Philippines. Within a month's time the Japanese had coopted many of Manila's most illustrious Filipinos—José Yulo, José P. Laurel, and Claro M. Recto among them—to MacArthur's dismay on Corregidor.

But after the fall of Bataan and Corregidor, numerous guerrilla organizations in the Philippines—from Quezon's own guerrillas under Vicente Umali to the Chinese Volunteer Guerrillas—sprang up throughout the archipelago. Some harbored distinctly anti-American sentiments, such as the socialist-communist Hukbong Bayan Laban a Hapon (People's Army Against Japan); others provided valuable intelligence for the Southwest Pacific Area Command. "The nucleus of intelligence operations" in the Philippines was G-2's own Military Intelligence Service (MIS), organized in early January 1942 under the command of Brigadier General Simeon de Jesus.

The groundwork for the resistance had been laid by the Allied Intelligence Bureau (AIB) in Brisbane, which had established a network of spies covering all of Southeast Asia before the war. Colonel Charles A. Willoughby remained the head of G-2 after MacArthur and his staff fled Corregidor and set up GHQ in Melbourne in April 1942. Jockeying for position was Colonel Courtney A. Whitney, in charge of the Philippine Regional Section of AIB, who convinced MacArthur to lend his support to a squadron of all American and Filipino spies in the islands, known as SPYRON.

Between 1942 and 1944 as many as 180,000 guerrillas operated in the Philippines. On Luzon alone there were eighteen different units. One of them, Major Robert Lapham's Luzon Guerrilla Armed Forces (LGAF), numbered 13,000 men. Ramsey's ECLGA swelled to 40,000.

Guerrilla units in the Philippines engaged Japanese forces, liquidated informants, acted as coast watchers and plane spotters, and observed troop movements. They raided Japanese garrisons and disrupted supply and communication lines. Eventually they controlled thirty-six of the archipelago's forty-eight provinces, not including strategically important Manila and Davao.

At first, intelligence was relayed to local commanders of guerrilla organizations by runners who relied on the "bamboo telegraph" and traveled by sailboat and *banca* between the islands. But to reach Australia, high-frequency radio was required. Guerrilla commander Colonel Marcario Peralta on Panay had contacted MacArthur in Australia with an eye on expanding his command from Panay to the Visayas and Luzon. Then in late 1942, 2nd Lieutenant Robert V. Ball of the Signal Corps pounded out a message on an old cylindrical encoding device for Lieutenant Colonel Wendell W. Fertig, a former mining engineer turned guerrilla leader in Mindanao. Fertig was also trying to lay down a line to

Australia. The translated message was vintage Fertig: **WE HAVE THE HOT DOPE ON THE HOT YANKS IN THE HOT PHILIPPINES.**

The message was picked up by a U.S. Navy signalman at Radio Station KFS, San Francisco, and relayed to Washington. Once Washington was able to verify Fertig's identity, the War Department gave Fertig the call sign WYZB and told him, on Valentine's Day 1943, that he would hear next from KAZ, the net control station for the Southwest Pacific Area Command in Darwin, Australia. One week later, in the first of many radio messages he received from MacArthur, Fertig was appointed commander of the 10th Military District.

Meanwhile, Major Jesus Villamor arrived in Mindanao via the submarine USS *Gudgeon* with the first of MacArthur's espionage teams from Australia, code-named "Planet." The former commander of the 6th Pursuit Squadron of the Philippine Army Air Corps, Villamor had been evacuated to Australia after the fall of Bataan and was trained in intelligence. Villamor established a network of agents from northern Luzon to southern Negros, from Sorsogon in the east to Panay in the west.

Mindanao was easier to access than Luzon by submarine, so guerrilla units in the southern Philippines reaped more of the supplies that SWPA was able to send: arms, ammunition, food, medical supplies, 3BZ radio transceivers, currency (both real and counterfeit), and American cigarettes. Colonel Arthur Fischer, who became executive director of the American Cinchona Plantation, was called upon to share with guerrillas his homemade recipe—"as simple as making tea"—for extracting totaquine from cinchona bark by using the juice of wild lemons or guavas as an acetic acid and lye or ashes as an alkaline. Ever modest, MacArthur made sure that two million books of matches in wax-coated covers were distributed, bearing the crossed American and Philippine flags on one side and the motto "I Shall Return" on the other.

On March 5, 1943, the USS *Tambor* surfaced in Pagadian Bay, Mindanao, with another load of special cargo from Australia that included intelligence agent Lieutenant Commander Charles "Chick" Parsons, and Captain Charles Smith, who had escaped from Samar after the surrender of the Philippines. One of their objectives was to establish contact with their old friend Fertig and create a chain of command among the other guerrilla organizations. The promise of arms, supplies, and back pay was a strong incentive.

Fertig had promoted himself to brigadier general of the Mindanao-Visayan Force, USFIP. With his shaved head, goatee, and Moro hat, Fertig had gone native; he looked more Asian than American. After Parsons hooked up with him at his unassuming headquarters in the barrio of Es-

peranza, he stripped Fertig of his rank and reminded him of his reporting responsibility to GHQ if he didn't want to be relieved of his command. Then he presented Fertig with two radio sets for intelligence
purposes. Per AIB's plan, a network of coast watcher stations would be
established from the Surigao Strait, northeast of Mindanao, to Davao in
the southeast, in order to monitor Japanese ship movements.

The major guerrilla armies had their own radio stations and call
signs. Lapham received his radio set directly from Bob Ball, who on
Smith's instructions sailed up the Tayabas coast from the Visayas and
into Dibut Bay. Anderson and Major Russell W. Volckmann of the U.S.
Army Forces in the Philippines, North Luzon (USAFIP NL) also obtained transmitters. Not until August 31, 1944, did the USS *Narwhal*
slip into Dibut Bay with thirty tons of supplies for LGAF units.

By then, more than 150 frequencies were in use throughout the
Philippines bearing as many as fifty messages each day or more. Guerrilla
formations maintained contact with KAZ in Australia and with the War
Department through KFS, the radio station of the Signal Intelligence
Division of the Western Defense Command in Half Moon Bay, California. If direct communication between the guerrillas and MacArthur was
impossible, KFS served to monitor and relay traffic.

Orders to guerrilla leaders were issued over KAZ or via Fertig. In
June 1944 alone Fertig's unit sent over 1,076 messages and received
1,057. Thirty-two code men were required to monitor five separate frequencies eighteen hours a day, and one was manned around the clock.
Colonel Willoughby considered the "air, ground and naval intelligence
data . . . efficiently correct and, therefore, of great value in the preparation and successful prosecution of Allied plans in the Philippine area."

The ECLGA covered five districts: Manila, Bataan, Bulacan, Pampanga, and Pangasinan-Tarlac. Each district had its own regiment and
commander who reported to Ramsey. Aircraft warning and naval observation posts were perched on Mt. Balagbag where, with the aid of a tele-
scope, Ramsey claimed, enemy activities were watched with "pinpoint"
precision. To evade American submarines, Japanese merchant convoys
hugged the coast. But many were unable to escape detection by American and Filipino coast watchers.

Guerrilla radio operators faced the danger of having their location
pinpointed by Japanese radio direction finding (DF) stations. First, each
Japanese DF station would determine the direction, or line bearing, of
an active guerrilla radio transmitter from its own location. When these
stations obtained sufficient bearings, a Japanese controller would draw
the bearings on a map. The point at which all the bearings intersected

was the location of the guerrilla radio station. This technique was known as triangulation.

Japanese counterintelligence in the Philippines closely monitored guerrilla wireless communications and at various times penetrated guerrilla codes. They eavesdropped on Peralta on Panay, Fertig on Mindanao, and Major Ralph Praeger of the Cagayan-Apayao Forces (CAF) in northern Luzon, and they intercepted plain-language messages transmitted from MacArthur in Australia. They even intercepted messages concerning submarine movements, though they admitted "it is very difficult to decipher the meaning because of the especial codes used." "Generally speaking," said one Japanese report documenting guerrilla messages in the first ten days of February 1943, "the growth in frequency of communication is a phenomenon which must be noted as an indication of effective action based on liaison between the various enemy guerrilla groups and AMERICAN contact with the PHILIPPINES." Another report of April 28, 1943, made the barbed comment: "While maintaining close liaison with each other by wireless and other means, they report information to AMERICA and AUSTRALIA, especially to MACARTHUR, deluded by belief [sic] in the arrival of a relieving force." On August 30, 1943, Praeger was captured by the Japanese, and the CAF was dissolved.

The radio at Ramsey's camp was set up behind headquarters on "Signal Hill" and operated by Lieutenant Leopoldo Guillermo. But initially Ramsey couldn't reach SWPA directly. To do that he first had to obtain a navy codebook from Peralta, the designated head of the 6th Military District in Panay. Then he had to encode the messages before they could be sent from Signal Hill to WYZB, which became the major control station in the Philippines. The messages were decoded by Fertig's cryptographers, analyzed by Fertig, recoded, transmitted to AIB in Brisbane where they were decoded, and finally delivered by courier to MacArthur's headquarters in Melbourne. Or they were sent via Lieutenant Colonel Edwin Andrews, a close friend of Villamor who took over Station 4E7 after Villamor was recalled to Australia.

According to Jimmy Carrington, several of Ramsey's Filipino guerrillas witnessed the loading of American POWs onto unmarked Japanese transport ships in Manila and actually counted the number of prisoners departing. Carrington himself had seen the hand clickers they used. He guessed that "at least" five or six Japanese merchant vessels were surveilled with POWs on board. Ships were unnamed, but in May 1943 training for the Philippine Regional Section included four and a half hours of ship and aircraft recognition. In February 1944 GHQ issued the "Philippines Intelligence Guide," which was illustrated to facilitate identification of Japanese aircraft, and war and merchant ships. Ship tonnage was estimated by the bridge, stack, and mainmast design, and the number and placement of lifeboats.

G-2 remained oddly uninterested in the increasing surveillance of the Port Area, where "American POWs were exclusively employed on piers," Fertig reported on December 21, 1943. There was a wonderful opportunity, he proposed, to obtain information on shipping by using Filipino agents as dock hands, which would eliminate any danger posed to American POWs, who were closely watched by the Japanese. But at the bottom of Fertig's message, Courtney Whitney remarked at GHQ/SWPA:

```
Action taken: None.
Action recommended: None.
```

There was an obvious lag time between the observation of land and ship movements and the transmission of information to SWPA. The delays back and forth, Fertig confessed to MacArthur, could be "heartbreaking." To save time, ship information sometimes went straight to Naval Intelligence in Perth, which passed it along to Operations, which in turn notified only the commanders of American submarines in the area. According to Lloyd Waters, one of Fertig's radio operators, "we'd send all the messages . . . to MacArthur." The control station of the 10th Military District even tried communicating directly with a submarine commander in the vicinity on a prearranged schedule in addition to sending regular dispatches to SWPA. If the intelligence that guerrilla units provided to SWPA helped it track and target enemy vessels, presumably it could have been used to prevent Japanese merchant ships carrying Allied POWs from being attacked by U.S. Navy planes and submarines. As early as 1943, MacArthur was aware of such a possibility. On February 19, 1943, Praeger had radioed the general:

```
UNCONFIRMED REPORT AMERICAN OFFICERS FIELD
GRADE AND ABOVE TAKEN MANILA OCT 1ST SHIPMENT
JAPAN.
```

On March 4, 1944, Lieutenant Colonel Andrews, a mestizo who had been a ranking officer in the Philippine Army Air Corps and who worked hand in hand with Salipada Pendatun, radioed MacArthur that a German seaman who escaped from a blockade runner seized by the Japanese

```
SAW AMERICAN WAR PRISONERS FORCED TO STEVEDORE
NIP SHIPS, WHILE IN TRANSIT THEY ARE LOCKED IN
HOLDS TO PREVENT ESCAPE IF TORPEDOED.
```

On June 10, 1944, Fertig contacted MacArthur:

> DAVAO PROVINCE, 6 JUNE: 39 TRUCKLOADS OF MEN
> (POW) EMBARKED AT BUNAWAN WHARF ON TRANSPORT
> BELIEVED FOR MANILA. BLINDFOLDED AND BOUND
> DURING TRIP TO SHIP.

At the bottom of the message was a comment from G-2:

> IT IS POSSIBLE THAT ALL [POW] WERE EVACUATED
> FROM MINDANAO--MAY SUGGEST A MOVEMENT OF
> PRISONERS TO JAPAN ITSELF. ACTION: FERTIG
> INSTRUCTED TO SECURE MORE INFO ON POW
> EVACUATION.

Five weeks later, on July 18, MacArthur heard from Major Bernard L. Anderson, commanding officer of a guerrilla band in Tayabas Province, northeast of Manila:

> LARGE GROUP OF AMERICAN AIR CORPS POW LEFT
> MANILA 02 JULY FOR JAPAN.

The removal of Air Corps prisoners to Japan, the G-2 comment read this time, is a "*significant development.*"

On August 18 a Japanese naval message was intercepted from Manila to Tōkyō that divulged the route of a Japanese cargo ship, the *Shinyō Maru*:

> SHINYO MARU IS TO PROCEED FROM ZAMBOANGA TO
> CEBU AND THEN TRANSPORT SOMETHING ON TO
> MANILA."

A message of September 6 referred to the "something" as "750 troops for Manila via Cebu." The "troops" were really POWs from Davao.

Meanwhile Tom Mitsos, a cryptographer who was in charge of the code room at Fertig's 10th Military District Radio Station in Waloe, Mindanao, received a message from Davao coast watchers that a Japanese freighter loaded with POWs had departed from Davao City in a small convoy. According to Mitsos, the message was relayed to SWPA, which in turn notified the U.S. Navy. A "do not attack this convoy" order was issued to all submarines in the area as the ship steamed toward Zamboanga City, a passage known to cryptographers as "Torpedo Alley."

The unknown ship arrived in Zamboanga late in the afternoon of August 24. Don LeCouvre, who led an American guerrilla group in the Zamboanga area under Fertig, reported its safe arrival to Waloe. But unbeknownst to LeCouvre, the POWs were transferred on September 4 to a second ship, the Manila-bound *Shinyō Maru*. The original prison ship left Zamboanga City unmolested. When the *Shinyō Maru* sailed from Zamboanga, LeCouvre dutifully radioed the information. Not until the morning of September 7, however, did LeCouvre learn that the POWs had been moved to the *Shinyō Maru*. He immediately sent a priority message to Waloe, which in turn transmitted it to Australia, but it was too late. At 1647 on September 7 a submarine off of Sindangan Point, the USS *Paddle*, deftly zeroed in on the *Shinyō Maru* and blew it apart. Six hundred sixty-seven POWs out of 750 men died—the bulk of whom were from the Mindanao-Visayan Force that had reluctantly surrendered under Generals Fort and Sharp in May 1942. Many of the POWs who survived the blast were machine-gunned in the water by the Japanese. Fertig kept MacArthur apprised of the entire incident.

```
                    S E C R E T
                           17 SEPTEMBER 1944
    TO: GENERAL MACARTHUR
    FROM: FERTIG
    NR 855 17 SEPTEMBER
    PRISONER OF WAR MCGEE REPORTS: 750 AMERICANS
    ON PRISON BOAT TORPEDOED OFF LILOY 07
    SEPTEMBER. 83 SURVIVORS, 26 OF WHOM ARE
    OFFICERS. ALL NOW IN SIMDANGAN [sic]. 30 WOUNDED
    AND TWO HAVE GANGRENE. DO YOU WISH NAMES OF
    SURVIVORS BY RADIO OR ALL OF FACTS BY PICK
    UP/ INFORMATION STILL INCOMPLETE.
       HAVE INSTRUCTED BOWLER TO RUSH MEDICINE AND
    DOCTORS THERE.
```

Once Fertig debriefed two of the survivors, he contacted Australia:

```
                           05 OCTOBER 1944
                    S E C R E T
    TO: GENERAL MACARTHUR
    FROM: FERTIG
    NR 5 05 OCTOBER
       POW LT RICHARD COOK AND STAFF SGT JOSEPH
    COE, SERIAL 7000444, HAVE REMAINED WITH
```

CORPS. THEY DELIVERED FULL DETAILS OF
ATROCITIES PRACTICED ON PRISONERS BEFORE
AND DURING SINKING.

MacArthur professed a particular interest in escaped POWs. By June 1943 the general realized that the officers to whom Major Praeger had in all likelihood referred in his message of February 19, 1943, had actually been transported even earlier from the Philippines—in the summer of 1942—and arrived safely in either Formosa or Japan. When he met Dyess, Mellnik, and McCoy in July 1943 and heard Dyess's account of Japanese atrocities on the march from Mariveles to San Fernando, MacArthur assured him: "Captain, I'm afraid the people back home will find it hard to believe you. I believe you because I know the Japs."

But many POWs who suffered under the Japanese would suffer still more at the hands of the Americans. In the early morning hours of September 12, 1944, the *Rakuyō Maru* was traveling in a convoy from Singapore to Japan with 1,318 POWs aboard. Armed with intelligence from FRUPAC, the USS *Sealion II* opened fire with three Mark XIV steam torpedoes and sank the ship. Later that night the USS *Pampanito* took aim at another vessel in the same convoy carrying 900 POWs. The ship was the former *President Harrison*, which had been captured two years earlier and renamed the *Kachidoki Maru*. The "kill" occurred at 3,800 yards, nearly the maximum range of the Mark XVIII electric torpedo. Three days later, while surface patrolling the waters southeast of Hainan Island, the *Pampanito* picked up 73 survivors, and the *Sealion* rescued 54 men. The *Sealion* radioed ComSubPac, and the submarines were granted permission to evacuate to the closest Allied base, which was some 1,800 miles away on Saipan. In the space of two attacks, 1,635 POWs died. Among them were British and Australian POWs who had slaved on the infamous Siam-Burma "Railway of Death" along the River Kwae Noi in Thailand. They had survived one nightmare, only to perish in another.

From guerrilla messages based on eyewitness reports transmitted to SWPA, from radio traffic that FRUPAC and FRUMEL intercepted from Japanese vessels such as the *Kenwa Maru* (which counted Fred, John, and Murray among its passengers in March 1944), and from firsthand testimony of POWs who braved torpedo attacks by U.S. Navy submarines, MacArthur and the War Department gained ample evidence that the Japanese were using unmarked merchant ships to transport POWs to Japan and that Allied POWs were at grave risk. If the navy could target enemy vessels with deadly accuracy, why couldn't they pinpoint those ships that cried out for safe passage?

To be sure, the logistical challenges of relaying information to SWPA, FRUPAC, and FRUMEL quickly and acting on it effectively were formidable. The same ships that transported POWs also transported Japanese troops. The vessels traveled in convoys of warships, and their ship numbers were changed regularly. In September 1944 the *Kenwa Maru* was sunk by American planes in the Visayan Sea carrying not POWs but the 353rd Independent Infantry Battalion of the Japanese Army, an ULTRA intercept revealed. Moreover, withholding fire from POW transports might tip off the Japanese that the Americans had cracked their codes.

But the problems were not insurmountable. In spite of MacArthur's avowed sympathy for the plight of Allied POWs, the military objective of destroying the Japanese Navy and merchant fleet took precedence over their fate. "Absolutely there were people in the Port Area," said Ramsey, "and if they saw POW transport activities, this information would have been forwarded." But that wasn't the primary objective of guerrilla intelligence, which was to collect information on Japanese troops, armaments, and ship movements. As Secretary of the Navy James Forrestal later acknowledged: "Even though our intelligence began to establish the fact that the Japanese were transporting American prisoners in their ships, the great necessity for destroying Japan's vital lifeline of shipping gave us no choice but to sink all Japanese ships encountered."

The POWs leaving the Philippines for Japan in early October 1944 were staring down a gauntlet. On one side, U.S. Navy bombers from Admiral Halsey's Task Force 38 were aiming to reduce Japanese air power in the Philippines, Formosa, and Okinawa in preparation for the Leyte landings. On the other, Rear Admiral Lockwood's submarines were on the prowl for major Japanese fleet movements between Tōkyō Bay and Luzon Strait.

On October 11, 1944, the Military Intelligence Service in Manila sent its daily dispatch to GHQ in Australia:

```
STREETCAR USED TO TRANSPORT CARGOES FROM PORT
AREA AT 2100 H. AMERICAN PRISONERS AND
INTERNEES BOARDED A 9,000-TON SHIP (NAME
CONCEALED) OUT OF BREAKWATER.
```

MIS overestimated the ship's tonnage, but the report of its human cargo was right on target.

Action taken: none.

21

The *Arisan Maru*

AT 1600 ON THE AFTERNOON of October 11, 1944, George Ferguson was among 1,800 Allied POWs and civilian internees waiting to board a Japanese merchant ship at Manila's bomb-damaged Pier 7. The men were divided into six drafts of 300 apiece and represented all ranks and service branches—the army and navy, the 4th Marines and Far East Air Force. There were officers and enlisted men, doctors and corpsmen, and survivors from Bataan and the siege of Corregidor. The 100 or so civilians were British, Dutch, and American. Tired, hungry, and sick, they came from camps all over the Philippines—Cabanatuan, Palawan Barracks—and the Davao Penal Colony on Mindanao. They had filtered through Bilibid Prison prior to their departure, but only the woolen shirts and trousers issued by the Japanese hinted at their destination: Manchuria, Korea, or Japan. Wherever they were headed, George and his former Bilibid patient Corporal Donald E. Meyer agreed, it was bound to turn out okay.

An air raid siren sounded in the Port Area, and the POWs were hustled belowdecks into the upper half of No. 2 hold, a compartment fifty feet wide by seventy-five feet long that could reasonably accommodate 200 to 300 people. When they complained that there wasn't enough room, Japanese guards entered swinging their rifle butts. Men were pressed so tightly together, they couldn't breathe. Knees buckled; bodies remained upright only by the crush of flesh. Sweat streaming, they stripped off their woolens, gasped for air, and begged for water. Japanese guards kept their machine guns trained on the entrance to the hold. By 1630 the ship was under way, heading south for the Palawan Islands in a convoy led by the *Kokuryū Maru*.

Captain Sugino Minemaru commanded the crew. First Lieutenant Funatsu Toshio was transportation officer. Second Lieutenant Yamaji Kiyoshi, a former English professor at the University of Tōkyō, served as the POW guard officer.

The 6,886-ton vessel, which had first sailed out of the Mitsui

Tamanao shipyards in Okayama Prefecture in June 1944, was known as the *Arisan Maru*, named after a mountain in Formosa. A Type 2A freighter, the ship had three large holds, and was used primarily to carry coal along the Japan Sea coast. The No. 3 hold contained tons of nickel ingots and boxes of airplane parts. There was still a mound of coal in the No. 1 hold.

Before being pressed into service to transport prisoners of war from Manila, the *Arisan Maru* had ferried 6,000 troops from the Guandon Army in Pusan, Korea, to Okinawa. The inside of the ship was fitted with three tiers of bunks, each a little more than three feet high. Many of the men were doubled over with dysentery. Almost all of them suffered from diarrhea. The Japanese handed the POWs eight five-gallon oil cans with the tops removed, but they quickly overflowed with waste. There was a constant drip of urine and fecal matter from the upper to the lower bunks. Soon the deck was slick with excrement. The temperature soared to 120 degrees. "The filth and stench," said Staff Sergeant Philip Brodsky, an army corpsman, were "indescribable." In some places the sides of the hold were literally "too hot to touch," remarked 2nd Lieutenant Robert S. Overbeck, a civilian engineer who had been captured on Corregidor.

The American doctors and corpsmen tried to set up a makeshift hospital in the rear of the hold, where they administered whatever medicine remained in their pouches. "If only we could get some medical supplies," said one doctor, "we would be able to relieve the suffering of our men." The Japanese had Red Cross medical supplies on board. First Sergeant Calvin Graef of the 515th Coast Artillery had seen them being loaded at Pier 7. But in only one instance did he see a doctor, Lieutenant Colonel Dwight Deter, gain access to them. The Japanese offered no further assistance.

By evening, the *Arisan Maru* had lost contact with its flagship and headed in a southwesterly direction. The next day, carrier planes from Admiral Halsey's Task Force 38 swept over Formosa in 1,378 sorties, and Rear Admiral Lockwood dispatched two wolf packs—*Sawfish*, *Icefish*, *Drum*, and *Snook* and *Shark*, *Blackfish*, and *Seadragon*—to blockade Luzon Strait. The *Arisan Maru* sneaked into a cove in one of the Palawan Islands to the south. Philip Brodsky, who had been imprisoned in Palawan Barracks, thought it was Coron, a small island southwest of Mindoro. By then, nearly a hundred men had collapsed from heat exhaustion and dehydration. Hundreds of others, according to Sergeant Avery E. Wilber, went insane.

On October 13, the Japanese agreed to move 600 men from the middle No. 2 hold to the forward No. 1 hold, which served as a coal bunker and had been used for the transportation of tanks and ordnance from

Korea to the Philippines. George Ferguson remained in the No. 2 hold. Don Meyer went into the forward hold, where the POWs were so crazed with thirst that they drank the dirty bilge water, "which had run off the coal into the scuppers of the hold." Lack of space forced them to take turns sleeping. The vessel stayed put for several days "hiding from the U.S. Air Force," as Private 3rd Class Glenn Oliver put it.

In the early morning hours of October 15, Major Robert B. Lothrop, a former post engineer on Fort Mills, asked to go to the latrine. A West Point gymnast, Lothrop wriggled out of a porthole and landed in the water. A sentry sounded the alarm, and Lothrop was killed as he swam away from the *Arisan Maru*, after taking four direct hits. The Japanese sent a launch to retrieve his body and gave the thirty-seven-year-old major—the father of an eight-year-old daughter back home—a formal burial at sea.

Within the first forty-eight hours, five men—not including Lothrop— had died. The first three were taken topside and dispatched without ceremony. The other two corpses remained in the hold for an entire day. Later, one dead man sat next to Sergeant Avery Wilber for two days before the Japanese removed him. The death toll increased until "there were dead all over," said Private Anton E. Cichy. "I had seen so many dead every morning—thirty, thirty-five every morning—I figured, well, maybe next morning I'd be dead." The POWs were allowed to dispose of their dead only at night.

On October 19, the *Arisan Maru* circled back to Manila, where it was loaded with rice, green bananas, papayas, and sugar. Initially the prisoners were given dry rice to eat—a quarter canteen cup twice a day—and a few ounces of stale, rusty water. Calvin Graef had worked in the kitchen at Davao and was allowed topside with the other POW cooks, where they were permitted to steam rice in 85-gallon vats. Half canteen cups were served three or four times a day for a total daily ration of 250 grams. Men passed their mess kits as the rice ration was lowered down into the hold by rope, but there was no guarantee that they would get them back. They were given no salt, no sugar, no dry rations, and no legumes. Occasionally rotten vegetables were doled out for the sick.

By contrast, the crew of the *Arisan Maru* was fed 600 grams of rice a day, in addition to 100 grams of pumpkin, some sugar, biscuits, 2.5 pints of water, and plenty of tea with their meals. Sometimes they couldn't resist a little bonbon of the chocolate they had stolen from the POWs' Red Cross supplies. The hatches were kept closed during the day, though the Japanese finally relented and allowed some of the sick to come up on deck for fresh air.

At midnight on October 20, the eve of MacArthur's landing on

Leyte, the *Arisan Maru* resumed her journey. The ship was now part of MATA-30, a twelve-vessel convoy bound for Formosa, escorted by three destroyers. The largest of them was the flagship *Harukaze*, which Fred Berley and Butch Parker had been invited aboard four years earlier as Japan celebrated its mythical 2,600th anniversary.

MATA-30 labored up the west coast of Luzon, hoping to reach Takao on October 24, but the convoy was widely dispersed in four rows. The *Arisan Maru* and the *Kimikawa Maru*, which had earlier been damaged by an enemy torpedo, were the two slowest vessels, their top speed a mere seven knots. Around October 23, Matsuo Chuneji, the chief steward, ordered the chief mate to offer the POWs as much water and food as was available. They could resupply in Takao. At noon the Japanese supplied the POWs with cotton life preservers. There were no markings to indicate that the *Arisan Maru* was a prisoner of war transport ship. The reason, according to the captain, was "a security matter."

Convoy MATA-30 was moving slowly, too slowly through the swift current of the Bashi Channel. But Suzuki Shō, chief navigator of the *Harukaze*, knew it would be difficult to pick up the sound of enemy propellers by hydrophone if the destroyer were moving at a faster speed. The *Harukaze* was tasked with locating hostile submarines, luring them away from the convoy, and if possible destroying them. If for some reason the *Harukaze* was unable to fire, at least it could make it impossible for the enemy to strike. A submarine wouldn't move if its captain knew it had been detected.

The convoy was an emergency configuration. The bombing of Manila had forced the Japanese to leave in such a hurry that Suzuki couldn't remember there being the usual "convoy meeting" before embarkation. But his route up the Bashi Channel was all too familiar. American submariners knew it so well that they called the waters between Luzon and Formosa "Convoy College," a campus where "wolf packs" took lessons in picking off their prey. It was little help that the vessels in MATA-30 operated at varying speeds.

Wolf packs of two or more boats represented a change in strategy for the U.S. submarine offensive against the Imperial Japanese Navy and merchant marine. Japanese convoys were larger, stronger, and better defended. Wolf packs carried more firepower and had greater maneuverability, and their number allowed for diversionary tactics. Their skippers received intelligence from ULTRAs, they used short-range radio sparingly, and when there was TBS (talk between ships), it was in code.

The *Kokuryū Maru*, a passenger ship, seemed the most obvious target to Suzuki. He navigated a zigzag course from the beginning. Once the ships approached the southern end of Luzon Strait, the plan was for five of them—the *Kimikawa Maru, Kokuryū Maru, Kikusui Maru, Ryōfu Maru,* and *Shikisan Maru*—to proceed at top speed, leaving the others to follow in their wake.

At 0600 on October 23 the Japanese destroyers picked up radio signals from enemy submarines. Three hours later, when MATA-30 was approximately 200 miles west of Cape Bojeador, the *Harukaze* intercepted more signals. South of the *Tang* in Formosa Strait, three American wolf packs lay in wait: the *Snook* and the *Cobia;* the *Icefish, Drum,* and *Sawfish,* known as "Banister's Beagles"; and the *Blackfish, Seadragon,* and *Shark II,* or "Blakely's Behemoths." The *Harukaze* accelerated to seven knots.

At 1730 the *Sawfish* unleashed a torpedo at the port side of the *Kimikawa Maru,* causing a terrific explosion in the No. 7 hold. A converted seaplane tender, it sank in less than three minutes. Then just after midnight on October 24 the *Snook* ripped into the *Shinsei Maru.* The torpedo was a dud, but the hole it caused forced the passenger-cargo ship to slow down. Before the next hour was out, the *Kokuryū Maru* was nailed in her starboard side and engine room.

Convoy MATA-30 was in disarray. The ships spread out, but the attacks only gained in ferocity. At 0315 the *Snook* fired another dud, this time at the starboard side of the tanker *Kikusui Maru,* then made up for the embarrassment with a shot that exploded in her bow and a third that set the boiler room area on fire. For an encore, the *Snook* stopped the *Tenshin Maru* dead in her tracks at 0605, slamming her port side with one torpedo and tearing open the wound with another. The ship split in two forward of the bridge and disappeared below the waves in a mere two minutes.

College was going well, and there was only a day's worth of classes before graduation. In the next eight hours the *Drum* sank the passenger-cargo ship *Shikisan Maru* in less than two minutes. The *Seadragon* sent the *Taiten Maru* up in flames and down stern first. Then she finished off the ailing *Shinsei Maru.* At 1405, just as the *Eikō Maru* was rescuing the last survivors of the *Shinsei Maru,* the *Sealion* roared back and buried the cargo ship in a paupers' grave.

In less than twenty-four hours the U.S. Navy had sunk eight of the twelve vessels in convoy MATA-30. A total of 41,228 tons of merchant shipping had been destroyed. Now it was Commander Ed Blakely's turn.

It was late afternoon. The South China Sea was flecked with whitecaps. The wind was blowing from the west as the *Arisan Maru* steamed through the Bashi Channel off southern Formosa. Most of the POWs on board were unaware of the damage that American submarines had inflicted on MATA-30. But the captain was. The *Arisan Maru* sailed under radio silence. A few of the men on the cooking and water detail saw wreckage in the water and survivors who appeared to be Japanese, thought Calvin Graef. They tried to get a better look but were cracked on the head for doing so.

Just before 1700, the time of the evening meal, Japanese sailors and guards suddenly began sprinting for the bow. Graef glanced over the starboard side of the ship and saw the rippling wake of a torpedo as it sped toward the stern, barely missing it. Seconds later another torpedo raced toward the bow from the opposite direction, sending the Japanese scrambling back to the stern. It missed "by inches," Graef said.

Sirens wailed. The Japanese shunted the cooking detail down into the hold. "C'mon, *navy!*" the men below bellowed. Some prayed to die. A chaplain gave absolution. Resolution would be such a relief. One of the 5-inch guns on deck had just begun firing when George Ferguson and the men in the No. 2 hold felt a terrific concussion. A torpedo from the *Shark* had slashed into the starboard side of the No. 3 hold. The *Arisan Maru* trembled, her engines stopped. Her aft mast crumpled, and the sternpost rudder split apart. Water flooded through the jagged holes made by the torpedo.

The *Arisan Maru* buckled amidship but remained afloat. The bow stayed level for roughly two and a half hours. The stern, which carried depth charges, began to go down first.

Joined in its fury by the *Take*, the *Harukaze* went after the *Shark* with a vengeance. The two destroyers fired multiple depth charges. The U.S. Navy Security Station in Washington, D.C., known as OP-20-G, was listening in on messages from the *Harukaze*, which at 1739 "attacked on sound, the submarine which torpedoed the *Arisan Maru*. Sinking generally confirmed." Heavy oil, clothing, and cork floated to the surface.

"Tried to contact *Shark*, unable to raise her," reported the *Seadragon*. "*Shark* cannot be contacted," confirmed the *Snook*. Ed Blakely and his crew were never heard from again.

The *Harukaze* and the *Take* returned to the *Arisan Maru* seven or eight miles away, searching for survivors. First Lieutenant Funatsu Toshio wanted to machine-gun the POWs. That would be chaos, said the captain, Sugino Minemaru. There were only fifteen or so armed guards on board. An interpreter told the POWs to remain where they were. Then the Japanese cut the bamboo and rope ladders leading down into hold No. 1 and slammed the hatch covers over the No. 2 hold.

There was panic at first, but before long a strange calm fell over the men. The relief some had prayed for had arrived with irrevocable force.

"Remember just one thing," said Major Paul M. Jones of the 26th

Cavalry Regiment, Philippine Scouts, and a native Tennesseean: "We're American soldiers. Let's play it that way to the very end of the script."

An army chaplain began to recite: "O Lord, if it be Thy will to take us now, give us the strength to be men. . . ."

They could hear the Japanese running back and forth above on the steel deck, but within an hour they had abandoned ship. The Japanese took with them the only two lifeboats on board, which had a capacity of sixty men apiece. The situation seemed hopeless, and it was this realization that finally spurred many of the POWs to action, seized by a desperate desire to live.

Men shinnied up the huge stanchions in the No. 1 hold and dropped ladders down for their buddies below. They lowered one of the long wooden hatch covers into the No. 2 hold, propping it up against a bulkhead, so others could climb out onto the deck. They even managed to evacuate the sick until no POWs remained in the holds. A few Japanese who missed the departing lifeboats remained topside. They had no means of escaping except by jumping overboard. "We took care of them," said Graef coolly. The POWs had no lifeboats and no life rafts, but there were plenty of kapok life belts. The waves were cresting ten to fifteen feet high from a lingering typhoon. The air was cold. The wind continued to blow from due west.

At the sight of other ships in the convoy, some immediately leaped into the sea, medical officers and chaplains among them. They clung to spars, crates, oil cans—anything they could get their hands on. Others had only one thing on their minds: food. They ransacked the galley, gorging themselves like dogs at a bowl of scraps before almost certain death. They stuffed their mouths with fists full of rice and sugar, guzzled bottles of catsup, furiously smoked two or three cigarettes at a time, only to vomit and cramp up once they hit the water.

Second Lieutenant Robert Overbeck was one of the first to swim out of the torpedo hole in the sinking ship. About forty other POWs headed toward the two Japanese destroyers in the area, shouting, waving, crying for help. The *Harukaze* was 500 yards away. Overbeck crawled up the iron rings on the sides of the ship and had almost made it to the deck when six Japanese beat him back down with the long bamboo poles they used to push men under water. His left arm was cut, and on approaching the *Take*, he met with a similar reception. Calvin Graef had a piece of his right ear nipped off in greeting, but he managed to get away. When Don Meyer saw that the Japanese were bent on rescuing only the Japanese, he and another POW threw a plank overboard and used it as a life raft. Several Japanese seaplanes surveyed the scene.

Once her boilers exploded, the *Arisan Maru* sank quickly at 1940. Her position was 20.00N 118.44E, southeast of the Pratas Reefs. The nearest land was Quantung Province, China, 250 miles away.

The *Harukaze*, meanwhile, took on board fifteen Japanese survivors but no POWs. "Am discontinuing sweep," the captain said in a message intercepted by OP-20-G. "Have 11 patients who should be hospitalized." At the bottom of the intercept, GI, the file and information section, noted: "Above despatch [*sic*] suggests HARUKAZE remained behind to pick up survivors of ARIYAMA MARU [*sic*] disaster and continue sweeping for enemy submarines while the convoy went on to port."

By then "it was dark," explained Fukuyama Tsuyoshi, the destroyer's commanding officer, "and hard to see anyone in the water." He had ordered his executive officer, Ueyanagi Isamu, not to rescue any prisoners of war, an order that was passed on to the assistant torpedo officer on the quarterdeck. The *Take* took on board another 347 Japanese survivors before steaming toward Takao. Shiga Hiroshi, the ship's torpedo officer, could hear the POWs adrift at sea, whistling through their fingers, pleading to be rescued as the destroyer departed.

Overbeck saw a half-submerged lifeboat that had been cast off by the Japanese as they boarded one of the destroyers. The current carried it away, but Overbeck swam after it, removing his life preserver so he could swim faster. The boat was stripped of its equipment and supplies, except for one keg that was filled with salt water and another that contained a little fresh water. Overbeck, who had directed the excavation of tunnels and bomb shelters on Corregidor, stood up so that men who were calling out for help in the darkness would be able to locate him.

He was giving one POW directions when a large crate drifted into the side of the boat. He lifted the lid and saw, as if by a miracle, a sail and an anchor inside, as well as emergency rations from a Japanese lifeboat. He wrapped the canvas around himself to keep warm. Sergeant Avery Wilber was the first POW Overbeck helped on board. He had been wounded in the left arm from the explosion on the *Arisan Maru* and had been floating on a four-by-four for four or five hours. Overbeck shared the canvas with him. Then around midnight, as the moon was high, came Private Anton Cichy, paddling on a plank. At dawn the three men were joined by 1st Sergeant Calvin Graef and Corporal Donald Meyer, whom they spotted fifty yards away on a ramshackle bamboo raft.

All hands got to work. They bailed out the lifeboat and rigged a mast. Then at around 0900 they spotted a Japanese destroyer. They quickly took the rigging down and pretended to be dead. The destroyer circled the lifeboat like a shark. Guns were trained on the men as the vessel loomed within 100 yards, circling them again. The ship pulled away, and once it was out of sight, Overbeck raised the sail and set out northwest by west, using the sun as his guide and at night the stars. Wilber sat in the stern, steering the boat by tiller. In the meantime a keg of potable water had floated toward their lifeboat. The men hauled it aboard. They now had food, water, and the consolation of one another. During the next two days two Japanese planes flew overhead, but at an altitude high enough, Meyer hoped, to make identification impossible.

On the evening of October 26, after two days at sea, they caught sight of the East China coast. The weather was poor, and instead of trying to reach the mainland themselves, they pulled alongside a large fishing junk. Several Chinese families were on board—men, women, and children. The POWs were thrown a rope and invited on one at a time. The nine-man crew spoke no English, but the captain caught their drift. The POWs wanted to contact Chiang Kai-shek's or American forces, if possible. "We go china to day," the captain scribbled. But did he mean today, the POWs wondered, or in two days? Then he wrote down the words "American or British." Wilber pointed to "American." The captain smiled.

The Chinese made sure to destroy the lifeboat and any Japanese evidence. The captain's wife fried some fish, boiled some rice, and prepared tea for the weathered survivors. They were even given tobacco and rolling papers. Then, once the nets were hauled in, the POWs ate again. They were treated to a bath and pampered with clean, warm clothes. They slept on deck that night, and when it began to rain, they were moved down to the crew's quarters.

The next morning the captain took them by sampan to Kitchioh, in Kwangtung Province on the China coast. A Chinese magistrate named Mr. Lee, who spoke English, contacted Hai-feng, the site of a weather station operated by the Air and Ground Forces Resources and Technical Staff (AGFRTS) for the 14th Air Force. AGFRTS had been set up by the Office of Strategic Services to gather intelligence and disseminate propaganda in Japanese-occupied China. On the afternoon of October 28, Corporal Francis J. Baron of AGFRTS arrived in Kitchioh, and the POWs were escorted to the temporary headquarters of General Yu Yung Kee, a former aide of General Stilwell's in Burma, who advised them to leave in the morning. They had landed on the only five-mile stretch of coast that wasn't controlled by the Japanese. There were no roads out of Kitchioh, only footpaths. A security detail and a Chinese interpreter would assist them.

On October 29 they began a twelve-day journey in country. Disguised as natives, they were feted along the way by Chinese villagers who threw banquets for them, entertained them, and plied them with liquor. By foot, bicycle, *jiaozi* (sedan chair), and weapons-carrier, they traveled from Lu-feng to Hingning and Namyung. The Americans there radioed General Claire L. Chennault's headquarters in Kunming to evacuate the POWs by plane. They left Namyung at noon on November 12 on a DC-3. When they arrived in Kunming, General Chennault, architect of the American Volunteer Group (better known as the Flying Tigers) and commander of U.S. air power in China, stood by to welcome them personally. From Kunming they flew over the Hump and on to New Delhi, where they caught sight of the Taj Mahal, then crossed Persia, North Africa, and the Atlantic, landing in New York on December 1, 1944. They reached their final destination of Washington, D.C., the very next day.

It didn't seem possible, said Calvin Graef, that there were any other survivors of the *Arisan Maru*. The weather had been bitter and the seas high; the men were in poor condition; and there had been little wreckage to keep them afloat.

But while Overbeck had been one of the first men to abandon the sinking *Arisan Maru* on October 24, army corpsman Philip Brodsky and army doctor Corporal Russell L. Lash viewed the scene with almost surreal detachment from topside. Brodsky had broken his hand earlier down in the No. 2 hold when he punched a fellow POW in the face for stealing his rice ration. Once on deck he and Lash made sure they got their fair share of rice and sugar from the galley. Then they waited. The ship was listing from its starboard side, and Brodsky calmly waited for it to sink so the suction could pull him beneath the waves. What was the point in struggling anymore? He had suffered enough.

The aft deck of the *Arisan Maru* had peeled off from port to starboard. You could peer down into the bowels of the boat, see water sloshing around, and hear the groan of steel whenever a wave rolled by. Around dusk the stern of the *Arisan Maru* broke off, pointing straight up, and the ship began to sink quickly. A loud explosion followed, and men dropped into the water. To Brodksy's surprise, there was little suction. He slid off as easily as if he'd been on a raft at the beach in Atlantic City, New Jersey, where he'd enlisted in the army. Several hundred feet away in the water, Private 3rd Class Glenn Oliver saw "quite a few men still on the ship, some sitting, some standing and holding on to the rail" as she went under. Among them were dozens of men who had gathered around a chaplain and were praying.

Brodsky was an experienced swimmer, but his weight had dropped from 170 to 120 pounds, and he was hampered by a hurting hand. Lash weighed a mere 100 pounds, and within seconds Brodsky heard him calling. They found the remains of a *benjo* with a dozen other men clinging to it, each jostling for a better position. Then they spotted two wooden hatch covers, about ten by two feet. Brodsky found a four-foot plank, laid it down crosswise, and draped his body over it to hold the raft together. The friction tore at the skin of his arms. At night, he heard the sounds of men crying for help, and then the cries disappeared into the inky darkness. He and Lash remained together until dawn, when Lash decided that they should part company. Brodsky wanted him to stay; three hands were better than one, but he didn't want to hinder Lash. He watched Lash swim away on his hatch cover until he lost sight of him at daylight. There were thirty or forty men in the distance and Brodsky called out to them, but he heard no one answer.

Around 1000 Brodsky saw the first sign of hope: a Japanese cruiser was heading toward him. Sailors were lined up along the deck railing. He pleaded with them in English and the little Japanese he had picked up from prison camp. The ship came within thirty feet. One of the sailors tossed an empty cigarette package at him as the cruiser passed by. He watched it disappear over the horizon. He was alone in the middle of the ocean, 250 miles from the coast of China, draped over two pieces of wood, a crucifix on the water.

He had all but given up hope when at noon he saw another figure on a raft that was made from two hatch covers in the shape of a wedge. Brodsky called out to him. Would it be okay if he joined him? "Sure," came the reply, "come on over." It was Glenn Oliver, and the men made a pact: they wouldn't kill each other, and they wouldn't eat each other. They tried tying their three hatch covers together to form a triangle, but the lines kept coming undone.

The wind picked up at night, and in the darkness Oliver made out four waterlogged life rafts about six feet in length. They were tied bow to stern with a thick two-inch hauser. Oliver climbed onto one, while Brodsky grabbed another. They stretched out for the first time in thirty-six hours, but the rafts were half-submerged. They tried stacking them, but it took all of their energy to sandwich just two together. They completed the task in the morning, lashing the four rafts with manila rope. They were tired, parched, and hungry, but afloat.

Around noon Brodsky saw a body in a life jacket 150 yards away. Perhaps there was a canteen on it. He took off his underpants, gave them to Oliver to wave as a flag so he wouldn't lose sight of him over the swells, and swam. Just before he reached it, the corpse slipped out of the life jacket. There was no canteen. Brodsky used the life jacket as a pillow. He and Oliver looked for other corpses that day. They didn't say what they were thinking, but they knew they'd resort to cannibalism if they found another body. They'd had no food and hardly any water for three days. When it rained, they held up Brodsky's shirt and wrung it out to drink the water from it. When they finally came across a dead minnow on their raft, they split it, sucking on each piece "for about an hour."

On the morning of October 28 Oliver saw six columns of smoke. A convoy was zigzagging in the distance. Brodsky waved his long-sleeve white shirt back and forth. An enemy destroyer, with the insignia E-146 on its bow, pulled out of formation and came within twenty yards of the men. Brodsky swam for the ship. The Japanese tossed him a tie-line, but he couldn't make it up the Jacob's ladder without help. He scraped himself badly on the barnacles that clung to the hull. Oliver dog-paddled to a life ring but was also too weak to climb the ladder. He fell back into the water but was thrown some rope by the Japanese and then hoisted on deck. It was 1:07 P.M., he saw on the wristwatch of a Japanese seaman.

The two POWs were nearly naked, badly sunburned, and dehydrated. Brodsky weighed a mere 89 pounds and was covered with open sores. He was urinating pus. The Japanese gave them *fundoshi* to wear. Brodsky had to beg for water. Finally he found some steaming hot broth on deck and drank it. Later they were handed a small portion of *lugao*. The temperature plunged at night, and Brodsky shook so severely that his teeth chattered. The petty officer issued them blue serge uniforms. The wool chafed at Brodsky's skin. He couldn't get comfortable, but he slept as best as he could on the steel deck by the bridge.

Around 0700 the next day the destroyer pulled into Takao, where the security detail of the *Arisan Maru* had also arrived. Brodsky and Oliver were escorted to a large building, where they were interrogated by the Kempeitai. The men were blindfolded, and their hands were tied behind their backs. They were taunted with the threat of execution. The Japanese stroked their bare necks with sword blades and bolted their rifles as if forming a firing squad. The Kempeitai were furious at Brodsky and slapped him every time he denied being a submariner. Once their blindfolds were removed, Brodsky and Oliver encountered another survivor of the *Arisan Maru* in the room. It was Warrant Officer Martin Binder of the USS *Pigeon*, the submarine rescue ship that had been based in Cavite.

Binder had survived by clinging to a raft with ten other men. After a day at sea, half of them had found bits of flotsam that they decided to pin their lives on. After three days only Binder and one other *Arisan Maru* survivor remained. But drinking sea water drove the man out of his mind. He tore off his life jacket and in spite of Binder's entreaties said "he was going to swim for it." Binder was left by himself to bat away sharks with his water-filled canteen. Eventually he was picked up by a Japanese transport and taken to Takao for interrogation.

Brodsky, Oliver, and Binder were loaded onto a truck and imprisoned in a bamboo cell for the night. In the morning they met a fourth survivor of the *Arisan Maru*, Private Charles W. Hughes of the Coast Artillery Corps. They were transferred to a freighter in the harbor, where Brodsky recognized several POWs from O'Donnell and Palawan, but they were forbidden to speak to one another. They were confined on deck for nearly a week before the ship set sail for Japan. This time the POWs were locked in the aft hold. They'd never make it out alive if they were targeted by the Americans. The vessel departed on November 8, but returned to Formosa a mere twenty-four hours later; the waters were too dangerous. The sickest men were evacuated to a hospital at the Shirakawa POW Camp, where Hughes died. Brodsky, Oliver, and Binder were transferred with 400 POWs to Toroku in central Formosa. When American planes began bombing the area in December 1944, the prisoners were moved yet again by ship. Brodsky ended up in Taihoku, a coal mining camp in the mountains of northern Formosa, populated mostly by British POWs from Singapore. Binder had the good fortune to be consigned to a camp where the Japanese commandant refused to let POWs work because "he believed it too dangerous." Glenn Oliver was transported to Moji and then Ōsaka, where he was imprisoned in a camp well known to John Bookman: Wakayama.

Brodsky, Oliver, and Binder found it inconceivable—as did Calvin Graef—that there had been any other survivors of the *Arisan Maru*. Indeed, of the 1,800 POWs who boarded the *Arisan Maru* on October 11, 1944, only eight survived: Robert Overbeck, Avery Wilber, Anton Cichy, Calvin Graef, Donald Meyer, Philip Brodsky, Glenn Oliver, and Martin Binder. George Ferguson was but one of 1,792 POWs lost at sea. One Japanese soldier and four civilians died. It was a tragedy whose proportions surpassed those of the *Titanic* and *Lusitania*, marking the greatest loss of American lives in a single maritime disaster.

Lucy Ferguson wouldn't learn of George's fate for months. When Fred, John, and Murray heard a rumor about him in Kōbe, they simply refused to believe it.

———

The greatest naval engagement of World War II, the Battle for Leyte Gulf, ended triumphantly for the United States. In spite of Halsey's reckless pursuit of Ozawa's ships, Admiral Toyoda's ruse failed, leaving the Seventh and Third Fleets exposed. With less than half the airplanes he needed in the face of overwhelming Allied power, Vice Admiral Ōnishi

Takijirō, commander of the Japanese First Air Fleet, resorted to a devious and desperate tactic: arming the single-engine Zero fighter with a 557-pound bomb and targeting enemy carriers. "Human bombs," Commander Tamai Asaichi described them to Lieutenant Seki Yukio, who led the first surprise attack with his five Sacred Eagles. Formed into Special Attack Forces, they were known as *tokkōtai*. Navy recruits were called *shinpū*, or "God's wind," a name that harks back to the typhoons that miraculously prevented Mongol ships from landing in Japan in 1274 and 1281. Outside Japan they were known as kamikaze.

The kamikaze had little strategic impact on the Battle for Leyte Gulf but enormous symbolic significance. As Lieutenant Seki wrote in a farewell letter to his family before crashing into Rear Admiral Clifton Sprague's carrier *St. Lo* on October 25, 1944, "Nothing can be a greater honor" than to sacrifice oneself "for the sake of Japan."

But victory eluded the Japanese at Leyte; their losses—four carriers, three battleships, ten cruisers, and eleven destroyers—effectively crippled their fleet. On October 26, 1944, less than a week after the American landings, *The New York Times* crowed: "U.S. DEFEATS JAPANESE NAVY; ALL FOE'S SHIPS IN ONE FLEET HIT; MANY SUNK; BATTLE CONTINUES."

That same month marked the peak of Japanese merchant ship losses and proved the most deadly for American POWs being transported from Manila to Japan. In the seven weeks from the sinking of the *Rakuyō Maru* on September 6 to the sinking of the *Arisan Maru* on October 24, 1944, a total of 10,716 Allied POWs died at the hands of U.S. submariners.

By late December the island of Leyte had fallen. Luzon would be next. Dr. Ōhashi himself was convinced Japan would lose the war. He admitted as much to Hinomoto Teruko, the seventeen-year-old daughter of one of his wife's friends, as they walked one day from her house in Toyonaka, a suburb of Ōsaka, to the train station.

The Americans had routed the Japanese at sea and slashed the last supply line between the Philippines and East Asia. Now they would target the Japanese Home Islands—from the air.

22

Fire from the Sky

THEY WERE YOUNG, handsome, fearless, and a little foolish, from the mountains and the plains, small towns and big cities. An eleven-man crew might originate from eleven different states. They were teenagers, many of them, in their twenties if they were officers, eager for experience, out to test their mettle. Some were in college, like Ed Keyser and nineteen-year-old Ed Levin. Some were teaching college, like John Ciardi. Others were in girl trouble and had barely made it through high school. They became pilots and bombardiers, navigators and flight engineers, radio operators and central fire control gunners, blister and tailgunners for a brand-new bird, the B-29: the Superfortress. They were the boys of the 73rd Bomb Wing, the initial bomb wing of the XXI Bomber Command. "Kids," their thirty-eight-year-old commander, Brigadier General Emmett "Rosie" O'Donnell called them. Based in Saipan, their mission was first to destroy Japan's principal engine manufacturers, its aircraft component and assembly plants, and then to incapacitate Japan's port areas. In short, their goal was to burn to the ground Japan's six most important cities: Tōkyō, Yokohama, Kawasaki, Nagoya, Ōsaka—and Kōbe.

They had heard the stories of the Bataan Death March. They had watched Darryl F. Zanuck's *The Purple Heart* on Saipan and recoiled in horror when the Japanese scooped out the eyeballs of Jimmy Doolittle's intrepid airmen. They'd had relatives who had fought in the Pacific, brothers who'd been captured in the Philippines. And they would never forget Pearl Harbor.

"I hated the Japanese," said Sergeant Jules Stillman, the dapper right blister gunner for the *Beau Bomber II*, who in civilian life decorated candy store windows in New York City for a living. "They showed us a picture of a Japanese officer, sword in hand, beheading a B-29 pilot shot down over Japan. This was a Japanese propaganda photo. So I vowed that if I was ever captured, I'd kill as many Japanese officers as I could,

and then shoot myself. I didn't think too much about what we were doing. You just did your job."

Private 1st Class John Davidson, Jr., affixed personalized notes to
the 2,000-pound bombs he loaded into B-29s on Saipan. "Here's to you,
Tōjō," he wrote, "payback time." And indeed it was payback time for the
Japanese, who on December 7, 1941, had dared to tell the "Goddam
Americans" in leaflets that had fluttered to the ground over Oahu to "all
go to hell." Now the most technologically sophisticated country on earth
would spare neither military installations nor residential neighborhoods
in the most sustained bombing of a single nation in the world's history,
even if the bombing of civilians constituted war crimes under the
Geneva Convention.

In February 1944, after the conquest of the Gilbert and Marshall Islands, U.S. forces launched Operation Forager to capture the Marianas—
Saipan, Tinian, and Guam. Twelve hundred miles from Japan, Saipan
was a vital operational center for the Japanese. A few miles to the south,
Tinian held a 9,000-strong garrison under the command of Admiral
Kakuta Kakuji. Guam, the southernmost island, 150 miles away, had
been the headquarters of Admiral Ozawa's Striking Force.

The Marianas were of strategic importance to the U.S. Army Air
Forces (USAAF) because they could put the Superforts within striking
distance of Japan's Home Islands. On June 15, 1944, just as the invasion
of Saipan was being launched, B-29s from the XX Bomber Command's
air base in Chengtu, China, struck the Imperial Iron and Steel Works at
Yawata in Kyūshū. But Kyūshū was the maximum range for the planes
executing Project Matterhorn, the campaign to attack Japan from the
Asian mainland. Those raids continued through early 1945, and their
targets included Manchukuo, Korea, China, Formosa, and Southeast
Asia, but they had limited effect. Henceforth the Marianas would form a
base of operations for the long-range bombing of Japan, with airfields
for B-29s, P-51 fighter escorts, and headquarters of the XXI Bomber
Command on Guam.

The assault on Saipan was one of the bloodiest campaigns in the Pacific. In mid-June 1944 Saipan's 32,000-strong garrison under Vice Admiral Nagumo Chūichi, commander of the Japanese carrier force that
attacked Pearl Harbor, faced an invasion force of 127,571 American
troops, two-thirds of whom were marines. In the first forty-eight hours
U.S. Marines suffered 4,000 casualties at the hands of Lieutenant General Saitō Yoshitsugu's 31st Army. What was supposed to be a three-day
campaign turned into an agonizing three-week battle.

"Come out and surrender!" one American is alleged to have demanded of a Japanese soldier in a cave.

"Come and get me, you souvenir-hunting sonovabitch!" came the reply in flawless English.

On June 24 Imperial General Headquarters determined that Saipan was a lost cause. Better that its defenders should choose *gyokusai* than surrender, and they did. On July 6 Nagumo and Saitō committed suicide after Saitō ordered the largest *banzai* charge of the war. Every man was sworn to "take seven lives to repay our country." Forced to retreat to the northern end of the island, hundreds of Japanese civilians, including pregnant women and young children, leaped to their deaths from Marpi Point, some of them clinging to the necks of Japanese soldiers as they plunged into the sea. The Americans called it Suicide Cliff. When the smoke had cleared, 31,000 Japanese soldiers and 22,000 civilians were dead. The Americans suffered 3,426 losses. "It was obvious that Japan had no hope at all of regaining supremacy on the sea or in the air," wrote a Japanese trainee pilot. Navy Seabees (Construction Battalion) celebrated the U.S. victory by displaying the heads of dead Japanese impaled on spikes.

In August 1944, the 73rd Bomb Wing commenced operations on Saipan and was assigned to the Twentieth Air Force. The aviation engineers were already working day and night to build an 8,500-foot runway from coral clawed out of Saipan's mountains. Four airfields were supposed to be ready by the time General Haywood S. "Possum" Hansell of the XXI Bomber Command arrived on October 12. They weren't. But by November the 73rd Bomb Wing was there in full force. With twenty planes per squadron, three squadrons per bomb group, and four groups per wing—497th, 498th, 499th, and 500th—it comprised, including ground echelons, some 12,000 men.

On November 24 the first B-29s rolled down Isley Field on their way to Target 357: Tōkyō. More than 100 Superforts, led by *Dauntless Dotty* with Brigadier General Emmett O'Donnell in the pilot's seat, flew over the ocean at around 1,500 feet. They raised their altitude as they approached the IP (Initial Point) 100 miles or so from the mainland, passed snow-draped Mt. Fuji, and from 27,000 to 33,000 feet bombed the Musashino engine plant of the Nakajima Company in northwest Tōkyō, ten miles from the Imperial Palace. The Japanese responded by launching retaliation raids against Saipan's "new management," as the Americans facetiously referred to themselves, from Iwo Jima 725 miles away.

Three days later "Piss-Call Charlie came over at midnight," Sergeant John Ciardi wrote in his Saipan diary. "Four Betty's sneaked in under the radar net by riding in on the wave tops" and targeted the 499th dispersal area as B-29s were being readied for another raid. Ciardi, a gunner, had the bunk right next to Tech Sergeant Ed Levin.

Eight to ten Zero fighters strafed the air base in the face of ferocius antiaircraft fire. Then one plane peeled away, fingering the Americans' quonset hut with eerie red tracers and opening up with a .20-caliber machine gun. Bullets flew within inches of Ciardi's head.

"Words can't describe the feeling when a tracer comes after you," said Levin, "a flash of light as if it's aimed just at you. That was more terrifying than being wounded."

There were no foxholes near the air base on Saipan because you were scratching coral just a few inches beneath the topsoil. Sandbag shelters sat aboveground like bees' nests that had fallen off trees. A slight man, Levin wrestled with the six-foot-tall Ciardi to get under, of all things, a canvas cot. On another occasion airmen dove for cover at the sound of what they thought was an air raid alarm over the public address system. It turned out to be the opening glissando of Gershwin's *Rhapsody in Blue*. They laughed about it afterward, but the fear was real: three B-29s had gone up in flames, and a total of twenty had been knocked out of commission.

"They shot hell out of our ships," wrote 2nd Lieutenant Robert E. Copeland, who was eager for action. Four Japanese planes paid the price. He went down to the 883rd area where one of the Zekes was blown into pieces no larger than its propeller. He came upon the remains of the first dead man he'd ever a seen, he noted in his diary—a pilot, like himself.

A few nights later Japanese fighter-bombers returned, killing some men while maiming others as they tried to extinguish fires or move Superforts that were perched like sitting ducks on their hardstands.

The capture of Iwo Jima on February 19, 1945, was a huge relief. It meant there were fighter escorts on some B-29 missions as well as a place to land 627 miles north of Saipan in case of an emergency. Radio transmitters could now guide bombers along the "Hirohito Highway" to Tōkyō and back. Not a bad thing, either, to have air-sea rescue support from lifeguard submarines and surface vessels at preestablished coordinates along the 1,400-mile route from the Marianas to Honshū in case you had to ditch. The submarines were protected by "SuperDumbos," armed B-29s that were equipped with life rafts, survival gear, and droppable radio buoys.

But fear shadowed you. It was hard not to get a little nervous when you heard, at your preflight briefings, the words "fierce," "intense," and "accurate" to describe the flak you were about to encounter over your bombing target. Hard not to be a little apprehensive when you put on your gloves, steel helmet, jacket, Mae West, laminated flak vest, crash harness, and safety while preparing for takeoff. Hard not to feel as if an eternity were passing when the bomb bay doors were open for just one or two minutes, "because that's when we're most vulnerable," wrote Copeland in a letter to his mother. But you had a job to do, you were part of an eleven-man team, and you had to lose your fear to function effectively. For most of the men in the 73rd Bomb Wing, there was no other choice. As Ciardi put it simply: "We functioned."

Second Lieutenant Ed Keyser of the 499th Bomb Group was an exception. It wasn't fear but conscience that made him refuse to participate in his first fire raid. S-2 (Intelligence) claimed that Japanese homes were being used to make shells and machine parts, that civilians were being turned into active enemies. Keyser didn't entirely buy it. His grandfather had been a conscientious objector in the Civil War, living just a few miles from Appomattox. Keyser also chose to object. The only way to get out of a mission was to go to church, which he did on his first scheduled fire raid. But he saw the handwriting on the wall, and pacifism gave way to pragmatism. If he wanted to go home, he would have to complete his thirty-five missions, which meant flying on incendiary bombing raids.

Crews were as closely knit as families. It might be a day or several days between missions. They slept fitfully, maybe five, six hours a night. They attended classes in tactics, navigation, ordnance, and bombardment. When they weren't studying, the enlisted men chugged beer, the officers drank booze, and they both played poker. From the Chamorro natives who helped guard the Japanese POW camp on Saipan, they learned how to make hooch by taking the eye out of a coconut, inserting seven to nine raisins, plugging it back up, and waiting for fermentation. They ate too much Spam and complained about the amount of Australian "laaaaaaamb," as they called it. They played handball and baseball, went hiking, and planted gardens. At night they listened to KSAI-Radio Saipan, eyed the grass-skirted Kanaka Dancers, ogled stars such as Betty Hutton at USO shows, relished Irving Berlin's "This Is the Army" extravaganza, or caught a movie at the open-air Surfside Theater, where they sat on sandbags or the metal crates that bombs were shipped in.

Sweltering heat and driving rains made life miserable for the ground echelon during the early days of operations, though once the weather cleared up, Saipan could be quite pleasant. A new chemical known as DDT, which eliminated mosquitoes and the consequent risk of malaria, had been field-tested in Castel Volturno, north of Naples, in May 1944. DDT made its Pacific debut on Saipan. Before that the marines had called the island Flypan, so plagued had it been with flies.

Airmen were prohibited from keeping flight logs on their person in case they were captured, but many took notes of their missions afterward. Ed Keyser kept his in *Esquire's Date Book*, opposite the dates he had gone on in the prior year with Candy and Molly. John Ciardi kept a more expansive diary and wrote poems inspired by his experience on Saipan: "Poem for My Twenty-Ninth Birthday," "Visibility Zero," and "Elegy for a Cave Full of Bones—Saipan, Dec. 14, '44."

The planes were beautiful, marvels of technology nearly 100 feet long, with 142-foot wings for takeoff and landing at lower speeds, pressurized compartments, and a computerized central-fire-control (CFC) gunnery system that choreographed an armament of twelve .50-caliber machine guns and a 20mm cannon in the tail. They came equipped with a radar unit to help locate targets, boasted a maximum 16,000-pound bomb load capacity, and had a record range of 5,333 miles. Seven thousand gallons of gas—a small railroad tank car—would take you to Japan and back.

Until 1945, when the order came down to remove the nose art, the women who adorned the planes were beautiful too—outrageous, salacious, and curvaceous. Scantily clad in bikinis and diaphanous negligees or just plain naked, they had lips that invited kisses, breasts that shamelessly beckoned, and names that left nothing to the imagination: *Supine Sue, Salvo Sally, Shady Lady, Helion, Stripped,* and *Poison Lil,* who was topless and held in her left hand a martini glass with a bomb in it.

As alluring as they were, the B-29s were riddled with problems—like takeoff and landing. These birds were so big and weighed so much when combat loaded—138,000 pounds—that you held your breath as they strained to get off the ground. Isley Field on Saipan was about 500 feet above the sea, so when B-29s thundered down the runway at 160 mph, they dropped off the edge of the island so close to the ocean you could see ripples in the water from the propeller wind or feel waves slap the underbelly as you prayed your pilot maintained a steady course and built up enough speed until, after a harrowing forty seconds that seemed like a lifetime, he nudged the control column, tilted the nose up, and the plane was airborne. Some Superforts didn't make it.

"You dreaded the takeoff more than the actual bombing," said 1st Lieutenant Walter Sherrell, an airplane commander with the 498th Bomb Group. Two miles away the airstrip at Tinian was more like a boat ramp than a runway; every day a plane seemed to be lost before it was even airborne.

The engines overheated, the oil pumping system failed to feed the top cylinders, and valves were "swallowed," which meant the engine had to be shut down and the propeller "feathered." Some bombardiers considered the Norden bombsight completely ineffective at high altitudes, and blisters proved another liability. Many of the spherical windows that enabled the side gunners to see were blown out in combat, which could send a plane tumbling to earth. On one occasion a gunner was ejected into the atmosphere at 30,000 feet, dangling from an extended seat harness before he was finally hauled back inside the cabin.

Then there was the discovery of the Jet Stream. "We were on a bomb run for forty minutes where we had an airspeed of 200 mph," said Sergeant Ronald Routhier, a top gunner with the 499th Bomb Group, "and a ground speed of 40 to 45 mph. You'd drop your bombs and miss your targets altogether. And you'd burn up a tremendous amount of fuel." In the first mission over Tōkyō, planes were caught in a 140 mph headwind. Whenever Jules Stillman made it safely back to Saipan after a bombing run, he kissed the ground.

But modifications were continually made, kinks were ironed out, and the B-29's idiosyncrasies became as familiar as a horse's bad habits. Which didn't mean that the strategy for which they were intended always yielded the desired results. Nearly a dozen raids over Tōkyō and Nagoya between November 1944 and January 1945 targeting the Japanese aircraft industry demonstrated poor bombing accuracy, unacceptable abort ratios, and steep ditching rates. The winds were tremendous, and cloud cover frequently obscured targets. Radar equipment was initially inadequate, and positions were frequently misread. In January 5.7 percent of airborne B-29s were lost. Flying at high altitudes also required a larger fuel load, and a corresponding reduction in the size of the payload. In short, high-level daylight precision bombing proved to be anything but precise.

The Japanese called the Grumman fighters *kumabachi*, meaning "bear wasps." B-29s were literally *B-nijūku*, but they would prove to have a far deadlier sting. First, however, USAAF demanded a radically new bombing strategy.

On January 21, 1945, General Henry "Hap" Arnold, the USAAF commander who had vowed to avenge the deaths of the Doolittle raiders by destroying Japan's "inhuman war lords," relieved General Hansell as commanding general of the XXI Bomber Command. His replacement was Major General Curtis LeMay, who arrived in the Marianas from Kharagpur, India, where he headed the XX Bomber Command in the China-Burma-India theater.

Gruff, daunting, and demanding, the Cigar, as LeMay was called for invariably chomping on a stogie, was a champion of incendiary bombing. He knew from the great fire that had devoured Tōkyō after the earthquake of 1923 that the city was an ideal target. LeMay had been in Europe a few weeks before the bombing of Hamburg and had arrived in the Pacific theater shortly before the bombing of Dresden. Doolittle, who commanded the U.S. Army Eighth Air Force, protested that attacks against civilians were tantamount to terrorism. It was a long-simmering argument within the Army Air Force Command, but such reservations were brushed aside. If Churchill himself had scruples about bombing defenseless German cities, he endorsed the strategy relentlessly pursued by Air Marshal Sir Arthur Travers "Bomber" Harris, chief of the British Bomber Command, on the grounds "that those who have loosed these horrors upon mankind will now in their homes and persons feel the shattering strokes of just retribution." Churchill wanted to overwhelm German civil authorities with a tide of refugees. General Carl "Tooey" Spaatz, commander of U.S. Strategic Air Forces in Europe, and "Bomber" Harris, having learned well the lesson of the Luftwaffe's attack on Coventry in November 1940, stood ready to execute his wishes.

Many German and Japanese cities were actively engaged in war work. Dresden was celebrated for its beauty and its artistic treasures and as a manufacturer of luxury goods. But Dresden also contained hundreds of factories, the most important of which were in optical and electrical communications. On the night of February 13, 1945, Dresden went up as "a single column of flame," said the young American POW Kurt Vonnegut, Jr., who was forced to recover bodies in the aftermath of the bombing. "Corpse mining," his protagonist Billy Pilgrim called it in the novel *Slaughterhouse Five*. An estimated 25,000 to 40,000 died at the hands of the RAF and the U.S. Army Eighth Air Force. The city once known as "Florence on the Elbe" lay like a frame with its canvas burned out.

Two-thirds of Japanese industry was scattered between homes and small factories that employed thirty workers or less. Industrial targets were frequently surrounded by residential neighborhoods. Homes were made of wood, *shōji* (paper) screens separated rooms, and *tatami* mats lay on the floor like sawdust. Japan's cities were far more combustible than those in Germany, and for the most part they were poorly defended. Model Japanese urban areas had been constructed and tested in the United States at Dugway Proving Ground and Eglin Field, Florida. The results were encouraging, according to an Air Intelligence study of October 1943. Seventeen hundred tons of incendiaries could reduce Japan's twenty largest cities to rubble.

The bombs themselves were relatively harmless-looking. Twenty inches long, three inches in diameter, and hexagonally shaped, they weighed a mere 6.2 pounds and were known as M-69 incendiaries. They had been developed by National Defense Research Council scientists back in 1942, and their destructive capability was unique. On impact, a delayed-action fuse detonated a TNT charge that sprayed magnesium particles through gasoline gel, igniting any combustible surface within reach. When bundled in packages of nineteen, M-69s formed cluster bombs. When the bomb recipe was 5 percent aluminum napthene, 5 percent aluminum palmitate, and 0.5 percent carbon black mixed in with gasoline, it was known as napalm. Thirty-eight M-69s were clustered into a single 500-pound bomb. One B-29 was capable of carrying forty such clusters—or 1,520 firebombs.

"The primary purpose of these attacks," explained the *Air Intelligence Report*, a publication of the XXI Bomber Command, "is to destroy/damage the factories making the weapons, equipment and supplies needed by the Japanese to carry on the war. . . . Unfortunately for the Japanese many of the objectives . . . lie within or immediately adjacent to known highly inflammable sections of their few principal cities." Less unfortunate, the report suggested, was the fact that "thousands of little shops often located in a front or back room of individual residences" played a "tremendous part" in war production. Their role in that effort, whether voluntary or compulsory, "invited" incendiary attack. A Pentagon report compiled by the Incendiary Subcommittee had already concluded that successful area attacks on Tōkyō, Yokohama, Kawasaki, Nagoya, Ōsaka, and Kōbe would destroy 70 percent of the houses in those cities and reduce by 20 percent one year's production of "frontline" military equipment.

LeMay wanted to test incendiary bombing at high altitudes. He chose Nagoya first and Kōbe second. For the Kōbe raid, LeMay substituted 500-pound incendiaries topped with frag clusters instead of the M-69s, which were used in Nagoya. And for the first time, B-29s from the 313th Bomb Wing on Tinian were sent over Japan in a dual-wing mission. On February 4, 1945, sixty-nine planes in a radar-directed attack bombed the industrial waterfront of southwestern Kōbe, where war production factories were concentrated. In one of the first daylight raids, 159.2 tons of incendiaries were dropped and 13.6 tons of frags from 24,500 to 27,000 feet. Despite stiff resistance from some 200 Japanese fighter planes, 1,039 buildings were damaged or destroyed. A total of 4,350 people were rendered homeless. Brigadier General Lauris Norstad, chief of staff, Twentieth Air Force, considered the results "inconclusive." The Japanese did not. Two days later Obata Tadayoshi, a statesman well connected to the cabinet, declared: "The expression 'sure victory' is misleading" because it is "identical with sure death. . . . Our leaders should frankly reveal the real state of affairs, while our people on their part must be ready for any emergency."

Precision bombing raids followed on Nakajima's Ōta aircraft assembly plant and then on Tōkyō on February 25—after American forces had landed on Iwo Jima. The assessment of the Tōkyō raid was more encouraging, but LeMay remained unimpressed. "This outfit has been getting a lot of publicity without having really accomplished a hell of a lot in bombing results," he quipped to public relations officer and staff press censor Lieutenant Colonel St. Clair McKelway on March 6, 1945.

LeMay switched tactics: have the B-29s fly at altitudes of 5,000 to 8,000 feet, and combine M-69s with high-explosive bombs; strip the planes of guns and ammunition except tail-gun positions; bring along only the waist- and tail-gunners; eliminate the bomb-bay fuel tanks, and a B-29 could carry six tons of incendiaries. Three hundred B-29s flying over Japan was almost equivalent to 1,000 B-17s over Europe. The B-17 had a bomb capacity of only two tons on long missions. "Boys," the word went around Saipan, "throw your oxygen masks away, for LeMay is here to stay."

Weather conditions were better at low altitudes, winds ranged from 28 to 40 mph (compared to 140 to 200 mph at 25,000 to 30,000 feet), and radar was more effective. Automatic weapons fire tended to be ineffective above 5,000 feet, and the accuracy of flak was reduced below 10,000. True, there was a greater chance of low-level attacks from the enemy. Fall out of formation, and you risked getting rammed by kamikaze. But the risk was reduced if you carried out the raids at night. "These missions had to be completed," said a report issued in the Marianas entitled *Turning Point: General LeMay's Great Decision*, "in time for the B-29's to coordinate their efforts with the naval strike at Okinawa," which was scheduled to begin on March 23. The results were diabolically effective. Fire rained down upon Japan's major cities.

On March 9, 1945, 334 B-29s took off from the Marianas on a "maximum effort" mission code-named Meetinghouse. Planes from the 314th Wing left Guam at 1735, followed by the 73rd Wing from Saipan and the 313th Wing from Tinian forty minutes later. From a blister on the *Mary Ann*, pilot Chester W. Marshall of the 73rd could see the battle raging on Iwo Jima below. Their altitude was low, around 2,000 feet. North of Iwo they switched off their navigation lights for fear of being spotted by enemy ships.

The lead planes, "pathfinders," were armed with 180 seventy-pound M-47 napalm bombs. Then came the B-29s loaded with 24 five-hundred-pound M-69 clusters. Each plane carried on average 912 firebombs. Visibility was near zero. Navigators had to rely on radar to avoid midair collisions. The Superforts climbed to bombing altitude and just after midnight began to arrive over Tōkyō.

The pathfinders raced in at 300 mph, just under 5,000 feet, dropping bombs to illuminate a three-by-four-mile rectangle next to the city's most important industrial zone. Giant searchlights scanned the sky, hoping to lock onto a B-29 for the antiaircraft gunners below. It was "a beautiful but horrifying sight," said 1st Lieutenant Marshall. "You knew that its crew could be shot out of the sky any minute, but the silver B-29 gleamed a ghostly white, and you prayed that the people inside would make it through another minute or two." Red and white tracers exploded around the aircraft, followed by bursts of flak as the planes neared their target. But the B-29s were flying at such low altitudes that most of them eluded antiaircraft fire, and they remained out of range of small-caliber automatic weapons.

The 73rd Bomb Wing targeted Asakusa Ward, west of the Sumida River, and Honjo Ward to the east. Clusters spilled out of bomb bays and split open 100 feet aboveground, spewing napalm in a deadly bolus and branding Tōkyō with a giant flaming *X.* For the next three hours wave after wave of B-29s saturated the imperial city with 1,665 tons of incendiaries from 4,900 to 9,200 feet—8,333 magnesium bombs per square mile. Strong spring gusts blowing from the north and west fanned thousands of individual fires not into a firestorm but into something even more lethal—a "sweep conflagration" that soared to a temperature of 1,800 degrees Fahrenheit. The searing heat softened glass, melted metal, and turned asphalt back into tar. Smoke and debris were "hurled upward to more than 15,000 feet," said Marshall.

"Going into northwest Tōkyō at the end of the fire raids," remarked 1st Lieutenant Vernon V. Piotter, a navigator in the 869th Squadron of the 497th Bomb Group, "the thermal drafts took you up like an elevator. The altimeter spun around, and within seconds we went from from 6,000 to 24,000 feet." The G-force pinned airmen to their seats. "The turbulence flipped the plane on its back, then the plane dove, but our pilot was able to pull us out of it."

The Japanese fired shells, rockets, and tracers at oncoming aircraft, hitting forty-two planes and downing nine. Hundreds of thousands of rounds poured into the sky, but many gunners died at their batteries.

In some sections of the city the first air raid alarms *(kūshū keiho!)* didn't sound until minutes after the first bombs fell. Six thousand firefighters were deployed on 843 fire trucks, but they were helpless before the conflagration. Houses exploded, buildings burned like ovens, and entire city blocks ignited. The heat turned shallow canals into boiling cauldrons. Water from fire hoses simply vaporized. Men, women, and children ran from flames that surged down city streets as if a dam had burst its locks. They threw themselves into water tanks and stood on rooftops, only to be incinerated or to collapse from asphyxiation as the fires consumed the oxygen in the air. The radiant heat caused dehydration, respiratory collapse, and agonizing death. People crumpled like puppets to two-thirds their normal size. The Germans had a word for it—*Bombenbrandschrumpfleichen*—meaning "incendiary bomb shrunken bodies." Corpses piled up beneath the Kototoi Bridge like thousands of mannequins.

Across the Sumida River in Asakusa, the police and civilian fire wardens urged residents to form bucket brigades, to remove food and valuables from their homes, and to take cover in the nearby air raid shelters. But the fires devoured everything in their path—wood, paper, *tatami,* air raid shelters, clothing, hair, flesh. Hundreds crowded into the 200-year-old Kwan Yin Buddhist temple, dedicated to the goddess of mercy, which had miraculously protected them during the 1923 earthquake, but magnesium firebombs quickly penetrated its roof. Rafters dripping with flames collapsed into the crowds below, setting entire families alight. Those who escaped faced shrapnel and magnesium sparks streaming down from the sky. There was no sanctuary to be had, neither aboveground nor underground, not in Sumida Park nor in the Sumida River.

"The very streets were rivers of fire," said police photographer Ishikawa Takeo. "Everywhere one could see flaming pieces of furniture exploding in the heat, while the people themselves blazed like matchsticks." Tōkyō's citizens died naked, blackened, shrunken in size, their flesh split open like overcooked meat. The police found bodies that had literally melted into one another. Others perished, as Ishikawa's photographs revealed, like the victims of Pompeii, in medias res, their last living gestures petrified in disbelief, mouths agape, silently screaming, hands raised in supplication, knees bent, heads shielded by the crook of an arm, as if trying to hide from the horror, as if trying to go to sleep.

"If you could look down in hell," said Ronald Routhier, "that's just what it would look like."

As he headed back toward Guam, 2nd Lieutenant Bernard Greene, a bombardier from the 314th Bomb Wing, could see "a reddish glow 185 miles out to sea and the curvature of the earth because of it." When Ed Keyser and the boys from the 499th Bomb Group touched down at Isley Field on Saipan, Chaplain William Bray stood by the runway and made the sign of the cross, as he always did at takeoff and landing.

LeMay already knew from Brigadier General Thomas S. Power that the mission had been a "total success," but the airmen weren't entirely aware of the extent of the damage they had inflicted on Tōkyō. Except for one thing: B-29s weren't pressurized when the bomb bays were open. At high altitude, crewmen put on their oxygen masks. At low altitude, the cabin filled with whatever was in the air. And what was in the air over Tōkyō in the early morning hours of March 10, 1945, was the acrid odor of burned human flesh.

"Excellent results," wrote Jules Stillman in his diary. "Biggest and best raid of the season."

An AP article that ran in the Sunday, March 11, edition of *The New York Times* could only wonder at "how many perished in the holocaust." But Secretary of War Stimson, acutely aware of the uproar that had followed the bombing of Dresden, told J. Robert Oppenheimer, director of the Manhattan Project, that he "thought it appalling that there should be no protest in the United States over such wholesale slaughter."

LeMay had no qualms. "We knew we were going to kill a lot of women and kids when we burned that town," he said bluntly. "Had to be done." General Arnold radioed that he was "exceptionally well pleased" with the results.

"I believe that all those under my command on these island bases have by their participation in this single operation shortened this war," LeMay announced in a press release that very day. Churchill had used the same justification for bombing Dresden.

The American firebombing of Tōkyō left 83,793 dead, and 40,918 wounded. A total of 267,171 buildings were destroyed; 1,008,005 people were homeless. Of the city, 15.8 square miles were burned, including 17 percent of Tōkyō's industrial area and 63 percent of its commercial district. The pulse of the city's residential area was stilled. In one night an area more than two-thirds the size of Manhattan had been wiped out.

"Even after all the bones were buried," said Kobayashi Hiroyasu, when it rained over Tōkyō, "a blue flame burned. From the phosphorus. Soldiers stationed there used to say, 'Maybe they'll come out tonight.' Thinking of the ghosts and the blue flames."

It took almost a month to remove the dead from Tōkyō. In the meantime, the XXI Bomber Command launched a strike against Nagoya on March 11, followed by Ōsaka on March 13. Then came Kōbe.

23

Total War

THE INCENDIARY RAIDS demonstrated the woeful inadequacy of Japanese air defense and fire-control systems. For each town *chōkai* (village assocations) were organized, which were divided into *tonari-gumi* (neighborhood associations) of fifteen to thirty households in Kōbe and broken down still further into *rimpo,* organizations of five to ten houses for neighbors' mutual assistance. Families were taught how to extinguish fires, run bucket relays, weather blackouts, and take shelter during bombings. Each home was supposed to be equipped with 40-gallon water tanks, 2.5-gallon buckets, straw mats with which to beat out fires, sand, fire prevention pumps, fireproof clothes, ropes, shovels, and portable ladders. It was recommended that the heads of households study the flow of water from rivers, canals, and ponds.

In December 1944 local municipalities distributed *The Anti–Air Raid Guidelines for Families and Tonari-gumi.* Men were advised to wear steel helmets and leggings during air raids. Women dressed in *monpe* and donned padded *bōkō zukin,* cotton caps that were supposed to "protect the head from the sky," as did their children. Badges identified individual blood types, and emergency boxes were issued that contained parched beans, preserved foods, and first aid. Another government publication, *An Outline for Building Air Raid Shelters,* instructed residents on how to construct their own three-foot-deep shelters beneath the floors of their houses, or build open and covered trenches.

The air raid warning signal (one long blast) and the alarm (a continuous wail) "went off so often it was like the boy crying wolf," said Araki Kiyoshi, who was thirteen at the time. "You trusted it less and less." Schoolchildren were told to get under their desks and cover their eyes and ears during air alerts. They learned how to distinguish enemy carrier-based planes and were taught to run at right angles to evade a fighter's line of fire. Posters denouncing the "American and British beasts" were hung throughout Kōbe, and straw effigies of Roosevelt and

Churchill were woven to allow passersby to stab them with bamboo spears.

But the air raid precautions were as useless against incendiaries as primitive superstitions. Bomb shelters became death traps. Municipal services were overwhelmed by the ferocity of the B-29 assaults. In Kōbe, all the fire battalion chiefs were policemen, and many of those in fire-fighting positions had no fire-prevention training whatsoever. Fire departments lacked CO_2 extinguishers, foam, water tanks with booster pumps, and salvage and wrecking equipment. Kōbe's industries developed their own factory air raid protection forces but were short on fire pumps as well. The city's water supply system was insufficient even under normal conditions.

Only the two and a half miles of tunnels that were feverishly being dug into the slopes of the Rokkō Mountains were safe. Throughout Japan, more than 10 million people would leave the cities for the countryside to escape the American firebombings. Indeed, tens of thousands of women, children, elderly, and infirm fled Kōbe in 1944–45. But by January 1945, an estimated 784,000 people remained behind. Wedged between the mountains and the sea on a strip of land ten miles long, Kōbe made an ideal incendiary target.

"I'm not afraid to fly in combat, but on each mission I become more and more aware of the insipid foolishness of war," pilot Robert Copeland wrote to his mother before the raid. "I don't want to kill anyone. I want to be free to live my life in peace, doing the things I like to do most. . . . It hurts very deeply to have that which is paramount to me connected with fear, pain and even death."

On the night of March 16–17, 1945, 370 B-29s carried out Mission No. 43 over Kōbe from 6,800 feet. *Miss Leading Lady* led the way. The planes were armed with the $M_{17}AI$, a 500-pound cluster of 110 four-pound magnesium thermite incendiaries because stocks of M-69s and M-47s were running low.

The Superforts swept Kōbe from west to east, and then from south to north, dropping a record 2,355 tons of bombs in two hours. It was the most concentrated bombardment to date and the first in which the B-29s encountered fighter opposition from the Japanese. Flak was medium to heavy and close enough for Sergeant Stillman's taste, ripping into the No. 3 engine of the *Beaubomber* and splintering the right front bomb bay door. The Japs were "waking up," as Stillman put it. Three hundred and fourteen enemy fighters—Irvings, Zekes, Tonys, Tōjōs, and Oscars—made ninety-three separate passes at American bombers, but to little effect.

Around midnight the men at the Kōbe POW Hospital were awakened by the short blasts of air raid sirens. They parted the black air raid curtains and looked up in amazement. The B-29s were flying in so low, you could see their identification numbers as searchlights flashed on them. "It was the most spectacular and yet awesome sight we had so far been privileged to see," said Stan Smith. The Americans had finally come. They had rescued POWs in a daring Ranger raid on Cabanatuan on January 29, 1945. They had liberated Manila after a ferocious battle waged by General Krueger's Sixth Army, during which 100,000 civilians died. They had thrown open the gates of Bilibid Prison on February 4, "the most unforgettable day of all of our lives," remarked Pharmacist's Mate Robert W. Kentner. And they had launched the campaign to take back the Rock in a courageous airborne and amphibious assault executed by the 503rd Regimental Combat Team. Now the U.S. Army Air Force dominated the skies over Honshū.

Thank God the B-29s were targeting the waterfront, Fred Berley sighed with relief. The planes were heading to the southwest. The sight of them whipped one Japanese sergeant into a fury. He randomly started beating prisoners with a stick, whacking Fred and Murray between the shoulders. Ōhashi apologized for his behavior. The man was shell-shocked, he explained. Murray thought he must have lost a friend or relative in one of the earlier air attacks.

At Kōbe House the POWs were dressed and standing by as ordered, "waiting for our own building to be hit," said John Lane, an Australian who had been with the 2nd 4th Machine Gun Battalion at the fall of Singapore. Hundreds of antiaircraft guns fired into the nighttime sky. Murray saw one B-29 get caught in the glare of searchlights over the harbor and plunge from the sky. He couldn't help but wonder about the fate of its crew. Then at 0300 Harold Mason, a civilian at Futatabi Internment Camp, watched another B-29 break into pieces over Mt. Futatabi, two miles north of central Kōbe. The Superfort had been rammed by a "Tony"—a Kawasaki Ki-61 army fighter—and burst into flames. Two parachutes mushroomed to the ground. The tail section fell 500 yards from the camp.

Radio operator Robert Doty's plane was one of the last over Kōbe, a "tail-end Charlie." Suddenly a searchlight locked on to it, and the cabin lit up like the Fourth of July. The tail-gunner screamed that a kamikaze was closing in fast, but the gunners had no ammunition. The pilot spotted a dark cloud and dove into it after the bombs were dropped, but it turned out to be smoke from the ground fires over Kōbe. Thermal updrafts bounced the plane around "like a feather in a windstorm. We did everything but turn over. Two minutes later we emerged at 25,000 feet." A whole section of the B-29's floorboards had been torn loose. Staff

Sergeant Doty ended up in the belly of the B-29, still strapped to his chair and secured to the floor, but between two alternators and with a toilet slowly leaking over his head. The plane reeked of smoke.

By the time the raid was over, one-fifth of Kōbe was burned out, including the eastern half of the business district and an industrial sector to the southeast. Five hundred industrial buildings were destroyed, and 162 were damaged, among them the Kawasaki shipyards, which had produced some 2,000 submarines for the Imperial Japanese Navy. A total of 65,951 homes were in ruins; 2,669 people were killed; 11,289 were injured; and 242,468 were left homeless. The Japanese press deliberately downplayed the air attacks and the destruction caused by them. But those on the ground during the raid on Kōbe weren't so easily fooled.

Fujimoto Toshio was sixteen years old, but he went to bed early on the night of March 16. He lived on the east side of Yakusenji Temple in the Minami-Sakasegawa section of Hyōgo Ward in Kōbe. It was a neighborhood of small shops, a movie theater, a playhouse, and numerous temples. Toshio worked during the day as an apprentice at Mitsubishi Electric. After dark the air raid corps made their rounds to urge people to observe the blackout. Oddly, Toshio hadn't heard the air raid siren that night. He awoke to the rumble of aircraft. When he went outside to investigate, he saw what appeared to be a rope falling from the sky. Suddenly night turned into day. It was a flare from *Miss Leading Lady*. Toshio woke his family immediately. They had agreed beforehand that in the event of an air raid, they would meet under the Ōwada bridge. The bridge was reinforced with steel plates to protect it from horse hooves. Toshio had seen POWs unloading cargo there from barges in Hyōgo Canal.

His mother, younger brother, and sister were the first to leave the house. Then a bomb broke through the roof, and Toshio started to run. When he reached the bridge, smoke was pouring out from the passageway beneath it. Toshio was surrounded by flames. He leaped into the canal and landed in a boat. The sea air was cool, but above him flames reached for the sky. This is hell, Toshio thought. The wind picked up, and the boat caught fire. Toshio jumped into a lighter beside it and lost consciousness.

When he awoke, dawn was breaking. Toshio found himself on the shore, pinned beneath an overturned boat. He struggled to get free. There was no one moving anymore on the bridge. A pitch-black corpse lay in a toilet nearby. Half a dozen people were clustered together, burned to death. One of them, he thought, was his younger sister. Toshio suffered compound fractures in both legs. His mother and

brother were badly burned on the arms and legs. His parents were never able to identify his sister's remains.

Thirteen-year-old Tsuji Hideko had been evacuated from Kōbe but returned so she could attend her graduation. Her family lived in a residential sector of Hyōgo Ward, sandwiched between a Kawasaki and Mitsubishi factory. They were startled awake in the early morning hours of March 17 and found themselves in the midst of exploding bombs, their house on fire. Hideko's father, Shimada Kaichi, shouted to the children to dunk their cotton sleeping mats in a pail of water to protect their heads. Her older sister, Kayoko, threw five-year-old Shūji onto her back. Her mother grabbed the baby, Tsuruyo. One-year-old Tadahiro was killed instantly.

They ran toward the Ōwada bridge, but fires licked the sky, drew breath from their own perimeters, and then billowed out into a raging firestorm. Hideko's nine-year-old brother, Masaru, burst into flames. Only his shoes remained. Her mother and father, badly burned on the face, arms, and legs, collapsed at the bridge. Hideko begged a man on the street for help. She was dying. Wouldn't he please help her? He pushed her away, and she fell over her father, who lay unconscious. A blackened body lay nearby. She recognized the change purse—it was her mother's. The force of Hideko's fall woke Kaichi, and together they tried to tamp down the flames with their bare hands. They ran toward the canal, taking little Tsuruyo with them, but the canal was a sheet of fire. Before losing consciousness, Hideko remembered being evacuated by a military vehicle. When she came to, she was in an aid station at Dojo Elementary School. Her skin was so badly burned, it simply peeled off. Her scalp wouldn't stop bleeding. Her mother was dead. Her siblings Masaru, Shūji, and Tadahiro were dead. And now she realized that Tsuruyo must have been dead before she and her father carried him from the Ōwada bridge. His back was blackened. His stomach was untouched, the pale white of a baby's belly.

Mikitani Hiroko was a busy little toddler who had helped her mother, Kimiko, bury the family's possessions in the ground to protect them from air raids. Kimiko's husband, Yashirō, was visiting a nephew in Ōsaka where he worked in the Kawasaki Aircraft Takasago factory. Kimiko was seven months pregnant.

On March 17 their house in Kōbe received a direct hit from a B-29. Kimiko went up onto the roof and tried to toss off the bombs, burning herself badly. Then she grabbed Hiroko while her aunt, Nakahashi

Reiko, ministered to her disabled grandfather. The streets were corridors of flames. The Kempeitai urged residents to "Stay! Protect your homes!" Reiko wanted Kimiko to leave Hiroko with her, but Kimiko refused and carried her on her back. Reiko covered her head and face with a scarf, and when she reached the Ōwada bridge, she jumped. She ended up floating downstream in Hyōgo Canal instead of landing on a barge, as she had hoped. Kimiko stayed where she was. She feared she was going mad. The heat from the firestorm was intense. She couldn't hear or see. Her cries were answered with silence. Then she blacked out. On waking, she found piles of bodies burning near her. She swung Hiroko around to her side. The child was dead. Kimiko prayed for her. She wanted to die with her. She needed to find her sister, her grandfather. She needed to go home, and when she somehow arrived where her house once stood, she found Yashirō, as if he had been waiting for her all the time. He took her to a hospital for treatment, but the doctor didn't believe that the baby in her womb, Masako, would survive.

———————

Only three B-29s were lost in the March 16–17 raid. One was shot down over the town of Oshibe. Another disappeared at sea. By morning, the Japanese located the wreckage of the third plane that had exploded over Mt. Futatabi.

You never heard much about the airmen who didn't make it back. "For a saving grace, we didn't see our dead / Who rarely bothered coming home to die / But simply stayed away out there / In the clean war, the war in the air," wrote the poet Howard Nemerov, an RAF Coastal Command pilot. Not until several days later did Ed Keyser hear about Z □ 8.

Known as *St. Bernard* for coming to the aid of disabled planes, Z □ 8 of the 881st Squadron, 500th Bomb Group had been flying alone at an altitude of 3,300 feet when it was caught in enemy tracers. In the predawn darkness a Tony rammed it from behind. There was a burst of light, a wing fluttered down, and two airmen bailed out before the Superfort went into free fall. The bodies of the other crewmen, said eyewitness Fukada Kaoru, looked as if they had dropped from the aircraft as it disintegrated in the sky.

Five airmen in the tail assembly of the plane were killed instantly. Four others were found below the Futatabi civilian internment camp. A Japanese flight boot was discovered in the debris belonging to ace fighter pilot Captain Ogata Jun'ichi of the Army's 56th Sentai, one of the two main intercept groups in the Ōsaka-Kōbe area. The two survivors were Sergeant Algy S. Augunus, who had a broken leg, and 2nd Lieutenant Robert W. Nelson, a freckle-faced kid from Kansas who walked with

such a proud military bearing that it looked, said his friend Ed Keyser, as if his back were in a brace. The body of the twenty-year-old pilot, 2nd Lieutenant Robert E. Copeland, lay near the point of impact. The letter he wrote to his mother remained unsent among his belongings on Saipan.

The captured fliers were transferred to the Ōsaka Military Prison in Ishikari, where the Central Army had its headquarters. Their fate had already been decided by the Ōsaka Kempeitai. A military tribunal found them guilty of the "indiscriminate bombing" of Ōsaka and Kōbe. The sentence, under the "Enemy Airmen's Act," was death. Asked if he had any last words, Sergeant Augunus stated simply: "I don't hate none of you, because you did your duty as I did my duty, only what I want to say is that this damn war will be over soon and there will be peace forever. That is all."

After a botched beheading that the Japanese tried to cover up, the two Americans were shot in the head at point-blank range.

The winter of 1944–45 was the coldest on record in Japan in more than half a century. Spring arrived with sudden force. Soon it was cherry blossom season, traditionally a time to worship Yama-no-Kami, the mountain deity who was the most powerful god in ancient Japanese cosmology and whose domain was the preserve of mountain cherries (*yamazakura*). The cherry blossoms (*sakura*) were believed to augur the size of the autumn rice crop. The longer the blooms lasted, the more bounteous was fall's reward.

But at the Kōbe POW Hospital that spring, there was growing anxiety among the Japanese. After the first raid in February, the Japanese behaved as if nothing had happened. Ōhashi had arranged a meeting for the American doctors with Kinosita Ryōjun of the pathology department of Ōsaka University. Kinosita had been educated in England, was married to an Englishwoman, and spoke excellent English. The meeting took place as scheduled in Ōhashi's office, but there was no mention whatsoever of the B-29 attack that had preceded it. Their silence was, in itself, alarming.

The March raid was different. The camp administration made the POWs build shelters to protect Japanese personnel and supplies. One was a simple hole dug into the ground, three by four feet, covered with timber and a sheet of tin, and then raked over with soil. Another was built into the side of a terrace and was large enough to stand up in.

Fred thought such measures were useless and only inflamed fears. Besides, the boys in the B-29s were their friends. The POWs could see the raids over Ōsaka across the bay and pooled their money, placing bets on

where the Superforts would strike next. They called it "bombing for yen." Murray felt somewhat differently: there was no such thing as a friendly bomb.

Soon Colonel Murata submitted plans to the Chubu-gun chief and the Ministry of the Army for the relocation of POWS from the Kōbe-Ōsaka area. The idea was to transfer them to camps in the mountains that were considered safe from the American bombings. The subcamps Chikkō, Kōbe, Naruo, Taishō, Yodogawa, Sakurujima, and Umeda were emptied first. All the officers at Kōbe House, with the exception of the medical officers, were moved. Three groups of Australian POWs from Kōbe House would be transferred to Fukuoka and Hiroshima, until only seventy-six members of the original J Force remained as stevedores. The POWs at Ōsaka No. 1 Headquarters Camp and the doctors and staff of the Kōbe POW Hospital stayed behind.

In late March 1945 the Allies could almost taste victory. "The greatest naval armada in history," as *New York Times* military editor Hanson Baldwin described it, was bearing down on Okinawa. The central island in the Ryūkyū archipelago in the East China Sea, Okinawa was the key to an Allied invasion of the Japanese Home Islands. Three hundred forty miles from Kyūshū, Okinawa would serve as an advance naval base and airbase for medium-range bombers. To secure it, the United States committed 1,213 ships—aircraft carriers and submarines, battleships and destroyers, gunboats and oilers—and 170,000 troops in an operation code-named Iceberg.

The Japanese High Command had anticipated enemy attacks against Okinawa, Formosa, Shanghai, and the southern coast of Korea. The purpose of defending them was to wage a war of attrition. The strategy, as explained in the *Outline of Army and Navy Operation*, was "to reduce his [the enemy's] preponderance in ships, aircraft and men, to obstruct the establishment of advance bases, to undermine enemy morale, and thereby to seriously delay the final assault on Japan."

Seventy-seven thousand soldiers from the Thirty-second Japanese Army stood ready to defend Okinawa, augmented by 20,000 Okinawan militia, including young men of the Blood and Iron paramilitary unit, high school girls, and even children. Senior staff officer Colonel Yahara Hiromichi was the man who designed the Japanese operational plan for "the inevitable showdown." It was a plan, he admitted, that was "doomed from the start."

In a frantic attempt to destroy the Allied invasion force as it advanced toward Okinawa, Admiral Toyoda launched Operation Ten-go. Bettys from the 5th Air Fleet swept in from Kyūshū to bomb enemy transports.

Kamikaze were unleashed in mass attacks called *kikusui* or "floating chrysanthemums." Suicidal pilots were strapped to 4,700-pound rocket-propelled bombs that hurtled through the air at speeds up to 600 mph. The Japanese named them *oka,* meaning "cherry blossom"; the Americans called them *baka,* for "screwball." By month's end the carriers *Franklin, Enterprise,* and *Yorktown* were crippled. The *Indianapolis,* flagship of Admiral Raymond A. Spruance's Fifth Fleet, was struck; the destroyer *O'Brien* was badly damaged; and the minesweeper *Skylark* sank after hitting two mines.

On Sunday, April 1, Vice Admiral Marc A. Mitscher's Task Force 58 celebrated Easter by pounding Okinawa with a devastating barrage of rockets and mortars to ease the way for the landings on the island's southwest coast. Sixty thousand men met suspiciously little resistance and were ashore by nightfall. The Americans quickly secured two airfields to the east. Three marine divisions drove south as the 6th Marines forayed north. By April 4 the newly formed U.S. Tenth Army, under Lieutenant General Simon Buckner, had pushed the back of General Ushijima Mitsuru's Thirty-second Army up against the southern city of Shuri. Two days later 700 kamikaze came screaming out of bases in Kyūshū and Formosa to zero in on the U.S. Fifth Fleet, sinking thirteen destroyers. Inland, the Japanese were safely holed up in an extensive network of limestone caves. In spite of stepped-up bombardment, the XXIV Army Corps faced a standoff.

Five days after the Battle of Okinawa began, Hirohito removed Prime Minister Koiso Kuniaki and appointed seventy-eight-year-old retired admiral Suzuki Kantarō, a hard-line imperialist, as head of a new government. On April 8 the Imperial Japanese Army issued Directive No. 2438, "Outline of Preparations for the Ketsugō Operation." In this plan each army—from the First and Second General Armies, to the Air General Army, the China Expeditionary Army, and the Fifth and Seventeenth Area Armies—"will make combat preparations and conduct operations in the overall operation to repel the American invasion of the Homeland, Korea, Karafuto and adjacent waters." Seven areas of operation were designated, from Chishima and the Northern Military District to the Korea Military District. The Kōbe-Ōsaka region was part of the Central Military District. The task of the Fifteenth Area Army, under the control of the Second General Army, was to defend approaches to the Inland Sea in order to keep shipping lanes open.

The objective of Ketsugō was simple: "The Imperial Army will rapidly establish a strategic disposition aimed at the ultimate annihilation of the enemy by strengthening its combat preparations and will encounter the American invasion at key areas on the Japanese homeland."

Turning the homeland into a battlefront called for the stockpiling of arms, ammunition, fuel, and—at the expense of the civilian population—food. *"Ichioku ichigan,"* the slogan went; "one hundred million as one bullet." Or, as the cockpit manual that accompanied Japanese pilots on their kamikaze missions exhorted: "Transcend life and death. When you eliminate all thoughts about life and death, you will be able to totally disregard your earthly life." U.S. intelligence estimated that 6,700 Japanese planes would be available for kamikaze pilots to defend the Home Islands. The actual number exceeded 12,700. To the very end, Army Minister Anami Korechika maintained that the chances of a Japanese victory were "considerable."

———————

The POWs sensed not only a change of mood in the Japanese but a change in behavior. At the Kōbe POW Hospital, the Japanese began to practice *kendō* (the way of the sword). One day a guard asked Murray if he wanted to spar. Murray had fenced in high school, and when he saw the armor (*bōgu*), which consists of a face mask (*men*), chest protector (*dō*), hip and groin protector (*tare*), and padded leather gloves (*kote*), he figured, why not? He would have to get clobbered to get hurt.

Fred thought he was crazy. You didn't challenge the Japanese. During the war with China the Japanese had used Chinese soldiers and civilians for "killing competitions," bayonet and beheading practice. What was Murray thinking?

Murray pushed the line between reason and risk, politesse and provocation. He took pleasure in verbal jousting and the game of one-upmanship. He was skilled at psychologically unbalancing others and then analyzing reactions once defenses broke down. There was an element to his behavior at once playful and controlling, and if John saw the humor in it, others were less amused. Perhaps it was simply egotism that made him think he would be okay; perhaps it was a necessary defense against the reality of his present predicament. He had a natural distrust of authority, whereas Fred respected it—indeed, represented it—though he certainly wasn't afraid to challenge what struck him as bunkum. But Fred had his limits, and Murray's went beyond them, which made the senior medical officer as uncomfortable as if he were watching a less experienced swimmer stray too far from the beach. As far as Murray was concerned, Fred was overreacting. He'd be just fine.

The guard held his wooden sword (*bokken*) with two hands. Murray held it in one hand, as if it were a foil, and went on to explain how points were scored in fencing. When he tapped the guard's chest with the tip of his *bokken,* he was met with a look of incomprehension commingled with fear. Surely the guard knew *kendō,* a requirement for Japanese boys since 1939. But fencing, as it was practiced in Europe and America, was a complete mystery to him. Murray made certain that whatever hybrid sport they were playing in this tournament of East against West, the guard won. He may have been something of a provocateur, but he was nobody's fool. It would have been a terrible loss of face for the guard, with potentially brutal consequences.

Ōhashi himself was on edge. He noticed that Fred, always well groomed, had shaved his head. He called Fred into his office. What did he mean by it? Fred worried that he was losing his hair, which was not uncommon on a slow starvation diet. Ōhashi worried that Fred knew of an impending attack because he had cut off his hair just as Kōbe's citizens had been advised to shear their locks and keep themselves covered during air raids. Fred had had no idea. It was pure coincidence, he replied. Suddenly the ground began to shake. Ōhashi looked at Fred with eyes as wide as saucers, and then he jumped out the window. *Jishin!* Fred followed suit. Kōbe sat on the edge of the Eurasian Plate in an active fault zone. *Jishin!* It was an earthquake.

The firebombings forced the Ōhashis to move from their house in Ōsaka to Nishinomiya, northeast of Kōbe, where the Miyazakis had a large family home. Eighteen-year-old Miyazaki Shunya, who had feared Japan couldn't possibly win a war with America when he first heard the news of the Pearl Harbor attack, had decided to become an engineering student to escape conscription. Shunya suffered from a stubborn case of tuberculosis that resisted Ōhashi's attempts to treat it. One day Ōhashi brought Shunya to the Kōbe POW Hospital, where Page took him on as his patient. Page cured Shunya of his TB, but there was little he could do to improve the food situation in Japan.

"Today there was a ration of beef," read the February 25, 1945, diary entry of Hata Sen'ichirō as it appeared in the *Kōbe Shimbun*. "Happiness. It's been more than a month. Beef on the black market goes for more than 25 yen for 100 *momme* [13.2 ounces]. Sugar goes for 70 yen, though the official price is about 1.5 yen."

In 1944 the average daily intake for Japanese civilians was 1,900 calories. Wheat and dry noodles—substitutes for rice—accounted for 26 percent of the ration. They were then replaced by soybeans, corn, sorghum, and other rough grains imported from Manchuria. Until March 1945 residents of Ōsaka consumed 1,920 calories per day, which was virtually unchanged from three years earlier. But once the firebombings began, rations were reduced by 10 percent and the quality of the food declined. At Ōsaka University students lunched on a little rice, half a potato, a salted plum, and twenty or thirty locusts—caught in nearby fields the day before by lower classmen—boiled in soy sauce and sake. The air raids of March 16–17 had destroyed Kōbe's rationing headquarters, so emergency distribution centers were set up in the western part of the city. By then, rice substitutes constituted 40 percent of the ration, and pumpkin became the staple.

Whether it was rice or a rice substitute, the food was avidly consumed by the POWs down to the last grain. The Dutch prolonged their dining experience by molding rice balls the size of marbles, which they ate over a period of hours. The POWs paid Ōhashi in yen for seeds, and at Kōbe planted a vegetable garden with eggplant, cucumbers, and tomatoes. The vegetables were fertilized with *daiben*—night soil—so they were always cooked, never eaten raw. On one occasion Murray saw a recuperating British POW strolling along with a cane and proudly smoking a pipe when there was no tobacco to be found. Back home Murray had been partial to unfiltered Camels, two packs a day.

"What are you smoking?" he inquired.

"Cherry blossom petals," the man replied with more than a whiff of self-satisfaction.

The cherry trees were nourished just like the vegetables—with night soil.

Better wait for a cigarette, Murray thought with a smile.

———

On April 12, 1945, President Franklin Delano Roosevelt died suddenly of a cerebral hemorrhage, and Vice President Harry S. Truman assumed the presidency of the United States. British and American armies bore down on Germany from the west, and Soviet forces advanced from the east, then converged at the Elbe River on the twenty-fifth. After five years, eight months, and six days, the war in Europe came to a crashing end. German resistance in Italy collapsed, Mussolini was killed by Italian partisans on April 28, and two days later Hitler commited suicide in his Berlin bunker. General Gustav Jodl, the new chief of staff of the German Army, signed an unconditional surrender for Germany that took effect on May 8, which President Truman declared V-E Day, for Victory in Europe.

The news of the fall of Berlin was covered by Harold King in a Reuters dispatch that appeared in Japan's leading newspaper, *Asahi Shimbun* (Morning Sun). The Tripartite Pact was in shreds. The swastika at the German embassy in Kōbe flew at half mast. The "Land of the Gods" no longer seemed invincible. No longer was *Yamato damashii* (the spirit of Japan) sufficient to ensure victory.

Celebrations broke out across America, from the Brooklyn Bridge to the Golden Gate. "THE WAR IN EUROPE IS ENDED!" exclaimed the headline of *The New York Times* on May 8, 1945. There were parades, block parties, and prayers of thanksgiving. Car horns blared, and tickertape poured out of Wall Street windows, while across the country shots were fired and church bells chimed in jubilation. Times Square turned into New Year's Eve at midmorning. But the joy was tempered by those mourning Roosevelt's death and the realization that, as the battle for Okinawa raged, the road to Tōkyō was fraught with peril.

The Combined Chiefs of Staff had assumed that Japan's defeat hinged on an invasion of the Home Islands. At the Anglo-American conference in Yalta in February 1945, they considered the possibility that it might have to be delayed until 1946. In April 1945 the JCS designated MacArthur commander in chief of U.S. Army Forces, Pacific (AFPAC), and in May he was charged with the responsibility for the invasion of Kyūshū. Nimitz was assigned the "conduct of naval and amphibious phases." GHQ/AFPAC would be operational in Manila within a month.

MacArthur's plan, code-named Operation Downfall, was divided into two ninety-day campaigns: Operation Olympic called for the invasion of Kyūshū, and Operation Coronet for the assault on Honshū. General Walter Krueger's Sixth Army, which had liberated Luzon, would spearhead Olympic on November 1, 1945. Coronet would follow on March 1, 1946. The Eighth and Tenth Armies were to land at Sagami Bay, while the First Army was to establish a beachhead on the Kujūkuri coast for a massive assault on the Kantō Plain. Olympic called for 766,700 troops ashore; Coronet required a staggering 1,026,000.

The Allies had crushing air and naval superiority, but in defense of the homeland, Willoughby estimated in March 1945, the Japanese could muster a ground force of 937,000. That same month Japan's cabinet adopted the Decisive Battle Educational Measures Guidelines. With the exception of grades one through six, classes were suspended so schoolchildren could engage in preparations for the final battle. Soon Japan enacted the People's Volunteer Corps Law, which enabled the government to draft or organize into militias all men between fifteen and sixty and all women from seventeen to sixty years of age. Instilled with the "Spirit of Three Million Spears," women were trained to defend themselves with bamboo staves against an American invasion. In one remote prefecture, high school girls were taught to protect their honor with carpenter's awls. "You must aim at the enemy's abdomen," a teacher warned. "Understand? If you don't kill at least one enemy soldier, you don't deserve to die!"

It was total war.

A slew of patients were admitted to the Kōbe POW Hospital in May. Among Murray's cases were Henry Severian Hardt, a civilian worker from Wake who suffered from such severe retinitis, he couldn't see his own fingers within ten inches of his face; William Henry Lidington, a telegraphist with the Royal Navy, whose acute glomerulonephritis turned his urine a sickly reddish-brown and accounted for his grotesque edema and hypertension; Fate O'Brien Bolgiano, another Wake Islander who was physically fit but displayed a host of neurotic symptoms, which gradually disappeared once he was put to work at the hospital; John Roger Hill, an Australian ill with pulmonary tuberculosis; James Frank Lupton, a U.S. Navy Seaman 2nd Class; and Corporal John Edgar Goddard, a 60th Coast Artillery man from Imperial, Nebraska, who also suffered from pulmonary tuberculosis.

One of the more unusual cases was a young POW from Kōbe House who had injured his toe while working as a stevedore. The Japanese neglected to give him a tetanus injection. He was John's patient, but the guards wouldn't let him stay in the hospital. Two days later they brought him back with a terrific infection—the early stages of tetanus. The slightest vibration triggered a spasm so violent that his back arched until his feet nearly touched his head. Ōhashi was able to obtain some tetanus serum from another hospital, but John had to sedate him first so Ōhashi could administer it. After a few weeks the patient began to recover. Rabies at Bilibid, now tetanus at Kōbe: the three navy doctors had never seen such diseases before.

Hunger drove men to extremes. Pharmacist's Mate 3rd Class Russell D. Chamberlin had a psychiatric patient in his charge and was supposed to make sure he was bathed, clothed, and fed. Word got around that Chamberlin was simply feeding himself. What if other corpsmen got the same idea? The worst thing that could happen would be for the men to start turning on one another, Fred thought; he'd make an example of Chamberlin. He took the corpsman downstairs into the cellar and began beating the daylights out of him.

Murray ran after them. "Fred," he admonished, "you can't do that!"

Fred was beside himself. Stealing food from a sick POW? How low could you go? And a corpsman to boot? The son of a bitch. Rage cast reason aside. Discipline collapsed at the sight of its own weakness. Page and John Bookman couldn't believe the scene unfolding before their eyes.

"I can't?" Fred challenged Murray.

"No, you can't," Murray shot back.

"Well, who's going to stop me?" goaded the Golden Gloves champion.

"I am," countered Murray, who was a good half-foot taller, "because I'm a helluva lot bigger than you are."

Fred backed down, abashed at his own behavior. Afterward the doctors drafted a court-martial for Chamberlin and replaced him with Pharmacist's Mate 1st Class Richard L. Bolster.

On another occasion a British POW was accused of stealing Spam but refused to admit it; Fred decided to find out for himself the truth of the matter. He forced a stomach pump down the man's throat and tendered up the incriminating evidence. Stealing food was forbidden, trading food was forbidden, and swapping tobacco—which assuages the appetite but has no nutritional value—was forbidden, but none of the acts excused, Fred felt more keenly than anyone, his own lapse in judgment.

Chamberlin's counterpart was a Japanese orderly named Saki, who kept track of parcels received and distributed to POWs. Private Allen Beauchamp, who had served with the 3rd Battalion, 4th Marines, worked in Saki's office and saw for himself the packages that had been pilfered. But theft was hardly confined to Japanese enlisted men.

Over in Nishinomiya, the Miyazakis were reduced to living on beans, millet, pumpkin, and sweet potatoes. They purchased what was available on the black market and supplemented their diet with fruit and vegetables from the Ōhashi family farm in Wakayama. Shunya remembered Ōhashi bringing back items he had lifted from Red Cross parcels at the hospital: Spam, crackers, grape jelly, Jell-O, Camel cigarettes, even toilet paper. Surely it was wrong, but what else could you do if your family was hungry? The army generals, Dr. Ōhashi told Shunya, were bringing Japan to the brink of catastrophe.

POW corpsmen stealing from their patients. POW doctors beating their orderlies. Japanese guards stealing from their prisoners. Japanese officers stealing what their guards stole. Breaches of discipline on the part of the medical staff at the Kōbe POW Hospital were exceedingly rare, but they showed how thin the moral fabric of camp life was wearing.

Japan was resolved on fighting to the bitter end, the *Mainichi Shimbun* reported after V-E Day. "The Japanese people must be turned into war power," declared Admiral Ōnishi, "and if the enemy should land, they should take up arms and defeat him even if they suffer losses of three and five million. This is not impossible."

Ōhashi saw it differently. "Soon you will be going home," he confided to Fred. The B-29 precision attack on the Kawanishi aircraft plant that spilled over into eastern Kōbe on May 11 reinforced his point: America's technological advantage was incontestable.

But what was home for a man who had been away from it for three and a half years? What was home for someone whose family and friends were not relatives or acquaintances but fellow prisoners? What remained of the life that you had loved and left behind?

―――――――

It had been a long time since Murray had heard from Laura Reade. When he received a letter from her at the Kōbe POW Hospital in May 1945, he opened it with anticipation, silently read it, and kept the contents to himself. She had met someone.

She had been singing up at an Adirondack resort, and one summer afternoon a fellow in the audience had heard her perform *"Là ci darem la mano"* (Give me your hand) from Mozart's *Don Giovanni*. He was smitten.

When he ran into her at the front desk where she handled the incoming mail, he had asked, "Is there anything for me?"

"What's your name?" Laura inquired.

"Blank," he said.

She laughed and asked: "But what's your *real* name?"

"Gerald Blank," he replied.

Gerald didn't think he stood a chance with Laura—she was wild for the camp athletic director. But she agreed to go on a few dates with him back in New York City. They didn't have much money, but they had enough for the movies and cheap seats at the opera. And they got along wonderfully well. She told Gerald she had been dating Murray, and when she referred to a restaurant she and Murray had once gone to, Gerald felt a twinge of envy; he couldn't afford to take her there. She mentioned to Gerald that Murray had gone overseas to the Philippines and was now a POW. Poor guy, Gerald thought, and thought no more about him. He proposed to Laura casually before leaving for basic training down at Camp Jackson near Columbia, South Carolina.

"Do we have any kind of understanding?" he asked her in a taxi.

She replied just as casually, "Oh well, okay."

They were married in May.

Murray could hardly believe the words on the page. He'd been waiting for years, waiting for something. *Absence makes the heart grow fonder.* Waiting for nothing. *Out of sight, out of mind.* It was over, over before he'd even had a fair shot at a beginning. Was that why it had been so long since he had heard from her? It was humbling to recall the thoughts he had had about Laura during his years of captivity, humbling to imagine what she had been thinking about him—if she thought about him at all. He had no way of knowing, of course, that she had remained in contact with the Navy Department, anxiously awaiting word of his whereabouts and well-being. He had never thought she would find someone else to love as he felt she had loved him. She still signed her letters, "Love, Laura," but it was a different Laura, wasn't it? And he was a different person, too, because someone else had claimed his place. She never told him the actual date of the wedding. It was May 28, 1942.

In May 1945 the XXI Bomber Command began dropping tons of propaganda pamphlets over Japanese cities warning civilians of the B-29 raids to come. The leaflets had been prepared in Washington, D.C., and on Guam, written in Japanese, loaded into the bomb bays of weather planes, and released from a high altitude, to be dispersed over as wide an area as possible. Some showed a photograph of Truman; others pictured B-29s littering Nagoya with bombs. One of the most disturbing images was a graphic color illustration of a man being consumed by flames. Another featured a mother dressed in a kimono, weeping before the corpses on the ground. A leaflet entitled "The Living Hell After a Bombardment" read:

> Japanese Citizens!
> From the safety of their splendid air-raid shelters, the military clique boldly urges you to resist. However, your air-raid shelters are nothing but the entryway to death. If you continue your resistance, every day will only bring greater fear into your lives. Bombs will open great craters in your cities, bombs that are dropped on factory districts will destroy your homes while you run around frantically in search of nonexistent shelter, and incendiary bombs will cause great fires that will envelop you in flames and burn you to ashes. All of the bombers will leave terror in their wake.
> You can absolutely not escape. There is no place you can hide, and resistance only means terrifying death.
> Demand the cessation of this hopeless resistance, that is the only path to saving your country.

Allied POWs in Japan had little if any information about impending bombings, unless they gleaned it from the Japanese. Once, when hospital guards saw a squadron of USAAF planes in the distance, they exclaimed: "No! No bombs for Kōbe! Bomb for Yokohoma."

Nor were American airmen briefed in much detail on how to comport themselves in the event of their capture. "Now, if you are taken prisoner—*never*—repeat *never* call a Jap a Jap," they were warned before the March 9

Tōkyō raid. "It is always a Japanese, and say it with respect. Give him some lip or call him a Jap and he'll take your head right off." They were instructed to avoid the emperor's palace and historic Kyōto, the ancient city that housed 253 Shintō shrines and 1,600 Buddhist temples. But they were told nothing about POW camps in their target areas. "And it was a good thing we didn't know," said 1st Lieutenant Leslie E. Hodson, an airplane commander with the 499th Bomb Group of the 73rd Bomb Wing. "We would have tried to avoid them, even though there was little chance of it."

On June 1, 1945, the men at the Kōbe POW Hospital watched 458 B-29s pummel the port facilities and petroleum installations of Ōsaka. They watched with fascination and detachment, thrilled that it was "them" and not "us," while acutely aware that Kōbe was bound to be targeted again. The bombers were armed with incendiaries as well as T_4E_4 frag clusters, which were dropped first to deter any attempts at firefighting. An escort of P-51 fighters accompanied them. A total of 2,788 tons of bombs fell over Ōsaka from 18,000 to 28,500 feet. A relatively small area—only 3.15 square miles—was burned out, but the damage was massive.

The POWs in Kōbe could not see the buildings that collapsed like sand castles, the houses that ignited as quickly as *tatami* mats and *shōji* screens, the mangled, carbon-coated bodies of men, women, and children burned to death as they tried to escape a conflagration that devoured block after city block, neighborhood after neighborhood. In the spectacle of the moment, they watched with as little feeling for the human lives lost as if they were witnessing a forest fire across the bay, in awe of the deadly Superforts, engines of their vengeance, portents of their freedom. The curtain of smoke drawn over the city obscured the cruel reality of 136,107 homes and 4,222 factories destroyed, 3,960 people killed or missing, 218,682 souls left homeless.

Ōsaka No. 1 Headquarters Camp was located in a military zone, bordering the city's industrial district. The camp was equipped with air raid shelters and blackout curtains; the prisoners were drilled in fire prevention. Japanese civilians sought refuge there, believing it would be safe from attack. According to Sawamura Masatoshi, a Red Cross flag was raised atop a bamboo pole. Sawamura acted as a lookout in a guard tower for the B-29s, sounding the alarm when planes approached and signaling the all-clear after they departed. But as Chief Medical Officer David Hochman put it in his diary: "It was very obvious that the area we were in had to be levelled, and so it was." Two incendiaries and one demolition bomb hit the camp, setting off fires that "spread at an amazing speed with terrific heat and intensity," said Hochman. Sawamura found himself surrounded by flames and had to be rescued by Japanese Navy and camp personnel. Within thirty minutes Colonel Murata's headquarters was burned to the ground. Stray chickens and rabbits were roasted alive. POWs suffered injuries but no fatalities. Most of the men were out on work details unloading military equipment, iron ore, bauxite, salt, and foodstuffs from ships in the bay, or they had been evacuated to the Sumitomo pier. The camp galley staff, led by the English Quartermaster Dix, managed to salvage hundreds of sacks of rice, beans, sugar—which was fortunate, Murata let it be known, because no more food was forthcoming from government stores.

The colonel's daughter, Kiyoko, was in Ōsaka at the time of the raid. The force of a concussion threw her on her back, cracking a vertebra. Her hair caught on fire. A dozen women near her lay dead. Corpses floated in the moat around Ōsaka Castle. She remembered fighter planes shooting at anything that moved—women, children, horses, trains, even laundry set out to dry. Kiyoko was taken home to Kyōto, and Dr. Ōhashi paid her a visit, but he had nothing with which to treat her burns except a poultice and vinegar.

The next day Archbishop Marella visited Ōsaka No. 1 Headquarters Camp to survey the damage. An Italian who resided in Tōkyō, Marella was an apostolic delegate. The Vatican was technically neutral during the war, but Italy had been an Axis power until the Fascist Party was dissolved and the armistice was proclaimed on September 8, 1943. Murata had let Marella bring priests into camp for Catholic services. Marella, in turn, commended Murata and Sawamura for their efforts on the prisoners' behalf. But the fate of the POWs under Murata hung by a slender thread.

In the pouring rain, the POWs from Ōsaka No. 1 Headquarters Camp were moved to Tsumori Subcamp No. 13-B. Some 500 men were squeezed into a two-story building that could barely accommodate 150 people. Camp conditions were abysmal, yet Murata threatened to withhold food from the prisoners unless they increased their productivity. The colonel confided to David Hochman that he had received orders from Tōkyō that no prisoners were to be repatriated by their own forces. So that was the plan, thought Hochman. Kill the POWs. He had wondered what might happen to them should Japan be invaded, but he preferred not to dwell on it.

In fact, Tōkyō had issued guidelines concerning the "final disposition" of POWs nearly a year earlier. On August 1, 1944, the chief of staff of the Taihoku Headquarters Camp on Formosa was advised:

Under the present situation if there were a near explosion or fire; shelter for the time being could be had in nearby buildings such as the school, a warehouse, or the like. However, at such time POW's [*sic*] will be concentrated and confined in their present location and under heavy guard the preparation for the final disposition will be made.

The time and method of the disposition are as follows:

(1) The Time.
Although the basic aim is to act under superior orders, individual disposition may be made in the following circumstances:
(a) When an uprising of large numbers cannot be suppressed without the use of firearms.
(b) When escape from the camp may turn into a hostile fighting force.
(2) The Methods.
(a) Whether they are destroyed individually or in groups, or however it is done, with mass bombing, poisonous smoke, poisons, drowning, decapitation, or what, dispose of them as the situation dictates.

The order was not without precedent. On December 13, 1937, the Japanese 66th Battalion in Nanking was directed to execute "all POWs."
In December 1944 the Japanese carried out those plans on the southern Philippine island of Palawan in the Sulu Sea. Fearing an American landing, General Terada Seichi, commander of the Second Air Division, instructed Captain Kojima to dispose of the 150 American POWs at Puerto Princesa Prison Camp. For nearly three years the prisoners there had slaved over building an airfield. To the delight of the POWs, American B-24 Liberators quickly destroyed it on October 28, 1944. The Japanese responded by cutting their rations and forcing them to fill in the bomb craters and dig their own shelters. On the morning of December 14, Kojima heard from headquarters that an American convoy was bound for Palawan. He recalled the men from work, let them have their noonday meal, and then told them that they were about to die. At the sound of an air raid bell, Lieutenant Satō urged the POWs to take cover. But the Americans could see only two P-38s, and they were flying away from the island. Minutes later a second air raid alarm went off, though only one American bomber was in the distance. The prisoners were herded into log-covered shelters, which were surrounded by barbed-wire fences and armed guards. Then the guards poured in gasoline and

torched them. The explosions were nearly instantaneous. Fires raced along the line of liquid, turning the shelters into raging ovens. Black smoke billowed from the earth. POWs ran screaming outside, their hair, clothes, and flesh in flames, only to be machine-gunned or bayoneted to death. Eleven POWs survived the massacre by crawling beneath the fence on the southeast side and scrambling down a sixty-foot cliff to the beach below.

Three months later, on March 17, 1945, the War Ministry produced "Army Secret No. 2257," in which the vice minister of war informed field commanders: "As the war situation has become very critical, I have been ordered to notify you not to make any blunders in the treatment of prisoners of war based upon the attached *Outline for the Disposal of Prisoners of War According to the Change of Situation* when the havocs of war make themselves felt in our imperial homeland and Manchuria."

When Murata told Hochman that no prisoners were to be repatriated, Hochman couldn't believe that the colonel would execute his orders. He'd always gotten along with him. But he kept Murata's words to himself—they would only upset the other POWs.

Japanese plans for the disposition of civilians were no less chilling. In June 1945 the Ōsaka police chief issued a directive: "Due to the nation-wide food shortage and the imminent invasion of the home islands, it will be necessary to kill all the infirm old people, and the very young, and the sick. We can't allow Japan to perish because of them."

———

On June 5, the XXI Bomber Command resumed its campaign to level Japan's major cities with Mission No. 188, a "maximum effort attack" involving the 58th, 73rd, 313th, and 314th Bombardment Wings. The target was the Kōbe urban area. The weather over the Pacific was cloudy with intermittent showers, but it cleared up once the Superforts reached the coast of Japan. Okino Island, in Ōsaka Bay, was the IP (Initial Point). Flying at a ground speed averaging 325 mph and at altitudes ranging from 13,650 to 18,000 feet, the various groups were spaced within four minutes of one another to saturate Kōbe's antiaircraft and firefighting defenses. It was a perfect day for bombing.

The air raid alarms were such a common occurrence at the Kōbe POW Hospital that at 0700 the staff was having breakfast as usual in spite of the fact that sirens had sounded as the sun began to rise. Then at 0730 waves of planes, led by Major Ray Brashear's *Betty Bee* of the 878th Squadron, 499th Bomb Group, began to fly in over the port city on a northeasterly heading. By 0815 they were directly overhead.

"This is it!" Fred said, running through the halls. "This is the big one!"

Doctors and corpsmen hurried their patients down to the main floor and into Ward No. 2. They isolated the tuberculars in a hole in the ground that was covered with a sheet of corrugated tin. They handed out blankets that had been doused in the camp's reservoirs. Red Cross food, clothing, medicine, and equipment were moved into a dugout, and sacks of millet, barley, soy butter, and dried fish were piled nearby. Then they grabbed their medical kits. Murray brought his few worldly possessions outside, hoping they'd survive the raid.

An Australian POW named Mariencek called down to the TB patients in the shelter, "What's wrong with you blokes? You all scared or something?"

A voice came back, "Hell no, I ain't scared."

"Will that bloke who ain't scared please come out and let someone in who is scared?" he replied.

For Sergeant Paul S. Haemmelgar, one of the nonambulatory patients, the situation was anything but funny. Page and Fred had performed an emergency appendectomy on him the night before. Corpsmen carried him to the cooks' quarters. Fred would never forget the look on the marine's face: sheer terror.

Waves of B-29s darkened the sky. The planes first blanketed the harborfront, then swept up toward the Rokkō Mountains. Ernie Irvin thought they might be Russian. He was used to the old USAAF insignia—a white star in a blue circle—and didn't recognize the white bars outlined in blue that had been added to it in mid-1943.

"They're dropping leaflets!" Louis Indorf exclaimed.

"Leaflets, hell," Fred replied. "Those are bombs!"

To the POWs, it was a beautiful sight, hundreds of B-29s flying in perfect V-shaped formations with a terrible kind of majesty. Prisoners emerged from buildings and peered up at the sky as if they were castaways at sea who had spotted a ship on the horizon. The Superforts looked almost dark blue, and were so close together that they seemed to overlap. "It made us feel proud," Murray said, "as if we were not some poor, starved bastards the Japanese could spit on." And it made the Japanese cringe.

"*B-nijōku! B-nijōku!*" they exclaimed. *B-29s! B-29s!*

The same guard with whom Murray had fenced after the mid-March raid grabbed his hand, as if he could somehow stop the bombs from falling and protect them both. The doctors moved over in front of Ward No. 2. Stan Smith went inside the OR.

"When they hit, they exploded with a great big 'whoosh' and tremendous flame, spattering jellied gasoline," Fred recalled. "It was nothing like a bomb blast." Metal, tin, and spent bullets sputtered down from the sky, shrapnel from antiaircraft guns.

Ten 500-pound cluster bombs blasted the grounds, hitting the hospital, the shelter, and the cooks' quarters. Incendiaries fluttered onto the upper floor of Ward No. 2, igniting it instantaneously. Fire breathed out of the hole where the TB patients were huddled and from the dugout where provisions were stored. Stan Smith saw "a blinding flash" and blacked out just as the OR caved in. When he came to, he struggled to free himself from timbers and debris before the entire building was consumed by flames.

A line of fires now ran from the hospital down to the sea. The Japanese stood by as doctors and corpsmen raced through the wards trying to free trapped patients. Murray searched for John Akeroyd in Ward No. 2, only to discover that he had already been evacuated. An Englishman, Sydney Chapman, came staggering out, his clothes ablaze. Ernie Irvin tackled him to smother the flames, burning himself in the process. E. S. Williams was in the passageway to Ward No. 3 when an entire wall buckled, and hearing cries, he dashed in to rescue James Lupton, who was badly burned on the face and hands. Thomas Lyall was buried by a staircase in Ward No. 1, dug himself out, and managed to extricate Bluey Ashworth with the help of Stan Smith and John Page, who had been struck on the back by a fallen beam. A fallen beam was all that saved Dixie Dean when the ceiling collapsed and timbers tumbled down around him in the shape of a wooden tepee. Murray ran back inside Ward No. 2 to make sure they hadn't forgotten any patients. He found one last POW with a leg in a cast cheerfully waiting to be rescued as flames threatened one side of the ward. Murray hoisted him onto his back and carried him, like a father removing a wounded child, from the hospital compound.

Down at Kōbe House the guards took cover so quickly they forgot to unlock the side gate of a building where the POWs were confined, and the building was on fire. As John Lane put it: "When we had been caught in a mortar barrage on Singapore Island, I had been petrified. Waiting for a torpedo to slice through the thin hull of the *Wales Maru* had left me terrified. Now, with a little more maturity, I was merely shitscared." Fortunately a bomb blast enabled the men to escape through a breach. They scrambled to save the contents of the quartermaster store and stocks of medicine. Kōbe House was obliterated, but only one POW was lost. Three Japanese guards died when their shelter was splashed with incendiaries.

A plume of smoke rose 22,000 feet high as fires roared through downtown Kōbe. Bombs landed on a streetcar, incinerating straphangers. A friend of Ferid Kilki, a young Muslim who lived near the Kōbe POW Hospital, was tapped on the shoulder by an incendiary and instantly reduced to carbon. Dozens of women and children walked into a reservoir, only to drown.

Meanwhile, the fires in the hospital compound were burning out of control. POWs threw buckets of water onto the wards and a building nearby. Their efforts were mostly futile, though without realizing it, they had helped save Kōbe's art museum.

Staff evacuated patients up the hill, where Japanese civilians were sitting, lying, and moaning beside the road. Doctors and corpsmen administered first aid, liberally giving injections of morphine to alleviate the searing pain suffered by burn victims. Then, from their perch above Kōbe, they watched Japan's most cosmopolitan city disintegrate before their eyes.

From Kasugano Avenue, the B-29s looked to Tomonaga Kiyoko like a swarm of dragonflies. Her husband had told her to run for safety when the first incendiary bombs sprinkled down "like a shower." Tugging her four-year-old daughter by the hand and carrying her one-and-a-half-year-old son on her back, she fled westward to an elevated road. By the time she reached Wakana Elementary School, people were climbing wooden utility poles trying to escape the flames. The sea was scarlet; the very mountains seemed to be on fire. Burning bodies clung to one another, writhing on the ground. The pavement was so hot that it was difficult to walk. Kiyoko's children were too scared to cry.

Over in Higashi Nada Ward the air raid corps was fighting a losing battle. Araki Kiyoshi threw buckets of water on the entryway to his house and ran. He saw the mother of a classmate get hit by an incendiary and feared he would be next. There were no ambulances in operation. Casualties were rushed to the Minato Minami Hospital on planks, boards, doors—anything that could be used as a litter.

The B-29s departed by heading southeast over the water. In their wake they left buildings stripped to their foundations. Utility wires hung as limply as loose strings. Bottles lay on the ground deformed by the heat. Entire neighborhoods were reduced to embers. Then the rains came, black with ash. Kiyoshi would never forget one burn victim whose body had turned the color of coal: "Under the air-raid hood, the skin had peeled away. It looked like a boiled octopus."

Once the air raid warnings were over, the people of Kōbe began to emerge from the ruins of their city. Men, women, and children carried whatever possessions they could salvage from their homes in baskets and boxes, on their shoulders or atop bicycles. But over on Mt. Nunobiki, in the northeastern part of the city, they saw an ominous sight: a strange red glow in the darkened sky that they feared was another terrible weapon. They panicked at its approach, breaking into a run as it seemed to get nearer and larger. Only when they looked back did they realize what they were fleeing: the sun.

By late afternoon the fires in Kōbe had died down, and the POW doctors returned to the site of their hospital. Paul Haemmelgar was dead; only his torso was recovered. Two tubercular patients were killed, identifiable by their remains: Private Samuel J. Byall, a 4th Marine who had been stationed at Cavite, and Aubrie Arthur Knight. Seventeen POWs sustained first-, second-, and third-degree burns; four others suffered cuts, bruises, and abrasions. It was a miracle that the casualties to POW patients and staff alike were so light.

The OR was gone. The meticulously kept patient records were gone. Most of the food, medicine, and supplies were gone, except for sixty sulfa tablets and four emergency medical kits. The few belongings Murray had tried to save by storing them outside were gone. Ōhashi's office was left standing, and he allowed Fred, John, and four corpsmen to use it as a temporary aid station. The seriously injured were moved into the hospital morgue. The doctors worked until 1800 that evening tending the wounded.

In less than an hour and a half, 473 B-29s had dropped 3,006 tons of incendiaries and 71 tons of high explosives over Kōbe. Within the city 4.35 square miles were leveled; 51,399 buildings were destroyed; 3,614 people were killed; 10,064 were injured; and 179,980 were left homeless. Opposition was the stiffest to date. Between 150 and 160 Japanese interceptors made 647 atttacks. Ray Brashear's *Betty Bee* was rammed and lost its right horizontal elevator. In all, nine B-29s were missing due to fighters and flak and two due to mechanical problems; another 176 were damaged. Mission No. 188 had been an unqualified success.

"Good results," Ed Keyser jotted nonchalantly in his notepad on the way back to Saipan. "Mod. Acc. Flak. Mod. Agg. Ft'rs." To his entries in *Esquire's Date Book* he added, "Huge fires on M.P.I. [main point of impact]."

Since the bombing campaign began, almost nine square miles of Kōbe—a city the size of Baltimore—had been burned out. Nearly three-quarters of its residences and more than half of its industrial structures had been razed to the ground. The largest urban area attack in the region, the June 5, 1945, raid eliminated Kōbe from the list of incendiary targets for the XXI Bomber Command.

Murray refused to believe the casualty figures when he later learned them. It seemed impossible that so many had survived. You couldn't even recognize the city's downtown except for the confluence of streetcar tracks, though some buildings in the industrial area stood out from the path of destruction. "I couldn't tell where we were," he said, "because everything was burned down." Kōbe was a wasteland. When Murray gazed at it from the slopes of the Rokkō Mountains, he saw a city of the dead.

24

Darkness Before Dawn

IT WAS COLD that night. They slept on the ground, many without blankets. The next morning, June 6, 1945, Page and Murray led fifty-seven ambulatory patients on an eight-mile trek to Maruyama, a POW camp in the hills northwest of Kōbe. Any wounded Japanese they came across they treated as if they were their own men. They feared retaliation for the bombings.

The burn wounds were horrendous. Skin ignites because of hydrocarbons in fat that make bodies blaze like fuel. Flesh bubbles with blisters. Noses and ears melt down to cartilage. In second-degree burns, a breath of air can cause unbearable pain. In third-degree burns, limbs char or turn a ghostly white. Patients in such cases are almost beyond pain because the nerve endings themselves have been destroyed. Shock, renal failure, and septicemia are the greatest perils. Without hospitalization, serious burn cases will die.

The POW doctors had no saline solution for fluid replacement. They had no tannic acid or silver nitrate to prevent infection. They had no sterile cotton applicators. They had only morphine to relieve pain. The Japanese were grateful. They welcomed help of any kind. They knew the difference between the POWs and their attackers.

An eerie quiet fell over Kōbe. Smoke rose from ruins as far as the eye could see. Rooftops lay at jagged angles, exposing iron girders twisted from the heat. Lone chimneys poked up through the rubble like the pilings of abandoned wharves. The streets were deserted, littered with burned-out trucks, cars, and trolleys.

Fred and John remained behind with corpsmen Bolster, Hildebrand, and Williams, and Private Allen Beauchamp. There were thirty-nine stretcher cases and thirteen patients who could walk only with assistance—men suffering from malnutrition and tuberculosis and recovering from surgery. Seventeen of them had second- and third-degree burns. The doctors needed help with the evacuation, and they needed food. Fred requested the services of 200 POWs from Kōbe House. In the meantime, they scavenged through a few homes that had escaped the bombing, but found nothing to eat. They picked some green tomatoes that were growing by the creek and made a meal of watery soup. The skies were threatening, and by evening the wind began to blow, presaging rain.

Just as the patients were bedded down for the night, Sergeant Usui Sōcho, assistant to Dr. Ōhashi, arrived with ten soldiers, three litters, and 100 POWs from Kōbe House. Usui told them they had to leave—at once. The corpsmen improvised six stretchers from doors the stevedores brought with them, so now they had a total of nine. Then Fred had to make one of the most difficult decisions in his life: choose who would be carried and who would have to walk, winnowing out the weak from the weakest.

By 2200 the rain turned into a downpour and the wind into a gale. They wandered for miles through the darkness, a pathetic procession of sick and wounded, the half-starved and half-dead, tuberculars who looked like skeletons in the faint glow of embers.

It took four men to bear a stretcher; others shouldered the infirm like human crutches. The guards urged the patients on. Fred pleaded with Ōhashi to slow down.

"Dr. Berley," Ōhashi turned to him and said, "this is one night you will never forget."

"No," Fred swore, "I will never forget it."

They stumbled through the gloom, counting off paces, fighting off sleep. Condemned men, shackled to responsibility, weighed down by adversity. A slip on a rock, a misstep over a root, and you felt like you might break apart because you were shivering with cold, you were caked with mud, you were bone-tired—and hungry.

In the middle of the night Corpsman Richard Bolster was overcome with despair. Hope seemed to have passed him by. This truly was the valley of the shadow of death, he thought, but he found no solace in Scripture. And yet they couldn't stop, they couldn't let their patients down. They could no more ignore the sounds of their suffering than they could turn a deaf ear to a child's cries for help. There was little consolation in company. But through a last summoning of will, through some unknown inner reserve of strength, the doctors and corpsmen shepherded the sick to safety.

Four hours later they arrived at the Kawasaki train station. Ōhashi roused the stationmaster from his sleep so they could take an electric up the toughest part of the grade. When they got off, they faced a steep hike up a narrow, winding street. At 0400 on June 7 the last refugees from the Kōbe POW Hospital finally arrived at Maruyama.

The nightmarish journey had a deleterious effect. A British POW named Cook expired almost immediately. Fred collapsed onto the floor and fell into a deep asleep.

Later that day 458 B-29s returned to hammer the east-central section of Ōsaka. Planes from the 58th Wing carried 1,000-pound high-explosive bombs to knock out the Ōsaka Army Arsenal; 2,540 tons of bombs consumed another 2.21 square miles of the city and destroyed 55,333 buildings. The Ōhashi family home was one of them.

Maruyama means "a circle of mountains." Also known as Kawasaki, the camp was established on December 8, 1942, to house Australian C Force POWs, who helped build an aircraft carrier at the Kawasaki shipyard. Unlike the wood shingle buildings that composed the Kōbe POW Hospital or the brick godowns of Kōbe House, Maruyama consisted of three barracks made from bamboo frame and mud, a guardhouse, a kitchen, and a hospital ward. The compound was surrounded by a twelve-foot board fence.

There had been a shortage of water and food but no shortage of cruelty. The Japanese guards lived up to their nicknames: Dog Face, Black John, Ragged Ass, and Snake. The sole Negro POW in the camp was beaten continually, kept in the guardhouse, and eventually starved to death. As the food situation deteriorated throughout Japan, the POWs were fed "navy stew," a concoction of rice, fish, fish bones, matchboxes, and cigarette butts. Two POWs who had been caught stealing food were strung up by their thumbs from a tree until their feet barely touched the ground; then they were thrashed by the guards in front of the entire camp. The punishment stopped only when the men lost consciousness.

Retribution came from another direction on June 15, 1945, when 444 B-29s dropped 3,157 tons of bombs over Ōsaka and Amagasaki, destroying 1.9 square miles of the former and 0.59 mile of the latter. After three months of bombing raids, 53 percent of Ōsaka—a city the size of Chicago—was wiped out. Two million residents were forced to flee to the countryside. Phase 1 of the urban area program of the XXI Bomber Command was complete. Japan's six most important industrial cities had been burned to the ground. In Phase 2 the Superforts turned their wrath on sixty of Japan's smaller cities, with populations ranging from 100,000 to 350,000. Sometimes they hit as many as four targets in one day.

Ten more patients died as a result of the march from Kōbe to Maruyama. The death toll might have been worse had it not been for Ōhashi's efforts. On June 17, 1945, the POW doctors wrote a letter of appreciation for his assistance under circumstances that beggared description:

Dear Dr. Ohashi

We, the medical officers of the Kobe Prisoner of War Hospital, acting on behalf of the staff and patients of the hospital, wish to offer our deep appreciation and gratitude to you and your staff for the very considerate and kind treatment accorded to us during the past two weeks during which time our hospital has come to such an unhappy end.

Knowing full well of the extent of the disaster which the people of Kobe have experienced and the difficulties which have arisen as a result, we have nothing but praise and thanks for the sincere and untiring efforts which were made by the Nipponese Hospital and Medical Authorities to feed and house us, and to make the sick and injured comfortable.

In our long years spent as Prisoners of War this experience has been one of the most tragic, but its discomforts and hardships have to a very great extent been alleviated by the care which has been given to us.

We therefore hope sincerely for the personal safety and welfare of yourself and your staff and that the future will bring about an early end to this state of danger and anxiety.

We remain, Dr. Ohashi,
Yours sincerely,

John A. Page, Surg. Lieut. Cmdr, R. N.
Stanley W. Smith, Lt. (DC) U.S.N.
Ferdinand V. Berley, Lt. (MC), U.S.N.
Louis Indorf, R.M.O.II., Dutch Army.
M. Glusman, Lt. (jg) MC, U.S.N.R.
J. Bookman, Lt. (jg), MC, U.S.N.R.
E.M. Gonie, R.M.O. II, Dutch Army.

That same day Imperial General Headquarters issued a statement that read, "The day is near when the 100,000,000 people as one man will be in active resistance to the enemy who does not allow any consideration of humanity and of cultural values to stand in the way of establishing a hegemony over the world."

The British and Australian POWs from Kōbe House stayed at Maruyama less than two weeks. On June 19 they were transferred to Wakinohama, a former primary school on the Kōbe-Ōsaka highway, in front of the Kawasaki Steel Rolling Mill and near the railway tracks that ran toward the docks. Flanked on one side by a tank factory with forty-eight chimneys and on the other by a gas works and railway viaduct, Wakinohama had survived the bombing of Kōbe unscathed. Thereafter the Kōbe POW Hospital staff and patients remained the sole inhabitants of Maruyama.

The camp was plagued with problems. It was filthy, sewage flowed freely into an open pit, and the roofs leaked. There was a shortage of potable water, while an infestation of fleas made it impossible to get any rest at night. So the doctors hung their blankets on clotheslines and shook them out before using them. Instead of turning in on beds or bays, they slept on top of tables after placing the table legs in cans of water to deter the fleas. At least there weren't any lice—fleas sucked the blood out of the pesky parasites before they could feed on human hosts.

"We had no medicines, bandages, soap, mess gear—well, in fact we had nothing," said Fred, whose notes on the June 5 air raid were written in the only ink at his disposal: methylene blue dye.

But they knew from Bilibid, Cabanatuan, Tsumori, and Ichioka exactly what they had to do, and after two weeks the buildings had all been scrubbed down, the garbage was collected and burned, the sewage pit was covered, and a fly-catching campaign was under way. Rags were used as bandages, then washed and dried in the sun so they could be used again every three or four days. When the doctors discovered maggots inside wounds, they were at first repulsed and then amazed at how effective the creatures were at debriding, dissolving dead tissue, and stimulating healing. One British burn victim, Tom Taylor of the Royal Navy, later reported to Fred that his maggot-cleansed wound had left "just a few small scars here and there." The larvae of blowflies, maggots were indefatigable, but once they began to nibble on raw flesh and nerve endings, it became "extremely uncomfortable for the poor patients," noted Fred.

By the summer of 1945 the average daily caloric intake for Japanese civilians had plummeted to 1,680. By then the government had reduced the staple food ration from 1,160 to 1,040 calories a day. Nearly a quarter of Japan's urban population was afflicted with serious nutritional deficiencies.

In contrast, POWs at Maruyama consumed roughly half the national average. Fred took to bending a pin into a hook to catch finger-sized fish from the camp pond, which he gave to the sick. There was little else the doctors could do to improve their lot. Without access to the black market, the money they had was useless. Food stocks were kept in reserve for the military. Civilians were told to supplement their meals with weeds—chickweed, mugwort, plantain, and thistle. Elsewhere in Japan children were literally starving to death.

POWs received 70 grams of millet a day, a small bun and a half, and either a small squash or a portion from eight eggplants that were divided among 129 men. For an entire week, the daily intake at Maruyama hovered around 800 calories. At that rate the body begins to consume itself. In Western Europe during the winter of 1944–45, the diet had been even less, but it was comparatively rich in whole grain breads and vegetables. Undernourished since MacArthur officially implemented half rations in January 1942, the navy doctors estimated that they had six to eight weeks to live.

"So many could only be described realistically," said Stan Smith, "as healthy-looking cadavers."

Fred, whose weight had dropped from 150 to 110 pounds, was so exhausted that all he could do was make his sick calls in the morning, lie down and rest, make another round of sick calls in the afternoon, and rest again. Murray's weight had plunged from 200 to 159 pounds. John went from 150 to less than 112 pounds. Akeroyd, who in good health was a robust 260 pounds, weighed less than 100, and Allen Beauchamp checked in at 85. A loss of 25 to 30 percent of original body weight constitutes severe semistarvation. Most human beings won't survive weight losses exceeding 35 to 40 percent.

Starvation lowers blood pressure, weakens the pulse, and causes a decrease in the basal metabolic rate. Desperate for sustenance, the body burns tissue for fuel. Your neck thins, your shoulders lose their padding. Fat around the buttocks and abdomen melts away. Your waistline cinches. Ribs and vertebrae poke through a taut envelope of skin. Your bones actually grow thinner, and your skeleton may shrink. As your muscles atrophy—conspicuously on the upper arms and thighs—your vital organs and glands get smaller. The hair on your head turns coarse, but facial hair feels silky soft—babylike. Fingernails no longer grow as quickly as they used to, your face may discolor, and your urine might turn pale. Movement takes greater effort, muscles ache, and extremities can tingle with heat or cold. But while you have less energy, less strength, and less endurance, and you may suffer a loss in visual acuity, your brain remains unaffected until you lapse into unconsciousness.

The POWs grew anxious, irritable, and depressed. They fought over rations and stole from one another. They bartered for morsels and debased themselves before their captors. Some gulped down their food. Others played with it or squirreled it away to make it last as long as possible. They no longer dreamed at night. They no longer fantasized. They lost their faith in God. All day long a queasy emptiness gnawed at their stomachs, though in the final stages of starvation, you experience no hunger at all.

Some POWs were suspicious of one another, fearful and angry. They sniffed out food wherever they thought there might be something edible, convinced that others were getting more while they had less. Sometimes they were right.

One day the Japanese quartermaster embarked on an eight-mile trek with two Americans, two Englishmen, and one Australian for a salvage detail at the former Kōbe POW Hospital. Their reward, said the quartermaster, would be a noontime meal. It was a lovely summer day, but hunger clutched at their stomachs. They grated on one another, knowing what a man would say before he even said it—or at least thinking they knew—and wishing he would shut up. But they always shared their tobacco.

By the time they arrived at the old hospital at 1400, they still hadn't eaten. With hope and hesitation in their voices, they asked the quartermaster when they would have their promised meal.

He smiled, baring broken teeth, and said, "*Ima,*" meaning now. "*Meshi, meshi,*" he added, meaning food, or rice.

"How much?" asked the corpsmen.

"*Takusan,*" he replied, or plenty.

The word, said Richard Bolster, "threw us into ecstasy."

The scene took on a luminous quality. Hope shone through the destruction around them. The evergreens on the slopes, the soft afternoon sky, the harbor shimmering in the distance. "A beautiful rosebush clung bravely to a trellis," remarked Bolster, "both adjacent to a tree that had been scorched. I thought then how inseparable are life and death, but it was still a rosebush and still alive and therefore still beautiful."

The quartermaster led them to a rusty cauldron and a sack of rice. Almost simultaneously the five POWs burst into laughter. Suddenly everything seemed all right. Tensions relaxed, animosities were forgotten, and friendships were rekindled because there was food, and plenty of it for everyone. They cleaned the rice, set a fire, scoured the cauldron, and then watched the grains turn plump and soft in the boiling water until they were cooked to delectation.

"Rice was life," affirmed Bolster, "and we had *takusan.*" After a second bowlful, they saved the leftovers in a wooden bucket, placed it in a hand-held cart beside the burned hospital blankets they recovered, and began the journey back to Maruyama. They were halfway home by dusk when they stopped for a break. The quartermaster advised them not to eat in front of Japanese civilians. So much food was bound to raise questions when so many had so little. The moon was high by the time they climbed the last steep hill to Maruyama. A dog barked in the distance. Birds chirped in the pine trees. Said Bolster:

I remember musing that somewhere, people walked arm in arm and found love and beauty in each other, things that we had all but forgotten. The camp seemed right for us. It was a dim dream that we had ever been free men. It was an even stranger fantasy that we would ever be free again, though we sensed that enough. . . .

Right then we had had enough and still had enough rice. That was the important thing.

But enough for some wasn't enough for everyone. One day Fred, John, and Murray watched a cat crawl over a fence. A symbol of healing in ancient Egypt, a gastronomic delicacy in China, a beloved house pet in the West, it was something a hawk might swoop down on and devour if one were spotted unawares on a country road, something a coyote might kill, a dog might attack—certainly not what an American, even one mired in poverty, would consider consuming. But the doctors were far beyond any such consideration. They had no moral or ethical qualms, no shred of feline affection, no gustatory contempt. They saw one thing only: food.

"You could see the same thought cross our faces at the same time," John said. They trapped the cat, "expertly disemboweled it, as you would expect of doctors," he added, and tossed it into a pot of water, which was brought to a boil on a hot plate wired by one of the POWs from Wake Island. They added a few greens, cooked it until tender, and ate it. Fred couldn't stomach the broth, but meat was meat, even if, to Murray's taste, it was "gamey as hell."

The guards at Maruyama had become more belligerent and were practicing their swordstrokes. This time Murray had the good sense not to join them. Fred had found four iron rods and told John, Murray, and Richard Bolster about them. They also located in the floor of a deserted building a tunnel that they believed ran outside the camp. An escape hatch, if they needed one. In fact, two POWs—Private Rodaway and Private Smith—had attempted escape from Maruyama in June. They were caught, tried, and sentenced to fifteen years in Ōsaka Military Prison. The navy doctors shared their secret with only a few other POWs. Fred assumed the Japanese would kill them all should the Americans invade Japan—if they hadn't starved to death in the meantime. And the Americans were tantalizingly close to achieving that goal.

Okinawa was the Normandy of the Pacific. Operation Iceberg succeeded in securing the island as a stepping-stone for the invasion of Kyūshū.

American casualties were high; Japanese losses were catastrophic. General Ushijima's ill-conceived counteroffensive of May 5 alone cost 5,000 Japanese lives. Native Okinawans searched desperately for cover as the two lines grew closer together. Mothers in hiding were told to hush their babies: the Americans, who rooted out the Japanese with flamethrowers in cave-to-cave fighting, would hear them. On May 31 Shura was captured, and on June 21 Ushijima issued his final order for the continuation of a guerrilla war. Then he committed suicide.

Should the Americans capture Okinawa, "every man will be killed, flattened under bulldozers, every woman will be raped and re-raped," *heitai-san* (friendly soldiers) warned students of the Okinawa First Girls' High School who had been mobilized as nurses. Captain Akamatsu Yoshiji ordered the islanders to commit mass suicide. Thousands leaped to their deaths from Mabuni Cliff.

In the Battle for Okinawa 7,830 Japanese planes were downed. The Thirty-second Army was decimated. The mighty *Yamato*, the world's largest battleship, was sunk. As many as 110,000 to 150,000 civilian lives were lost, including 1,105 high school boys and 263 girls. An unprecedented 11,000 Japanese were eventually taken captive; 12,500 Americans were killed—more than the entire American contingent on Corregidor—among them Lieutenant General Simon Buckner, four days short of his objective of capturing the island. Celebrated war correspondent Ernie Pyle died in a hail of machine-gun fire during the fight for Ie-Shima. Some 49,000 Americans were wounded.

"If Okinawa is lost," Colonel Yahara heard Japanese officers say during the final stage of fighting, "Japan will certainly fall." But Yahara himself believed there would be one last battle for the homeland.

On July 26, 1945, the United States, Britain, and China delivered Japan an ultimatum that had been drawn up in Potsdam, Germany, over the preceding two weeks. The Potsdam Declaration was a thirteen-point proclamation that called for the elimination of "the authority and influence of those who have deceived and misled the people of Japan into embarking on world conquest"; adherence to the Cairo Declaration of November 1943, confining Japanese sovereignty to the four main islands, Honshū, Hokkaidō, Kyūshū, Shikoku; the prosecution of Japanese war criminals; the removal by the Japanese government of any hindrance to democracy; and "the unconditional surrender of the Japanese armed forces." "The alternative for Japan," the Potsdam Declaration concluded, "is prompt and utter destruction."

MacArthur was never consulted by the Allied leadership before the

terms of the Potsdam Declaration were aired. Had his advice been solicited, he would have made his position clear: the Japanese people had
to be reassured that the emperor would remain on the throne.

The response of Japan's Supreme War Leadership Council to the
Potsdam Declaration was divided. Foreign Minister Tōgō Shigenori
thought the terms were less severe than the Cairo Declaration, which demanded the "unconditional surrender of Japan." That view was supported by Navy Minister Admiral Yonai and Prime Minister Suzuki.
Through the "good offices" of the Soviet Union, they hoped to achieve
an honorable peace. But General Anami Korechika, the army minister,
General Umezu Yōshijirō, the army chief of staff, and Admiral Toyoda
Soemu, navy chief of staff and a member of Umezu's family clan, dis-
sented. They were resolved to prosecute the war unless their terms were
met: the Allies had to acknowledge the emperor's inviolability; there
could be only minimal occupation of Japan, from which Tōkyō was exempt; and Japan would disarm herself and try her own war criminals. At
a July 29 press conference, Suzuki announced only, "We will simply
mokusatsu it," meaning "kill it with silence." His ominous ambiguity was
interpreted as a flat-out rejection of the Allied ultimatum.

General Anami had expected the United States to invade the Japanese mainland as early as July, then revised his estimate to August 1945.
The Imperial Japanese Army's strategy was to amass a force twice the size
of the enemy's in the hopes of destroying two-thirds of the invaders at
sea and on the beaches and the remaining one-third inland.

U.S. Army Chief of Staff George Marshall estimated Japanese troop
strength in Kyūshū and the Ryūkyū Islands (not including Okinawa) at
half a million. In southern Kyūshū alone, the number of Japanese soldiers had increased from 80,000 to 206,000 men, according to a report
received by MacArthur's headquarters on July 29, "with no end in sight."

Marshall had originally projected Japanese Army, Navy, and Air
ground forces on Kyūshū at 350,000 by November 1, 1945, but the
Japanese had attained that number more than a month before Potsdam.
By August 2 the U.S. War Department's Military Intelligence Service
put Japanese manpower on Kyūshū at 534,000, a figure that would be
revised to 549,000 and then to 600,000. In actuality, the Japanese had
assigned 900,000 troops to the defense of Kyūshū alone. The final estimate for the combined strength of Japanese forces in the Home Islands,
according to the Joint Intelligence Committee of the Joint Chiefs of
Staff, was raised to 2.6 million men.

In spite of upwardly revised estimates of Japanese manpower, Marshall held to an American-led invasion force of 766,700. American casualties were estimated "at a minimum a quarter of a million," Truman

wrote, quoting Marshall. This was nearly twice the casualty figure for MacArthur's campaigns in the Philippines, Iwo Jima, and Okinawa combined. Japanese military and civilian deaths on Kyūshū have since been conservatively projected at 580,000 to 630,000. But before the wording of the Potsdam Declaration was even finalized, Truman made a fateful decision.

———

On August 8, 1945, the cooks at Maruyama went out of the camp for provisions and returned with a copy of the *Asahi Shimbun* that ran a tantalizing headline: "ENEMY DROPS NEW-TYPE BOMB ON HIROSHIMA. AIR RAID CONDUCTED BY SMALL NUMBER OF B-29S. CONSIDERABLE CASUALTIES; PARTICULARS UNDER INVESTIGATION." The subhead added: "Attached to a Parachute, Exploded in Mid-Air. A Savage New Bomb with a Disregard for Humanity." Based on an Imperial General Headquarters communiqué, the full text of the article ran as follows:

A little after 8 a.m. on the 6th, a small number of enemy B-29s penetrated Hiroshima and dropped a small number of bombs. As a result, a considerable number of buildings in the city were destroyed, while fires broke out all over the city. It appears the enemy used a new-type bomb in this attack, and it appears that this bomb was dropped with a parachute and exploded in mid-air. Investigation is under way regarding the power of the bomb, but it cannot be taken lightly.

In using this new-type bomb, the enemy has openly undertaken a scheme to kill and maim innocent people. We must not overlook the fact that impatience with the course of the war lies behind the enemy venturing to engage in this inhumane action. The enemy that has engaged in such inhumane savagery has no right to immediately resume talking about justice and humanity.

It is expected that the enemy will use similar bombs in the future, and the authorities will provide direction concerning countermeasures, but until then it is necessary to accelerate existing anti–air raid measures, namely, the rapid evacuation of cities, as well as the preparation of underground air-raid shelters and other measures. As we have seen in this latest enemy attack, although it was a raid by a small number of planes, it is dangerous to treat such an attack too lightly.

In conjunction with the first use of the new-type bomb, the enemy has engaged in all kinds of exaggerated propaganda, and it appears that Truman has already made an announcement concerning the use of a new-type bomb. We must not be distracted by this, but every one of us, each with his own strong spirit of enmity, must intensify his air-raid precautions.

The account in the English-language *Mainichi Shimbun,* "A National Newspaper for International Readers," was nearly as brief as the official one:

> A small number of enemy B-29s penetrated into Hiroshima on August 6 shortly after 8 a.m. and dropped a number of explosive bombs, as a result of which a considerable number of houses in the city were destroyed and fire broke out in various places.
>
> It seems that the enemy dropped new-type bombs attached to parachutes which exploded in the air. Although details are still under investigation, their explosive power cannot be made light of.

What neither newspaper stated because of a dearth of information was that 118,661 civilians had been killed in a flash, and an additional 79,130 were injured. The lack of details, coupled with a seriousness of tone on the one hand and moral castigation on the other, signified an event of extraordinary magnitude that was utterly without precedent.

The news was puzzling to the POWs in Maruyama. A small number of planes? A small number of bombs? It could mean only one thing, thought Murray, who had minored in physics and was well aware of Ernest Rutherford's experiments in splitting the atom. Surely, he told Fred, it was an atom bomb.

Hiroshima lies 150 miles from Kōbe. Less than twenty-four hours before the bombing, theoretical physicist Mimura Yoshitaka of Hiroshima Bunri University was lecturing 600 army officers from the Hiroshima garrison.

"Could you tell us, sir, what the atomic bomb is?" asked a young lieutenant colonel. "Is there any possibility that the bomb will be developed by the end of this war?"

"Well, it's difficult to say," the professor replied, after explaining that Dr. Nishina Yoshio and scientists at the Tōkyō Institute of Physics and Chemistry had solved the mystery of nuclear fission. "But I can tell you this much: not before the end of this war."

In Tōkyō, Foreign Minister Tōgō Shigenori advised Hirohito that the Potsdam Declaration should be accepted as soon as possible on the dubious grounds that it would not compromise His Majesty's sovereignty. The emperor instructed Tōgō to inform Prime Minister Suzuki that the war should be terminated without delay. Japan could not risk another tragedy such as Hiroshima. But an emergency meeting of the Supreme War Leadership Council was mysteriously postponed because one of its members had to attend to "more pressing business."

Back in Washington, Truman warned that "a rain of ruin from the air, the like of which has never been seen on earth," would ensue if Japan did not accept the Allied terms of surrender. MacArthur, who like Nimitz learned of the atom bomb only shortly before it was deployed, felt that it was "completely unnecessary from a military point of view" to effect a Japanese surrender.

That same day in Moscow Soviet foreign minister Vyacheslav Molotov divulged to Japanese ambassador Satō Naotake that "the Soviet Government declares that from tomorrow, that is from August 9, the Soviet Union will consider herself in a state of war against Japan."

On August 9, three months after Germany's surrender, the USSR invaded Manchuria. Later that morning an emergency meeting of the Supreme War Leadership Council was convened. At 1102, while the meeting was in session, the B-29 known as *Bock's Car* unleashed a plutonium bomb 1,540 feet over Nagasaki.

William L. Laurence of *The New York Times* accompanied the mission. "Does one feel any pity or compassion for the poor devils about to die?" he asked. "Not when one thinks of Pearl Harbor and of the Death March on Bataan." As a result, 73,884 people perished and 74,909 were injured.

Laurence watched an entire city vanish beneath a pillar of fire that in a matter of seconds rose 60,000 feet in the air. Yet his words reflected the national sentiment as articulated by President Truman:

> Having found the bomb, we have used it. We have used it against those who attacked us without warning at Pearl Harbor, against those who have starved and beaten and executed American prisoners of war, against those who have abandoned all pretense of obeying international laws of warfare. We have used it in order to shorten the agony of war, in order to save the lives of thousands and thousands of young Americans.

Prime Minister Suzuki, Foreign Minister Tōgō, and Navy Minister Admiral Yonai argued in favor of accepting the Potsdam Declaration on condition that the imperial house and throne be preserved. Army Minister General Anami and the chiefs of staff of the army and navy, General Umezu and Admiral Toyoda, refused to make any further concessions. The conference was deadlocked. Just before midnight a full-dress meeting was held before the emperor in a bomb shelter beneath the Imperial Palace. Finally, at 0200 on August 10, Suzuki rose and said softly:

> Gentlemen, we have spent hours in deliberation without coming to a decision and yet agreement is not in sight. You are fully aware that we cannot afford to waste even a minute at this juncture. I propose,

therefore, to seek the imperial guidance and substitute it for the decision of this conference.

Then the forty-five-year-old emperor made his "sacred decision," or *seidan*. "That it is unbearable for me to see my loyal troops disarmed goes without saying," Hirohito acknowledged. "But the time has come to bear the unbearable." Japan would surrender "with the understanding that the said declaration does not comprise any demand which prejudices the prerogatives of His Majesty as a Sovereign Ruler."

Washington replied through a San Francisco broadcast that reached Tōkyō around 0400 on August 12. The formal American response arrived in Tōkyō from Secretary of State James Byrnes via the Swiss government on the morning of August 13. The ruling authority of the emperor and of the government of Japan was to be "subject to the Supreme Commander of Allied Powers who will take such steps as he deems proper to effectuate the surrender terms." The emperor would be required to order the Japanese Army, Navy, and Air Force "to cease active operations" and lay down their arms. In addition,

> Immediately upon the surrender the Japanese Government shall transport prisoners of war and civilian internees to places of safety, as directed, where they can quickly be placed aboard Allied transports.
>   The ultimate form of government of Japan shall, in accordance with the Potsdam Declaration, be established by the freely expressed will of the Japanese people.

Washington's response did not explicitly accept Tōkyō conditions. In the meantime Truman ordered the continuation of the bombing of Japan. Amagasaki, near Ōsaka and Kōbe, was targeted on August 10–11. Tsuchizaki, 95 percent of which had been destroyed, was scheduled for August 14–15. Between August 11 and August 14, B-29 attacks caused another 1,250 deaths and 1,300 injuries. Tōkyō would be the next target, Truman hinted to the Duke of Windsor on August 14, with a third plutonium-type bomb if Japan did not unconditionally agree to the Allies' terms. The American reply had to be accepted immediately, Hirohito told Tōgō, a demand he reiterated at a joint imperial conference of the cabinet ministers and the Supreme War Leadership Council on the morning of August 14:

> If we do not terminate the war at this juncture, our unique national structure will be destroyed and our nation will suffer extermination.

If we save anything, be it ever so little, we could yet hope to rebuild the nation in the future. I urge upon you, therefore, to accept the reply at once and save the nation, alleviating their untold sufferings.

"The Emperor was in tears when he pronounced his verdict," said Kase Toshikazu of the Japanese Foreign Office. Hirohito made no mention of the "untold sufferings" of Allied prisoners of war in Japan.

At noon on August 15, 1945, the guards at Maruyama were huddled over a radio. The sight struck Fred Berley as distinctly odd. They were listening to a high, reedy voice they had never heard before, the sacred Voice of the Crane. In a six-minute recorded broadcast, the emperor, in formal court language, read the Imperial Rescript Ending the War:

> After pondering deeply the general trends of the world and the actual conditions obtaining in our Empire today we have decided to effect a settlement of the present situation by resorting to an extraordinary measure.
>
> We have ordered our Government to communicate to the Governments of the United States, Great Britain, China, and the Soviet Union that our Empire accepts the provisions of their joint declaration.

The speech presented Hirohito as a pacifist and antimilitarist and adumbrated a new role for him in postwar Japan. Japan's aggression against America and Britain, the emperor explained, was never meant "to infringe upon the sovereignty of other nations or to embark upon territorial aggrandizement." On the contrary, it was intended "to ensure Japan's self-preservation and the stabilization of East Asia." But despite nearly four years of "gallant fighting . . . the war situation," he said with stunning understatement, "has developed not necessarily to Japan's advantage, while the general trends of the world have all turned against her interest." In the first official acknowledgment of the atomic bomb's destructive power, he admitted that those trends included the enemy's deployment of "a new and most cruel bomb" resulting in the loss of "many innocent civilian lives."

Hirohito expressed neither regret to the peoples that Japan had vanquished nor remorse to his conquerors, only appreciation to his East Asian allies; that is, to his collaborators in Malaya, Indochina, and the Dutch East Indies. Nearly three million Japanese lay dead as a result of the war. While the emperor conceded that continued fighting would result in Japan's complete destruction, the nation's choice to cease hostilities, he suggested, was a noble sacrifice that would prevent "the total extinction of human civilization."

> We are keenly aware of the inmost feelings of all you, our subjects. However, it is according to the dictates of time and fate that we have resolved to pave the way for a grand peace for all the generations to come by enduring the unendurable and suffering what is insufferable. Having been able to save and maintain the structure of the Imperial State, we are always with you, our good and loyal subjects, relying upon your sincerity and integrity.
>
> Beware most strictly of any outbursts of emotion that may engender needless complications, and of any fraternal contention and strife that may create confusion, lead you astray and cause you to lose the confidence of the world.
>
> Let the entire nation continue as one family from generation to generation, ever firm in its faith in the imperishableness of its divine land, and mindful of its heavy burden of responsibilities, the long road before it. . . .
>
> All you, our subjects, we command you to act in accordance with our wishes.

The words "surrender" and "defeat" were never even mentioned.

Hirohito's words were heard by millions throughout Japan. Men and women openly wept. They knelt and bowed in the direction of the Imperial Palace to apologize for losing the war. Others were left scratching their heads. Radio announcer Wada Shinken reread the rescript in ordinary language. What did it mean? Wada made it clear when he remarked: "We ourselves invited a situation in which we had no choice but to lay down our arms. . . . Since the situation has developed this way, the nation will unite and, believing in the indestructibility of the divine land, put all of its energies into rebuilding for the future." Few realized that in the predawn darkness there had been an army plot to seize Hirohito and free him from the hands of the defeatists; that the commanding general of his personal guard division had been assassinated; or that troops had surrounded the Imperial Palace in an attempt to impound his recorded message and enable him to prosecute the war.

The POWs at Maruyama had no idea why the camp guards had been listening so intently to the radio. Fred merely saw an opportunity to steal an ear of corn from the garden directly in front of where the guards were sitting. He shared it with John and Murray, and they ate the corn, cob and all.

Ōhashi seemed to have disappeared. When he called the POW doctors into his office, they knew something unusual had happened. Ordinarily Ōhashi wore an undershirt and house slippers. Today he was dressed in full military regalia. He sat behind his desk, his pallor wan, his demeanor dejected. In halting English he said, "For you—I have good news." He trembled as he held a piece of paper. "The war is now past!"

Page put a hand to his forehead and staggered back. By God, it was true.

But the very phrasing of Ōhashi's announcement suggested that the news was anything but good for the Japanese doctor.

Ōhashi proceeded to call a camp assembly and address the POWs at large. They were tense with anticipation. Could it be what they had hoped?

Ōhashi was brief and to the point. "The war is now over!" he said in heavily accented English. "There are three reasons. The emperor has ordered all countries to cease fighting."

The POWs chuckled at that one.

"The Americans have invented some kind of atomic bomb."

There were murmurs of acknowledgment.

"And," he concluded, "we have no more navy!"

The POWs roared with laughter. They whooped with joy, waved their arms, and slapped one another on the back. The Americans broke into "The Star-Spangled Banner," the English and Australians joined in with "God Save the Queen," and the Dutch followed with "Wilhelmus." The waiting and yearning, the scheming and dreaming, the abuse and neglect were finally over.

The Britishers quickly raised over the camp a Union Jack that they had stitched together from remnants of clothing. Down at Wakinohama flags from four nationalities—American, British, Dutch, and Chinese—flew overhead, to the annoyance of the Japanese. Old grudges were forgotten, old debts forgiven as the men anticipated their homecomings, made plans that they knew, this time, they could realize: the first home-cooked meal they'd eat, the first girl they'd call, the first movie they'd see.

And when the excitement died down, when their voices were hoarse from shouting, and when the thrill of the moment had tempered into reflection, they thought of their buddies left behind in the Philippines. Like George. But they'd be seeing him soon enough, right? It was only a rumor they'd heard about him, and by now they'd heard so many that they didn't believe any. They'd have that blowout in San Francisco after all, and at Murray's expense!

The night before, more than a full week after the destruction of Hiroshima, the Japanese Foreign Office had sent a telegram to the Allied powers informing them that "His Majesty the Emperor has issued an Imperial rescript regarding Japan's acceptance to the provisions of the Potsdam declaration." Truman received the message from Secretary Byrnes via the Swiss chargé d'affaires in Washington on the afternoon of August 14. The State Department had anxiously awaited a response from Tōkyō. After a hastily called press conference at 7:00 P.M. that sent reporters scrambling to relay the news, the president addressed the crowds gathered in front of the White House lawn.

"This is a great day," Truman announced, "the day we've been waiting for. This is the day for free governments in the world. This is the day when fascism and police government ceases in the world."

Half a million people swarmed through the capital to celebrate. Civilians and servicemen snaked into conga lines in Lafayette Square. Throngs of people descended on San Francisco's Market Square. In Manhattan, when the words "OFFICIAL—TRUMAN ANNOUNCES JAPANESE SURRENDER" flashed across the electric sign on the Times Tower at 7:03 P.M., a deafening roar rose from spectators who had waited hours for the news. Cars honked, truck horns blared, and revelers tossed hats and flags into the air. Caution was thrown to the winds as servicemen swept pretty girls off their feet and kissed perfect strangers, and the strangers kissed them back. Hawkers began selling whistles and V-J (for "Victory over Japan") buttons. Five thousand tons of streamers and confetti paper poured onto New York City streets. The garment district was draped in strips of brightly colored fabrics, buttons, and even feathers. By 10:00 P.M. the police estimated the crowd at 2 million.

Walking down Houston Street, Murray's sister Estelle watched neighborhood residents lean out of windows and dance on the sidewalk, yelling, cheering, "The war is over! The war is over!" As *The New York Times* succinctly wrote the next morning, August 15, 1945: "World War II became a page in history last night."

The POWs were free to come and go as they pleased, so long as they signed themselves in and out. The camp logbook became a public diary for expressing, in shorthand, feelings they had bottled up for years. They fabricated names—"URA Bastard," or "Go T. Hell"—to let the Japanese know just what they thought of them, though direct confrontations were rare.

Liberty was intoxicating; the taste of real food wasn't bad either. There were no officers in charge of the British POWs down at Wakinohama. Some of them showed up at Maruyama in civilian clothing bearing mouthwatering tales of how they had broken into warehouses, loaded up on sugar and tobacco, and distributed goods to the Caucasian population of Kōbe, including the White Russians. They brought with them provisions for a veritable banquet of dried eggs, ham, and powdered milk. A feast indeed, and it quickly caused an outbreak of diarrhea. The doctors were given the keys to the food store and immediately doubled the POW rations. Guards quietly stacked their rifles.

On August 17 Hirohito issued the Rescript to Soldiers and Sailors ordering the army and navy throughout the Asian and Pacific theaters to lay down their arms "in order to maintain our glorious national polity." All across Japan and its occupied territories POW guards and commandants slipped away before the dawn of the American occupation. They shed their uniforms, changed names, and switched identities to evade prosecution for war crimes. They were only following orders.

A memo from the chief of POW camps in Tōkyō authorized "personnel who mistreated prisoners of war and internees or who are held in extremely bad sentiment by them . . . to take care of it by immediately transferring or by fleeing without trace. Moreover, documents which would be unfavorable for us in the hands of the enemy are to be treated in the same way as secret documents and destroyed when finished with."

John and Murray were amazed at how quickly the attitudes of officers and guards changed, as if the emperor had waved a wand and said, "Let there be peace," and so it was. One minute the Japanese were slapping you silly, punishing you, berating you, and stealing your food. The next moment they greeted you with fawning subservience, as if three and a half years of maltreatment could suddenly be forgiven. The balance was tipped in the other direction, and it was oddly disorienting. You had to practice certain behaviors all over again, recover responses that had long been in abeyance. It was like learning to walk after being physically restrained, learning to see after being confined to the darkness. Power was handed to you with no prior warning, something to be used, something to be wary of as you adjusted your vision to the bright lights of freedom.

On August 21 Colonel Murata "crawled" into Maruyama, as Page put it. In the first of several attempts to rewrite his biography as commandant of the Ōsaka area camps, he thanked the lieutenant commander and the former medical staff of the Kōbe POW Hospital for their good work.

Page would have none of it. He told Murata exactly how he thought he had mismanaged POW rations and medical supplies. He accused him of "unnecessary brutality and beatings" and of driving "sick men to work always in the face of protests from the medical officers."

Murata replied that the problem was a shortage of Japanese doctors. Page countered by telling him his opinion "of Jap doctors in general and my experience with several individuals in particular."

Murata apologized. He hoped the Americans would forgive such behavior. Page let him know that indeed it would not be forgotten.

Murata tried another tactic. He invited Page and Fred to Wakinohama for supper, and they accepted. The camp was in disarray. During a predinner conversation, Murata explained that Lieutenant Takanaka, the commandant, was unable to maintain order. There was only W. O. Challiss, a British Army noncom in charge of all of the POWs, and the situation verged on chaos. "The sound of orders in English," said John Lane, "was almost embarrassing." Ex-POWs were commandeering taxis, hijacking trucks, stealing sugar and flour from godowns, and trading food for liquor. Drinking led to drunkenness, drunkenness erupted into brawls, and the brawls invited reprisals from Japanese civilians and the military. Murata stated repeatedly that he was responsible to the Allied forces for the safety of the former POWs, but he was afraid that disorder would descend into mob rule. He asked Page, the senior Allied medical officer in the Kōbe-Ōsaka area, "to write a letter absolving him of this responsibility."

Just then a British stevedore burst into their meeting and began cursing a blue streak at Murata until he'd used up almost every expletive known to the Royal Navy, Army, and Air Force combined, and then he left.

To Murata's chagrin, Page explained that he knew full well the terms of the Potsdam Declaration and that he viewed Murata's request as nothing more than a craven attempt to obtain documentation that might absolve him of war crimes. Murata, who was technically responsible for all of the Ōsaka-area POW camps. Murata, who allowed the crazed Nosu to act as a medical officer even though he himself found his behavior "strange." Murata, who surely knew of the sympathectomies performed on POW patients without their consent and of the fatalities that were the tragic result. Murata, whose staff included camp guards such as Bandō Bunhachi, who at Ichioka went from bay to bay beating POWs while shrieking like a madman: "All men die, jōtō [good]! All men die!" Murata, who denied prisoners adequate food, clothing, shelter, and forced sick men to work until they literally dropped dead. In separate interviews with the ICRC, Murata apologized for "regrettable occurrences" involving POWs, which were due to "differences of language" and "Japanese Army habits to enforce discipline," he maintained. Asked if he had any information pertaining to captured American airmen, the colonel responded with "an immediate stiffening of his attitude."

"I saw no reason why I should accept the burden of his responsibilities on my shoulders," said Page.

He told Murata he could do little to curtail the activities of the men once they were outside of Wakinohama; they had a right to food stores since food wasn't being provided by the Japanese. He reminded Murata that ex-POWs were no longer subject to Japanese military law and that guards should be bearing arms only to protect them. Civil law was now the rule, and violators were to be apprehended by the civil police force, brought back into camp, and detained until they could be tried by the occupation authorities. Should ex-POWs start receiving food from the Japanese, Page would try to stop them from raiding the warehouses. But right now Page and his staff had their hands full with their patients at Maruyama. He suggested that Murata bring back Allied officers from the outlying camps to take charge of Wakinohama. Then he demanded the release of Private Rodaway and Private Smith from Ōsaka Military Prison, a request Murata granted the next day.

The food situation began to improve at Maruyama, but the doctors were still without medical supplies. And one by one their patients were dying. Murray's patient John Edgar Goddard had succumbed to pulmonary tuberculosis on July 9. Fred's charge, Jack Hill, had expired on July 20. A Dutch POW named Nielant died on July 23, followed by a British patient, Lydington, on July 26.

Something had to be done quickly, or Maruyama would turn into another mortuary.

On August 15 Truman appointed General Douglas MacArthur Supreme Commander for the Allied Powers in Japan (SCAP). MacArthur moved promptly to revise Operation Blacklist, the "blueprint" for the nonmilitary occupation of Japan and southern Korea. Per his instructions, a sixteen-man Japanese delegation, led by Lieutenant General Kawabe Torashirō, deputy chief of the Imperial Army General Staff, arrived in Manila on the evening of the nineteenth. Lieutenant General Sutherland, Major General Willoughby, Deputy Chief of Staff Major General Richard J. Marshall, and Colonel Sidney F. Mashbir of the Allied Translator and Interpreter Section (ATIS) attended the night-long conference. MacArthur deliberately excused himself from it.

The purpose of the meeting was for the Japanese to review the various surrender documents so the Americans could be assured of compliance with the Allies' demands; to assist in plans for the first phase of the American occupation by establishing a Central Liaison Office; and to provide a complete list of POW camps throughout Japan and their locations so B-29s could airdrop food, clothing, and medical supplies. The Americans demanded that the Japanese remove all troops from the Tōkyō Bay area; repair Atsugi air base, fifteen miles west of Yokohama; and remove the propellers of aircraft that remained on the field where

MacArthur would land in order to preempt any kamikaze attacks. The Japanese asked the Americans to postpone their arrival until September 8 so they had time to execute their orders, rein in the armed forces, and restore calm to the capital city. Their request was denied.

Initially, an advance American echelon from Okinawa was to arrive at Atsugi on August 23. But there was streetfighting in Tōkyō instigated by Japanese military units opposed to the surrender. Kamikaze from the 302nd Airborne based at Atsugi maintained the emperor would never surrender in spite of his proclamation. Beneath Atsugi was an underground labyrinth that contained an arsenal as well as barracks for more than 1,000 men, machine shops, and even printing presses that could roll out suicide instruction manuals. Sutherland decided to reschedule the landing for 0900, August 26. The 11th Airborne Division would start homing in from Okinawa two days later.

Prior to the surrender, the Allies had known of only forty-three POW camps in the Far East. The Tōkyō Delegation drew up a list of 102 POW camps in Japan alone. On the basis of that information, ATIS prepared a detailed "Map Locating Prisoner-of-War Camps and Places Where Prisoners Are Employed." But in reality there were more than 300 Japanese POW camps in the Far East, and neither on the Tōkyō delegation's list, nor on the ATIS map, was Maruyama to be found.

Locating the camps was one thing; evacuating them was another, and that responsibility fell to Lieutenant General Robert L. Eichelberger's Eighth Army. "Mercy teams" organized by the Recovered Personnel Section in Okinawa, whose headquarters would move to Yokohama, were to accompany the advance airborne echelons into Atsugi. Special urgency was attached to seizing from the most notorious inland camps documents that could be used in the prosecution of war crimes.

The original plan in Operation Blacklist called for the evacuation of 200 to 250 POWs a day. At that rate it would take at least four months to liberate the estimated 32,000 POWs in Japan. Operation Blacklist did not prioritize those POWs who had to be evacuated first because of their health.

Meanwhile, the Tōkyō branch of the International Committee of the Red Cross had begun to go into POW camps on its own. Dr. Marcel Junod, chief delegate of the ICRC in the Far East, arrived in Manchuria on July 28 and in Japan on August 8. Junod was disconcerted by rumors of a generals' revolt against the emperor, by the leaflets dropped over Yokohama calling on the Japanese to fight to the bitter end, and by the violence that had broken out to the south. He wanted to get Red Cross representatives into the seven most important camps at once to ensure the safety of the POWs. Junod and seven delegates met in Tōkyō on

August 17 and immediately asked the Japanese government to arrange a conference with the Foreign Office, War Ministry, Prisoner of War Information Bureau, and Railway Office to facilitate the evacuation of POWs. E. H. Brunner was the ICRC delegate, M. A. Casal was the Swiss Legation delegate, and Per Bjoerstedt was the Swedish Legation delegate assigned to the Ōsaka area.

While the Japanese Prisoner of War Information Bureau preserved its prisoner lists, many officials, observed Junod, "seemed more occupied in burning tons of papers, propaganda sheets and compromising documents." In Tōkyō, he said, "we saw papers being destroyed in the streets." Records in the War Ministry offices on Ichigaya Hill, at army and navy installations throughout Japan, and at Kempeitai units were put to the torch to destroy evidence of war crimes. "You are instructed to be certain that of secret documents that required destruction," read one Tōkyō order, "not a single sheet be left behind."

Junod wired MacArthur in Manila that the ICRC was ready to serve as a liaison between GHQ and Japanese authorities at every port from which POWs were to be repatriated. GHQ had already issued instructions for "PW" to be painted on camp rooftops in block letters so planes could airdrop food and supplies. B-29s from bases in China and the Marianas began searching for POW camps, scattering pamphlets that read:

ALLIED PRISONERS

The JAPANESE Government has surrendered. You will be evacuated by ALLIED NATIONS forces as soon as possible.

Until that time your present supplies will be augmented by air-drop of U.S. food, clothing and medicines.

Fifty-five-gallon steel drums were packed with goods. Some of them contained C-rations, hospital supplies, canned fruit, dehydrated soup, vegetable puree, bouillon, and vitamin tablets. There were instructions on feeding 100 men, and warnings: "DO NOT OVEREAT OR OVERMEDICATE" and "FOLLOW DIRECTIONS." But there were no warnings as to how deadly the canisters, welded together, could be when their parachutes failed to open because the planes were flying as low as 200 feet at 250 mph.

POWs waved their arms and T-shirts at the sight of the B-29s, whose crews could see how emaciated they were from the air. But bounty took its toll when the care packages exploded on impact, hurtled through rooftops, and careened into shower stalls, causing more than a dozen deaths. The wastage ratio of supplies dropped was "extremely high," noted the ICRC. "They're killing us with kindness," the POWs said. Men who gorged on food gained up to two pounds a day; a few literally ate themselves to death.

The rooftops of Maruyama were emblazoned with "PW" so low-flying planes could spot the camp. But none of the airdrops contained the medicines and supplies the doctors needed most. They were in a race against time.

25

Mission of Mercy

THE THREE NAVY DOCTORS were tired of waiting, tired of seeing men ravaged by disease. For three and a half years they had tried their best to repair broken bodies, nurse them back to health, cure them of an array of illnesses, and relieve them of pain. Healers in a world of hurt, they were deprived of the very tools they needed most. The diseases were not terminal, at least most of them weren't, but the conditions created by the Japanese made many of them so. Sometimes, John felt, frustration gnawed at him almost as much as hunger itself as he watched once-healthy men turn into effigies of human beings, straw men who rotted, decomposed, and turned literally into waste.

Murray and Fred hatched a scheme. They would go to Tōkyō to alert MacArthur and the advance American forces of the extreme situation at Maruyama. If the tubercular patients weren't evacuated quickly, they'd never make it home. Page thought it was "a rum idea." John was also cool to the plan; it seemed an unnecessary risk. Besides, his ankle still hurt from the night he had rolled off the table he was sleeping on in an attempt to outflank Maruyama's fleas. Stan Smith volunteered to accompany Murray and Fred in his place.

To Fred their journey was "a mission of mercy." To Murray, it was also a unique opportunity to obtain the proper medicine and equipment to treat and study patients suffering from a full menu of nutritional deficiencies. And to a man there was one thing they couldn't wait to see: the Pacific Fleet of the U.S. Navy, which was due to arrive in Sagami Bay on August 26, 1945.

The men were heady with excitement. It was an outlandish idea—inspired, courageous, and potentially dangerous. Three American navy doctors venturing into Tōkyō unarmed, unescorted, before U.S. occupation forces had landed. Imperial Japanese forces numbered 6,983,000, stretching from Manchuria to the Solomon Islands and the Southwest Pacific; 2,576,085 of them were stationed in the Home Islands alone.

Haggard and homeless, the ex-POWs didn't own so much as the clothes on their backs. Fred borrowed John's navy hat and wore a khaki shirt with a Marine Corps insignia on it. Murray's only pair of trousers had been sewn out of light canvas by a British patient. Smith sported a civilian cap. They had no luggage, except their razors and a few provisions from B-29 food drops.

On Saturday, August 25, they left on the electric tram from Kawasaki and arrived at the Kōbe rail terminus around 1700. The wind began to blow, and a hard rain fell, but it failed to dampen their spirits. The ticket agent was taken aback by their request to go to Tōkyō. In spite of the B-29 raids, the railway network to Tōkyō was intact. But travel was severely restricted due to disrupted service, the masses of Japanese military men being demobilized, and emissaries carrying out SCAP directives. The city had been zoned, she said; only those with special military permits were allowed to enter it.

The doctors explained their mission in broken Japanese. "Baseball? Baseball?" inquired Japanese children on seeing the Americans. Then, as if he had stepped out of a short story, a well-dressed gentleman, briefcase in hand, overheard the doctors' request. He spoke fluent English and switched back into Japanese to persuade the agent that they were indeed authorized to go to Tōkyō. He accompanied them to the designated track, and together they boarded the train for Ōsaka at 2100, which would take them to Tōkyō via Yokohama. The gentleman removed three peaches from his briefcase, one for each of them. He said he was glad the war was over. Americans and Japanese could now be friends.

Before the war, Ōsaka to Tōkyō was a twelve-hour train ride. The doctors wouldn't arrive in the capital until 1415 Sunday afternoon. The platform at Ōsaka's Umeda Station was mobbed with Japanese soldiers. Their packs, laden with blankets and raincoats, mess kits and shelter halves, were nearly as big as they were. When the train pulled in, they threw their possessions in first and then swarmed through the doors and windows. They were filthy, their uniforms stank, and their belongings piled up like dirty laundry in the crowded aisles. The air was stale with the smell of distilled sweat.

Murray and Stan Smith sat together. Fred was behind them, next to a Japanese marine who shared his hardtack with him. The Americans talked freely in English, speaking a language they assumed no one could understand. After several hours a Japanese soldier across the aisle asked, "You are POWs?"

They were startled by his perfect English, and their response was deliberately disingenuous. They were doctors, they said, noncombatants according to the Geneva Convention, who did not qualify as prisoners of war.

"Then you have been, let us say, detained by the Japanese military?"

All of a sudden it seemed warm—hot, in fact—even with the train's windows open.

Yes, they replied, they had been "detained," first in the Philippines and then in Japan.

"Ah, yes." The interlocutor paused before continuing his line of inquiry. "Are you not then still to be considered in the control of the military?" he prodded.

The Japanese military had guaranteed the safety of POWs to MacArthur, the doctors asserted. Colonel Murata Sōtarō himself had granted them their freedom.

This seemed to satisfy the stranger. "Now there is a typhoon approaching," he informed them. "The initial landing in Tōkyō Bay has been delayed two days."

A typhoon had raged through the Ryūkyūs and swept into southern Japan. That meant the first U.S. soldiers wouldn't be on Japanese soil until August 28. That meant the three American navy doctors would arrive in Tōkyō two days before MacArthur landed at Atsugi air base.

Fred, Murray, and Stan were utterly alone as they traveled through a country still "impressively beautiful," as one writer described it, with "mountains and waterfalls and green rice paddies, and peasants in bamboo hats." But its cities were in ruins, and some 9 million Japanese were left homeless. The only Westerners in a sea of Asian faces, they were a curiosity to those who had never before seen—much less encountered—an American.

They arrived in Yokohama in the dark, switched trains, and slept until dawn. At stop after stop soldiers returning home debarked until, by the time the navy doctors reached Tōkyō, it felt as if they were the only passengers aboard.

It was an overcast afternoon. The eastern half of the city, from Ueno and Tōkyō Stations to the Arakawa Drainage Channel, was a wasteland. Seven hundred thousand structures had been destroyed in the B-29 raids. Since the March 9 bombing, homes that had been reduced to ashes and buildings ground to gravel had been neatly swept up. Streets stretched like runways through a plain of desolation, identifiable by occasional standing structures and their relation to the Sumida River. The Low City was ravaged, as it had been by the fires after the 1923 earthquake, but the path of destruction was even wider; some wards were nearly wiped off the map. The great Kannon Temple, the main building of the palace, and the municipal library in Hibiya Park were now a part of history. The parks along the river were cemeteries. Tōkyō's population had shrunk from 7 million in February 1945 to less than 3 million. One in ten residents, the police estimated, lived in temporary shelters. Thousands roamed the city in search of food, sifting through ruins, inhabiting the subways. And yet the damage in Tōkyō seemed far less to the navy doctors than what they had seen in Kōbe.

There were no other ex-POWs on Tōkyō's streets, though 1,200 Allied prisoners remained locked up at Ōmori Main Camp on an island in Tōkyō Bay that was connected to the mainland by a wooden causeway. Nor was there any U.S. military presence. The first American echelon had yet to touch down at Atsugi, and Admiral Halsey's landing force was still offshore of Yokosuka.

On leaving the train station, the navy doctors were met with stares of surprise, indifference, and hatred. They were strangers in a land that was foreign to its own inhabitants, where women stilll dressed in wartime *monpe*, where the defeated were just beginning to confront the consequences of surrender.

Japan's militarist leaders bathed in the blood of remorse and recrimination. "By disemboweling myself," said Admiral Ōnishi, architect of the kamikaze units, "I cannot apologize sufficiently." On the morning of August 15, Army Minister General Anami committed ritual seppuku. Major Hatanaka Kenji shot himself in the forehead with the pistol he had used to murder Lieutenant General Mori Takeshi, commander of the Konoye Division. Lieutenant Colonel Shiizaki Jirō, also from the Military Affairs Section of the Ministry of War, sliced open his belly and then blew his brains out as he knelt facing the Imperial Palace. Major Koga Hidemasa, an associate of Hatanaka and Shiizaki, met the tip of his sword on the parade ground outside the Imperial Guards Division headquarters. There were rumors of a "government of resistance" and plans to occupy the Imperial Palace at midnight on August 20. On August 24 Eastern District Army Commander General Tanaka Shizuichi, the man who had quashed the coup, put a bullet to his head. Inspired by the Atsugi insurrection, more than a dozen rightist youths in Atagoyama linked arms in groups of three and detonated hand grenades "for our sins in disobeying the Imperial Rescript." By month's end more than 1,000 officers and members of the imperial armed forces had taken their own lives. But in spite of the millions of imperial troops bearing weapons, the resistance came to naught. Hirohito's emissaries succeeded in persuading the Japanese military to disarm. As ultranationalist and underground boss Kodama Yoshio put it: "Defeat and unconditional surrender . . . also signified national death."

No one knew what to expect from the occupation. Families hid their possessions; women and children were secreted in the countryside. On August 19 the Home Ministry instructed municipal governments to set up "comfort facilities" or "Recreation and Amusement Associations" using national treasury monies, in order "to hold back the mad frenzy [of the occupying troops] and cultivate and preserve the purity of our race long into the future." Interim prime minister Prince Higashikuni appointed Kodama Yoshio as a cabinet councilor to oversee the burgeoning sex trade. Ōhashi Hyōjirō made sure his daughters shaved their heads for fear that they would be raped by American soldiers.

In the twilight hours between surrender and occupation, the three American doctors were certain of their mission but less confident of its success.

The killing of Allied POWs did not end with Japan's capitulation. In Manchuria, 600 Chinese and Manchurian laborers who were used as experimental subjects in Unit 731 laboratories at Pinffan near Harbin were gassed to death or poisoned with potassium cyanide. At Fukuoka, guards marched sixteen American POWs to a glade, where they were stripped and then hacked to death to the amusement of the guards' girlfriends. In North Borneo, more than 2,700 British and Australian POWs who were constructing an airfield were herded into the jungle; all but six were either killed or died. In Ōsaka, hours after the entire Ōsaka Kempeitai had gathered to hear the emperor's speech, five American airmen were executed at the Sanadayama Military Cemetery (two of them were unsuccessfully beheaded). As Fujioka Hideo, chief of the department of Special Police Business, later explained, "We still had the spirit as officers to carry on and not let the war end in defeat."

They walked and walked until they flagged down a lone Japanese Army truck with two soldiers in it. The Americans asked if they would take them to the Imperial Hotel in the Hibiya District, where the Imperial Palace, the Diet, the central government offices, and the diplomatic embassies were located. Redesigned by Frank Lloyd Wright as a grand hotel that could compete with the Waldorf-Astoria in New York, the Ritz in Paris, and the Carlton in London, the Imperial had been completed in 1923. Fred and Stan had stayed there before hostilities began when it was the epitome of elegance in the East, drawing politicians, foreign dignitaries, celebrities, and movie stars, from Babe Ruth to Charlie Chaplin and Helen Keller.

The hotel had survived the great Kantō earthquake of 1923 and the March 1945 firebombing, but the war had taken its toll. Radiators were stripped from guest rooms. Fans, fixtures, carpet runner rods, and even cooking utensils had been handed over to the government in accordance with the 1943 law ordering the collection of metals. An aerial attack against Tōkyō on May 25–26, 1945, gutted the south wing and damaged the banquet rooms, the famous Peacock Room, and the annex. The interior needed painting; the lobby was darkened by walls made from brown tile and green Oya tuff; and the furniture was as shabby as the staff's uniforms. The windows looked out on a city in ruins, and at night the hallways were alive with vermin. But to Fred, Murray, and Stan, the Imperial was a palace.

They walked downstairs and into the men's lavatory to wash up. Then they went to the front desk and asked for rooms. The clerk couldn't believe what he was hearing. Rooms? He sucked in his breath through clenched teeth.

The hotel was preparing to accommodate the new Foreign Office, which was going to meet with the occupying powers, he explained. Okazaki Katsuo, a Ministry of Foreign Affairs official who had served with the Tōkyō delegation in Manila, had instructed the manager, Inumaru Tetsuzō, of the advance echelon's needs. They were closely involved with plans at Atsugi air base that were being coordinated by Lieutenant General Arimatsu, chairman of the reception committee. But it was August 26. The first American forces weren't due until the twenty-eighth. Who were these men?

"We're doctors from the Kōbe POW Hospital," Fred replied.

And they wanted rooms? the clerk asked.

"Yes," Fred affirmed.

That would be difficult, the clerk said, but he would see what could be done. In the meantime, perhaps the Americans would like to wait in the mezzanine.

Stan thought they were being brushed off until either the Foreign Office or the Kempeitai could be notified of their presence. Sure enough, Major Fujisaki of the Foreign Office arrived and began interrogating them in English.

Fred explained that they had come from Maruyama outside Kōbe, where 120 ex-POWs were in need of food and medicine. They had made the trip to Tōkyō so they could inform MacArthur of their patients' plight and also see the Pacific Fleet.

Fujisaki found Fred's story hard to believe. First of all, American POWs were still technically under the control of the Japanese. Second, it would have been extraordinarily risky for any Americans to travel all the way from Kōbe to Tōkyō given the unstable situation in Japan. Why

would they go to all that trouble just for their patients? The story didn't
add up. There must be another motive.

"Didn't people throw stones at you, stare at you, attempt to molest
you?" he asked. "We are daily confining hundreds of avowed fanatics
who would gladly have taken your lives in one last gesture of revenge."

That might be true, Fred replied, but here they were, in Tōkyō. Now
could they please get a room and something to eat?

Finally their request was granted. Fred and Murray shared one room;
Stan stayed in another. Soon they were served their first complete meal
in three and a half years: breaded veal cutlets, rice, a fresh vegetable
salad, bread and butter, rice cakes and tea for dessert. They ate on real
plates, used knives, forks, and spoons, drank from glass goblets, and
dabbed their mouths with cloth napkins. They bathed with soap and
dried off with cotton towels. They tested the mattresses on their beds
and the plushness of chair cushions as if they were discovering such
amenities for the first time. Boy, this was the life! Or it would have been,
had they not been placed under guard.

Sakagami Jin'ichirō, a young English-speaking Japanese who had
been a college student at the time of the Pearl Harbor attack, sat by the
window of Fred and Murray's room guarding the hotel's unexpected
guests. Sakagami casually provided them with a wealth of information
about Japanese plans to annihilate the American invasion force. Thousands of kamikaze had been waiting for the call to arms, he said. Ten
thousand volunteers were prepared to act as live mines to destroy incoming landing craft, he asserted. He was pleased the war was over. He was
eager to visit the United States.

Effectively under house arrest, the ex-POWs had limited freedom of
movement in the hotel. Murray noticed that the room next to theirs had
its door slightly ajar. That was odd, he thought. He ventured inside and
found himself staring at a bank of electronic surveillance equipment.
They were being bugged as well. The Japanese clearly thought their
"mission of mercy" story was a ruse. The doctors were in Tōkyō not to
enlist aid but to report war crimes. If they contacted MacArthur before
the signing of the surrender treaty, the terms of the surrender might be
even harsher for the Japanese people.

For several days the Japanese Foreign Office tried to persuade the
doctors to return to Kōbe. If the Americans agreed to leave, Fujisaki
promised, the Foreign Office would deliver their message. The navy doctors didn't buy it. They insisted on handing over the roster of
Maruyama's patients directly to MacArthur's staff. The Japanese tried another tactic. They called in the Kempeitai.

The Kempeitai were the military police of the Imperial Japanese Army. They were feared as much by Japanese citizens and subjects of the Co-Prosperity Sphere as by officers and enlisted men who breached military discipline. Like their German counterpart, the Gestapo, the Kempeitai were trained in counterintelligence and the art of coercion. Their policy was one of intimidation, and their tactics were officially sanctioned by the Japanese Army training manual, *Notes on the Interrogation of Prisoners of War*, which described various forms of physical and psychological torture. There were more than 10,000 Kempeitai in Japan alone. They stood guard in war plants. They tapped telephones. They harassed so-called enemies of the state. They trafficked in narcotics, counterfeited, supplied women for military brothels, and participated in the notorious activities of Unit 731. They swaggered through the streets of Kōbe and Ōsaka on horseback, searching for aliens, neutrals, spies, quislings, or simply violators of wartime regulations. Caucasians were immediately suspect. As Max Pestalozzi, an ICRC delegate in Yokohama, put it: "We never knew whether we were privileged with diplomatic prerogatives or whether we would land in jail." Above and beyond the law, the Kempeitai were loathed for their arrogance, intolerance, and excessive use of force. They had power over local POW camp commandants, and the army allowed them to apprehend, prosecute, and sentence captured American fliers on its behalf. The Kempeitai, in short, were both judge and jury. The Tōkyō headquarters building was just across from the Imperial Palace, and it was there that eight of Doolittle's raiders were imprisoned for some forty-five days and tortured before three of them were condemned to death.

On the afternoon of Tuesday, August 28, Captain Nakamura of the Tōkyō Kempeitai strode into the Imperial Hotel. Solidly built, he was brusque, belligerent, and he spared the ex-POWs any pleasantries.

"Who knows you're here?" Nakamura barked through an interpreter, Nakao Kiyoaki, a Japanese schoolteacher who had been schooled at Catholic University in Dayton, Ohio.

It was a curious question, but his meaning was clear: *Who would know if you disappeared? Who would know if we killed you? Who would ever find your remains? Who would care?*

Nakao took a softer approach in the translation. He explained to the doctors that their request to contact American authorities had been denied by the Foreign Office.

But Murray knew enough Japanese to get the message. He stepped forward to reply, looked Nakamura in the eye, and said, poker-faced, "The entire camp knows we're here."

It was a bluff. Only John knew of their whereabouts. They hadn't even bothered to say goodbye to Page.

"Why did you come to Tōkyō? What is the real purpose of your trip?" the captain demanded.

They were threats, not questions, uttered with the same contempt that the camp guards had shown when they shrieked commands at POWs, as if nobody had told the Kempeitai that the war had ended, as if their behavior were guided by an uncontrollable urge to abuse the power the Imperial Japanese Army had conferred upon them when the army itself was in the process of disbanding.

But the doctors weren't prisoners anymore. From the balcony of their hotel room that morning, they watched fighter planes usher in the vanguard of the Allied staff to Atsugi air base. C-54s followed in the afternoon, with the advance echelon of the 11th Airborne Division. As Murray listened to Nakamura, he could see carrier planes from Admiral Halsey's Third Fleet skim Tōkyō's treetops. The sky belonged to the Americans, and the sight of it was emboldening. No more would the ex-POWs have to submit to Little Speedo or Big Speedo, Air Raid or Donald Duck, Mad Butcher or Dumb Shit. No more would they have to bow at the waist or fear being slapped or beaten as a Japanese officer strode by in leather boots, vitamin stick in hand. No more would they have to wonder where their next meal would come from, or what indignity tomorrow would bring.

Yet here were the Kempeitai telling them in so many words that they were worth no more than the dirt beneath their heels. Murray felt the years of rage, resentment, and wounded pride well up in him. He drew himself up to his full six feet, jabbed his finger at Captain Nakamura, and said:

"Listen, you goddamned son of a bitch. We won the war. And if you don't treat us with the respect that is our due as officers of the United States Navy, I'll see to it that your ass is strung from the highest lamppost in Tōkyō!"

The victor commanded the vanquished, his language torn from the mouths of the Japanese. Fred looked at Murray in amazement. Had he gone mad? He was the junior navy medical officer and had no authority whatsoever to say what he had. Were he the senior medical officer, he still would have had no right to make such a threat. For God's sake, Fred thought, we'll all be shot! A moment of stunned silence followed. The Kempeitai blanched. Seconds felt like hours. Then Nakamura did an about-face and abruptly left the room.

The army washed its hands of the ex-POWs, and the Foreign Office took over. After much haggling, the doctors agreed to return to Kōbe if they could first contact the Swiss consulate in Tōkyō, the official representative of U.S. interests in Japan. Fujisaki escorted them to the American embassy building, where the consulate had temporary quarters.

There they were greeted by Dr. Erwin Bernath, whom they remembered from his visit to the Kōbe POW Hospital in October 1944. Fred handed over the roster of Maruyama POWs to Bernath, who promised to deliver to Allied headquarters the doctors' request to evacuate their tubercular patients. He would also reassure the families of the POW doctors that they were safe. Bernath then rounded up his staff associates, called some friends (including the Swedish delegate, Per Bjoerstedt, who lived in Shioya), and threw a small party to celebrate the arrival of the Americans.

The next day, August 29, the doctors checked out of the Imperial Hotel. The tab came to 115.20 yen for rooms and 138.30 yen for meals. Charge it to the U.S. Navy, they told the hotel clerk. They left Tōkyō by train under Kempeitai escort. Nakao Kiyoaki kicked four Japanese soldiers out of their seats so he and the Americans could sit down on the journey back to Ōsaka. Once settled in, he explained that had the Kempeitai failed to prevent the ex-POWs from meeting with MacArthur, only seppuku could have absolved them from shame.

Murray was struck by how able-bodied and healthy the Japanese seemed. Whether raw recruits or returning veterans, they were well fed and in high spirits. Two and a half million soldiers, claimed Nakao, had been ready to defend an American landing on Japan. When the train passed Yokohama, the doctors had their first glimpse of the U.S. Navy in nearly four years. The sight of the Third Fleet in Sagami Bay, the help that had finally made its way—battleships, cruisers, and destroyers—brought tears to their eyes. They were going home.

———

There was a race within the American military to be the first to set foot on the Japanese Home Islands. Lieutenant General Eichelberger, commander of the Eighth Army, asked MacArthur if he could precede his arrival in Japan by two days to ensure his safety in Yokohama. MacArthur gave him two hours. On August 30 hundreds of C-47s from Okinawa bearing the bulk of the 11th Airborne Division arrived in three-minute intervals at Atsugi, followed by the 27th Infantry Division. To secure the Yokosuka Naval Base, the American fleet brought in the 6th Marine Division and the 4th Marine Regimental Combat Team, whose predecessors had so valiantly defended Corregidor. Then around 1400 that afternoon "a beautiful plane" touched down at Atsugi named *The Bataan*.

As the 11th Airborne's military band struck up "Ruffles and Flourishes," out stepped MacArthur, clenching a long corncob between his teeth.

"He hesitated a moment," remarked one Japanese observer, "and gazed upward toward the horizon from left to right and took a momentary Napoleon-like pose, reminding viewers of a victor and a conqueror."

"Bob," MacArthur said to Eichelberger, "this is the payoff."

Eichelberger agreed, though he "wasn't quite sure what the payoff would be." Just a few days before, "bitter fighting" had erupted at Atsugi when the Japanese Army, deeply distrustful of the kamikaze pilots, removed all of the propellers from their planes. American soldiers had arrived in Japan, but they were outnumbered "thousands to one." Entire divisions of Japanese soldiers still hadn't demobilized. The local navy air force—the Sagamihara Air Corps—was determined to engage American forces, while the Special Attack Corps vowed to attack the battleship USS *Missouri* in Tōkyō Bay, until dissuaded by Prince Takamatsu, an emissary of the emperor.

The reception at Atsugi was gracious and went off without incident. Sandwiches had been prepared by the kitchen staff of the Imperial Hotel.

Before he arrived in Japan, MacArthur had formulated fifteen objectives for the American occupation. Many of the principles had already been articulated and argued over by the State-War-Navy Coordinating Committee (SWNCC) and its Far East Subcommittee during the previous two years in Washington and were formalized in the directive entitled "United States Initial Post-Surrender Policy for Japan," sent to MacArthur by the Joint Chiefs of Staff.

First destroy the military power. Punish war criminals. Build the structure of representative government. Modernize the constitution. Hold free elections. Enfranchise the women. Release the political prisoners. Liberate the farmers. Establish a free labor movement. Encourage a free economy. Abolish police oppression. Develop a free and responsible press. Liberalize education. Decentralize political power. Separate church from state.

The New Grand Hotel in Yokohama quickly became the nexus for army, air force, and navy officers, as well as the international press. The old Customs House, which had been painted black to avoid detection during air raids, served as the advance GHQ/AFPAC, which had jurisdiction over U.S. troops in the Far East and Japan, composed primarily of the 200,000-man-strong Eighth Army. A separate headquarters organization, GHQ/SCAP, would be established in Tōkyō to oversee the civil administration of Japan.

Following on MacArthur's heels was the Recovered Personnel Section from Okinawa, charged with finding and repatriating 32,624 ex-POWs throughout Japan. Once located and evacuated, they were no longer ex-POWs, they were Recovered Allied Military Personnel, or RAMPs. Their new name reflected the new lives they had just begun.

Technically, the liberation of POWs was the responsibility of the Eighth Army, but when the Recovered Personnel Section showed up at Ōmori, they discovered that the navy had liberated the camp twelve hours earlier. At a conference aboard the *Missouri* on the morning of August 29, the navy's top brass decided that although the naval landings were not scheduled until August 30, the POWs in camps around Tōkyō Bay should be released immediately. The seriously ill would be transferred to the hospital ship, the USS *Benevolence*, which was about five miles offshore in Tōkyō Bay.

Commodore Joel T. Boone, medical officer of the Third Fleet, won the distinction of being the first American officially ashore in the Tōkyō environs after the capitulation of Japan. Temporarily designated medical officer of Task Force 31, Boone was in charge of all medical officers and corpsmen assisting in the evacuation of ex-POWs. That afternoon Boone left the USS *San Juan* by LCVP (landing craft, vehicle personnel) with Commodore R. W. Simpson, commander of Task Group 30.6; Commander Harold E. Stassen, Simpson's chief of staff; Dr. Junod of the ICRC; and Chaplain Robinson of the *Missouri*, who served as interpreter. They were guided to Ōmori by navy planes flying overhead. As they approached the camp, they saw ex-POWs standing on the dock naked. Men dove into the water and began swimming toward the LCVP, but the officers on board urged them back to shore, fearful of causing injury. When the landing party reached Ōmori, they found a Swedish Red Cross representative waiting at the camp gate, having been denied entry. The Americans demanded to see the commandant, Colonel Sakaba, and informed him that they were there to liberate the POWs. Sakaba replied that the War Ministry had not instructed him to release them. A heated argument ensued, in which Commodores Simpson and Boone, who were unarmed, explained that they represented Admiral William F. Halsey, commander of the U.S. Third Fleet. Sakaba continued to object until Simpson and Boone simply shoved him aside and entered the various camp buildings, beginning with the dispensary. Boone described the scene:

> The excitement of the prisoners was a never-forgettable sight. Many of them were unclad, some clad merely with a G-string, others with trunks, while some others were dressed in non-descriptive apparel. . . . Commodore Simpson, Commodore Boone and Commander Stassen circulated among the prisoners of the camp and into the various buildings to appraise the situation and to inform the prisoners that they were free. The scene was one of wild exultation.

Once the situation was under control, Boone went to Shinagawa, the hospital camp for the Tōkyō area that he had heard about from Dr. Junod and which was just a few miles north of Ōmori. He waved when he saw POWs in the windows, but there was no response. They had no idea the moment of liberation had come. When they finally recognized Boone as an American officer, "those that were able to, ran out of doors and jumped through windows, running toward him, hugging him, yelling and literally kissing him and falling at his feet in their excitement."

The conditions at Shinagawa were horrific. POWs were emaciated, and the buildings that housed them were filthy. They lived on mud floors and had no blankets. As Simpson radioed Halsey's headquarters on entering the camp, "There has never been a blacker hellhole than the prisoner-of-war hospital that we are now evacuating."

Of the first group of prisoners screened aboard the *Benevolence*, Boone reported that 85 percent of them suffered from severe malnutrition, while there were numerous cases of beriberi and tuberculosis. The signs of intense suffering, emotional distress, and fear were unmistakable. Boone was shocked at their condition. "Nobody came out of Japan hating the Japs more than I did," he remarked, "and I say that as a physician and a man who was born a Quaker."

Fred, Murray, and Stan spent the night at Ōsaka No. 1 Headquarters Camp, which was still under the supervision of Colonel Murata. The next day a young Russian commandeered a car and drove them to Maruyama. The camp was deserted except for a few cooks. While the navy doctors were in Tōkyō, the Kōbe municipal police department had arranged for food and supplies to be sent into the compound. The ICRC hadn't made it there yet. Then on August 29, after Fred, Murray, and Stan appealed to Erwin Bernath in Tōkyō for emergency medical assistance, patients and staff were evacuated by bus and ambulance from Maruyama to a wing of the Ōsaka Red Cross Hospital. There were beds with clean sheets, plenty of medical supplies, and patients were tended by Japanese nurses who couldn't have been more cooperative. To all appearances, the "mission of mercy" had been a success.

Under the stewardship of Chief Surgeon Dr. Hara, the Ōsaka Red Cross Hospital began receiving patients from subcamps within a fifty-mile radius. Ōhashi was pleased to see his old friends again. Page remained cool over their violation of protocol. In the next few days, so many planes made area food drops that Page signaled the pilots to stop. One canister killed a woman next door after it crashed through her roof. The hospital itself was hit, though no injuries were sustained.

Food, clothing, books, copies of *Life* magazine, Lucky Strikes, and news sheets had been air-dropped by navy Grummans from the USS *Randolph* and planes from the U.S. Far Eastern Air Force. Over at Waki-nohama, RAMPs opened packages that included messages from American pilots such as "See You in New York," "Texas Is Proud of You," and "Never a Dull Moment."

The navy doctors spent the night on the roof of the Ōsaka Red Cross Hospital, but they were too excited to sleep. Fred stayed up with William McGaffin, a foreign correspondent for the *Chicago Daily News*. He peppered the reporter with questions. So much was new to him—the helmets of the occupation forces, their carbines and Jeeps, the K-rations he was tasting for the first time. He pored over magazine advertisements, reminisced about dancing in the Forest Room of the Drake Hotel in Chicago, and worried that "everyone back there is so far ahead of us now." He wondered who this new kid singer Frank Sinatra was.

When McGaffin told him he'd be returning to "a world of squawking juke boxes," Fred inquired, "What's a juke box?"

Meanwhile General Albert C. Wedemeyer, commander of American forces in China, proposed that Lieutenant General Jonathan M. Wainwright, recently freed from Sian, Manchuria, be invited to attend the formal surrender ceremony on September 2. General Douglas MacArthur readily agreed. The occasion was rich in symbolism and drama.

On an overcast Sunday morning, the haggard general beloved by his troops on Bataan and Corregidor stood behind MacArthur on the hot quarterdeck of the battleship *Missouri* in Tōkyō Bay. To his left was Lieutenant General Arthur E. Percival, the British commander when Singapore fell to the Japanese. Behind them was a phalanx of Allied admirals and generals in khaki against the backdrop of the greatest armada in the world. The thirty-one-starred flag from Commodore Perry's flagship, *Mississippi*, lay in a glass case atop a bulkhead. The canvas and leatherbound surrender documents rested on a table nearby. The battleship's flagstaff flew the same Stars and Stripes that had waved from the Washington Capitol on December 7, 1941, while the colors of Great Britain, the Soviet Union, and China fluttered above the veranda deck. Sailors leaned over railings, stood on gun turrets, and sat on masts craning for the best view as the navy band struck up "Anchors Aweigh."

A hush descended over the *Missouri* as the Japanese delegation came on board. Foreign Minister Shigemitsu Mamoru, who had lost a leg in an assassination attempt fifteen years before in Shanghai, walked gin-

gerly on an artificial limb and seated himself with difficulty at a mess table covered with green baize. He was dressed in a swallowtail coat,
striped pants, a silk top hat, and yellow gloves. No words were exchanged between Shigemitsu and MacArthur. General Umezu, chief of
the Imperial Army General Staff, wore formal military garb. To Kase
Toshikazu, a member of the Foreign Office educated at Amherst and
Harvard, it was "the torture of the pillory." Said 2nd Lieutenant
Sakamoto, a nisei linguist: "The whole scene was as if a huge lion had
cornered a tiny, helpless-looking mouse in a cage. If ever there was a
scene that brought home to me how sad a defeated nation can be—this
scene was it." MacArthur finally spoke:

> It is my earnest hope, and indeed the hope of all mankind, that from
> this solemn occasion a better world shall emerge out of the blood and
> carnage of the past—a world dedicated to the dignity of man and the
> fulfilment of his most cherished wish for freedom, tolerance and
> justice.

Suddenly the battleship's quarterdeck, recorded Kase, was trans-
formed "into an altar of peace." At precisely 9:03 A.M. Shigemitsu signed
the instrument of surrender on behalf of Emperor Hirohito, followed by
Umezu for the Imperial General Staff. Then MacArthur added his signature on behalf of the Allied powers, but not before handing Wainwright
one of the pens he used and giving Percival another; he completed his
signature with a small red fountain pen of Mrs. MacArthur's. After a
mere twenty minutes the ceremony was declared over. In a final salute
400 B-29s and 1,500 carrier planes roared over the *Missouri*. Then, in
what seemed poetic justice to some and an act of divine intervention to
others, "the sun burst through low-hanging clouds," reported *The New
York Times*, "as a shining symbol to a ravaged world now done with war."
    The *Missouri* had no broadcast facilities, so MacArthur stepped up to
another microphone for a recording that was rushed to the communications ship *Ancon* and transmitted around the world:

> Today the guns are silent. A great tragedy has ended. A great vic-
> tory has been won. . . . As I look back upon the long, tortuous trail
> from those grim days of Bataan and Corregidor, when an entire
> world lived in fear, when democracy was on the defensive every-
> where, when modern civilization trembled in the balance, I thank a
> merciful God that he has given us the faith, the courage and the
> power from which to mold victory. We have known the bitterness of

defeat and the exultation of triumph, and from both we have learned there can be no turning back. We must go forward to preserve in peace what we won in war.

Ōhashi considered the surrender ceremony a disgrace. It was laughable, he wrote in his diary, to think of General Umezu, who had been so adamantly opposed to the Potsdam Declaration, taking part in it. As for General Yamashita Tomoyuki, the "Tiger of Malaya," who had lost most of the Philippines to American forces by June 1945, he should have killed himself rather than capitulate.

The good doctor was tormented by feelings of humiliation and he was anxious for Colonel Murata, whose fate under the Allied occupation could easily be linked to his own. He was most concerned about his family. In the first week of occupation, newspapers recorded 931 offenses by American soldiers in Yokohama, ranging from armed robbery to rape. In Kanagawa Prefecture alone, 1,336 rapes by American GIs were reported in the first ten days.

Outwardly Ōhashi was gracious and dignified. He invited Page and Fred to the Miyazaki home in Nishinomiya, where he still lived with his family. He introduced them to his wife, Yukako, and his eldest daughter, Yasuko, who let the Americans choose a Japanese doll from her collection. Ōhashi presented Page with an ancestral sword. He gave Fred a kimono for his mother along with his personal fan, which he explained was a symbol of life.

Sensō owari. The war is over.

Most RAMPs were evacuated by railroad to Yokohama's Central Station. Early arrivals were greeted by the IX Corps band, an honor guard, high officials in military regalia, and Mrs. MacArthur, who was a regular presence. The army was less than cordial to the ICRC, whose "preliminary work—which in some ways has facilitated theirs and could have served to greater advantage if we had been consulted in the least," bristled one report, "was ignored."

The Recovered Personnel Section had taken over a warehouse, where RAMPs were bathed, clothed, and fed hot food, given physical exams, and provided with bedrest, if necessary. Four tables were set up where the newly liberated filled out Red Cross reports and were allowed to send telegrams home. Behind a battery of typewriters, clerks typed out names, ranks, and serial numbers for airplane manifests. There were litter-bearers and nurses on staff, whose lovely smiles and natural compassion led to the first contact that most of the men had had with a Western woman in years. But by and large the Recovered Personnel Section had little idea of just how poor the health was of the ex-prisoners of the Japanese.

John Plath Green, an intelligence officer with the Eighth Army, was horrified by the situation at Ōmori. He drew up plans for the accelerated evacuation of POWs, which he presented to American and Japanese officials as well as to Marcel Junod of the ICRC. Junod had urged that POWs in Hokkaidō be rescued first because of the conditions in the coal mining camps. But there were also an estimated 10,000 POWs in southern Honshū and on the island of Shikoku, to the southeast. Green's idea was to create small mobile units consisting of a commanding officer, an officer's assistant, and three or four enlisted men who could fan out over the Home Islands. But he was short on personnel. He asked Lieutenant Travis J. Smith, a former Ōsaka POW he had met in Yokohama, if he'd be interested in helping establish a district headquarters for the Eighth Army Recovery Personnel at the New Ōsaka Hotel for processing RAMPs. Smith took up the challenge and enlisted seventy-five RAMPs as volunteers for recovery teams. Within eighteen days the Eighth Army liberated 23,985 Allied POWs in Hokkaidō, Honshū, and Shikoku, and many of them were recovered by RAMPs.

The POWs at the Ōsaka Red Cross Hospital had one thing on their minds: going home. On September 6, 1945, an American recovery team arrived at the hospital, and on September 7, the day MacArthur officially assumed control of the occupation, Ōhashi selected Fred, John, and four corpsmen to evacuate forty-seven patients on a special Pullman train, outfitted with sleeping berths and bound for Yokohama. Page, Stan Smith, and Murray followed the next day along with the remaining patients and personnel.

It was hard to say goodbye. The fall of Bataan. The siege of Corregidor. The prison hospital in Bilibid. The farm at Cabanatuan. The voyage of the "sugar ship." That hellhole Ichioka. The American firebombing of Kōbe. Fred, John, and Murray had been through so much together that words were inadequate to the occasion. Maybe they'd catch up with one another for that blowout in San Francisco. Maybe not.

On arriving at Yokohama's Central Station, Fred recognized Admiral Richard Byrd, surrounded by a throng of marines, bayonets at the ready. Byrd was in Japan as a confidential adviser to the navy. He had been on Okinawa at the time of its capitulation, attended the surrender ceremony on the *Missouri*, and remained in Japan to help inspect the atomic bomb damage at Hiroshima and Nagasaki for the United States Strategic Bombing Survey. Fred introduced himself to the admiral, told him about the trainload of sick RAMPs from Ōsaka, and asked him if he would come aboard so they could catch sight of the celebrated polar explorer. Byrd agreed and shook the hand of every last man.

In Yokohama they saw a city that had been 80 percent destroyed by the firebombing of May 29, 1945. The chimneys of bathhouses and the steel safes of businesses were all that remained standing in some neighborhoods. The brick and concrete buildings that survived near the waterfront, like the old Customs House, still wore black camouflage. The seven-story Yamato department store had crumpled like an accordion. A nation starving for scrap metal had devoured Yokohama's bridges, railings, stanchions, and gas main covers. Thousands of bicycles lay in heaps of twisted metal. Stores were bereft of consumer goods.

The Recovered Personnel Section handed Fred and John khaki shirts, trousers, underwear, socks, shoes, and shaving gear. It issued them repatriation identification numbers. The Americans were transferred to ships returning to the States via Guam, or they were flown from Atsugi to San Francisco with stopovers in Guam, Kwajalein, and Honolulu. Page was repatriated to England by way of Okinawa and Manila. Akeroyd was flown to Australia. Those unfit for air travel were placed aboard LSTs (landing ship, tank) and taken to the hospital vessels, the HMS *Tjitjilengka*, the USS *Marigold*, or the USS *Rescue*. Stan Smith returned to the States aboard the *Rescue*, which processed 6,300 RAMPs alone.

Fred and John left Yokohama on an LST that had been converted into a small hospital ship. The staff physicians spoke of their new patients with great interest but failed to ask a single question of the ex-POW doctors. They speculated as to why so many men had edema, then permitted them to stand on the chow line for twenty-four hours, which only made them sicker.

Maybe Fred wasn't interested in talking anyway. It was so damned hard, he now found, to control your emotions, to put into perspective what had just happened, what had been happening for the past three and a half years. As the ship chugged toward the Marianas, movies were shown on board. Fred found himself sitting alone in a corner, bawling like a baby.

Once back in San Francisco, the RAMPs did the craziest of things. At Letterman General Hospital they saluted officers who wore hospital clothes. They wandered into the administration building day and night to check on the status of their orders. They consumed enormous quantities of food, eating six to twelve hamburgers at a time. They used a spoon for every dining purpose, as they had during the years of their confinement.

Murray was flown to the States, so he saw the Golden Gate before either Fred or John. Prior to his departure he spent the night on the USS

Iowa, the battleship that had supported air strikes against Luzon during MacArthur's landing on Leyte, and served as Admiral William F. Halsey's flagship in the surrender ceremony. When the captain, Charles Wellborn, Jr., heard that Murray had been assigned to the 16th Naval District in Cavite, he invited him to his quarters. It was like being invited back into a gentlemen's club after a long hiatus. Wellborn handed Murray some aerial reconaissance photographs of the Cavite Navy Yard after it had been bombed by the Americans during the Battle for Manila. It turned out that they knew many men in common. Wellborn was eager to know who had survived, who had not, who had become a POW, and who had eluded capture. So much in war, the captain agreed, was the luck of the draw. He could just as easily have been in Murray's place.

Several officers on the *Iowa* noticed the peculiar hand-sewn canvas trousers and army-issue boots that the young navy doctor wore, and pitched in to buy him a new pair of shoes. It was a gracious gesture and prompted Murray, not yet thirty, to look back on the life he had loved and lost after boarding the *President Garfield* more than four years earlier. And as his plane took off from Atsugi air base on September 8, 1945, he couldn't help but wonder about the life that lay ahead as he watched Japan fade away.

Coming Home

"So you see," my father said, "I had nothing. The Japs made us feel like the lowest of the low. We dressed, ate, and acted like tramps. We smoked cigarette butts like tramps. I was garbage. And when I returned to the States, it was as if I had landed in a foreign country. I hadn't heard of DDT. I'd never seen penicillin. I knew nothing about modern medicine. I had been on ice for four years, and I couldn't shake this feeling of being different from everyone else."

It is nighttime on Bataan. The air is heavy with humidity. From our hotel in Mariveles, we can see flashes of lightning and hear thunder rolling across Manila Bay. Normally reserved, my father has spoken to me more honestly during our trip to the Philippines, more freely about himself, than at any time in my life. Stories bubble up like waves filling tidepools.

The heat is brutal, but it slows us down little. My father is remarkably active for a man eighty-six years of age. We visit the site of the old Cavite Navy Yard, now as quiet as a cemetery; search for the tunnel above Sisiman Cove where he holed up with John Bookman; try to find Cell Block No. 3 in Bilibid Prison, once again Manila's municipal jail; and step onto the beach at Lingayen, where Japanese forces landed on Luzon.

There are times when my father seems happier than I have ever seen him, excavating and explicating his past, as if my presence, my interest in it confers legitimacy on his experience. At one point he begins to sing Kipling: "On the road to Mandalay / Where the flyin'-fishes play / An' the dawn comes up like thunder outer China 'crost the Bay!" I cannot remember ever having heard him sing before. There are moments, too, of sober reflection, as we look for names we know on the Wall of the Missing at Manila's American Cemetery; hunt for the site of Hospital No. 2 in the thickets of Bataan; or pause before the Pacific War Memorial on Corregidor, which is designed so that every year on May 6 the noontime sun casts a halo of light around a commemorative plaque that reads: "Sleep, My Sons, Your Duty Done . . . For Freedom's Light. Come Sleep in the Silent Depths of the Sea, or in Your Bed of Hallowed Sod— Until You Hear at Dawn the Low, Clear Reveille of God."

He is determined to find his bivouac position in Government Ravine, but the roads on Corregidor differ from the ones blown off the Rock nearly sixty years ago, and the scorched earth has been reclaimed by jungle. We never do find the exact spot, the juncture that divides his life neatly into two: before he became a prisoner of war and after.

Conversation peels away layer after layer of the past. At times he speaks in a whisper, as if afraid his words will be overheard. Some scenes are as clear as day; others are mistakenly remembered or, as he admits, missing entirely. His story reads like a bildungsroman in reverse, a tale not of development, I realize, but of unbecoming.

———

It didn't feel right to stay in San Francisco, especially after he had received, on September 14, 1945, a radiogram at the Aiea Heights Hospital in Honolulu:

```
OVERJOYED TO HEAR FROM YOU ALL WELL
IMPATIENTLY AWAITING YOUR ARRIVAL
HAPPY AND HEALTHY NEW YEAR--
MOTHER DAD FAMILY.
```

But it didn't feel right to be back in New York, either.

The homecomings were strange for so many of the men. There were no brass bands, no parades, no welcoming committees to greet them as they landed on native ground. In the end, the defense of Bataan and Corregidor, which had slowed but could not halt the Japanse juggernaut in the Pacific, had more symbolic than strategic significance. But symbols ring hollow once removed from their context. As Murray put it, "We lost our part of the war."

He was pale, thin, and withdrawn. He was moody, his sister Estelle said, and he had a hair-trigger temper. He grew furious when he heard one doctor describe the hardships Americans had suffered under rationing on the home front. He was mystified as to why the story of an Army Air Corps B-25 bomber crashing into the seventy-ninth floor of the Empire State Building the previous July had seized the city's imagination. He had no job and no home he could call his own, and he discovered that every girl he had ever dated was now married. Having had so little control over his life in captivity, he was confounded by his hard-earned freedom.

He contacted the parents of Fred and John to assure them of their sons' safety. As much as he wanted to turn his back on the war, as much as he wanted to forget, he was obliged to write to the loved ones of those who never made it back. It was understood that if you witnessed someone's death, you would notify the next of kin at the earliest opportunity. Relatives replied asking for more details, a parting gesture, a final word. There were family members who stayed in touch for years seeking consolation.

"Was John Edgar cheerful?" Mrs. Goddard wanted to know from Imperial, Nebraska.

> *Did he give you my address or did you get it from records?*
> *Had he been ailing long before coming to the hospital or would you know?*
> *Did he talk about coming home?*
> *Did he know he wasn't going to live?*
> *Did he have anything to say about any one or thing in particular?*
> *Was his teeth good and was his hair still black?*

Sometimes Murray wondered if the war would ever end. And he couldn't help but wonder about George.

It was the summer of 1945 when the mailman brought a letter addressed to Lucille Ferguson from Commander H. B. Atkinson, the officer in charge of the Casualty Section at the Bureau of Naval Personnel in Washington, D.C. She was at her parents' home in Wausau, Wisconsin, and knew at once that something was wrong. She refused to open the envelope. Her uncle read the letter himself, then passed it on to her. There was no mention of the *Arisan Maru* by name. There was no mention of the total number of dead. There was no mention of the fact that the Japanese freighter had been sunk by an American submarine. The only explanation offered was that the ship "bore no mark to indicate it was carrying prisoners of war."

Atkinson concluded: "The Navy Department shares in your loss and extends sincere sympathy to you in your loss. It is hoped that you may find comfort in the knowledge that your husband gave his life for his country, upholding the highest traditions of the Navy."

So it was over. It had been nearly five years since she had last seen George, five years during which she had been planning, hoping, and dreaming of the life they would begin together. Five years of waiting. Perhaps there had been a mistake.

"Records maintained by the Japanese authorities in the Philippine Islands have come into the possession of United States Naval personnel," Atkinson had said, "and these records reveal that your husband did not survive the sinking."

But what if the records were wrong? She knew there had been survivors.

She wrote to Avery Wilber, asking if he knew George.

"He was of medium build, had dark hair and eyes, and very dark, heavy eyebrows. Would you remember whether or not he was on your ship?" she asked.

She wrote to Donald Meyer.

"He was a very good friend of mine," Meyer replied. "I thought very highly of him. . . . Everybody liked him."

She clung to the hope, as did George's mother, that he was somewhere, somehow, alive. There were so many questions and so few answers, but as time went by, there appeared to be only one certainty: George was gone.

For nearly a year after his death, Lucille Ferguson continued to receive those little POW postcards from her husband in the Philippines invariably listing his health as "excellent."

It was a story whose end was anything but clean.

None of the three other navy doctors could accept George's fate. On October 18, 1945, Fred wrote Lucy from the U.S. Naval Training Center in Great Lakes, Illinois, telling her to keep her chin up "and hang on us as long as there is a spark of hope." In Guam he had met Warrant Officer Martin Binder, one of the *Arisan Maru* survivors. George had been in excellent physical condition, Binder reported, and had had plenty of time to get off of the sinking ship. "I have not given up hope that he made it," Fred affirmed, "possibly to some obscure place in China—or island off the China coast for I am sure that if there was anybody on that ship that could do it—it would be George."

But that month belief hardened into cold fact. Murray was the last of the three doctors to write:

November 22, 1945

Dear Lucy—

I've wanted very much to write to you ever since I got back to the States—a little over a month ago—but I've hesitated because I've been so intimately associated with your husband George. I was afraid anything I might say would be re-opening an old wound. However I understand from Johnny Bookman that he has written to you and that Fred Berley has written to you & that there'd be no harm in my writing too. I don't know whether you've heard from Carey Smith but George, Fred, Jake, Carey & I were all part of an intimate group who lived, ate &

slept together while we were prisoners for a period of 2 years. We were together on Corregidor after the surrender, at the Bilibid POW hosp. & at the Cabanatuan POW Camp. We shared everything, our food, cigarettes, money, clothing—even our mail. So you see we got to know each other very well & I don't think I've ever met a finer person than George. Fred, Jake & I were together in Kobe when we first heard rumors about that ship George was on—& it was a terrific blow to us—we refused to believe it at first—claiming that it was just rumor & we heard all sorts of rumors while we were prisoners. But Jake & I were in Wash. a couple of weeks ago—& they were pretty definite about their information. . . .

We knew about you—George had told us. I knew all about your wedding—George had told the whole story—about his being worried at coming late—etc. But then I'd told George all about my girl & we knew all about Fred's, Carey's & Jake's families. We used to watch George pull out a couple of letters from you—time after time—while we were at Bilibid—& we were green with envy. He was the only one of the group who'd received mail at that time—& boy were we jealous.

So I've known you for a long time Lucy—since I've known George so well I've an idea how you must have felt.

Believe me—& I mean every word of this—if there is ever anything at all I can do for you—don't hesitate to get in touch with me—You see we're old friends.

  Sincerely,
  Murray Glusman

It could have been Fred, John, or Murray. It could have been any of them. Of the fourteen navy doctors whose narrative histories had been written up by Commander Hayes in his "Report on Medical Tactics," which had been buried—along with his diary and notes—in hermetically sealed containers beneath Bilibid Prison's commissary, half were dead. In addition to medical officers Lieutenant George T. Ferguson and Lieutenant George P. Hogshire, nearly 100 corpsmen were lost on the *Arisan Maru*. Of the 277 Navy Medical Department men on duty in China and the Philippines when hostilities erupted, 154 died, only 7 of them during combat. The mortality rate of navy medical personnel exceeded 55 percent.

———

Hayes's premonition came true. On the afternoon of December 13, 1944, 1,619 Bilibid POWs boarded the 7,362-ton *Oryoku Maru*, the last group of prisoners to evacuate the Philippines. Thin, ragged, and weakened by nearly three years of confinement, they were the last survivors of the Bataan Death March, defenders of Corregidor and Mindanao. Two-thirds of them were senior officers—combat unit commanders as well as doctors from Bilibid and Cabanatuan. Captain Nogi Naraji, director of the Bilibid hospital, supervised the boarding, which included Japanese women and children. General Kou Shiyoku, commandant of the prisoner of war camps in the Philippines, stood on deck while men were packed so tightly below that they collapsed from suffocation. There were no portholes in the holds, no ventilation except the hatch. The prisoners begged for water, but their requests were repeatedly denied. First Lieutenant Toshino Junsaburō, the guard from Cabanatuan known as "Liver Lips" who executed Robert Huffcutt, was in charge of the transport. His interpreter, a hunchback named Wada Shūsuke, carried out his orders.

The *Oryoku Maru* sailed the next morning, and the POWs soon encountered their greatest threat—Admiral Halsey's Task Force 38. During the day, carrier planes from the USS *Hornet* and USS *Hancock* made several passes, leaving Fred's friend, Marion Wade, and Murray's corpsman, Cecil Peart, with shrapnel wounds. Jack Schwartz and the medical staff were allowed to treat the injured, Japanese women and children among them. Then they were beaten in revenge for the attack.

That night was "the most horrible period of my life," said Colonel Beecher of the 4th Marines. The hatches were closed, and men went insane from dehydration and lack of oxygen. They stripped off their clothes to let the pores of their skin breathe. They slit their own veins to drink blood. They slit the veins of others to drink more blood. They knifed, strangled, or beat fellow prisoners to death with empty canteens in search of water. They ate feces out of honey buckets, swallowed urine to slake their thirst. By dawn, the ship had drifted aground, and "even those who had not lost control of themselves," said Beecher, "looked like demons."

The steering gear of the *Oryoku Maru* was shattered, and on the morning of December 15 the *Hornet*'s planes found the ship off of Olongapo. Six rockets and a 500-pound bomb exploded in the aft hold, where the highest-ranking officers were confined. Two hundred fifty were killed instantly. The Japanese civilians had been quietly evacuated during the night, and many of the crew followed their lead. There were no life preservers left for the prisoners, who began to abandon ship once they realized they were no longer under guard. Jack Schwartz couldn't swim; he held on to Lieutenant Kenneth Wheeler as they jumped thirty feet down to the water. Three or four hundred yards off Olongapo Point, the men made a desperate bid for shore. One U.S. Navy pilot strafed six Japanese in a lifeboat, careful to avoid the two Americans sitting in the stern. Another waggled his wings in recognition as he flew over the thin white bodies struggling in the water. A Japanese naval landing party had positioned a machine gun in front of the old Olongapo Naval Station and began picking off survivors drifting away from the beach. Hayes set up a small aid station on the seawall. The navy bombers returned. Having knocked out the bases's anti-aircraft gun, they bombed and sank the ghost ship.

The 1,333 prisoners who reached land were penned up for five days in a concrete tennis court that measured sixty by a hundred feet and was surrounded by a fifteen-foot-high chicken-wire fence. Raw from sunburn, they shivered with cold at night and were given only a few tablespoons of raw rice for meals. Navy corpsmen draped two bedsheets over a "hospital" area at one end of the court. Hayes and Cecil Welch worked alongside Jack Schwartz, who successfully amputated the gangrenous arm of a U.S. Marine corporal using a razor and without anesthesia. Dozens perished from injuries and exposure.

The POWs were trucked in two groups to San Fernando, Pampanga. The fifteen sickest men, Wada said, were to be removed to Manila for hospitalization. Instead, on the night of December 23, they were driven to a small cemetery outside San Fernando where, in the presence of Wada and Toshino, they were bayoneted, decapitated, and buried in a mass grave. The next day the prisoners were packed into a train bound for San Fernando, La Union. Wada told the wounded to ride atop the boxcars so they could wave their bandaged limbs at American pilots to ward off attack. "How shall I ever forget this Christmas Eve," Cecil Peart asked. Once in San Fernando, the men were marched to Lingayen Gulf, where they spent two days and bitterly cold nights on the beach. Their nightmare resumed on December 27, when 1,070 prisoners boarded the *Enoura Maru*, and the remaining 250 were herded onto the 5,860-ton *Brazil Maru*, rejoining their comrades on the *Enoura Maru* once they reached Takao, Formosa.

Hayes died on the *Enoura Maru* on January 6, 1945. On January 9, the day U.S. forces launched the invasion of Luzon, a bomb tore through the ship's forward hold, killing 300 men, many of whom were medics. "The carnage," said Major John M. Wright, Jr., of the Coast Artillery Corps, "was beyond description." "I felt that . . . we were beyond prayer," said corpsman Loren Stamp. The survivors were transferred back to the *Brazil Maru* and, after a forty-seven-day journey, finally reached Moji, Japan, on January 29.

Of the 1,619 POWs who had boarded the *Oryoku Maru* on December 13, 1944, 300 died; 316 more perished on the *Enoura Maru*, and another five on the *Brazil Maru*. Roughly half the army doctors who had served at Manila's Sternberg Hospital and Hospital No. 2 on Bataan—including Lieutenant Colonel William Riney Craig—died. More than three-quarters of the marine officers who embarked that day from Manila died. Max Schaeffer of the Headquarters and Service Company died. William "Hogey" Hogaboom of Battery A died. Willy Holdredge of Battery C died. Robert Chambers, Jr., of Company O died.

"Fidgety Frank" Bridget of Patrol Wing 10 died. The ranks of Bilibid's medical staff were ravaged. Marion Wade died. Gordon Lambert died. Maurice Joses died. Clyde Welsh and Cecil Welch died. Chaplain Cummings died. The poet Henry G. Lee survived the attack against the *Oryoku Maru*, only to die on the *Enoura Maru*. His poem "Group Four," penned more than a year before in Cabanatuan on Armistice Day, November 11, 1943, reads like an epitaph for the hellship victims:

> We'll have our small white crosses by and by,
> Our cool, green lawns, our well-spaced, well-cared trees,
> Our antique cannons, muzzles to the sky,
> Our statues and our flowers and our wreaths.
> We'll have our bold-faced bronze and copper plaques
> To tell in stirring words of that we saved
> And who we were, with names and dates; our stacks
> Of silent rifles, spaced between the graves.
> We'll have our country's praise, here below
> They'll make a shrine of this small bit of hell
> For wide-eye tourists; and so few will know
> And those who know will be the last to tell
> The wordless suffering of our lives as slaves,
> Our squalid deaths beneath this dripping sky,
> The stinking tangle of our common graves.
> We'll have our small white crosses by and by.

Carey Smith, who used to sing "We'll be free in '43 / No more war in '44 / Hardly a man alive in '45," was one of the few navy doctors who survived.

———

Months after the war some still didn't know if Murray had made it home. One former patient wrote to his father:

> *Dear Mr. Glusman*
> *The last time I saw Dr. Glusman was in March 44 on a Nip tramp*
> *steamer. I told him that I'd write—Please let me know if he is OK—*
> *Because I'm almost sure the doctor saved my life.*
> > *Alway* [sic] *your friend*
> > *Sgt. Stevens.*

But what had survived, really, when you felt you had nothing left, when your perspective on life had been so distorted that the world was unrecognizable, when conversation was detached from reality, and when the landscape of the heart was so charred by the fires of hatred that you wondered if you could ever love again, ever feel as intensely again, ever find someone who would be able to find you beneath the ruin of your former self?

Intellectually he knew it wasn't true. His life had been put on hold, not taken away. On the scale of horrors, the Japanese had dealt far more harshly with Chinese, Filipino, and Korean captives than they had with Caucasian POWs. Their treatment of the Javanese, Burmese, Malayan, and Indian slave laborers working the notorious Siam-Burma Railway was even worse. According to one estimate, 31.4 percent, or 60,600 of 193,000 Allied POWs, died compared to 48.3 percent, or 290,000 native prisoners out of 600,000. E. M. Gonie and Louis Indorf, officers of the Royal Dutch East Indian Army, left three and a half years of captivity only to watch Indonesia catapult into four years of war in its struggle for independence, after which they found themselves at once without a country and orphaned by the Dutch home government. There were concentration camp survivors and refugees from Germany and occupied Eastern Europe who had lost their businesses, their homes, and their families. Prisoners of war lived in fear of death, not, like some of Murray's relatives in the Ukraine, under threat of generational extinction. They suffered from systematic abuse and neglect, not the orchestrated attempt to annihilate an entire people.

The three navy doctors were lucky: lucky to have survived the bombing of the Cavite Navy Yard, lucky to have escaped the Bataan Death March by mere hours, lucky to have endured the siege of Corregidor, lucky to have left the Philippines on the *Kenwa Maru*, lucky to have emerged unscathed from the American firebombing of Kōbe. Unlike the prison doctors of Nazi Germany, they were never forced to engage in experimental medical procedures; nor did their diagnoses result in inmates being sent to the gas chamber. But comparing your own lot with that of someone whose was worse was no palliative. To the contrary, it forced you to wonder why chance favored you and not others, why you deserved to live and they didn't. Instead of confirming self-worth, it called it into question.

Captain L. B. Sartin, who was liberated from Cabanatuan in February 1945, welcomed Murray back to the realm of the living.

> *Naval Hospital*
> *New Orleans, La.*
> *November 18, 1945*

Dear Murray:
I was delighted to see your name among the survivors who were liberated in Japan. I am thankful that as many got through the awful ordeal as did. Of course the terrible part is that so many perished during the last few weeks, just when liberation was in sight. . . .

I hope that you will enjoy your leave, and I know you will. The transition from prison life will take a while, I know from experience. Everything was so strange when I first returned. I felt like I was in a new world. I have gained about fifty pounds and can no longer get in the clothes I purchased when I first returned.

Let me hear from you from time to time and if I can do anything for you let me know.

Kindest regards.

Sincerely,

L. B. Sartin

John eased back into civilian life. When he arrived at the Brooklyn Navy Yard on October 5, 1945, after convalescing at the U.S. Naval Hospital in Oakland, a medical officer told him he would have to remain there for rehabilitation. "No way," he replied with a resoluteness born from his experience. He took a taxi to 21 East 87th Street in Manhattan, where his parents gave him "a royal welcome," as they put it. He was happy to see his family, but he was noticeably subdued. Thirty-three pounds heavier since liberation, he was still underweight, and at one meal, he polished off a dozen eggs. His ankles were swollen from edema, and his night vision was shot. He was circumspect in speaking of his wartime experience, and his reticence tended to deflect questions about it. By New Year's Eve he was engaged to Ruth Lowe, whom his sister Edith had decided was the girl for him, and he was working as an assistant resident at Bellevue Hospital. He was married in April 1946, by which time he had begun his residency at Mount Sinai Hospital.

Fred, meanwhile, was as angry as a hornet. He was irritable and restless. He couldn't understand the questions people asked him about POW camp life, couldn't grasp that they didn't already know the answers. He set his sights on a fellowship in surgery at Cook County Hospital and hoped the navy would at least pay for his coursework in anatomy and pathology at Northwestern University. The business of writing condolence letters, drafting reports, and submitting commendations for medals and decorations helped focus his energies.

November 25, 1945

Dear Murray,

I am certainly very happy to have heard from you—I understand perfectly how you feel about this readjustment business—I had one helluva time myself when I first got back. . . .

I'm afraid that I was an awful fizzle for the various reporters that interviewed me because I just could not talk about the past—but now it doesn't bother me too much altho [sic] it is very difficult to tell a story because there is so much there.

You undoubtedly remember me mentioning the psychoanalyst that I knew whose daughter I used to go with—well, I've been to his home for dinner and was over just the other night for cocktails. I mentioned your name to him and some of the work you did with hysteria at Kobe and he almost knocked me over when he told me that he had already heard about you. I don't want to tell you what to do, but I feel very strongly, and John does too, that your field is Neuropsychiatry rather than Neurosurgery.

It was a damned shame that we couldn't have met in Frisco, but in some ways it was just as well because I know that the way John and I felt—we just didn't have any desire to go out. I finally broke down and took a cute little nurse out the night before I left. Felt like a high school kid on his first date but finally calmed down and had a grand time. Thanks a lot for calling the folks when you got home—they appreciated it very much as I do.

Well, Murray, that's about all the scuttle for now—keep in touch with me and let me hear from you and some day the three of us will have that party together.

Fred

Many returning veterans suffered from fear and anxiety, listlessness and depression, and were tormented by flashbacks and nightmares in which they relived traumatic events. The doctors had not been engaged in actual combat; nor did they have to live with the consequences of having killed anyone. But they had been subjected to five months of horrific warfare before enduring three and a half years of captivity, and they were haunted by those they had been unable to save. The syndrome came to be known as "post-traumatic stress disorder."

Symptoms of the disorder were first noted in 1871 by Jacob Mendes Da Costa, a Civil War army surgeon who described it as "soldier's heart." In 1919 British cardiologist Sir Thomas Lewis observed a similar affliction in veterans of World War I. That same year Scottish psychiatrist Dr. William Rivers became one of the first doctors to treat veterans by having them recall their traumatic experiences, a technique he used with his most celebrated patient, the war poet Siegfried Sassoon. American psychoanalyst Abram Kardiner went a step further by positing, in 1941, a psychological as well as a physiological basis to war neurosis. In *War Stress and Neurotic Illness*, which he wrote with Herbert Spiegel, Kardiner described five characteristics of war neurosis: a heightened startle response and general irritability; a proclivity for aggressive outbursts; a fixation on trauma; emotional constriction and a reduced level of personality functioning; and an atypical dream life.

But the experience of POWs in World War II, like that of concentration camp survivors, was utterly new to stateside psychoanalysts. Systematic, quantitative studies on the psychological effects of captivity, on the threat of imminent death, and on starvation were rare. Ancel Keys, the creator of the K-ration, launched a pioneering project with Josef Brozek, Austin Henschel, Olaf Mickelsen, and Henry Longstreet Taylor to help prepare for the massive relief efforts in war-torn Europe. Called the Minnesota Experiment, it tracked the effects of controlled starvation on thirty-six conscientious objectors in 1944–45. But their complete findings didn't appear until *The Biology of Human Starvation* was published in 1950. Given the paucity of reliable information, analysts treated postwar psychological disorders with varying degrees of success. As Kardiner and Spiegel admitted, "The real drawback . . . lies in the absence of a consistent psychopathology, which alone can furnish the directives for therapy."

Lacking empirical data, psychiatrists could listen, girlfriends and spouses could offer consolation, but their understanding hinged on the willingness of their patients, lovers, and husbands to talk. And many of them wouldn't because they were psychically numb. Others remained silent because they didn't want pity, they didn't want anyone else to see them in the degraded position to which they had been reduced. The problem was finding a common language, and the only ones who spoke it were their fellow ex-POWs.

Murray dear,

I want to tell you again how wonderful it was to see you, and what a good evening it was last night—

I have some tickets for Maggie Teyte, a most luxurious singer of French songs, for Town Hall, December 19th. Can I take you? It's only fitting, no?

Suppose you call and let me know very soon—I'll be disappointed if you can't make it.

By the way, my mother is most anxious to say hello to you— Perhaps we can arrange that soon?

Love,
Laura

She was living uptown, eager to find an apartment that she and Gerald could move into the next month. Murray was staying with his

mother and father. Had he heard of anything available? Would he keep
an eye out for her and let her know? Murray exploded.

"Where the hell do you think I've been all these years?" he fumed.
"Now I'm supposed to be looking out for you?"

Laura realized her mistake and apologized immediately.

In January 1946 Gerald was discharged from the army, and Laura invited Murray to their new place at 230 East 32nd Street. A husband, a
wife, and her ex-lover. Reality staring four years of yearning in the face.
Murray was polite, but in the pauses between conversation, in the stolen
looks and averted glances, he could only wonder why Laura had married
Gerald instead of waiting for him. How could he not feel abashed for
dreaming of a life that might have been? Didn't she realize that the very
idea of her had sustained him, that she was the girl about whom he had
spoken with Fred, George, and John throughout their captivity? Of
course not. And of course he would never tell her.

The couple had tickets for a concert later that evening, and as they
parted, it struck Gerald that Murray had no place to go.

It was time to move on—and Murray did, without ever seeing Laura
again.

Soon Fred was engaged to Camille Pascale, "a wonderful person," he
wrote Murray. "So now—it is up to you to do your stuff. 1st Jake—then
me—now you?—After all—you are the youngest."

If the war confirmed Fred's intention of becoming a navy surgeon
and clarified John's decision to go into internal medicine with a sub-
specialty in metabolic diseases—particularly diabetes—it had, perhaps,
the most direct influence on the path taken by my father.

Shortly after his repatriation, he began psychoanalysis to cope with
the problems of reintegration. Then he entered the field of psychiatry itself. An indifferent medical school student, he worked feverishly to make
up for lost time. After completing a neurology residency at the New York
Neurological Institute, part of the Columbia University College of
Medicine, he attended the Menninger Foundation School of Psychiatry
in Topeka, Kansas, as a fellow. There he met Louise Johns, a stunning
young doctor whom he married in 1950.

His postwar career in neurological research was launched at New
York State Psychiatric Institute, and he won a position as an assistant
professor of clinical psychiatry at Columbia. His research took off, and
in a double promotion he leaped over an associate professorship to become a full professor. He used his training in neurology to specialize in
behavioral physiology, with a focus on the neural mechanisms in the

brain that trigger responses with which he was all too familiar: fear, anxiety, and aggression.

The effects of the war lingered. He agonized over his papers for publication. An eloquent correspondent, he found himself staring at a blank page in a typewriter when it came time to publicly present his work. He obsessed over grammar, syntax, and spelling as if, like a starving man hoarding a few grains of rice, he was afraid to let go of all that he had left: words. He was riven with self-doubt. Was it good enough? Did it express what he meant to say? Did he speak with the authority he once had, or could readers sense that it had been stolen from him? He feared that his inadequacy, the paucity of ideas, his lack of self-worth, would be exposed. He couldn't write.

Like many POWs, he rarely revealed his wartime experiences to his family. Having created the world anew by having children, were he and his fellow ex-POWs trying, like so many parents, to preserve a halo of innocence around them? Or was burying the past simply the most effective way of dealing with painful memories? Contrary to the basic tenets of traditional analysis—the "talking cure," as it was known in its early days—there is a growing body of research, including studies of Holocaust survivors by Hanna Kaminer and Peretz Lavie, that supports the idea of repression as a means of helping survivors "to seal off the atrocities that they experienced."

"We wanted to get on with our lives," explained John. "We didn't want people to feel sorry for us simply because we had been prisoners of war. We wanted to make it on our own."

Murray and John became the very best of friends, and they remained lifelong friends with Fred. Reunions among the three of them were infrequent, though they were always glad to see one another, always glad to be, simply, present. "A man who has succeeded in living a day without physical suffering should consider himself perfectly happy," wrote the poet Czeslaw Milosz in *Visions of San Francisco Bay*, and they were—as much as they could be. Invariably their war stories were accompanied by laughter. Lazarus-like, it emerged from the recesses of the past. But if laughter, as Viktor Frankl remarked in *Man's Search for Meaning*, is "one of the soul's weapons in the fight for self-preservation," it can also be exclusive, defensive, the language of secret sharers: a dam shoring up tears.

If he can never never forgive Japan for its treatment of POWs in the Pacific, he finds the actions of the U.S. government almost as enigmatic: failing to prosecute Hirohito as a war criminal; drafting and signing the

1951 San Francisco Peace Treaty, which waived "all reparations claims of the Allied Powers and their nationals arising out of any actions taken by Japan"; and continuing to uphold the treaty in spite of the fact that Great Britain, the Isle of Man, Australia, the Netherlands, Norway, and New Zealand all passed legislation to compensate former POWs themselves.

The treaty, the reasoning went, was an assurance that Japan would be a bulwark against Communist aggression in Korea and elsewhere. The U.S. used the same rationale to exonerate Class A war criminals and to commute the sentences of those convicted of war crimes. Peggy and Sterling Seagrave have suggested a darker motive: secretly drafted by John Foster Dulles, the treaty enabled Washington to protect several billion dollars of Japanese war booty seized in the form of "gold, platinum, and barrels of loose gems . . . to create a covert political worldwide action fund."

Undaunted, a group of American ex-POWs who were defenders of Bataan and Corregidor filed suit seeking remuneration from Japanese industrialists who had exploited them as slave laborers in World War II. In November 2003 the California Fourth Appellate District Court of Appeals ruled that "the 1951 treaty is express in not allowing the claims of the plaintiffs." In spite of its ruling, the court acknowledged that "this does not in any way diminish the heroism of these plaintiffs."

But of course it does when you consider that in 1948 the U.S. government gave ex-POWs a paltry $1 for every day they were deprived of adequate rations and added another $1.50 per diem allowance in 1950 as reparations for forced labor and inhumane treatment. Fifty years after the war, by contrast, every Japanese-American interned in the United States—an egregious violation of civil liberties, to be sure—was awarded $20,000, even if interned for only a day. In 2001, Britain finally reached into its own coffers to pay former prisoners of the Japanese £10,000 apiece. Shortly afterward, the U.S. government handed over the back pay it owed ex-POWs for their promotions in captivity. By then, many veterans had died, which spared them the indignity of being compensated in wartime dollars, though their widows and families were not.

It is the principle, not a desire for profit, that chafes at my father. Of course cash settlements cannot compensate for suffering and loss, but they do constitute an admission of guilt and a token attempt at historical restitution. According to the late Iris Chang, Japan has forked over less than 1 percent of the war reparations paid by Germany, which recently awarded $401 million—roughly $3,000 per person—to Jewish survivors of the Holocaust who worked as slave laborers under the Third Reich. Sixty years after the end of World War II, the thinning ranks of American ex-POWs have received neither compensation for their slave labor under the Rising Sun nor an apology from Japan.

My father has never used his POW experience as a marker or signifier in his own life. He would describe himself neither as a survivor, nor as a victim, nor as a veteran. His perspective is informed by a Kafkaesque sense of the absurd, a learned distrust of authority and a distinct distaste for the pomp and circumstance that attend it. Which is not to say that he is free of residual anger.

While John resisted speaking Japanese as a POW, he taught his children how to count from one to ten, how to say please, thank you, and you're welcome. My father had no qualms about using the language of the conqueror, but I never heard him utter a word of it until we were in Tōkyō's Narita Airport en route to the Philippines in 2001. It was his first trip to Japan since the end of the war. He purchased a fifth of duty-free Stolichnaya, twisted off the cap, and took a long swig of warm vodka as we waited for our connecting flight. An eighty-six-year-old man chugging booze out of a brown paper bag. A man, I might add, who was never a heavy drinker.

Once in Tōkyō, he tried to adjust his wartime memory of the city to the cosmopolis it has become. Our suite at the Imperial Hotel was elegant, the service solicitous. When I informed the general manager's assistant that my father was an ex-POW who had last stayed in the Imperial Hotel in August 1945, he paused, shook his head, and said, "War is very, very bad." I don't think my father believed he was sincere. A part of him would have been just as happy, he admitted, to see Tōkyō razed to the ground.

He is convinced that dropping the atomic bomb was the most expedient way of ending the war in the Pacific, that it saved lives, American and Japanese. I am convinced that had the war not ended when it did, Fred Berley, John Bookman, my father, and thousands of other Allied POWs as well as Asian noncombatants would not have survived.

"My God, what have we done?" wrote airplane commander Captain Robert A. Lewis in his log as the *Enola Gay* circled the mushroom cloud that blossomed up from Hiroshima on the morning of August 6, 1945. What had we done, indeed.

I cannot find any moral justification for bombing a civilian population, any more than I can justify an artillery assault against a hospital or a submarine attack against an enemy transport carrying prisoners of war. But morality, of course, is the first casualty of war. German U-boats targeted British merchant shipping in World War I. Japan bombed China's cities in the second Sino-Japanese War. The Condor Legion of the German Luftwaffe, under the command of General Francisco Franco, destroyed 70 percent of the Basque town of Guernica in the Spanish Civil War. Germany's blitz of Britain's cities, from London to Liverpool, resulted in 40,000 civilian deaths in World War II. The RAF retaliated with night raids on German cities, the handiwork, screamed the Nazi press, of Churchill's "criminal clique."

Before World War II, the U.S. castigated Germany's policy of unrestricted submarine warfare, and Secretary of State Cordell Hull denounced "the use of incendiary bombs which inevitably and ruthlessly jeopardize non-military persons and property." America changed course with a vengeance. The firebombing of Japanese cities was quickly branded "slaughter bombing" by Japanese Radio. According to Martin Caidin, in the six months of American firebombing beginning with the March 9, 1945, raid on Tōkyō, Japanese "civilian casualties were more than twice as great as total Japanese military casualties in forty-five months of war." It was brutal, unethical, and immoral, but it also "clinched victory and almost certainly shortened the war in the Far East," concluded historian Richard Overy.

The war ended the Japanese Empire and "precipitated everywhere the downfall of western power in Asia," remarked Peter Calvocoressi and Guy Wint. But the atomic bomb also sealed humanity's fate. To wish that it hadn't been dropped is to wish that my father hadn't lived.

I am not so much a baby boomer as a child of Hiroshima and Nagasaki.

Between 34 and 37 percent of American POWs of the Japanese died in captivity. The mortality rate for German POWs of the Russians was 45 percent, while that of Russian POWs captured by the Germans soared to 60 percent.

By contrast, the mortality rate for American POWs in the Mediterranean and European theaters was less than 1 percent. Historians have long used the high mortality rate of American POWs in the Pacific to emphasize the barbarity of the Japanese. But the picture changes when you take into account the fact that 93 percent of Allied POW deaths at sea in the Pacific theater were not due to ill treatment at the hands of the Japanese but were rather a "direct result," according to Gregory F. Michno, "of Allied bullets, bombs, or torpedoes." A staggering 19,000 POW deaths were caused by friendly fire, nearly a third of the total number of American casualties during the Vietnam War.

Those who survived were more than twice as likely to die in their first two years of freedom as World War II veterans who did not experience incarceration. Three and a half years in a Japanese prison camp, it has been estimated, aged a man by ten to fifteen years, though the Veterans Administration was painfully slow to recognize prison camp–related disabilities, whether physical or psychological.

The scars of the survivors bear witness. Otis King, the 4th Marine who swam from Bataan to Corregidor, still suffers from edema. He wears a size fourteen shoe to accommodate his size eleven feet when they swell up in the morning. His legs balloon, and you can press your fingers into his calves, leaving deep indentations as if his flesh were putty. His buddy Ted Williams lost his eyesight to xerophthalmia and corneal ulcers. Fiery John Kidd, Admiral Hart's assistant in Manila, experienced a lifetime of medical complications following the abdominal sympathectomy that he was forced to undergo without anesthesia at Ichioka. Leatherneck James Fraser walks on two feet without toes, having amputated them after he developed gangrene while trying to relieve the symptoms of "burning feet" by burying them in the snow. On the back of Mike Christle's head you can feel the deep indentation from where he was beaten with a shovel for cheering on American B-29s as they flew over Notogawa POW Camp. The hands of his pal, Everett Reamer, are gnarled from holding buckets of sand in front of him for days on end without food and water at Ōsaka No. 1 Headquarters Camp.

One study found that as many as 78 percent of former POWs of Japan still showed signs of peripheral neuropathy twenty to thirty-five years after the war. Then there are the psychiatric problems that have dogged ex-POWs, who were prone to elevated rates of suicide, accidental death, and hospitalization for psychoneuroses. John Nardini, who later became head of the Neuropsychiatric Branch of the Navy's Bureau of Medicine and Surgery, was so bottled up with anger after the Japanese surrender that he contemplated killing a Japanese guard or staff member—any Japanese would do—until he weighed the practical consequences. According to one VA study conducted between 1968 and 1981, 82 percent of Pacific POWs experienced some kind of psychiatric impairment. Depression was three to five times that of the general population. Another study found that, forty years after the war, 70 percent of POW survivors "fulfilled the criteria for a current diagnosis of PTSD and 78% for a lifetime diagnosis compared to 18% and 29% respectively, of combat veterans" of the Pacific theater. Not only do the psychiatric disorders persist among ex-POWs, but according to a third study, they have shown a marked increase in the last two decades, after peaking in the immediate postwar years and reaching an all-time low in the 1970s. In many cases their resurgence coincided with retirement, a time to reflect, reassess, and revisit the wartime years.

I speak with these men, who allow me into their fraternity as the son of a former POW. In their seventies, eighties, and nineties, they take me, a stranger, into their confidence at the veterans' conventions where we meet, in the elevators, in the hallways, in their hotel bedrooms. They tell me they don't know why they are telling me the things they do: humorous tales, episodes of bravery, brutality, humiliation, and perseverance. Their eyes well up with tears; their memories rouse them to anger. They tell me of nightmares that have suddenly come back after being in abeyance for years. They are surprised that anyone cares.

John Bookman always struck me as the most mild-mannered of men: soft-spoken, even-keeled, someone who would immediately win your trust as a physician. After the war he embarked on an illustrious career in medicine as an internist and then went on to become chief of the Diabetes Clinic at Mount Sinai Hospital. The war, he maintained, had no lasting effect on him. It was a part of his life that was over. But the suffering he witnessed and the Japanese indifference to it continued to affect him. He confided to me in the very apartment he came home to in the fall of 1945: "Every once in a while I have a Japanese patient, and when I examine her throat, the thought goes through my mind of choking her." Six months before John died suddenly in 1986 at the age of seventy-six, he began experiencing the symptoms of "burning feet." The imprint of the past would never be erased.

Of the three surviving POW doctors, Fred Berley was the most willing to forgive the Japanese. A navy surgeon who retired as a rear admiral, he approached his life and work with military vigor. In December 1946 he sent a Christmas card to Ōhashi in which he spoke of his desire to visit the doctor in Wakayama, where Ōhashi had established a new practice. Ōhashi wrote back expressing "a heavy heart with penitence and thanks." Fred would eventually visit Japan, entertain Japanese guests in his home, and even play host to Japanese foreign exchange students.

He would forgive, but he would never forget what he believed was the uniqueness of Japanese cruelty. "I wish we were fighting against Germans," John Hersey quoted a marine on Guadalcanal as saying. "They are human beings, like us. . . . But the Japanese are like animals." Indeed, Japan's language, culture, and political heritage, even its conception of time, tied to the emperor's reign, are unique. In the context of its history, Japan's fifteen years of war were unique. But Japanese cruelty, I would argue, was not.

The Germans slaughtered 6 million Jews and 20 million Russians in World War II. From 1931 to 1945 the Japanese were responsible for 17,222,500 deaths, according to historian Robert Newman, many of whom were ethnic Chinese. The systematic ruthlessness forged by a modern military ethos that bent political and civilian life to its will was unique in the history of Japan. But in the larger context of the twentieth century, whose catalog of horrors began with the Philippine-American War and ended in Kosovo, a century that witnessed gruesome trench warfare in World War I, the Spanish Civil War, the Holocaust, the fire-bombing of Dresden and Tōkyō, the dropping of the atomic bomb on Hiroshima and Nagasaki, the extermination of 1.65 million Cambodians by the Khmer Rouge, the Iraq-Iran war, the extermination in Rwanda of 800,000 Tutsis by the Hutu majority, the extermination of 7,000 Muslims in Srebenica by Bosnian Serbs, civil wars in Angola, Algeria, the Congo, Sudan, and Sierra Leone, a century in which 100 million people died in wars, was Japanese cruelty unique? It was unique insofar as there were standing orders to Japanese soldiers to take no captives, and insofar as cruelty to civilians and noncombatants, if not explicitly sanctioned by the state as in Nazi Germany, was tacitly approved by Hirohito's failure to uphold the imperial rescripts of his father and grandfather that respected international law and the rights of prisoners of war.

What was most disturbing to Fred Berley, John Bookman, and my father, I suspect, was ultimately not the ease with which the Japanese carried out the most heinous of acts, or the scale of them, but the reflection those acts cast on human nature. They subscribed to the Western notion espoused by Aristotle and Aquinas that human beings are, in essence, benevolent. To them, neglecting the sick and killing the wounded was "unnatural." It defied the very reason they became doctors. It ran counter to the rules of war as they understood them, and contrary to their conception of who and what people are. The war shattered their weltanschauung, or worldview. It turned their moral universe upside down, called into question their very idea of humanity. At the same time they subscribed to the notion, as the former head of statistical analysis for the Twentieth Air Force, Robert S. McNamara, put it, that "in order to do good, you may have to engage in evil."

History, Chris Hedges reminds us, is revised, denied, exaggerated, and fabricated for political purposes. The Turkish government refuses to acknowledge the Armenian genocide of 1915, in which one million died. Croatian strongman Franjo Tudjman asserted that the Germans killed one million Jews in the Holocaust, not six million. Japanese nationalists such as Ishihara Shintarō, a former cabinet minister and coauthor with Watanabe Shōichi of *The Japan That Can Say No*, maintain that the Rape of Nanking is "a story made up by the Chinese."

Historical grievances may be transmitted from one generation to another, argues psychiatrist Vamik Volkan, whether it is Czechs sustaining the memory of the Battle of Bilá in 1620, which marked their absorption into the Habsburg monarchy for 300 years; Scots reliving the Battle of Culloden and Bonnie Prince Charlie's ill-fated attempt to restore a Stuart to the English Crown in 1746; or Chinese soccer fans burning the Japanese flag at a game in Beijing's Worker Stadium and chanting: "May a big sword chop off the Japanese heads!" Transgenerational trauma, Hedges adds, can also be invented. Palestinian refugees in Gaza camps identify themselves with villages where they never lived and that no longer even exist.

The writer Eva Hoffman, whose parents were Holocaust survivors, rejects the idea of a "second generation" who consider themselves victims of victims "damaged by calamities that had been visited on somebody else." The role of succeeding generations is not, as I see it, to incorporate the pain of one's parents in a vain attempt to relieve it, but to understand the origin of the trauma and its subsequent manifestations.

My father eats chicken until there is only a nest of bones left on his plate; then he consumes the bones. He would rather do without than drink green tea. He hoards his mail. For years he would not buy Japanese products. When my older brother, out of childish curiosity, once got his hands on the razor my father had used while a POW and accidentally nicked its edge, he "blew his stack," as my mother called his periodic outbursts.

When I was twenty-four years old, a friend of mine was diagnosed with a primary tumor of the liver. She died six months later. It was my first encounter with the death of a contemporary.

"That's the way the ball bounces," my father said.

I asked him if that was all he had to say.

"I've seen football fields of men go down," he offered by way of explanation.

It was an interesting choice of words, a sports metaphor: life as a game to be played, war as a test of mettle and manliness, with clear winners and losers. "Play the greater game and join the Football Battalion," urged one British recruiting poster during World War I. He had been referring to those who perished on the hellships, and at the time the association couldn't have been more foreign to me. I had never so much as heard of George Ferguson or a hellship, and without understanding the context of the remark, I was unable to read the message struggling for articulation.

"They seemed to lose emotional regard for their fellow prisoners," said army doctor Lieutenant Colonel Norman Q. Brill on the basis of neurological and psychiatric examinations of 4,617 RAMPs who had been confined in Japan for thirty-nine months or more. "One man reported waking when light returned in the hold of the prison ship and seeing his friend's throat cut and his canteen gone. This did not move him at all."

My father was moved by the story of my friend's death; he simply couldn't express it. What he was trying to say was: I know what it's like to lose a dear friend.

In Western culture, the enormity of the Holocaust has overshadowed the experience of Allied POWs of the Far East. There is no literary work comparable to Elie Wiesel's *Night*, or to Primo Levi's *Survival in Auschwitz*, no civilian diaries that speak to us with the urgency of Anne Frank or Etty Hillesum, no fiction with the imaginative power of Thomas Mann's *Dr. Faustus* or Günter Grass's *The Tin Drum*.

In Japan, Tasaki Hanama's novel *Long the Imperial Way*, Noma Hiroshi's *Zone of Emptiness*, Ooka Shohei's *Fires on the Plain*, and Senō Kappa's *A Boy Called H* offer powerful portraits of Japanese military culture and of the deprivations experienced on the home front. In his novel *The Sea and the Poison*, Endō Shūsaku, a Catholic, writes chillingly of the lack of conscience displayed by a Japanese doctor who assists in a lethal medical experiment on an American POW. But the two literary masterpieces to emerge from the Pacific theater remain John Hersey's nonfiction work *Hiroshima* and Ibuse Masuji's novel *Black Rain*, also about Hiroshima. The suffering of Pacific POWs has dimmed in the afterglow of the atomic bomb, as the country paved over its past with the tacit approval of its American occupiers and revised its history from that of aggressor to that of victim in charting and building its future.

Ask a Japanese veteran, such as Arakawa Tatsuzō of the 3rd Battalion, 20th Regiment, about atrocities committed against prisoners of war on Bataan, and the subject will quickly change to the civilian deaths caused by the American incendiary campaign over Japan and the dropping of the atomic bomb. In 1993 Prime Minister Hosokawa Morihiro—whose grandfather, Prince Konoe Fumimaro, evaded responsibility as prime minister during the Nanking massacre and the signing of the 1940 Axis Pact by committing suicide in 1945 after being charged as a Class A war criminal—acknowledged that Japan had waged "an aggressive war and a wrong war." Less than a decade later Prime Minister Koizumi Jun'ichirō authorizes new history textbooks that glorify Japan's imperial past and visits Yasukuni Shrine, an altar of Japanese militarism that houses the remains of Class A war criminals and memorializes the Kempeitai, Japan's military police. Konishi Yukio, the priest at Juganji Temple outside Ōsaka, where the ashes of 1,086 Allied POWs repose, tells me that during his time no government officials have attended the annual memorial ceremony he holds for Allied servicemen who died on Japanese soil during World War II.

There has been no public discourse in Japan about its role in the Pacific War comparable to that in Germany over the causes and consequences of Nazism, no recognition of the plight of Allied POWs, no gesture as powerful as former West German chancellor Willy Brandt's when, after the Berlin Wall was toppled, he got down on his knees in the former Warsaw Ghetto to beg forgiveness for his country's past. The Rape of Nanking is briefly described in every Japanese history textbook approved by the Ministry of Education and is taught to high school seniors, and the plight of POWs on the notorious Burma-Siam Railway is referred to in some of them. But the ordeal of American and Filipino POWs on the Bataan Death March is mentioned in only a few— *Nippon-shi B* (History of Japan), *Shin Nippon-shi B* (New History of Japan), and *Waido Nippon no Rekishi* (Wide History of Japan)—and the entries run no more than a single sentence. Asian neighbors, China and Korea, have successfully pressed their cases for Japan's accountability during World War II; the United States has not. The story of Allied POWs under the Japanese is entirely absent from *Senshi Sōsho*, the official Japanese military history of World War II. Is this the difference, Ian Buruma has asked, between what anthropologist Ruth Benedict called a "shame culture" in Japan and a "guilt culture" in Germany? Or is it the legacy of Hirohito's absolution, for which the Americans must be held accountable? Sixty years after Tōkyō feverishly tried to destroy evidence of war crimes before the first occupation troops landed on the Home Islands, Japan has yet to officially acknowledge the extent of its wartime culpability.

I bear no ill will toward the Japanese people. Sadness over their role in World War II, yes, but not anger. I am encouraged by independent organizations such as the Center for Research and Documentation on Japan's Wartime Responsibility, the POW Research Network, and the Ōsaka International Peace Center, a museum that offers simple but powerful presentations on Japan's fifteen-year war of aggression, as well as the American firebombing campaign and the dropping of the atomic bomb on Hiroshima and Nagasaki. Yet as I walk the streets of Kōbe and Ōsaka, I cannot find a single historical marker indicating the existence of

Tsumori, Ichioka,Wakayama, Kōbe House, the Kōbe POW Hospital, Wakinohama, or even Ōsaka No. 1 Headquarters Camp. Over the site of Maruyama rises a gleaming white condominium complex.

———————

As Colonel Murata's eldest daughter, Inoue Kiyoko, demonstrates the art of Japanese tea (*cha-do*) for me at her 100-year-old house in Kyōto, she tells me that her father never spoke of his work as commandant of the Ōsaka area camps. She never knew the location of Ōsaka No. 1 Headquarters Camp. He was a good man, she says, who had a hard life. Hadn't he established the Kōbe POW Hospital? Hadn't he received a commendation from Archbishop Marella for letting priests minister to prisoners and looking after the safety of POWs during air raids? She speaks in a voice at once plaintive, imploring, and keening, as if she were in mourning. She cannot accept the idea that he was responsible for the maltreatment of Allied POWs, much less for any prisoner's death.

When I meet Nakato Masako and her family in Kōbe, they tell me I am the first Westerner to step inside their home. Masako is the head of an unofficial organization known as the Kōbe Bombing Victims group. Tsuji Hideko, one of the group's members and sixty-nine years of age, tells me the story of the March 15–16 fire raid from the perspective of a thirteen-year-old girl. When she is finished, she raises a trouser leg to reveal a large discolored scar from where she was burned. Then she lowers her head, parts her hair, and exposes a bald spot, at the center of which is an ugly keloid scar. Red, raised, shaped like a crab from the build-up of keratonin, it is a daily reminder to her of the terror she experienced that fateful night in 1945. Masako adds her own graphic account, even though she was a fetus in her mother's womb at the time. Her teenage daughter Atuko listens spellbound. She has never heard her mother mention a word about the firebombing of Kōbe, words that really belong to her dead grandmother.

When I finally meet Ōhashi Yoshihisa in Takarazuka, a suburb of Ōsaka, it is like meeting an old friend. By pure coincidence he works in Sunshine City, a huge office complex built on the site of Sugamo Prison, where the grandfather he never knew was imprisoned for suspected war crimes. He hosts a lunch for me with his aunts—Dr. Ōhashi's daughters—his mother, and his children. Miyazaki Shunya, the sickly teenager whom Lieutenant Commander Page treated for tuberculosis at the Kōbe POW Hospital—now in his late seventies—also attends. We raise a glass to our forebears, avidly exchange information, and thumb through carefully preserved photo albums of the Ōhashi family dating back to Meiji-era Japan. There are wedding pictures and formal family portraits, shots of Dr.

Ōhashi in the army and in the operating room. But I find myself providing captions to an image that seems to have been torn from the pages of history. While Yoshi had seen, as a child, the official photograph of the medical staff of the Kōbe Prisoner of War Hospital dated November 1944, his father rarely spoke about his own father's wartime experiences. Indeed, Yoshi could identify only one man in it, his grandfather Dr. Ōhashi; the POWs themselves were anonymous. Neither he nor his aunts, Yasuko and Kazuko, were aware of the circumstances of that group portrait, one of two extant photographs of my father as a prisoner of the Japanese, without which I would never have been able to locate the Ōhashi family.

We are sitting on the terrace of the Corregidor Inn, each sipping a bottle of San Miguel beer. From our perch my father and I have a view of the former 92nd Garage Area, now a sandy beach. It is a beautiful day, and the island, densely foliated after sixty years with *kupan* trees and white *luan,* bamboo and mangrove, evokes a Pacific paradise. I try to picture the Japanese attack of December 29, 1941. I don't have to look far because the fire-blackened remains of barracks such as Middleside, vaunted with Ozymandias-like arrogance for its invincibility, stand on Corregidor to this day. Bombed first by the Japanese and then by the Americans during the island's liberation, they look like ancient ruins, a maze of stairways leading to the sky, window frames gaping into thin air, slabs of concrete dangling from twisted, rusted steel rods, a concrete skeleton blackened by a hatred that transcends race, nationality, culture, and time.

Wars divide, they damage, they destroy. It is a commonplace that they also foster camaraderie, forge unlikely friendships, and link men to one another as "blood brothers," as POWs called the ten-men shooting squads at Cabanatuan. The irony is not lost on me that what has brought me closer to my father at the end of his life is the war that took him captive at the beginning of it. Memory yields to historical record as I learn things about him, his friends, and the world in which they lived that he himself never knew. Our roles as father and son, teacher and student, have been inverted. Or if not inverted, as Wordsworth would have it, at least they have achieved a kind of parity. We are each other's own best audience, hungry for information, eager to share. I detect the young man in the old man he thought he would never become.

"Those who have not lived through the experience," Elie Wiesel wrote, referring to the Nazi death camps, "will never know; those who have will never tell; not really, not completely." Indeed, if war remains the palimpsest behind the narrative of my father's life, there are inevitably elisions in the manuscript, scenes forgotten, episodes omitted, questions that remain all the more compelling for their having gone unanswered: resonance from irresolution.

In the telling, his story has become our story, but our story will always be their story, of four American doctors and their fight for life as prisoners of the Japanese, a small chapter in the history of World War II, to be handed down from one generation to the next.

Epilogue

ON A COLD, RAINY DAY in November 1945, a letter arrived at the Ōhashis' new house in Kizuyama that stunned the doctor and his wife. By order of GHQ Memorandum AG 000.5 concerning the "Apprehension and Detention of Certain Individuals," Ōhashi Hyōjirō was to be interrogated for suspected war crimes.

Yukako had no idea of what her husband had done. Their children couldn't understand why their father was leaving home. Ōhashi dutifully packed a small bag, put on his uniform, and on November 27 was escorted by a member of the Japanese Liaison Office to Tōkyō's Sugamo Prison, a complex of squat, featureless buildings containing 700 cells. He was photographed front and profile, fingerprinted, and confined to Cell No. 3. The former POW camp commandant was now a prisoner. He had been charged with no crime.

Article 10 of the Potsdam Declaration declared that "stern justice shall be meted out to all war criminals, including those who have visited cruelties upon our prisoners." Within days of MacArthur's arrival in Japan, SCAP began rounding up cabinet ministers and military officers, career diplomats and government advisers, POW camp commandants, doctors, orderlies, guards, and interpreters. Thousands of suspects were caught in the American dragnet, from ex–Prime Minister Tōjō, who bungled his own suicide just before he was apprehended, to former Naval Chief of Staff Admiral Nagano Osami, from Foreign Minister Shigemitsu to Colonel Murata Sōtarō, commandant of the Ōsaka area camps.

On January 19, 1946, MacArthur announced the formation of the International Military Tribunal for the Far East (IMTFE) in Tōkyō, which would prosecute not only conventional war crimes but "crimes against peace." The court consisted of eleven justices; the charter governing the Tōkyō trials was based on the Nuremberg Charter. Because so much incriminating evidence had been destroyed by the Japanese immediately following the surrender, affidavits and statements of ex-POWs played a key role in the prosecution of war criminals. Convictions carried sentences that ranged from imprisonment to death.

The defendants were categorized as Class A for those who conspired to wage war "in violation of international treaties"; Class B for those who violated "the laws and customs of war"; and Class C for those who committed atrocities against prisoners of war or withheld "medical treatment and/or supplies necessary for survival."

The emperor's role, MacArthur argued—over British, Australian, and Soviet objections, as well as a joint resolution passed by the U.S. Congress in late September 1945—was vital for Japan's transition to a democratic society. "Destroy him," he cautioned Eisenhower by telegram on January 25, 1946, "and the nation will disintegrate."

Hirohito remained immune from prosecution, as did General Ishii Shirō and his cohorts in Unit 731, which was responsible for bacteriological and medical experiments on more than 3,000 Allied prisoners of war. The Joint Chiefs of Staff and MacArthur were as eager to obtain the details of Japan's biological weapons program and its experiments on live human subjects as they were to prevent the data from falling into Communist hands.

The Allied chief prosecutor was Joseph Keenan, who declared: "In this very courtroom will be made manifest to the Japanese people themselves the elements of a fair trial which, we dare say, perhaps they may not have enjoyed in the fullness—in all of their past history." To which Senator Robert A. Taft countered: "The trial of the vanquished by the victors cannot be impartial no matter how it is hedged about with the forms of justice."

Twenty-eight of Japan's political and military leaders designated Class A criminals were named in the fifty-five-count indictment of April 29, 1946, and found guilty of a "criminal conspiracy to wage wars of aggression." Some 5,100 Japanese were accused of Class B and Class C war crimes.

General Yamashita Tomoyuki, the "Tiger of Malaya" and commander of all Japanese forces in the Philippines; General Homma Masaharu, whose troops brutalized American and Filipino POWs on the infamous Bataan Death March; and General Kou Shiyoku, commandant of the prisoner of war camps in the Philippines, were swiftly tried by the five-man U.S. Military Commission in Manila and executed. General Curtis LeMay himself admitted to Robert McNamara that "if we'd lost the war, we'd all have been prosecuted as war criminals."

Habe Toshitarō of Tsumori POW Camp was sentenced to eight years' hard labor. Bandō Bunhachi of Ichioka ("All men die, jōtō [good]! All men die!") was sentenced to six years of hard labor. His sidekick, Katō

Masayoshi, faced twenty-five years of hard labor. Nosu Shōichi, the "Mad Butcher," was never brought to trial, Lieutenant David Hochman believed, for reason of insanity due to tertiary syphilis. Colonel Murata received a lifetime of hard labor. Uchiyama Eitarō, Yamanaka Norio, Ono Buicho, Matsumori Hideo, Ogiya Yorio, Nakamichi Kanji, and Kunitake Michio, all of whom were tried in connection with the execution of Sergeant Algy S. Augunus and 2nd Lieutenant Robert W. Nelson, received sentences ranging from three years to thirty years of hard labor, while death by hanging was the punishment meted out to Ōtahara Kiyotomi, the former head of the Judicial Section of the Fifteenth Area Army. Wada Shūsuke, the interpreter aboard the *Oryoku Maru*, stared at a lifetime of hard labor. His superior, Toshino Junsaburō, was executed on August 18, 1948, as was "Air Raid" Ihara. The charges against Fukuyama Tsuyoshi, commanding officer of the *Harukaze*, and Ueyanagi Isamu, his executive officer, for refusing to rescue POWs from the sinking *Arisan Maru*, were dropped "in view of the tactical situation, i.e., the close proximity of hostile forces." The case was closed.

Ōhashi Kazuko knew that her father's incarceration must have something to do with the treatment of Allied prisoners of war. One former POW, Corporal Foster H. Templon of the 24th Pursuit Group, had already given testimony against Ōhashi for purloining Red Cross parcels "for his own use" and that of his staff at the Kōbe POW Hospital.

Months passed. His cell was small, furnished with a *tatami* mat, table, electric lamp, and toilet. Inmates were responsible for keeping their quarters clean and were assigned prison duties. There were gardens outside, a library inside, and a doctor available twenty-four hours a day. The practice of religion was encouraged. A Japanese priest, Dr. Hanayama Shinshō, presided over a separate Buddhist altar. But while living conditions at Sugamo had improved from the days when it held political prisoners, security had also been tightened. A ten-foot-high barbed-wire fence was erected around a newly created outer compound, not so much to prevent escapes as to deter cold and hungry Japanese citizens from stealing food and fuel from the Americans.

Ōhashi lost weight. He grew a thin, scraggly beard. Depressed, he suffered from diarrhea and had trouble sleeping. Yasuko was allowed to bring him books to read, most of which were of a religious nature. In February 1946 Kazuko consulted a Japanese lawyer who told her, "They are very strict. . . . But if he has done nothing wrong you can only wait and believe that he will be declared innocent."

Ōhashi met Tōjō in Sugamo, but the former prime minister preferred fraternizing with the guards rather than with his fellow prisoners. The

Japanese doctor turned to Buddhist writings for solace. He copied numerous sutras and kept a diary. "To that higher dignity which alone
benefits the sacred purpose we are about to serve," he wrote in English
on the first page. He also tried his hand at haiku:

> The moon is bright
> Brilliant sunset-burned clouds
> Darken its light.

His family didn't know what they could do to help him, but Ōhashi
thought of one thing: the letter the POW doctors had written on
June 17, 1945, expressing "nothing but praise and thanks for the sincere
and untiring efforts which were made by the Nipponese Hospital and
Medical Authorities to feed and house us, and to make the sick and injured comfortable."

On April 27, 1946, a guard approached Ōhashi and spoke the words
he had been waiting months to hear: "You may go home."

The good doctor bowed, palms pressed together.

"Is it true?" he asked. "I cannot believe it."

The guard showed him his discharge papers. Ōhashi Hyōjirō was no
longer a suspected war criminal. He was to be released and returned to
his former status. He was free.

───────────

Nogi Naraji, the former director of the hospital at Bilibid Prison, was
not so lucky. He was also far from blameless. Technically Nogi had been
in charge of all medical units in the prisoner of war camps throughout
the Philippines from November 11, 1942, until the Japanese surrendered the archipelago. He had watched 100 men die of diphtheria at
Bilibid before administering antitoxin. At Santo Tomás he had once insisted that the internee medical staff delete the words "malnutrition" and
"starvation" from eight death certificates because they reflected unfairly
on the Japanese administration. "World conditions," he had asserted,
"were such that everybody was suffering from a shortage of food." He
had authorized the dispatch of POWs on the Oryoku Maru when many
of them were clearly unfit for the voyage and had selected the drugs and
medical supplies that were to accompany them, even though this was the
responsibility of the shipping transport unit.

But Nogi's sentence of twenty-five years at hard labor for failing to
provide proper food, clothing, housing, and medical care to POWs,
when food and housing were the responsibility of the supply officer,
struck dozens of ex-POWs as unfair. Lieutenant Colonel Walter Waterous was a key witness against him. Lieutenant Colonel Jack Schwartz, an

Oryoku Maru survivor, "chided" Waterous for his testimony and hoped he would recant. Nogi's defense attorney, Ellis Filene, launched a campaign to free him and collected statements and affidavits on his behalf from Schwartz, Manila schoolteacher Nancy Belle Norton, 4th Marine Ted Williams, and Chaplain Perry O. Wilcox of Bilibid, among others, which he submitted to GHQ. Nogi was freed after serving nine years of his twenty-five-year sentence.

Meanwhile, U.S. Army sergeant John David Provoo was tried and found guilty of four acts of treason, which included contributing to the death of Captain Burton C. Thompson on Corregidor. The U.S. Supreme Court overturned the conviction on the grounds that Provoo—also known as Nichijo Shaka—had been denied the right to a speedy trial.

In January 1957, four years after Provoo's conviction, Ōhashi Hyōjirō died of cancer. He never had a chance to entertain Fred Berley in Wakayama, and he never had a chance to visit America. By December 1958 all of Japan's convicted war criminals were pardoned by the United States, and the gates of Sugamo Prison were closed forever. But the doors of Juganji Temple, where the remains of Allied POWs are kept along with hundreds of family letters, photographs, and mementos, are still open.

"Each day," Konishi Yukio said to me from the peaceful shrine on Mt. Ikoma that overlooks Ōsaka, "I pray that this tragedy is not repeated."

ACKNOWLEDGMENTS

Conduct Under Fire originated as an essay I wrote for the late Staige Blackford at the *Virginia Quarterly Review.* An article on Corregidor for Sheila Glaser, then at *Travel + Leisure,* enabled me to visit the Philippines with my father in 2001. My agent, David Black, encouraged me to extend my journey into a book, for which I will always be thankful.

Michael and Beth Norman, coauthors of the forthcoming history of the Bataan Death March, *Tears in the Darkness,* were selfless supporters of this project from the beginning and provided essential advice for research both in the United States and in the Philippines. Frank Gibney of the Pacific Basin Institute kindly put me in touch, via Hijino Shigeki, with Ishii Shinpei, who handled my Japanese research. Shinpei tracked down original documents, key interview subjects, and the locations of many of the Japanese POW camps described herein, and he introduced me to a team of sleuths dedicated to documenting the experience of Allied POWs in the Pacific War, the POW Research Network in Japan. John Dower was an early advocate and rightly recommended John Junkerman as a translator of Japanese texts.

My gratitude to the following archivists and academics, writers and researchers: Jan K. Herman, historian of the Navy Medical Department at the Bureau of Medicine and Surgery in Washington, D.C., was generous with BUMED's historical materials, read the manuscript, and made many useful suggestions; Kenneth Schlesinger and Barry Zerby of the Modern Military Records Branch of the National Archives conscientiously pursued arcane document requests; Richard Long, the retired curator and historian of the Marine Corps History and Museums Division, unearthed useful records of the 4th Marines; Dr. Richard J. Sommers of the Military History Institute steered me to fascinating U.S. Army and ATIS reports; Ricardo Trota Jose, historian at the University of the Philippines, was a gracious host in Quezon City, and an invaluable reader of the manuscript, which benefited greatly from his review; Andrew Miller, historian of the American Defenders of Bataan and Corregidor, kindly vetted sections on Bataan, Corregidor, and Cabanatuan; Roger Mansell proved a valuable critic and a fount of information on POWs in the Far East with a Web site (www.mansell.com) as impressive as Sallyann Wagoner's for the 73rd Bomb Wing (home.att.net/~sallyann2/ 73bomb-wing-data.html); Robert J. Hanyok, senior historian at the National Security Agency Center for Cryptologic History, hunted down guerrilla messages between the Philippines and Australia and explained the intricacies of their radio networks on Luzon and Mindanao; Rear Admiral Donald Showers patiently described for me the daily activities of FRUPAC, FRUMEL, and the role of ULTRA intelligence; Gregory F. Michno, author of the definitive *Death on the Hellships*, shared radio intercepts and notes from the Submarine Force Library in Groton, Connecticut; Colonel Rafael Estrada of the Filipino Defenders of Bataan and Corregidor was our distinguished guide to the old Cavite Navy Yard and Bilibid Prison; Edna Binkowski helped locate the old navy tunnels in Mariveles and Hospital No. 1 on Bataan; and Ibuki Yuka, Nagasawa Nori, Hirata Noriko, and Miyazaki Shunya found original documents, oral testimony, and photographs pertaining to wartime Kōbe and Ōsaka. Toru Fukubayashi, a founding member of the POW Research Network in Japan, along with Utsumi Aiko and Sasamoto Takeo, uncovered crucial GHQ/SCAP documents on Ichioka, Tsumori, and Wakayama.

My appreciation extends to Kathy Lloyd of the Washington Navy Yard; Archie Difante of Maxwell Air Force Base; James Zobel of the MacArthur Memorial Archive; Fabrizio Bensi of the Historical Archives Unit of the International Committee of the Red Cross in Geneva; Tsunemoto Hajime of the Ōsaka International Peace Center; Dr. Claire Panosian, professor of medicine and infectious diseases at the UCLA Medical Center; Dr. Andrew Spielman, professor of tropical public health at Harvard University's School of Public Health; Dr. Harvey N. Himel of the William Randolph Hearst Burn Center at New York Presbyterian Hospital; and Linda Goetz Holmes, author of *Unjust Enrichment*.

Karen Broderick performed valuable photo research. Anne Fadiman kindly granted permission on behalf of the estate of Annalee Jacoby Fadiman for the use of Melville Jacoby's haunting wartime photographs of Bataan and Corregidor in the Time, Inc., Picture Collection. Michael Emmerich was a conscientious second reader for Japanese style, usage, and consistency. Karen Coeman graciously translated Dutch military records for me, and Deanna Heikkinen, correspondence in Spanish.

Joe Vater welcomed me into the veterans' organization, the American Defenders of Bataan and Corregidor, whose valiant members could not have been more forthcoming with their stories, as were the 4th Marines, thanks to Martin Christie. Especial thanks to Ted Williams for his detailed recollections of Cavite and Mariveles; Jimmy Carrington for his descriptions of ELGFA guerrilla activities; Philip Brodsky for his remarkable account of the *Arisan Maru* sinking; and John Cook, John Kidd, Dr. David Hochman, and Duane Heisinger for sharing unique manuscript and research materials. Ed Keyser invited me to the annual reunion of the 73rd Bomb Wing Association, where I was introduced to the world of the B-29 bomber and the men who flew their missions over Japan. June Faubion of the Defenders of Wake, Guam, and Cavite directed me to important sources of information on Tsumori POW Camp.

Conduct Under Fire could not have been written without the cooperation of numerous World War II ex-POWs, veterans, and their families, who opened their lives to me in spite of memories that were at times difficult to share. Foremost among them are Fred and Camille Berley; Lucille Ferguson and Jane Klecan, the widow and sister of George Ferguson, respectively; the late John Bookman and his son, Richard, and daughter, Ann; Gerald Blank, the widower of the late Laura Reade; Ali Arnold-Brown and the late Christopher Page, daughter and son of the late John Allison Page; Margaret Mace, daughter of the late John Akeroyd; Duane A. Smith, son of the late Stanley L. Smith; Jennifer Eastberg, daughter of the late Ralph Hibbs; Dale Wilber, whose father, the late Avery Wilber, was an *Arisan Maru* survivor; Bill Bowen, whose father perished on the *Arisan Maru*; Keeney Hayes, granddaughter of Thomas Hirst Hayes, who unhesitatingly offered information that proved essential to my understanding of the medical activities of the 4th Marines on Bataan and Corregidor; Ōhashi Yoshihisa and his family for opening up the world of Ōhashi Hyōjirō for me and allowing me to touch a piece of history that I assumed had vanished long ago; and of course, my mother, Louise, my father, Murray, and my aunt, Estelle.

The late Roger Straus, renowned publisher, colleague, inspiration, and friend, never missed an opportunity to remind me that editors are supposed to edit, not write, all the while wholeheartedly endorsing this project. Jonathan Galassi, a brilliant publisher, editor, translator, and poet in his own right, understands what it takes to write a book while working full time, and he couldn't have been more accommodating. My associate, Aodaoin Ofloinn, ran my office effortlessly in both my absence and my presence and was an unflagging source of encouragement and help. Steve Brown offered book-saving technical support with deadpan panache. Dear friends Sarah and Avo Reid were warm hosts to numerous research trips of mine to Washington, D.C. Kathryn Court is one of the great editors in the world of publishing, and it is a privilege to be published by her and her talented colleagues in the Penguin Group.

Ali Bothwell Mancini was a rigorous editor, offered many valuable suggestions, and smoothly shepherded the book through production.

Lastly, I would like to thank my wife, Emily, for her unwavering support, for assuming the lion's share of family responsibilities while I was holed up writing or traveling for research, and for still being able to toss together a gourmet dinner late at night and after a long day at the office, only to rise early the next morning to tackle a job far more demanding than mine.

To all of you, my deepest thanks.

NOTES

Some abbreviations frequently used in the Notes and Bibliography:

ACICR — Archives of the International Committee of the Red Cross (Archives du Comité International de la Croix-Rouge), Geneva, Switzerland

AFHRC — Air Force Historical Research Center, Maxwell Air Force Base, Alabama

ATIS — Allied Translator and Interpreter Section

BUMED — Bureau of Medicine and Surgery, Washington, D.C.

GHQ/SCAP — General Headquarters/Supreme Commander of Allied Powers

MCHC — Marine Corps Historical Center, Washington Navy Yard, Washington, D.C.

MHI — Military History Institute, Carlisle Barracks, Pennsylvania

MMA — Douglas MacArthur Memorial Archive, Norfolk, Virginia

MR — Microfilm roll

NARA — National Archives Records Administration, College Park, Maryland

NHC — Naval Historical Center, Washington Navy Yard, Washington, D.C.

RAC — Rockefeller Archive Center, Sleepy Hollow, New York

RG — Record Group

UNTOHC — University of North Texas Oral History Collection, Denton, Texas

USSBS — United States Strategic Bombing Survey

WCO/JAG — War Crimes Office, Judge Advocate General's Department, U.S. War Department

Prologue

1 **With the fall:** James H. Belote and William M. Belote, *Corregidor: The Saga of a Fortress* (New York: Harper and Row, 1967), p. 75.

2 **Fifty million lives:** I.C.B. Dear and M.R.D. Foot, eds., *The Oxford Companion to World War II* (New York: Oxford University Press, 1995), p. 291.

2 **2.35 million Japanese:** ibid., p. 290.

2 **406,000 Americans:** American Battle Monuments Commission, Washington, D.C.

2 **Between September 1940:** Mark Jonathan Harris, Franklin D. Mitchell, and Steven J. Schecter, *The Home Front: America*

During World War II (New York: G.P. Putnam's Sons, 1984), p. 46.

2 **Nearly 2 million American women:** David M. Kennedy, *Freedom from Fear: The American People in Depression and War, 1929–1945* (New York: Oxford University Press, 1999), p. 778.

2 **59,000 women joined:** Judith A. Bellafaire, "The Army Nurse Corps in World War II," U.S. Army Center of Military History.

2 **Some 56,000 physicians:** Albert E. Cowdrey, *Fighting for Life: American Military Medicine in World War II* (New York: Free Press, 1994), p. 101.

2 **Mobile Army Surgical Hospital:** The
Mobile Army Surgical Hospital, or MASH,
was added to the U.S. Army Medical Service
Corps in 1948. See Richard V. N. Ginn, *The
History of the U.S. Army Medical Service Corps*
(Washington, D.C.: Office of the Surgeon
General and U.S. Army Center of Military
History, 1997), p. 200.

2 **"Barbarians of the Pacific":** John H.
Crider, "Unity Is Stressed," *New York Times*,
September 17, 1944, p.1.

2 **Such language bore:** John W. Dower,
*War Without Mercy: Race and Power in the
Pacific War* (New York: Pantheon, 1986),
p. 221.

3 **As *shidō minzoku:*** ibid., p. 203.

3 **"Eight Corners of the World Under
One Roof":** ibid., p. 274.

3 **The Pacific POW:** E. Bartlett Kerr,
*Surrender and Survival: The Experience of
American POWs in the Pacific, 1941–1945*
(New York: William Morrow, 1985), p. 297.

3 **Of the approximately 193,000:** Van
Waterford, *Prisoners of the Japanese in World
War II: Statistical History, Personal Narratives
and Memorials Concerning POWs in Camps
and on Hellships, Civilian Internees, Asian Slave
Laborers and Others Captured in the Pacific
Theater* (Jefferson, N.C.: McFarland, 1994),
p. 146.

3 **Their fate hinged on:** J. E. Nardini,
"Survival Factors in American Prisoners of War
of the Japanese," *American Journal of Psychiatry*
109, no. 4 (October 1952).

3 **It was a war in which:** See Leo Braudy,
*From Chivalry to Terrorism: War and the
Changing Nature of Masculinity* (New York:
Alfred A. Knopf, 2003), p. 471.

3 **Forty-two percent of the 25,580 U.S.
Army:** Mary Ellen Condon-Rall and Albert E.
Cowdrey, *The Medical Department: Medical
Service in the War Against Japan,* in *United
States Army in World War II: The Technical
Services* (Washington, D.C.: Center of Military
History, 1998), p. 383.

4 **In *Civilization and:*** Sigmund Freud,
Civilization and Its Discontents, trans. and
ed. James Strachey (New York: W. W. Norton,
1961), p. 97n.

1: The Prettiest Girl in the World
6 **He had little knowledge:** Saburō Ienaga,
The Pacific War, 1931–1945 (New York:
Pantheon, 1978), p. 29.

6 **Japan's historic animosity:** Ronald

Spector, *Eagle Against the Sun* (New York: Free
Press, 1985), p. 44.

6 **Kansas City:** Workers of the Writers'
Program of the Works Projects Administration
in the State of Missouri, *The WPA Guide to
1930s Missouri* (Lawrence: University Press of
Kansas, 1986), pp. 241–59.

8 **By December 12:** Iris Chang, *The Rape of
Nanking* (New York: Basic Books, 1997),
p. 101.

8 **sank the USS *Panay:*** Kemp Tolley,
Yangtze Patrol: The U.S. Navy in China
(Annapolis, Md.: Naval Institute Press, 1971),
p. 247.

8 **Japanese brutality:** Chang, *Rape of
Nanking*, pp. 144, 155–57.

8 **The sinking of:** Tolley, *Yangtze Patrol,*
p. 251.

9 **On the other side:** Harriet Sergeant,
*Shanghai: Collision Point of Cultures,
1918–1939* (New York: Crown, 1990), p. 12.

9 **The largest port:** ibid., pp. 1–2, 4–5.

9 **"Everywhere one jostled":** Harold
Acton, *Memoirs of an Aesthete* (London:
Methuen, 1948), p. 290.

9 **Shanghai was hot:** ibid., p. 291.

9 **Chinese laborers:** Han Suyin, *A Mortal
Flower: China: Autobiography, History*
(London: Granada, 1982), p. 2:264.

10 **That same year:** ibid., p. 2:198.

10 **By 1935 average:** ibid., p. 2:264.

10 **It was not uncommon:** Jan K.
Herman, "Yangtze Patrollers—Bilibid POWs,"
U.S. Navy Medicine, November–December,
1985.

10 **The Japanese occupied:** Edwin
P. Hoyt, *Japan's War, 1853–1952* (New York:
McGraw-Hill, 1986), pp. 98–99.

10 **The International Settlement:** William
R. Evans, *Soochow and the 4th Marines* (Rogue
River, Ore.: Atwood, 1987), p. 3, map of
"Defense Sectors in Shanghai—1937."

10 **The two-battalion regiment:** Kenneth
W. Condit and Edwin T. Turnblad, *Hold High
the Torch: A History of the 4th Marines*,
Historical Branch, G-3 Division,
Headquarters, U.S. Marine Corps (Washington, D.C., 1960), p. 144; Evans, *Soochow,*
pp. 1–6.

10 **If things got hot:** James W. Carrington,
author interview, May 16, 2002, San Antonio,
Tex.

10 **"We were lovers":** Alton C. Halbrook,
interview, no. 122, March 21–April 18, 1972,
UNTOHC.

10 **"This town would":** Barbara W. Tuchman, *Stilwell and the American Experience in China, 1911–45* (New York: Macmillan, 1971), p. 88.

10 **The social hub:** Cecil J. Peart, "Asiatic Reminiscences of a Navy Corpsman with the Marines," pp. 6–8. RG 389, Box 2177, NARA.

11 **Cecil Jesse Peart:** ibid., p. 7.

11 **Sex was the:** W. Patch Hitchcock, *Forty Months in Hell* (Jackson, Tenn.: Page, 1996), p. 6.

11 **By 1934:** Sergeant, *Shanghai,* pp. 31–33.

11 **The women worked:** Hitchcock, *Forty Months,* pp. 8, 10, 12.

11 **Between nights on:** ibid., p. 21.

12 **From the rooftop:** Sergeant, *Shanghai,* p. 101.

12 **The *Guam* was:** Tolley, *Yangtze Patrol,* p. vii.

12 **The objective of:** ibid., p. 5ff.

13 **Unlike the *Luzon*:** Tolley, *Yangtze Patrol,* p. 220.

14 **"This was Kipling's":** ibid., p. 125.

14 **In Hankow:** George Ferguson to Lucille Ferguson, November 29, 1939.

14 ***pretty* good":** George Ferguson to Lucille Ferguson, December 28, 1939.

15 **"of rascality and sobriety":** James O'Rourke to Lucille Ferguson, n.d.

15 **"I've never seen":** George Ferguson to Lucille Ferguson, March 12, 1939.

15 **But there were:** George Ferguson to Lucille Ferguson, n.d.

16 **"a group of Japanese":** George Ferguson to Lucille Ferguson, December 14, 1939.

16 **"Walked through a door":** George Ferguson to Lucille Ferguson, January 1, 1940.

16 **"best event in":** George Ferguson to Lucille Ferguson, January 5, 1940.

16 **In 1939:** See William Glassford, "Narrative of Events in the Far Eastern Theatre, 1939–1942," May 1950, p. 12. Asiatic Defense Campaign, 1941–42, NRS, 1984-33, MR #1, NHC.

16 **That didn't stop:** ibid., p. 4.

17 **"not very humorous":** George Ferguson to Lucille Ferguson, June 27, 1940.

17 **"War news":** George Ferguson to Lucille Ferguson, July 6, 1940.

17 **"I love you":** George Ferguson to Lucille Ferguson, August 12, 1940.

17 **By late August 1940:** David H. Grover and Gretchen G. Grover, *Captives in Shanghai: The Story of the President Harrison,* (Napa Calif.: Western Maritime Press, 1989), pp. 30–31.

17 **Japan joined Germany:** Thomas C. Hart, "Narrative of Events, Asiatic Fleet, Leading up to War and From 8 December 1941 to 15 February 1942." Asiatic Defense Campaign, 1941–42, NRS, 1984-33, MR #1, NHC.

17 **"Do you remember":** George Ferguson to Lucille Ferguson, December 11, 1940.

18 **"remain in Hankow":** George Ferguson to Lucille Ferguson, March 17, 1941.

18 **Some 20,000 to:** J. Michael Miller, "From Shanghai to Corregidor: Marines in the Defense of the Philippines" (Washington, D.C.: Marine Corps Historical Center, 1997), p. 1.

18 **Soon his letters:** Grover and Grover, *Captives in Shanghai,* p. 8.

18 **"Maybe we'll have":** George T. Ferguson, *Diary,* p. 9, BUMED.

19 **The Japanese had:** Hoyt, *Japan's War,* p. 192.

19 **On July 24:** D. Clayton James, *The Years of MacArthur,* vol. 1, *1880–1941* (Boston: Houghton Mifflin, 1970), p. 589; W. G. Winslow, *The Fleet the Gods Forgot: The U.S. Asiatic Fleet in World War II* (Annapolis, Md.: Naval Institute Press, 1982), p. 5.

19 **The American, British, Chinese, and Dutch:** Asahi Shimbun, *The Pacific Rivals: A View of Japanese-American Relations* (New York: Weatherhill/Asahi, 1972), p. 88.

19 **"Isn't there a song":** George Ferguson to Lucille Ferguson, August 30, 1941.

19 **In the field:** Alain Batens, "The Geneva Convention Brassard," at steinert/geneva_convention_brassard.htm; Alain Batens, "The WWII Medical Department," at steinert/wwii_medical_department.

19 **"load a rifle":** George Ferguson to Lucille Ferguson, September 3, 1941.

20 **The security of:** Grover and Grover, *Captives in Shanghai,* p. 25.

20 **Plans were:** Glassford, "Narrative of Events," pp. 12–17.

20 **Then in November:** James Leutze, *A Different Kind of Victory: A Biography of Admiral Thomas C. Hart* (Annapolis, Md.: Naval Institute Press, 1981), pp. 219–20.

20 **Colonel Howard prepared:** Grover and Grover, *Captives in Shanghai,* p. 27.

20 **On the journey north:** ibid., p. 29.

20 **The *Madison* and:** ibid., p. 34.

20 **a regiment of some:** Miller, "Shanghai to Corregidor," p. 1.

20 **On the evening of:** ibid., p. 2.

20–21 **"Outwardly we":** Grover and Grover, *Captives in Shanghai,* p. 35.

21 **As novelist J. G. Ballard:** ibid., p. 31.

21 **On November 24:** Ferguson, *Diary,* p. 17.

21 **Shortly after midnight:** Winslow, *Fleet the Gods Forgot,* p. 53.

22 **One Japanese destroyer:** Alfred Littlefield Smith, "Guest of the Emperor," interview by Jan K. Herman, *U.S. Navy Medicine,* January–February 1986, p. 17.

22 **The *Finch:*** Winslow, *Fleet the Gods Forgot,* p. 56.

23 **Al Smith watched:** Smith, "Guest of the Emperor," p. 17.

23 **The forward hold:** Frank Hoeffer, Journal, "Hard Way Back," at www.wtv-zone .com/califPamela/memorial-Page-5.html.

23 **And then, in:** This account is based on Glassford, "Narrative of Events."

23 **Under clear skies:** Tolley, *Yangtze Patrol,* p. 282.

23 **The *President Harrison:*** See Grover and Grover, *Captives in Shanghai,* p. 37; Ferguson, *Diary,* p. 17; Hart, "Narrative of Events," p. 31.

2: Pearl of the Orient

26 **And when he was a resident:** William B. Breuer, *Sea Wolf: The Daring Exploits of Navy Legend John D. Bulkeley* (Novato, Calif.: Presidio Press, 1989), p. 20.

26 **Houston Street was:** William Crozier et al., comps. and eds., "On the Lower East Side: Observations of Life in Lower Manhattan at the Turn of the Century," Preface, p. 2, www.tenant.net/Community/LES/contents .html.

26 **Eighty-two thousand people:** Irving Howe, *World of Our Fathers* (New York: Harcourt Brace Jovanovich, 1976), pp. 69, 149.

26 **The clash of:** Federal Writers Project Guide to 1930s New York, *The WPA Guide to New York City* (New York: Random House, 1939), pp. 108–24.

27 **The first recorded telephone:** Paul Starr, *The Social Transformation of American Medicine* (New York: Basic Books, 1982), p. 69.

28 **Tamiment was founded:** Author unknown, "Camp Tamiment History," in People's Educational Camp Society, Box 3, Tamiment Library and Robert F. Wagner Labor Archives, Elmer Holmes Bobst Library, New York University.

28 **Sylvia Fine:** Martha Schmoyer LoMonaco, *Every Week, A Broadway Revue: The Tamiment Playhouse, 1921–1960* (Westport, Conn.: Greenwood Press, 1992), pp. 2, 70–71.

29 **Jerome Rabinowitz:** Greg Lawrence, *Dance with Demons: The Life of Jerome Robbins* (New York: G. P. Putnam's Sons, 2001), pp. 1, 32–33, 35, 544n35. See program for "The Tamiment Players Present," July 22, 1939, for use of this stage name, in People's Educational Camp Society, Box 3, Tamiment Library and Robert F. Wagner Labor Archives, Elmer Holmes Bobst Library, New York University.

29 **The songs, skits, and:** Richard Corliss, "Peter Pan Flies Again," *Time,* March 6, 1989.

31 **At low tide:** Paul Ashton, *And Somebody Gives a Damn!* (Santa Barbara, Calif.: Ashton, 1990), p. 17.

31 **Pier 7 was:** Nick Joaquin, *Manila, My Manila* (Manila, Philippines: City of Manila, 1990), p. 164.

31 **Manila Hotel:** James, *Years of MacArthur,* pp. 1:495.

31 **Across Luneta Park:** Ralph Emerson Hibbs, *Tell MacArthur to Wait* (Quezon City, Philippines: Giraffe Books, 1996), p. 29.

31 **The streets of Manila:** Dorothy Cave, *Beyond Courage: One Regiment Against Japan, 1941–45* (New Mexico: Yucca Tree Press, 1992), p. 51.

32 **Tagalog:** Joaquin, *Manila,* p. 5.

32 **Sternberg General Hospital:** Ginn, *Army Medical Service Corps,* pp. 20, 35n117.

32 **Colonel Percy J. Carroll:** Condon-Rall and Cowdrey, *Medical Department,* pp. 48–49.

32 **The Army Medical Department:** Ginn, *Army Medical Service Corps,* p. 6.

32 **The Navy Medical Department:** Harold D. Langley, *A History of Medicine in the Early U.S. Navy* (Baltimore, Md.: Johns Hopkins University Press, 1995), p. 359.

33 **Corpsmen were responsible:** Peter B. Land and Richard W. Byrd, interview with

Danny Thomas, October 26, 1999, p. 20, #1296, UNTOHC.

33 **"Candy asses":** Jan K. Herman, "Life as a Hospital Corpsman at Naval Hospital Cañacao, Philippine Islands, 1940–41," *U.S. Navy Medicine*, March–April 1998, p. 15, personal notation by Ernie J. Irvin.

33 **In the field:** Alain Batens, "Field Equipment of a WWII Corpsman," pp. 1–2, 6, at home.att.net/~corpsman/field_equipment_of_a_wwii_corpsm.htm.

33 **Medical officers were:** David Steinert, "Equipment of a WWII Combat Medic," at home.att.net/~steinert/newpage2.htm.

33 **Murray, meanwhile:** Memorandum, Thomas C. Hart, Commander in Chief, U.S. Asiatic Fleet, to Lieutenant junior grade Murray Glusman, September 5, 1941.

34 **Cavite was the:** Stanley Karnow, *In Our Own Image: America's Empire in the Philippines* (New York: Ballantine Books, 1989), p. 167; Joaquin: *Manila*, pp. 106–8.

34 **Twenty-five years:** Warren Zimmerman, *The First Great Triumph: How Five Americans Made Their Country a World Power* (New York: Farrar, Straus and Giroux, 2002), pp. 300–302.

34 **He was in Singapore:** George Dewey, *Autobiography of George Dewey, Admiral of the Navy*, ed. Eric McAllister Smith (Annapolis, Md.: Naval Institute Press, 1987), p. 215.

34 **A native-led insurrection:** Zimmerman, *Triumph*, p. 303.

34 *Cavitismo*, **as it:** Joaquin, *Manila*, pp. 106, 121, 133.

34 **On May 1, 1898:** Dewey, *Autobiography*, p. 186.

34 **the enemy was spotted:** ibid., p. 191.

35 **With Spain's defeat:** Karnow, *Our Own Image*, p. 130.

35 **America gained:** Zimmerman, *Triumph*, p. 321.

35 **Dewey unofficially supported:** Dewey, *Autobiography*, p. 216.

35 **A reluctant imperialist:** Karnow, *Our Own Image*, p. 134; Zimmerman, *Triumph*, pp. 318–19.

35 **But McKinley was:** Karnow, *Our Own Image*, p. 134; Zimmerman, *Triumph*, pp. 318–19.

35 **To Aguinaldo:** Karnow, *Our Own Image*, pp. 134–35.

35 **It was a bloody:** ibid., p. 179.

35 **The Americans tortured:** ibid., p.178.

35 **Rudyard Kipling's:** Quoted in Dower, *War Without Mercy*, p. 151.

36 **To retaliate for:** Brian McAllister Linn, *The Philippine War, 1899–1902* (Lawrence: University Press of Kansas, 2000), pp. 314–15.

36 **By year-end, more than 750:** Linn, pp. 313–14.

36 **The "war of insurrection":** Ricardo Trota Jose, *The Philippine Army, 1935–1942* (Manila, Philippines: Arenco de Manila University Press, 1992), pp. 14–15.

36 **"There must be two Americas":** Mark Twain, "To the Person Sitting in Darkness," in *Mark Twain: Collected Tales, Sketches, Speeches, and Essays, 1891–1910*, ed. Louis J. Budd (New York: Library of America, 1992), p. 467.

36 **With the U.S. victory:** Quoted in Dower, *War Without Mercy*, p. 151.

36 **As if to atone:** Joaquin, *Manila*, pp. 139–51.

36 **The city's most illustrious:** Karnow, *Our Own Image*, p.16.

36 **William Howard Taft:** ibid., p. 214.

36 **By then relations:** Alan Schom, *The Eagle and the Rising Sun: The Japanese-American War, 1941–1943* (New York: W. W. Norton, 2004), p. 174.

37 **"internal autonomy":** Karnow, *Our Own Image*, p. 15.

37 **In the spring:** Richard Connaughton, *MacArthur and Defeat in the Philippines* (Woodstock and New York: Overlook Press, 2001), p. 18.

37 **Nothing if not confident:** Jose, *Philippine Army*, pp. 23–25.

37 **But the primary role:** James, *Years of MacArthur*, pp. 1:502–03.

37 **It was a fact:** Quoted in Connaughton, *MacArthur and Defeat*, p. 191.

37 **Since the Russo-Japanese War:** Karnow, *Our Own Image*, p. 263.

37 **Manila was some:** Louis Morton, *The War in the Pacific: The Fall of the Philippines* (Washington, D.C.: Government Printing Office, 1953), pp. 4, 7.

37 **Strategists argued that:** Edward S. Miller, *War Plan Orange: The U.S. Strategy to Defeat Japan, 1897–1945*, (Annapolis,

Md.: Naval Institute Press, 1991),
pp. 53–56.

38 **In its war plans:** ibid., p. 1.

38 **The strategy to:** Leutze, *Different Kind of Victory*, p. 158.

38 **The Philippines relied:** Tuchman, *Stilwell*, p. 44.

38 **General MacArthur, however:** Morton, *War in the Pacific*, p. 27.

38 **The "citadel type defense":** ibid., pp. 65, 67.

38 **The War Department agreed:** ibid., pp. 11–12, 50, 68; Alvin P. Stauffer, *United States Army in World War II, The Technical Services, The Quartermaster Corps: Operations in the War Against Japan* (Washington, D.C.: Office of the Chief of Military History, Department of the Army, 1956), p. 6.

38 **George Catlett Marshall:** Miller, *War Plan Orange*, pp. 61–62.

39 **Albert Winterhalter:** ibid., pp. 55, 395n15.

39 **Machine shops:** "Map of U.S. Navy Yard, Cavite, P.I., Showing Conditions on June 30, 1936," courtesy Ricardo Trota Jose; Winslow, *Fleet the Gods Forgot*, p. 85.

39 **Seven hundred tons:** Miller, "Shanghai to Corregidor," p. 7.

39 **The high water level:** Rear Admiral Francis W. Rockwell, USN, "Narrative of Naval Activities in Luzon Area, December 1, 1941 to March 19, 1942," RG 38, Box 1732–1733, NARA.

40 **An SCR-270B:** "Disposition and Employment of U.S. Marines on the Asiatic Station During the Initial Stages of the War," April 6, 1942, RG 127, Box 309, NARA.

40 **This was radar:** Ted Williams, author interview, March 20, 2002.

40 **The 270B was:** Miller, "Shanghai to Corregidor," p. 16.

40 **The army's air warning:** James, *Years of MacArthur*, p. 1:612; Williams interview.

40 **Admiral Hart had:** Connaughton, *MacArthur and Defeat*, p. 116.

40 **They had layouts:** ibid., pp. 144, 146.

40 **maps of coastal:** Schom, *Eagle and Rising Sun*, pp. 126–27.

41 **Then again, the 16th Naval District:** Leutze, *Different Kind of Victory*, p. 180; Hart, "Narrative of Events," p. 4.

41 **A Chicagoan:** Federal Writers' Project Guide to 1930s Illinois, *The WPA Guide to Illinois* (New York: Pantheon Books, 1983), pp. 264–72.

43 **"A well trained":** "Report on the Fitness of Officers, Berley, Ferdinand V., May 14, 1941–August 15, 1941."

43 **The new Fleet Surgeon:** Ferdinand V. Berley to Guy and Rosa Berley, August 23, 1941.

43 **"The prevention of":** *Handbook of the Hospital Corps, U.S. Navy 1939* (Washington, D.C.: Government Printing Office, 1939), p. 576.

44 **In Chefoo, China:** John F. Kidd with Erwin C. Winkel, *Twice Forgotten* (unpublished).

44 **prophylactic station:** Connaughton, *MacArthur and Defeat*, p. 137. See also Ted Williams, *Rogues of Bataan II: Memoirs of a Marine* (privately printed, 2004), p. 11; Richard M. Gordon, *Horyo: Memoirs of an American POW* (St. Paul, Minn.: Paragon House, 1999), p. 39; and Eric Morris, *Corregidor: The American Alamo of World War II* (New York: Stein and Day, 1981), p. 8.

44 **Venereal disease:** Robert G. Davis, *Diary: Covering Period 8 December 1941– 7 September 1945*, p. 8, RG 389, Box 2176, NARA.

45 **"tropical hours":** John Bumgarner, *Parade of the Dead* (Jefferson, N.C.: McFarland, 1995), p. 48.

46 **Filipino women:** Hibbs, *Tell MacArthur*, p. 22.

46 **The stream of luminaries:** Geoffrey Perret, *Old Soldiers Never Die: The Life of Douglas MacArthur* (New York: Random House, 1996), p. 236.

46 **By late November 1941:** Rockwell, "Narrative," p. 1.

46 **On November 27:** James, *Years of MacArthur*, p. 1:615.

46 **"An aggressive move":** Morris, *Corregidor*, pp. 49–50.

46 **The Philippines:** Kennedy, *Freedom from Fear*, p. 525.

46 **"state of readiness":** Rockwell, "Narrative," p. 3.

46 **The windows of:** Thomas Hirst Hayes to Thomas Hayes, Jr., July 26, 1944, entry in *Diary*, p. 17, courtesy Keeney L. Hayes.

46 **"three-day readiness":** Rockwell, "Narrative," p. 3

47 **"AIR RAID ON":** Edwin P. Hoyt, *The Lonely Ships* (New York : David McKay, 1975), p. 141.

47 **"Japan started":** Grover and Grover, *Captives in Shanghai*, p. 49.

47 **Major General Richard K. Sutherland:** Morton, *War in the Pacific*, p. 79.

47 **At 0530:** Jan K. Herman, *Battle Station Sick Bay: Navy Medicine in World War II* (Annapolis, Md.: Naval Institute Press, 1997), p. 37.

47 **"Japan attacks America":** Clark Lee, *They Call It Pacific* (New York: Viking Press, 1943), p. 33.

47 **The Japanese had attacked:** Melville Jacoby, "War Hits Manila," in *Reporting World War II*, vol. 1, *American Journalism 1938–1944* (New York: Library of America, 1995), p. 253; "Philippine Epic," *Life* 12, no. 15 (April 13, 1942), p. 27; Ian Sayer and Douglas Botting, "America's Secret Army: The Untold Story of the Counter Intelligence Corps," Congressional Record, January 30, 1996.

47 **Shopkeepers piled:** Lee, *Pacific*, pp. 5–37.

47 **At Nielson Field:** Morton, *War in the Pacific*, pp. 80–84.

47 **But Brereton couldn't:** Perret, *Old Soldiers*, p. 250.

48 **Then at 1225:** John Toland, *The Rising Sun: The Decline and Fall of the Japanese Empire, 1936–1945* (New York: Random House, 1970), pp. 1:292–93.

48 **"The sight which met us":** Quoted in Connaughton, *MacArthur and Defeat*, p. 169.

48 **Air raid sirens:** Allison Ind, *Bataan: The Judgment Seat* (New York: Macmillan, 1944), p. 99.

48 **A second wave:** Connaughton, *MacArthur and Defeat*, p. 170.

48 **Forty miles to:** Morton, *War in the Pacific*, pp. 85–87; Ind, *Bataan*, pp. 101–04.

49 **In little more:** Morton, *War in the Pacific*, p. 88.

49 **The strength of:** Frank O. Hough, Verle E. Ludwig, and Henry I. Shaw, Jr., *Pearl Harbor to Guadalcanal: History of U.S. Marine Corps Operations in World War II* (Washington, D.C.: Historical Branch, G-3 Division, Headquarters, U.S. Marine Corps), p. 1:163.

49 **"Damn it have":** Ferguson, *Diary*, December 8, 1942, entry.

49 **Few in the Philippines:** Dear and Foot, *Oxford Companion*, p. 872.

49 **Eighteen warships:** John Keegan, *Encyclopedia of World War II* (Middlesex, England: Hamlyn, 1977), p. 198.

49 **It was "a date which will":** Franklin Delano Roosevelt, "Joint Address to Congress Leading to a Declaration of War Against Japan," December 8, 1941. Franklin Delano Roosevelt Library and Museum, www.ourdocuments.gov.

49 **"So far," the president:** Russell D. Buhite and David W. Levy, eds., *FDR's Fireside Chats* (Norman, Okla.: University of Oklahoma Press, 1992), p. 199.

Chapter 3: Red Sunset

50 **"Today, December 8":** Robert J. C. Butow, *Tojo and the Coming of the War* (Princeton, N.J.: Princeton University Press, 1962), p. 407.

50 **Young women in Kazuko's:** Ōhashi Kazuko, author interview, July 13, 2002, Takarazuka, Japan.

50 **Taiheiyō Sensō:** Frank Gibney, ed., *Sensō: The Japanese Remember the Pacific War: Letters to the Editor of "Asahi Shimbun,"* trans. Beth Cary (Armonk, N.Y.: M. E. Sharpe, 1995), p. 123.

50 **Kazuko's father:** Miyazaki Shunya, author interview, July 13, 2002, Takarazuka, Japan.

50 **"Truly it is time":** Quoted in Haruko Taya Cook and Theodore F. Cook, *Japan at War: An Oral History* (New York: New Press, 1992), p. 69.

51 **Japanese novelist Dazai Osamu:** Quoted in Dower, *War Without Mercy*, p. 242.

51 **In 1941 U.S. steel:** Richard Overy, *Why the Allies Won* (New York: W. W. Norton, 1995), p. 195.

51 **But twenty years:** Belote and Belote, *Corregidor*, p. 32.

51 **"The Philippine situation":** Overy, *Why the Allies*, p. 202.

51 **At the beginning:** Spector, *Eagle Against Sun*, pp. 45–46.

51 **The twin-engine Mitsubishi:** Schom, *Eagle and Rising Sun*, p. 214.

51 **a superior 47mm antitank gun:** Constant Irwin, interview, August 7, 1942, Louis Morton Papers, Box 2, pp. 6–8, MHI.

51 **50mm grenade launcher:** Mike Yaklich, "Japanese Ordnance Material of World War II," at www.wlhoward.com/japan.htm, p. 16.

51 **portable 70mm gun:** John Hersey, *Men on Bataan* (New York: Alfred A. Knopf, 1942), pp. 296–99.

51 **By contrast, the armament:** Robert A. Clement, "Some of My Life Experiences," p. 15, Personal Papers Collection, MCHC.

52 **the 1903 Springfield:** Yaklich, "Ordnance Material," p. 11.

52 **"lacked even obsolete":** Jonathan M. Wainwright, *General Wainwright's Story*, ed. Robert Considine (Garden City, N.Y.: Doubleday, 1945), p. 26.

52 **Infantrymen were:** Spector, *Eagle Against Sun*, p. 73; Donald Knox, *Death March: The Survivors of Bataan* (New York: Harcourt Brace Jovanovich, 1981), p. 29.

52 **Shoddy American-issue:** Jose, *Philippine Army*, p. 205.

52 **For the defense of northern Luzon:** Schom, *Eagle and Rising Sun*, p. 219.

52 **45th and 57th Infantry:** Knox, *Death March*, p. 30.

52 **The 31st Infantry:** Connaughton, *MacArthur and Defeat*, p. 135.

52 **But their reputation was:** Gavin Daws, *Prisoners of the Japanese: POWs of World War II in the Pacific* (New York: William Morrow, 1994), p. 268.

52 **Conditioned by:** ibid., p. 152.

52 **Fred had seen:** Ferdinand V. Berley, interview by Jan K. Herman, pp. 10–11.

53 **Japanese battleships:** Ienaga, *Pacific War*, p. 146.

53 **Prewar medical mobilization:** Mary Ellen Condon-Rall, "U.S. Army Medical Preparations and the Outbreak of War: The Philippines, 1941–6 May 1942," *Journal of Military History* 56 (January 1992), p. 41.

53 **Once Rainbow 5:** Wibb E. Cooper, "Medical Department Activities in the Philippines from 1941–6 May 1942," p. 47, RG 389, Box 2176, NARA.

53 **Twenty surgical teams:** James O. Gillespie, "Malaria and the Defense of Bataan," in Leonard D. Heaton, John Boyd Coates, Jr., Ebbe Curtis Hoff, and Phebe M. Hoff, *Preventive Medicine in World War II*, vol. 6, *Communicable Diseases: Malaria* (Washington, D.C.: Office of the Surgeon General, 1963), p. 500.

54 **Filipino Medical Corps:** Cooper, "Medical Department," p. 49.

54 **Rizal Station:** Morton, *War in the Pacific*, p. 120.

54 **Captain Robert G. Davis:** Cooper's paraphrase of Davis in Cooper, "Medical Department," p. 50.

54 **Trenches and air raid:** James W. Keene, "First Separate Marine Battalion, Marine Barracks, Navy Yard, Cavite, Philippine Islands," p. 7, Personal Papers Collection, MCHC.

54 **But the location of:** Condon-Rall, "Army Medical Preparations," p. 45.

54 **Estado Mayor:** Thomas Hirst Hayes to Thomas Hayes, Jr., August 12, 1944, entry in *Diary*.

54 **another desirable target:** Cooper, "Medical Department," p. 51.

54 **Nonetheless patients and staff:** Hayes to Hayes, Jr., August 12, 1944, entry in *Diary*.

54 **one of five:** Condon-Rall and Cowdrey, *The Medical Department*, p. 21.

55 **At 0300 on:** Davis, *Diary*, p. 1.

55 **The submarine tender *Canopus*:** "All Hands Book Supplement," Ships' History Section, Navy Department, June 1960, p. 58.

55 **Women employees:** Rockwell, "Narrative," p. 4.

55 **George Ferguson was assigned:** Ferguson, *Diary*, p.17.

55 **The duty radioman:** Miller, "Shanghai to Corregidor," p. 16; author interview with Ted Williams, March 8, 2002.

55 **The same finding:** Samuel Eliot Morison, *History of United States Naval Operations in World War II*, vol. 3, *The Rising Sun in the Pacific, 1931–April 1942* (Edison, N.J.: Castle Books, 2001), p. 171.

55 **At 1235:** William Hogaboom, "Action Report, Bataan," *Marine Corps Gazette*, April 1946, p. 25.

56 **They were oddly beautiful:** See A.V.H. Hartendorp, *The Japanese Occupation of the Philippines* (Manila, Philippines: Bookmark, 1967), p. 1:63; George Burlage, interview by Ronald Marcello, November 18, 1970, p. 18, #63, UNTOHC; W. L. White, *They Were Expendable* (Cleveland, Ohio: World, 1944), p. 14.

56 **The paint locker:** John Toland, *But Not in Shame* (New York: Random House, 1961), p. 69.

56 **Waves of Japanese bombers:** Gwinn U. Porter, "Antiaircraft Defense of Corregidor," monograph, School of Combined Arms, p. 14, Louis Morton Papers, Box, 15, MHI.

56 **But Japanese fighters:** U.S. War Department, *Handbook on Japanese Military Forces* (Washington, D.C.: Government Printing Office, reprinted by Baton Rouge: Louisiana State University Press, 1991), pp. 56–57.

56 **Out at Battery C:** Hough, Ludwig,

and Shaw, *Pearl Harbor*, p. 163. See also "Battery A—lst Separate Marine Battalion," p. 3, Personal Papers Collection, MCHC.

57 **A bomb rattled:** "Pigboat Doc" by Wheeler Lipes, in Herman, *Battle Station Sick Bay*, pp. 46–47; Hoyt, *Lonely Ships*, pp. 153–55; Winslow, *Fleet the Gods Forgot*, pp. 86–88; "USS Bittern—War damage received, and report of abandoning of," from Comanding Officer to Secretary of the Navy, December 13, 1941, Asiatic Defense Campaign, 1941–42, NRS, 1984-33, MR #1, NHC.

57 **Inflammable liquid:** "History of the USS *Peary*," Navy Department, Office of the Chief of Naval Operations, Division of Naval History, Ships' Histories Section, p. 1, Asiatic Defense Campaign, DesDiv 59, NRS 237, MR, NHC.

57 **Erickson:** Fredrik de Coste, "U.S. Navy Doctor Who Survived 37 Soul-Shaking Months in Japan Prisoner of War Camp Relates Experiences," *Star and Herald* (Panama), June 10, 1945.

57 **Out of fright:** Loren E. Stamp, *Journey Through Hell* (Jefferson, N.C.: McFarland, 1993), p. 12.

57 **The wounded straggled:** James L. Kent, interview by Ronald E. Marcello, May 11, 1972, #127, UNTOHC; Alton C. Halbrook, interview by Ronald E. Marcello, March 21–April 18, 1972, p. 36, #122, UNTOHC.

57 **One woman had:** White, *Expendable*, p. 20.

57 **Another civilian ran:** Williams, *Rogues of Bataan II*, p. 22.

57 **Over at the garage:** ibid., p. 23.

57 **One headless corpse:** Hartendorp, *Japanese Occupation*, p. 1:64.

57 **High winds fanned:** Morison, *Naval Operations*, pp. 3:171–74; Miller, "Shanghai to Corregidor," pp. 7–9.

58 **At 1600.:** Hartendorp, *Japanese Occupation*, p. 1:65; K. E. Lowman, "Fleet Surgeon's Activities—U.S. Asiatic Fleet, a Resume, 1941–45," p. l, BUMED; Thomas Hirst Hayes, "Report on Medical Tactics, 4th Regiment, USMC, Medical Personnel, Manila Bay Area, 12-7-41 to 5-6-42," p. 12, Hospital Corps Archives Memo 268-45, Folder 15-B, BUMED.

58 **Durward Allen Laney:** Hayes, "Report

on Medical Tactics," p. 17; Stamp, *Journey*, p. 127.

59 **"brought up to us":** Thomas Hirst Hayes, notes from December 8–December 10, 1941, written in Bilibid Prison, August 5, 1944, in *Diary*, BUMED.

59 **285 patients passed:** Mark Murphy, "You'll Never Know!" *New Yorker*, June 12, 1943, p. 46.

59 **Some 300 bombs:** John Wilkes, "The Commander Submarines, U.S. Asiatic Fleet to Commander in Chief, U.S. Fleet and Chief of Naval Operations, April 1, 1942," p. 7, Asiatic Defense Campaign, 1941–42, NRS, 1984-33, MR #1, NHC.

59 **Five hundred people:** Clay Blair, *Silent Victory: The U.S. Submarine War Against Japan* (Annapolis, Md.: Naval Institute Press, 1975), p. 134.

59 **MacArthur's wife:** John Costello, *The Pacific War, 1941–1945* (New York: Quill, 1982), p. 160.

59 **The naval base:** Toland, *But Not in Shame*, p. 69.

59 **In the coda:** Hartendorp, *Japanese Occupation*, p. 1:2.

59 **Hundreds of canines:** Hayes to Hayes, Jr., August 12, 1944, entry in *Diary*; M. M. Champlin, "Narrative," p. 19, Asiatic Defense Campaign, 1941–42, NRS, 1984-33, MR #1, NHC.

59 **The smell of:** Raymond G. Deewall to Director of Naval Intelligence, July 11, 1944, p. 4, Asiatic Defense Campaign, 1941–42, NRS, 1984-33, MR #2, NHC.

59 **Murray and Gordon:** Hayes, "Report on Medical Tactics," p. 90.

60 **The road to Manila:** Hayes to Hayes, Jr., August 6, 1944, entry in *Diary*.

60 **Bloodied and dirty:** Robert W. Kentner, *Kentner's Journal: Bilibid Prison, Manila, P.I., from 12-8-41 to 2-5-45*, p. 4, RG 389, Box 2177, NARA.

60 **"before too much":** Hayes to Hayes, Jr., August 12, 1944, entry in *Diary*.

60 **Events were unfolding:** Hayes to Hayes, Jr., August 12, 1944, entry in *Diary*. See also A. M. Barrett, *Casus Belli*, p. 17, BUMED.

60 **To become some:** Hayes to Hayes, Jr., August 12, 1944, entry in *Diary*.

60 **Davis seemed more:** Hayes to Hayes, Jr., August 21, 1944, entry in *Diary*.

60 **As a result:** Davis, *Diary*, p. 1.

61 **There they could treat:** Hayes, "Report

on Medical Tactics," p. 11; Ferguson, *Diary*, p.18.

61 **In the meantime:** Keene, "First Separate Marine Battalion," p. 7.

61 **It was a grisly:** Hayes, "Report on Medical Tactics," p. 18.

61 **Laney's remains:** ibid., p. 77.

61 **"red sunset":** James L. Kent, interview by Ronald E. Marcello, May 11, 1972, pp. 13–14, #127, UNTOHC.

Chapter 4: Invisible Enemies

62 **In the densely:** Andrew Spielman and Michael D'Antonio, *Mosquito: A Natural History of Our Most Persistent and Deadly Foe* (New York: Hyperion, 2001), pp. 95–96.

62 **Malaria flourished:** Fred H. Mowrey, M.D., "Statistics of Malaria," in John Boyd Coates, Jr., and W. Paul Havens, Jr., eds., *Internal Medicine in World War II*, vol. 2, *Infectious Diseases* (Washington, D.C.: Office of the Surgeon General, 1963), pp. 449–50.

62 **In the 1930s:** Robert J. T. Joy, "Malaria in American Troops in the South and Southwest Pacific in World War II," *Medical History* 43 (1999): 193.

63 **On the flat:** James O. Gillespie, "Malaria and the Defense of Bataan," in Heaton, Coates, Hoff, and Hoff, *Preventive Medicine*, p. 6:498.

63 **MacArthur himself:** James, *Years of MacArthur*, pp. 1:89–90.

65 **Towering monkey pod:** Hibbs, *Tell MacArthur*, p. 77.

65 **You learned not:** Robert E. Haney, *Caged Dragons: An American P.O.W. in WWII Japan* (Ann Arbor, Mich.: Sabre Press, 1991), p. 24.

65 **The climate:** Hibbs, *Tell MacArthur*, p. 135.

65 **Dewey himself:** Dewey, *Autobiography*, p. 13.

65 **On the southern slopes:** Karl C. Dod, *United States Army in World War II: The Technical Services, the Corps of Engineers: The War Against Japan* (Washington, D.C.: Office of the Chief of Military History, 1966), pp. 86–87.

65 **As far back:** Rockwell, "Narrative," p. 2.

66 **The spur on the pincer:** John Foreman, *The Philippine Islands*, 3rd ed. (1905); Ashton, *Somebody Gives*, p. 104.

66 **Legend has it:** "The Harbor Defenses of Manila and Subic Bays, 1937," booklet

compiled "primarily for the information of incoming personnel about to begin a first tour with the Coast Artillery in the Philippine Islands," based on an article in *The New York Times* by Robert Aura Smith, July 24, 1932, in the Belote Collection, Box 2, p. 6, MHI. For a different version of this story see Foreman, *Philippine Islands*.

66 **Mariveles was little more:** Leutze, *Different Kind of Victory*, p. 157.

66 **But the work:** Jose, *Philippine Army*, pp. 187–88.

66 **On December 8:** D. Clayton James, *The Years of MacArthur*, vol. 2, *1941–1945* (Boston: Houghton Mifflin, 1975), p. 27.

66 **By December 10:** Morton, *War in the Pacific*, pp. 161–62.

66 **There were 66,000 Filipino:** Connaughton, *MacArthur and Defeat*, p. 215.

67 **When G-3:** James, *Years of MacArthur*, p. 2:28.

67 **A troop withdrawal:** Connaughton, *MacArthur and Defeat*, p. 215.

67 **Fifteen thousand tons:** Morton, *War in the Pacific*, p. 256.

67 **The army procured:** Stauffer, *Army in World War II*, p. 9.

67 **There were 2,295,000 pounds:** Morton, *War in the Pacific*, p. 254.

67 **By agreement:** Stauffer, *Army in World War II*, p. 8.

67 **Five thousand tons:** ibid., p. 9.

67 **There were enough field rations:** Morton, *War in the Pacific*, p. 255.

67 **WPO-3 had:** ibid., pp. 256–67.

67 **MacArthur didn't:** James, *Years of MacArthur*, p. 2:27; across the international dateline it was December 11.

68 **A malaria survey:** Persis Putnam to Paul Russell, November 7, 1929, RG 1.1, Series 242I, Box 6, Folder 64, RAC.

68 **First applied in 1927:** Victor G. Heiser to Frederick F. Russell, January 31, 1930, RG 1.1, Series 242I, Box 6, Folder 66, RAC.

68 **Victor Heiser:** Heiser to Russell, May 8, 1928, RG 1.1., Series 242I, Box 6, Folder 2, RAC.

68 **Russell arrived:** Russell to Heiser, February 20, 1932, RG 1.1, Series 242I, Box 6, Folder 67, RAC; Russell to Heiser, September 22, 1931, RG 1.1, Series 242I, Box 6, Folder 66, RAC.

68 **Having visited thirty-six provinces:** Paul F. Russell, "Memorandum Regarding a New Plan for the Control of Malaria in the

Philippines," p. 2, RG 1.1, Series 242I, Box 6, Folder 67, RAC.

68 **plasmochin:** Mark Honigsbaum, *The Fever Trail: In Search of the Cure for Malaria* (New York: Farrar, Straus and Giroux, 2001), p. 218.

69 **"few foot trails":** Richard C. Mallonée, "Bataan Diary," vol. 2: "The Defense of Bataan," p. 1, Richard C. Mallonée Papers, Box 1, MHI.

69 **Malaria as well as dysentery:** Cowdrey, *Fighting for Life,* p. 7.

69 **"would be extremely difficult":** Walter H. Waterous, "Statement of Experiences and Observations Concerning the Bataan Campaign and Subsequent Imprisonment," p. 38, Louis Morton Papers, Box 6, MHI.

69 **"Costly and time-consuming":** Paul F. Russell, "Appendix A, Third Quarterly Report, Malaria Investigations, Philippines Islands," RG 5, IHB/D, Box 71, RAC.

69 **"no *practical* control":** Russell to Heiser, April 4, 1932, RG 1.1, Series 242I, Box 6, Folder 67, RAC.

70 **By 1936 Fischer was:** Honigsbaum, *Fever Trail,* p. 220.

70 **"There lies our disease threat":** Hayes to Hayes, Jr., July 28, 1944, entry in *Diary.*

70 **The disease would peak:** John Jacob Bookman, "Medical Notes," p. 1. Courtesy Richard Bookman.

70 **Lieutenant Colonel Curtis Thurston Beecher:** Curtis Thurston Beecher, "Experiences in the Fighting on Corregidor," p. 7. Courtesy Douglas County Historical Society, Roseburg, Ore.

70 **Because there were few:** Lee, *Pacific,* p. 190.

70 **A barrier net:** Malcolm McGregor Champlin, "Narrative," recorded September 5, 1944, p. 6, Asiatic Defense Campaign, 1941–42, NRS, 1984-33, MR #2, NHC.

70 **Clockwise as:** E. L. Sackett, handdrawn map of Mariveles, in Earl Le Roy Sackett Special Collections, American Heritage Center, University of Wyoming.

70 **The *Maryanne*:** Nancy Russell Young, "Reflections on Bob and Jessie Russell," September 17, 1981 (unpublished), p. 23.

71 **Beecher knew:** Beecher, "Experiences," p. 12.

71 **When lumber came in:** Dower, *War Without Mercy,* pp. 263–64.

71 **The marine guard:** Ted Williams, interview, March 8, 2002.

71 **By late 1941:** Beecher, "Experiences," p. 9.

71 **Which was a good:** Paul F. Russell, "Final Report on the Malaria Investigations of the International Health Division of the Rockefeller Foundation in the Philippines Islands, 1921–1934," p. 14, RAC.

Chapter 5: Exodus

72 **The Americans had:** Lee, *Pacific,* p 43.

72 **A thousand Japanese:** Morton, *War in the Pacific,* pp. 115–16.

72 **A mirror tied:** Carl Mydans, *More Than Meets the Eye* (New York: Harper and Brothers, 1959), pp. 65–66.

72 **A secret radio:** Morton, *War in the Pacific,* p. 117.

72 **The truth was:** Connaughton, *MacArthur and Defeat,* p. 102.

72 **One marine remembered:** George Burlage, interview by Ronald E. Marcello, November 18, 1970, p. 13, #63, UNTOHC.

72 **Nurses at Sternberg:** Hibbs, *Tell MacArthur,* p. 25.

72 **"suffered from nervous":** James O. Gillespie, "Recollections of the Pacific War and Japanese Prisoner of War Camps, 1941–1945," p. 6, RG 389, Box 2177, NARA.

72 **"What ward are you":** Ferguson, *Diary,* p. 18.

72 **A statement issued:** Stanley W. Smith, *Prisoner of the Emperor: An American POW in World War II* (Niwot, Colo.: University Press of Colorado, 1991), p. 17.

72 **Manila was bombed:** Blair, *Silent Victory,* p. 135.

72 **A radio tower:** Hoyt, *Lonely Ships,* p. 163.

73 **The two doctors:** Ferguson, *Diary,* pp. 18–19; Miller, "Shanghai to Corregidor," p. 9; Hayes, "Report on Medical Tactics," p. 11, lists sixteen dead.

73 **Blackouts in Manila:** Thomas Hirst Hayes to Thomas Hayes, Jr., August 12, 1944, entry in *Diary.*

73 **That night a marine:** Williams, *Rogues of Bataan II,* pp. 20–21; Miller, "Shanghai to Corregidor," p. 8; Ferguson, *Diary,* p. 19.

73 **The next day:** Carter Berkeley Simpson, *Diary,* pp. 6–7, BUMED.

73 **MacArthur formally:** Hough, Ludwig, and Shaw, *Pearl Harbor,* pp. 2:165–66; 165n38.

73 **The marines and navy:** Connaughton, *MacArthur and Defeat,* p. 203.

74 **"Come on, Douglas":** Leutze, *Different Kind of Victory*, p. 164.

74 **Hart outranked MacArthur:** ibid., pp. 133–34.

74 **MacArthur complained:** James, *Years of MacArthur*, p. 2:20.

74 **Hart complained:** ibid., p. 21.

74 **But the Far East Air Force:** Morton, *War in the Pacific*, p. 146n1.

74 **So the two fastest ships:** ibid., p. 154.

74 **MacArthur ordered tanks:** Toland, *But Not in Shame*, p. 92.

74 **Hart sent four submarines:** Winslow, *Fleet the Gods Forgot*, p. 112.

74 **Torpedoes ran:** Leutze, *Different Kind of Victory*, pp. 241–42.

74 **Opposition from:** Toland, *But Not in Shame*, pp. 93–94.

74 **To compound the problem:** ibid., p. 92.

75 **By December 22:** Morton, *War in the Pacific*, p. 125.

75 **Of them, 34,856 were:** Connaughton, *MacArthur and Defeat*, p. 200.

75 **Their only opposition:** Morton, *War in the Pacific*, p. 94.

75 **Homma would:** ibid., p. 144.

75 **"The enemy has landed":** Morris, *Corregidor*, p. 163.

75 **The next night:** Morton, *War in the Pacific*, p. 139.

75 **The area was defended:** Jose, *Philippine Army*, pp. 212–13.

75 **Homma's troops:** James, *Years of MacArthur*, p. 2:28.

75 **The rationale was:** Morton, *War in the Pacific*, p. 165.

75 **Engineers would dynamite:** Dod, *Army in World War II*, p. 82.

75 **Wainwright took:** Toland, *But Not in Shame*, p. 112.

76 **"the last ditch":** Wainwright, *Story*, p. 36.

76 **"an entirely unjustifiable":** Connaughton, *MacArthur and Defeat*, p. 193.

76 **"Everybody knows":** ibid., p. 194.

76 **It was a delaying action:** Wainwright, *Story*, p. 41.

76 **The North Luzon engineers:** Morton, *War in the Pacific*, pp. 166–69.

76 **But a single act:** Toland, *But Not in Shame*, p. 124.

76 **Homma, however:** ibid., p. 130.

77 **Simultaneous with:** Gillespie, "Malaria," in Heaton, Coates, Hoff, and Hoff, *Preventive Medicine*, pp. 6:499–500.

77 **Its components were:** Stauffer, *Army in World War II*, p. 10.

77 **Hospital No. 1 was:** Murphy, "You'll Never Know!" p. 48.

77 **There was one:** Alfred A. Weinstein, *Barbed-Wire Surgeon* (New York: Macmillan, 1948), p. 16.

77 **A second echelon:** Elizabeth M. Norman, *We Band of Angels: The Untold Story of American Nurses Trapped on Bataan by the Japanese* (New York: Random House, 1999), p. 39.

77 **Colonel James O. Gillespie:** Cooper, "Medical Department," pp. 57–59.

77 **The medical supply depot:** Gillespie in Heaton, Coates, Hoff, and Hoff, *Preventive Medicine*, p. 6:501.

77 **The irony is:** Condon-Rall, "Medical Preparations," pp. 35–36.

77 **Colonel Carroll escorted:** Ashton, *Somebody Gives*, pp. 26, 53.

77 **Floramund Fellmuth:** Norman, *Band of Angels*, p. 24.

77 **The eleven navy nurses:** ibid., p. 25.

77 **Meanwhile the evacuation:** Thomas Hirst Hayes to Thomas Hayes, Jr., August 20, 1944, entry in *Diary*.

78 **But back in:** Hayes, "Report on Medical Tactics," p.19.

78 **With the Japanese advancing:** Cooper, "Medical Department," p. 53.

78 **The navy did its best:** Lowman, "Fleet Surgeon's Activities."

79 **One complete battalion:** Thomas H. Hayes, "Report of the Medical Activities of the Fourth Regiment U.S. Marines and Attached Troops for the Period 1-1-42 to 5-6-42 on Corregidor, P.I.," p. 16, BUMED.

79 **Major Peter Kempf:** Cooper, "Medical Department," p. 78.

79 **Red Cross warehouses:** Hartendorp, *Japanese Occupation*, p. 1:5.

79 **Rizal Stadium was:** Daws, *Prisoners*, p. 64.

79 **On December 24:** Morris, *Corregidor*, p. 201.

79 **"to spare the Metropolitan area":** *Philippines Herald* 85, no. 121 (December 26, 1941), p. 1.

79 **Since Hart was transferring:** John Wilkes, "War Activities Submarines,

U.S. Asiatic Fleet, December 1, 1941–April 1, 1942," p. 11. Asiatic Defense Campaign, 1941–42, NRS, 1984-33, MR #1, NHC; Morison, *History of Naval Operations*, p. 3:198.

79 **It was Rockwell's last:** Rockwell, "Narrative," p. 6.

79 **In a separate meeting:** Morison, *History of Naval Operations*, p. 3:167.

80 **The *Canopus* was:** E. L. Sackett, "The History of the USS *Canopus*," p. 6, Louis Morton Papers, Box 19, MHI.

80 **Depth charges:** Thomas K. Bowers, "Personal Narrative of Philippine Campaign from 8 December 1941 to 29 April 1942," p. 4, Asiatic Defense Campaign, 1941–42, NRS, 1984-33, MR #1, NHC; "All Hands Book Supplement," June 1960, pp. 58–63.

80 **Hayes arrived in Mariveles:** Hayes to Hayes, Jr., August 12, 1944, entry in *Diary.*

80 **The Japanese had spotted:** Miller, "Shanghai to Corregidor," p. 15.

80 **John Bookman and:** George Ferguson, *Diary*, p. 20.

81 **"Just why they":** Hayes to Hayes, Jr., August 23, 1944, entry in *Diary.*

81 **Eight marines:** Beecher, "Fighting in Corregidor," pp. 9–10; Miller, "Shanghai to Corregidor," p. 15.

81 **"Life was a matter":** Hayes, "Report on Medical Tactics," p. 79.

81 **On Christmas Eve:** James, *Years of MacArthur*, p. 2:30.

81 **Manila's gold, silver, paper money:** Amea Willoughby, *I Was on Corregidor: Experiences of an American Official's Wife in the War-Torn Philippines* (New York: Harper & Brothers, 1943), pp. 188–91.

81 **The *Canopus* steamed:** Sackett, "History of *Canopus*," p. 8.

81 **The Sangley Point radio station:** Hough, Ludwig, and Shaw, *Pearl Harbor*, p. 168.

82 **The district naval intelligence:** Mike Cheek, "War Diary," February 20, 1972, p. 5, Asiatic Defense Campaign, 1941–42, NRS, 1984-33, MR #2, NHC.

82 **The last directive:** L. B. Sartin, "Report of Activities of the United States Naval Hospital Unit in the Philippines from December 8, 1941 to January 30, 1945," MC USN, RG 389, Box 2178, NARA.

82 **But the army viewed:** Davis, *Diary*, p. 2.

82 **Around noon:** Hayes, "Report on Medical Tactics," p. 19.

82 **sending flames hundreds:** Hartendorp, *Japanese Occupation*, p. 1:3.

82 **Admiral Hart stole away:** Morton, *War in the Pacific*, p. 155.

82 **A banner was strung:** Lee, *Pacific*, p. 125.

82 **The newspapers carried:** Knox, *Death March*, pp. 42–43.

82 **Every boat:** Carlos Romulo, *I Saw the Fall of the Philippines* (New York: Doubleday Doran, 1943), pp. 78–79.

83 **When two vehicles:** Cave, *Beyond Courage*, p. 99.

83 **The dirt tracks:** See Mariano Villarin, *We Remember Bataan and Corregidor* (Baltimore, Md.: Gateway Press, 1990), p. 19.

83 **"black with people":** Lee, *Pacific*, p. 126.

83 **Philippine Army soldiers:** Knox, *Death March*, p. 46.

83 **Philippine Army engineers:** Dod, *Army in World War II*, p. 78.

83 **The Japanese had breached:** Duane Schulz, *Hero of Bataan: The Story of General Jonathan M. Wainwright* (New York: St. Martin's Press, 1981), pp. 112–13.

83 **In southern Luzon:** Morton, *War in the Pacific*, p. 191.

Chapter 6: Rendezvous

85 **As Chaplain William Thomas Cummings:** Romulo, *I Saw*, pp. 263–64.

85 **Five hundred dead:** See Lowman, "Fleet Surgeon's Activities."

85 **Like the rest:** Ferguson, *Diary*, p. 20.

86 **"What a Christmas":** ibid.

86 **The Section Base:** F. J. Bridget to Company Commander, "Positions of Forces," February 3, 1942, MR, NRS 159, Naval Campaign in the Orient Papers, NHC.

86 **To the southeast:** E. L. Sackett to Commandant, 16th Naval District, April 10, 1942, p. 2, Asiatic Defense Campaign, 1941–42, NRS, 1984-33, MR #1, NHC; Ted Williams, interview, March 8, 2002; Simpson, *Diary*, p. 7.

86 **Mariveles was now:** Hough, Ludwig, and Shaw, *Pearl Harbor*, p. 1:170.

86 **George replaced Nardini:** Hayes, "Report on Medical Tactics," p. 12.

86 **John and Murray:** Hayes to Hayes, Jr., August 21, 1944, entry in *Diary.*

87 **Hayes departed:** ibid.

87 **Three and a half miles long:** "The Harbor Defenses of Manila and Subic Bays," Belote Collection, Box 2, p. 5, MHI; Dewey, *Autobiography*, pp. 199–200.

87 **At the request of:** Paul D. Bunker, "Seaward Defense Commander's Report of Damage," 59th CA, Exhibit I, p. 1, in George F. Moore, "Report of Major General George F. Moore, U.S.A., Formerly Commanding the Philippine Coast Artillery Command and the Harbor Defenses of Manila and Subic Bays with Headquarters at Fort Mills, Corregidor, Philippine Islands, 14 February 1941–6 May 1942," Fort Monroe, Va., 15 December 1945, in George F. Moore Papers, MHI.

87 **Battery Way held:** ibid.

88 **Fort Hughes (Caballo):** Morris, *Corregidor*, p. 57.

88 **As a result of:** Dod, *Army in World War II*, pp. 101–06.

88 **Near Monkey Point:** Edward J. Drea, *MacArthur's ULTRA Codebreaking and the War Against Japan, 1942–45* (Lawrence: University Press of Kansas, 1992), pp. 10–11.

88 **On January 30:** Robert B. Stinnett, *Day of Deceit: The Truth About FDR and Pearl Harbor* (New York: Simon and Schuster, 2000), p. 23.

89 **MacArthur moved into a cottage:** Morris, *Corregidor*, p. 184.

89 **Leland D. Bartlett:** Leland D. Bartlett, interview by Ronald E. Marcello, September 13, 1972, p. 51, UNTOHC.

89 **High Commissioner Sayre:** Hartendorp, *Japanese Occupation*, p. 1:183.

90 **Corregidor was cooler:** Alfonso J. Aluit, *Corregidor* (Manila, Philippines: Lucky Press, 2001), pp. 7–8.

90 **the Rock was packed:** Cooper, "Medical Department," p. 80.

90 **Lieutenant Colonel William Riney Craig:** Hayes to Hayes, Jr., August 28, 1944, entry in *Diary*.

90 **Hayes had dual:** Hayes, "Report on Medical Tactics," p. 7.

91 **The Far East Air Force:** Hough, Ludwig, and Shaw, *Pearl Harbor*, p. 1:170.

91 **Japanese pilots raised:** J. W. Keene, "Philippine Defense 1941: Corrregidor."

91 **"They knew":** Hayes to Hayes, Jr., August 28, 1944, entry in *Diary*.

91 **"I wasn't afraid":** Ernest Bales, author interview, San Antonio, Tex., May 2002.

91 **"Here they come":** Hayes to Hayes, Jr., August 28, 1944, entry in *Diary*.

91 **At 1300:** Hough, Ludwig, and Shaw, *Pearl Harbor*, p. 1:170. See "Report of Commanding Officer of Antiaircraft Defense Command, Harbor Defenses of Manila and Subic Bays, Fort Mills, P.I.," p. 4, Exhibit F, George F. Moore Papers, MHI.

91 **The last group:** "All Hands Book Supplement," June 1960, pp. 58–60; Morison, *History of Naval Operations*, pp. 3:198–99; Sackett, "History of *Canopus*," p. 9.

92 **An estimated sixty tons:** Moore, "Antiaircraft Defense Command," p. 4.

92 **The electric trolley line:** "Proceedings of a Board of Officers Appointed to Evaluate War Damage to the Harbor Defenses of Manila and Subic Bays," Headquarters 14th Antiaircraft Command, APO 75, October 6, 1945, William C. Braly Papers, MHI.

92 **Two of the five:** John K. Borneman, interview by William M. Belote, November 4, 1964, p. 2, Belote Collection, Box 2, MHI.

92 **The Post Medical Inspector:** Hayes to Hayes, Jr., August 28, 1944, entry in *Diary*.

92 **The real target:** Belote and Belote, *Corregidor*, p. 50.

92 **"Well the Lord knows":** Ferguson, *Diary*, p. 21.

92 **But the Japanese:** Morton, *War in the Pacific*, p. 154.

92 **"I give to the people":** Quoted in Perret, *Old Soldiers*, p. 262.

92 **"Death Valley":** Ernest J. Irvin, "Wartime Reminiscences," interview by Jan K. Herman, p. 3, BUMED.

93 **The soil in:** Ind, *Bataan*, pp. 199–200.

93 **Most cases could:** Hayes, "Report on Medical Tactics," p. 20.

Chapter 7: Opening Salvos

94 **Thirty miles across:** Joaquin, *Manila*, p. 185.

94 **Then the Japanese flag:** Toland, *But Not in Shame*, pp. 146–47.

94 **Radiant red:** See David J. Lu, *Japan: A Documentary History*, vol. 1, *The Dawn of History to the Late Tokugawa Period* (Armonk, N.Y.: M. E. Sharpe, 1997), pp. 4–5.

94 **A newspaper advertisement:** *Manila Daily Bulletin*, Manila, Philippines, January 2, 1942, pp. 1–2, courtesy Curtis B. Brooks. See also Carlos Quirino, *Chick Parsons: America's*

Master Spy in the Philippines (Quezon City, Philippines: New Day, 1984), p. 9.

95 **The men on:** Lee, *Pacific*, p. 167.

95 **But the "Summer Brigade":** Toland, *But Not in Shame*, p. 149.

95 **By January 7:** Hough, Ludwig, and Shaw, *Pearl Harbor*, p. 1:172.

95 **Wainwright was in charge:** James, *Years of MacArthur*, pp. 2:48–49.

95 **At almost the same:** Morton, *War in the Pacific*, pp. 263–64.

96 **At dawn on January 10:** James, *Years of MacArthur*, pp. 2:52–53.

96 **"Where are your":** Wainwright, *Story*, pp. 49–50.

96 **Murray was driving:** Hayes, "Report on Medical Tactics," p. 21; Cheek, "War Diary," p. 13.

96 **"Sir: You are well":** Morton, *War in the Pacific*, pp. 268–69; Breuer, *Sea Wolf*, p 38.

97 **It was early evening:** George S. Clarke, interview by Perry G. E. Miller, August 14–15, 1942, Louis Morton Papers, Box 2, pp. 9–10, 15, MHI.

97 **In the meantime:** ibid., pp. 11–12, 24–25; Cheek, "War Diary," pp. 8–9.

97 **Between the soldiers:** James, *Years of MacArthur*, pp. 2:35.

97 **there were 110,000:** Morton, *War in the Pacific*, p. 401.

98 **Half-rations:** Dod, *United States Army*, pp. 13–14.

98 **A quartermaster bakery:** Harold A. Arnold, "The Lesson of Bataan," *Quarter-master Review*, November–December 1946.

98 **Their meat was tough:** Knox, *Death March*, p. 84.

98 **It is reported:** John H. S. Dessez, to All United Commanders, January 15, 1942, re: "Livestock, slaughter of," U.S. Asiatic Defense Campaign, 1941–42, NRS, 1984-33, MR #1, NHC.

98 **"If something is":** Quoted in Norman, *Band of Angels*, pp. 37–38.

98 **The area was under guard:** Williams, *Rogues of Bataan II*, p. 40.

99 **The twenty-year-old marine:** ibid., pp. 41–42.

99 **As 2nd Lieutenant Leona Gastinger:** Knox, *Death March*, pp. 67–68.

99 **"he and his assistants":** Bumgarner, *Parade*, p. 69.

100 **With the help of:** Fred H. Mowrey, M.D., "Statistics of Malaria," in Heaton,

Coates, and Hoff, *Preventive Medicine*, p. 6:459.

100 **For the site of Hospital No. 2:** Morton, *War in the Pacific*, p. 381.

100 **"We had wounded and sick":** Knox, *Death March*, p. 83.

100 **"I guess we are all":** Norman, *Band of Angels*, p. 66.

100 **One of the consequences:** Ancel Keys et al., *The Biology of Human Starvation* (Minneapolis: University of Minnesota Press, 1950), p. 1:14.

100 **Tunnel No. 4:** This description of Tunnel No. 4 is drawn, in part, from Ind, *Bataan*, pp. 242–43; Sackett, "History of Canopus," p. 11.

101 **First Lieutenant Carter Simpson:** Simpson, *Diary*, p. 10.

101 **Crippled in her:** Sackett, "History of Canopus," p. 18.

101 **Shortly after MacArthur's visit:** James, *Years of MacArthur*, pp. 2:55–58; Wainwright, *Story*, pp. 50–51.

102 **The men were hungry:** Knox, *Death March*, pp. 65–66.

102 **"the President [has] personally":** Perret, *Old Soldiers*, pp. 261–62.

102 **"Help is on the way":** Schulz, *Hero of Bataan*, p. 139.

102 **West of Mt. Natib:** Morton, *War in the Pacific*, p. 282.

102 **Acting on Sutherland's:** James, *Years of MacArthur*, pp. 2:55–58; Wainwright, *Story*, pp. 50–51; Schulz, *Hero of Bataan*, p. 141.

102 **In the haste of retreat:** Cooper, "Medical Department," p. 26.

102 **But the inexorable:** Norman, *Band of Angels*, p. 38.

102 **The very next day:** Cooper, "Medical Department," pp. 55–56; Norman, *Band of Angels*, p. 38.

102 **The Japanese knew:** International Federation of Red Cross and Red Crescent Societies, "Red Cross, Red Crescent: A History," at www.ifrc.org/who/history.asp.

103 **Wainwright's front:** Romulo, *I Saw*, p. 196.

103 **Francis J. Bridget:** Hough, Ludwig, and Shaw, *Pearl Harbor*, p. 1:175. See also Cheek, "War Diary," p. 7; Robert A. Clement, "Brief History of C Battery, Fourth Marine Regiment, Anti-Aircraft," unpublished ms., p. 13. Courtesy of Gladys Irwin.

104 **So was Bulkeley's MTB Squadron 3:** White, *Expendable*, p. 27.

104 **Kelly appealed:** White, *Expendable*, pp. 76–77.

104 **On the night of January 22:** Breuer, *Sea Wolf*, p. 47.

104 **Bulkeley hoisted them:** White, *Expendable*, pp. 76–84; Breuer, *Sea Wolf*, pp. 46–49.

105 **Two barges of:** Rockwell, "Narrative," p. 14; Belote and Belote, *Corregidor*, p. 62.

105 **Platoon Sergeant Robert "Duke" Clement:** This account is based on Robert A. Clement, "The Naval Battalion of Bataan, May 3, 1994," unpublished ms., pp 7–11; Miller, "Shanghai to Corregidor," pp. 20–21; Sackett, "History of *Canopus*," p. 14.

106 **"the new type of suicide squads":** Sackett, "History of *Canopus*," p. 14.

107 **Six navy men:** Miller, "Shanghai to Corregidor," p. 22.

107 **When Mensching:** Chick Mensching, author interview, April 3, 2002.

107 **The naval battalion needed help:** Hough, Ludwig, and Shaw, *Pearl Harbor*, p. 1:178.

107 **That same day:** Bunker, "Seaward Defense Commander's Report of Damage," p. 1.

107 **"the first firing":** Moore, "Report of Major General," p. 31.

107 **Four rounds hit:** Hogaboom, "Action Report," p. 29.

107 **The fires were:** Paul D. Bunker, *Bunker's War: The World War II Diary of Col. Paul D. Bunker*, ed., Keith A. Barlow (Novato, Calif.: Presidio Press, 1996), p. 44.

107 **The descending shells:** Irvin, "Wartime Reminiscences," p. 2.

107 **Colonel Paul D. Bunker:** Bunker, *Bunker's War*, p. 46.

108 **"We were terrified":** Moore, "Report of Major General," p. 31.

108 **They climbed into:** Bunker, *Bunker's War*, p. 48.

108 **They burrowed into:** Robert D. Scholes, "Mop Up Operation in Vicinity of Longoskawayn Point," February 1, 1942, p. 2, Asiatic Defense Campaign, 1941–42, NRS, 1984-33, MR #2, NHC; Clement, "Naval Battalion," p. 10, with Irvin's marginalia; Morton, *War in the Pacific*, pp. 306–07.

108 **The next day the Scouts:** Morton,

War in the Pacific, p. 307; Hough, Ludwig, and Shaw, *Pearl Harbor*, p. 1:179.

109 **"lost without a trace":** Quoted in Morton, *War in the Pacific*, p. 312.

109 **Combined losses:** Hough, Ludwig, and Shaw, *Pearl Harbor*, p. 1:180.

109 **Three days later:** Morton, *War in the Pacific*, p. 318.

109 **"Scores of Japs":** William E. Dyess, *The Dyess Story* (New York: G.P. Putnam's Sons, 1944), p. 43.

109 **"proffer of honorable":** Wainwright, *Story*, p. 57.

109 **MacArthur's headquarters:** Morton, *War in the Pacific*, p. 323; Sayer and Botting, "America's Secret Army."

109 **"The old rules of war":** Wainwright, *Story*, p. 57.

110 **But the tactic backfired:** Dod, *Army in World War II*, pp. 93–96.

110 **But after ten minutes:** Dyess, *Dyess Story*, pp. 44–45.

110 **On January 26:** Villarin, *We Remember*, pp. 77–82.

110 **"There was so much killing":** Hibbs, *Tell MacArthur*, p. 84.

111 **"When surrounded":** Training Bulletin 14, November 2, 1942, Headquarters 41st Infantry Division, APO 41, Asiatic Defense Campaign, 1941–42, NRS, 1984-33, MR #2, NHC.

111 **The field hospitals:** Hersey, *Men on Bataan*, pp. 53–54; Melville and Annalee Jacoby, "Bataan Wounded Lived with Pain," *Life* 12, no. 16 (April 20, 1942), pp. 32–35.

111 **The ragtag naval battalion:** Morison, *History of Naval Operations*, pp. 3:200–01; Belote and Belote, *Corregidor*, p. 64; Winslow, *Fleet the Gods Forgot*, pp. 106–07; Sackett, "History of *Canopus*," p. 62.

111 **The navy doctors experienced:** W. Philip Giddings and Luther H. Wolff, "Factors of Mortality," in John Boyd Coates, Jr., and Michael E. DeBakey, *Surgery in World War II*, vol. 2, *General Surgery* (Washington, D.C.: Office of the Surgeon General, 1955), pp. 213–21.

112 **"wild-eyed with terror":** Weinstein, *Barbed-Wire Surgeon*, p. 37.

112 **Of several dozen:** Hayes, "Report on Medical Tactics," pp. 84–85.

112 **Second-generation Japanese-Americans:** Dower, *War Without Mercy*, p. 80.

112 **The fact that no evidence:** Peter Irons,

Justice at War: The Story of the Japanese American Internment Cases (Berkeley: University of California Press, 1993), p. 59.

113 **"a Jap is a Jap":** Dower, *War Without Mercy*, p. 80.

113 **Over the next eight:** Irons, *Justice at War*, p. 49.

113 **Admissions to Hospitals Nos. 1:** Harold W. Glattley, March 6, 1942, to Surgeons, 21st and 41st Divisions, p. 1, Louis Morton Papers, Box 9, MHI.

113 **This was the first stage:** Henry K. Beecher, "Resuscitation of Men Severely Wounded in Battle," in Coates and DeBakey, *Surgery in World War II*, pp. 2:9–10.

113 **At Hospital No. 1 the army:** Hayes, "Report on Medical Tactics," p. 85.

113 **Ann Bernatitus:** Murphy, "You'll Never Know," pp. 46, 48, 51.

114 **The most unusual patient:** Hartendorp, *Japanese Occupation*, p. 1:181.

114 **The "angels of Bataan":** Cooper, "Medical Department," pp. 64–65; Ashton, *Somebody Gives*, p. 68.

114 **A shortage of fuel:** Cooper, "Medical Department," pp. 25–27.

114 **The policy of:** ibid., pp. 32–33.

114 **For that reason:** ibid., p. 34.

114 **Snafu:** Gillespie, "Recollections," pp. 16–17.

116 **Hibbs was furious:** Hibbs, *Tell MacArthur*, p. 52.

116 **There were twenty-eight men:** ibid., p. 54.

116 **Once casualties made it:** See Melville Jacoby, "Philippine Epic," *Life* 12, no. 15 (April 13, 1942), p. 35.

116 **Most wounds were:** Morton, *War in the Pacific*, p. 381; U.S. War Department, *Handbook on Japanese Military Forces*, pp. 190–91.

116 **Remarkably:** Cooper, "Medical Department," p. 61.

Chapter 8: Never Surrender

117 **Senjinkun:** Yuki Tanaka, *Hidden Horrors: Japanese War Crimes in World War II* (Boulder, Colo.: Westview Press, 1996), p. 208.

117 **Bound by the honor:** *The Official Journal of the Japanese Military Administration*, ed. The Japanese Military Adminstration (Manila, Philippines: Niti Niti Shimbum Sha, 1942), pp. 237–42.

118 **Yamagata's directive:** Quoted in

Ohtani Keijiro, *The POWs*, trans. Kan Sugahara (Tosho Shuppan, 1978), pp. 32–46; Itō Masanori, *The Military Caste's Ups and Downs*.

118 **"Meditation on inevitable":** Yamato Tsunetomo, *Hagakure: The Book of the Samurai*, trans. William Scott Wilson (New York: Kodansha, 1983), p. 164.

118 **Historically the emperor:** Donald Keene, *Emperor of Japan: Meiji and His World, 1852–1912* (New York: Columbia University Press, 2002), p. 366.

118 **she saw the Indian:** Edwin O. Reischauer and Marius B. Jansen, *The Japanese Today: Change and Continuity* (Cambridge, Mass.: Belknap Press/Harvard University Press, 1978), p. 78.

118 **After U.S. Navy Commodore:** ibid.

118 **But it was Japan's:** ibid., p. 239.

119 **Japan learned from:** ibid., p. 81.

119 **In the Nihou Shoki:** Lu, *Japan*, pp. 1:3–4.

119 **"extend the line":** Quoted in Hoyt, *Japan's War*, p. 2.

119 **The early Japanese:** Reischauer and Jansen, *Japanese Today*, p. 42.

119 **The gods were:** William Theodore De Bary et al., eds., *Sources of Japanese Tradition: From Earliest Times to 1600*, 2nd ed. (New York: Columbia University Press, n.d.), pp. 17–18.

119 **"the supreme command":** Reischauer and Jansen, *Japanese Today*, p. 240.

119 **Seven years earlier:** Keene, *Emperor of Japan*, p. 367.

119 **The military man's loyalty:** Quoted in Emiko Ohnuki-Tierney, *Kamikaze, Cherry Blossoms, and Nationalisms: The Militarization of Aesthetics in Japanese History* (Chicago: University of Chicago Press, 2002), p. 13.

119 **Japanese militarists believed:** Reischauer and Jansen, *Japanese Today*, p. 241; Tanaka, *Hidden Horrors*, p. 208.

119 **With the military:** ibid.

119 **In the four decades:** Toshikazu Kase, *Journey to the "Missouri"* (New Haven, Conn.: Yale University Press, 1950), p. 1.

119 **Japan was at a crossroads:** Ramon H. Myers and Mark R. Peattie, eds., *The Japanese Colonial Empire, 1895–1945* (Princeton, N.J.: Princeton University Press, 1984), p. 6.

120 **the Liaotung Peninsula:** Zimmerman, *First Great Triumph*, p. 470.

120 **Port Arthur:** Myers and Peattie, *Colonial Empire*, p. 17.

120 **"naturally paved the way"**: Kase, *Journey*, pp. 2, 21.

120 **Coupled with the:** Irons, *Justice at War*, pp. 10–11.

120 **In October 1906:** ibid.

120 **Anti-American rioting:** Zimmerman, *The First Great Triumph*, p. 471.

120 **exclusionist fervor:** Miller, *War Plan Orange*, p. 21.

120 **Privately Roosevelt admitted:** Asahi Shimbun, *The Pacific Rivals: A View of Japanese-American Relations* (New York: Weatherhill/Asahi, 1972), p. 60.

120 **While the president refused:** Miller, *War Plan Orange*, p. 21.

120 **A key feature of:** ibid., p. 61.

120 **By 1921:** ibid., p. 74.

121 **On the heels of:** Spector, *Eagle Against Sun*, pp. 20–21; Belote and Belote, *Corregidor*, pp. 21–22.

121 **The trend would:** Kennedy, *Freedom from Fear*, p. 388.

121 **In Japan, militarists:** Arnold C. Brackman, *The Other Nuremberg: The Untold Story of the Tokyo War Crimes Trials* (New York: William Morrow, 1987), p. 192.

121 **"The Ministry could do":** Asahi Shimbun, *Pacific Rivals*, p. 76.

121 **Six years before:** Braudy, *Chivalry to Terrorism*, p. 467.

121 **"a flower no less":** Inazo Nitobe, *Bushido: The Soul of Japan* (Boston: Tuttle, 2001), p. 1.

121 *Bushidō* **was:** Asahi Shimbun, *Pacific Rivals*, pp. 62–63.

121 **"bridge of transpacific":** Irons, *Justice at War*, p. 12.

122 **By then Japan:** Asahi Shimbun, *Pacific Rivals*, p. 68.

122 **Japanese silk reelers:** ibid., p. 69.

122 **"I left on each":** ibid., p. 64.

122 **In 1933 Japan:** Herbert P. Bix, *Hirohito and the Making of Modern Japan* (New York: HarperCollins, 2000), p. 317.

122 **Her colonial conquests:** ibid., pp. 10–11.

Chapter 9: "Help is on the way"

123 **Homma was indisputably:** See Lawrence Taylor, *A Trial of Generals: Homma, Yamashita, MacArthur* (South Bend, Ind.: Icarus Press, 1981), pp. 40–53.

123 **Having graduated from:** Major General Francis Stewart Gildercy Piggott, affi-

davit, in *U.S.A. vs. Masaharu Homma*, Records of the Judge Advocate General (Army), War Crimes Branch, 1945–46, RG 177, Vol. 28, Box 5, p. 3275, NARA.

123 **was fluent in:** Prince Higashi Kuni, affidavit, in *U.S.A. vs. Masaharu Homma*, RG 153, Vol. 28, Box 5, p. 3262, NARA.

123 **In the meantime:** Arthur Swinson, *Four Samurai: A Quartet of Japanese Army Commanders in the Second World War* (London: Hutchinson, 1968), p. 40.

123 **In 1922 Homma:** Masaharu Homma, testimony, in *U.S.A. vs. Masaharu Homma*, RG 153, Vol. 26, Box 5, p. 3030, NARA.

123 **Then he fell in love:** Swinson, *Four Samurai*, p. 41.

123 **In 1927 Homma:** Masaharu Homma, testimony, in *U.S.A. vs. Masaharu Homma*, RG 153, Vol. 26, Box 5, p. 3030, NARA.

123 **Many Japanese considered:** Shiro Ozaki, affidavit, in *U.S.A. vs. Masaharu Homma*, RG 153, Vol. 28, Box 5, pp. 3247–48, NARA.

124 **He was opposed:** Schom, *Eagle and Rising Sun*, p. 76.

124 **Homma's views:** Taylor, *Trial of Generals*, pp. 40–53.

124 **After Nanking fell:** Toland, *But Not in Shame*, p. 92.

124 **Homma had been:** Masaharu Homma, testimony, in *U.S.A. vs. Masaharu Homma*, RG 153, Vol. 26, Box 5, p. 3034, NARA.

124 **Instead, he was:** Swinson, *Four Samurai*, pp. 40–41.

124 **whose unit code:** Ricardo Trota Jose to author, November 21, 2004.

124 **"A paper genius":** Taylor, *Trial of Generals*, pp. 40–53.

124 **daring to take them:** See Masaharu Homma, testimony, in *U.S.A. vs. Masaharu Homma*, RG 153, Vol. 28, Box 5, p. 3116. "Q. Now, were you confident, in your talks with your staff officers concerning these conditions in prisoner of war camps, that your officers were doing everything in their power to alleviate the conditions? A. That was my impression at the time. Now I come to know the many things since I came here, I am not so sure about it."

124 **Army Chief of Staff:** Morton, *War in the Pacific*, p. 263.

124 **The Japanese, boasted Tōjō:** Gregory F. Michno, *Death on the Hellships: Prisoners at*

Sea in the Pacific War (Annapolis, Md.: Naval Institute Press, 2001), p. 1.

124 **"Japan is no":** Quoted in Hoyt, *Japan's War*, p. 247.

124 **But twice in:** Bix, *Hirohito*, p. 447.

125 **While Major Kimura:** These figures are from January 6–March 1, 1942. See Morton, *War in the Pacific*, p. 349.

125 **An unsettling lull:** Hough, Ludwig, and Shaw, *Pearl Harbor*, p. 1:180.

125 **"My people entered":** Manuel L. Quezon to George C. Marshall, February 8, 1942, Louis Morton Papers, Box 2, MHI.

126 **"The troops have":** Louis Morton Papers, Box 2, MHI.

126 **"I have only":** Franklin D. Roosevelt to Commanding General, U.S. Army Forces in Far East, February 10, 1942, Louis Morton Papers, Box 2, MHI.

127 **"so long as there remains":** ibid.

127 **His imperatives were:** Connaughton, *MacArthur and Defeat*, p. 278.

127 **"magnificently exceeded":** Buhite and Levy, *Fireside Chats*, p. 212.

127 **"I urge every Filipino":** Charles A. Willoughby and John Chamberlain, *MacArthur, 1941–1951* (New York: McGraw-Hill, 1954), p. 55.

127 **"I cannot stand":** ibid., pp. 55–56.

127 **It took hours:** Simpson, *Diary*, p. 13.

127 **But remarkably little:** Hayes, "Report on Medical Tactics," p. 22.

128 **When fodder ran out:** Champlin, "Narrative," pp. 95–96, 103.

128 **"We ate the":** Knox, *Death March*, p. 84.

128 **Horses along with:** Stauffer, *Army in World War II*, p. 14.

128 **The only real chance:** ibid., p. 19.

128 **The 1,000-ton *Legaspi*:** ibid., pp. 19–20.

128 **Air deliveries:** Charles M. Wiltse, *Medical Supply in World War II* (Washington, D.C.: Office of the Surgeon General, 1968), pp. 404–06.

128 **Except for a few:** Stauffer, *Army in World War II*, pp. 20–21.

129 **"We're the battling bastards":** Toland, *Rising Sun*, pp. 1:355–56.

129 **Bob Kelly had:** White, *Expendable*, pp. 116–17.

129 **That evening:** Perret, *Old Soldiers*, p. 276.

129 **"My pirates":** Breuer, *Sea Wolf*, p. 56.

129 **General Tōjō:** James, *Years of MacArthur*, pp. 2:100–01.

129 **"Let me die":** Breuer, *Sea Wolf*, p. 64.

130 **"By guess and":** Quoted in Toland, *But Not in Shame*, p. 271.

130 **MacArthur was so grateful:** Breuer, *Sea Wolf*, p. 64.

130 **"The President of":** Willoughby and Chamberlain, *MacArthur*, p. 64.

130 **"God have mercy":** Toland, *But Not in Shame*, p. 277; James, *Years of MacArthur*, p. 2:109.

130 **Before he left:** Toland, *But Not in Shame*, p. 270.

131 **Songs and snipes:** James, *Years of MacArthur*, pp. 2:125–26.

131 **"Dugout Doug MacArthur":** Schulz, *Hero of Bataan*, p. 202.

131 **"I've been in General":** Hibbs, *Tell MacArthur*, p. 85.

131 **"I am going":** James, *Years of MacArthur*, p. 2:126.

131 **"We told you so":** Hersey, *Men on Bataan*, p. 260.

131 **One day in February 1942:** Kidd, *Twice Forgotten*, p. 54.

132 **Private 1st Class Richard T. Winter:** Richard Winter, author interview, May 23, 2003, Albuquerque, N.M.

132 **Captain Roland G. "Roly" Ames:** Belote and Belote, *Corregidor*, p. 54.

132 **AP correspondent Clark Lee:** Lee, *Pacific*, p. 170.

132 **He had, after all:** Schom, *Eagle and Rising Sun*, pp. 182–83.

132 **That perception was:** James, *Years of MacArthur*, p. 2:129.

132 **The fact that Roosevelt:** ibid.

132 **"His utter disregard":** ibid., p. 2:132.

132 **The citation was:** ibid., p. 2:131.

132 **MacArthur was made a hero:** Schom, *Eagle and Rising Sun*, p. 149.

132 **Marshall was indefatigable:** ibid., p. 150.

133 **"the assumption":** Quoted in ibid., p. 136.

133 **Streets, bridges, buildings:** James, *Years of MacArthur*, pp. 2:133–35.

133 **Several weeks earlier:** Morris, *Corregidor*, p. 359.

133 **"Mine eyes have seen":** Otis J. King,

Alamo of the Pacific (Fort Worth, Tex.: Branch Smith, 1999), p 52.

133 **In the meantime:** Wainwright, *Story*, p. 69; Schulz, *Hero of Bataan*, p. 202.

133 **Wainwright appointed:** Wainwright, *Story*, p. 73.

133 **Wainwright was enormously:** Morris, *Corregidor*, p. 329.

134 **he rectified:** Denys W. Knoll, "Intelligence Report, 16th Naval District, March 12–May 3, 1942," p. 31, Louis Morton Papers, Box 19, MHI.

134 *"Your Excellency"*: Schulz, *Hero of Bataan*, pp. 208–09; Norman, *Band of Angels*, p. 74.

134 **In late March:** Stauffer, *Army in World War II*, pp. 28–29.

134 **"like eating your little":** Alton C. Halbrook, interview by Ronald E. Marcello, March 21, 1972, and April 18, 1972, p. 64, #122, UNTOHC.

134 **They picked mangoes:** Ashton, *Somebody Gives*, pp. 95–96; Waterous spells it *nomia*, "Statement of Experiences," p. 53.

135 **They went fishing:** This technique is recounted in R. C. Sheats, "Diving as a 'Guest of the Emperor,' " in Ashton, *Somebody Gives*, p. 241.

135 **They washed down:** Weinstein, *Barbed-Wire Surgeon*, pp. 25–47; Waterous, "Statement of Experiences," p. 54; Bumgarner, *Parade*, p. 68.

135 **There was a "favored":** Allen C. McBride, "Notes on the Fall of Bataan," pp. 90, 111–12, Louis Morton Papers, Box 14, MHI.

135 **"From the standpoint":** Quoted in Morton, *War in the Pacific*, p. 383.

135 **Unless food stocks:** Stauffer, *Army in World War II*, p. 30.

135 **Standard treatment was:** Gillespie in Heaton, Coates, Hoff, and Hoff, *Preventive Medicine*, pp. 6:503–04; Benjamin M. Baker, "The Suppression of Malaria," in ibid., pp. 2:465–68.

135 **When the supply:** Hibbs, *Tell MacArthur*, p. 79; Ashton, *Somebody Gives*, p. 197.

135 **A dearth of mosquito bars:** Cooper, "Medical Department," p. 22.

135 **Filipino civilians:** Morton, *War in the Pacific*, p. 378n55; William J. Kennard, "Observations on Bataan, notes taken at conference held by Lt. Col. Roger G. Prentiss, Jr., 22 August 42," pp. 5–6.

135 **Filipino Brigadier General Vicente Lim:** Quoted in Romulo, *I Saw*, pp. 106–07, 267.

136 **By early March:** Gillespie, "Malaria," in Heaton, Coates, Hoff, and Hoff, *Preventive Medicine*, p. 6:507.

136 **Ward No. 2 handled:** Bumgarner, *Parade*, p. 69.

136 **Indeed, the man:** Gillespie, "Malaria," in Heaton, Coates, Hoff, and Hoff, *Preventive Medicine*, p. 6:506.

136 **"It is my candid":** Cooper, "Medical Department," Tab 1.

136 **By late March:** Gillespie, "Malaria," in Heaton, Coates, Hoff, and Hoff, *Preventive Medicine*, p. 6:507.

136 **Chick Mensching:** Chick Mensching, author interview, April 3, 2002.

136 **quinine dihydrochloride:** Ashton, *Somebody Gives*, p. 79.

136 **Compounding the malaria problem:** Waterous, "Statement of Experiences," p. 7.

136 **The men ate:** Bumgarner, *Parade*, p. 69.

136 **Sanitary conditions:** Waterous, "Statement of Experiences," pp. 42, 102; Cooper, "Medical Department," pp. 76–77.

137 **"Patients are being":** Norman, *Band of Angels*, p. 55.

137 **"Had to clear":** ibid., p. 78.

137 **Infected plasma:** Bumgarner, *Parade*, p. 62.

137 **When the bacillus antitoxin:** ibid.

137 **The day of the visit:** Gillespie, "Recollections," p. 21.

137 **Both Hospitals Nos. 1:** Norman, *Band of Angels*, p. 38.

137 **ammunition dump:** Weinstein, *Barbed-Wire Surgeon*, p. 41.

138 **In the early morning:** Hayes, "Report on Medical Tactics," p. 85.

138 **Twenty-three were killed:** Romulo, *I Saw*, p. 262.

138 **"We regret the unfortunate":** Norman, *Band of Angels*, p. 79.

138 **Weinstein was convinced:** Weinstein, *Barbed-Wire Surgeon*, pp. 42–43.

138 **Hospital No. 1 managed:** ibid., p. 29; Norman, *Band of Angels*, p. 62.

138 **"Romances flourished":** Weinstein, *Barbed-Wire Surgeon*, pp. 30–31.

138 **Three nurses were married:** Norman, *Band of Angels*, p. 62.

138 **Captain Dyess:** Dyess, *Dyess Story*, pp. 50–51.

138 **The self-published broadside:** *Jungle Journal*, February 25, 1942, in Ashton, *Somebody Gives*, pp. 55–56.

139 **"like baseball cards":** Ashton, *Somebody Gives*, p. 67.

139 **"Don't Wait to Die":** T. C. Parker, "The Epic of Corregidor—Bataan, December 24, 1941–May 4, 1942," *United States Naval Institute Proceedings* 69, no. 1 (January 1942), pp. 17–18.

139 **Japanese-controlled KZRH:** Hoeffer, "Hard Way Back," p. 6.

139 **"It is cherry blossom time":** Morton, *War in the Pacific*, p. 386; Sayer and Botting, "America's Secret Army."

139 **on March 27:** Knox, *Death March*, pp. 90–91.

139 **Some of the frontline:** Daws, *Prisoners*, p. 71

139 **"Hunger and disease":** Quoted in Morton, *War in the Pacific*, p. 384.

139 **The standard-issue:** ATIS, "Organization of Medical Units in the Japanese Army," Research Report No. 83, July 29, 1944, pp. 10–11, microfiche, MHI.

139 **There was aspirin:** U.S. War Department, *Handbook on Japanese Military Forces*, pp. 345–46.

140 **Medics were responsible:** ATIS, "Organization of Medical Units," p. 3.

140 **They carried their:** ibid., p. 28.

140 **Field hospitals were:** ibid., pp. 7, 29.

140 **Standard daily rations:** Morton, *War in the Pacific*, p. 412.

140 **and consisted of:** Masaharu Homma, testimony, in *U.S.A. vs. Masaharu Homma*, RG 153, Vol. 27, Box 5, 3122, NARA.

140 **But by January 1942:** Gillespie in Heaton, Coates, Hoff, and Hoff, *Preventive Medicine*, pp. 6:509–10.

140 **The Japanese 14th Army:** ibid.

141 **Japanese hospitals on Bataan:** See Morton, *War in the Pacific*, p. 412.

141 **It was hard:** Wada Kinsuke, author interview, July 9, 2002, Kyōto, Japan.

141 **"I call upon every":** Romulo, *I Saw*, p. 231.

141 **Once Quezon reached:** James, *Years of MacArthur*, p. 2:112.

141 **He was now responsible:** ibid., pp. 2:119–21.

141 **The fate of the garrison:** Belote and Belote, *Corregidor*, p. 90; Wainwright, *Story*, p. 114; Kenneth R. Wheeler, interview by

William M. Belote, November 9, 1963, p. 1, Belote Collection, Box 1, MHI.

142 **The troops were ravaged:** Hayes, "Report on Medical Tactics," p. 22.

142 **By April 1:** Morton, *War in the Pacific*, p. 404n62.

Chapter 10: "Wherever I am . . . I still love you"

143 **there were only 9,000:** Stauffer, *Army in World War II*, p. 28.

143 **But little of Corregidor's:** James, *Years of MacArthur*, p. 2:64.

143 **which meant valuable:** Stauffer, *Army in World War II*, p. 28.

143 **Officers and men:** Lee, *Pacific*, p. 160.

145 **By early January 1942:** Belote and Belote, *Corregidor*, pp. 42–43.

146 **The air smelled:** Amea Willoughby, *I Was on Corregidor*, p. 109.

146 **Respiratory ailments:** Cooper, "Medical Department," p. 83.

146 **The absence of daylight:** John W. Gulick, "Memoirs of Battery C, 91st CA PS," p. 122, MHI.

146 **"Tunnels, dust, heat":** Belote and Belote, *Corregidor*, p. 72

146 **John Nardini was:** Hayes, "Report on Medical Tactics," p. 4.

147 **The Office of the Regimental Surgeon:** "Notes on the 1st Battalion, Fourth Marines, Fort Mills, Corregidor, P.I.," author unknown, courtesy Richard A. Long; Cecil Peart, correspondence with author, March 25, 2003.

147 **Few preparations had been made:** "A Report of the Medical Activities of the Fourth Regiment U.S. Marines and Attached Troops for the Period 1/1/42 to 5/6/42 on Corregidor, Philippine Islands," BUMED, p.1; Beecher, "Experiences," pp. 16–17; Samuel L. Howard, "Report on the Operation, Employment and Supply of the Old 4th Marines from September 1941 to the Surrender of Corregidor, May 6, 1942," p. 15, RG 127, Box 309, Folder A-21, NARA; Hanson Baldwin, *Battles Lost and Won: Great Campaigns of World War II* (New York: Konecky and Konecky, 1966), p. 124.

147 **An estimated two miles:** Moore, "Report of Commanding Officer," Exhibit E, p. 3.

147 **Colonel Lloyd E. Mielenz:** Dod, *Army in World War II*, pp. 58, 102.

147 **The antiaircraft batteries:** Belote and Belote, *Corregidor*, pp. 77–78.

148 *"Woke up other day"*: Ferguson, *Diary*, p. 28.

148 **Two miles of additional:** Moore, "Report of the Commanding Officer," Exhibit E, p. 3.

148 **"tunnelitis":** Belote and Belote, *Corregidor*, p. 70.

149 **On February 17:** Hough, Ludwig, and Shaw, *Pearl Harbor*, p. 1:180; Miller, "Shanghai to Corregidor," p. 23.

149 **George estimated that:** Hayes, *Diary*, p. 30.

149 **An acute infection:** "Shigellosis," in Mark H. Beers and Robert Berkow, eds., *The Merck Manual of Diagnosis and Therapy* (Whitehouse Station, N.J.: Merck Research Laboratories), 1999, pp. 1164–65; "Amebiasis," in ibid., pp. 1255–57.

149 **In the absence:** Charles G. Roland, *Long Night's Journey into Day: Prisoners of War in Hong Kong and Japan, 1941–1945* (Waterloo, Ont.: Wilfrid Laurier University Press, 2001), p. 172.

150 **The bombs bursting:** "Narrative Report of Action During War, from November 1, 1941–May 5, 1942, from Battery C, 60th Coast Artillery to Commanding Officer, 60th Coast Artillery," pp. 76, 83, RG 407, Box 124, Folder 3, NARA; Belote and Belote, *Corregidor*, p. 47; Moore, "Report of the Commanding Officer," Exhibit F, p. 7.

150 **the *Seadragon*:** Blair, *Silent Victory*, p. 173.

150 **But 50 percent of enemy:** Porter, "Antiaircraft Defense," p. 14.

150 **At first the Japanese:** "Narrative Report of Action During War," pp. 67–68, 73–74.

151 **Photo Joe teased:** Stamp, *Journey*, p. 22.

151 **on February 6:** Morton, *War in the Pacific*, pp. 485–86.

151 **"I wonder what it's like":** Ferguson, *Diary*, p. 29.

151 **Planes swept in:** Moore, "Report of the Commanding Officer," pp. 45–46.

151 **the house that Wainwright:** Wainwright, *Story*, p. 74.

151 **"the largest air raid":** Moore, "Report of the Commanding Officer," Exhibit F, p. 9.

152 **One day Wainwright:** Ferdinand V. Berley, interview by Jan K. Herman, 7, 21, 27 February, 6 March, 3, 10, 24 April, and 1 May 1995, p. 18.

152 **The batteries on Corregidor:** E. L. Barr, "Diary: History of Battery M—60th Coast Artillery," p. 3, RG 407, Box 125, Folder 7, NARA.

152 **"I dare you":** Hanson Baldwin, " 'The Rock': The Fall of Corregidor," in Baldwin, *Battles Lost and Won*, p. 133.

152 **But he remembered:** Borneman interview, p. 3.

152 **The *Seadragon* left:** Moore, "Report of Commanding Officer," p. 33; Bunker, *Bunker's War*, p. 58; Blair, *Silent Victory*, p. 173.

Chapter 11: "We are not barbarians"

154 **"I see no gleam":** Henry G. Lee quoted in Calvin Ellsworth Chunn, *Of Rice and Men: The Story of Americans Under the Rising Sun* (Los Angeles/Tulsa, Okla.: Veterans' Publishing Company, 1946), pp. 186, 473.

155 **Homma's artillery:** Hough, Ludwig, and Shaw, *Pearl Harbor*, p. 1:182.

155 **"Shock Absorbers":** Romulo, *I Saw*, p. 199.

155 **"comfort girls":** Ienaga, *Pacific War*, p. 184.

155 **"came from a San Francisco":** Masaharu Homma, interview by Walter E. Buchly, p. 7, Louis Morton Papers, Box 8, MHI.

155 **His intelligence:** Condon-Rall, "Medical Preparations in the Philippines, 1941–42," p. 2.

155 **"total chaos":** Quoted in Gillespie, "Malaria," in Heaton, Coates, and Hoff, *Preventive Medicine*, p. 6:20.

155 **Once Mt. Samat:** Morton, *War in the Pacific*, p. 415.

155 **"There is no reason":** Toland, *Rising Sun*, p. 1:359.

155 **One hundred and fifty pieces of artillery:** ibid.

155 **Some 3,000 casualties:** Ashton, *Somebody Gives*, p. 67.

156 **"Every vehicle that":** Abie Abraham, *Oh God Where Are You?* (New York: Vantage Press, 1997), p. 37.

156 **"to cut the traction ropes":** Juanita Redmond, *I Served on Bataan* (New York: Garland, 1984), p. 107.

156 **Lieutenant (j.g.) Claud Mahlon Fraleigh:** Murphy, "You'll Never Know," p. 53.

156 **"I heard myself":** Redmond, *I Served*, p. 109.

156 **Corrugated tin roofs:** Toland, *But Not in Shame*, p. 288; see also Richard S. Roper, *Brothers of Paul: Activities of Prisoner of War*

Chaplains in the Philippines During World War
II (Odenton, Md.: Revere, 2003), pp. 87–94.

156 **Ten bombs:** Cooper, "Medical Department," p. 57.

156 **Smith, Fraleigh:** Hartendorp, *Japanese Occupation*, pp. 1:181–82.

156 **Later that day:** Toland, *Rising Sun*, 1:360.

157 **Full rations:** McBride, "Fall of Bataan," p. 117.

157 **Major General King returned:** Knoll, "Intelligence Report," p. 12.

157 **"We didn't know":** Knox, *Death March*, p. 94.

157 **"The worst day":** ibid., pp. 98–99.

157 **"Your U.S. convoy":** Moore, "Report of the Commanding Officer," p. 51.

157 **"under any circumstances":** Morton, *War in the Pacific*, p. 455.

157 **"Already our hospital":** Quoted in Condon-Rall, "Medical Preparations in the Philippines, 1941–42," p. 52.

157 **With 75,500 men still:** There were 78,000 men officially on Bataan on April 3, 1942, but roughly 75,500 on April 9, 1942, according to historian Ricardo Trota Jose, due to deaths incurred in the meantime and escapes to Corregidor. Letter to the author, February 14, 2005.

157 **The Radio Intercept Tunnel:** Parker, "Epic of Corregidor," p. 18.

158 **"Tell him not":** Toland, *Rising Sun*, p. 1:365.

158 **King had already:** Major General Edward P. King, Jr., affidavit, in *U.S.A. vs. Masaharu Homma*, WCO/JAG, 1945–46, RG 177, Vol. 28, Box 5, p. 3285, NARA.

158 **Thousands of troops:** Morton, *War in the Pacific*, p. 454.

158 **General King ordered:** Hayes, "Report on Medical Tactics," p. 86.

158 **The nurses of Hospital No. 1:** Romulo, *I Saw*, pp. 278–86.

158 **Major Achille C. Tisdelle, Jr.:** testimony, in *U.S.A. vs. Masaharu Homma*, WCO/JAG, 1945–46, RG 177, Vol. 28, Box 4, p. 2302, NARA.

158 **On April 6:** Sackett, "History of Canopus," p. 63.

159 **"demolition of everything":** E. L. Sackett, memorandum, from the Commander, Mariveles Area, to the Commandant, 16th Naval District, April 10, 1942, Asiatic Defense Campaign, 1941–42, NRS, 1984-33, MR #1, NHC.

159 **That included arms:** G. W. Hirsch, comments, on McBride's "Notes on the Fall," p. 130.

159 **The *Dewey* dry dock:** See Wilkes, "War Activities Submarines."

159 **"Transportation other":** Commanding Officer, Naval Force, Mariveles Area, to Officers on Duty in Mariveles Area, April 9, 1942, Asiatic Defense Campaign, 1941–42, NRS, 1984-33, MR #1, NHC.

159 **Soldiers, civilians:** Knox, *Death March*, p. 101.

159 **"Where ya going":** Irvin, "Wartime Reminiscences," p. 4.

159 **Ammunition dumps:** Moore, "Report of the Commanding Officer," p. 50.

159 **Soldiers smashed:** Dod, *Army in World War II*, pp. 100–01; Cave, *Beyond Courage*, p. 147.

159 **Throughout the night:** Moore, "Report of the Commanding Officer," p. 50.

160 **"You could have":** Dyess, *Dyess Story*, p. 65.

160 **They jumped into tugs:** Otis King, author interview, May 22, 2003, Albuquerque, N.M.

160 **"sick at heart":** Redmond, *I Served*, p. 126.

160 **John Kidd:** Hayes, "Report on Medical Tactics," p. 86.

160 **The mountainside trembled:** Kidd, *Twice Forgotten*, p. 58.

160 **Huge rocks were hurled:** Sackett, memorandum, from the Commander, Mariveles Area, p. 22; Hayes, "Report on Medical Tactics," p. 22.

160 **Bataan looked as if:** Parker, "Epic of Corregidor," quoted in Hough, Ludwig, and Shaw, *Pearl Harbor*, p. 1:183.

161 **At 0500:** Charles B. Brook, interview by William M. Belote, October 23, 1963, p. 1, Belote Collection, Box 1, MHI.

161 **Three more bombing:** Moore, "Report of the Commanding Officer," p. 52.

161 **The officers and crew:** Hayes, "Report on Medical Tactics," p. 50.

161 **At 0900 Major General King:** Toland, *Rising Sun*, p. 1:366.

161 **Nakayama would not:** Major Achille C. Tisdelle, testimony, in *U.S.A. vs. Masaharu Homma*, WCO/JAG, 1945–46, RG 177, Vol. 28, Box 4, p. 2305, NARA.

161 **"My forces":** Toland, *Rising Sun*, p. 1:366.

161 **Homma had anticipated:** Stanley L.

Falk, *Bataan: The March of Death* (New York: Curtis Books, 1962), p. 137.

161 **Filipinos accounted for:** Of the 75,500 men captured on Bataan on April 9, 1942, historian Ricardo Trota Jose estimates that 64,104 were Filipinos, and 11,446 were Americans. Letter to the author, February 14, 2005.

161 **"begged for a halt":** Associated Press, "What Tokyo Reports," *New York Times*, April 10, 1942.

161 **Indeed, the fall of:** Toland, *But Not in Shame*, p. 310.

161 **In late March:** Toland, *Rising Sun*, p. 1:366.

162 **"Rest areas":** Richard C. Mallonée, *The Naked Flagpole: Battle for Bataan*, ed. Richard C. Mallonée II (San Rafael, Calif.: Presidio Press, 1980), pp. 144–45.

162 **Kawane had only:** ibid., p. 145.

162 **Thousands upon thousands:** Toland, *Rising Sun*, p. 1:366.

162 **"patients rather than prisoners":** Quoted in Falk, *Bataan*, p. 187.

162 **"I thought it was":** ibid., p. 188.

162 **"There were far more":** Hitome Junsuke, author interview, July 12, 2002, Kyōto, Japan.

162 **By the afternoon of:** Dyess, *Dyess Story*, p. 76.

162 **The scene made:** Knox, *Death March*, p. 119.

162 **Privates were mixed:** ibid., p. 127.

162 **Only later, at Limay:** Falk, *Bataan*, p. 111.

162 **"marveled at how it was":** E. B. Miller, *Bataan Uncensored* (Long Prairie, Minn.: Hart, 1991), p. 219.

162 **"kill all prisoners":** Toland, *Rising Sun*, p. 1:368.

162 **But other Japanese:** Ricardo Trota Jose to author, November 21, 2004.

163 **Tsuji had been:** Toland, *Rising Sun*, p. 1:367.

163 **The killings began:** Ashton, *Somebody Gives*, p. 184.

163 **Private Blair Robinett:** Knox, *Death March*, p. 121.

163 **Armed with bayonet-tipped rifles:** ibid.

163 **Artesian wells ran:** ibid., pp. 132, 138.

163 **"They'd bayonet you":** Bert Bank, *Back from the Living Dead* (Tuscaloosa, Ala.: privately published, 1945), pp. 21–22.

163 **The Japanese looted:** ibid., p. 24.

163 **Men chewed sugarcane:** Falk, *Bataan*, p. 132.

163 **Stragglers were clubbed:** ibid., p. 108.

163 **forced to bury:** ibid., p. 132.

163 **"If you fell":** Knox, *Death March*, p. 136.

163 **The roadside was strewn:** Bank, *Living Dead*, p. 23.

163 **"the Jap guards went":** Dyess, *Dyess Story*, p. 90.

163 **Dysentery ran rampant:** ibid., p. 134.

164 **"Dear friends":** Daws, *Prisoners*, p. 74.

164 **The Japanese drew:** ibid., p. 75.

164 **Those who survived:** Dyess, *Dyess Story*, p. 94.

164 **From there they:** Hough, Ludwig, and Shaw, *Pearl Harbor*, p. 1:183.

164 **It was a designation:** Falk, *Bataan*, p. 169.

164 **Between 5,000:** Knox, *Death March*, p. 154.

164 **Up to 1,100:** U.S. Historical Center, Fort McNair, Washington, D.C.

164 **In total, more Fil-Americans:** Toland, *Rising Sun*, p. 1:375.

Chapter 12: "I go to meet the Japanese commander"

165 **"every last one of them":** Wainwright, *Story*, p. 81.

165 **Corregidor struck them:** Cooper, "Medical Department," p. 83; Hartendorp, *Japanese Occupation*, p. 1:183.

165 **These served as wards:** Amea Willoughby, *I Was on Corregidor*, p. 108.

165 **Several small radios:** Hartendorp, *Japanese Occupation*, p. 1:184.

165 **"Bataan has fallen!":** quoted in Dean Schedler, "Dazed, Weary Troops Reach Corregidor Under Foe's Fire," *New York Times*, April 11, 1942, p. 1.

166 **"Probably never before":** Hayes, *Diary*, p. 28.

166 **Hayes complained:** Hayes, "Report on Medical Tactics," p. 6.

166 **During bombing raids:** Amea Willoughby, *I Was on Corregidor*, p. 108.

166 **Morale was so low:** Knoll, "Intelligence Report," p. 21.

166 **"If the Japanese can":** Morris, *Corregidor*, p. 409.

166 **Corregidor needed:** Baldwin, *Battles Lost and Won*, pp. 422–23n21. See also

Hough, Ludwig, and Shaw, *Pearl Harbor*,
p. 1:171; Howard, "Report on the Operation,"
p. 18.

166 **George watched:** Hayes, "Report on
Medical Tactics," p. 14.

167 **The chocolate bars came:** "Notes on
the 1st Battalion, 4th Marines," p. 1.

167 **Highly concentrated:** Stauffer, *Army
in World War II*, p. 304.

167 **First Battalion troops:** "Notes on the
1st Battalion, 4th Marines," p. 1.

167 **The chalk V:** Toland, *Rising Sun*,
1:387.

167 **Then there was:** B. H. Chamberlain,
Things Japanese, quoted in R.W. Burchfield, *A
Supplement to the Oxford English Dictionary*
(Oxford: Clarendon Press, 1976), p. 2:1211.

167 **"Chief Tomas picked":** J. E. Lighter,
ed., *Random House Historical Dictionary of
American Slang* (New York: Random House,
1997), pp. 2:251, 669.

168 **The marines were nearly:** Beecher,
"Experiences," p. 18.

168 **Scoured out of:** Hayes, "Report on
Medical Tactics," p. 13.

168 **"Couple casualties":** Ferguson, *Diary*,
p. 33.

168 **They were, though:** William C. Braly,
"Corregidor Log," p. 2:1, Braly Papers, Box 3,
MHI.

168 **That afternoon a column:** McBride,
"Notes on the Fall," p. 109.

168 **They were confined:** Waterous, "Statement of Experiences," pp. 112–13.

168 **Apparently one of Matsuii's officers:**
Norman, *Band of Angels*, p. 94; Weinstein,
Barbed-Wire Surgeon, pp. 49–52.

168 **The surrender at Hospital No. 2:**
Gillespie, "Recollections," p. 24.

168 **"Anyone caught":** Bumgarner, *Parade*,
p. 78.

168 **A guard was posted:** William J.
Priestly, "57 Infantry PS, Diary," Book 2,
"Chronology from Col. Wm. Craige—
Med Report," Louis Morton Papers, Box 9,
MHI.

169 **Battery personnel moved:** Colonel
William D. North, testimony, in *U.S.A. vs.
Masaharu Homma*, RG153, Entry 177, Vol. 7,
Box 2, p. 808, NARA.

169 **The Americans had raised:** Melvyn H.
McCoy, S. M. Mellnik, and Welbourn Kelley,
Ten Escape from Tojo (New York: Farrar and
Rinehart, 1944), p. 17.

169 **On April 22:** Gillespie, "Recollections," p. 27.

169 **The day after:** Walter H. Waterous,
testimony, in *U.S.A. vs. Masaharu Homma*,
RG 153, Entry 177, Vol. 7, Box 2, p. 763,
NARA.

169 **Those who wanted:** ibid.

169 **A few were:** ibid.

169 **Japanese soldiers:** Cooper, "Medical
Department," p. 173.

169 **The patients at Hospital No. 2:**
Waterous, "Statement of Experiences," p. 84.

169 **Sekiguchi's men had:** Walter H.
Waterous, testimony, in *U.S.A. vs. Masaharu
Homma*, RG 153, Entry 177, Vol. 7, Box 2,
p. 757, NARA.

169 **When the American:** Colonel William
D. North, testimony, ibid., p. 809, NARA.

170 **Despite repeated requests:** Gillespie,
"Recollections," p. 20.

170 **"We got nothing":** ibid., p. 26.

170 **A medical detachment:** ibid., p. 28.

170 **"Many of us turned":** Quoted in
Norman, *Band of Angels*, p. 95.

171 **The area, known as:** This account is
based on Patrick Clancey, "The Siege and
Capture of Corregidor," p. 5. www.jatoga.
net.au/~witman/chs_41-42/marines.htm

171 **"0800—On the morning":** Moore,
"Report of the Commanding Officer," p. 53.

171 **By mid-April:** "Proceedings of a Board
Appointed," p. 70.

171 **For every shell:** C. L. Irwin,
"Corregidor in Action," *Coast Artillery Journal*,
January–February 1943, p. 11, MHI.

171 **But they were oddly uninformed:**
Colonel Walter E. Buchly, interview of
Japanese Lieutenant General Masaharu
Homma, p. 5, Louis Morton Papers, Box,
MHI, p. 5; Dyess, *Dyess Story*, p. 74.

172 **The Japanese preferred:** Sami
Korhonen, "The Battles of the Winter,"
www.winterwar.com, pp. 1–12; "Proceedings
of a Board Appointed," p. 70.

172 **The reason was simple:** Homma interview, p. 8.

172 **the number surged to 30,600:**
Morton, *War in the Pacific*, p. 324.

172 **Homma had requested:** ibid.

172 **300,000 tablets:** ibid., p. 324.

172 **May 5 was:** ibid., pp. 523–25.

172 **What a change:** Ferguson, *Diary*,
p. 33.

173 **On April 13:** Andrew Miller, letter to

author, July 7, 2004. Belote and Belote, *Corregidor*, identify the plane as a B-25, but Miller was an eyewitness, and the plane bore the number 41-2447.

173 **In a direct plea:** Stauffer, *Army in World War II*, pp. 30–31.

173 **By April 14:** Baldwin, *Battles Lost and Won*, p. 139.

173 **"life on Corregidor took":** Leon M. Gurrero, "The Last Days of Corregidor," *Philippine Review* (May 1943), quoted in Morton, *War in the Pacific*, p. 542.

173 **On April 18:** Wainwright, *Story*, pp. 90–91.

174 **What none of them:** F.A.P., "The Flag of Corregidor," *Coast Artillery Journal*, May–June 1942, MHI.

174 **Lieutenant Colonel James H. Doolittle:** Spector, *Eagle Against Sun*, pp. 154–55.

174 **the effect was galvanizing:** Hartendorp, *Japanese Occupation*, p. 1:185.

174 **Of the captured fliers:** Geoffrey Perret, *Winged Victory: The Army Air Forces in World War II* (New York: Random House, 1993), p. 153.

174 **In revenge for:** Hoyt, *Japan's War*, p. 279.

174 **"We hope we raised hell":** Bunker, *Bunker's War*, p. 134.

174 **Then on April 24:** Belote and Belote, *Corregidor*, pp. 118–20.

175 **Fort Drum fired:** William C. Braly, *The Hard Way Home* (Washington, D.C.: Washington Infantry Journal Press, 1947), p. 69.

175 **"You would hear":** quoted in Schultz, *Hero of Bataan*, pp. 261–62.

176 *Night Hawk:* Moore, "Report of Commanding Officer," Part C, p. 28; William C. Braly, "Corregidor Log," Vol. 2, unpaginated, Braly Papers, Box 3, MHI.

176 **The next day:** Moore, "Report of Commanding Officer," p. 60.

176 **A string of bombs:** Bunker, *Bunker's War*, p. 138.

176 **"Wet, oily, slick":** Ferguson, *Diary*, p. 36.

177 **maybe a romantic stroll:** Romulo, *I Saw*, p. 170.

177 **Sometimes a voice:** Norman, *Band of Angels*, p. 98.

177 **Suddenly at 2158:** Moore, "Report of Commanding Officer," p. 60.

177 **the concussion slammed shut:** Morris, *Corregidor*, p. 440.

177 **Arms and legs:** Redmond, *I Served*, pp. 145–46.

177 **One army nurse:** Norman, *Band of Angels*, p. 101.

177 **"We worked all that night":** Redmond, *I Served*, p. 145.

177 **"Net result 14 dead":** Ferguson, *Diary*, p. 36.

177 **Ten days earlier:** Moore, "Report of Commanding Officer," p. 56.

178 **Some marines:** Simpson, *Diary*, p. 17.

178 **Shrapnel had:** Hayes, "Report on Medical Tactics," p. 24.

178 **The problem:** Wainwright, *Story*, p. 92.

178 **"People of Malta":** Charles A. Jellison, *Besieged: The World War II Ordeal of Malta, 1940–1942* (Hanover, N.H.: University Press of New England, 1984), p. 167.

178 **"The officers and":** Wainwright, *Story*, pp. 98–99.

179 **The morning of April 29:** *Fourteenth Army Operations*, vol. 1, *Japanese Studies in World War II*, pp. 45–46, Historical Section, G-2, GHQ, FEC, MHI.

179 **"While the enemy artillery":** ibid., p. 1:51.

179 **At 0730 three:** "Proceedings of a Board Appointed," p. 31.

179 **Both the North and South:** Braly, "Corregidor Log," Vol. 2.

179 **Artillery mauled:** Morris, *Corregidor*, p. 445.

179 **"Another intensive bombardment":** Ferguson, *Diary*, p. 37.

179 **Cheney and James Ravines:** Barr, "Diary: History of Battery M," pp. 13–14.

180 **Fort Drum fired:** Peart, "Asiatic Reminiscences," p. 17.

180 **The roar of the Rock:** J.W. Keene, "Philippine Defense 1941: Corregidor."

180 **Seventy-five-millimeter:** Stephen M. Mellnik, "How the Japs Took Corregidor," *Coast Artillery Journal*, March–April 1945, p. 10, MHI.

180 **The only respite:** Simpson, *Diary*, p. 16.

180 **"During the day":** Beecher, "Experiences," p. 30.

180 **Then Japanese artillery:** Bunker, *Bunker's War*, p. 136.

180 **"I guess my life":** Ferguson, *Diary*, p. 35.

180 **Rations left men:** Bunker, *Bunker's War*, p. 142.

180 **reserve stocks:** Belote and Belote, *Corregidor*, p. 140.

180 **"Pardon me":** William C. Braly, interview by William M. Belote, June 24, 1964, p. 1, Belote Collection, Box 2, MHI.

180 **Cordite fumes:** Belote and Belote, *Corregidor*, pp. 126–27.

180 **Fifty feet underground:** Hartendorp, *Japanese Occupation*, p. 1:184.

180 **Lieutenant (j.g.) Charles B. Brook:** Charles B. Brook, interview by William M. Belote, October 23, 1963, pp. 1–2, Belote Collection, Box 1, MHI.

181 **"You'll never get":** Hartendorp, *Japanese Occupation*, p. 1:184.

181 **On April 17:** Schultz, *Hero of Bataan*, p. 269.

181 **The moon was full:** Norman, *Band of Angels*, p. 105.

181 **kissed Wainwright:** Schultz, *Hero of Bataan*, p. 102.

181 **Batteries Way and Geary:** Morris, *Corregidor*, p. 446.

181 **Explosion followed explosion:** Moore, "Report of Commanding Officer," p. 65.

181 **There were enough shells:** Schultz, *Hero of Bataan*, p. 272.

181 **The noise on:** Valentine P. Foster, interview by William M. Belote, November 29, 1963, p. 4, Belote Collection, Box 2, MHI.

181 **Wainwright himself had:** Schultz, *Hero of Bataan*, p. 264.

181 **"My head suddenly felt":** Wainwright, *Story*, p. 100.

181 **The blast from:** Alex Davies, "Acoustic Trauma: Bioeffects of Sound," schizophonia.com/installation/trauma/trauma_thesis.

182 **By the late afternoon:** Barr, "Diary: History of Battery M," pp. 15–16.

182 **Even disabled guns:** Belote and Belote, *Corregidor*, p. 128.

182 **This was George's territory:** Ferguson, *Diary*, p. 37.

182 **A 240mm shell breached:** Moore, "Report of the Commanding Officer," p. 65.

182 **"as big as your":** Hayes, "Report on Medical Tactics," p. 24.

182 **John, just a few:** Miller, "Shanghai to Corregidor," p. 27.

182 **sixty-man pit crew:** Belote and Belote, *Corregidor*, pp. 128–30.

182 **"when an enemy shell":** Calvin E. Chunn, *Diary*, the Louis Morton Papers, Box 3, MHI.

183 **Williams and Shofner:** Miller, "Shanghai to Corregidor," p. 27.

183 **By day's end:** "Procedings of a Board Appointed," pp. 71–72.

183 **A garrison of:** Wainwright, *Story*, p. 86.

183 **With the increased patient load:** Hayes, *Diary*, p. 18.

183 **Surprisingly there were:** ibid., p. 6.

183 **"there was no zone":** Cooper, "Medical Department," p. 84.

183 **That didn't stop:** Hayes, *Diary*, p. 7.

183 **"There was dust":** Miller, "Shanghai to Corregidor," p. 27.

183 **blinded Corregidor's:** Moore, "Report of the Commanding Officer," p. 66.

183 **"more like the Mojave":** Parker, "Epic of Corregidor," p. 20.

184 **Almost anywhere:** Baldwin, *Battles Lost and Won*, p. 129.

184 **"Situation here is":** Schultz, *Hero of Bataan*, pp. 274–75.

184 **"They relieved themselves":** quoted in ibid., p. 277.

184 **"3rd May 1942 Sunday":** Ferguson, *Diary*, p. 37.

184 **What was in:** Miller, "Shanghai to Corregidor," pp. 27–28.

184 **They would be:** ibid.

184 **Lieutenant General Kitajima:** ibid., pp. 22–23.

185 **The next night:** ibid., p. 28.

185 **Led by the:** Morton, *War in the Pacific*, p. 552.

185 **"The vital points of":** *Fourteenth Army Operations*, p. 2:53.

185 **At 2130:** Blair, *Silent Victory*, pp. 196–97.

185 **Colonel Pete Irwin:** Wainwright, *Story*, p. 108.

185 **Footlockers full:** Blair, *Silent Victory*, pp. 196–97.

185 **By 22:30:** Norman, *Band of Angels*, p. 110.

185 **Fifty-four army:** ibid., p. 111.

185 **Prior to:** Irvin, "Wartime Reminiscences," p. 6.

185 **Planes dive-bombed:** Mellnik, "How the Japs," p. 10.

186 **"With morale at":** Schultz, *Hero of Bataan*, p. 278.

186 **The Japanese directed:** Morton, *War in the Pacific*, p. 553.

186 **"Expect enemy landing":** Miller, "Shanghai to Corregidor," p. 28.

186 **A Philippine Army officer:** Wainwright, *Story*, p. 114.

186 **Antitank barricades:** McCoy, Mellnik, and Kelley, *Ten Escape*, p. 14.

186 **On the morning:** William C. Braly, interview by William M. Belote, June 24, 1964, p. 2, Belote Collection, Box 2, MHI.

186 **Colonel Howard decided:** Miller, "Shanghai to Corregidor," p. 28.

186 **"Damn that full moon":** Braly interview, June 24, 1964, p. 2.

186 *"5th May Tuesday 1942":* Ferguson, *Diary*, pp. 37–38.

187 **In one extraordinary:** McCoy, Mellnik, and Kelley, *Ten Escape*, p. 17.

187 **At 1447 the Rock:** Moore, "Report of the Commanding Officer," p. 71.

187 **Wainwright was lounging:** Beebe, *Diary*, p. 17, RG 389, Box 2176, NARA

187 *"Prepare for probable":* Moore, "Report of the Commanding Officer," p. 71.

187 **Ten minutes later:** Miller, "Shanghai to Corregidor," p. 29.

188 **On Kindley Field:** Belote and Belote, *Corregidor*, p. 146.

188 **The stragglers who:** ibid., pp. 146–47.

188 **Some begged:** ibid., pp. 146–47.

188 **It was a massacre:** Baldwin, *Battles Lost and Won*, p. 144.

188 **By 2315 what:** Miller, "Shanghai to Corregidor," p. 29.

188 **Battery Way:** W. Massello, Jr., interview by William M. Belote, Belote Collection, Box 1, MHI; Belote and Belote, *Corregidor*, pp. 127, 159.

188 **"a spectacle that confounded":** Kazumarō Unō, *Corregidor: Isle of Delusion*, p. 19, quoted in Morton, *War in the Pacific*, 556.

188 **Marines hidden in:** Belote and Belote, *Corregidor*, pp. 148, 150.

188 **Eight out of:** Miller, "Shanghai to Corregidor," pp. 31–32.

188 **Shortly before midnight:** Clancey, "Siege and Capture," p. 12.

189 **At 0020 a Marine:** Moore, "Report of the Commanding Officer," p. 72.

189 **A battle line:** Belote and Belote, *Corregidor*, p. 154.

189 **At 0100 Joe Williams's:** ibid., p. 14.

189 **"Well, we opened":** Ferguson, *Diary*, p. 38.

189 **Malinta was filled:** Brook, interview, p. 3.

189 **The remaining nurses:** Hartendorp, *Japanese Occupation*, p. 1:185.

189 **By then one part:** Morton, *War in the Pacific*, p. 557.

189 **At 0200 the two:** Miller, "Shanghai to Corregidor," p. 34.

190 **"YOU AND YOUR DEVOTED":** Wainwright, *Story*, p. 118.

190 **At 0430 Colonel Howard:** Morton, *War in the Pacific*, pp. 557–58.

190 **"untrained in infantry tactics":** Beecher, "Experiences," p. 33.

190 **"wiped out":** Wainwright, *Story*, p. 118.

190 **In the chaos of:** Miller, "Shanghai to Corregidor," p. 33.

190 **"Joe, what in":** ibid., p. 37.

191 **At 0600 Williams:** Wainwright, *Story*, p. 18.

191 **Williams was "a tiger":** Brook interview, p. 2.

191 **The machine gun nest:** Miller, "Shanghai to Corregidor," p. 39.

191 **Two old leathernecks:** Baldwin, *Battles Lost and Won*, p. 146.

191 **At dawn the Japanese:** Belote and Belote, *Corregidor*, p. 157.

191 **Batteries Way and Stockade:** Moore, "Report of the Commanding Officer," p. 73.

191 **Barges were blown:** Mellnik, "How the Japs," p. 10.

191 **"My God":** quoted in Morton, *War in the Pacific*, p. 560.

192 **At daybreak, the:** Belote and Belote, *Corregidor*, p. 158.

192 **Then Lieutenant Otis E. Saalman:** J. Michael Miller, "Shanghai to Corregidor," p. 40.

192 **Casualties on Corregidor:** Clancey, "Siege and Capture," p. 11.

192 **The wounds resulted:** Luther H. Wolff, M.D., Samuel B. Childs, M.D., and W. Philip Giddings, M.D., "Wounding Agents," in Coates and DeBakey, *Surgery in World War II*, pp. 2:97–101.

192 **"felt a small explosion":** Brook interview, p. 3.

193 **Captain Chunn:** Belote and Belote, *Corregidor*, p. 165.

194 **There were no antitank guns:** Lewis Charles Beebe, "Personal Experience Sketches," p. 19, MHI.

194 **Enemy artillery fire:** Miller, "Shanghai to Corregidor," p. 41.

194 **By 1000 Wainwright:** Morton, *War in the Pacific*, p. 561.

194 **"It was the terror":** Wainwright, *Story*, p. 119.

194 **Between April 29:** Porter, "Antiaircraft Defense," p. 13.

194 **Six to eight hundred:** Morton, *War in the Pacific*, p. 560.

194 **Most of the officers:** Mellnik, "How the Japs," p. 10.

194 **The toll on the Japanese:** ibid., p. 11.

194 **Hayes estimated:** Baldwin, *Battles Lost and Won*, p. 151.

194 **"One hundred and seventy-three":** ibid., p. 147.

194 **The transmission was:** Blair, *Silent Victory*, p. 197.

194 **The Rock's defenders:** Moore, "Report of the Commanding Officer," Exhibit F, p. 17.

194 **Firing pins were:** Stamp, *Journey*, p. 30.

195 **Top secret maps:** Braly, *Hard Way Home*, pp. 4–5.

195 **The tunnel had been designed:** Moore, "Report of the Commanding Officer," Exhibit E, p. 4.

195 **Leland D. Bartlett:** Leland D. Bartlett, interview by Ronald E. Marcello, September 13, 1972, p. 56, UNTOHC.

195 **"They are not near":** Mellnik, "How the Japs," p. 11.

196 **Wainwright chose midday:** Braly interview, p. 4.

196 **Brigadier General Beebe had already:** Beebe, *Diary*, p. 20.

196 **"With broken heart":** Wainwright, *Story*, pp. 122–23.

196 **At 1200:** General Jonathan M. Wainwright, deposition, in *U.S.A. vs. Masaharu Homma*, RG 153, Box 3, Vol. 16, p. 2286, NARA.

196 **"My God," said:** Schultz, *Hero of Bataan*, p. 289.

196 **The Japanese continued:** Rudolfo B. Parra, testimony, in *U.S.A. vs. Masaharu Homma*, RG 153, Vol. 16, Box 3, pp. 2246–47, NARA.

196 **even though the:** ibid., p. 2250.

196 **Later that afternoon:** Wainwright, *Story*, p. 127.

196 **There were 40,000 men:** Connaughton, *MacArthur and Defeat*, p. 289.

197 **The blood of:** Wainwright, *Story*, p. 132.

197 **"A tremendous artillery":** General Jonathan M. Wainwright, in deposition, in *U.S.A. vs. Masaharu Homma*, RG 153, Vol. 18, Box 4, p. 2382, NARA.

197 **Wainwright tendered:** Deposition of General Jonathan M. Wainwright in *U.S.A. vs. Masaharu Homma*, RG 153, Vol. 16, Box 3, p. 2291, NARA. See also Schultz, *Hero of Bataan*, pp. 304–5.

197 **George Ferguson sat:** Ferguson, *Diary*, p. 38.

Chapter 13: Limbo

198 **"a minor epic in":** Hanson W. Baldwin, "Bataan's Epic of Valor," *New York Times*, April 10, 1942.

198 **"gallant effort":** Frank Kluckhohn, "Foe Says Wainwright Agrees to Full Philippine Surrender," *New York Times*, May 8, 1942.

199 **"To comply":** "No Information on Kin," *New York Times*, May 8, 1942.

199 **By then the idea:** David M. Kennedy, "On the Home Front: What Is Patriotism Without Sacrifice?" *New York Times*, February 16, 2003, sec. 4, p. 3.

200 **H. Ford Wilkins's:** *New York Times*, December 9, 1941, p. 1.

200 **Twenty-four-year-old John Hersey:** Hersey's pieces on Bataan were beautifully crafted, but they relied so heavily on the reporting of Melville and Annalee Jacoby and "the early cables of Carl and Shelley Mydans" that he dedicated his first book, *Men on Bataan*, to the four reporters, "partly so they won't charge me with grand larceny." He then arranged for *Time* to pay the Jacobys $450 for the unauthorized use of their work. See Anne Fadiman, *Ex Libris: Confessions of a Common Reader* (New York: Farrar, Straus & Giroux, 1998), pp. 109–11. According to Fadiman, the daughter of Annalee Jacoby, the Jacoby's dispatches became "the nearly verbatim basis for about half of Hersey's best-selling *Men on Bataan*."

200 **In fact, one could:** See "Japanese Report Manila Air Blows," *New York Times*, December 12, 1941.

201 **Even then it was:** See "Philippine Epic," *Life* 12, no. 15 (April 13, 1942).

201 **Two days after:** Romulo, *I Saw*, p. 81.

201 **Carl and Shelley Mydans:** Mydans, *More Than Meets*, p. 71.

201 **Royal and Pontifical University:** Hartendorp, *Japanese Occupation*, p. 1:8.

201 **H. Ford Wilkins:** ibid., p. 1:xiv.

201 **When Clark Lee:** Lee, *Pacific*, p. 246.

The rumor was false. Beliel was interned in Santo Tomás Internment Camp, where he became circulation manager of STIC's newsletter, *Internews*. He made his first broadcast after the liberation of Santo Tomás to the United States on February 7, 1945, for the Mutual Broadcasting System.

201 **Carlos Romulo:** Romulo, *I Saw*, pp. 272, 305.

202 **Private Everett D. Reamer:** Everett D. Reamer, author interview, July 1, 2003; see also Everett D. Reamer, *Sanity Gone Amuck: World War II: Pacific 1941–1945* (privately printed, 1998), pp. 42–43.

202 **Wainwright was on:** General Jonathan M. Wainwright deposition, in *U.S.A. vs. Masaharu Homma*, RG 153, Vol. 16, Box 3, pp. 2291–92, NARA. See also testimony of Colonel John R. Pugh in *U.S.A. vs. Masaharu Homma*, RG 153, Vol. 18, Box 4, p. 2400, NARA.

202 **The transmission was:** Schultz, *Hero of Bataan*, p. 313.

202 **In Santo Tomás:** Hartendorp, *Japanese Occupation*, p. 1:106.

202 **Wainwright and his staff:** Deposition of General Jonathan M. Wainwright in *U.S.A. vs. Masaharu Homma*, RG 153, Vol. 16, Box 3, pp. 2293–94, NARA.

202 **"How many airplanes are":** Braly, *Hard Way Home*, pp. 6–7.

202 **Corpses were piled:** Ferdinand V. Berley, interview by Jan K. Herman, p. 19; James L. Kent, interview by Ronald E. Marcello, May 11, 1972, p. 28, #127, UNTOHC.

203 **One American work detail:** Halbrook interview, March 21, 1972, pp. 110–12; Melvyn McCoy and S. M. Mellnik, "Death Was Part of Our Life," *Life*, February 7, 1944, p. 21.

203 **"to clean up the battlefield":** Bartlett, *Casus Belli*, pp. 64–65.

203 **The next day a long line:** Belote and Belote, *Corregidor*, pp. 178–79.

203 **The Japanese set:** John M. Wright, *Captured on Corregidor: Diary of an American POW in World War II* (Jefferson, N.C.: McFarland, 1988), p. 7.

203 **Then roughly 12,000:** Cooper, "Medical Department," p. 84.

203 **Some 800 cases:** Belote and Belote, *Corregidor*, p. 178.

204 **Men were so cramped:** Braly, *Hard Way Home*, p. 8.

204 **there was no shelter:** Beecher, "Experiences," pp. 34–35.

204 **Water was stored:** Andrew Miller, letter to author, July 7, 2004.

204 **Officers and enlisted men:** Cooper, "Medical Department," pp. 84–85.

204 **"This was the example":** Alton C. Halbrook, interview by Ronald E. Marcello, March 21 and April 18, 1972, pp. 98–101, #122, UNTOHC.

204 **He begged Private John R. Brown:** Braly, *Hard Way Home*, p. 9.

204 **The Japanese took:** M. L. Daman, interview by Ronald E. Marcello, September 29 and October 6, 1973, p. 34, UNTOHC.

205 **All of the captives:** McCoy, Mellnik, and Kelley, *Ten Escape*, p. 18.

205 **"queer for boots.":** Halbrook interview, p. 124.

205 **Compared to the conduct:** Noel Barber, *A Sinister Twilight: The Fall of Singapore* (Boston: Houghton Mifflin, 1968), pp. 241–43.

205 **"They dreaded coming onto":** Loren H. Brantley, interview by Ronald E. Marcello, November 19, 1971, p. 24, UNTOHC.

205 **"almost jovial":** McCoy, Mellnik, and Kelley, *Ten Escape*, p. 18.

205 **On one detail:** Haney, *Caged Dragons*, p. 79.

205 **The newly captured:** Hoeffer, "Hard Way Back," pp. 10–11.

206 **The Americans bathed:** Braly, *Hard Way Home*, p. 10.

206 **A system was devised:** Beecher, "Experiences," pp. 34–35.

208 **With a little medicine:** Cooper, "Medical Department," p. 85.

208 **"It was like plunging":** Beecher, "Experiences," pp. 36–37.

209 **By then nearly 12,000:** Braly, *Hard Way Home*, p. 15.

209 **"in the most suffocating":** McCoy, Mellnik, and Kelley, *Ten Escape*, p. 22.

209 **On the morning of:** Braly, *Hard Way Home*, p. 16.

209 **But the barges stopped:** Beecher, "Experiences," p. 38.

209 **Garden hoses were:** Sergeant Thomas H. Bogie, testimony, *U.S.A. vs. Masaharu Homma*, RG 153, Vol. 12, Box 3, pp. 1655–56, NARA.

210 **"From twelve o'clock":** May Harries, *Philippine Postscripts*, December 1945, quoted in Braly, *Hard Way Home*, p. 17.

210 "**31st May 1942**": Ferguson, *Diary*, p. 40.

211 **Provoo had once:** Sayer and Botting, "America's Secret Army."

211 **Thompson told the corpsman:** This account is based on Berley and Halbrook's recollections. Sayer and Botting claim the reason was that Provoo had "relayed their orders that all sick and wounded Americans should be moved out at once so that Japanese wounded could be hospitalized there. When he heard this order Captain Thompson of the Medical Service Corps told Provoo: 'Tell them to go to hell, the men are too sick to be moved.' " In fact, many of the wounded had already been moved to the 92nd Garage Area, and the hospital at Topside was considered far preferable to what remained of the one in Malinta Tunnel. Otis H. King tells yet another version of this story, in which "the Captain asked for supplies, Provoo refused and Captain Thompson threatened him with a court martial." King, *Alamo of the Pacific*, p. 186.

211 **The next morning:** Robert S. LaForte, Ronald E. Marcello, and Richard L. Himmel, eds., *With Only the Will to Live: Accounts of Americans in Japanese Prison Camps, 1941–1945* (Wilmington, Del.: Scholarly Resources, 1994), p. 68; Halbrook, interview by Marcello, pp. 116,122; Halbrook, author interview, March 27, 2003.

211 **The old Fort Mills:** Cooper, "Medical Department," p. 87.

211 **Life at Topside:** Ferguson, *Diary*, p. 42.

212 **"a large iced cake":** Norman, *Band of Angels*, p. 139.

212 **One Japanese doctor:** Thomas Hirst Hayes, *Bilibid Notebook*, book I, *July 1942*, p. 41, BUMED.

212 **One week later:** Kentner, *Journal*, p. 30.

212 **They were responsible:** Stamp, *Journey*, p. 37.

212 **On July 2:** Michno, *Hellships*, p. 39.

212 **Fred enlisted a:** Clarence Shearer, *Journal*, 29 May 1942–8 July 1943, Companion Document to Sartin, *Bilibid Letter Book, 1942*, p. 15, RG 389, Box 2178, NARA.

212 **In the morning:** Kentner, *Journal*, p. 30.

213 **It was early afternoon:** Ferguson, *Diary*, p. 42.

213 **"a nice Jap":** Norman, *Band of Angels*, p. 140.

213 **The nonambulatory patients:** Hartendorp, *Japanese Occupation*, p.1:186.

213 **women were separated:** Barrett, *Casus Belli*, p. 38.

213 **At 1500 they arrived:** Hayes, *Bilibid Notebook*, book I, *July 1942*, pp. 2–3.

213 **"a dirty filthy mess":** Ferguson, *Diary*, p. 42.

Chapter 14: *Horyo*

214 **"shades of the prison-house":** William Wordsworth, "Ode: Intimations of Immortality from Recollections of Early Childhood," v. 67, in *Wordsworth: Poetical Works*, ed. Thomas Hutchinson and Ernest de Selincourt (Oxford: Oxford University Press, 1969), p. 460.

214 **Bilibid looked like:** A.E.W. Salt and H.O.S. Heistand, "The Street Names of Manila and Their Origins," *Historical Bulletin* 15 (1971), p. 266; Mauro Garcia and C. O. Resurreccion, eds., *Focus on Old Manila* (Manila: Philippine Historical Association, 1971).

214 **Aguinaldo had been:** Bumgarner, *Parade*, p. 82.

214 **"I sincerely believe":** Ramón Victorio, "Prison System in the Philippine Islands," lecture to the American Prison Congress, Salt Lake City, August 15–22, 1924, p. 2, in Philippine Department of Justice, Bureau of Prisons, *Catalogue of Products of the Industrial Division of Bilibid Prison and General Information Relative to the Bureau of Prisons* (Manila: Bureau of Printings, 1927).

214 **Like the spokes:** Paul Ashton, *Bataan Diary* (privately published, 1984), pp. 240–41.

215 **Before headquarters of:** Rockwell, *Narrative*, p. 6.

215 **Since their capture:** Davis, *Diary*, p. 5.

215 **Bilibid was enclosed:** Ashton, *Somebody Gives*, p. 304.

215 **Davis and his staff:** Davis, *Diary*, p. 5.

215 **After the Japanese robbed Davis:** ibid., p. 23.

215 **One evening the:** ibid., p. 26.

215 **When some 300:** ibid., p. 27.

215 **One week later:** Philippine Department of Justice, Bureau of Prisons, *Catalogue*, p. 19.

216 **Wainwright would soon:** Schulz, *Hero of Bataan*, p. 318.

216 **"Anything," said Davis:** Davis, *Diary*, p. 28.

216 **Prison conditions:** Gillespie, "Recollections," p. 33.

216 **Plumbing and electrical:** Shearer, *Journal*, p. 1.

216 **"accommodating place":** Barrett, *Casus Belli*, pp. 52–55.

216 **They constructed a:** *Handbook of the Hospital Corps, U.S. Navy 1939*, pp. 540–41.

216 **"coolator":** Shearer, *Journal*, p. 9.

216 **With materials from:** ibid., pp. 2–3.

217 **Officers had quarters:** Kentner, *Journal*, p. 27.

217 **Bilibid's patient census:** Barrett, *Casus Belli*, p. 37.

217 **The army medical officers:** Shearer, *Journal*, p. 8.

217 **But some of the:** ibid., p. 15.

217 **"Here are piled":** Hayes, *Bilibid Notebook*, 1:5.

218 **Bilibid became the:** Davis, *Diary*, p. 28.

218 **There were a total:** Waterford, *Prisoners*, pp. 250–65, 187–211.

218 **Officially, it was:** Barrett, *Casus Belli*, p. 56.

218 **That was Sartin:** ibid., p. 101.

218 **Nogi was ultimately:** "Channels of PW Camp," RG 331, Box 1576, NARA.

218 **His colleague:** Naraji Nogi, testimony to Investigating Officer Jerome Richard, War Crimes Investigating Detachment, October 23, 1945, RG 331, Box 1908, NARA.

219 **"All right, you":** Barrett, *Casus Belli*, p. 52.

219 **Horyo Jōhōkyoku:** Daws, *Prisoners*, p. 52.

219 **For the approximately 324,000:** Waterford, *Prisoners of the Japanese,* p. 146.

219 **The Horyo Jōhōkyoku was in charge:** Arthur L. Lerch, "Japanese Handling of American Prisoners of War," reprinted in *Tokyo Trial Materials: Documents of POW Information Bureau* (Gendai Shiryo Shuppan, 1999), pp. 304–5.

219 **The Geneva Convention:** Reprinted in Kerr, *Surrender and Survival*, pp. 329–34.

219 **The International Committee of the Red Cross:** Lerch, "Japanese Handling," p. 316.

219 **Japan had its own:** Falk, *Bataan*, p. 208.

219 **This was to:** Tanaka, *Hidden Horrors*, p. 72.

219 **Article 2:** Falk, *Bataan*, p. 208.

220 **The rules were revised:** Lerch, "Japanese Handling," p. 310.

220 **By and large Japan's:** Tanaka, *Hidden Horrors*, p. 72.

220 **Japan Red Cross Society:** Sumio Adachi, "A Process to Reaffirmation of International Humanitarian Law: A Japanese View," *Law and Order* 5 (September 25, 1983), p. 22.

220 **This stood in marked contrast:** David Haward Bain, *Sitting in Darkness: Americans in the Philippines* (Boston: Houghton Mifflin, 1984), pp. 84–87.

220 **Boer refugees:** Thomas Packenham, *The Boer War* (New York: Avon Books, 1979), pp. 531–32, 549, 581.

220 **"to conform to the discipline":** Falk, *Bataan*, p. 10.

220 **Article 6 stipulated:** ibid., p. 209.

220 **The Japanese prescribed:** Lerch, "Japanese Handling," p. 313.

220 **There was no due process:** Bix, *Hirohito*, pp. 27–28.

220 **This marked a:** Kita Yoshito, "The Japanese Military's Attitude Toward International Laws and the Treatment of Prisoners of War," Nihon University, part 2.

221 **Japan was a party:** Bix, *Hirohito*, p. 361.

221 **1929 Geneva Convention:** Sumio Adachi, "Unprepared Regrettable Events: A Brief History of Japanese Practices on Treatment of Allied War Victims during the Second World War," Studies of Cultural and Social Science, No. 45 (Hashirimizu, Yokosuka, Japan: The National Defense Academy, 1982), p. 283.

221 **Whether this was:** Adachi, "Process to Reaffirmation," p. 31.

221 **But disdain for:** Bix, *Hirohito*, pp. 360–65.

221 **On February 4:** Quoted in Brackman, *Other Nuremberg*, p. 250.

221 **Less than a month:** Yoshito, "Japanese Military's Attitude," part 2.

221 **420 grams of:** L. De Jong, *The Collapse of a Colonial Society: The Dutch in Indonesia During the Second World War* (Leiden: KITLV Press, 2002), p. 291.

221 **Army Minister Tōjō Hideki:** Lord Russell of Liverpool, *The Knights of Bushido: A Short History of Japanese War Crimes* (London: Cassell, 1958), p. 141.

222 **"all prisoners of war to engage":**
Brackman, *Other Nuremberg*, p. 264.

222 **Instructions to this:** ibid., p. 290.

222 **In early August 1942:** ibid., p. 291.

222 **But in some cases:** ibid.

222 **A first lieutenant:** Kentner, *Journal*, p. 96.

222 **"as interpreted by":** Sartin, "Report of Activities," p. 63.

223 **"The best possible care":** Barrett, *Casus Belli*, pp. 58–59.

223 **"The Army doctors condone":** Simpson, *Prisoners*, p. 22. See also Hayes, *Bilibid Notebook*, p. 1:3, and Daws, *Prisoners*, p. 109.

223 **"We will never forget":** Hayes, *Bilibid Notebook*, p. 1:3.

223 **He arrived at Bilibid:** ibid., p. 12.

223 **Like Pavlov's dogs:** Barrett, *Casus Belli*, pp. 116–17.

224 **"To sweat and boil":** Hayes, *Bilibid Notebook*, p. 1:36.

224 **The Japanese were obsessed:** Kentner, *Journal*, p. 33.

224 **Fred and John:** Daws, *Prisoners*, p. 102.

224 **Men were dying:** See Shearer, *Journal*, "List of Deaths."

224 **The rice itself:** Shearer, *Journal*, pp. 10–11.

224 **Once the Japanese:** Smith, *Prisoner of Emperor*, p. 51.

224 **"There is so much":** Shearer, *Journal*, p. 10.

225 **"You are unfortunate":** Hayes, *Bilibid Notebook*, p. 2:16.

225 **Tayabas, wrote Paul Russell:** Paul Russell, "Philippine Islands, Malaria: 1931 Annual Report, Narrative and Statistical," by p. 13, RAC.

225 **Those who survived:** Ashton, *Somebody Gives*, p. 205; Ashton, *Bataan Diary*, pp. 215–21.

225 **"covered with scabies":** Paul Reuter, author interview, October 30, 2001.

225 **"This afternoon at":** Ferguson, *Diary*, p. 43.

226 **Who, if he cried:** See Rainer Maria Rilke, "The First Elegy," *The Selected Poetry of Rainer Maria Rilke*, ed. and trans. Stephen Mitchell (New York: Random House, 1982), p. 151.

226 **"He always got on":** Jeanne Gier Fisher, author interview, November 19, 2001.

226 **Thirty to forty POWs:** Sartin, "Report of Activities," p. 8.

226 **"At this rate":** Ferguson, *Diary*, pp. 44–45.

226 **Most of the prisoners:** Kerr, *Surrender and Survival*, p. 65.

226 **More than 2,000:** Waterford, *Prisoners*, 253.

226 **before the 14th:** Kerr, *Surrender and Survival*, p. 65.

226 **Homma Masaharu hadn't:** Masaharu Homma, testimony, in *U.S.A. vs. Masaharu Homma*, RG 153, Vol. 27, Box 5, p. 3144, NARA. See also the deposition of Charles F. Lewis, Jr., Medical Corps, in *U.S.A. vs. Masaharu Homma*, RG 153, Vol. 11, Box 2, NARA, pp. 1456–57.

226 **much less to:** ibid., p. 3114.

226 **excessive mortality rate:** Around June 10, 1942, Homma received a report that over 16,000 POWs had died at Camp O'Donnell (see ibid., p. 3145). The actual number was much higher.

226 **John escaped malaria:** Patrick Manson, *Tropical Diseases: A Manual of the Diseases of War Climates* (Birmingham, Ala.: Classics of Medicine Library, 1984), pp. 175–76.

227 **"down to skin and bones":** Hayes, *Bilibid Notebook*, pp. 1:5, 19.

227 **But the Japanese:** ibid., p. 2:106.

227 **Men clamored to:** Beecher, "Experiences," p. 40.

227 **Soon two corpsmen:** Smith, *Prisoner of Emperor*, pp. 51–52.

227 **an American schoolteacher:** ibid., pp. 52–53.

227 **Lieutenant Walter H. Waterous:** Barrett, *Casus Belli*, p. 148. See also *U.S.A. vs. Masaharu Homma*, R6 153, Entry 177, Vol .7, Box 2, pp. 775–76, NARA.

227 **His associate, Maxima Villanueva:** Waterous, "Statement of Experiences," pp. 148–50.

227 **she managed to smuggle:** Ashton, *Somebody Gives*, p. 273.

227 **Ralph Hibbs:** Hibbs, *Tell MacArthur*, pp. 128–33.

227–28 **Other POWs pilfered:** Ashton, *Somebody Gives*, p. 276.

228 **So the men began:** Chunn, *Of Rice and Men*, p. 22.

228 **"27th August Thursday":** Ferguson, *Diary*.

228 **"the ravages of poor diet":** Kentner, *Journal*, p. 38.

228 **The symptoms were:** Hayes, *Bilibid Notebook*, p. 2:106.

228 **"scourge of the American":** Alan M. Kraut, *Goldberger's War: The Life and Work of a Public Health Crusader* (New York: Hill and Wang, 2003), pp. 4–5.

228 **Xerophthalmia and optical:** Barrett, *Casus Belli*, p. 62.

228 **But of all the:** Ralph E. Hibbs, "Beriberi in Japanese Prison Camp," *Annals of Internal Medicine* 25, no. 2 (August 1946), p. 270.

Chapter 15: "The last thin tie"

230 **The sole navy doctor:** Hayes, *Bilibid Notebook*, p. 1:4.

230 **All of the medical:** Stamp, *Journey*, p. 38.

230 **He also served as:** *Handbook of the Hospital Corps, U.S. Navy 1939*, pp. 737, 740.

230 **fishing with dynamite:** Stamp, *Journey*, p. 43.

231 **Twenty tons of gold:** Blair, *Silent Victory*, p. 207.

232 **The motor pool:** Stamp, *Journey*, p. 51.

232 **Little more than 2 million:** This story is based on R. C. Sheats, "Diving as a 'Guest of the Emperor,' " in Ashton, *Somebody Gives*, pp. 236–45.

233 **He was an artist:** Hayes to Hayes, Jr., July 26, 1941, entry in *Diary*.

233 **He even tried:** Barrett, *Casus Belli*, p. 101.

233 **"my closest comrade":** Hayes to Hayes, Jr., August 12, 1944, entry in *Diary*.

233 **"Emaciated carcasses":** Hayes, *Bilibid Notebook*, p. 1:5.

233 **"the stuffed shirt":** ibid., p. 1:10.

233 **"like Haitian zombies":** ibid., p. 1:43.

233 **"I knew when I left":** ibid., p. 1:34.

233 **He feared that:** ibid., p. 1:92.

233 **"we will be bombing":** ibid., p. 1:96.

234 **"heroic, modest":** Hayes, "Report on Medical Tactics," p. 15.

234 **"worthy of the best":** ibid., p. 27.

234 **"It was inspiring":** Hayes, *Bilibid Notebook*, p. 3:47.

234 **Hayes was a stickler:** Hayes, *Diary*, p. 40.

234 **"a Mayo Clinic isn't":** Hayes, *Bilibid Notebook*, p. 1:8.

234 **"Osler has said":** John Bookman, "Medical Notes," p. 1.

234 **But what John:** ibid., pp. 1–2.

235 **no shortage of patients:** Hayes, *Bilibid Notebook*, p. 2:4.

235 **37 percent of all:** Kentner, *Journal*, p. 41.

235 **Tunics were cut:** James E. McCall, *Santo Tomás Internment Camp: STIC in Verse and Reverse STIC-toons and STIC-tistics* (Lincoln, Neb.: Woodruff, 1945), p. 35.

235 **Santo Tomás, the:** Kentner, *Journal*, p. 41.

235 **Those on work parties:** Daws, *Prisoners*, p. 112.

235 **The men reused:** Hayes, *Bilibid Notebook*, p. 2:96.

235 **The POWs had access:** Kentner, *Journal*, p. 40.

236 **Volleyball and baseball:** Hayes, *Bilibid Notebook*, p. 3:74.

236 **Saturday nights the POWs:** Barrett, *Casus Belli*, p. 134.

236 **"They break up my":** Hayes, *Bilibid Notebook*, p. 2:11.

236 **The punishment for:** ibid., pp. 18, 36.

236 **When Corporal Robert C. Barnbrook:** Sartin, "Report of Activities," p. 65; Kentner, *Journal*, pp. 40, 67.

236 **When two army colonels:** Hayes, *Bilibid Notebook*, p. 2:86.

236 **Rumor had it that:** ibid., p. 2:66.

237 **"November seems to be":** Ferguson, *Diary*, p. 8.

237 **"Well, another month":** ibid., n.p.

237 **the strange rumor:** Hayes, *Bilibid Notebook*, p. 2:90. In all likelihood, Hayes was referring to the *Lisbon Maru*, which departed Hong Kong on September 27, 1942, with 1,816 Allied POWs and was torpedoed by the American submarine USS *Grouper* on October 1, 1942. Eight hundred and forty-two prisoners either drowned or were shot by the Japanese in their efforts to escape the sinking ship. The survivors resumed their journey from Shanghai on the *Shinsei Maru* and three days later arrived in Moji, Japan. See Michno, *Hellships*, pp. 43–47.

237 **Nearly 500 operations:** Barrett, *Casus Belli*, p. 160.

237 **Others were quarantined:** Shearer, *Journal*, p. 34.

237 **Pellagra continued:** Kentner, *Journal*, p. 42.

237 **Dengue accounted for:** Sartin,

"Report of Activities," p. 76; Kentner, *Journal*, p. 41.

237 **Ted Williams was:** Williams, *Rogues of Bataan II*; Ted Williams, author interview, March 26, 2003.

238 **Thirteen men died:** Shearer, *Journal*, pp. ii–iii.

238 **The Japanese permitted:** Kentner, *Journal*, p. 41.

238 **Murray arrived at:** ibid., p. 49.

238 **Eighty percent of the hospital patients:** ibid., p. 48.

238 **When Sartin appealed:** Hayes, *Bilibid Notebook*, p. 2:107.

238 **Ishii recommended that:** ibid., p. 3:9.

238 **"Had we been obliged":** ibid., p. 2:93.

239 **"Really increased":** Ferguson, *Diary*, December 23, 1942, entry.

239 **Less than two weeks:** *Prisoners of War Bulletin* 1, no. 6 (November 1943), in John E. Olson Papers, Box 1, MHI.

239 **The packages weighed:** Hayes, *Bilibid Notebook*, p. 3:65.

239 **The corned beef:** Chunn, *Of Rice and Men*, p. 28.

239 **On the other hand:** Cecil Peart, letter to author, March 25, 2003.

239 **One sailor died:** Ferdinand V. Berley, author interview, September 2001, p. 37.

239 **The Japanese were:** Beecher, "Experiences," p. 76.

240 **"A public act":** Sartin, "Report of Activities," p. 74.

240 **Even with such restrictions:** Ferguson, *Diary*, p. 4.

240 **But only fifteen letters:** Hayes, *Bilibid Notebook*, p. 3:176.

240 **"Very few people":** Ferguson, *Diary*, July 1, 1942, entry.

241 **As a result:** Lerch, "Japanese Handling," p. 6.

242 **It was a foolish taunt:** Rena Krasno, *That Last Glorious Summer, 1939, Shanghai to Japan* (Hong Kong: Old China Hand Press, 2001), p. 66.

242 **Anti-Comintern Pact of 1936:** ibid., pp. 141–43.

242 **And they could only:** Hayes, *Bilibid Notebook*, p. 3:165.

242 **Corporal Lloyd D. Adams:** Ferdinand V. Berley, author interview, September 2001; Kentner, *Journal*, p. 55; Ted Williams, author interview, April 1, 2003; Hayes, *Bilibid Notebook*, p. 3:98.

242 **Corporal Donald E. Meyer:** C. M. Smith to Lucille Ferguson, March 7, 1946.

243 **"I knew he would":** Donald E. Meyer to Lucille Ferguson, August 9, 1945.

243 **"painful feet":** Glusman, *Diary*, p. 2.

243 **Nogi was so:** Hayes, *Bilibid Notebook*, p. 3:77.

243 **The incidence of:** ibid., p. 3:97.

243 **When the plague:** Thucydides, *The Peloponnesian War*, trans. Rex Warner (Harmondsworth, U.K.: Penguin Books, 1954), p. 155.

243 **"In the midst of":** quoted in Thomas G. Bergin, *Boccaccio* (New York: Viking Press, 1981), p. 291.

243 **"The inner man is":** Hayes, *Bilibid Notebook*, p. 2:28.

243 **"place":** See "Taking One's Proper Station" in Ruth Benedict, *The Chrysanthemum and the Sword: Patterns of Japanese Culture* (Boston: Houghton Mifflin, 1946).

243 **The emphasis on:** Reischauer and Jansen, *Japanese Today*, pp. 149–50.

244 **"If we act as a hospital":** Hayes, *Bilibid Notebook*, p. 1:43.

244 **Toyo no Gaika:** Ashton, *Somebody Gives*, p. 269; Irvin E. Alexander, "Recollections of Bataan & After," p. 189, Louis Morton Papers, Box 3, MHI.

244 **"Across the Sea":** translation quoted in Gibney, *Sensō*, p. 37.

245 **"majoring in Spanish":** Hayes, *Bilibid Notebook*, p. 2:46.

245 **"I suppose there is":** quoted in Chunn, *Of Rice and Men*, p. 22.

245 **"Schweizer informed Yakashisi":** Hayes, *Bilibid Notebook*, p. 3:105.

245 **food deficiency cases decreased:** Bookman, "Medical Notes," p. 3.

246 **"in hellish shape":** Hayes, *Bilibid Notebook*, p. 3:130.

246 **In May, Memorial:** Kentner, *Journal*, p. 61.

246 **A six-piece camp orchestra:** ibid.

246 **"the wounded playing":** Glusman, *Diary*, p. 8.

246 **"a welcome relief":** Bookman, *Diary*, May 22, 1943.

246 **"very thin camote soup":** ibid., July 20, 1943.

246 **In peacetime the:** *U.S.A. vs. Naraji Nogi*, Defense Exhibit D, January 20, 1947: Segundo G. Jao to Robert Cohn, January 11, 1947, RG 389, Box 2177, NARA. See also McCall, *Santo Tomás*, p. 111.

247 **Before the war:** Bruce F. Johnston, with Mosaburo Hosado and Yoshio Kusumi, *Japanese Food Management in World War II* (Stanford, Calif.: Stanford University Press, 1953), p. 277.

247 **Ninety-five percent of:** ibid., pp. 70–71, 277.

247 **Rice and bread:** Joaquin, *Manila*, pp. 189–90.

247 **"stand in the sun":** Hayes, *Bilibid Notebook*, p. 3:121.

247 **"Most of the people":** Glusman, *Diary*, p. 10.

248 **"They still haven't been":** ibid., p. 12.

248 **The POWs built:** Hayes, *Bilibid Notebook*, pp. 3:90, 159.

248 **"I can hear the":** ibid., p. 1:31.

248 **Herthneck was isolated:** Kentner, *Journal*, p. 65.

248 **"My one shipmate:** Hayes, *Bilibid Notebook*, p. 3:173.

248 **"Two letters from you":** ibid., p. 3:174.

250 **The very month that:** Murphy, "You'll Never Know," p. 46.

250 **Bernatitus described her:** ibid., p. 55.

251 **"I would kind of":** ibid., p. 56.

251 **He had been humiliated:** Kentner, *Journal*, p. 68.

251 **Blau was sentenced:** ibid.

252 **"1. Strict observance":** ibid., pp. 80–81.

252 **a patient census:** ibid., p. 80.

252 **The foursome said goodbye:** Barrett, *Casus Belli*, pp. 93–96.

Chapter 16: The Good Doctor

253 **Sunday afternoons:** Ōhashi Kazuko and Ōhashi Yasuko, author interviews, July 13, 2002, Takarazuka, Japan.

253 **Weimar Berlin:** Ian Buruma, *Inventing Japan, 1853–1964* (New York: Modern Library, 2003), p. 67.

254 **sixty-six POWs per boxcar:** Waterous, "Statement of Experiences," pp. 122–23.

254 **"mostly closing down":** Bookman, *Diary*, October 11, 1943, entry.

254 **It took eight hours:** Hibbs, *Tell MacArthur*, p. 137.

254 **The "*Carabao* Railway Express":** ibid.

255 **"The place looks like":** Bookman, *Diary*, October 11, 1943, entry.

255 **But instead of tents:** Cooper, "Medical Department," p. 114.

255 **The Japanese posted:** Hibbs, *Tell MacArthur*, p. 142.

255 **The navy doctors had:** Vince Taylor, *Cabanatuan: Japanese Death Camp* (Waco, Tex.: Texian Press, 1985), p. 76.

255 **Cabanatuan originally consisted:** American Battle Monuments Commision, "Cabanatuan American Memorial," at www.abmc.gov/c.htm; Andrew Miller, "The Historian's Corner," *Quan* 50, no. 4 (February 1996), p. 6; 50, no. 5 (April 1996), pp. 12–13; 51, no. 1 (July 1996), pp. 4–5.

255 **The camp's westernmost side:** See the hand-drawn map of Cabanatuan in Chunn, *Of Rice and Men*.

255 **Each *bahay*:** M. L. Daman, interview by Ronald E. Marcello, September 29, 1973, and October 6, 1973, p. 65, UNTOHC.

256 **The Americans organized:** Beecher, "Experiences," pp. 50–51, 60.

256 **Until September 1942:** Gillespie, "Recollections," p. 45.

256 **Colonel Mori was:** Memorandum to the Prosecution Section (Report No. 93), GHQ, U.S. Army Forces, Pacific Theater, WCO/JAG, RG 331, Box 1118, Folder 4, NARA.

256 **Major Iwanaka:** Beecher, "Experiences," p. 112.

256 **The Japanese medical:** Naraji Nogi depostion, October 23, 1945, p. 3, RG 331, Box 1908, NARA.

256 **"while better than those":** Dyess, *Dyess Story*, p. 126.

256 **"rarely reached 1,000":** Eugene C. Jacobs, *Blood Brothers: A Medic's Sketchbook* (New York: Carlton Press, 1985), p. 51.

256 **Overflowing pit latrines:** Condon-Rall and Cowdrey, *Medical Department*, p. 370.

256 **There was no quinine:** Chunn, *Of Rice and Men*, p. 37.

256 **"Inching their way":** Gillespie, "Recollections," p. 50.

257 **a commissary:** Ashton, *Somebody Gives*, p. 263.

257 **In all, 250 medical:** Gillespie, "Recollections," p. 38.

257 **Thirty wards designed:** Jacobs, *Blood Brothers*, pp. 55–56.

257 **When the buildings:** Ashton, *Somebody Gives*, p. 259.

257 **Isolated from other:** Jacobs, quoted in Taylor, *Cabanatuan*, p. 85; Cooper, "Medical Department," p. 116.

257 **no blankets:** Gillespie, "Recollections," p. 40.

257 **Some couldn't make it:** ibid.

257 **Zero Ward took:** John Bumgarner, author interview, December 20, 2001, Greensboro, N.C.

257 **The Japanese wouldn't set foot:** Cooper, "Medical Department," p. 16.

257 **In June 1942:** Gillespie, "Recollections," p. 44.

257 **To control diarrhea:** Hibbs, *Tell MacArthur*, p. 158.

257 **They advised dysentery:** Jacobs, *Blood Brothers*, p. 49.

258 **They cultivated soybean:** ibid., pp. 154–55.

258 **They fermented rice:** See Samuel C. Grashio and Bernard Norling, *Return to Freedom* (Tulsa, Okla.: NCN Press, 1982), p. 60.

258 **one set of dentures:** Alexander, "Recollections," p. 186.

258 **"in every case":** Ashton, *Somebody Gives*, p. 262.

258 **Loren E. Stamp:** Stamp, *Journey*, p. 65.

258 **"the Taj Mahal":** Hibbs, *Tell MacArthur*, p. 152.

258 **Fifteen hundred men:** Cooper, "Medical Department," pp. 114–18.

258 **Some of the POWs:** ibid., p. 144.

258 **The final insult:** ibid., p. 141.

258 **"A kindly word":** Weinstein, *Barbed-Wire Surgeon*, pp. 118–20.

258 **In the early months:** Alfred C. Oliver, Jr., "The Japanese and Our Chaplains," RG 389, Box 2177, NARA.

258 **They buried the deceased:** Andrew Miller, letter to author, July 7, 2004.

258 **During the torrential rains:** Gillespie, "Recollections," p. 45.

258 **"Pits were always":** Waterous, "Statement of Experiences," p. 133.

259 **"I'm going to die":** Calvin Chunn, "Notebooks," p. 76, RG 407, Box 128, Folder 9, NARA.

259 **The youngest POWs:** Stephen C. Sitter and Charles J. Katz, M.D., "American POWs Held by the Japanese," p. 14, BUMED.

259 *Quanning* **boosted morale:** Chunn, "Notebooks," p. 32.

259 **Religious belief:** Sitter and Katz, "POWs," p. 23.

259 **Nardini stocked:** Dr. John Nardini,

interview by Gavin Daws, September 22, 1984, Gavin Daws Papers, MHI.

259 **"Self-pity":** Ernest Bales, author interview, May 2002, San Antonio, Tex.

259 **As on Bataan:** Sitter and Katz, "POWs," p. 48.

259 **two reported suicides:** Gillespie, "Recollections," p. 48.

259 **"Men generally degenerated":** ibid., pp. 48–49.

260 **Nardini made the decisions:** ibid., p. 70.

260 **The Japanese made POWs:** Waterous, "Statement of Experiences," p. 66.

260 **Around September 1, 1942:** Alexander, "Recollections," p. 174.

260 **After forty-eight hours:** Beecher, "Experiences," p. 65.

260 **One night Beecher:** Alexander, "Recollections," pp. 73–74.

261 **In April 1943:** Chunn, *Of Rice and Men*, p. 102.

261 **The Japanese were furious:** ibid.

261 **Trujillo was a:** Beecher, "Recollections," p. 75.

261 **"three distinct sounds":** Chunn, "Notebooks," p. 31.

261 **Henry G. Lee wrote:** Henry G. Lee, "An Execution," quoted in Gillespie, "Recollections," pp. 42–43. See also Chunn, *Of Rice and Men*, pp. 211–12.

261 **"Red in the":** quoted in Gillespie, "Recollections," pp. 42–43.

261 **"shooting squads":** Chunn, *Of Rice and Men*, pp. 100–1.

262 **By the time:** Bookman, *Diary*, October 11, 1943, entry.

262 **The camp was divided:** Cooper, "Medical Department," p. 122.

262 **Except for John Nardini:** Smith, *Prisoner of Emperor*, p. 67.

262 **"No work, no eat":** Beecher, "Experiences," p. 112.

262 **"slapped around":** Weinstein, *Barbed-Wire Surgeon*, pp. 116–17.

262 **The POWs' work:** Waterford, *Prisoners*, p. 347.

262 **equipment operators:** Beecher, "Experiences," pp. 91–92.

262 **Some enlisted men:** Taylor, *Cabanatuan*, p. 95.

262 **"honey detail":** Chunn, "Notebooks," p. 60.

262 **movie detail:** ibid., p. 61.

262 **A Japanese sergeant:** Beecher, "Experiences," p. 88.

263 **"Do not oppose":** quoted in Hampton Sides, *Ghost Soldiers: The Forgotten Story of World War II's Most Dramatic Mission* (New York: Doubleday, 2001), p. 162.

263 **If the count fell short:** Hibbs, *Tell MacArthur*, p. 144.

263 **You'd say *arigatō*:** Hartendorp, *Japanese Occupation*, p. 2:586.

263 **Occasionally it was:** Hibbs, *Tell MacArthur*, p. 149.

263 **Many men wore *nothing*:** Hartendorp, *Japanese Occupation*, p. 2:587.

263 **They walked down:** Glusman, *Diary*, October 15–20, 1943, entry.

264 **Steal a *camote*:** Eugene Forquer, "Cabanatuan Concentration Camp, Nueva Ecija, Luzon, Philippine Islands," RG 389, Box 2177, NARA; Chunn, "Notebooks," p. 33.

264 **Private Walter R. Connell:** Chunn, "Notebooks," p. 2.

265 **beriberi peripheral neuritis:** Hibbs, "Beriberi in Japanese Prison Camp," p. 275.

265 **"rice brain":** Hibbs, *Tell MacArthur*, p. 159.

265 **You couldn't write:** Gillespie, "Recollections," p. 41.

265 **In time the POWs:** Beecher, "Experiences," p. 100.

265 **The men grew eggplant:** Weinstein, *Barbed-Wire Surgeon*, p. 139.

265 **Fred was lucky:** Beecher, "Experiences," p. 89.

265 **Food was cooked:** Taylor, *Cabanatuan*, p. 94.

265 ***kawas*:** Morris, *Corregidor*, p. 487.

265 **On at least one occasion:** Ferdinand V. Berley, author interview, September 2001, Jacksonville, Fla., p. 42.

266 **One prisoner made:** Weinstein, *Barbed-Wire Surgeon*, p. 143.

266 **Fred himself carved:** Berley interview, p. 42.

266 **With scrap lumber:** Weinstein, *Barbed-Wire Surgeon*, pp. 130–31.

266 **Corporal Holliman:** ibid., pp. 134–35.

266 **Sergeant John Katz:** Stamp, *Journey*, p. 67.

266 **Called the Cabanatuan Cats:** Jacobs, *Blood Brothers*, p. 70.

266 **Cabanatuan Mighty Art Players:** Weinstein, *Barbed-Wire Surgeon*, p. 163.

266 **Audiences of 3,000 to 4,000:** Beecher, "Experiences," p. 107.

266 **Lieutenant Colonel D. S. Babcock:** Chunn, "Notebooks," p. 65.

266 **The most popular periodical:** Andrew Miller, letter to author, July 7, 2004.

266 **When the books became:** Chunn, *Of Rice and Men*, p. 84.

266 **movies:** Chunn, "Notebooks," p. 7.

266 **Personal items were:** Taylor, *Cabanatuan*, pp. 113–15.

267 **Substitute coconut fuel oil:** Beecher, "Experiences," p. 103.

267 **a touch of peppermint:** Weinstein, *Barbed-Wire Surgeon*, p. 140.

267 **Cornmeal for:** Beecher, "Experiences," p. 103.

267 **Eventually Major Iwanaka:** ibid., p. 102.

267 **Within three months:** Wright, *Captured*, pp. 55, 63.

267 **The men eagerly consumed:** Hibbs, "Beriberi," p. 182.

267 **Lieutenant Robert Huffcutt:** Hartendorp, *Japanese Occupation*, p. 2:588. This incident occurred on August 11, 1944. Huffcutt was the last man to die in Cabanatuan out of a total of 2,656 deaths, according to Andrew Miller, historian of the American Defenders of Bataan and Corregidor.

267 **When he went to retrieve:** Beecher, "Experiences," p. 118.

267 **There was a schedule:** Robert Taylor, interview, November 2, 1974, and January 16, 1975, pp. 91,119, #255, UNTOHC.

267 **no rabbi:** Roper, *Brothers of Paul*, p. 19.

267 **Dice were made:** Weinstein, *Barbed-Wire Surgeon*, p. 134.

268 **A 1916 British recruiting:** Sandy Balfour, *Vulnerable in Hearts: A Sentimental Journey* (New York: Farrar, Straus & Giroux, in press).

268 **High Commissioner Sayre:** Amea Willoughby, *I Was on Corregidor*, p. 175.

268 **"So far":** Bookman, *Diary*, November 17, 1943, entry.

268 **"May '42 made":** ibid., September 1, 1943, entry.

268 **sexual favors:** Berley interview, p. 42.

269 **Wish fulfillment fed:** Gillespie, "Recollections," p. 47.

269 **The officers from Bataan:** Chunn, "Notebooks," pp. 37–42.

269 **defanged cobra:** Jay Kent, interview by Ronald E. Marcello, May 11, 1972, p. 46, UNTOHC.

269 **"Taiwans":** Beecher, "Experiences," p. 96.

269 **The behavior of the:** Tanaka, *Hidden Horrors*, pp. 202–3.

269 **"The discipline was":** Kawasaki Masaichi, author interview, July 2002, Wakayama, Japan.

269 **"The Lieutenant slapped":** Hanama Tasaki, *Long the Imperial Way* (Boston: Houghton Mifflin, 1950), p. 45.

270 **A slap in the face:** Beecher, "Experiences," p. 98.

270 **But the violence that:** Tanaka, *Hidden Horrors*, pp. 206–7.

270 **"until the wretched body":** Giles Milton, *Samurai William: The Englishman Who Opened Japan* (New York: Farrar, Straus & Giroux, 2003), pp. 180, 228.

270 **With their "red":** Reischauer and Jansen, *Japanese Today*, p. 397.

270 **They were *ijin*:** ibid., p. 402.

270 **five to ten times:** U.S.A. Historical Center, Fort McNair, Washington, D.C.

270 **Sundays were Sundays again:** Chunn, "Notebooks," p. 29.

270 *Gyokusai:* Tanaka, *Hidden Horrors*, p. 9.

271 **"take no prisoners":** ibid., p. 74; Daws, *Prisoners*, p. 276.

271 **nothing to fear:** Chang, *Rape of Nanking*, pp. 4, 6. See "Iris Chang: Obituary," in *The Economist*, November 27, 2004, p. 91, for a summary of the controversy surrounding these figures.

271 **Or the British:** Michno, *Hellships*, p. 42; Hoyt, *Japan's War*, p. 250.

271 **Or the Australian:** Tanaka, *Hidden Horrors*, pp. 82–86.

271 **"In one notorious":** Cowdrey, *Fighting for Life*, p. 196.

271 **They even cannibalized:** Tanaka, *Hidden Horrors*, pp. 120–23.

271 **"Cannibalism was a":** ibid., pp. 126, 128.

271 **Along with the mail:** Joseph D. Harrington, *Yankee Samurai* (Detroit: Pettigrew Enterprises, 1979), p. 193, cited in Gerald F. Linderman, *The World Within War: America's Combat Experience in World War II* (New York: Free Press, 1997), p. 183.

271 **One infamous photograph:** Dower, *War Without Mercy*, p. 65.

271 **The Allies executed:** ibid., pp. 66–67. See Blair, *Silent Victory*, pp. 383–85.

271 **On Bataan, said:** James L. Kent, interview by Ronald E. Marcello, May 11, 1972, p. 33, #127, UNTOHC.

271 **"This is explained":** James C. Blanning, "War Diary," pp. 79–80. Courtesy John Fagan.

271 **When Japanese soldiers:** Ienaga, *Pacific War*, p. 292; See also Cook and Cook, *Japan at War*, p. 380.

271 **Dr. Marcel Junod:** "Notes on a talk given by Dr. Marcel Junod," p. 4.

272 **Many Japanese POW camp:** Tanaka, *Hidden Horrors*, p. 38.

000 **They asserted their authority:** ibid., p. 162.

272 **"so emaciated that their skins":** Alexander, "Recollections," p. 164.

272 **By year end more than:** Cooper, "Experiences," pp. 114–18.

272 **Diphtheria broke out:** Hibbs, *Tell MacArthur*, p. 187.

272 **for treatment and prevention:** Gillespie, "Recollections," p. 39.

272 **Waterous feared an:** Waterous, "Statement of Experiences," pp. 141–51.

273 **One POW:** C. M. Graham, *Under the Samurai Sword* (Privately printed, 1998), pp. 96–97.

273 **While diphtheria was common:** Crawford F. Sams, *"Medic": The Mission of an American Military Doctor in Occupied Japan and Wartorn Korea* (Armonk, N.Y.: M. E. Sharpe, 1998), p. 102.

273 **Sometimes anything seemed:** Beecher, "Experiences," p. 100.

273 **They smuggled in shoes:** Hartendorp, *Japanese Occupation*, p. 2:592.

273 **Mut's principal agent:** Harold K. Johnson to Recovered Personnel Division Headquarters, U.S. Army Forces Western Pacific, September 10, 1946, reprinted in Ashton, *Bataan Diary*, pp. 383–84; J. E. Kramer to Recovered Personnel Division, August 2, 1946, reprinted in Ashton, *Bataan Diary*, p. 402.

273 **Chaplain's Aid Association:** Weinstein, *Barbed-Wire Surgeon*, p. 153; Beecher, "Experiences," p. 92.

273 **And they welcomed:** Hartendorp, *Japanese Occupation*, pp. 2:593–94.

273 **The Philippine Women's Federation:** Weinstein, *Barbed-Wire Surgeon*, p. 109; Alfred A. Weinstein, August 8, 1947, to M. H. Marcus, Record Personnel Division, quoted in Ashton, *Bataan Diary*, pp. 421–23.

274 **A Philippine Red Cross:** Waterous, "Statement of Experiences," p. 139.

274 **reputed morphine addict:** Colonel Jack W. Schwartz, testimony, September 16, 1945, RG 331, Box 1118, Folder 4, NARA.

274 **Pilar Campos:** E. Carl Engelhart to Board Concerning Services Rendered American POWs, July 18, 1947, reprinted in Ashton, *Bataan Diary*, p. 431.

274 **Peggy Doolin:** Margaret Utinsky, *"Miss U"* (San Antonio, Tex.: Naylor, 1948), pp. 10, 52, 63, 70.

274 **Claire Phillips:** Taylor, *Cabanatuan*, p. 102; Jacobs, *Blood Brothers*, p. 65.

274 **She managed to:** Sides, *Ghost Soldiers*, p. 187.

274 **"The medicines and foodstuffs":** Harold K. Johnson, August 8, 1946, reprinted in Ashton, *Bataan Diary*, pp. 397–99.

274 **But there were entire segments of:** Daws, *Prisoners*, p. 163.

274 **Inside Cabanatuan:** Bunker, *Bunker's War*, pp. 94–95; Alexander, "Recollections," pp. 186–87.

274 **He even had:** Daws, *Prisoners*, p. 282.

275 **But Hutch wanted:** Jan K. Herman, "Guest of the Emperor," p. 21.

275 **"We were never":** Weinstein, *Barbed-Wire Surgeon*, p. 150.

275 **they raided the:** Beecher, "Experiences," pp. 90–91.

275 **"tons of food":** Weinstein, *Barbed-Wire Surgeon*, p. 127.

275 **The purchasing power:** Andrew Miller, author interview, Albuquerque, N.M., May 23, 2003.

275 **sulfathiazole pills:** Hibbs, *Tell MacArthur*, pp. 163, 151, 176, 181; Weinstein, *Barbed-Wire Surgeon*, pp. 85–86. See Stamp, *Journey*, p. 58, in which a navy corpsman uses baking soda for the same purpose; Beecher, "Experiences," p. 78.

275 **counterfeit drugs:** Waterous, "Statement of Experiences," p. 178.

275 **Naomi Flores:** Hartendorp, *Japanese Occupation*, p. 2:589.

275 **They imprisoned Miss U:** Utinsky, *"Miss U,"* p. 115.

276 **Guzman:** Johnson, reprinted in Ashton, *Bataan Diary*, p. 383.

276 **Father Buttenbruck from visiting:** Beecher, "Experiences," p. 80; Chunn, "Notebooks," p. 31.

276 **Treatt, Jack Schwartz:** Beecher, "Experiences," p. 93.

276 **Prices escalated:** ibid., p. 114.

276 **Father Buttenbruck was:** E. Carl Engelhart to Board Concerning Services Rendered American POWs, July 18, 1947, reprinted in Ashton, *Bataan Diary*, pp. 429–34; Hartendorp, *Japanese Occupation*, 2:496.

276 **One prisoner was:** Chunn, "Notebooks," p. 11.

276 **faked the symptoms:** Beecher, "Experiences," p. 84.

276 **Sergeant Jack C. Wheeler:** Chunn, "Notebooks," p. 1.

276 **Warrant Officer C. A. Price:** ibid.

276 **the most heinous:** Stamp, *Journey*, p. 70.

276 **men verbally emasculated:** Dower, *War Without Mercy*, pp. 81–88.

276 **There was "Little Speedo":** Beecher, "Experiences," p. 97.

276 **"Big Speedo":** Alexander, "Recollections," pp. 166–67.

277 **"Air Raid" Ihara:** Chunn, *Of Rice and Men*, pp. 96–97; Chunn, "Notebooks," p. 59; M. L. Daman, interview by Ronald E. Marcello, September 29, 1973, and October 6, 1973, p. 52, UNTOHC.

277 **There was Koshinaga:** Chunn, *Of Rice and Men*, p. 54; Taylor, *Cabanatuan*, pp. 96–97.

277 **Told he was named:** Karl A. Bugbee, interview by Ronald E. Marcello, December 8, 1971, p. 42, UNTOHC.

277 **"Dumb-Shit":** Hibbs, *Tell MacArthur*, p. 150.

277 **They removed the newspapers:** Chunn, "Notebooks," p. 8.

277 **"redolent of heaven":** Glusman, *Diary*, p. 20.

277 **gynecomastia:** Ralph E. Hibbs, "Gynecomastia Associated with Vitamin Deficiency Disease," *American Journal of the Medical Sciences* 213, no. 2 (February 1947), pp. 176–77.

277 **Japanese headquarters strictly:** Beecher, "Experiences," p. 77.

277 **Drugs became dollars:** ibid., p. 79.

277 **As the black market:** Wright, *Captured*, p. 62.

277 **Granulated fish:** Cooper, "Medical Department," p. 121.

277 **Inflation increased:** Alexander, "Recollections," pp. 197–98.

278 **They rooted through:** Daman interview, pp. 53, 59.

278 **cut up corncobs:** Stamp, *Journey*, p. 70.

278 **The signs were clear:** Alexander, "Recollections," pp. 191–92.

278 **According to such accounts:** ibid.

278 **"was celebrated as beautifully":** Wright, *Captured*, p. 62.

278 **The International Committee of the Red Cross:** Chunn, "Notebooks," p. 12.

278 **Major Paul Wing:** Caption for Signal Corps photograph 265335, Cabanatuan, December 25, 1943, RG111, Box 116, Still Picture Branch, NARA.

278 **By mid-January:** Sitter and Katz, "POWs," p. 50.

278 **Then talking and smoking:** Chunn, "Notebooks," p. 13.

279 **"We have arranged":** Glusman, *Diary*, p. 21.

279 **Almost the entire navy:** ibid.

279 **As early as September 1942:** Linda Goetz Holmes, *Unjust Enrichment: How Japan's Companies Built Postwar Fortunes Using American POWs* (Mechanicsburg, Pa.: Stackpole Books, 2001), pp. 149–50.

279 **They were loaded onto:** ibid., pp. 151–56.

280 **The medical detachment:** Weinstein, *Barbed-Wire Surgeon*, p. 171.

280 **cases of amoebic dysentery:** ibid.

280 **One of Craig's corpsmen:** John Cook, author interview, May 18, 2002, El Paso, Tex.

281 **atoll of Truk:** Blair, *Silent Victory*, pp. 560–61.

281 **Operation Hailstone:** Butow, *Tojo*, p. 427.

Chapter 17: "The Japanese will pay"

282 **"JAP ATROCITIES":** *Chicago Daily Tribune*, January 28, 1944, p. 1.

282 **"Bataan Death March":** Dyess, *Dyess Story*, pp. 11, 170–71.

282 **"The Japanese will pay":** quoted in James, *Years of MacArthur*, p. 2:512.

282 **But their story was:** Michno, *Hellships*, p. 91.

283 **"The period of our defensive":** quoted in Butow, *Tojo*, p. 425.

283 **On May 8, 1943:** Spector, *Eagle Against Sun*, pp. 253–54.

283 **Quadrant conference:** James, *Years of MacArthur*, p. 2:331.

283 **Rabaul:** ibid., p. 2:332.

283 **Once Germany was:** quoted in Costello, *Pacific War*, p. 443.

283 **There was little reason:** ibid., pp. 442–46.

283 **not superiority but supremacy:** Kennedy, *Freedom from Fear*, p. 618.

283 **B-17s, B-24s, and B-29s:** ibid., pp. 654–55.

283 **For 1942–43:** ibid., p. 618.

283 **Wartime production as:** Alan S. Milward, *War, Economy and Society, 1939–1945* (Berkeley: University of California Press, 1979), p. 63.

284 **Military procurement surged:** Kennedy, *Freedom from Fear*, p. 645.

284 **The 96,318 military:** ibid., p. 654.

284 **In Japan wartime spending:** Milward, *War, Economy*, p. 84.

284 **Japan's imports of:** ibid., p. 167.

284 **In 1937 Japan:** Schom, *Eagle and Rising Sun*, p. 61.

284 **The Axis powers:** Kennedy, *Freedom from Fear*, p. 654.

284 **Through eight loan drives:** "Brief History of World War Two Advertising Campaigns: War Loans and Bonds," in the John W. Hartman Center for Sales, Advertising, and Marketing History, at http://scriptorium.lib.duke.edu/adaccess/warbonds.html.

284 **Millions of Americans volunteered:** Harris, Mitchell, and Schecter, *Home Front*, pp. 62–64.

284 **Companies and corporations:** These advertisements appeared variously in *Life* magazine issues: December 15, 1941; March 30, 1942; April 13, 1942; April 20, 1942; and February 7, 1944.

285 **"Why aren't there":** quoted in Richard Lingeman, *Don't You Know There's a War On? The American Home Front 1941–1945* (New York: Thunder's Mouth Press/Nation Books, 2003), pp. 198–99.

285 **combat documentaries:** ibid., p. 189.

285 **Of the seven movies:** Dower, *War Without Mercy*, pp. 15–17.

285 **The accounts were:** McCoy and Mellnik, "Death Was Part of Our Life."

286 **Their sons were:** See Commander Walter Karig, USNR, and Lieutenant Welbourn Kelley, USNR, *Battle Report: Pearl Harbor to Coral Sea* (New York: Farrar & Rinehart, 1944), pp. 361–487, for a state-by-state listing of action casualties in the first six months of war in the Pacific theater.

286 **John Bookman, previously reported:** Memorandum from Navy Department, Bureau of Naval Personnel, to Dr. and Mrs. Samuel Bookman, May 7, 1943, re: Officers Reported as Prisoners of War.

286 **Operation 1 was:** Drea, *MacArthur's ULTRA*, pp. 73–74.

286 **On November 23:** Dear and Foot, *Oxford Companion*, p. 1103.

286 **In January 1944:** Costello, *Pacific War*, pp. 448–53.

286 **strikes against the Marianas:** Blair, *Silent Victory*, pp. 560–61.

287 **Tōjō was right:** H. P. Willmott, *The Second World War in the Far East* (London: Cassell, 1999), p. 126.

287 **They thought they:** Ashton, *Bataan Diary*, pp. 240–41.

287 **Fifty percent of Bilibid's:** Kentner, *Journal*, p. 101.

287 **"winter clothing":** ibid., p. 104.

287 **"Can 'Yanks and tanks":** Hayes, *Bilibid Notebook*, January 11, 1944, entry.

287 **In July 1940:** Joan Beaumont, "Victims of War: The Allies and the Transport of Prisoners-of-War by Sea, 1939–45" (Australian War Memorial), p. 1.

287 **On August 8, 1942:** ibid.

288 **The ICRC proposed:** ibid., p. 2.

288 **Britain balked:** ibid., p. 3.

288 **"In view of the":** ibid., p. 88.

288 **Seven weeks earlier:** Michno, *Hellships*, p. 47.

288 **As far as the Combined Chiefs:** ibid., pp. 87–88.

288 **"Execute Unrestricted Air":** William Tuohy, *The Bravest Man: The Story of Richard O'Kane and U.S. Submariners in the Pacific War* (Gloucestershire, UK: Sutton, 2001), p. 50.

288 **With no sea lanes:** Blair, *Silent Victory*, pp. 83–84, 841–42.

288 **a radar set:** Joan and Clay Blair, Jr., *Return From the River Kwai* (New York: Simon and Schuster, 1979), p. 226; Blair, *Silent Victory*, p. 322.

288 **Japanese ship movements:** Drea, *MacArthur's ULTRA*, pp. 73–74; Blair, *Silent Victory*, p. 294.

289 **U.S. Navy cryptanalysts:** Drea, *MacArthur's ULTRA*, pp. 12–13.

289 **The Ship Movement Code:** See Stinnett, *Day of Deceit*, pp. 71–72.

289 **"The Japanese were meticulous":** Donald Showers, author interview, February 4, 2003.

289 **To prevent ULTRA data:** Tuohy, *The Bravest Man*, pp. 62–63.

289 **The Australia-based:** ibid., p. 66.

289 **"he chose to ignore":** Donald Showers, interview by Bill Alexander, March 13, 1998, p. 56, #1257, UNTOHC.

289 **"ULTRA tip-off messages":** ibid., p. 64.

289 **The Japan-Truk shipping:** Blair, *Silent Victoy*, p. 509.

290 **Inspired by the:** Theodore Roscoe, *United States Submarine Operations in World War II* (Annapolis, Md.: Naval Institute Press, 1949), pp. 240–42.

290 **In February 1944:** "Statistical Summary: Attrition War Against Japanese Merchant Marine," from U.S. Strategic Bombing Survey, "The War Against Japanese Transportation," reprinted in Roscoe, *United States Submarine Operations in World War II*, pp. 523–24.

290 **On February 25:** Michno, *Hellships*, pp. 152–56, 294, 314.

290 **They marched from Azcarraga:** Kentner, *Journal*, pp. 104–5.

290 **Tied up at:** Weinstein, *Barbed-Wire Surgeon*, pp. 170–81.

290 **What a difference:** Bumgarner, *Parade*, p. 138.

291 **The civilians walked:** Weinstein, *Barbed-Wire Surgeon*, p. 182.

291 **The *benjo* hung:** Bumgarner, *Parade*, p. 142.

291 **Ernie Irvin volunteered:** Irvin, "Wartime Reminiscences," p. 7.

291 **On more than one:** ibid., p. 143.

291 **"Msg Manila to Tokyo":** RG38, Box 1220, NARA.

292 **"MATA":** Ricardo Trota Jose to author, November 21, 2004.

292 **"Msg Manila to Hiroshima":** ibid.

292 **They pushed such thoughts:** Weinstein, *Barbed-Wire Surgeon*, p. 182.

292 **"I was seized":** Bumgarner, *Parade*, p. 143.

292 **Only one POW had:** No less than five separate accounts describe this incident; See Weinstein, *Barbed-Wire Surgeon*; Smith, *Prisoner of Emperor*; Bumgarner, *Parade*; Berley author interview; and Irvin, "Wartime Reminiscences," p. 7. Yet this sinking cannot be confirmed in Roscoe, *Submarine Operations*.

292 **But the only American submarine:** I am grateful to Gregory Michno for this point, which he described in an e-mail dated April 28, 2002.

292 **The skies turned:** Bumgarner, *Parade*, pp. 144–45.

293 **"Mesg Takao to Hiroshima":** ibid.

293 **While the *Kenwa Maru*:** Bumgarner, *Parade*, p. 145.

293 **The bags were hoisted:** Weinstein, *Barbed-Wire Surgeon*, p. 184.

293 **The sugar was unrefined:** Irvin, "Wartime Reminiscences," p. 6.

293 **They added sugar:** ibid., p. 7.

293 **Or they ate:** Smith, *Prisoner of Emperor*, p. 80.

293 **"The sugar ship":** Weinstein, *Barbed-Wire Surgeon*, p. 184.

294 **Army surgeon Alfred Weinstein:** H. L. Cleave, "Medical Report on Shinagawa Camp," September 11, 1945, p. 1, RG 407, Box 148, NARA.

294 **Lieutenant Nosu Shōichi:** Perpetuation of Testimony of Dr. David Hochman, June 18, 1946, "In the Matter of Atrocities Committed at POW Camps in the Osaka area, Between November 1942 and July 1945, by Lt. Nosu, Chief Medical Administrator," WCO/JAG, p. 2, RG183, Case File W33-53-21, NARA.

294 **"I, Dr. Nosu":** quoted in Smith, *Prisoner of Emperor*, pp. 90–91.

294 **Murray tried engaging:** ibid., p. 91.

Chapter 18: Bridge over Hell

295 **In 1600:** Grant K. Goodman, *Japan: The Dutch Experience* (London: Athlone Press, 1986), pp. 4–5.

295 **In 1630:** ibid, p. 34.

295 **From 1640 until:** ibid., pp. 10–12, 18.

295 **inevitably, Japanese interpreters:** ibid., pp. 32–33.

295 ***rangakusha*:** ibid., pp. 5–6.

295 **They were keen:** ibid., p. 37.

296 **Classical Chinese medicine:** Marius

B. Jansen, *The Making of Modern Japan* (Cambridge, Mass.: Harvard University Press, 2000), p. 210.

296 **The interpreters learned:** Goodman, *Japan*, pp. 38–40.

296 **Their contributions, notably:** Donald Keene, *The Japanese Discovery of Europe, 1720–1830*, rev. ed. (Stanford, Calif.: Stanford University Press, 1969), pp. 21–24. See also Shigehisa Kuriyama, "Between Mind and Eye: Japanese Anatomy in the Eighteenth Century," in Charles Leslie and Allan Young, eds., *Paths to Asian Medical Knowledge* (Berkeley: University of California Press, 1992), pp. 21–43.

296 ***Kaitai Shinsho*:** a translation by Sugito Gempako and Maeno Ryotaku of *Tafel Anatomica* by Johann Adam Kulmus.

296 **Subcamp No. 13-B:** Lassiter A. Mason, statement, December 1, 1945, p. 3, RG331, Box 1192, NARA.

296 **"drab-looking buildings":** Smith, *Prisoner of Emperor*, p. 92.

296 **"Put your gear":** ibid., pp. 92–93.

296 **Lieutenant Jack George put:** ibid.

297 **Ōsaka, the second-largest:** Kazuo Nishida, *Storied Cities of Japan* (Tōkyō: John Weatherhill, 1963), pp. 251–52.

297 **The city was celebrated:** ibid., pp. 250–51.

297 **a major supplier of wartime:** W. F. Craven and J. L. Cate, eds., *The Army Air Forces in World War II*, vol. 5, *The Pacific: Matterhorn to Nagasaki, June 1944 to August 1945* (Chicago: University of Chicago Press, 1953), p. 619.

297 **Hochman reported to Nosu:** Hochman testimony, p. 2; See also Mason statement.

298 **fifty-three-year-old Murata:** Inoue Kiyoko, author interview, July 12, 2002, Kyōto, Japan.

298 **"Our people will not":** Quoted in William McGaffin, "The Price of Victory: Japs More Cruel to Yanks Than to Other Captives," *Chicago Daily News*, September 8, 1945, p. 2.

298 **Ōsaka No. l:** Philip E. Sanders, statement, May 1, 1946, in *U.S.A. vs. Sotaro Murata*, Case #155, Headquarters Eighth Army, United States Army, Office of the Staff Judge Advocate, Yokohama, Japan, February 16, 1949, RG 331, Box 994, NARA.

298 **"Nosu couldn't do anything":** Kobayashi Kazuo, author interview, July 11, 2002, Ōsaka, Japan.

298 **frequent drills:** Daws, *Prisoners*, p. 101

298 **a special latrine for diarrhea:** See Signal Corps photograph, SC-225182, September 21, 1945: "Latrine used by men at Tsumori prison camp. The diarrhea sign was placed on the door by the American doctor but soon lost its significance for all men had diarrhea." Still Photo Collection, NARA.

299 **POWs hauled rocks:** Mason statement, p. 4.

299 **Some were so:** Joseph Astarita, author interview, June 4, 2003.

299 **Rice, or barley:** Gus Priebe, author interview, June 6, 2003.

299 **permission to bake bread:** Sam Silverman, author interview, June 4, 2003.

299 **practice dentistry:** Smith, *Prisoner of Emperor*, p. 94.

299 **Down in the shipyards:** Ienaga, *Pacific War*, pp. 98–101.

300 **secret shortwave radios:** Frank Gross, author interview, June 24, 2003.

300 **B.H.J. Boerboom:** GHQ/SCAP Records, Investigation Division Report No. 134, RG 331, Box 1765, Folder 13, NARA.

300 **The prisoners' clothing:** Gross interview.

300 **"make them strong":** Smith, *Prisoner of Emperor*, p. 95.

300 **When Samuel Silverman:** Silverman interview, June 4, 2003.

301 **Tsukioka Yoshio used:** Tsukioka Yoshio, author interview, July 11, 2002, Ōsaka. In 1952 Juganji Temple was moved to Mount Ikoma in Higashi, Ōsaka, to make way for the expanded Tanimachi subway line. See Kahorl Sakane, "Foreign WWII Soldiers Rest in Peace at Ōsaka Temple," *Daily Yomiuri*.

301 **Like other residents:** Milward, *War, Economy*, pp. 256–57; Cook and Cook, *Japan at War*, p. 177.

301 **Rationing began:** Thomas R. H. Havens, *Valley of Darkness: The Japanese People and World War II* (New York: W. W. Norton, 1978), p. 50.

301 **The Basic Necessities:** Ienaga, *Pacific War*, pp. 193–94.

301 **By early 1942:** Cook and Cook, *Japan at War*, p. 172. For research on food in Japanese culture, I am indebted to Nakao Tomoyo, who kindly shared her Japanese publications with me. See *"Sensō horyo mondai no hikaku bunkateki kōsatsu: 'Shoku' no mondai*

o chûshin ni" (Comparative Cultural Aspects of the POW Problem: Focusing on the Isssue of "Food"), in *Sensō sekinin kenkyū* (War Responsibility Studies) no. 22 (Winter 1998), no. 23 (Spring 1999), and no. 26 (Winter 1999).

301 **The nutritional standard:** Ienaga, *Pacific War*, p. 193.

302 **Military rations were:** Milward, *War, Economy*, pp. 257–58.

302 **gas stations:** ibid., p. 319.

302 **Women and high school:** ibid., pp. 257–58.

302 **But coal and charcoal:** Havens, *Valley of Darkness*, p. 122.

302 **"a ratio of one hundred":** Asahi Shimbun, *Pacific Rivals*, pp. 100–101.

302 **To augment dwindling:** Gibney, *Sensō*, pp. 180–81.

302 **To conserve energy:** Havens, *Valley of Darkness*, p. 122.

302 **Sweet potatoes were:** ibid., p. 123.

302 **And to save leather:** ibid., p. 120.

302 **Extravagance, associated with:** ibid., p. 15.

302 **"Luxury Is the Enemy":** ibid., p. 18.

302 **Books and magazines:** ibid., p. 23.

302 **Foreign films:** Mainichi Newspapers, *Fifty Years of Light and Dark: The Hirohito Era* (Tōkyō: Mainichi Newspapers, 1975), p. 111.

302 **Freedom of speech:** Ienaga, *Pacific War*, p. 99.

303 **Habeas corpus was:** ibid., p. 98.

303 **"People's bars":** Havens, *Valley of Darkness*, pp. 151, 152.

303 **Neighborhood associations:** Cook and Cook, *Japan at War*, p. 171.

303 **Members dug trenches:** ibid., p. 340.

303 **As of 1943:** Ienaga, *Pacific War*, p. 195.

303 **Boys as young:** ibid., p. 198.

303 **the minimum age:** See Cook and Cook, *Japan at War*, pp. 173–75.

303 **By 1944 millions:** Havens, *Valley of Darkness*, p. 103.

303 **In Kōbe third- and fourth-year students:** See Kappa Senoh's autobiographical novel, *A Boy Called H: A Childhood in Wartime Japan*, trans. John Bester (New York: Kodansha International, 1999), p. 279.

303 **Schoolgirls helped:** Ōsaka International Peace Museum, Exhibition Hall A.

303 **The elderly were:** Havens, *Valley of Darkness*, p. 104.

303 **Children were expected:** Gibney, *Sensō*, p. 7.

303 **"imperial likenesses":** See Senoh, *Boy Called H*, p. 99.

303 **From the sixth edition:** Ienaga, *Pacific War*, p. 107.

303 **Japan was a divine:** Havens, *Valley of Darkness*, p. 29.

303 **For years the curriculum:** ibid., p. 27.

303 **At one school:** Cook and Cook, *Japan at War*, p. 468.

303 **Imperial General Headquarters:** Kase, *Journey*, p. 74.

303 **official wire service:** Cook and Cook, *Japan at War*, p. 62.

303 **Radio broadcasts boasted:** ibid., p. 253.

304 **Even when the Left:** Buruma, *Inventing Japan*, p. 231.

304 **The *kokutai*:** Ienaga, *Pacific War*, p. 231.

304 **"Truly it is time":** quoted in Cook and Cook, *Japan at War*, p. 69.

304 **Ringed by the:** Milward, *War, Economy*, p. 259.

304 **It was a small camp:** "Investigation of the Wakamaya Prisoner of War Camp," January 31, 1946, GHQ/ SCAP, p.1.

305 **The kitchens at Wakayama:** Perpetuation of Testimony of John Jacob Bookman, "In the Matter of Inadequate Medical Supplies and Food Furnished prisoners of war at Wakayama Prisoner of War Camp and Kobe Prisoner of War Hospital, from April 1944 to June 1945," WCO/JAG, p. 2, RG 331, Box 954, Folder 17 [OS-204-J-16], NARA.

305 **Okazaki Isojirō:** ibid.

305 **Wakayama Iron Works:** "Report on Wakayama Camp," GHQ/SCAP, Investigation Division Report No. 143, January 31, 1946, RG 331, NARA.

305 **But John and the other:** Nakamura Ryuichiro, author interview, July 9, 2002, Wakayama, Japan.

305 **The hospital was:** Michno, *Hellships*, pp. 46–47.

306 **A stone walkway:** Jan Hendrik Ritsma, affidavit, 11 June 1946, RG 331, Box 994, NARA.

306 **These weren't humans:** Ferdinand V. Berley, interview by Jan K. Herman, pp. 28–29; see also "Plan of the Ichioka Prisoner of War Camp, Ichioka Hospital Ward," prepared by Hiroyuki Morita, attached to statement of Yoshiro Nakata, January 18, 1946, Investigation Division Report No. 125. RG 331, Box 1765, Folder 4, NARA.

306 **The POWs at Ichioka:** GHQ/SCAP, Investigation Division Report No. 125, RG 331, Box 1765, NARA.

306 **Together they had:** Michno, *Hellships*, pp. 83–84.

306 **At first Surgeon-Lieutenant:** Roly Dean, autobiographical narrative (unpublished), p. 219.

306 **"Our first reaction":** letter to Joe Vater (unpublished), 1995.

307 **two bodies fit:** Roly Dean, letter to author, June 11, 2002.

307 **Then the barrels:** Jack Hughieson, letter to author, November 23, 2001.

307 **soaked the rice overnight:** Clayton Woodrow Atwood, affidavit, October 29, 1945, RG 331, Box 994, NARA.

307 **They made tea:** Dean narrative, p. 231.

307 **stole them outright:** Leslie George Kelly, statement, October 14, 1946, RG 331, Box 994, NARA.

307 **For surgery, Jackson:** Charles Anthony Jackson, affidavit, "In the Matter of Japanese War Crimes and in the Matter of the Ill-Treatment of Prisoners of War and Conditions at Ichioka Hospital Camp, Osaka, Japan," RG 331, Box 994, NARA.

307 **Once Jackson resorted:** Clinton D. Metzler, deposition, September 25, 1945, RG 331, Box 994, NARA.

307 **From November 1942:** Jackson affidavit.

308 **The sick received:** ibid., p. 1.

308 **First Lieutenant Matsuyama:** John Quinn, statement, September 7, 1945, RG 407, Box 148, NARA.

308 **"four of the victims":** Jackson affidavit, p. 1.

308 **The guards:** Hendrik Jan Ritsma, statement, June 11, 1946, p. 2, RG 331, Box 994, NARA.

308 **"you took a bashing":** Dean narrative, p. 235.

308 **"piss tin and bedpan":** ibid., p. 227.

309 **In April 1944:** John Quinn, "Anglo American Solidarity," unpublished recollection, April 1984.

309 **They gave buckets:** John Quinn, "49 Top Hats," unpublished recollection, April 1984.

309 **John Quinn:** ibid.

310 **The game was:** Ricardo Trota Jose to author, November 21, 2004.

310 **"There we stood":** Quinn, "Anglo-American Solidarity," pp. 2–3.

310 **"we always made sure":** Dean narrative, p. 227.

310 **Jackson would have:** ibid., 232.

310 **To cure diarrhea:** Hochman testimony, "In the Matter of Atrocities."

310 **primary erythromelalgia:** Jackson affidavit.

311 **Kidd was so bloated:** Kidd, *Twice Forgotten*, pp. 85–96.

312 **absorbent chromic catgut:** Dr. John Kirkup, letter to the author, July 14, 2003.

313 **"Suitably" meant killing:** "Killing of POWs in Osaka," *Mainichi Shimbun*, August 13, 1998, p. 17, trans. for the author by John Junkerman.

313 **The Japanese suspected Jackson:** John Finch Akeroyd, statement, Australian War Memorial, October 10, 1942.

313 **Moreover, he had:** Dean narrative, p. 238.

314 **"It is important to note":** Murray Glusman, "Discharges and Deaths," in "Medical Notes."

314 **Nor could they:** Robert Jay Lifton, *The Nazi Doctors: Medical Killing and the Psychology of Genocide* (New York: Basic Books, 2000), p. 269.

315 **"The Japs took it":** Smith, *Prisoner of Emperor*, p. 100.

315 *Tenko* **was scheduled:** Joseph W. Wright, testimony "In the matter of I.T. Scott, USN," November 25, 1946, p. 3, RG 331, Box 994, NARA.

315 **Akeroyd saluted:** Ferdinand V. Berley, testimony, "In the Matter of the Beating of Patients and Staff Members at Ichioka Stadium Hospital, Osaka, Japan, 8 May 1944, 15 February 1946," p. 3, RG 331, Box 994, NARA.

315 **Kitamura joined the fray:** ibid.; John Finch Akeroyd, statement, n.d., RG 331, Box 994, NARA.

315 **They slapped, punched:** Ritsma statement, p. 2.

315 **Sometimes three Japanese:** E.M. Gonie, affidavit, Investigation Division Report No. 125, June 20, 1947, RG 331, Box 1765, Folder 4, NARA.

316 **"All men die":** Akeroyd statement, p. 2; Thomas Rhodes, notes, September 7, 1945, Red Cross Hospital, Ōsaka.

316 **There would be no:** Gonie affidavit.

316 **John Allison Page:** J. A. Page, "Report On Period Served as Prisoner of War of the Imperial Japanese Army from 25th December 1941 to 8th September, 1945," p. 2, CMAC, GC/131/18, Acc. No. 413, Papers of Surgeon/Commander J.A. Page, RN, Wellcome Trust Library for the History and Understanding of Medicine, London.

316 **Page had been captured:** ibid., p. 1.

316 **"The Royal Navy blokes":** Dean narrative, p. 239.

316 **an X-ray of Akeroyd's:** Sams, *"Medic,"* p. 144.

317 **Fred figured:** Berley interview by Herman, p. 30.

317 **On July 10:** p. 3. See Lionel Wigmore, *The Japanese Thrust* (Canberra: Australian War Memorial, 1957), pp. 620–25.

Chapter 19: Bad Timing and Good Luck

318 **"the vestibule of the country":** *City of Kobe: Its Evolution and Enterprises* (Corporation of the City of Kobe, 1929), p. 6.

318 **with a population:** U.S. Strategic Bombing Survey, "Effects of Air Attack on Osaka-Kobe-Kyoto," Urban Areas Division, June 1947, MR #A117, p. 149, AFHRC.

318 **Japanese girls were:** Buruma, *Inventing Japan*, p. 66.

318 **Japanese men wore:** ibid.

318 **Jazz was:** Asahi Shimbun, *Pacific Rivals*, p. 78.

318 NO PHOTOGRAPHING: Krasno, *Last Glorious Summer*, p. 62.

319 **Nippon Airplane:** U.S. Strategic Bombing Survey, "Effects of Air Attack on Osaka-Kobe-Kyoto," Urban Areas Division, June 1947, MR #A1157, p. 156, AFHRC.

319 **Kawasaki Shipbuilding Yards:** U.S. Strategic Bombing Survey, "Field Report Covering Air-Raid Protection and Allied Subjects in Kobe Japan," Exhibit G, February 1947, p. 105, Civilian Defense Division, MR #A1115, AFHRC.

319 **Kōbe Steel turned:** U.S. Strategic Bombing Survey, "Effects of Air Attack on Osaka-Kobe-Kyoto," pp. 191, 212.

319 **The hospital occupied:** Sotaro Murata, message, August 27, 1945, p. 2, Archives générales 1918–1950, Groupe G [Generalités: affaires operationnelles] 1939–1950, G 3/51, M. Junod, Japón, Box 219 [1], ACICR.

319 **Equipment was Japanese:** Page, "Report on Period," p. 3.

319 **There was a communal bath:** Erwin Bernath, "Report on the Visit Made on October 4, 1944, by a Delegate of the Swiss Legation at Tokyo, to Hospital No. 30 Dependent upon Prisoner of War Camp Kobe No. 31," RG 331, Box 952, NARA.

319 **By July 1944:** De Jong, *Collapse*, p. 291.

319 **At the Kōbe POW Hospital:** H. C. Angst, "Report on Kōbe POW Hospital Visit, August 18, 1944," ICRC, p. 2, RG 331, Box 952, NARA.

319 **Captain C. R. Boyce:** Wigmore, *Thrust*, p. 624.

320 **more serious cases:** C. R. Boyce, "Medical Report," Section 2, Admin. & Dis. Book Kobe House POW Camp 09.06.1943–06.09.1945, Australian War Memorial 54, Written Records 1939–1945 War, 554/15/2.

320 **The Japanese refused:** Beaumont, "Victims of War," pp. 2–3.

320 **"because they always":** "In the Matter of Inadequate Means of Transportation," p. 3.

320 **On June 6:** Dear and Foot, *Oxford Companion*, pp. 974–95.

321 **"Victory on the March":** Japanese caption quoted from photograph 179026, in RG 80-G, General Records of the Department of the Navy, General Photographs, 1918–45 (Prints), 178750-179177, Still Picture Branch, NARA.

321 **The seriousness of:** Sam Sofer, "Narrative," unpublished manuscript, p. 35; Jack Hughieson, letter to author, September 21, 2001.

321 **daily air raid drills:** John Lane, *Summer Will Come Again*, at www.summerwill-come-again.com, p. 5:3.

321 **"most suitable":** Angst, "Report on Kōbe POW Hospital Visit."

321 **"SATISFACTION GRATITUDE":** Report No. 1199, Kōbe Prisoner of War Hospital, September 18, 1944, RG 331, Box 952, NARA.

321 **"I command!":** Smith, *Prisoner of Emperor*, p. 104.

321 **"Difficulty grows":** quoted in Waterford, *Prisoners of Japanese*, p. 21.

322 **"principles of humanity":** Lane, *Summer*, p. 5:3.

322 **Or at Ōsaka:** Philip Earl Sanders, testimony, 1 May 1946, p. 3, RG 331, Box 994, NARA.

322 **Private Everett D. Reamer:** This account is based on Reamer, *Sanity*, pp. 65–70, and Reamer interviews, June 2003, Albuquerque, N.M.

324 **In 1870, two years:** John Z. Bowers, *Medical Education in Japan: From Chinese Medicine to Western Medicine* (New York: Harper and Row, 1965), p. 35.

324 **Pathological anatomy:** William Johnston, *The Modern Epidemic: A History of Tuberculosis in Japan* (Cambridge, Mass.: Council on East Asian Studies/Harvard University, 1995), p. 46.

324 **The emperor Meiji:** Keene, *Emperor of Japan*, p. 798n5.

324 **Hashimoto went on:** ibid.

324 **By the late nineteenth century:** Bowers, *Medical Education*, pp. 35–37.

324 **At the same time:** Quoted in Starr, *Social Transformation*, p. 113.

325 **Germany was preeminent:** ibid., pp. 113–14.

325 **Lectures and rote memorization:** Sams, *"Medic,"* p. 121.

325 **Hopkins made a:** Starr, *Social Transformation*, p. 115.

325 **The medical curriculum:** Bowers, *Medical Education*, pp. 38–39.

325 **There was no written:** Sams, *"Medic,"* p. 121.

325 **Before World War II:** ibid.

325 **They were allowed:** ibid., p. 132.

325 **Second-class doctors:** ibid., p. 121.

325 **In the Russo-Japanese:** Hans Zinsser, *As I Remember Him: The Biography of R.S.* (Boston: Little, Brown, 1940), p. 394.

325 **In 1940 Shiga was:** ibid., p. 390.

325 **But the same government:** Margaret M. Lock, *East Asian Medicine in Urban Japan: Varieties of Medical Experience* (Berkeley: University of California Press, 1980), p. 15.

325 *Kanpō,* **as it:** Bowers, *Medical Education*, p. 37.

325–26 **With little understanding:** Roland, *Long Night's Journey*, p. 191.

326 **"Arrangements to send":** ATIS, "Survey of Japanese Medical Units," Research Report No. 124, January 17, 1947, p. 10, microfiche, 10-RR-124, MHI.

326 **Japanese doctors were:** ibid., pp. 11–12.

326 **Forward-area hospitals:** "Fake Hospital Ship," RG 389, Box 2176, NARA.

326 **"The man was tied":** ATIS, "Japanese Medical Units," p. 10.

326 **In Mukden, Manchuria:** Tanaka, *Hidden Horrors*, pp. 137–39.

327 **He even assisted Fred:** Ferdinand V. Berley, statement, n.d., RG331, Box 952, NARA.

327 **The disease haunted Japan:** Johnston, *Modern Epidemic*, p. 41.

327 **By the late nineteenth century:** ibid., pp. 25, 63.

327 **During the war:** Johnston, Hosodo, and Kusumi, *Japanese Food Management*, p. 52.

327 **surpassing even the number:** See Sams, *"Medic,"* p. 109. In 1945 the death rate among Japanese civilians from tuberculosis was 282 per 100,000, which exceeded, according to Sams, "the number who died from all of the bombing, the fire raids, and the two atomic bombs."

327 **artificial pneumothorax:** Katherine Ott, *Fevered Lives: Tuberculosis in American Culture Since 1870* (Cambridge, Mass.: Harvard University Press, 1996), pp. 7, 95–97.

328 **A lieutenant colonel:** Dean narrative, pp. 347–48.

329 **Beriberi was a:** Johnston, Hosodo, and Kusumi, *Japanese Food Management*, p. 91.

329 **beriberi actually declined:** ibid., p. 164.

329 **John drafted a:** John Jacob Bookman, "Diarrhea and Dysentery Among POWs," in "Medical Notes."

329 **In extreme cases:** Keys et al., *Biology*, p. 2:588.

329 **"painful feet":** J. A. Page, "Painful-Feet Syndrome Among Prisoners of War in the Far East," *British Medical Journal* 2 (August 24, 1946), p. 260. See also Murray Glusman, M.D., "The Syndrome of 'Burning Feet' (Nutritional Melalgia) as a Manifestation of Nutritional Deficiency," *American Journal of Medicine*, Vol. III, No. 2, August 1947, pp. 211–23.

329 **Fourth Marine James Fraser:** James Fraser, author interview, Albuquerque, N.M., May 2003.

329 **Symptoms of the disease:** Robert B. Lewis, " 'Painful Feet' in American Prisoners of War," *U.S. Armed Forces Medical Journal* 1, no. 2 (February 1950), p. 146.

330 **"there were quite a lot":** Staff of the Kobe POW Hospital, "Painful Feet," February–March 1945. This manuscript was the basis of a paper published after the war under the sole authorship of J. A. Page as

"Painful-Feet Syndrome Among Prisoners of War in the Far East" (above).

331 **In his "Memorandum on":** Ernest Jones, *The Life and Works of Sigmund Freud*, ed. Lionel Trilling and Steven Marcus (New York: Basic Books, 1961), pp. 393–95.

331 **And he had read:** Sigmund Freud and Josef Breuer, *Studies on Hysteria*, trans. and ed. James Strachey (New York: Avon Books, 1966), p. 42.

331 **"each individual symptom":** ibid., pp. 40–41.

332 **One evening in:** Blair and Blair, *Return from the River*, pp. 250, 212, 272–74.

332 **secondary syphilis:** Dean narrative, pp. 349–50.

333 **"as thick as two planks":** ibid., p. 240.

333 **They themselves were:** Daws, *Prisoners*, p. 262.

333 **Indian POWs:** Dean narrative, p. 226.

334 **"This is *Humanity Calls*":** Kerr, *Surrender and Survival*, pp. 189–90.

334 **The *Prisoners of War Bulletin*:** ibid., pp. 185–88.

334 **At Kōbe, recording:** Smith, *Prisoner of Emperor*, p. 107.

335 **Between 1942 and 1945:** "Record of Number of Requests for Visiting POW Camps by the Protecting Powers and Their Acceptance and Permission," June 19, 1946, Archives générales 1918–1950, Groupe G [Généralités: affaires operationnelles] 1939–1950, G 3/51, M. Junod, Japón, Box 219 [2], ACICR.

335 **"In Germany particularly":** "Notes on a Talk Given by Dr. Marcel Junod," p. 11.

335 **Three thousand calories was:** Johnston, Hosado, and Kusumi, *Japanese Food Management*, p. 277.

335 **Even at Colonel Murata's:** Page, "Painful-Feet Syndrome," pp. 2–3.

335 **Fish and meat:** ibid.

335 **robust condition:** Lane, *Summer*, pp. 2:1, 3:9.

335 **They forged keys:** ibid., p. 5:3.

336 **patients stole food:** Jack Hughieson, letter to author, November 23, 2001.

336 **It must have been special:** Smith, *Prisoner of Emperor*, pp. 106–7.

336 **If such visits were staged:** Page, "Report on Period Served," p. 3.

337 **Christmas shopping:** *Kōbe-shi shi, Dai-san shu: Shakai bunka hen* (*Kōbe City History*, vol. 3, *Society and Culture*), n. d., pp. 10–15.

337 **Fish and beef:** ibid., pp. 30–33.

338 "M'ARTHUR INVADES": *New York Times*, October 20, 1944, p. 1.

339 **A total of:** "The Battle for Leyte Gulf," at www.angelfire.com/fm/odyssey/LEYTE-GULF-Summary-of-the-Battle-htm, pp. 1–12.

339 **more than 1,000 planes:** ibid., p.154.

339 **In the SHO-GŌ:** Dear and Foot, *Oxford Companion*, p. 688. See Keegan, *Encyclopedia*, pp. 153–54.

339 **The Battle for Leyte Gulf:** James, *Years of MacArthur*, p. 2:539.

339 **"People of the Philippines":** ibid., p. 557.

Chapter 20: "Action Taken: None"

340 **"Many are the lessons":** Simpson, *Diary*, p. 54.

340 **By early May:** William Riney Craig, "Medical Notes," p. 10. Courtesy John Cook.

340 **Riney Craig:** ibid., p. 20.

340 **Thousands of civilians:** Dr. Segundo G. Jao, "Average Diet of the Civilian Population in Manila During the Years 1942 to 1945," to Robert Cohn, January 11, 1947, Defense Exhibit D, *U.S.A. vs. Naraji Nogi*, 20 January 1947, NARA.

340 **Japanese quartermaster depots:** Michno, *Hellships*, p. 91.

340 **the *Teia Maru*:** ibid., p. 91.

340 **"Evidence is accumulating":** Edwin Andrews to Douglas MacArthur, NR243, February 7, 1944, RG 496, Entry 109, Box 571; Jesus Villamor to Douglas MacArthur, vol. 3, NARA.

340 **Also included with:** *Prisoners of War Bulletin* 1, no. 6 (November 1943), John E. Olson Papers, Box 1, MHI.

341 **What you earned:** Craig, "Medical Notes," p. 10.

341 **"We are now approaching":** Simpson, *Diary*, p. 2:7.

341 **"all the time":** Craig, "Medical Notes," p. 26.

341 **The *Taikoku Maru*:** Michno, *Hellships*, pp. 314–15.

341 **"now pronounced fit":** Beecher, "Experiences," p. 126.

341 **"So long, see you later":** quoted in Jan K. Herman, "Guest of the Emperor," p. 21.

342 **It was cloudy:** Craig, "Medical Notes," p. 28.

342 **Among them were twenty:** Waterous, "Statement of Experiences," p. 172; Nancy Russell Young, "Reflections on Bob and Jessie Russell," September 17, 1981, unpublished manuscript, p. 55.

342 **At 1700 they:** Kentner, *Journal*, p. 122. Note that Kentner counted 206 men in this draft.

342 **The resistance to disease:** Hayes, *Bilibid Notebook*, final part, p. 71.

342 **The average daily:** Kentner, *Journal*, p. 121.

342 **"looks like we":** Hayes, *Bilibid Notebook*, final part, p. 58.

342 **Even the pigs:** ibid., p. 35.

342 **Air raid drills:** Kentner, *Journal*, p. 118.

342 **Japanese air force:** Hayes, *Bilibid Notebook*, final part, p. 96.

342 **At 0930 on:** Hartendorp, *Japanese Occupation*, pp. 2:365–66.

342 **Internees at Santo Tomás:** Hartendorp, *Japanese Occupation*, pp. 2:365.

342 **Up at Cabanatuan:** Calvin Robert Graef with Harry T. Brundidge, "We Prayed to Die," *Cosmopolitan* 118, no. 4 (April 1945).

342 **"black with planes":** Hayes, *Bilibid Notebook*, final part, pp. 140–41.

343 **Jimmy Carrington:** This story is based on interviews with James W. Carrington and Joseph E. Dupont on May 15, 2002, in San Antonio, Tex., and in May 2004 in Orlando, Fla., as well as Hayes's *Bilibid Notebook*, April 15–16, 1944, entries.

344 **many of the POWs:** Hayes, *Bilibid Notebook*, April 15, 1944, entry.

344 **Parker had hit the wire:** Ashton, *Bataan Diary*, p. 254.

344 **Marking's guerrillas:** Robert Lapham and Bernard Norling, *Lapham's Raiders: Guerrillas in the Philippines, 1942–1945* (Lexington: University Press of Kentucky, 1996), p. 70.

344 **"an able, amiable soldier":** Edwin Price Ramsey and Stephen J. Rivele, *Lieutenant Ramsey's War* (New York: Knightsbridge, 1990), p. 247.

344 **When the Japanese Army:** Cortes, Boncan, and Jose, *Filipino Saga*, p. 358.

344 **As President Quezon's executive secretary:** David Joel Steinberg, *Philippine Collaboration in World War II* (Ann Arbor: University of Michigan Press, 1967), pp. 37, 190n71; Cortes, Boncan, and Jose, *Filipino Saga*, p. 359.

345 **But after the fall of:** Cortes, Boncan, and Jose, *Filipino Saga*, p. 367.

345 **Jockeying for position:** Quirino, *Chick Parsons*, p. 21.

345 **Between 1942 and 1944:** James, *Years of MacArthur*, p. 2:507.

345 **Guerrilla units in:** ibid., pp. 507–8.

345 **Robert V. Ball:** Ira Wolfert, *American Guerrilla in the Philippines* (New York: Simon and Schuster, 1945), p. 134.

346 **"WE HAVE THE":** John Keats, *They Fought Alone* (Philadelphia and New York: J.P. Lippincott, 1963), p. 171.

346 **One week later:** ibid., p. 187.

346 **Meanwhile, Major Jesus:** Allison Ind, *Allied Intelligence Bureau: Our Secret Weapon in the War Against Japan* (New York: David McKay, 1958), pp. 125–26.

346 **Villamor established:** ibid., p. 157.

346 **Colonel Arthur Fischer:** Arthur F. Fischer, "Memorandum for Major General Richard J. Marshall, Deputy Chief of Staff, GHQ, Southwest Pacific Area," May 20, 1944, RG 16, Box 65, Folder 6, "Philippine Sub Division Administration, July 1944," MMA.

346 **Ever modest, MacArthur:** B. M. Fitch to Michael L. Stiver, August 20, 1943, RG 16, Box 64, Folder 1, "P.R.S., Administration, December 1943," MMA.

346 **On March 5, 1943:** Quirino, *Chick Parsons*, p. 40.

346 **Fertig had promoted himself:** ibid., p. 31.

347 **Then he presented:** ibid., p. 29 .

347 **Per AIB's plan:** Ind, *Allied Intelligence Bureau*, p. 167.

347 **Lapham received his:** Lapham and Norling, *Lapham's Raiders*, pp. 144, 148.

347 **Not until August 31:** ibid., p. 151.

347 **By then, more than:** "Messages Between U.S./Philippine Guerrilla Forces and HQ, SWPA, December 1942–November 1943." SRH-220, Part I, p. 27, RG 457, Records of the National Security Agency, Central Security Service, Entry 9002, "Study of the Historical Background of the Signal Service, 1776–1939."

347 **If direct communication:** ibid.

347 **Orders to guerrilla:** Quirino, *Chick Parsons*, pp. 28–30.

347 **1,076 messages:** RG 16, Box 31, Folder 2, "Fertig Messages—July 1944," MMA.

347 **Thirty-two code men:** Lloyd Waters, author interview, June 17, 2002.

347 **"air, ground, and naval":** cited in

Thomas Mitsos, "Guerrilla Radio" unpublished ms., chap. 5, p. 3. Courtesy Clyde Childress.

347 **The ECLGA covered:** Ramsey and Rivele; *Lieutenant Ramsey's War*, pp. 176–77.

347 **Aircraft warning:** Edwin P. Ramsey, "USAFFE Luzon Guerrilla Army Forces, HQ, East Central Luzon Guerrilla Area in the Field," May 15, 1945, in *Intelligence Activities in the Philippines During the Japanese Occupation, Documentary Appendices (II)*, vol. 2, *Intelligence Series*, RG-23A, Box 12, Folder 10, Willoughby Papers, MMA.

347 **To evade American submarines:** See Wendell Fertig to Douglas MacArthur, NR 426, 04 July 1944, RG 16, Box 31, Folder 2, "Fertig Messages—July 1944," MMA.

347 **Guerrilla radio operators:** Edwin Price Ramsey, author interview, February 10, 2003.

348 **They eavesdropped on:** ATIS, "Japanese Ten Day Period Reports on Monitoring of Allied Wireless Communications in the Philippines," No. 31, March 29, 1945, p. 6, SRH-231, RG 457, Records of the National Security Agency, Central Security Service, Entry 9002, "Study of the Historical Background of the Signal Service, 1776–1939."

348 **messages transmitted from MacArthur:** ibid., p. 86 .

348 **"it is very difficult":** ibid., p. 44.

348 **"Generally speaking":** ATIS, "Japanese Ten Day Period Reports," p. 6.

348 **"While maintaining close":** ibid., p. 50.

348 **On August 30:** Lapham and Norling, *Lapham's Raiders*, pp. 209, 229.

348 **The radio at Ramsey's:** Ramsey and Rivele, *Ramsey's War*, pp. 247–48.

348 **The messages were decoded:** Wendell Fertig to Douglas MacArthur, October 23, 1944, RG 16, Box 31, Folder 5, "Fertig Messages, October 1944," MMA.

348 **Or they were sent:** Ind, *Allied Intelligence Bureau*, p. 157.

348 **According to Jimmy Carrington:** James W. Carrington, author interview, May 24, 2002, San Antonio, Tex.

348 **Ships were unnamed:** Allison W. Ind, "Personnel Procurement and Training Scheme," May 4, 1943, RG 16, Box 65, Folder 2, MMA.

348 **In February 1944:** "Philippines Intelligence Guide," February 10, 1944, in

Intelligence Activities in the Philippines During the Japanese Occupation.

349 **"Action taken":** #1400, December 21, 1943, 508, Fertig, RG 16, Box 18, Folder 1, "Fertig—December 1943," MMA.

349 **There was an obvious:** RG 16, Box 31, Folder 2, "Fertig Messages—July 1944," MMA.

349 **To save time:** Ind, *Allied Intelligence Bureau*, pp. 177, 211.

349 **"we'd send all the messages":** Lloyd Waters, author interview, June 17, 2002.

349 **The control station:** Charles A. Parsons, "Report on Conditions in the Philippine Islands as of June 1943," in Quirino, *Chick Parsons*, p. 137.

349 **"UNCONFIRMED REPORT AMERICAN":** Ralph Praeger to Douglas MacArthur, NR25 S-229, February 19, 1943, RG 496, "Records of the General Headquarters Southwest Pacifc Area and U.S. Armed Forces Pacific," Entry 109, Box 564, "Praeger to MacArthur," NARA.

349 **On March 4, 1944:** Keats, *They Fought Alone*, pp. 124–25.

349 **"SAW AMERICAN WAR":** Andrews to Douglas MacArthur, NR 251, March 4, 1944, RG 496, Entry 109, Box 571, "Villamor to MacArthur, Vol. 3," NARA.

350 **"DAVAO PROVINCE, 6 JUNE":** Wendell Fertig to MacArthur, NR 251, June 10, 1944, RG 496, Entry 109, Box 527, "Vol. 9, Fertig to MacArthur," NARA.

350 **The removal of Air Corps:** Bernard Anderson to MacArthur, NR 40, July 18, 1944, RG 496, Entry 109, Box 538, "Vol. 1, Anderson to MacArthur," NARA.

350 **Meanwhile, Tom Mitsos:** Mitsos, *Guerrilla Radio*, chap. 10, pp. 10–12.

351 **The unknown ship arrived:** ibid. Note that Mitsos dates the message from Davao "around the first of September 1944" and also mistakes the date of this ship's arrival.

351 **Not until the morning of September 7:** ibid., chap. 10, p. 12.

351 **At 1647 on September 7:** Lee A. Gladwin, "American POWs on Japanese Ships Take a Voyage into Hell," *Prologue* (NARA quarterly) 35:4 (Winter 2003), p. 33.

351 **a submarine off:** Keats, *They Fought Alone*, p. 397; Morton, *War in the Pacific*, pp. 576–77.

351 **Many of the POWs:** Michno, *Hellships*, p. 230.

351 **"PRISONER OF WAR MCGEE":** RG 16, Box 31, Folder 5, "Fertig: Messages—October 1944," MMA.

352 **By June 1943:** WYZB to Douglas MacArthur, NR 143, June 1943, Entry 109, Box 523, "Vol. 2, Fertig to MacArthur," NARA.

352 **"Captain, I'm afraid":** William Edwin Dyess as told to Charles Leavelle, "Dyess' Own Story," *Chicago Sunday Tribune*, January 30, 1944, p. 1.

352 **In the early morning:** Blair and Blair, *Return from the River*, pp. 113–14; see Michno, *Hellships*, pp. 201–7.

352 **Later that night:** Blair and Blair, *Return from the River*, p. 172.

352 **Three days later:** Tuohy, *Bravest Man*, pp. 303–4.

352 **The *Sealion* radioed:** Blair and Blair, *Return from the River*, p. 218.

352 **From guerrilla messages:** Manila to Cebu, October 6, 1944, RG 38, Box 1220, NARA.

353 **"Absolutely there were":** Interview with Edwin Price Ramsey, February 10, 2003.

353 **"Even though our intelligence":** James Forrestal to David I. Walsh, October 16, 1945, courtesy Lucille Ferguson.

353 **down a gauntlet:** Blair, *Silent Victory*, pp. 745–46. For security reasons, U.S. Navy submarine skippers were not even informed of the imminent invasion of Leyte. See Blair, *Silent Victory*, p. 751.

353 **U.S. Navy bombers:** ibid., pp. 745–46.

353 **"STREETCAR USED TO":** Military Intelligence Service, Appendix 19, "History of the Military Intelligence Service, USAFFE," in *Intelligence Activities in the Philippines During the Japanese Occupation*, p. 10.

Chapter 21: The *Arisan Maru*

354 **The *Arisan Maru*:** The following account of the *Arisan Maru*'s journey draws on Michno, *Hellships*, pp. 249–58; interviews with survivors; GHQ/SCAP Records; Manny Lawton, *Some Survived: An Epic Account of Japanese Captivity During World War II* (Chapel Hill, N.C.: Algonquin, 1984); and Dale Wilber, "The Last Voyage of the 'Arisan Maru' " (unpublished).

354 **At 1600 on the:** "Escape in China Sea, Mr. Robert S. Overbeck, U.S. Engineering Department," EX-Report No. 483, prepared by MIS-X Section, CPM Branch, December 1944, p. 3, RG 153, Box 1431, NARA.

354 **An air raid siren:** Perpetuation of the Testimony of Calvin Robert Graef, WCO/JAG, April 27, 1946, p. 2, RG 153, Box 1431, NARA.

354 **When they complained:** Perpetuation of the Testimony of Anton Ervin Cichy, WCO/JAG April 30, 1946, p. 1, RG 153, Box 1431, NARA.

354 **Men were pressed:** Calvin R. Graef, Donald E. Meyer, Anthony E. Cichy, and Avery E. Wilber, joint statement, December 6, 1944, p. 1, RG 153, Box 1431, NARA.

354 **Japanese guards kept:** "Maryland Survivor Says 1800 Lost on Prison Ship," *Washington Post*, February 17, 1945.

354 **By 1630 the ship:** Funatsu Toshio, statement, GHQ/SCAP Records, Investigation Division Reports No. 479, RG 331, Box 1780, Folder 4, NARA, hereinafter referred to as GHQ/*Arisan Maru*; Michno, *Hellships*, p. 250.

354 **Captain Sugino Minemaru:** Robert E. Miller, report, GHQ/*Arisan Maru*.

354 **The 6,886-ton vessel:** Noma Hisashi, *The Story of Mitsui and O.S.K. Liners Lost During the Pacific War* (Tōkyō: Hisaski Noma, 2002), pp. 399–401; Abe Tadashi, interview by Ishii Shinpei, February 12, 2002, trans. for the author by John Junkerman.

355 **A Type 2A freighter:** Wilber, *Last Voyage*, p. 191.

355 **The inside of the ship:** "Data Sheet— Case No. AP 119," RG 153, Box 1431, NARA.

355 **The Japanese handed:** Graef testimony, p. 4.

355 **"The filth and stench":** Philip Brodsky, statement, January 25, 1946, GHQ/*Arisan Maru*.

355 **"too hot to touch":** Robert S. Overbeck, deposition, June 13, 1946, in response to letter dated April 9, 1946, from Director, Civil Affairs Division, War Department, Washington, D.C., file 105-46, subject, Request for Interrogation.

355 **The American doctors:** Calvin Robert Graef with Harry T. Brundidge, "We Prayed to Die," *Cosmopolitan* 118, no. 4 (April 1945), p. 177.

355 **"If only we could":** Graef testimony, p. 4.

355 **1,378 sorties:** Samuel Eliot Morison, *History of United States Naval Operations in World War II*, vol. 12, *Leyte: June 1944–January 1945* (Edison, N.J.: Castle Books, 2001), p. 91.

355 **dispatched two wolf packs:** Blair, *Silent Victory*, p. 746.

355 **Brodsky, who had:** Brodsky statement.

355 **Hundreds of others:** "U.S. Told 1,800 Americans Died in Japanese Prison Ship Sinking," *New York Times*, February 17, 1945.

355 **On October 13:** Wilber, *Last Voyage*, p. 191.

356 **"which had run off":** Donald Ernest Meyer, affidavit, "In the Matter of the Atrocities Committed in Connection with the Sinking of the Japanese Prisoner of War Ship, *Arisan Maru* in the Bashi Channel, by an American Submarine on 24 October 1944," May 20, 1946, p. 2.

356 **Major Robert B. Lothrop:** Richard Huston, Casualty Data Officer, USA CILHI, to Mrs. Joanne Loomis Crandall, September 18, 2000. Courtesy Mrs. Joanne Loomis Crandall.

356 **Within the first forty-eight:** Glenn Oliver, unpublished memoir, p. 163. Courtesy Mrs. Glenn Oliver.

356 **The first three:** Graef, "We Prayed to Die," p. 177.

356 **"there were dead all over":** Chuck Haga, "Survivor's Tale," *Minneapolis Star Tribune*, October 23, 1994.

356 **Calvin Graef had:** Graef, "We Prayed to Die," p. 177.

356 **Half canteen cups:** Roberta Graef, author interview, January 22, 2002; sworn statement of Donald Ernest Meyer, May 23, 1946, Exhibit B in GHQ Investigation Division Reports No. 479, "Arisan Maru," RG 331, Box 1780, Folder 4, NARA.

356 **Occasionally rotten vegetables:** Graef testimony, p. 5.

356 **By contrast, the crew of:** interrogation of Nishikawa Keizo in GHQ Investigation Division Reports No. 479, "Arisan Maru," RG 331, Box 1780, Folder 4, NARA.

356 **The hatches were:** Wilber, *Last Voyage*, p. 190.

357 **MATA-30:** ibid., p. 195.

357 **The *Arisan Maru* and:** Michno, *Hellships*, p. 250.

357 **Around October 23:** Wilber, *Last Voyage*, pp. 198–99.

357 **At noon the Japanese:** Donald Ernest Meyer, affidavit, "In the Matter of the Atrocities Committed in Connection with the Sinking of the Japanese Prisoner of War Ship *Arisan Maru* in the Bashi Channel, by an American Submarine on 24 October 1944,"

May 22, 1946, p. 2, RG 153, Box 1431, NARA.

357 **There were no markings:** Graef testimony.

357 **"a security matter":** Wilber, *Last Voyage*, p. 196.

357 **Wolf packs carried:** Blair, *Silent Victory*, p. 509.

357 **Their skippers received:** ibid., p. 542.

357 **The *Kokuryū Maru*:** Suzuki Shō, interview by Ishii Shinpei, March 19, 2002, trans. for the author by John Junkerman.

358 **three American wolf packs:** Michno, *Hellships*, p. 250.

358 **A total of 41,228 tons:** Tonnage calculated from Roscoe, *United States Submarine Operations*, p. 524; "Japanese Naval and Merchant Vessels Sunk During World War II by United States Submarines," pp. 527ff; "kills" taken from Michno, *Hellships*, pp. 250–51.

358 **The wind was blowing:** Toshio Funatsu, testimony GHQ/*Arisan Maru*.

359 **A few of the men:** Graef testimony.

359 **Graef glanced over:** Graef, "We Prayed to Die," p. 178.

359 **"C'mon, *navy!*":** ibid.

359 **A chaplain gave:** Philip Brodsky, interview by George Burlage, December 13, 1989, p. 22, #815, UNTOHC.

359 **One of the 5-inch guns:** Graef testimony.

359 **a terrific concussion:** Perpetuation of Testimony of Philip Brodsky, WCO/JAG, September 5, 1946, p. 2, RG 153, Box 1431, NARA.

359 **A torpedo from:** Avery E. Wilber, statement, December 5, 1944, RG 407, Box 146, NARA.

359 **The bow stayed level:** Graef, Meyer, Cichy, and Wilber joint statement, p. 2.

359 **The stern, which:** Tadashi interview.

359 **The U.S. Navy Security Station:** RG 38, Box 1152, NARA.

359 **Heavy oil, clothing:** Blair, *Silent Victory*, p. 770.

359 **"Tried to contact":** Snook, SS 279, 7th Patrol Report, and *Seadragon*, SS 194 , 11th Patrol Report, Submarine Force Library, Groton, Conn., courtesy Gregory F. Michno.

359 **Ed Blakely and:** Michno, *Hellships*, pp. 253–54.

359 **First Lieutenant Funatsu Toshio:** Graef testimony, p. 6.

359 **Then the Japanese cut:** Graef, Meyer, Cichy, and Wilber joint statement, p. 2.

359 **"Remember just one thing":** Graef, "We Prayed to Die," p. 178.

360 **An army chaplain:** ibid.; see Wilber, *Last Voyage*, p. 208 and Roper, *Brother of Paul*, pp. 203–5.

360 **They could hear the:** Oliver memoir.

360 **The Japanese took with:** Tadashi interview.

360 **"We took care of them":** Graef testimony, p.6.

360 **The waves were:** Robert S. Overbeck, statement, December 6, 1944, p. 4.

360 **At the sight:** Brodsky interview, p. 23.

360 **They ransacked the:** Brodsky testimony, p. 3.

360 **Overbeck crawled up:** *The Washington Post*, "Maryland Survivor Says 1800 Lost."

360 **His left arm was:** Overbeck deposition.

360 **Calvin Graef had:** Graef testimony, p. 7.

360 **When Don Meyer saw:** Donald Ernest Meyer, testimony GHQ/*Arisan Maru*.

360 **Several Japanese seaplanes:** Wilber, *Last Voyage*, p. 209.

361 **Once her boilers:** Graef testimony, p. 7.

361 **at 1940:** Wilber, *Last Voyage*, p. 204.

361 **Her position was:** Shinshichiro Komamiya, *Senji Yuso Sendan Shi* (Wartime Transportation Convoys History), part 1, trans. William G. Somerville (Tōkyō: Shuppan Kyodosha, 1987).

361 **The nearest land:** Avery E. Wilber, statement, December 5, 1944, p. 1.

361 **"Am discontinuing sweep":** I am grateful to Rear Admiral Donald M. Showers, U.S. Navy (Ret.), for attributing sources to these messages, February 22, 2003.

361 **"ARIYAMA MARU":** "ariyama" should have read "arisan." In all likelihood there was a mistake in decoding by the American cryptanalyst, or the code group that spelled "san" was garbled during transmission by the Japanese.

361 **"it was dark":** Fukuyama Tsuyoshi, testimony in GHQ/*Arisan Maru*.

361 **He had ordered:** Ueyanagi Isamu, testimony in GHQ/*Arisan Maru*.

361 **The *Take* took on:** Kimata Jiro, *Zanson Suru Teikoku*, p. 369.

361 **Shiga Hiroshi:** Shiga Hiroshi, *Saigo no nebi bru* (1980), chap. 10.

361 **Overbeck saw a:** Graef, Meyer, Cichy, and Wilber, joint statement, p. 2.

361 **He lifted the lid:** Perpetuation of Testimony of Avery E. Wilber, WCO/JAG, May 2, 1946, RG 153, Box 1431, NARA.

361 **Sergeant Avery E. Wilber:** Wilber statement; Wilber, *Last Voyage*, p. 211.

361 **Then at around 0900:** Graef testimony, p. 8.

362 **Wilber sat in the:** Wilber, *Last Voyage*, p. 213.

362 **In the meantime:** ibid.

362 **During the next:** Meyer affidavit, p. 4.

362 **The weather was:** Gene Weeks, "Five Came Back," *Hence* (July–August–September 1946), William H. Owne Papers, MHI.

362 **The POWs were:** Calvin R. Graef, statement, December 5, 1944, p. 5.

362 **The POWs wanted:** Cichy statement.

362 **"We go china":** Wilber, *Last Voyage*, p. 215.

362 **The Chinese made:** Meyer affidavit, p. 5.

362 **They slept on deck:** Graef statement, p. 6.

362 **On the afternoon of:** Graef testimony, p. 8.

362 **They had landed:** Michno, *Hellships*, p. 256.

362 **A security detail:** Graef testimony, p. 7

363 **When they arrived in Kunming:** www.cia.gov/cia/publications/oss/art09.htm.

363 **General Chennault:** Wilber, *Last Voyage*, p. 222.

363 **From Kunming they:** Graef testimony. Overbeck gives December 1, 1944, as the date of arrival in Washington, D.C.

363 **It didn't seem possible:** Graef statement.

363 **The ship was listing:** Lawton, *Some Survived*, p. 117.

363 **The aft deck of:** Oliver memoir, p. 164.

363 **"quite a few men":** ibid.

363 **Among them were:** Donald Meyer quoted in Tracy Seipel, "Echoes of World War II," *Denver Post*, October 23, 1994.

363 **Brodsky was an:** Brodsky testimony, p. 3.

364 **There were thirty or forty:** Lawton, *Some Survived*, p. 119.

364 **a Japanese cruiser was heading:** "Japanese Ship Torpedoed, Brodsky Fished from Sea," *Polyscope* 2, no. 20 (Woodrow Wilson General Hospital, Staunton, Va.) (November 16, 1945), p. 1.

364 **"come on over":** Brodsky testimony, p. 4.

364 **they wouldn't kill:** Philip Brodsky, author interview, November 24, 2001, Cherry Hill, N.J.

365 **They'd had no food:** Sally MacDonald, "He Survived," *Seattle Times*, October 24, 1994, sec. F, p. 1.

365 **When they finally:** Lawton, *Some Survived*, p. 128.

365 **Around 0700 the:** Wilber, *Last Voyage*, p. 220.

365 **He tore off:** statement of Boatswain Martin Binder, July 31, 1946, Liaison and Research Branch, American Prisoner of War Information Bureau.

366 **The sickest men:** Lawton, *Some Survived*, p. 135.

366 **Brodsky ended up:** Brodsky testimony, pp. 4–6.

366 **Binder had the:** Binder statement, p. 3.

366 **Glenn Oliver was:** Oliver memoir.

366 **One Japanese soldier:** "Translated Extracts from Japanese Records," vol. 2, "General Notes," para. 4, Exhibit H, GHQ/*Arisan Maru*.

367 **"Human bombs,":** Mainichi Newspapers, *Fifty Years of Light and Dark*, p. 127.

367 **Special Attack Forces:** See Ohnuki-Tierney, *Kamikaze*, pp. 159–60; *Fifty Years of Light and Dark*, pp. 127–28.

367 **"Nothing can be a greater":** *Fifty Years of Light and Dark*, p. 128.

367 **But victory eluded:** "Battle for Leyte Gulf," p. 11.

367 **"U.S. DEFEATS":** *New York Times*, October 26, 1944, p. 1.

367 **That same month:** Statistical Summary: Attrition War Against Japanese Merchant Marine, from U.S. Strategic Bombing Survey, "The War Against Japanese Transportation," reprinted in Roscoe, *Submarine Operations*, p. 524.

367 **In the seven weeks:** Compiled from Michno, *Hellships*, p. 316.

367 **By late December:** Keegan, *Encyclopedia*, p. 154.

367 **The Americans had:** U.S. Strategic Survey (Pacific), Naval Analysis Division, *The Campaign of the Pacific War* (Washington, D.C.: Government Printing Office, 1946), p. 289.

Chapter 22: Fire from the Sky

368 **They were young:** St. Clair McKelway, "A Reporter with the B-29s," Part 1, *New Yorker*, June 9, 1945, p. 56.

368 **Based in Saipan:** Martin Caidin, *A Torch to the Enemy: The Story of the Devastating Fire Raid Against Tokyo—March 10, 1945* (New York: Ballantine Books, 1960), pp. 45ff.

368 **"I hated the Japanese":** Jules Stillman, author interview, May 16, 2003, Charlotte, N.C.

369 **"Here's to you":** John Davidson, Jr., author interview, May 17, 2003, Charlotte, N.C.

369 **"Goddam Americans":** Caidin, *Torch to Enemy*, p. 20.

369 **In February 1944:** Dear and Foot, *Oxford Companion*, p. 718.

369 **On June 15, 1944:** Caidin, *Torch to Enemy*, p. 32.

369 **Those raids continued:** Dear and Foot, *Oxford Companion*, p. 1076.

369 **The assault on Saipan:** Keegan, *Encyclopedia*, pp. 216–17.

369 **In the first forty-eight:** Dear and Foot, *Oxford Companion*, p. 974.

370 **"Come out and surrender!":** quoted in Caidin, *Torch to Enemy*, p. 41.

370 **On June 24:** "The Tragedy of *Banzai* Cliff," Ōsaka International Peace Center, Ōsaka, Japan.

370 **On July 6:** Keegan, *Encyclopedia*, p. 217.

370 **"take seven lives":** Caidin, *Torch to Enemy*, p. 44.

370 **Forced to retreat:** Previous estimates have been as high as 4,000. Historian Richard B. Frank, in *Downfall: The End of the Imperial Japanese Empire* (New York: Random House, 1999), states "the actual number of suicides probably did not much exceed one thousand" (p. 30).

370 **Suicide Cliff:** Keegan, *Encyclopedia*, p. 217.

370 **"It was obvious":** quoted in Overy, *Why the Allies*, p. 301.

370 **Navy Seabees (Construction Battalion):** Daws, *Prisoners*, p. 278.

370 **In August:** Craven and Cate, *Army Air Forces*, p. 517.

370 **The aviation engineers:** Caidin, *Torch to Enemy*, p. 48.

370 **On November 24:** "Brief History of 497th Bombardment Group, 1943–46," AFHRC, 1957, p. 8.

370 **More than 100:** Craven and Cate, *Army Air Forces*, p. 558.

370 **"Piss-Call Charlie":** John Ciardi, *Saipan: The War Diary of John Ciardi* (Fayetteville: University of Arkansas Press, 1988), p. 23.

371 **Eight to ten:** Robert E. Copeland, *Diary*, November 27, 1944, entry, sallyann2/copeland1.html.

371 **Then one plane:** See U.S. War Department, *Handbook on Japanese Military Forces*, pp. 53–75.

371 **"Words can't describe":** Ed Lawson (né Levin), author interview, May 17, 2003, Charlotte, N.C.

371 **There were no foxholes:** Chester Marshall, Lindsey Silvester, and Scotty Stallings, eds., *The Global Twentieth* (Memphis, Tenn.: Global Press, 1988), p. 3:251.

371 **three B-29s had gone:** McKelway, "Reporter with B-29s."

371 **"They shot hell":** Copeland, *Diary*, November 27, 1944, entry.

371 **Iwo Jima:** Prentiss Burkett, *The Unofficial History of the 499th Bomb Group (VH)* (Temple City, Calif.: Historical Aviation Album, 1981), p. 13.

371 **Radio transmitters could:** Caidin, *Torch to Enemy*, p. 108.

371 **"SuperDumbos":** Chester Marshall, *Final Assault on the Rising Sun* (London: Airlife, 1995), pp. 75–78.

371 **But fear shadowed you:** "H. L. Peterson, 1st Sqdn., 9th Bomb Group, 'The Kobe Premonition,' " in Marshall, Silvester, and Stallings, *Global Twentieth*, pp. 4:222–23.

371 **Hard not to be:** ibid.

372 **Hard not to feel:** Robert E. Copeland to Norma Copeland, n.d., courtesy William Copeland.

372 **"We functioned":** Ciardi, *Saipan*, p. 23.

372 **Ed Keyser:** James B. Grim, in Marshall, Silvester, and Stallings, *Global Twentieth*, p. 2:111.

372 **From the Chamorro natives:** Davidson interview.

372 **A new chemical:** Heaton, Coates, and Hoff, *Preventive Medicine*, pp. 6:8–9.

373 **Ed Keyser kept:** Ed Keyser, *Diary*, courtesy Ed Keyser.

373 **The planes were beautiful:** Caidin, *Torch to Enemy*, p. 31.

373 **They came equipped:** Chester Marshall, *B-29 Superfortress* (Osceola, Wisc.: Motorbooks, 1993), p. 19; Caidin, *Torch to Enemy*, p. 29.

373 **As alluring as they:** Caidin, *Torch to Enemy*, p. 104.

373 **Isley Field on Saipan:** ibid., pp. 106–7.

373 **"You dreaded the takeoff":** Walt Sherrell, author interview, May 17, 2003, Charlotte, N.C.

373 **plane seemed to be lost:** William C. Campbell, *Journal of My Military Life, B-29 Aircraft Commander, 497th Group, 73rd Bomb Wing* (privately printed), p. 35.

373 **The engines overheated:** ibid., p. 20.

374 **"We were on a bomb run":** Ronald Routhier, author interview, May 17, 2003, Charlotte, N.C.

374 **Whenever Jules Stillman:** Stillman interview.

374 **Nearly a dozen raids:** U.S. Strategic Bombing Survey, "The Effects of Air Attack on Japanese Urban Economy: Summary Report," Urban Areas Division, March 1947, App. A, p. 44, MR #A1157, AFHRC.

374 **B-29s were literally:** "Japs Slander Our Planes," *20th Bomber Command Special Reports*, June 16, 1945, XX Bomber Command archive, MR # A7811, AFHRC.

374 **On January 21, 1945:** "War News Summarized," *New York Times*, April 22, 1943, p. 1.

374 **relieved General Hansell:** Alan D. Coox, "Strategic Bombing in the Pacific," in R. Cargill Hall, ed., *Case Studies in Strategic Bombardment* (Washington, D.C.: Air Force History and Museums Program, Government Printing Office, 1998), p. 311.

374 **Major General Curtis LeMay:** Craven and Cate, *Army Air Forces,* p. 560.

374 **Gruff, daunting, and demanding:** St. Clair McKelway, "A Reporter with the B-29s," Part 3, *New Yorker*, June 30, 1945, p. 26.

374 **LeMay had been:** Sven Lindqvist, *A History of Bombing* (New York: New Press, 2001), p. 107.

374–75 **Doolittle, who commanded:** Perret, *Winged Victory*, p. 369.

375 **"that those who have loosed":** Quoted in W. B. Sebald, *On the Natural History of Destruction*, trans. Anthea Bell (New York: Random House, 2003), p. 19.

375 **But Dresden also contained:** Frederick Taylor, *Dresden: Tuesday, February 13, 1945* (New York: HarperCollins, 2004), pp. 148–49, 414–15.

375 **An estimated 25,000 to 40,000:** ibid., p. 401.

375 **Two-thirds of Japanese industry:** Peter Wyden, *Day One: Before Hiroshima and After* (New York: Simon and Schuster, 1984), p. 134.

375 **Industrial targets were:** Craven and Cate, *Army Air Forces*, p. 610.

375 **Seventeen hundred tons of incendiaries:** ibid.

375 **The bombs themselves:** Coox, "Strategic Bombing," p. 316.

375 **When the bomb recipe:** Lindqvist, *History of Bombing*, p. 107.

376 **"The primary purpose":** "Effects of Incendiary Attacks," *Air Intelligence Report* 1, no. 4 (March 29, 1945), p. 1352, MR #C0036, AFHRC.

376 **A Pentagon report:** E. Bartlett Kerr, *Flames over Tokyo: The U.S. Army Air Forces' Incendiary Campaign Against Japan, 1944–1945* (New York: Donald I. Fine, 1991), p. 77.

376 **On February 4, 1945:** Craven and Cate, *Army Air Forces*, pp. 569–70.

376 **Brigadier General Lauris Norstad:** Kerr, *Flames over Tokyo*, p. 134.

376 **"The expression 'sure victory' ":** Havens, *Valley of Darkness*, p. 161.

377 **"This outfit has been":** McKelway, "Reporter with B-29s," Part 3, p. 27.

377 **LeMay switched tactics:** Prentiss Burkett, *The Unofficial History of the 499th Bomb Group (VH)* (Temple City, Calif.: Historical Aviation Album, 1981), p. 14.

377 **strip the planes:** Coox, "Strategic Bombing," p. 317.

377 **The B-17 had:** McKelway, "Reporter with B-29s," Part 3, p. 33

377 **"Boys," the word:** ibid., p. 27.

377 **Weather conditions were:** *XXI Bomber Command Operations*, March 22, 1945, p. 1317, MR #71810, AFHRC.

377 **"These missions had":** Caidin, *Torch to Enemy*, pp. 76, 78.

377 **On March 9, 1945:** Wyden, *Day One*, p. 183.

377 **Planes from the 314th:** Craven and Cate, *Army Air Forces*, p. 615.

377 **From a blister:** Marshall, *B-29 Superfortress*, p. 86.

377 **The lead planes, "pathfinders":**
Craven and Cate, *Army Air Forces*, p. 614.
377 **The pathfinders raced:** Caidin, *Torch to Enemy*, p. 110.
378 **"a beautiful but":** Marshall, *B-29 Superfortress*, p. 86.
378 **Red and white:** Kerr, *Flames over Tokyo*, p. 180.
378 **The 73rd Bomb Wing:** ibid., p. 172.
378 **Clusters spilled out:** Caidin, *Torch to Enemy*, p. 110.
378 **For the next:** ibid., p. 113.
378 **Strong spring gusts:** ibid., pp. 117–18.
378 **The searing heat:** Marshall, *Final Assault*, p. 130.
378 **"Going into northwest Tōkyō":** Vernon Piotter, author interview, May 17, 2003, Charlotte, N.C.
378 **In some sections of:** Edward Seidensticker, *Tokyo Rising: The City Since the Great Earthquake* (Cambridge, Mass.: Harvard University Press, 1991), p. 141.
378 **Six thousand firefighters:** Kerr, *Flames over Tokyo*, p. 190.
378 **Houses exploded:** This description is based on Caidin, *Torch to Enemy*, pp. 135–52, and Kerr, *Flames over Tokyo*, pp. 189–214.
379 **"The very streets":** quoted in Wyden, *Day One*, p. 185.
379 **Tōkyō's citizens died:** Takeo Ishikawa, *Tokyo in Raiders' Ordeal*, trans. Dr. and Mrs. William D. Bray.
379 **"If you could look":** Routhier interview.
379 **"a reddish glow":** Bernard Greene, author interview, April 2003.
379 **LeMay already knew:** Wyden, *Day One*, p. 184.
379 **Except for one:** Robert Doty, author interview, May 17, 2003, Charlotte, N.C.
380 **"Excellent results":** Julius Stillman, *Combat Diary*, November 1944–August 1945 (privately printed), p. 20.
380 **"thought it appalling":** quoted in Kerr, *Flames over Tokyo*, p. 213.
380 **"We knew we":** quoted in Lindqvist, *History of Bombing*, p. 109.
380 **"exceptionally well pleased":** quoted in Kerr, *Flames over Tokyo*, p. 212.
380 **"I believe that all":** ibid., p. 212.
380 **The American firebombing:** Craven and Cate, *Army Air Forces*, p. 617.
380 **Of the city:** ibid., p. 616.
380 **In one night:** McKelway, "Reporter with B-29s," Part 3, p. 36.

380 **"Even after all the":** quoted in Cook and Cook, *Japan at War*, p. 353.
380 **It took almost a month:** Dower, *War Without Mercy*, p. 41.

Chapter 23: Total War
381 **The incendiary raids demonstrated:** U.S. Strategic Bombing Survey, "Field Report Covering Air-Raid Protection and Allied Subjects in Kobe Japan," February 1947, p. 8, MR #A1154, AFHRC.
381 **Families were taught how:** "Preparation for an Air Raid," Ōsaka city circular, trans. for the author by Ibuki Yuka.
381 **In December 1944:** *The Anti-Air Raid Guidelines for Families and Tonari-gumi*, Ōsaka International Peace Center, Exhibit A, Ōsaka, Japan.
381 **Another government publication:** ibid.
381 **"went off so often":** Araki Kiyoshi, interview by Ishii Shinpei, Kōbe, March 17, 2002, trans. for the author by John Junkerman.
382 **In Kōbe all:** USSBS, "Field Report Covering Air-Raid Protection," p. 16.
382 **Fire departments lacked:** ibid., p. 19.
382 **Kōbe's industries developed:** ibid., p. 22.
382 **Only the two and a half miles of tunnels:** ibid., p. 68.
382 **Throughout Japan:** Havens, *Valley of Darkness*, p. 167.
382 **Indeed, tens of thousands:** USSBS, "Field Report Covering Air-Raid Protection," p. 24.
382 **But by January:** USSBS, "Effects of Air Attack on Osaka-Kobe-Kyoto," Urban Areas Division, June 1947, MR A1177, p. 149, AFHRC.
382 **"I'm not afraid":** Robert E. Copeland to Norma Copeland. Courtesy William Copeland.
382 **On the night of March 16–17:** Craven and Cate, *Army Air Forces*, p. 622.
382 **The planes were armed:** ibid.
382 **stocks of M-69s:** Kerr, *Flames over Tokyo*, p. 217.
382 **The Superforts swept:** Charles F. Gregg, *Diaries, 1941–45*, p. 171, ID CSUZ89056-A. Courtesy Hoover Institute for the Study of War and Peace.
382 **"waking up":** Stillman, *Combat Diary*, p. 23.
383 **"It was the most spectacular":** Smith, *Prisoner of Emperor*, p. 110.

383 **They had thrown:** quoted in Kerr, *Surrender and Survival*, p. 250.

383 **And they had launched:** ibid., pp. 524–25.

383 **At Kōbe House:** Lane, *Summer*, p. 5:7.

383 **Then at 0300:** Harold J. Mason, affidavit, December 28, 1945, GHQ/SCAP Records, Investigation Division Report No. 12, March 1947–June 1948, RG 331, Box 1758, Folder 13, NARA.

383 **Radio operator Robert Doty's:** Robert Doty, author interview, May 17, 2003, Charlotte, N.C.

384 **The Japanese press:** See Senoh, *Boy Called H*, p. 390: "A considerable number of fires were started within the city as a result of bombing by a force of approximately sixty B29s, but they were almost all brought under control by 10:00 a.m."

384 **Fujimoto Toshio was:** Fujimoto Toshio, interview by Ishii Shinpei, March 17, 2002, Kōbe, Japan, trans. for the author by John Junkerman.

385 **Mikitani Hiroko:** Nakata Masako, interview, July 10, 2002, Kōbe, Japan.

386 **Only three B-29s:** *XXI Bomber Command Air Intelligence Report*, vol. 1, no. 4 (March 29, 1945), p. 4, MR #C0036, AFHRC.

386 **One was shot down:** Fukubayashi Toru, "Allied Airplanes Lost over the Japanese Mainland—Chuba Army District" (unpublished).

386 **By morning, the:** Suchiro Ito, interrogation by First Lieutenant Joseph J. Henderson, GHQ/SCAP, Investigation Division Report No. 12, January 13, 1948, p. 9.

386 **"For a saving grace":** Howard Nemerov, "The War in the Air," in Harvey Shapiro, ed., *Poets of World War II* (New York: Library of America, 2003), pp. 141–42.

386 **In the predawn darkness:** Koji Takaki, "Captain Junichi's Last Combat," p. 1, Sallyann2/copeland7.html (July 8, 2004).

386 **The bodies of:** Koji Takaki to William Copeland, May 19, 2000. Courtesy William Copeland.

386 **Five airmen in:** Friar Marcian Pellet to Norma Copeland, Novmber 7, 1945. Courtesy William Copeland.

386 **A Japanese flight boat:** Takai, "Captain Junichi's Last Combat," p. 1.

387 **The body of:** Harold K. Brinkerhoff to Norma Copeland, December 19, 1945. Courtesy William Copeland.

387 **The captured fliers:** "Execution of Lt. Nelson and Sgt. Augunus," March 2, 1946, p. 1, GHQ/SCAP, Legal Section Investigation Division, RG 331, Folder 21, NARA.

387 **Their fate had:** ibid., p. 2.

387 **A military tribunal:** *U.S.A. vs. Eitaro Uchiyama et al.*, Headquarters Eighth Army, U.S. Army, Office of the Staff Judge Advocate, Case #123, Yokohama, July 1, 1948, pp. 22–23.

387 **The sentence, under:** ibid., pp. 17–18, 20.

387 **Asked if he:** Takao Mori, testimony, in *U.S.A. vs. Eitaro Uchiayama et al.*, RG 331, Box 994, OS-202 (L-48), p. 12, NARA.

387 **a botched beheading:** ibid.

387 **the Japanese tried:** ibid., p.17.

387 **Americans were shot:** ibid., p.16

387 **Soon it was cherry:** Ohnuki-Tierney, *Kamikaze*, p. 29.

388 **Soon Colonel Murata:** " 'Message' of Colonel Sotaro Murata," 27 August 1945, Commander Osaka POW Camp, p. 5, Archives générales, 1918–1950, Groupe G [Généralities: affaires opérationelles], 1939–1950, G 3/51, M. Junod, Japón, Box 219 [1], ACICR.

388 **All the officers:** Wigmore, *Thrust*, p. 624.

388 **"The greatest naval":** Baldwin, *Battles Lost and Won*, p. 368.

388 **To secure it:** Dear and Foot, *Oxford Companion*, p. 836.

388 **"to reduce his":** Samuel Eliot Morison, *History of United States Naval Operations in World War II*, vol. 14, *Victory in the Pacific, 1945* (Edison, N.J.: Castle Books, 2001), p. 92.

388 **"the inevitable showdown":** Hiromichi Yahara, *The Battle for Okinawa: A Japanese Officer's Eyewitness Account of the Last Great Campaign of World War II*, trans. Roger Pineau and Masatoshi Uehara (New York: John Wiley, 1995), pp. 144, 196.

389 **Kamikaze were unleashed:** ibid., p. 181.

389 **named them** *oka:* ibid., p. 100.

389 **Five days after:** Bix, *Hirohito*, p. 493.

389 **In this plan:** Headquarters, USAFFE and Eighth U.S. Army (Rear), "Homeland Operations Record," Japanese Monograph No. 17, p. 201, MHI.

389 **The Kōbe-Ōsaka region:** ibid., p. 65.

389 **"The Imperial Army":** ibid., p. 204.

390 **Turning the homeland:** ibid., pp. 219ff.

390 *"Ichioku ichigan":* Hoyt, *Japan's War*, p. 320.

390 **"Transcend life and":** Albert Axell and Hideaki Kase, *Kamikaze* (London: Longman, 2002), quoted in *Harper's Magazine*, December 2002, p. 20.

390 **U.S. intelligence estimated:** See D. M. Giangreco, "Operation DOWNFALL: U.S Plans and Japanese Counter-Measures," p. 7, from "Beyond Bushido: Recent Work in Japanese Military History" symposium, University of Kansas, February 16, 1998.

390 **To the very end:** Frank, *Downfall*, p. 196.

390 **Murray had fenced:** Richard Cohen, *By the Sword: A History of Gladiators, Musketeers, Samurai, Swashbucklers, and Olympic Champions* (New York: Modern Library, 2002), p. 162.

390 **During the war:** Chang, *Rape of Nanking*, pp. 56–57.

391 **"Today there was":** quoted in *Kōbe-shi shi, Dai-san shū: Shakai bunka hen* (*Kōbe City History*, vol. 3, *Society and Culture*), n.d., trans. for the author by John Junkerman.

391 **Until March 1945:** Havens, *Valley of Darkness*, p. 126.

391 **At Ōsaka University:** Tūjii Tomō, "Locusts and Beef," in Professors and Staff of Ōsaka Prefectural University, *My War Experiences* (Ōsaka, 1985), pp. 38–39, trans. for the author by Ibuki Yuka.

391 **Whether it was rice:** Smith, *Prisoner of Emperor*, p. 103.

392 **On April 12, 1945:** Harris, Mitchell, and Schecter, *Home Front*, p. 206.

392 **The news of:** Lane, *Summer*, p. 5:9.

392 **"THE WAR IN":** Lingeman, *Don't You Know*, p. 354.

393 **The Combined Chiefs:** James, *Years of MacArthur*, p. 2:521.

393 **At the Anglo-American:** ibid., p. 2:711.

393 **In April 1945:** ibid., pp. 2:724–26.

393 **Nimitz was assigned:** Spector, *Eagle Against Sun*, p. 542.

393 **GHQ/AFPAC would be:** Eiji Takemae, *Inside GHQ: The Allied Occupation of Japan and Its Legacy*, trans. Robert Ricketts and Sebastian Swann (New York: Continuum, 2002), p. xxvii.

393 **MacArthur's plan:** ibid., pp. 37–38.

393 **Olympic called for:** Frank, *Downfall*, p. 136.

393 **The Allies had crushing:** ibid., p. 200.

393 **Decisive Battle:** ibid., p. 188.

393 **People's Volunteer Corps:** Takemae, *Inside GHQ*, pp. 38–39.

393 **"Spirit of Three Million Spears":** Havens, *Valley of Darkness*, pp. 189–90.

395 **Private Allen Beauchamp:** Bookman, "In the Matter of Inadequate Medical Supplies," p. 3.

395 **Shunya remembered Ōhashi:** Miyazaki Shunya, author interview, July 16, 2002, Takarazuka, Japan.

395 **Japan was resolved:** Smith, *Prisoner of Emperor*, p. 105.

395 **"The Japanese people must":** quoted in Hoito Edoin, *The Night Tokyo Burned: The Incendiary Campaign Against Japan, March–August 1945* (New York: St. Martin's, 1987), p. 171.

395 **The B-29 precision attack on:** USSBS, "Effects of Air Attack On Osaka-Kobe-Kyoto," p. 159.

397 **In May 1945 the XXI Bomber Command:** Don. R. Thurow, author interview, May 17, 2003, Charlotte, N.C.

397 **"Japanese Citizens!":** "The Living Hell After a Bombardment," Leaflet No. 2047, trans. for the author by John Junkerman.

397 **Allied POWs in Japan:** Dean narrative, p. 354.

397 **"Now, if you are taken":** quoted in Caidin, *Torch to Enemy*, p. 80.

398 **They were instructed:** Nishida, *Storied Cities*, p. 210.

398 **"And it was a":** Leslie Hodson, author interview, April 4, 2003.

398 **On June 1, 1945:** Craven and Cate, *Army Air Forces*, p. 640.

398 **An escort of P-51 fighters:** Kerr, *Flames over Tokyo*, p. 258.

398 **The curtain of smoke:** Craven and Cate, *Army Air Forces*, p. 641.

398 **Ōsaka No. l:** Philip Earl Sanders, testimony, May 1, 1946, RG 331, Box 994, NARA.

398 **According to Sawamura Masatoshi:** Sawamura Masatoshi, interview by Tsujikawa Atushi, Utsumi Aiko, and Fukubayashi Tōru, December 7, 1997, and January 25, 1998, trans. for the author by Ibuki Yuka.

398 **"It was very obvious":** Dr. David Hochman, *Diary*, June 1, 1945, entry, courtesy David Hochman.

399 **Within thirty minutes:** Hoeffer, "Hard Way Back," p. 20.

399 **Most of the men:** Sanders testimony, p. 3.

399 **The camp galley:** Hoeffer, "Hard Way Back," p. 20.

399 **The colonel's daughter:** Inouye Kiyoko, author interview, July 12, 2002, Kyōto, Japan.

399 **Some 500 men:** Hoeffer, "Hard Way Back," p. 20.

399 **Camp conditions were:** ibid.

400 **"Under the present situation":** Document No. 2701, certified as Exhibit O in Doc. No. 2687, from "Journal of the Taiwan POW Camp HQ in Taihoku," entry August 1, 1944, RG 238, Box 2015, NARA.

400 **On December 13, 1937:** Chang, *Rape of Nanking*, p. 41.

400 **In December 1944:** Kerr, *Surrender and Survival*, pp. 212–14. See also Sides, *Ghost Soldiers*, pp. 7–12.

401 **"Army Secret No. 2257":** quoted in Brackman, *Other Nuremberg*, p. 265.

401 **Hochman couldn't believe:** Dr. David Hochman, author interview, January 22, 2002, New York City.

401 **"Due to the nationwide food shortage":** Ienaga, *Pacific War*, p. 182.

401 **On June 5:** "Headquarters XXI Bomber Commmand APO 234, Report of Attack on Kobe on June 5, 1945," p. 1, MR #A 7095, AFHRC.

401 **Flying at a ground speed:** ibid., p. 2.

401 **The air raid alarms:** A. Ray Brashear, "Crisis over Kobe," in Marshall, Silvester, and Stallings, *Global Twentieth*, pp. 3:131–32.

403 **Ten 500-pound cluster:** XXI Bomber Command, "Tactical Mission Report," Mission No. 188, June 5, 1945, pp. 1–2, APO 234, MR #B0108, AFHRC. See also Ferdinand V. Berley's contemporaneous handwritten account, "Disposition of American Staff During Kobe POW Hosp. Fire, June 5, 1945."

403 **"a blinding flash":** Smith, *Prisoner of Emperor*, p. 114.

403 **A fallen beam:** Dean narrative, p. 356.

403 **"When we had been":** Lane, *Summer*, p. 5:9.

403 **Kōbe House was obliterated:** Wigmore, *Thrust*, pp. 624–25.

403 **A friend of Ferid Kilki:** Ferid Kilki, author interview, July 14, 2002, Kōbe, Japan.

404 **Their efforts were mostly:** Irvin, "Wartime Reminiscences," p. 7.

404 **From Kasugano Avenue:** Kiyoko

Tomonaga, "Running Away on the Elevated Road," Kōbe Municipal Archives, trans. for the author by Ibuki Yuka.

404 **Araki Kiyoshi threw:** Araki Kiyoshi, interview by Ishii Shinpei, March 17, 2002, Kōbe, Japan, trans. for the author by John Junkerman.

404 **But over on Mt. Nunobiki:** Shiun, "The Torn Talisman on My Chest," Kōbe Municipal Archives, Kōbe, Japan.

405 **By late afternoon:** Berley, "Kobe POW Hosp. Fire."

405 **In less than an hour:** Coox, "Strategic Bombing," p. 339.

405 **Between 150 and 160 Japanese interceptors:** Katchadoor Kapeghian, author interview, May 17, 2003, Charlotte, N.C.

405 **In all, nine B-29s:** Craven and Cate, *Army Air Forces*, p. 641.

405 **Since the bombing:** USSBS, "Effects of Air Attack on Osaka-Kobe-Kyoto," p. 157.

405 **The largest urban area:** ibid., p. 159.

Chapter 24: Darkness Before Dawn

407 **Fred and John remained behind:** Bookman, "In the Matter of Inadequate Means of Transportation," p. 2.

407 **Seventeen of them:** Ferdinand V. Berley, interview by Jan K. Herman, p. 41.

408 **Fred pleaded with Ōhashi:** ibid.

408 **In the middle of:** Richard Bolster, "Rice Is Life," *Hospital Corps Quarterly* 20 (April–June 1947), pp. 3–6.

409 **Later that day:** Craven and Cate, *Army Air Forces*, pp. 641–42.

409 **Also known as Kawasaki:** Lane, *Summer*, p. 5:10.

409 **Two million residents:** Caidin, *Torch to Enemy*, p. 157.

409 **In Phase 2:** ibid.

409 **Ten more patients:** Bookman, "In the Matter of Inadequate Means of Transportation," p. 2.

410 **"The day is near":** Hoyt, *Japan's War*, p. 403.

410 **On June 19:** William McGaffin, "Captives Raise Flag in Osaka, Kobe," *Chicago Daily News*, September 7, 1945, p. 2.

411 **The camp was plagued:** *Investigation of Prisoner of War Camp Kawasaki Maruyama*, January 22, 1946, GHQ/SCAP Records, Investigation Division Report No. 166, January 1946–June 1948, RG 331, Box 1767, Folder 18, NARA.

411 **fleas sucked the blood:** Dr. Julien Goodman quoted in Waterford, *Prisoners of Japanese*, p. 204.

411 **When the doctors:** See W. S. Baer, "The Treatment of Chronic Osteomyelitis with the Maggot Larvae of the Blowfly," *Journal of Bone and Joint Surgery* 13 (1931), p. 438.

411 **The larvae of blowflies:** Ferdinand V. Berley, report, March 19, 1946, p. 9.

411 **By the summer of:** USSBS, *Summary Report Pacific War*, p. 20.

411 **By then, the government:** Johnston, *Japanese Food Management*, p. 164.

411 **Nearly a quarter:** Frank, *Downfall*, p. 351.

411 **Civilians were told:** Havens, *Valley of Darkness*, p. 129.

411 **Elsewhere in Japan:** Fukubayashi Toru, author interview, July 2002, Kyōto, Japan.

412 **POWs received 70 grams:** Bookman, "In the Matter of Inadequate Medical Supplies," p. 3.

412 **In Western Europe:** Keys et al., *Biology*, p. 1:xv.

412 **Undernourished since MacArthur:** Beecher, "Experiences," p. 9.

412 **A loss of 25 to 30 percent:** Keys et al., *Biology*, p. 1:106.

412 **Most human beings:** ibid., 1:18.

412 **Starvation lowers blood pressure:** See Keys et al., *Biology*, pp. 1:130–31, 138, 142, 170–71, 187–89; pp. 2:447, 665, 676, 691,693 695, 703, 706–7, 758, 762.

412 **The POWs grew anxious:** Norman Q. Brill, "Neuropsychiatric Examination of Military Personnel Recovered from Japanese Prison Camps," *Bulletin of the U.S. Army Medical Department*, April 1946, pp. 431–32.

413 **"A beautiful rosebush":** Bolster, "Rice Is Life," pp. 3–6.

414 **"I remember musing":** ibid.

414 **They were caught, tried:** Page, "Report on Period Served," pp. 5–6.

414 **Operation Iceberg succeeded:** Keegan, *Encyclopedia*, p. 190.

415 **The mighty *Yamato*:** Baldwin, *Battles Lost and Won*, p. 380.

415 **As many as:** Frank, *Downfall*, p. 188

415 **1,105 high school boys:** Mainichi Newspapers, *Fifty Years of Light and Dark*, p. 162.

415 **An unprecedented 11,000:** Frank B.

Gibney, epilogue, in Yahara, *Battle for Okinawa*, p. 199.

415 **"If Okinawa is lost":** ibid., p. 191.

415 **The Potsdam Declaration:** Quoted in David J. Lu, *Japan: A Documentary History*, vol. 2, *The Late Tokugawa Period to the Present* (Armonk, N.Y.: M. E. Sharpe, 1977), pp. 453–55.

415 **MacArthur was never:** James, *Years of MacArthur*, p. 2:775.

416 **The response of:** Brackman, *Other Nuremberg*, p. 34.

416 **They were resolved to:** ibid., p. 35.

416 **At a July 29 press:** Pacific War Research Society, *Japan's Longest Day* (New York: Kodansha International, 1980), pp. 16–17.

416 **His ominous ambiguity:** Mainichi Newspapers, *Fifty Years of Light and Dark*, p. 182.

416 **General Anami had:** Kase, *Journey*, p. 195.

416 **The Imperial Japanese Army's:** ibid.

416 **Army Chief of Staff:** Douglas J. MacEachin, "The Final Months of the War with Japan: Signals Intelligence, U.S. Invasion Planning, and the A-Bomb Decision," Center for the Study of Intelligence, Central Intelligence Agency, December 1998, p. 21.

416 **In southern Kyūshū:** Giangreco, "Operation DOWNFALL," p. 2.

416 **Marshall had originally projected:** MacEachin, "Final Months of the War with Japan," p. 15.

416 **By August 2:** ibid., p. 17.

416 **revised to 549,000:** ibid., p. 20.

416 **In actuality:** Drea, *MacArthur's ULTRA*, p. 222.

416 **The final estimate:** According to Richard Frank, on August 10, 1945, the Joint Intelligence Committee projected a combined force of 2.6 million men in defense of the Japanese Home Islands by October 15, 1945. See Frank, *Downfall*, p. 203.

416 **In spite of upwardly:** MacEachin, "Final Months of the War with Japan," p. 15.

416 **"at a minimum":** David McCullough, *Truman* (New York: Simon and Schuster, 1992), p. 437.

417 **This was nearly:** Frank, *Downfall*, p. 194.

417 **But before the wording:** MacEachin, "Final Months of the War with Japan," pp. 23–24.

417 **On August 8, 1945:** Mainichi Newspapers, *Fifty Years of Light and Dark*, p. 163.

417 **"A little after 8 a.m.":** *Asahi Shimbun*, August 8, 1945, trans. for the author by John Junkerman.

418 **"A small number of":** quoted in Mainichi Newspapers, *Fifty Years of Light and Dark*, pp. 163–64.

418 **What neither newspaper:** Dear and Foot, *Oxford Companion*, p. 531.

418 **Less than twenty-four:** quoted in Mainichi Newspapers, *Fifty Years of Light and Dark*, pp. 164–65.

418 **In Tōkyō, Foreign Minister:** Bix, *Hirohito*, pp. 503–4.

418 **"more pressing business":** Pacific War Research Society, *Japan's Longest Day*, p. 22.

418 **"a rain of ruin":** McCullough, *Truman*, p. 455.

419 **MacArthur, who like:** James, *Years of MacArthur*, p. 2:775.

419 **"the Soviet government":** McCullough, *Truman*, p. 22.

419 **"Does one feel":** William L. Laurence, "Atomic Bombing of Nagasaki Told by Flight Member," *New York Times*, September 9, 1945, in Douglas Brinkley, ed., *World War II: The Allied Counteroffensive, 1942–1945* (New York: Times Books, 2003), p. 380.

419 **73,884 people perished:** Dear and Foot, *Oxford Companion*, p. 773.

419 **Laurence watched an:** Laurence, "Atomic Bombing," p. 381.

419 **"Having found the bomb":** quoted in Bix, *Hirohito*, p. 502.

419 **Prime Minister Suzuki:** Pacific War Research Society, *Japan's Longest Day*, p. 25.

419 **The conference was deadlocked:** Kase, *Journey*, p. 233.

419 **"Gentlemen, we have spent":** quoted in ibid., p. 234.

420 **"sacred decision":** Bix, *Hirohito*, pp. 514–15.

420 **"That it is unbearable":** Pacific War Research Society, *Japan's Longest Day*, p. 34.

420 **"with the understanding":** ibid., p. 37.

420 **Immediately upon the surrender:** ibid., p. 241.

420 **In the meantime:** Horatio W. Turner III, "Last Mission—Air Offensive Japan," in Marshall, *Final Assault*, pp. 203–4.

420 **Between August 11 and August 14:** Takemae, *Inside GHQ*, p. 46.

420 **Tōkyō would be:** Jim B. Smith and Malcolm McConnell, *The Last Mission: The Secret Story of World War II's Final Battle* (New York: Broadway Books, 2002), p. 286.

420 **"If we do not terminate":** Kase, *Journey*, pp. 252–53.

421 **"The Emperor was in":** ibid., p. 253.

421 **"After pondering deeply":** Lu, *Japan*, pp. 2:457–58.

421 **The speech presented:** Bix, *Hirohito*, p. 527.

421 **Hirohito expressed neither:** ibid., p. 526.

421 **Nearly three million:** John W. Dower, *Embracing Defeat* (New York: W. W. Norton/New Press, 1999), p. 37.

422 **"We are keenly aware":** quoted in Lu, *Japan*, pp. 2:457–58.

422 **Hirohito's words were:** Bix, *Hirohito*, p. 527.

422 **"We ourselves invited":** quoted in ibid., pp. 527–28.

422 **Few realized that:** See Pacific War Research Society, *Japan's Longest Day*, and Smith and McConnell, *Last Mission*.

423 **"For you—I have good news":** Smith, *Prisoner of Emperor*, p. 118.

423 **The Britishers quickly:** "Preliminary Report No. 4," p. 2, G 3/51, M. Junod, Japón, Box 219 [I], ACICR.

424 **"His Majesty the Emperor":** Kase, *Journey*, p. 258.

424 **Truman received the message:** Arthur Krock, "Japan Surrenders, End of War! Emperor Accepts Allied Rule; M'Arthur Supreme Commander," *New York Times*, August 15, 1945, in Brinkley, *Final Counteroffensive*, p. 386.

424 **After a hastily called:** McCullough, *Truman*, pp. 461–62.

424 **"This is a great day":** Frederick R. Barkley, "President Joins Capital's Gaiety," *New York Times*, August 15, 1945, p. 4.

424 **In Manhattan:** Alexander Feinberg, "All City 'Lets Go,' " *New York Times*, August 15, 1945, p. 1.

424 **Five thousand tons of streamers:** Lingeman, *Don't You Know*, p. 355.

424 **"World War II became":** "World News Summarized," *New York Times*, August 15, 1945, p. 1.

425 **On August 17:** quoted in Bix, *Hirohito*, p. 530.

425 **"personnel who mistreated":** Document No. 2697, certified as Exhibit J in Doc. No. 2687 and referred to as Exhibit J in the affidavit of James Thomas Nehemiah

Cross, September 19, 1946, RG 238, Box 2011, NARA, at www.mansell.com/pow_resources/Formosa/Ex-J-txt.html, courtesy Roger Mansell.

425 **"unnecessary brutality and beatings"**: Page, "Report on Period Served," p. 6.

426 **Murata apologized:** ibid., p. 4.

426 **"The sound of orders in English":** Lane, *Summer*, p. 1:1.

426 **Murata, who was technically:** Akeroyd statement, NARA, p. 2; Thomas Rhodes, notes, September 7, 1945, Red Cross Hospital, Ōsaka.

426 **Murata, who denied:** *U.S.A. vs. Sotaro Murata*, Headquarters Eighth Army, U.S. Army, Office of the Staff Judge Advocate. Case #155, February 16, 1949, Yokohama.

426 **"regrettable occurrences":** "Preliminary Report No. 2: Evacuation: Chubugun District," G 3/51, M. Junod, Japón, Box 219 [I], ACICR.

427 **Then he demanded:** Page, "Report on Period Served," p. 6.

427 **The "blueprint" for:** Takemae, *Inside GHQ*, p. 39.

427 **Per his instructions:** James, *Years of MacArthur*, p. 2:778.

427 **The purpose of:** Takemae, *Inside GHQ*, p. 52.

428 **Beneath Atsugi was:** Arthur Veysey, "Find *Kamikaze* Workshops in Atsugi Tunnels," *Chicago Daily Tribune*, September 8, 1945, p. 5

428 **Prior to the surrender:** Marcel Junod, *Warrior Without Weapons* (London: Jonathan Cape, 1951), p. 277.

428 **On the basis:** Papers of HQ, United States Armed Forces Pacific Area Command, RG 4, Box 23, Folder 6, MMA.

428 **Locating the camps was:** James, *Years of MacArthur*, p. 2:778.

428 **"Mercy teams" organized:** Robert L. Eichelberger, *Our Jungle Road to Tokyo* (New York: Viking Press, 1950), pp. 265–66.

428 **evacuation of 200 to 250 POWs:** John Plath Green, interview by Ronald E. Marcello, February 6 and March 1, 1974, p. 141, #182, UNTOHC.

428 **Operation Blacklist:** ibid., p. 116.

428 **He wanted to get:** Junod, *Warrior*, p. 277.

429 **E. H. Brunner was:** "Delegates for Repatriation of Prisoners of War and Civilian Internees," Archives générales, 1918–1950, Groupe G (Généralités: affaires opérationelles), 1939–1950, G 3/51, M. Junod, Japón, Box 219 [1], ACICR.

429 **While the Japanese:** ibid., p. 278.

429 **"we saw papers":** "Notes on a Talk Given by Dr. Marcel Junod," p. 4.

429 **"You are instructed":** Brackman, *Other Nuremberg*, p. 40.

429 **POWs waved their arms:** Walter C. Epstein, "P.O.W. Flights," in Marshall, *Final Assault*, p. 212.

430 **The wastage ratio:** Ward W. Conquest, "Air Drops to Prisoners of War," September 2, 1945; G 3/51, M. Junod, Japón, Box 219 [I], ACICR.

Chapter 25: Mission of Mercy

431 **Imperial Japanese forces numbered:** Willoughby and Chamberlain, *MacArthur*, pp. 309–10.

432 **In spite of the B-29:** William McGaffin, "Writer Roves Japan, Safe as at Home," *Chicago Daily News*, September 10, 1945, p. 2.

432 **The city had been zoned:** Smith, *Prisoner of Emperor*, p. 120.

432 **"You are POWs?":** This dialogue is quoted from ibid. Courtesy Duane A. Smith.

433 **"impressively beautiful":** McGaffin, "Writer Roves Japan," p. 2.

433 **But its cities were:** Dower, *Embracing Defeat*, p. 47.

433 **The only Westerners:** McGaffin, "Writer Roves Japan," p. 2.

434 **Tōkyō's population had shrunk:** James, *Years of MacArthur*, p. 3:5.

434 **One in ten residents:** Seidensticker, *Tokyo Rising*, pp. 139–44.

434 **There were no:** "Notes on a Talk Given by Dr. Marcel Junod," p. 4.

434 **The first American:** Morison, *History of Naval Operations*, p. 14:360.

434 **"By disemboweling myself":** quoted in Brackman, *Other Nuremberg*, p. 43.

434 **"government of resistance":** Eiji, *Inside GHQ*, p. 56.

434 **On August 24,:** Smith and McConnell, *Last Mission*, pp. 266–67.

434 **By month's end:** Brackman, *Other Nuremberg*, p. 44.

434 **Hirohito's emissaries succeeded:** Takemae, *Inside GHQ*, p. 56.

434 **"Defeat and unconditional surrender":** Yoshio Kodama, *I Was Defeated* (Robert Booth and Taro Fukuda Publishers, Japan, 1951), p. 181; see also Sterling Seagrave and Peggy Seagrave, *Gold Warriors: America's Secret Recovery of Yamashita's Gold* (London

and New York: Verso Books, 2003), pp. 113–15, on Kodama's postwar relationship with Willoughby and the CIA.

435 **On August 19:** Dower, *Embracing Defeat*, pp. 124–25.

435 **"to hold back":** quoted in Bix, *Hirohito*, p. 538.

435 **Interim prime minister:** ibid., pp. 539–40.

435 **In Manchuria:** Daws, *Prisoners*, p. 336.

435 **At Fukuoka, guards:** ibid., p. 42.

435 **In North Borneo:** De Jong, *Collapse*, p. 292.

435 **In Ōsaka:** GHQ/SCAP Records, "Ikoma Shiuchi, Tomekichi Hamada et al., Osaka Kempei Tai," p. 10, Investigation Division Reports No. 479, April 22, 1947.

435 **"We still had the spirit":** Hideo Fujioka, testimony, April 18, 1946, p. 3, RG 331, Box 994, OS-152, NARA.

435 **The Americans asked:** See *The Imperial: The First Hundred Years* (Tōkyō: privately published, 1990), pp. 163–64.

436 **The hotel was preparing to:** ibid., p. 169.

437 **"Didn't people throw":** Smith, *Prisoner of Emperor*, p. 125.

437 **Soon they were served:** ibid.

438 **The Kempeitai were:** Lord Russell of Liverpool, *Knights of Bushido*, pp. 274–75.

438 **There were more:** Philip Jowett, *The Japanese Army 1931–45* (Oxford, England: Osprey, 2002), p. 16.

438 **They stood guard:** Overy, *Why the Allies*, p. 300.

438 **They trafficked in:** Jowett, *The Japanese Army*, p. 16.

438 **They had power:** ibid.

438 **Doolittle's raiders were imprisoned:** "Doolittle's Tokyo Raid: The Eight Who Were Captured," United States Air Force Museum, http://www.wpafb.af.mil/museum/history/wwii/cp6.htm

438 **"Who knows you're here?":** Smith, *Prisoner of Emperor*, p. 126.

440 **He would also reassure:** ibid., p. 128.

440 **Bernath then rounded:** ibid., p. 127.

440 **To secure the Yokosuka:** Takemae, *Inside GHQ*, p. 55.

440 **"He hesitated a moment":** Thomas T. Sakamoto, quoted in ibid., p. 54.

441 **Eichelberger agreed:** Eichelberger, *Our Jungle Road*, p. 262.

441 **Entire divisions of Japanese:** Kase, *Journey*, p. 264.

441 **Many of the principles:** James, *Years of MacArthur*, pp. 3:10–11.

441 **"First destroy the military power":** ibid., p. 3:10.

441 **The New Grand Hotel in:** Takemae, *Inside GHQ*, p. xvii.

441 **no longer ex-POWs:** Daws, *Prisoners*, p. 345.

442 **At a conference aboard:** Joel T. Boone, "Initial Release of Prisoners of War in Japan," p. 2, Joel T. Boone Papers. Courtesy Milton F. Heller, Jr.

442 **The excitement of the prisoners:** ibid., pp. 3-4.

443 **"those that were able":** ibid., p. 5.

443 **The conditions at Shinagawa:** Joel Boone, talk before the American Red Cross, January 16, 1946, p. 4, RG 389, Box 2176, NARA.

443 **"There has never been":** quoted in Robert R. Martindale, *The 13th Mission: The Saga of a POW at Camp Omori, Tokyo* (Austin, Tex.: Eakin Press, 1998), p. 239.

443 **Of the first group:** Boone, Red Cross, p. 8.

443 **"Nobody came out":** ibid., p. 4.

443 **While the navy doctors:** Page, "Report on Period Served," p. 6.

443 **The ICRC hadn't made:** "Preliminary Report No. 7: Evacuation—Chubugun District, Kōbe, August 29, 1945," G 3/51, M. Junod, Japón, Box 219 [l], ACICR.

443 **One canister killed a:** "Preliminary Report No. 12: Evacuation—Chubugun District," G 3/51, M. Junod, Japón, Box 219 [1], ACICR.

444 **Over at Wakinohama:** Lane, *Summer*, p. 2:3.

444 **"What's a juke box?":** William McGaffin, "Freed Captives Find Their New World a Strange Place," *Chicago Daily News*, September 10, 1945, p. 1.

444 **On an overcast Sunday morning:** Morison, *History of Naval Operations*, p. 14:362.

444 **The thirty-one-starred flag:** Takemae, *Inside GHQ*, p. 59.

444 **The canvas and leatherbound:** Morison, *History of Naval Operations*, pp. 14:362–63.

444 **Sailors leaned over railings:** Takemae, *Inside GHQ*, p. 58.

444 **A hush descended:** Homer Bigart, "Japan Signs, Second World War Is Ended Now," *New York Herald Tribune*, September 2,

1945, reprinted in *Reporting World War II* (New York: Library of America, 1995), p. 2:773.

445 **To Kase Toshikazu:** Kase, *Journey*, p. 7.

445 **"The whole scene":** Takemae, *Inside GHQ*, p. 58.

445 **"It is my earnest hope":** quoted in James, *Years of MacArthur*, p. 2:790.

445 **Suddenly the battleship's:** Takemae, *Inside GHQ*, p. 58.

445 **At precisely 9:03 A.M:** United Press dispatch quoted in "War Comes to End," *New York Times*, September 2, 1945, p. 1.

445 **Shigemitsu signed:** Kase, *Journey*, p. 1.

445 **Then MacArthur:** Wainwright, *Story*, p. 280.

445 **In a final salute:** ibid., p. 10.

445 **Then, in what seemed:** Wainwright, *Story*, p. 280.

445 **The *Missouri* had no:** "War Comes to End," *New York Times*, September 2, 1945, p. 1.

445 **"Today the guns are silent":** James, *Years of MacArthur*, p. 2:791.

446 **In the first week:** Takemae, *Inside GHQ*, p. 67.

446 **Outwardly Ōhashi:** Ōhashi Hyōjirō Prison Diary, p.1, trans. for the author by Ishii Shinpei.

446 **"preliminary work":** "Preliminary Report No. 15: Evacuation—Chubugun District," G 3/51, M. Junod, Japón, Box 219 [1], ACICR.

447 **John Plath Green:** Green, interview, pp. 118–26.

447 **Within eighteen days:** Eichelberger, *Our Jungle Road*, p. 266.

447 **Page, Stan Smith, and Murray:** Page, "Report on Period Served," p. 6.

447 **Byrd was in Japan:** Ohio State University Archives, Papers of Admiral Richard E. Byrd, RG 56.1, Folder 4138.

448 **In Yokohama they saw:** Takemae, *Inside GHQ*, p. 57.

448 **The brick and concrete buildings:** Sams, *"Medic,"* pp. 11–17.

448 **The Americans were transferred to:** Dorothy M. Davis, "Processing and Caring for Prisoners of War," *American Journal of Nursing* 46, no. 3 (March 1946), p. 152.

448 **Stan Smith returned to:** Smith, *Prisoner of Emperor*, p.129

448 **6,300 RAMPs alone:** Davis, "Processing and Caring for Prisoners," p. 152.

448 **Once back in San Francisco:** Norman Q. Brill, "Neuropsychiatric Examination of Military Personnel Recovered from Japanese Prison Camps," *Bulletin of U.S. Army Medical Department*, April 1946, p. 429.

Chapter 26: Coming Home

450 **"On the road to Mandalay":** Rudyard Kipling, "Mandalay," in Helen Gardner, ed., *The New Oxford Book of English Verse, 1250–1950* (New York: Oxford University Press, 1972), p. 811.

451 **In the end:** See Morton, *War in the Pacific*, p. 584.

453 **"He was of medium":** Mrs. George Theodore Ferguson to Avery Wilber, July 11, 1945. Courtesy Dale Wilber.

453 **"He was a very":** Donald E. Meyer to Mrs. G. T. Ferguson, August 9, 1945. Courtesy Lucille Ferguson.

453 **"I have not given up":** Ferdinand V. Berley to Lucille Ferguson, October 18, 1945. Courtesy Lucille Ferguson.

454 **Of the fourteen navy:** Barrett, *Casus Belli*, p. 166.

454 **Of the 277 Navy Medical Department:** Stamp, *Journey*, p. 131.

454 **On the afternoon of:** Daws, *Prisoners*, p. 293.

455 **General Kou Shiyoku:** Beecher, "Experiences," p. 141.

455 **First Lieutenant Toshino Junsaburō:** Kerr, *Surrender and Survival*, p. 218.

455 **carrier planes:** Cecil J. Peart, *Journal: Bilibid Prison to Manchukuo*, p. 2, RG 389, Box 2177, NARA.

455 **"the most horrible period":** Beecher, "Experiences," p. 140.

455 **The hatches were closed:** George Weller, "U.S. Prisoners Smothered in Hold of Jap Prison Ship," from "Cruise of Death," a fourteen-part series in the *St. Louis Post-Dispatch*, beginning November 11, 1945.

455 **They slit their own veins:** Weller, "Heroes of Bataan Battle for Lives," ibid.

455 **"even those who had":** Beecher, "Experiences," pp. 140–41.

455 **The steering gear:** Weller, "Yanks Machine-Gunned from Jap Prison Ship," from "Cruise of Death."

455 **Jack Schwartz couldn't:** Lawton, *Some Survived*, p. 166.

455 **One U.S. Navy pilot strafed six:** Weller, "Death Ship Goes Aground," from "Cruise of Death."

455 **Another waggled his wings:** Weller, "Yanks Machine-Gunned."

456 **The 1,333 prisoners who:** Wright, *Captured*, p. 96.

456 **Raw from sunburn:** Peart, *Journal*, p. 4

456 **Hayes and Cecil Welch worked:** Lawton, *Some Survived*, p. 173.

456 **The fifteen sickest men:** J. V. Crews and R. J. Hostetter, "Prisoners' Voyage of Doom," *Hospital Corps Quarterly* 20–21, (1947–48), p. 34.

456 **"How shall I":** Lawton, *Some Survived*, p. 6

456 **Once in San Fernando:** *U.S.A. vs. Junsaburo Toshino, Shusuke Wada, Kazutane Aihara, Shin Kajiyama, Suketoshi Tanou, Jiro Ueda, Hisao Yoshida*, February 25, 1947, SCAP File No. 014.13, Public Relations Informational Summary No. 510.

456 **On January 9:** Stamp, *Journey*, p. 93.

456 **"The carnage":** Wright, *Captured*, p. 123.

456 **"I felt that . . . we":** Stamp, *Journey*, p. 95.

456 **The survivors were transferred:** See Michno, *Hellships*, pp. 258–64.

456 **Of the 1,619 POWs who:** ibid., pp. 316–17.

456 **Roughly half:** Cowdrey, *Fighting for Life*, p. 18.

457 **"Group Four":** Henry G. Lee, "Group Four," in Chunn, *Of Rice and Men*, pp. 219–20. See also *Quan* 59, no. 2 (August 2004), pp. 8–9.

458 **On the scale of:** Brackman, *Other Nuremberg*, p. 253.

458 **According to one:** Waterford, *Prisoners of Japanese*, p. 146.

458 **E. M. Gonie and Louis Indorf:** See Daws, *Prisoners*, p. 384.

458 **Unlike the prison doctors:** Lifton, *Nazi Doctors*, pp. 214ff.

460 **Symptoms of the disorder:** This short history is based on "Post-Traumatic Stress Disorder: Evolution of a Diagnosis," *New York Times*, November 20, 2001.

460–61 **Kardiner described five:** ibid.

461 **"The real drawback":** Abram Kardiner and Herbert Spiegel, *War Stress and Neurotic Illness* (New York: Paul B. Hoeber, 1947), p. 5.

463 **there is a growing body of research:** see Christina Hoff Sommers, "The Republic of Feelings," American Enterprise Institute for Public Policy Research, posted January 1,

2001, www.aei.org/publications/pubID.12381/pub_detail.asp, p. 2.

463 **"one of the soul's":** Viktor E. Frankl, *Man's Search for Meaning: An Introduction to Logotherapy*, trans. Ilse Lasch (New York: Touchstone, 1984).

464 **Peggy and Sterling Seagrave:** Seagrave and Seagrave, *Gold Warriors*, pp. 3, 6.

464 **In November 2003:** Edward Jackfer, "Court Rules Against POW Lawsuits," *Quan* 58, no. 4 (February 2004), pp. 3–4.

464 **But of course:** Kerr, *Surrender and Survival*, pp. 296–97.

464 **Fifty years after:** Daws, *Prisoners*, p. 390.

464 **According to the late Iris:** Chang, *Rape of Nanking*, p. 12.

464 **Germany, which:** Clyde Haberman, "Putting Price on Holocaust? Not Even Close," *New York Times*, August 3, 2004, sec. B, p. 1.

465 **I am convinced:** See Frank, *Downfall*, p. 163.

465 **"My God, what have we done?":** Gordon Thomas and Max Morgan Witts, *Enola Gay* (New York: Stein and Day, 1977), pp. 264–65.

465 **German U-boats targeted:** ibid., pp. 88–89.

466 **Germany's blitz of Britain's cities:** ibid., p. 110.

466 **The RAF retaliated:** "Nazis See Battle As Fight to Finish," *New York Times*, September 11, 1940, p. 1.

466 **Before World War II:** Quoted in Spector, *Eagle Against Sun*, p. 487.

466 **The firebombing of:** Craven and Cate, *Army Air Forces*, p. 617.

466 **According to Martin Caidin:** Caidin, *Torch to Enemy*, p. 158.

466 **"clinched victory":** Overy, *Why the Allies*, p. 129.

466 **"precipitated everywhere":** Peter Calvocoressi and Guy Wint, *Total War: The Story of World War II* (New York: Pantheon Books, 1972), p. 881.

466 **Between 34 and 37 percent:** Condon-Rall and Cowdrey, p. 383.

466 **The mortality rate:** J. Segal, E. J. Hunter, and Z. Segal, "Universal Consequences of Captivity: Stress Reactions Among Divergent Populations of Prisoners of War and Their Families," *International Social Science Journal* 28, no. 3 (1976), p. 594.

466 **By contrast, the:** Calvocoressi and Wint, *Total War*, p. 881.

466 **But the picture:** Michno, *Hellships*, p. 292.

466 **A staggering 19,000:** ibid.

466 **Those who survived:** B. M. Cohen and M. Z. Cooper, "A Follow-up Study of World War II Prisoners of War," *VA Medical Monograph* (September), cited in Segal, Hunter, and Segal, "Universal Consequences," p. 597.

467 **Three and a half years in:** Daws, *Prisoners*, p. 388.

467 **Veterans Administration:** ibid., p. 385.

467 **One study found:** Chang-Zern Hong, M.D., "Peripheral Neuropathy in Former Prisoners of War," *Quan* 41, no. 5 (April 1987).

467 **psychiatric problems:** William Frank Page, *The Health of Former Prisoners of War: Results from the Medical Examination Survey of Former POWs of World War II and the Korean Conflict* (Washington, D.C.: National Academy Press, 1992), p. 98.

467 **John Nardini, who:** Dr. John Nardini, interview by Gavin Daws, September 22, 1984, tape 2, side 2, Gavin Daws Papers, MHI.

467 **According to one VA:** S. Oboler, "American Prisoners of War—An Overview," in T. Williams, ed., *Post-Traumatic Stress Disorders: A Handbook for Clinicians*, cited in Page, *Health of Former Prisoners*, p. 99.

467 **Depression was three:** ibid.

467 **"fulfilled the criteria":** P. B. Sutker, A. N. Allain, Jr., and D. K. Winstead, "Psychological and Psychiatric Diagnoses of World War II Pacific Theater Prisoner of War Survivors and Combat Veterans," *American Journal of Psychiatry* 150, no. 2 (February 1993), pp. 240–45.

467 **the psychiatric disorders:** Page, *Health of Former Prisoners*, p. 102.

467 **In many cases:** Cynthia Lindman Port, Brian Engdahl, and Patricia Frazier, "A Longitudinal and Retrospective Study of PTSD Among Older Prisoners of War," *American Journal of Psychiatry* 158 (September 2001), 1474–79.

468 **"a heavy heart":** Ōhashi Hyōjirō to Ferdinand V. Berley, n.d. (late 1946–early 1947).

468 **"I wish we were":** John Hersey, *Into the Valley*, quoted in Kennedy, *Freedom from Fear*, p. 561.

468 **Indeed, Japan's language:** John W. Dower, *Japan in War and Peace* (New York: New Press, 1993), p. 9.

468 **The Germans slaughtered:** Chalmers Johnson, "The Looting of Asia," *London Review of Books* 25, no. 22 (November 20, 2003), p. 3.

469 **But in the larger context:** Chris Hedges, *War Is a Force That Gives Us Meaning* (New York: Public Affairs, 1992), p. 13.

469 **to take no captives:** Bix, *Hirohito*, pp. 333, 360.

469 **"in order to do good":** See *The Fog of War*, directed by Errol Morris (Columbia TriStar, 2004).

469 **The Turkish government:** Hedges, *War Is a Force*, p. 127.

469 **Croatian strongman:** ibid., p. 70.

469 **Japanese nationalists:** quoted in Ian Buruma, *The Wages of Guilt: Memories of War in Germany and Japan* (New York: Farrar, Straus and Giroux, 1994), p. 122.

469 **Historical grievances may:** Vamik Volkan, *Blood Lines: From Ethnic Pride to Ethnic Terrorism* (New York: Farrar, Straus and Giroux, 1997), pp. 48–49.

470 **Chinese soccer fans:** Jim Yardley, "In Soccer Loss, a Glimpse of China's Rising Ire at Japan," *New York Times*, August 9, 2004, p. A3.

470 **Transgenerational trauma:** Hedges, *War Is a Force*, p. 72.

470 **"second generation":** Eva Hoffman, *After Such Knowledge: Memory, History, and the Legacy of the Holocaust* (New York: Public Affairs, 2004).

470 **"Play the greater game":** George L. Mosse, *Fallen Soldiers: Reshaping the Memory of the World Wars* (New York: Oxford University Press, 1990), p. 61.

470 **"They seemed to lose":** Brill, "Neuropsychiatric Examination of Military Personnel," p. 432.

471 **Ask a Japanese veteran:** Arakawa Tatsuzō, interview by Ishii Shinpei, March 19, 2002, Kyōto, Japan, trans. for the author by John Junkerman.

471 **Hosokawa Morihiro:** Buruma, *Wages of Guilt*, pp. 297–98.

471 **Less than a decade:** Herbert P. Bix, "Japan's New Nationalism," in *New York Times*, May 29, 2001.

471 **visits Yasukuni Shrine:** Stephanie Strom, "Japan's Premier Visits War Shrine,

Pleasing Few," *New York Times*, August 14, 2001.

472 **There has been no:** Buruma, *Wages of Guilt*, p. 243.

472 **The Rape of Nanking:** I am indebted to Fukubayashi Toru, a teacher at Kyōto Municipal High School and a founding member of the POW Research Network, for his research in this area.

472 **The story of Allied POWs:** Daws, *Prisoners*, pp. 24–25.

472 **Is this the difference:** Buruma, *Wages of Guilt*, p. 10.

473 **Hadn't he received:** *U.S.A. vs. Sotaro Murata*, Headquarters Eighth Army, U.S. Army, Office of the Staff Judge Advocate, Case #155, Yokohama, February 16, 1949, p. 20.

473 **She speaks in a voice:** Inoue Kiyoko, author interview, July 12, 2002, Kyōto, Japan.

473 **Masako adds her own:** Nakato Masako and Tsuji Hideko, author interview, July 10, 2002, Kōbe, Japan.

473 **When I finally meet:** Ōhashi Yoshihisa, author interview, Takarazuka City, Japan, July 13, 2002.

474 **It is a commonplace:** Jacobs, *Blood Brothers*, p. 7.

Epilogue

477 **Article 10 of the Potsdam:** Lu, *Japan*, p. 2:454.

477 **On January 19, 1946:** Dear and Foot, *Oxford Companion*, p. 347.

478 **The defendants were:** Brackman, *Other Nuremberg*, p. 46.

478 **Class B for:** ibid.

478 **and Class C:** John L. Ginn, *Sugamo Prison, Tokyo: An Account of the Trial and Sentencing of Japanese War Criminals in 1948 by a U.S. Participant* (Jefferson, N.C.: McFarland, 1992), p. 57.

478 **The emperor's role:** James, *Years of MacArthur*, p. 3:105.

478 **"Destroy him":** ibid., p. 3:106.

478 **The Joint Chiefs of Staff:** Bix, *Hirohito*, p. 617.

478 **Japan's biological weapons:** Brackman, *Other Nuremberg*, p. 200.

478 **into Communist hands:** Tien-wei Wu, "A Preliminary Review of Studies of Japanese Biological Warfare Unit 731 in the United States" (www.aiipowmia.com/731/7311study.html), p. 7.

478 **"In this very courtroom":** quoted in Richard H. Minear, *Victors' Justice: The Tokyo War Crimes Trial* (Princeton, N.J.: Princeton University Press, 1971), p. 74.

478 **Twenty-eight of Japan's:** Brackman, *Other Nuremberg*, p. 377.

478 **Some 5,100 Japanese:** James, *Years of MacArthur*, p. 3:102.

478 **"if we'd lost the war":** LeMay quoted in Nancy Ramsey, "Strangely Hopeful in a World of War and Caprice," *New York Times*, December 23, 2003, sec. E, p. 3.

479 **Uchiyama Eitarō:** *U.S.A. vs. Eitaro Uchiyama et al.*, Headquarters Eighth Army, U.S. Army, Office of the Staff Judge Advocate, Case #123, Yokohama, July 2, 1948, pp. 1–9.

479 **His superior, Toshino:** Ginn, *Sugamo*, p. 193.

479 **The charges against:** See the closing report by Miller, report, GHQ/*Arisan Maru*.

479 **His cell was small:** This description is based on an article in the August 1947 issue of *Stars and Stripes Review*, quoted in Ginn, *Sugamo*, pp. 7–9.

479 **A ten-foot-high:** Ginn, *Sugamo*, p. 6.

480 **"The moon is bright":** translation courtesy Peter Miller.

480 **On April 27, 1946:** Ōhashi Hyōjirō, *Diary*, trans. by Ishii Shinpei. Courtesy Ōhashi Yoshihisa.

480 **Ōhashi Hyōjirō was no longer:** GHQ/SCAP "Clarification of Status of Former Suspected War Criminals," RG 338, Far East Command, Sugamo Prison Files, File: Ohashi, Hyojiro, NARA.

480 **Nogi Naraji:** Hibbs, *Tell MacArthur*, p. 187.

480 **"World conditions":** Santo Tomás Internee Committtee memorandum, cited in Hartendorp, *Japanese Occupation*, p. 2:508.

480 **He had authorized the dispatch:** *U.S.A. vs. Naraji Nogi*. See "Statement of Dr. Naraji Nogi, Japanese Army Medical Corps," at www.oryokumaru.com/nogi.htm, p. 1.

480 **Lieutenant Colonel Jack Schwartz:** J. W. Schwartz to Ellis Filene, July 27, 1949.

481 **Nogi's defense attorney:** Lois Taylor, "A Man Who Cared Enough," in *Honolulu Star-Bulletin*, January 6, 1976.

481 **Meanwhile, U.S. Army:** Lisa Asato, "Treason Trial Shadows Ex-Soldier's Life," *Honolulu Star-Bulletin*, October 27, 2001.

481 **By December 1958:** Ginn, *Sugamo*, pp. 12–13.

481 **"Each day:** Konishi Yukio, author interview, July 15, 2002, Higashi, Japan.

SELECTED BIBLIOGRAPHY

Books

Acton, Harold. *Memoirs of an Aesthete*. London: Methuen, 1948.

Aluit, Alfonso J. *Corregedor*. Manila, Philippines: Lucky Press, 2001.

Asahi Shimbun. *The Pacific Rivals: A View of Japanese-American Relations*. New York: Weatherhill/Asahi, 1972.

Bain, David Haward. *Sitting in Darkness: Americans in the Philippines*. Boston: Houghton Mifflin, 1984.

Baldwin, Hanson. *Battles Lost and Won: Great Campaigns of World War II*. New York: Konecky and Konecky, 1966.

Beers, Mark H., M.D., and Robert Berkow, M.D., eds. *The Merck Manual of Diagnosis and Therapy*. Whitehouse Station, N.J.: Merck Research Laboratories, 1999.

Bell, Walter F. *The Philippines in World War II, 1941–1945: A Chronology and Select Annotated Bibliography of Books and Articles in English*. Westport, Conn.: Greenwood Press, 1999.

Belote, James H., and William M. Belote. *Corregidor: The Saga of a Fortress*. New York: Harper and Row, 1967.

Benedict, Ruth. *The Chrysanthemum and the Sword: Patterns of Japanese Culture*. Boston: Houghton Mifflin, 1946.

Bix, Herbert P. *Hirohito and the Making of Modern Japan*. New York: HarperCollins, 2000.

Blair, Clay. *Silent Victory: The U.S. Submarine War Against Japan*. Annapolis, Md.: Naval Institute Press, 1975.

Blair, Joan, and Clay Blair, Jr. *Return from the River Kwai*. New York: Simon and Schuster, 1979.

Bowers, John Z. *Medical Education in Japan: From Chinese Medicine to Western Medicine*. New York: Harper and Row, 1965.

Brackman, Arnold C. *The Other Nuremberg: The Untold Story of the Tokyo War Crimes Trials*. New York: William Morrow, 1987.

Braly, William C. *The Hard Way Home*. Washington, D.C.: Washington Infantry Journal Press, 1947.

Braudy, Leo. *From Chivalry to Terrorism: War and the Changing Nature of Masculinity*. New York: Alfred A. Knopf, 2003.

Breuer, William B. *Sea Wolf: The Daring Exploits of Navy Legend John D. Bulkeley*. Novato, Calif.: Presidio, 1989.

Brinkley, Douglas, ed. *World War II: The Allied Counteroffensive, 1942–1945*. New York: Times Books, 2003.

Budd, Louis J., ed. *Mark Twain: Collected Tales, Sketches, Speeches, and Essays, 1891–1910*. New York: Library of America, 1992.

Buhite, Russell D., and David W. Levy, eds. *FDR's Fireside Chats*. Norman, Okla.: University of Oklahoma Press, 1992.

Bumgarner, John, R. *Parade of the Dead*. Jefferson, N.C.: McFarland, 1995.

Bunker, Paul D. *Bunker's War: The World War II Diary of Col. Paul D. Bunker*. Edited by Keith A. Barlow. Novato, Calif.: Presidio, 1996.

Buruma, Ian. *Inventing Japan, 1853–1964*. New York: Modern Library, 2003.

———. *The Wages of Guilt: Memories of War in Germany and Japan*. New York: Farrar, Straus and Giroux, 1994.

Butow, Robert J. C. *Tojo and the Coming of the War*. Princeton, N.J.: Princeton University Press, 1962.

Caidin, Martin. *A Torch to the Enemy: The Story of the Devastating Fire Raid Against Tokyo— March 10, 1945*. New York: Ballantine Books, 1960.

Calvocoressi, Peter, and Guy Wint. *Total War: The Story of World War II*. New York: Pantheon, 1972.

Cave, Dorothy. *Beyond Courage: One Regiment Against Japan, 1941–45*. New Mexico: Yucca Tree Press, 1992.

Chang, Iris. *The Rape of Nanking*. New York: Basic Books, 1997.

Chunn, Calvin Ellsworth. *Of Rice and Men: The Story of Americans Under the Rising Sun*. Los Angeles/Tulsa, Okla.: Veterans' Publishing Company, 1946.

Ciardi, John. *Saipan: The War Diary of John Ciardi*. Fayetteville: University of Arkansas Press, 1988.

Clarke, Hugh V. *Twilight Liberation: Australian Prisoners of War Between Hiroshima and Home*. Sydney: Allen and Unwin, 1985.

Cohen, Richard. *By the Sword: A History of Gladiators, Musketeers, Samurai, Swashbucklers, and Olympic Champions*. New York: Modern Library, 2003.

Connaughton, Richard. *MacArthur and Defeat in the Philippines*. Woodstock and New York: Overlook Press, 2001.

Cook, Haruko Taya, and Theodore F. Cook. *Japan at War: An Oral History*. New York: New Press, 1992.

Cortes, Rosario Mendoza, Celestina Puyal Boncan, and Ricardo Trota Jose. *The Filipino Saga*. Quezon City, Philippines: New Day, 2000.

Costello, John. *The Pacific War, 1941–1945*. New York: Quill, 1982.

Cowdrey, Albert E. *Fighting for Life: American Military Medicine in World War II*. New York: Free Press, 1994.

Craven, W. F., and J. L. Cate, eds. *The Army Air Forces in World War II*, vol. 5, *The Pacific: Matterhorn to Nagasaki, June 1944 to August 1945*. Chicago: University of Chicago Press, 1953.

Daws, Gavin. *Prisoners of the Japanese: POWs of World War II in the Pacific*. New York: William Morrow, 1994.

Dear, I. C. B., and M. R. D. Foot, eds. *The Oxford Companion to World War II*. New York: Oxford University Press, 1995.

De Bary, William Theodore, et al., eds. *Sources of Japanese Tradition: From Earliest Times to 1600*. 2nd ed. New York: Columbia University Press, n.d.

De Jong, L. *The Collapse of a Colonial Society: The Dutch in Indonesia During the Second World War*. Leiden: KITLV Press, 2002.

Dewey, George. *Autobiography of George Dewey, Admiral of the Navy*. Edited by Eric McAllister Smith. Annapolis, Md.: Naval Institute Press, 1987.

Dower, John W. *Embracing Defeat: Japan in the Wake of World War II*. New York: W. W. Norton/Free Press, 1999.

———. *Japan in War and Peace: Selected Essays*. New York: New Press, 1993.

———. *War Without Mercy: Race and Power in the Pacific War*. New York: Pantheon, 1986.

Drea, Edward J. *MacArthur's ULTRA Codebreaking and the War Against Japan, 1942–45*. Lawrence: University Press of Kansas, 1992.

Dyess, William E. *The Dyess Story*. New York: G. P. Putnam's Sons, 1944.

Edoin, Hoito. *The Night Tokyo Burned: The Incendiary Campaign Against Japan, March–August 1945.* New York: St. Martin's, 1987.

Eichelberger, Robert L. *Our Jungle Road to Tokyo.* New York: Viking Press, 1950.

Endō, Shusaku. *The Sea and the Poison.* Translated by Michael Gallagher. New York: Taplinger, 1980.

Evans, William R. *Soochow and the 4th Marines.* Rogue River, Ore.: Atwood, 1987.

Fadiman, Anne. *Ex Libris: Confessions of a Common Reader.* New York: Farrar, Straus and Giroux, 1998.

Falk, Stanley L. *Bataan: The March of Death.* New York: Curtis Books, 1962.

Frank, Richard. *Downfall: The End of the Imperial Japanese Empire.* New York: Random House, 1999.

Frankl, Viktor E. *Man's Search for Meaning: An Introduction to Logotherapy.* Translated by Ilse Lasch. New York: Touchstone, 1984.

Freud, Sigmund. *Civilization and Its Discontents.* Translated and edited by James Strachey. New York: W. W. Norton, 1961.

Freud, Sigmund, and Josef Breuer. *Studies on Hysteria.* Translated and edited by James Strachey. New York: Avon Books, 1966.

Gibney, Frank, ed. *Sensō: The Japanese Remember the Pacific War: Letters to the Editor of "Asahi Shimbun."* Translated by Beth Cary. Armonk, N.Y.: M. E. Sharpe, 1995.

Ginn, John L. *Sugamo Prison, Tokyo: An Account of the Trial and Sentencing of Japanese War Criminals in 1948 by a U.S. Participant.* Jefferson, N.C.: McFarland, 1992.

Goodman, Grant K. *Japan: The Dutch Experience.* London: Athlone Press, 1986.

Gordon, Richard M. *Horyo: Memoirs of an American POW.* St. Paul, Minn.: Paragon House, 1999.

Grover, David H., and Gretchen G. Grover. *Captives in Shanghai: The Story of the "President Harrison."* Napa, Calif.: Western Maritime Press, 1989.

Haney, Robert E. *Caged Dragons: An American P.O.W. in WWII Japan.* Ann Arbor, Mich.: Sabre Press, 1991.

Harris, Mark Jonathan, Franklin D. Mitchell, and Steven J. Schecter. *The Home Front: America During World War II.* New York: G. P. Putnam's Sons, 1984.

Hartendorp, A. V. H. *The Japanese Occupation of the Philippines.* 2 vols. Manila, Philippines: Bookmark, 1967.

Havens, Thomas R. H. *Valley of Darkness: The Japanese People and World War II.* New York: W. W. Norton, 1978.

Hedges, Chris. *War Is a Force That Gives Us Meaning.* New York: Public Affairs, 2002.

Herman, Jan K. *Battle Station Sick Bay: Navy Medicine in World War II.* Annapolis, Md.: Naval Institute Press, 1997.

Hersey, John. *Hiroshima.* New York: Alfred A. Knopf, 1946.

———. *Men on Bataan.* New York: Alfred A. Knopf, 1942.

Hibbs, Ralph Emerson. *Tell MacArthur to Wait.* Quezon City, Philippines: Giraffe Books, 1996.

Holmes, Linda Goetz. *Unjust Enrichment: How Japan's Companies Built Postwar Fortunes Using American POWs.* Mechanicsburg, Pa.: Stackpole Books, 2001.

Holmes, Richard. *Acts of War: The Behavior of Men in Battle.* London: Weidenfeld and Nicolson, 2003.

Holmes, W. J. *Double-Edged Secrets: U.S. Naval Intelligence Operations in the Pacific During World War II.* Annapolis, Md.: Naval Institute Press, 1979.

Honigsbaum, Mark. *The Fever Trail: In Search of the Cure for Malaria.* New York: Farrar, Straus and Giroux, 2001.

Howe, Irving. *World of Our Fathers.* New York: Harcourt Brace Jovanovich, 1976.

Hoyt, Edwin P. *Japan's War, 1853–1952.* New York: McGraw-Hill, 1986.

———. *The Lonely Ships.* New York: David McKay, 1975.

Ibuse, Masuji. *Black Rain*. Translated by John Bester. Palo Alto, Calif.: Kodansha International, 1969.

Ienaga, Saburō. *The Pacific War, 1931–1945*. New York: Pantheon Books, 1978.

Ind, Allison. *Allied Intelligence Bureau: Our Secret Weapon in the War Against Japan*. New York: David McKay, 1958.

———. *Bataan: The Judgment Seat*. New York: Macmillan, 1944.

Irons, Peter. *Justice at War: The Story of the Japanese American Internment Cases*. Berkeley: University of California Press, 1993.

Jacobs, Eugene C. *Blood Brothers: A Medic's Sketchbook*. New York: Carlton Press, 1985.

James, D. Clayton. *The Years of MacArthur*. 3 vols. Boston: Houghton Mifflin, 1970.

Jansen, Marius B. *The Making of Modern Japan*. Cambridge, Mass.: Harvard University Press, 2000.

Jellison, Charles A. *Besieged: The World War II Ordeal of Malta, 1940–1942*. Hanover, N.H.: University Press of New England, 1984.

Joaquin, Nick. *Manila, My Manila*. Manila, Philippines: City of Manila, 1990.

Johnston, Bruce F., with Mosaburo Hosodo and Yoshio Kusumi. *Japanese Food Management in World War II*. Stanford, Calif.: Stanford University Press, 1953.

Johnston, William. *The Modern Epidemic: A History of Tuberculosis in Japan*. Cambridge, Mass.: Council on East Asian Studies/Harvard University, 1995.

Jones, Ernest. *The Life and Works of Sigmund Freud*. Edited by Lionel Trilling and Steven Marcus. New York: Basic Books, 1961.

José, F. Sionil. *Dusk*. New York: Modern Library, 1998.

Jose, Ricardo Trota. *The Philippine Army, 1935–1942*. Manila, Philippines: Ateneo de Manila University Press, 1992.

Junod, Marcel. *Warrior Without Weapons*. London: Jonathan Cape, 1951.

Kardiner, Abram, and Herbert Spiegel. *War Stress and Neurotic Illness*. New York: Paul B. Hoeber, 1947.

Karnow, Stanley. *In Our Own Image: America's Empire in the Philippines*. New York: Ballantine Books, 1989.

Kase, Toshikazu. *Journey to the "Missouri."* New Haven, Conn.: Yale University Press, 1950.

Keats, John. *They Fought Alone*. Philadelphia: J. P. Lippincott, 1963.

Keegan, John. *Encyclopedia of World War II*. Middlesex, England: Hamlyn, 1977.

Keegan, John, ed. *The Book of War: 25 Centuries of Great War Writing*. New York: Viking, 1999.

Keene, Donald. *Dawn to the West: Japanese Literature of the Modern Era: Poetry, Drama, Criticism*. New York: Columbia University Press, 1999.

———. *Emperor of Japan: Meiji and His World, 1852–1912*. New York: Columbia University Press, 2002.

———. *The Japanese Discovery of Europe, 1720–1830*. Rev. ed. Stanford, Calif.: Stanford University Press, 1969.

Kennedy, David M. *Freedom from Fear: The American People in Depression and War, 1929–1945*. New York: Oxford University Press, 1999.

Kenworth, Aubrey Saint. *The Tiger of Malaya: The Inside Story of the Japanese Atrocities*. New York: Exposition Press, 1953.

Kerr, E. Bartlett. *Flames over Tokyo: The U.S. Army Air Forces' Incendiary Campaign Against Japan, 1944–1945*. New York: Donald I. Fine, 1991.

———. *Surrender and Survival: The Experience of American POWs in the Pacific, 1941–1945*. New York: William Morrow, 1985.

Keys, Ancel, Josef Brozek, Austin Henschel, and Olaf Mickelson. *The Biology of Human Starvation*. Minneapolis: University of Minnesota Press, 1950.

Knox, Donald. *Death March: The Survivors of Bataan*. New York: Harcourt Brace Jovanovich, 1981.

Krasno, Rena. *That Last Glorious Summer, 1939, Shanghai to Japan.* Hong Kong: Old China Hand Press, 2001.

LaForte, Robert S., Ronald E. Marcello, and Richard L. Himmel, eds. *With Only the Will to Live: Accounts of Americans in Japanese Prison Camps, 1941–1945.* Wilmington, Del.: Scholarly Resources, 1994.

Langley, Harold D. *A History of Medicine in the Early U.S. Navy.* Baltimore, Md.: Johns Hopkins University Press, 1995.

Lapham, Robert, and Bernard Norling. *Lapham's Raiders: Guerrillas in the Philippines, 1942–1948.* Lexington: University Press of Kentucky, 1996.

Lawrence, Greg. *Dance with Demons: The Life of Jerome Robbins.* New York: G. P. Putnam's Sons, 2001.

Lawton, Manny. *Some Survived: An Epic Account of Japanese Captivity During World War II.* Chapel Hill, N.C.: Algonquin Books, 1984.

Lee, Clark. *They Call It Pacific.* New York: Viking Press, 1943.

Leslie, Charles, and Allan Young, eds. *Paths to Asian Medical Knowledge.* Berkeley: University of California Press, 1992.

Leutze, James. *A Different Kind of Victory: A Biography of Admiral Thomas C. Hart.* Annapolis, Md.: Naval Institute Press, 1981.

Lifton, Robert Jay. *The Nazi Doctors: Medical Killing and the Psychology of Genocide.* New York: Basic Books, 2000.

Lingeman, Richard. *Don't You Know There's a War On? The American Home Front, 1941–1945.* New York: Thunder's Mouth Press/Nation Books, 2003.

Linn, Brian McAllister. *The Philippine War, 1899–1902.* Lawrence: University of Kansas Press, 2000.

Lu, David J. *Japan: A Documentary History.* 2 vols. Armonk, N.Y.: M. E. Sharpe, 1997.

McCoy, Melvyn H., S. M. Mellnik, and Welbourn Kelley. *Ten Escape from Tojo.* New York: Farrar and Rinehart, 1944.

McCullough, David. *Truman.* New York: Simon and Schuster, 1992.

Mainichi Newspapers. *Fifty Years of Light and Dark: The Hirohito Era.* Tōkyō: Mainichi Newspapers, 1975.

Mallonée, Richard C. *The Naked Flagpole: Battle for Bataan.* Edited by Richard C. Mallonée II. San Rafael, Calif.: Presidio, 1980.

Manson, Patrick. *Tropical Diseases: A Manual of the Diseases of War Climates.* Birmingham, Ala.: Classics of Medicine Library, 1984.

Marshall, Chester. *B-29 Superfortress.* Osceola, Wisc.: Motorbooks, 1993.

———. *Final Assault on the Rising Sun.* London: Airlife, 1995.

Marshall, Chester, Lindsey Silvester, and Scotty Stallings, eds. *The Global Twentieth.* Memphis, Tenn.: Global Press, 1988.

Michno, Gregory F. *Death on the Hellships: Prisoners at Sea in the Pacific War.* Annapolis, Md.: Naval Institute Press, 2001.

Miller, E. B. *Bataan Uncensored.* Little Falls, Minn.: Military Historical Society of Minnesota, 1991.

Miller, Edward S. *War Plan Orange: The U.S. Strategy to Defeat Japan, 1897–1945.* Annapolis, Md.: Naval Institute Press, 1991.

Milton, Giles. *Samurai William: The Englishman Who Opened Japan.* New York: Farrar, Straus and Giroux, 2003.

Milward, Alan S. *War, Economy and Society, 1939–1945.* Berkeley: University of California Press, 1979.

Minear, Richard H. *Victors' Justice: The Tokyo War Crimes Trial.* Princeton, N.J.: Princeton University Press, 1971.

Morison, Samuel Eliot. *History of United States Naval Operations in World War II.* 14 vols., Edison, N.J.: Castle Books, 2001.

Morris, Eric. *Corregidor: The American Alamo of World War II*. New York: Stein and Day, 1981.

Morris, Norval, and David J. Rothman, eds. *The Oxford History of the Prison: The Practice of Punishment in Western Society*. New York: Oxford University Press, 1995.

Mosse, George L. *Fallen Soldiers: Reshaping the Memory of the World Wars*. New York: Oxford University Press, 1990.

Mydans, Carl. *More Than Meets the Eye*. New York: Harper and Brothers, 1959.

Myers, Ramon H., and Mark R. Peattie, eds. *The Japanese Colonial Empire, 1895–1945*. Princeton, N.J.: Princeton University Press, 1984.

Nishida, Kazuo. *Storied Cities of Japan*. Tōkyō: John Weatherhill, 1963.

Nitobe, Inazo. *Bushido: The Soul of Japan*. Boston: Tuttle, 2001.

Noma, Hiroshi. *Zone of Emptiness*. Translated by Bernard Frechtman. New York: World, 1956.

Norling, Bernard. *The Intrepid Guerrillas of North Luzon*. Lexington: University Press of Kentucky, 1999.

Norman, Elizabeth M. *We Band of Angels: The Untold Story of American Nurses Trapped on Bataan by the Japanese*. New York: Random House, 1999.

Official Journal of the Japanese Military Administration. Edited by the Japanese Military Administration. Manila, Philippines: Niti Niti Shimbum Sha, 1942.

Ohnuki-Tierney, Emiko. *Kamikaze, Cherry Blossoms, and Nationalisms: The Militarization of Aesthetics in Japanese History*. Chicago: University of Chicago Press, 2002.

Ooka, Shohei. *Fires on the Plain*. Translated by Ivan Morris. Boston: Tuttle, 1991.

Overy, Richard. *Why the Allies Won*. New York: W. W. Norton, 1995.

Pacific War Research Society. *Japan's Longest Day*. Palo Alto, Calif.: Kodansha International, 1968.

Page, William Frank. *The Health of Former Prisoners of War: Results from the Medical Examination Survey of Former POWs of World War II and the Korean Conflict*. Washington, D.C.: National Academy Press, 1992.

Perret, Geoffrey. *Old Soldiers Never Die: The Life of Douglas MacArthur*. New York: Random House, 1996.

————. *Winged Victory: The Army Air Forces in World War II*. New York: Random House, 1993.

Prados, John. *Combined Fleet Decoded: The Secret History of American Intelligence and the Japanese Navy in World War II*. Annapolis, Md.: Naval Institute Press, 1995.

Quirino, Carlos. *Chick Parsons: America's Master Spy in the Philippines*. Quezon City, Philippines: New Day, 1984.

Ramsey, Edwin Price, and Stephen J. Rivele. *Lieutenant Ramsey's War*. New York: Knightsbridge, 1990.

Redmond, Juanita. *I Served on Bataan*. New York: Garland, 1984.

Reischauer, Edwin O., and Marius B. Jansen. *The Japanese Today: Change and Continuity*. Enlarged ed. Cambridge, Mass.: Belknap Press/Harvard University Press, 1978.

Reporting World War II. 2 vols. New York: Library of America, 1995.

Roland, Charles G. *Long Night's Journey into Day: Prisoners of War in Hong Kong and Japan, 1941–1945*. Waterloo, Ont.: Wilfrid Laurier University Press, 2001.

Romulo, Carlos. *I Saw the Fall of the Philippines*. New York: Doubleday Doran, 1943.

Roscoe, Theodore. *United States Submarine Operations in World War II*. Annapolis, Md.: Naval Institute Press, 1949.

Lord Russell of Liverpool. *The Knights of Bushido: A Short History of Japanese War Crimes*. London: Cassell, 1958.

Sams, Crawford F. *"Medic": The Mission of an American Military Doctor in Occupied Japan and Wartorn Korea*. Armonk, N.Y.: M. E. Sharpe, 1998.

Schom, Alan. *The Eagle and the Rising Sun: The Japanese-American War, 1941–1943*. New York: W. W. Norton, 2004.

Schulz, Duane. *Hero of Bataan: The Story of General Jonathan M. Wainwright*. New York: St. Martin's Press, 1981.

Seagrave, Sterling, and Peggy Seagrave. *Gold Warriors: America's Secret Recovery of Yamashita's Gold*. London and New York: Verso Books, 2003.

Sebald, W. B. *On the Natural History of Destruction*. Translated by Anthea Bell. New York: Random House, 2003.

Seidensticker, Edward. *Tokyo Rising: The City Since the Great Earthquake*. Cambridge, Mass.: Harvard University Press, 1991.

Senoh, Kappa. *A Boy Called H: A Childhood in Wartime Japan*. Translated by John Bester. New York: Kodansha International, 1999.

Sergeant, Harriet. *Shanghai: Collision Point of Cultures, 1918–1939*. New York: Crown, 1990.

Shapiro, Harvey, ed. *Poets of World War II*. New York: Library of America, 2003.

Sides, Hampton. *Ghost Soldiers: The Forgotten Story of World War II's Most Dramatic Mission*. New York: Doubleday, 2001.

Smith, Jim, and Malcolm McConnell. *The Last Mission: The Secret History of World War II's Final Battle*. New York: Broadway Books, 2002.

Smith, Stanley W. *Prisoner of the Emperor: An American POW in World War II*. Niwot, Colo.: University Press of Colorado, 1991.

Spector, Ronald H. *Eagle Against the Sun: The American War with Japan*. New York: Free Press, 1985.

Spielman, Andrew, and Michael D'Antonio. *Mosquito: A Natural History of Our Most Persistent and Deadly Foe*. New York: Hyperion, 2001.

Stamp, Loren E. *Journey Through Hell: Memoir of an American Navy Medic Captured in the Philippines and Imprisoned by the Japanese*. Jefferson, N.C.: McFarland, 1993.

Starr, Paul. *The Social Transformation of American Medicine*. New York: Basic Books, 1982.

Stinnett, Robert B. *Day of Deceit: The Truth About FDR and Pearl Harbor*. New York: Simon and Schuster, 2000.

Swinson, Arthur. *Four Samurai: A Quartet of Japanese Army Commanders in the Second World War*. London: Hutchenson, 1968.

Takemae, Eiji. *Inside GHQ: The Allied Occupation of Japan and Its Legacy*. Translated by Robert Ricketts and Sebastian Swann. New York: Continuum, 2002.

Tanaka, Yuki. *Hidden Horrors: Japanese War Crimes in World War II*. Boulder, Colo.: Westview Press, 1996.

Tasaki, Hanama. *Long the Imperial Way*. Boston: Houghton Mifflin, 1950.

Taylor, Frederick. *Dresden: Tuesday, February 13, 1945*. New York: HarperCollins, 2004.

Taylor, Lawrence. *A Trial of Generals: Homma, Yamashita, MacArthur*. South Bend, Ind.: Icarus Press, 1981.

Taylor, Vince. *Cabanatuan: Japanese Death Camp*. Waco, Tex.: Texian Press, 1985.

Tenney, Lester I. *My Hitch in Hell: The Bataan Death March*. Washington: Brassey's, 2000.

Toland, John. *But Not in Shame: The Six Months After Pearl Harbor*. New York: Random House, 1961.

———. *The Rising Sun: The Decline and Fall of the Japanese Empire, 1936–1945*. 2 vols. New York: Random House, 1970.

Tolley, Kemp. *Yangtze Patrol: The U.S. Navy in China*. Annapolis, Md.: Naval Institute Press, 1971.

Tuchman, Barbara W. *Stilwell and the American Experience in China, 1911–45*. New York: Macmillan, 1971.

Tuohy, William. *The Bravest Man: The Story of Richard O'Kane and U.S. Submariners in the Pacific War*. Phoenix Mill: Sutton, 2001.

Utinsky, Margaret. *"Miss U."* San Antonio, Tex.: Naylor, 1948.

Villarin, Mariano. *We Remember Bataan and Corregidor*. Baltimore, Md.: Gateway Press, 1990.

Wainwright, Jonathan M. *General Wainwright's Story*. Edited by Robert Considine. Garden City, N.Y.: Doubleday, 1945.

Waterford, Van. *Prisoners of the Japanese in World War II: Statistical History, Personal Narratives and Memorials Concerning POWs in Camps and on Hellships, Civilian Internees, Asian Slave Laborers and Others Captured in the Pacific Theater*. Jefferson, N.C.: McFarland, 1994.

Weinstein, Alfred A. *Barbed-Wire Surgeon*. New York: Macmillan, 1948.

White, W. L. *They Were Expendable*. Cleveland, Ohio: World, 1944.

Willmott, H. P. *The Second World War in the Far East*. London: Cassell, 1999.

Willoughby, Amea. *I Was on Corregidor: Experiences of an American Official's Wife in the War-Torn Philippines*. New York: Harper and Brothers, 1943.

Willoughby, Charles A., and John Chamberlain. *MacArthur, 1941–1951*. New York: McGraw-Hill, 1954.

Winslow, W. G. *The Fleet the Gods Forgot: The U.S. Asiatic Fleet in World War II*. Annapolis, Md.: Naval Institute Press, 1982.

Wright, John M. *Captured on Corregidor: Diary of an American POW in World War II*. Jefferson, N.C.: McFarland, 1988.

Wyden, Peter. *Day One: Before Hiroshima and After*. New York: Simon and Schuster, 1984.

Yahara, Hiromichi. *The Battle for Okinawa: A Japanese Officer's Eyewitness Account of the Last Great Campaign of World War II*. Translated by Roger Pineau and Masatoshi Uehara. New York: John Wiley, 1995.

Yamamoto Tsunetomo. *Hagakure: The Book of the Samurai*. Translated by William Scott Wilson. New York: Kodansha International, 1983.

Zimmerman, Warren. *The First Great Triumph: How Five Americans Made Their Country a World Power*. New York: Farrar, Straus and Giroux, 2002.

Government Publications and Reports

Akeroyd, John Finch. Statement. Australian War Memorial, October 10, 1942.

Alexander, Irvin E. "Recollections of Bataan & After." Louis Morton Papers, Box 3, MHI.

Anderson, Robert S., and Ebbe Curtis Hoff. *Preventive Medicine in World War II*, vol. 9, *Special Fields*. Washington, D.C.: Office of the Surgeon General, 1969.

Arnold, Harold A. "The Lesson of Bataan." *Quartermaster Review*, November–December 1946.

Asiatic Defense Campaign. 1941–42, NRS 1984–33, MR #1–2, NHC.

Asiatic Defense Campaign. 1941–42, NRS 237, DesDiv 59, MR, NHC.

ATIS. "Enemy Publications." Research Report No. 321, February 21, 1945. "Regulations for Handling Prisoners of War." Microfiche, 10-EP-321, MHI.

ATIS. "Japanese Ten Day Period Reports on Monitoring of Allied Wireless Communications in the Philippines." Research Report No. 31, March 29, 1945, SRH-231, RG 457.

ATIS. "Organization of Medical Units in the Japanese Army." Research Report No. 83, July 29, 1944, Microfiche, MHI.

ATIS. "Self-Immolation as a Factor in Japanese Military Psychology." Research Report No. 76, Part I, April 4, 1944, Microfiche, 10-RR-76 (1-3), MHI.

ATIS. "Survey of Japanese Medical Units." Research Report No. 124, January 18, 1947, Microfiche, 10-RR-124, MHI.

Barr, E. L. "Diary: History of Battery M—60th Coast Artillery." RG 407, Box 125, Folder 7, NARA.

Barrett, A. M. *Casus Belli*. BUMED.

Beaumont, Joan. "Victims of War: The Allies and the Transport of Prisoners-of-War by Sea, 1939–45." Australian War Memorial.

Beebe, Louis C. *Diary*. RG 389, Box 2176, NARA.

Beecher, Curtis Thurston. "Experiences in the Fighting on Corregidor." Douglas County Historical Society, Roseburg, Ore.

Bellafaire, Judith A. "The Army Nurse Corps in World War II." U.S. Army Center of Military History.

Berley, Ferdinand V. Interview by Jan K. Herman. February 7, 21, 27, March 6, April 3, 10, 24, and May 1, 1995. BUMED.

Bookman, John Jacob. Testimony "In the Matter of Inadequate Means of Transportation Furnished Prisoners of War by the Japanese at Kobe Prisoner of War Hospital, on or about June 1945," WCO/JAG, January 17, 1946, p. 3, RG331, Box 984, Folder 17 [OS-204-J-16], NARA.

———. Testimony "In the Matter of Inadequate Medical Supplies and Food Furnished Prisoners of War by the Japanese at Wakayama Prisoner of War Camp and Kobe Prisoner of War Hospital, from April 1994 to June 1945," WCO/JAG, RG 331, Box 954, Folder 17 [OS-204-J-16], NARA.

Boone, Joel T. "United States Pacific Fleet Third Fleet, Initial Release of Prisoners of War in Japan." RG 389, Box 2176, NARA.

Bowers, Thomas K. "Personal Narrative of Philippine Campaign from 8 December 1941 to 29 April 1942." Asiatic Defense Campaign, 1941–42, NRS, 1984-33, MR #1, NHC.

Braly, William C. "Corregidor Log." Braly Papers, Box 3, MHI.

Bridget, F. J., to Company Commander. "Positions of Forces," February 3, 1942. MR, NRS, 159, Naval Campaign in the Orient Papers, NHC.

Brill, Norman Q. "Neuropsychiatric Examination of Military Personnel Recovered from Japanese Prison Camps." *Bulletin of the U.S. Army Medical Department*, April 1946.

Bunker, Paul D. "Seaward Defense Commander's Report of Damage," 59th CA, Exhibit I, in Moore, "Report of Major General."

Champlin, Malcolm McGregor. "Narrative," September 1944. Asiatic Defense Campaign, 1941–42, NRS, 1984-33, MR #1, NHC.

Cheek, Mike. "War Diary" of District Intelligence Officer to Director of Naval Intelligence, 16th Naval District, February 20, 1942. Asiatic Defense Campaign, 1941–42, NRS, 1984-33, MR #2, NHC.

Chunn, Calvin. *Diary*. Louis Morton Papers, Box 3, MHI.

———. "Notebooks." RG 407, Folder 9, Box 128, NARA.

Clement, Robert A. "Some of My Life Experiences." Personal Papers Collection, MCHC.

Coates, John Boyd, Jr., and Michael E. DeBakey. *Surgery in World War II*, vol. 2, *General Surgery*. Washington, D.C.: Office of the Surgeon General, 1955.

Coates, John Boyd, Jr., and W. Paul Havens, Jr., eds. *Internal Medicine in World War II*, vol. 2, *Infectious Diseases*. Washington, D.C.: Office of the Surgeon General, 1963.

Condit, Kenneth W., and Edwin T. Turnblad. *Hold High the Torch: A History of the 4th Marines*. Historical Branch, G-3 Division, Headquarters, U.S. Marine Corps. Washington, D.C., 1960.

Condon-Rall, Mary Ellen, and Albert E. Cowdrey. *The Medical Department: Medical Service in the War Against Japan,* in *United States Army in World War II*. Washington, D.C.: Center of Military History, 1998.

Cooper, Wibb E. "Medical Department Activities in the Philippines from 1941–6 May 1942." RG 389, Box 2176, NARA.

Coox, Alan D. "Strategic Bombing in the Pacific," in R. Cargill Hall, ed., *Case Studies in Strategic Bombardment*.

Davis, Robert G. *Diary: Covering Period 8 December 1941–7 September 1945*. RG 389, Box 2176, NARA.

"Disposition and Employment of U.S. Marines on the Asiatic Station During the Initial Stages of the War," April 6, 1942. RG 127, Box 309, NARA.

Dod, Karl C. *United States Army in World War II: The Technical Services, the Corps of Engineers; The War Against Japan*. Washington, D.C.: Office of the Chief of Military History, 1966.

Ferguson, George T. *Diary*. BUMED.

Forquer, Eugene. "Cabanatuan Concentration Camp, Nueva Ecija, Luzon, Philippine Islands." RG 389, Box 2177, NARA.

Fourteenth Army Operations, vol. 1, *Japanese Studies in World War II.* Historical Section, G-2, GHQ, Far East Command, MHI.

Gillespie, James O. "Recollections of the Pacific War and Japanese Prisoner of War Camps, 1941–1945." RG 389, Box 2177, NARA.

Ginn, Richard V. N. *The History of the U.S. Army Medical Service Corps.* Washington, D.C.: Office of the Surgeon General and U.S. Army Center of Military History, 1997.

Gladwin, Lee A. "American POWs on Japanese Ships Take a Voyage into Hell." *Prologue* (NARA quarterly) 35:4.

Glassford, William. "Confidential Diary." Asiatic Defense Campaign, 1941–42, NRS, 1984-33, MR #2, NHC.

———. "Narrative of Events in the Far Eastern Theatre, 1939–1942," May 1950. Asiatic Defense Campaign, 1941–42, NRS, 1984-33, MR #1, NHC.

Hall, R. Cargill, ed. *Case Studies in Strategic Bombardment.* Washington, D.C.: Air Force History and Museums Program, Government Printing Office, 1998.

Handbook of the Hospital Corps, U.S. Navy 1939. Washington, D.C.: Bureau of Medicine and Surgery, Government Printing Office, 1939.

Hart, Thomas C. "Narrative of Events, Asiatic Fleet, Leading Up to War and from 8 December 1941 to 15 February 1942." Asiatic Defense Campaign, 1941–42, NRS, 1984-33, MR #1, NHC.

Hayes, Thomas Hirst. *Bilibid Notebook.* BUMED.

———. *Diary;* includes "Report to Dept.," "Personal Record," "War Medicine," and letter to Thomas Hayes, Jr. BUMED.

———. "Report of the Medical Activities of the Fourth Regiment U.S. Marines and Attached Troops for the Period 1-1-42 to 5-6-42 on Corregidor, P.I." BUMED.

———. "Report on Medical Tactics, 4th Regiment, USMC, Medical Personnel, Manila Bay Area, 12-7-41 to 5-6-42." Hospital Corps Archives Memo 268-45, Folder 15-B, BUMED.

Heaton, Leonard D., John Boyd Coates, Jr., Ebbe Curtis Hoff, and Phebe M. Hoff. *Preventive Medicine in World War II,* vol. 6, *Communicable Diseases: Malaria.* Washington, D.C.: Office of the Surgeon General, 1963.

Herman, Jan K. "Life as a Hospital Corpsman at Naval Hospital Cañacao, Philippine Islands, 1940–41." *U.S. Navy Medicine,* March–April 1998.

———. "Yangtze Patrollers—Bilibid POWs." *U.S. Navy Medicine,* November–December 1985.

Hogaboom, William. "Action Report, Bataan." *Marine Corps Gazette,* April 1946.

Homma, Masaharu. Interview by Walter E. Buchly, March 1946. Louis Morton Papers, Box 8, MHI.

Hough, Frank O., Verle E. Ludwig, and Henry I. Shaw, Jr. *Pearl Harbor to Guadalcanal: History of U.S. Marine Corps Operations in World War II,* vol. 1. Historical Branch, G-3 Division, Headquarters, U.S. Marine Corps, 1958. Washington, D.C.

Howard, Samuel L. "Report on the Operation, Employment and Supply of the Old 4th Marines from September 1941 to the Surrender of Corregidor, May 6, 1942." RG 127, Box 309, Folder A-21, NARA.

"Intelligence Activities in the Philippines During the Japanese Occupation, Documentary Appendices" (II), vol. 2, Intelligence Series. RG 23A, Box 12, Folder 10, Willoughby Papers, MMA.

Irvin, Ernest J. "Wartime Reminiscences." Based on interviews by Jan K. Herman, February 25, March 24, and May 22, 1986. BUMED.

Irwin, C. L. "Corregidor in Action." *Coast Artillery Journal,* January–February 1943, MHI.

Keene, James W. "First Separate Marine Battalion, Marine Barracks, Navy Yard, Cavite, Philippine Islands." Personal Papers Collection, MCHC.

Kentner, Robert W. *Kentner's Journal: Bilibid Prison, Manila, P.I., from 12-8-41 to 2-5-45.* RG 389, Box 2177, NARA.

Knoll, Denys. "Intelligence Report, 16th Naval District, March 12–May 3, 1942." Louis Morton Papers, Box 19, MHI.

Lerch, Arthur L. "Japanese Handling of American Prisoners of War." Reprinted in *Tokyo Trial Materials: Documents of POW Information Bureau.* Gendia Shiryo Shuppan, 1999.

Lewis, Robert B. " 'Painful Feet' in American Prisoners of War." *U.S. Armed Forces Medical Journal* 1, no. 2 (February 1950).

Lowman, K. E. "Fleet Surgeon's Activities—U.S. Asiatic Fleet, a Resume, 1941–45." BUMED.

McBride, Allen C. "Notes on the Fall of Bataan." Louis Morton Papers, Box 14, MHI.

MacEachin, Douglas J. "The Final Months of the War with Japan: Signals Intelligence, U.S. Invasion Planning, and the A-Bomb Decision." Center for the Study of Intelligence, Central Intelligence Agency, December 1998.

Mallonée, Richard C. "Bataan Diary," vol. 2, "The Defense of Bataan." Richard C. Mallonée Papers, Box 1, MHI.

"Medical Organization, 4th Regiment, USMC, Defense of the Philippines, 1941–42." BUMED.

Mellnik, Stephen M. "How the Japs Took Corregidor." *Coast Artillery Journal*, March–April 1945, MHI.

Miller, J. Michael. "From Shanghai to Corregidor: Marines in the Defense of the Philippines." Washington, D.C.: Marine Corps Historical Center, 1997.

Moore, George F. "Report of Major General George F. Moore, U.S.A., Formerly Commanding the Philippine Coast Artillery Command and the Harbor Defenses of Manila and Subic Bays with Headquarters at Fort Mills, Corregidor, Philippine Islands, 14 February 1941–6 May 1942," December 15, 1945. George F. Moore Papers, MHI.

Morton, Louis. *The War in the Pacific: The Fall of the Philippines.* Washington, D.C.: Government Printing Office, 1953.

Nardini, John E. "Vitamin-Deficiency Diseases in Allied Prisoners of the Japanese." *Naval Medical Bulletin* 47, no. 2 (March–April 1947).

"Narrative Report of Action During War, from November 1, 1941–May 5, 1942, from Battery C, 60th Coast Artillery to Commanding Officer, 60th Coast Artillery." RG 407, Box 124, Folder 3, NARA.

Naval Camapign in the Orient Papers, NRS 159, MR, NHC.

"Notes on a Talk Given by Dr. Marcel Junod, Chief Delegate of the International Red Cross Committtee in the Far East, 21 June 1946." ACICR, Archives générales 1918–1950, Groupe G [Généralités: affaires opérationelles] 1939–1950, G 3/51, M. Junod, Japón, Box 219 [2].

"Notes on the 1st Battalion, Fourth Marines, Fort Mills, Corregidor, P.I." MCHC. Courtesy Richard A. Long.

Page, J. A. "Painful-Feet Syndrome Among Prisoners of War in the Far East." *British Medical Journal* 2 (August 24, 1946).

———. "Report on Period Served as Prisoner of War of the Imperial Japanese Army from 25th December 1941 to 8th September 1945." Box GC/131, Wellcome Trust Library for the History and Understanding of Medicine, London.

Parker, T. C. "The Epic of Corregidor—Bataan, December 24, 1941–May 4, 1942." *United States Naval Institute Proceedings* 69, no. 1 (January 1942).

Peart, Cecil J. "Asiatic Reminiscences of a Navy Corpsman with the Marines." RG 389, Box 2177, NARA.

Porter, Gwinn U. "Antiaircraft Defense of Corregidor." Monograph, School of Combined Arms. Louis Morton Papers, Box 15, MHI.

Priestly, William J. "57 Infantry PS, Diary." Louis Morton Papers, Box 9, MHI.

Prisoners of War Bulletin 1, no. 6 (November 1943), John E. Olson Papers, Box 1, MHI.

"Proceedings of a Board of Officers Appointed to Evaluate War Damage to the Harbor Defenses of Manila and Subic Bays." Headquarters 14th Antiaircraft Command, APO 75, October 6, 1945. William C. Braly Papers, MHI.

Records of the National Security Agency, Central Security Service, Entry 9002, "Study of the Historical Background of the Signal Service, 1776–1939."

"Report on *Arisan Maru*." GHQ/SCAP, Investigation Division Report No. 479. July 1945–April 1948. RG 331, Box 1780, Folder 4, NARA.

"Report on Ichioka Camp." GHQ/SCAP, Investigation Division Report No. 125. March 1946–September 1947. RG 331, Box 1765, Folder 4, NARA.

"Report on Maruyama Camp." GHQ/SCAP, Investigation Division Report No. 166. January 1946–June 1948. RG 331, Box 1767, Folder 18, NARA.

"Report on Tsumori Camp." GHQ/SCAP, Investigation Division Report No. 134. January 1946–April 1949. RG 331, Box 1765, Folder 13, NARA.

"Report on Wakayama Camp." GHQ/SCAP, Investigation Division Report No. 143. RG 331, NARA.

Rockwell, Francis W. "Narrative of Naval Activities in Luzon Area, December 1, 1941, to March 19, 1942." Asiatic Defense Campaign, 1941–42, NRS, 1984-33, MR #1, NHC.

Russell, Paul F. "Appendix A, Third Quarterly Report, Malaria Investigations, Philippines Islands." RG 5, IHB/D, Box 71, RAC.

———. "Final Report on the Malaria Investigations of the International Health Division of the Rockefeller Foundation in the Philippines Islands, 1921–1934." RAC.

———. "Memorandum Regarding a New Plan for the Control of Malaria in the Philippines." RG 1.1, Series 242I, Box 6, Folder 67, RAC.

———. "Philippine Islands, Malaria: 1931 Annual Report, Narrative and Statistical." RAC.

Sackett, E. L. "Evacuation of Mariveles Area, April 10, 1942." Asiatic Defense Campaign, 1941–42, NRS, 1984-33, MR #1, NHC.

———. Hand-drawn map of Mariveles in Earl Le Roy Sackett Special Collections, American Heritage Center, University of Wyoming.

———. "The History of the USS *Canopus*." Box 17, Louis Morton Papers, MHI.

Sartin, L. B. *Bilibid Letter Book, 1942: Papers Relating to the Establishment of a Naval Hospital Unit in Bilibid Prison, Manila, P.I.* RG 389, Box 2178, NARA.

———. "Report of Activities of the United States Naval Hospital Unit in the Philippines from December 8, 1941, to January 30, 1945." RG 389, Box 2178, NARA.

Sayer, Ian, and Douglas Botting. "America's Secret Army: The Untold Story of the Counter Intelligence Corps." *Congressional Record*, January 30, 1996.

Scholes, Robert D. "Mop Up Operation in Vicinity of Longoskawayn Point." February 1, 1942, Asiatic Defense Campaign, 1941–42, NRS, 1984-33, MR #2, NHC.

Segal, Julius. "Long-Term Psychological and Physical Effects of the POW Experience: A Review of the Literature." Center for POW Studies, Naval Health Research Center, San Diego, Calif.

Shearer, Clarence. *Shearer's Journal*. May 29, 1942–July 8, 1943. Companion Document to Sartin, *Bilibid Letter Book, 1942*, RG 389, Box 2178, NARA.

Simpson, Carter Berkeley. *Diary*. BUMED.

Sitter, Stephen C., and Charles J. Katz, M.D. "American POWs Held by the Japanese." BUMED.

Smith, Alfred Littlefield. "Guest of the Emperor." Interview by Jan K. Herman. *U.S. Navy Medicine*, January–February 1986.

Stauffer, Alvin P. *United States Army in World War II, the Technical Services, the Quartermaster Corps: Operations in the War Against Japan*. Washington, D.C.: Office of the Chief of Military History, Department of the Army, 1956.

XXI Bomber Command. "Tactical Mission Report," Mission No. 188, June 5, 1945. APO 234, MR #B0108, AFHRC.

U.S.A. vs. Eitaro Uchiyama et al. Headquarters Eighth Army, U.S. Army, Office of the Staff Judge Advocate. Case #123, Yokohama, July 1, 1948.

U.S.A. vs. Masaharu Homma, RG 153, Boxes 1–5, NARA.

U.S.A. vs. Naraji Nogi. June 8, 1946. RG 389, Box 1908, NARA.

U.S.A. vs. Sotaro Murata. Headquarters Eighth Army, U.S. Army, Office of the Staff Judge Advocate. Case #155, Yokohama, February 16, 1949.

U.S. Marine Corps. *The History of the Medical Department of the United States Navy in World War II*, vol.1. Fleet Marine Force Reference Publication 12-12. Washington, D.C., 1989.

U.S. Strategic Bombing Survey. "Effects of Air Attack on Japanese Urban Economy: Summary Report," March 1947. Urban Areas Division, MR #A1157, AFHRC.

———. "Effects of Air Attack on Osaka-Kobe-Kyoto," June 1947. Urban Areas Division, MR #A1157, AFHRC.

———. "Field Report: Covering Air-Raid Protection and Allied Subjects in Kobe Japan," February 1947. Civilian Defense Division, MR #A1154, AFHRC.

U.S. Strategic Bombing Survey [Pacific], Naval Analysis Division. *The Campaigns of the Pacific War.* Washington, D.C.: Government Printing Office, 1946.

———. *Interrogations of Japanese Officials*, vols. 1–2. OPNAV-P-03-100. Washington, D.C.: Government Printing Office, 1946.

U.S. War Department. *Handbook on Japanese Military Forces.* Washington, D.C.: Government Printing Office; reprinted by Baton Rouge: Louisiana State University Press, 1991.

Waterous, Walter H. "Statement of Experiences and Observations Concerning the Bataan Campaign and Subsequent Imprisonment." Louis Morton Papers, Box 6, MHI.

Wigmore, Lionel. *The Japanese Thrust.* Canberra, Australia: Australian War Memorial, 1957.

Wilkes, John. "War Activities Submarines, U.S. Asiatic Fleet, December 1, 1941–April 1, 1942." Asiatic Defense Campaign, 1941–42, NRS 1984-33, MR #1, NHC.

Wiltse, Charles M. *Medical Supply in World War II.* Washington, D.C.: Office of the Surgeon General, 1968.

Newspaper, Magazine, and Internet Articles

Adachi, Sumio. "A Process to Reaffirmation of International Humanitarian Law, a Japanese View." *Law and Order* 5 (September 25, 1983).

———. "Unprepared Regrettable Events: A Brief History of Japanese Practices on Treatment of Allied War Victims During the Second World War." *Studies of Cultural and Social Science*, no. 45. Hashirimizu, Yokosuka, Japan: National Defense Academy, September 1982.

Baldwin, Hanson W. "Bataan's Epic of Valor," *New York Times*, April 10, 1942.

Batens, Alain. "Equipment of a WWII Combat Medic." steinert/newpage2.htm.

———. "The Geneva Convention Brassard." steinert/geneva_convention_brassard.htm.

———. "The WWII Medical Department." steinert/wwii_medical_department.

"The Battle for Leyte Gulf." www.angelfire.com/fm/odyssey/LEYTE-GULF-Summary-of-the-Battle-htm.

Bolster, Richard. "Rice Is Life." *Hospital Corps Quarterly* 20 (April–June 1947).

Boone, Joel. "Talk Before the American Red Cross," January 16, 1946. RG 389, Box 2176, NARA.

"Brief History of World War Two Advertising Campaigns: War Loans and Bonds." John W. Hartman Center for Sales, Advertising, and Marketing History. scriptorium.lib.duke.edu/adaccess/warbonds.html.

Clancey, Patrick. "The Siege and Capture of Corregidor," p. 5. www/katpga/met/ai/~witman/chs_41-42/marines.htm.

Condon-Rall, Mary Ellen. "U.S. Army Medical Preparations and the Outbreak of War: The Philippines, 1941–6 May 1942." *Journal of Military History* 56 (January 1992).

Crozier, William, et al., eds. "On the Lower East Side: Observations of Life in Lower Manhattan at the Turn of the Century." www.tenant.net/Community/LES/contents.html.

Davies, Alex. "Acoustic Trauma: Bioeffects of Sound." schizophonia.com/installation/trauma/trauma_thesis.

Giangreco, D. M. "Operation DOWNFALL: U.S. Plans and Japanese Counter-Measures." From "Beyond Bushido" symposium, University of Kansas, February 16, 1998.

Glusman, John A. "Heroes and Sons: Coming to Terms." *Virginia Quarterly Review* 66, no. 4 (Autumn 1990).

———. "Tales of the Pacific." *Travel + Leisure* 32, no. 4 (April 2002).

Glusman, Murray, M.D., "The Syndrome of 'Burning Feet' (Nutritional Melalgia) as a Manifestation of Nutritional Deficiency," *American Journal of Medicine,* Vol. III, No. 2, August 1947, pp. 211–23.

Graef, Calvin Robert, with Harry T. Brundidge. "We Prayed to Die." *Cosmopolitan* 118, no. 4 (April 1945).

Hibbs, Ralph E. "Beriberi in Japanese Prison Camp." *Annals of Internal Medicine* 25, no. 2 (August 1946).

———. "Gynecomastia Associated with Vitamin Deficiency Disease." *American Journal of the Medical Sciences* 213, no. 2 (February 1947).

Hoeffer, Frank. "Hard Way Back." www.wtv-zone.com/califPamela/memorial-Page-5.html.

Jacoby, Melville. "Philippine Epic." *Life*, April 13, 1942.

Joy, Robert J. T. "Malaria in American Troops in the South and Southwest Pacific in World War II." *Medical History* 43 (1999): 192–207.

"Killing of POWs in Osaka." *Mainichi Shimbun*, August 13, 1998.

Kluckhohn, Frank. "Foe Says Wainwright Agrees to Full Philippine Surrender." *New York Times*, May 8, 1942.

McCoy, Melvyn, and S. M. Mellnik. "Death Was Part of Our Life." *Life*, February 7, 1944.

McGaffin, William. "The Price of Victory: Japs More Cruel to Yanks Than to Other Captives." *Chicago Daily News*, September 8, 1945.

McKelway, St. Clair. "A Reporter with the B-29s." *New Yorker*, June 16, 1945.

Miller, Andrew. "The Historian's Corner." *Quan* 50, no. 4 (February 1996), p. 6; 50, no. 5 (April 1996), pp. 12–13; 51, no. 1 (July 1996).

Murphy, Mark. "You'll Never Know!" *New Yorker*, June 12, 1943.

Nardini, J. E. "Survival Factors in American Prisoners of War of the Japanese." *American Journal of Psychiatry* 109, no. 4 (October 1952).

Osborn, Philip R. "Notes About Duty with the Yangtze Patrol 1939–1940." *Yangtze River Patroller* 13, no. 1 (March 1987).

Schedler, Dean. "Dazed, Weary Troops Reach Corregidor Under Foe's Fire." *New York Times*, April 11, 1942.

Segal, J., E. J. Hunter, and Z. Segal. "Universal Consequences of Captivity: Stress Reactions Among Divergent Populations of Prisoners of War and Their Families." *International Social Science Journal* 28 no. 3 (1976).

Weller, George. "Cruise of Death." A fourteen-part series in the *St. Louis Post-Dispatch,* beginning November 11, 1945.

"What Tokyo Reports." *New York Times*, April 10, 1942.

Wu, Tien-wei. "A Preliminary Review of Studies of Japanese Biological Warfare Unit 731 in the United States." www.aiipowmia.com/731/7311study.html.

Yaklich, Mike. "Japanese Ordnance Material of World War II." www.wlhoward.com/japan.htm.

Yoshito, Kita. "The Japanese Military's Attitude Toward International Laws and the Treatment of Prisoners of War." Nihon University.

Diaries, Letters, Manuscripts

Ashton, Paul. *And Somebody Gives a Damn!* Santa Barbara, Calif.: Ashton, 1990.

———. *Bataan Diary*. Privately published, 1984.

Bank, Bert. *Back from the Living Dead*. Tuscaloosa, Ala., 1945.

Berley, Ferdinand V. "Disposition of American Staff During Kobe POW Hosp. Fire, June 1945." Unpublished.

Bookman, John Jacob. *Diary* and "Medical Notes." Unpublished.

Clement, Robert A. "Brief History of C Battery, Fourth Marine Regiment, Anti-Aircraft." Unpublished. Courtesy Gladys Irvin.

———. "The Naval Battalion of Bataan, May 3, 1994." Unpublished.

Copeland, Robert E. *Diary.* sallyann2/copeland1.html.

Craig, William Riney. *Diary* and "Medical Notes" from Cabanatuan POW Camp. Unpublished. Courtesy John Cook.

Dean, Roly. Autobiographical narrative. Unpublished.

Ferguson, George. Letters to Lucille Ferguson. Unpublished.

Glusman, Murray. *Diary* and notes. Unpublished.

Graham, C. M. *Under the Samurai Sword.* Privately printed, 1998.

Heisinger, Duane. *Father Found: Life and Death as a Prisoner of the Japanese in World War II.* Privately published, 2003.

Hitchcock, W. Patch. *Forty Months in Hell.* Jackson, Tenn.: Page, 1996.

Irvin, Ernest J. "A Corpsman's Story." Unpublished. Courtesy Gladys Irvin.

Keyser, Ed. Personal flight log.

Kidd, John F., with Erwin C. Winkel. "Twice Forgotten." Unpublished.

King, Otis J. *Alamo of the Pacific.* Fort Worth, Tex.: Branch Smith, 1999.

Lane, John. *Summer Will Come Again.* www.summer-will-come-again.com.

McCall, James E. *Santo Tomás Internment Camp: STIC in Verse and Reverse STIC-toons and STIC-tistics.* Lincoln, Neb.: Woodruff, 1945.

Mitsos, Thomas. "Guerrilla Radio." Unpublished. Courtesy Clyde Childress.

Olson, John E., with Frank O. Anders. *Anywhere: Anytime; The History of the Fifty-seventh Infantry (PS).* San Antonio, Tex.: John E. Olson, 1991.

Quinn, John. "49 Top Hats." Unpublished. April 1984.

Reamer, Everett D. *Sanity Gone Amuck: World War II; Pacific 1941–1945.* Privately printed, 1998.

Roper, Richard S. *Brothers of Paul: Activities of Prisoner of War Chaplains in the Philippines in World War II.* Odenton, Md.: Revere, 2003.

Smith, Carey Miller. *Diary. Unpublished.* Courtesy Kathleen Hastings.

Stillman, Julius. *Combat Diary.* Privately printed.

Wilber, Dale. "The Last Voyage of the Arisan Maru." Unpublished.

Williams, Ted. *Rogues of Bataan II: Memoirs of a Marine.* Privately printed, 2004.

PHOTOGRAPH CREDITS

Frontispiece: National Archives (SC 334296). **Insert page 1,** *top:* Courtesy Navy Bureau of Medicine and Surgery Archives; *middle, bottom:* Lucille Ferguson, private collection. **Page 2,** *top left:* Ferdinand V. Berley, private collection; *top right:* Ann and Richard Bookman, private collection; *bottom left:* author's collection; *bottom right:* Gerald Blank, private collection. **Page 3:** National Archives (SC 130991). **Page 4,** *top:* official U.S. Navy photograph; *middle, bottom:* Melville Jacoby; reprinted by permission of the estate of Annalee Jacoby Fadiman. **Page 5,** *top:* Melville Jacoby; reprinted by permission of the estate of Annalee Jacoby Fadiman; *middle:* from *The War Against Japan: Pictorial Record, United States Army in World War II* (Washington, DC: Office of the Chief of Military History, Department of the Army, 1952), p. 44; *bottom:* National Archives (SC 334267). **Page 6,** *top:* from *The War Against Japan,* p. 35; *middle, bottom:* from *The War Against Japan,* p. 47. **Page 7,** *all:* Melville Jacoby; reprinted by permission of the estate of Annalee Jacoby Fadiman. **Page 8,** *top:* National Archives (SC 334296); *middle right:* author's collection; *bottom:* Courtesy Comité International de la Croix-Rouge (Hist-03185-27A). **Page 9,** *top, middle:* Courtesy Navy Bureau of Medicine and Surgery Archives; *bottom:* Ferdinand V. Berley, private collection. **Page 10,** *top:* Mikolski; National Archives (SC 203017); *middle left, bottom:* Courtesy Navy Bureau of Medicine and Surgery Archives. **Page 11,** *top:* National Archives (SC 265430); *bottom:* National Archives (SC 265335). **Page 12,** *top:* author's collection; *middle:* Ōhashi Yoshihisa, private collection; *bottom:* from Noma Hisashi, *Japanese Merchant Ships at War: Story of Mitsui and O.S.K. Liners Lost During the Pacific War* (2002). **Page 13,** *all:* Courtesy Kōbe Municipal Archives. **Page 14,** *top:* author's collection; *bottom:* National Archives (AC 57687). **Page 15,** *top:* Courtesy *Mainichi Shimbun; middle:* National Archives (AC 58995); *bottom:* author's collection. **Page 16,** *top:* Lieutenant C. F. Wheeler; National Archives (SG 348365); *middle:* Lieutenant C. F. Wheeler; National Archives (SG 348366); *bottom:* National Archives (SC 215252).

INDEX